W9-AXG-038

RIP FORD'S TEXAS

Personal Narratives of the West

John Salmon "Rip" Ford
Courtesy of Barker Texas History Center, University of Texas

RIP FORD'S
TEXAS

by
John Salmon Ford

Edited
With an Introduction and Commentary
by
Stephen B. Oates

UNIVERSITY OF TEXAS PRESS · AUSTIN

International Standard Book Number 0-292-77033-2 (cloth);
0-292-77034-0 (paperback)
Library of Congress Catalog Card Number 63-16057
Copyright © 1963, 1987 by Stephen B. Oates
All rights reserved
Printed in the United States of America

Second Paperback Printing, 1990

Requests for permission to reproduce material from this
work should be sent to Permissions, University of Texas
Press, Box 7819, Austin, Texas 78713-7819.

♾ The paper used in this publication meets the minimum
requirements of American National Standard for Information
Sciences— Permanence of Paper for Printed Library Materials,
ANSI Z39.48-1984.

For

H. Bailey Carroll

"As soon as you know the general outline of history of some period, it becomes agreeable and profitable to read the letters and memoirs of the time. Not only do they contain much intimate detail which makes it possible to realize that the men concerned really lived, but there is the advantage that the writers did not know what was going to happen, as the historians do."

BERTRAND RUSSELL

STATEMENT OF PURPOSE

By the Author

WHEN A MAN ASSUMES to place the matters connected with his career in life before the public, he is actuated by some motive. The real motives inducing the writer to tell his story are as follows: he has been an humble actor in the transaction of many affairs that happened in Texas from 1836 to almost the present date and believes that a large majority of the residents of this State are but little acquainted with the incidents which have given her people a reputation for gallantry in war and considerable insight in the management of public affairs; he knows that many men displayed a notable spirit of patriotism in the service of a noble State, and, feeling that they have been forgotten, he wants to offer something that will aid his fellow citizens to do justice to their memories and thus aid in arriving at the truth of history.

His main purpose will be to write the truth, to do injustice to no person, and to let the action of men be the facts by which we may judge them. The itching which some writers seem to feel to place themselves forward on all occasions will be avoided. The writer will not endeavor to become the hero upon all extraordinary events and to let the book speak of himself alone.

JOHN S. FORD
SAN ANTONIO, 1885

By the Editor

IN EDITING FORD'S MEMOIRS for publication, I had to make rather lengthy revision for several reasons. The original manuscript, now collecting dust in the Archives Division of the University of Texas Library, comprises nearly 1300 hand-written pages and is arranged by topical articles frequently without regard for chronology or outline. Also, many of the articles duplicate one another: for example, at about the midway point Ford wrote a terse, quite formal essay on the Civil War years in Texas; then later, after narrating the events of the Cortina War (1859–1860), he wrote a lively and detailed account of his experiences as a Confederate cavalry colonel in the lower Río Grande country. I reorganized much of the material so that it would read as a connected narrative, integrated articles that covered the same topic, corrected quoted material against the originals, corrected grammatical errors, but did not change the actual wording unless the diction was wrong or the phraseology was hopelessly obscure. In this reorganization I followed two rules of thumb: preserve Ford's style; and, if a sentence can be understood at all on first reading, don't fuss with it. In short, no matter what overhauling I did of Ford's sentences, they are still his: they are still his words, his ideas, his style, his thoughts, his criticisms, remarks, and anecdotes. I did, however, delete information that was superfluous or irrelevant to the course of the story, and took out those portions that covered events in which Ford did not himself participate. A few passages in the narrative required either rewriting or additional information before they made sense; these I enclosed in brackets.

It might be well now to describe in detail what I did in each of the six books that comprise this edition of Ford's memoirs.

Book One: "The Wilderness." In the original memoirs, the topical articles before the Mexican War are not arranged in any particular form or outline. I selected with care those articles dealing only with events in which Ford himself participated and organized them into topical chapters; in most cases Ford's original articles correspond to the numerical subdivisions within the chapters of this manuscript. A few of the original articles duplicated one another, in which case I did one of two things: (1) selected the article I deemed more informative and more readable and discarded the other; or (2) integrated them, choosing the best paragraphs of each and organizing them to read smoothly. Quite often I had to move a sentence from a paragraph where it was irrelevant or superfluous to a paragraph where it made some sense.

Book Two: "The Valley." I did not have to do much reorganization in the original account of the Mexican War (which a spot check will prove). Ford wrote about it in chronological form. I did relocate a few anecdotes that were out of place and put them where they logically belonged. I deleted lengthy battle reports and two accounts written by other men that covered events with which Ford had nothing to do.

Book Three: "The Trail." The chapters "West to El Paso" and "The Savage" are almost exactly as they appear in the original memoirs as topical articles. The four chapters about the Texas Rangers on the Nueces River are my organization. Ford discussed this Ranger action in his usual topical articles that ranged from one to thirty pages in length. I grouped these articles in what seemed to me to be reasonable chapters, the numerical subdivisions in each usually, but not always, corresponding to the topical articles themselves.

Book Four: "Between Two Rivers." The chapters "El Plan de la Loba" and "The Era of Suspicion" are topical articles as they appear in the original memoirs. The account of the Canadian River Expedition in the original manuscript was a mess. Since I could make little sense of the part that covers the actual fighting, I substituted Ford's official report to Governor Runnels. This is explained more fully in a note at the beginning of the chapter. The chapter "Sleepless Vigilance" is a collection of original topical articles that narrate Ranger activity after the Canadian River raid. I organized the four chapters covering the Cortina War the same way I put together the chapters on Ranger action along the Nueces.

Book Five: "Distant Horizons." Ford's two accounts of the Civil War in the original memoirs duplicate and often contradict one another, and both apparently were written in a hurry. In preparing them for publication, I had to adopt a rather radical editorial policy: first of all I omitted the forty-odd pages that were nothing but shapeless quotes from Oran Roberts' diary of the secession convention. Then I selected those topical articles that were relevant and organized them into chronological chapters, correcting errors in grammar and integrating articles that covered the same thing (they were numerous in this section) in the manner described above in connection with Book One. In radically revising the original account of this period, I followed my general editorial policy: to preserve Ford's style and to reorganize individual sentences only when they were beyond comprehension.

Book Six: "The Desert and Beyond." The first two chapters here are made up of topical articles that in the original manuscript were scattered around, some of them appearing in the sections on the Civil War, some in the section on the King and Kenedy enterprises. The last chapter, "The End of Innocence," is a collection of articles on the Davis-Coke controversy that Ford did not have arranged in any particular form.

The Appendices appeared midway in the original memoirs. I took them out of the main text for obvious reasons. Except for the omission of much irrelevant detail, each is organized exactly as it is found in the original manuscript.

I have followed the scholar's practice of adding in brackets the initials or first names of persons mentioned but have eschewed his habit of decorating memoirs like these with a multitude of pedantic footnotes. Ford, as an historian, ignored footnotes. He sought to convince his readers by clarity and literary verve rather than by prodigious citation. Only when there was doubt or confusion did I add notes to clarify or explain. Occasionally I inserted in a note a more detailed account of some obscure but irresistibly intriguing event which Ford only touched upon.

In short, our purpose—Ford's and mine—is to appeal to the specialist through truth and accuracy and to the general reader through lucidity in writing and economy in editing. That Ford would have approved of the changes I have made I am convinced. The manuscript as we have it was only the first draft of the history he intended to write. Ford was ill while he was compiling it, and he died before he could revise or reorganize his material.

Because Ford, extrovert that he was, said so little of himself in his memoirs and because his adopted daughter, after his death, appears to have taken the scissors to much of his early personal history in them, I thought it appropriate and useful to write a documented biographical sketch of him.

In preparing this book, I incurred heavy debts to several persons. I want to thank Dr. Llerena Friend, whose encyclopedic knowledge of Texas sources—a legend in itself—proved indispensable in the research stage of my work. Miss Pat Jones proofread the manuscript and offered helpful suggestions. I am heavily indebted to William John Hughes, who gave me valuable information about Ford's personal life, and to Dan Kilgore, who helped me on the lives of historical characters in the Corpus Christi area. Next I want to express my gratitude to Dr. H. Bailey Carroll and Dr. Harry H. Ransom, who collaborated in providing me with a special University of Texas research grant to fend off creditors while I wrote. Dr. Carroll in addition encouraged and assisted me throughout the project. I also owe much to Walter Prescott Webb. From this man I learned that history is not only compilation and synthesis but also an art and that the historical writer is an artist—not a scientist—who must strive to express original ideas with integrity and honesty and to present the past as a story of living people.

STEPHEN B. OATES, AUSTIN

Contents

BOOK 4: *Between Two Rivers*

BOOK 5: *Distant Horizons*

BOOK 6: *The Desert and Beyond*

Appendices

John Salmon "Rip" Ford

BY
STEPHEN B. OATES

>>

JOHN SALMON "RIP" FORD

When John Salmon Ford came to San Augustine, Texas, in the early summer of 1836, he had aspirations of becoming a great doctor. At twenty-one he was a tall, lean man with a ruddy complexion, piercing blue eyes, a Roman nose; and though he owned nothing beyond the rattling wagon he was riding in, he was full of youthful enthusiasm and confidence. Like thousands before him, he had come to Texas in hopes of making a new start in life. A republic now for nearly a month, Texas was a land of promise, of opportunity, where real estate and fortune were easy to get; its wild, robust character showed on the faces of friendly frontiersmen who waved at Ford and stared at an oak shingle, wired to the wagon sideboard, that read, *John Salmon Ford, Doctor.*

Perhaps during his first night in San Augustine Ford lay awake in his wagon, recalling his long trip from Tennessee: he had taken a steamboat down the Mississippi and up the Red River, then with the last of his money had bought the wagon and driven it across the border into Texas.

He probably recalled, too, with some nostalgia, the life he had left in Tennessee. Though a native of South Carolina, he had grown up on a small plantation in Lincoln County on the southern Tennessee border. There his father had taught him to ride and shoot, taught him the art of tilling the soil. But young Ford did not want to farm—he wanted an education; and, with the permission of his father, he enrolled in the county school. Like most rural schools in Tennessee, it was a small building: only one room with an earth floor and a few benches for eight grades of students whom the single teacher must instruct in spelling and arithmetic, in the classics and the Bible. John Salmon was a bright student. He finished the school's modest curriculum in five years. Then he read all the teacher's books and borrowed more from scholars in nearby Shelbyville to read at home after he had done the chores. At sixteen he was qualified to teach in a frontier school. Instead he went to Shelbyville to study medicine under Dr. James G. Barksdale. Ford met there a young girl named Mary Davis, whom he married and who, a year later, gave him twins—a girl and a boy. After that their marriage gradually fell apart and they were divorced just before his twenty-first birthday. He gained custody of the daughter, Fannie, whom he left with his mother and father when, wanting to make a fresh start, he set out for Texas. His parents hoped to follow him later.[1]

It was the beginning of a brilliant though rather erratic career as a public servant, for John Salmon would not only become a moderately successful doctor, but a lawyer, a surveyor, a respectable journalist, a trail blazer, a legislator of some distinction, a leading spirit in the annexation movement, an adjutant in the Mexican War, a state's righter, and one of the leading military men in the state, serving off and on as a Texas Ranger captain and in the Civil War as a colonel in the Confederate cavalry. An adventurer at heart, he was also involved in several misguided movements like the Know Nothing party, the Order of the Lone Star, the Knights of the Golden Circle, and many of the revolutionary movements along the Río Grande, not to mention the part he played in political wars such as the Davis-Coke controversy during Reconstruction. In addition

---

[1] Tom Lea, *The King Ranch*, I, 429–430; William John Hughes, "Rip Ford, Texan: The Public Life and Services of John Salmon Ford," ms., pp. 2–4. It should be remembered that a good many facts about Ford were gleaned from his memoirs. I obtained information about his personal life, particularly about his three marriages and his children, from William John Hughes, Ford's biographer, and from some of his living relatives: Guy B. Massey of Wilburton, Oklahoma, F. H. de Cordova of Corpus Christi, and L. R. Cowan of Brownsville. Short accounts of Ford's life not cited below are in *Biographical Directory of the Texan Conventions and Congresses; Biographical Souvenir of the State of Texas; Handbook of Texas;* and Sidney Smith Johnson, *Texans Who Wore the Gray.*

he served as mayor of two Texas towns and in his later years wrote and promoted Texas history. While he never rose to prominence in any one capacity except as a soldier, he was active in practically every important historical event from 1836 until he retired in 1883 to write the memoirs that follow this sketch.

Ford practiced medicine in San Augustine for some eight years. At first he made only night calls for folk who could not afford the higher prices of established doctors. The poor liked him. He listened to their troubles. He collected when they could pay. Once, in a dangerous and tedious operation, he removed a bone from a small boy's brain for a trifling charge. Word soon got around that he was a good doctor and before long his list of patients included some of the most prominent citizens in the county.

Though he often worked up to fifteen hours a day treating patients, the young doctor was active in community affairs. In 1838 he helped Isaac Ferguson organize a group of citizens to go out against a band of Indians who were raiding isolated homesteads north of San Augustine. After that he rode in other citizen companies commanded by Bill Kimbro and Jack Hays, a quiet little Tennessean who became one of Texas' most distinguished Indian fighters. Ford also found time to teach a Sunday School class, to participate in a local Thespian Corps, and to do some surveying near the Big Spring. Then he tried politics. He ran for representative in 1840 but lost to Sam Houston and H. W. Augustine.

For the next four years Ford concentrated on his medicine, earning enough money to pay his debts and to buy a larger office across the street from the local newspaper. He also developed an interest in law, studied it relentlessly at night after closing his office, and in a few months knew enough to pass the bar exams. According to the shingle above his door, Doctor Ford was also Lawyer Ford.

By now he had made friends with local political leaders and had impressed them with his frank opinion that Texas should join the Union, so he decided to run in the forthcoming election for representative. His short and fiery campaign called for annexation as soon as possible and for better protection of Texas' northwest frontier. He won handily over his two opponents and in the fall of 1844 set out for Washington-on-the-Brazos on a five-dollar mare.[2]

When Ford arrived in Washington, he found that annexation wasn't

---

[2] John S. Ford, "Dr. John S. Ford's Medical Journal" ms.; San Augustine *Red-Lander*, September 9, 1841, May 19, 1842, July 8, 1843, June 29, September 7, 1844; *Biographical Directory of the Texan Conventions and Congresses*, p. 30; George Lewis Crocket, *Two Centuries in East Texas*, pp. 244–245.

the only issue dominating political discussions. There was also a bitter controversy raging over the location of a permanent capital. Houston had moved it from Austin to Washington in 1842, but popular opinion now wanted it moved back to Austin. Ford agreed with Houston that Austin, situated as it was on the frontier, open to Indian incursions, was a risky place for a national capital. After Congress convened Ford helped draw up a resolution approving Houston's choice of Washington as capital, made a few pro-annexation speeches on the house floor, and served on five different committees, notable among them the Committee on Indian Affairs and the Committee on Education.

Wherever he went, Ford never tired of telling people that the possibility of another death struggle with Mexico and the inadequacy of frontier defense made it imperative that Texas join the United States immediately. In the special session of the Congress, young Ford was the man who introduced the resolution for Texas to join the Union, which was finally approved. Meanwhile, the United States Congress had passed a joint resolution approving annexation if Texas would write a constitution guaranteeing a republican form of government.[3]

Ford was not a delegate to the convention that assembled in Austin in the summer of 1845, but he was in the convention balcony every day as the official correspondent of the Texas National Register, a newspaper published at Washington-on-the-Brazos. While in Austin Ford also met and courted a young woman named Louisa Swisher who, though pale and fragile, seemed to have the kind of grace and inner beauty that John Salmon wanted most in a woman. There is no record of their courtship, but it must have been a short one: apparently they were married shortly after the annexation convention finished its work and Texas became the twenty-seventh state to join the Union.[4]

In the late summer of 1845, after the Fords had returned to San Augustine, John Salmon decided to give up medicine and go into the newspaper business. With a close friend, Mike Cronican, he left for Washington-on-the-Brazos to buy the Texas National Register and move the paper to Austin. By mid-November, 1845, the Fords were permanent residents of Austin; and Ford and Cronican were publishing a weekly, pro-Houston paper at the corner of Congress Avenue and Pecan Street.

Because the Register was pro-Houston, Austin readers gave it a cold

[3] Texas National Register (Washington-on-the-Brazos), December 7, December 14, 1844; Texas (Republic), Journals of the House of Representatives of the Ninth Congress, p. 5.
[4] Texas National Register (Washington-on-the-Brazos), July 24, August 7, 1845; Hughes, "Rip Ford, Texan," ms., pp. 18–20.

reception. The young editors had gall, lauding old Houston in a town where he was most unpopular. Austinites would not forget that he had strongly opposed the city as a capital and that three years before, when the Mexicans invaded Texas, he had tried to move the archives to Houston, having been stopped only by an angry mob threatening to shoot the "Dam old drunk Cherokee" and "every dam waggoner" who started with the papers.[5]

Ford and Cronican were soon getting anonymous threats to beat them up and dump all their machinery into the Colorado River if they didn't stop writing pro-Houston editorials. But the editors only wrote with more vigor in defense of Houston and his faction of the Democratic party. On January 17, 1846, they changed the name of the paper to the *Texas Democrat* indicating on page one their intent to pronounce "boldly and unreservedly upon political subjects" and "to advance the interests and disseminate the doctrines of the Democratic party."

Waging a campaign for better schools, better frontier defense, more doctors and books and lawyers and churches, the paper soon became one of the leading liberal journals in the state. In March the editors started publishing it semiweekly to give a more comprehensive and immediate political coverage.

Houston's friends in the legislature liked the way the tall journalist conducted himself. In April they showed their appreciation by electing Ford and Cronican state printers over a powerful opposition. Then in May, when a number of politicians met at the capitol to organize officially the Democratic party in Texas, they elected Ford and ten other prominent citizens to the state central committee. Ford was busy and outwardly happy.[6]

Then his wife fell sick. Ford doctored her himself; he almost never left her bedroom, dropping all his outside activities and leaving the management of the paper to Cronican. In August she lapsed into unconsciousness and soon died. John Salmon was stricken with grief. After the funeral services, he left Oakwood Cemetery feeling as if "the bosom of destruction" had passed "over his domestic hearth."

For many days he remained in his home refusing to see friends and

---

[5] Dorman H. Winfrey, "The Texan Archive War of 1842," *Southwestern Historical Quarterly*, LXIV, 171–184.

[6] *Texas National Register* (Austin), November 15, 1845, January 10, 1846; *Texas Democrat* (Austin), January 17, April 15, May 6, 1846; Hughes, "Rip Ford, Texan," ms., pp. 20–26; Ed Burleson Papers, ms.; Alexander W. Terrell, "The City of Austin from 1839 to 1865," *Quarterly of the Texas State Historical Association*, XIV, 113–128; Clarence J. Laroche, "Rip Ford: Frontier Journalist," ms., pp. 10–52; Ben C. Stuart, "The History of Texas Newspapers From the Earliest Period to the Present," ms., pp. 20–64.

well-wishers. But the loneliness, the pain, finally drove him from his solitude: once again he took up the dizzy pace of the public servant, arguing politics, writing vigorous editorials, making speeches, attending party meetings, and collecting data on frontier problems. He must never have slept or allowed himself a moment of relaxation when the memory of Louisa might have haunted him.

Nor did he feel any better when his mother and father with his ten-year-old daughter rode all the way from Tennessee to live with him. Even warm family love failed to revive him from the depths of his sorrow.

Meanwhile, the United States had gone to war against Mexico over the disputed Texas boundary, and many romantic youths were riding off to join General Zachary Taylor's army, now driving across the Río Grande. Ford too wanted to go, but he refrained. He was a newspaperman whose place in wartime was at his press. When he heard that Old Rough and Ready had captured Monterrey and had personally commended the action of Jack Hays' Texas Rangers, Ford, filled with envy, released his emotions by writing a poem for his editorial column:

> Down! tramp that pennon to the dust
> Strike, Texians, strike once more!
> Shall San Jacinto's glories rust?
> The God of battle is your trust,
> Strike as your sires of yore.[7]

When news came that Hays was calling for volunteers to fill out his regiment, Ford could restrain himself no longer. He told Cronican to take care of the paper for he was off to join Sam Highsmith's company of Hays' regiment. On May 10, 1847, Ford enlisted for six months, but word soon came that Taylor would receive no troops for less than twelve months. Highsmith's and several other companies then disbanded. Within weeks, however, Hays' recruiters had raised enough new companies to constitute a regiment—Hays' second regiment, as it was called. One of the first to re-enlist, John Salmon on July 7 was promoted to lieutenant and transferred to Hays' staff as regimental adjutant.[8] In August the command marched to Mier, Mexico, thence off to an amphibious landing at Veracruz and overland through a series of engagements to the ancient walls of Mexico City, where the Mexicans, after a frantic last stand, finally surrendered.

---

[7] *Texas Democrat* (Austin), December 9, 1846.
[8] *Ibid.*, July 24, 1847; U.S. War Department, Records Group No. 94, ms.

Hays and Adjutant Ford led the rangers into the heart of the city, well ahead of the main army.

"Los Diablos Tejanos!" "Los Diablos Tejanos!" cried the Mexicans as they crowded along the streets to get a look at the "Texas Devils." One war correspondent said they rode some standing upright, some sideways, some facing the rear, some by the reverse flank, some on horses, others on mustangs and mules; on they rode, pell-mell, wearing motley "uniforms" of almost every conceivable variety of pants and shirts, hats and caps ("caps made of the skins of . . . the dog, the cat, the bear, the coon, the wild cat . . . and each cap had a tail hanging to it"). And the frightened onlookers, not knowing whether to cheer or to run, believed the Texan to be "a sort of semi-civilized, half man, half devil, with a slight mixture of lion and the snapping turtle," and had "a more holy horror" of him than they had of "the evil saint himself."[9]

During the Mexico City campaign, Ford acquired two things that would stay with him for the rest of his life. One was malaria with its recurring chills and fever; the other was his famous nickname. As adjutant, Ford's main duty was to make reports of men killed in action. He had the habit of completing each report with "Rest in Peace" after his signature, but as the number of fatalities increased, he abbreviated the phrase to "R.I.P." A ranger noticed it and, to get back at Ford for giving every man in the outfit a nickname, called him "Old Rip" Ford.[10]

After the Mexicans surrendered, Ford and his comrades dispersed guerrilla bands operating around Mexico City, then rode to Veracruz, where they were mustered out of service, and sailed for home. When they landed at Port Lavaca they found a large crowd gathered to cheer them; in the eyes of the Texas public, Hays' rangers were national heroes, having conquered a country that for twenty years had suppressed the freedom and the natural rights of man, and had interfered with America's "Manifest Destiny" to rule these shores.

After attending an "elegant" ball in honor of the Texas Rangers, Ford returned to Austin and resumed the editorship of the *Texas Democrat*. But in a few months he was tired of newspaper work; he longed for the saddle and the wild life of a volunteer ranger. He told his partner Cronican how he felt, said he wanted to raise a volunteer company with which to patrol the frontier. Cronican said he understood and they sold their paper in January, 1849, to William H. Cushney.

---

[9] *Jack Hays, the Intrepid Texas Ranger*, p. 21.

[10] Ford's grandson, L. R. Cowan, of Brownsville, Texas, is the authority for the story of how Rip got his nickname. See Walter Prescott Webb, *The Texas Rangers: A Century of Frontier Defense*, p. 124 n.

Ford, however, failed to get permission from the state to raise a company—there simply was no money for such an enterprise—so he remained in Austin doing little except reading books on tactics and buying new items for his rapidly growing military library.[11]

Then came an exciting piece of news: a man named Sutter had discovered gold in California. Rumors flew. Bewhiskered prospectors were becoming millionaires almost overnight. First a few adventurers, then hundreds and thousands were heading west for a new life of wealth and well being. Texas businessmen were excited too, but for different reasons. The great exodus west, if it were channeled through Texas, might mean a fortune right here at home. They pored over old maps trying to find a suitable route across the state, but existing maps were inaccurate and incomplete. In February a group of merchants met at Austin and called on Rip Ford, who knew something about Texas geography, to draw up a report on the best overland route to California's gold via Austin and El Paso. Two days later Ford and a friend named Mullowney submitted a report based on an account by Jack Hays who had tried to reach El Paso the year before (unfortunately Hays' guide had gotten lost, the party had ended up somewhere in Mexico, and when it finally returned to civilization Texans knew no more about the region than they had before). Ford told the merchants that few fortune hunters would come through the state until a professional surveyor with a competent guide charted a route through the El Paso country.

At the same time an acquaintance of Ford's, Robert Simpson Neighbors, under orders from the United States Army, was planning to do just that. Hearing that Ford was interested in such a project, Neighbors came to Austin, and when the two men shook hands and sat down for coffee at Ford's small home, they were immediate friends. They were the same age, thirty-four, both over six feet and both with lean, powerful builds and blue eyes. Their personalities, however, were fairly dissimilar. Ford was loquacious and loud (his hands stroking and molding every phrase made his voice seem a bit louder than it really was); he was outgoing, with an electrifying vitality that drove him relentlessly through tasks no matter how difficult. He had wit too, a charming kind of humor that allowed him to poke fun at most anything without arousing a man's ire or injuring his pride. "The Major," as all Neighbors' friends knew him, also had wit: he knew more jokes than any man in the state, could tell them for hours, if he had listeners. His was a sarcastic wit: he never

---

[11] Frank Brown, "Annals of Travis County and of the City of Austin," ms., Chapter XI, p. 44.

smiled while telling his stories, he never smiled at all and wherever he went he stirred people with his stubborn pride, his solemn and determined air. When discussing business the Major was quiet and shrewd. In less than an hour he had persuaded Ford to accompany him to El Paso. They planned to leave on March 2, 1849, from Barnard's Trading Post near present-day Waco.[12]

It took them fifty-five days to cover the 1160 miles from San Antonio, Neighbors' headquarters, to El Paso and then back again. During that time Ford felt better mentally and physically than at any time since his wife's death. He made new friends too: Doc Sullivan, an impetuous and impish little man, always into mischief, and his constant companion, Alpheus D. Neal, and Delaware Jim Shaw and several other Indian scouts, all of whom accompanied the expedition; and out at El Paso Ford met a living Texas legend, the "Great Western," a huge, powerful woman who operated a hotel and gambling house. She could whip any man, fair fight or foul, could shoot a pistol better than anyone in the region, and at black jack could out play (or out cheat) the slickest professional gambler. The way the story had it, she had fallen in love with Zachary Taylor back in Florida and had followed him to Texas. When war began, and Old Rough and Ready led his army into Mexico, she came to El Paso and bought a hotel. One day a man fresh from the battle of Buena Vista came running into her hotel crying that Taylor had been badly defeated. The Great Western floored the courier with a powerful blow between the eyes as she bellowed: "You damned son of a bitch, there ain't Mexicans enough in Mexico to whip old Taylor!" According to the gossipers she was still in love with the general and would let no man touch her. Which was all right, they added, because it would require some mutation of man and gorilla to handle her anyway.[13]

When Ford returned to Austin in June, 1849, he published a report of the expedition in the *Texas Democrat* giving the exact route taken and describing in great detail the fertility of the soil and the abundance of natural resources in the west Texas region. He told everybody he met that Neighbors was one of the best trail blazers in the state.[14] The Major returned the compliment. "In Dr. John S. Ford," he told his army super-

---

[12] *Northern Standard* (Clarksville), February 10, 1849; *Texas Democrat* (Austin), February 24, 1849; Kenneth Franklin Neighbours, "Robert S. Neighbors in Texas, 1836–1859: A Quarter Century of Frontier Problems," ms., p. 9; Kenneth F. Neighbours, "The Expedition of Major Robert S. Neighbors to El Paso in 1849," *Southwestern Historical Quarterly*, LVIII, 36–59.

[13] George Washington Trahern (ed. by A. Russell Buchanan), "Texas Cowboy from Mier to Buena Vista," *Southwestern Historical Quarterly*, LVIII, p. 85.

[14] *Texas Democrat* (Austin), June 16, 1849.

visor, "I found an energetic and able assistant, the services rendered by him were important to the successful termination of the expedition. I cheerfully recommend him to your favorable notice."[15]

The opening of the El Paso route was a considerable achievement. It extended Texas' jurisdiction out to the Staked Plains, brought the eastern New Mexico region within reach of the Texas government (something that Texans had been trying to do since the tragic Santa Fé Expedition back in 1841) and, most important of all, facilitated the exodus west. In August alone over 4000 people passed through El Paso on their way to California. Then the Texas Legislature at its next session decided to act on the 1848 proposal to divide the area into counties and sent Major Neighbors to organize them.

That summer Ford decided to take up medicine again. For a small sum he bought an office on Pecan Street, but business was slow and his restless energy drove him to additional activities. He became a crusader, joined the Austin chapter of the Sons of Temperance, and traveled from town to town making speeches on the evils of alcohol. His campaigning did not go unappreciated. In a public ceremony a ladies' temperance committee named him workhorse of the year and presented him with a banner. After a brief acceptance speech, he left, unable to face the inevitable gossiping over tea and cake.[16]

He was extremely busy, yet somehow found time to teach in the Union Sunday School. His classes were composed of young men between fourteen and twenty. One of his students, Frank Brown, recalled later that Ford was conspicuous for his encyclopedic knowledge of the Scriptures. Every night, whether at home or in the field, he read the Bible, fulfilling a promise to his mother. As a teacher Ford was humorous and inspiring. Once he related to his class how Jeremiah got his name. It seemed that the prophet's original name was Jerry. One day Jerry was out walking and accidentally stumbled into a mud hole, extracting himself after considerable difficulty. When he returned to the village all covered with mud, everyone crowed with laughter. The prophet soon had a nickname, Jerry-Mire, and the scripture writers thinking this his true name corrected the spelling to Jeremiah. "This came near producing an explosion of laughter," Brown said, "which however we managed to repress to

[15] Robert S. Neighbors (ed. by Kenneth F. Neighbours), "The Report of the Expedition of Major Robert S. Neighbors to El Paso in 1849," *Southwestern Historical Quarterly*, LX, 532.
[16] *Texas Democrat* (Austin), July 21, August 4, 1849.

'sniggles,' by recalling to mind the sanctity of the place and our surroundings."[17]

When Ford quit teaching in August, 1849, General George M. Brooke of the United States Army called on him to raise a company of Hays' old rangers and lead them against renegade Indians and Mexican outlaws who during the past three years had outwitted the regular army with its book tactics and had terrorized the area between the Nueces and the Río Grande. Ford's rangers, sworn into United States service in Austin on August 23, were a wild bunch who drank heavily and had little regard for discipline or heel clicking; highly individualistic in the true sense of the term, they respected an officer only when he fought better than his men; armed with long-barreled Colts and huge bowie knives, dressed in motley and often outlandish garbs, they were deadly fighters.

Reaching the lower Río Grande country in mid-September, the rangers chased down several of the Indian bands and apprehended a number of Mexican outlaws. For the next two years "Ford's Old Company" kept peace and order in a region where the law had been how well you could shoot, or could ride.[18]

After the company disbanded in September, 1851, Ford and a few of his rangers crossed the border to help an old friend, José M. J. Carbajal, set up an independent and democratic republic along the Río Grande— "El Plan de la Loba," Carbajal called it. But the movement failed for lack of money and supplies, and Ford and Carbajal had to flee for their lives to Texas, an army of *Centralistas* in pursuit as far as the border.

Many influential Texans criticized the young ranger for getting involved in the Carbajal "fiasco." "A man has a right," Ford told them bluntly, "to assist a people who are resisting tyranny and battling for the exercise of their privileges as free men."

When Ford returned to Austin in January, 1851, he decided to return to politics. He announced his candidacy for interim senator to fill out the late Ed Burleson's term—won easily, indicating that not everybody disapproved of his recent activities. Rip's first effort in the Senate was an

---

[17] Frank Brown, "Annals of Travis County and of the City of Austin," ms., Chapter XI, p. 44, and Chapter XIII, p. 38.

[18] U.S. War Department, Records Group No. 94, ms.; *Texas State Gazette* (Austin), August 29, September 1, October 20, December 29, 1849, January 26, May 11, 1850; *Democratic Telegraph and Texas Register* (Houston), June 13, 1850; Brooke to Governor P. H. Bell, January 30, March 10, August 10, October 10, October 15, 1850, Governors' Letters, ms.; A. J. Sowell, "Colonel Rip Ford and Rangers Battle with the Indians," *Frontier Times*, IV, 24–28; Webb, *Texas Rangers*, p. 141.

impressive victory: he carried a bill defining the Austin city limits, out-
lining the method of establishing and collecting ad valorem taxes, and
compelling merchants who sold liquor to pay an additional five dollar
license fee. On the last day of the session he delivered a rambling oration
on the ridiculous state of frontier defense.

His crusading spirit returned. With loans from old friends, he bought
the *South-Western American* in November, 1852, announcing in his
first issue that he would push every "cause" vital to Texas interests.

Directly across Congress Avenue was a shrewd competitor, the *Texas
State Gazette*, edited by Wade Hampton and William R. Scurry, both
veteran newsmen. They welcomed the new enterprise, noting that "Ford
has the reputation of being a good writer and a courteous gentleman; he
is, besides, an old Texian, thoroughly acquainted with the history and resources of the state, and will be able to make his paper a very interesting
sheet. We welcome him to the ranks editorial right cordially."[19] Then in
the next issue of the *Gazette* Hampton impugned him for belonging to
a rival faction of the Democratic party.

Within a month Ford had endorsed a host of causes: his editorials
vindicated slavery and condemned the abolitionists, exposed corrupt
politicians without mercy, demanded state support of railroads, campaigned for temperance, called for a permanent ranger service, and denounced the rapidly growing Republican party as un-American. In the
1853 governor's race he supported Colonel M. T. Johnson, openly declaring war on the *Gazette*, which had announced for E. M. Pease.

One day in August the *Gazette* editors learned that Ford was planning
to leave for the Río Grande with a wagonload of campaign leaflets.
Hampton wrote an editorial accusing Ford of starting on a leaflet-spread-
ing campaign to persuade the uninformed Mexicans on the Río Grande
to vote for Johnson.

When Ford read this, he informed the *Gazette* that he was going
down there simply to get a testimony to his ranger service so that he could
collect back pay. He would take nothing beyond his horse, his Colts, and
maybe a saddlebag full of information about an "honest" gubernatorial
candidate. After Ford had gone, Hampton wrote that he didn't give much
of a damn what Ford took since he was "crazy" as a result of an old head
wound that had allowed his "not overly plentiful supply of brains to
leak out."[20]

---

[19] *Texas State Gazette* (Austin), November 13, 1852.
[20] *Southwestern American* (Austin), August 6, 1853. When Ford took over the paper,
he dropped the hyphen in Southwestern.

In the end Pease won the governorship, but Ford came out the better in his feud with Hampton. On December 31 Austin voters elected Rip mayor by a whopping majority, and the circulation of the *American* increased twofold as a result. Announcing that a city is governed best when governed least, Mayor Ford sought to clean up local politics by removing "extraneous" town offices and cutting salaries. Then over a strong opposition in the city council he rammed through an ordinance prohibiting liquor sales on Sunday and compelling peace officers to stay sober on the job.[21]

When the town marshal showed up drunk one morning, Ford fired him and assumed the duties himself. The next morning a gunman well known for his fighting abilities came to town for a spree. By noon he was deliriously drunk, shouting, knocking men down, embarrassing the ladies, and shooting out window panes with his six-shooters. Suddenly he faced a tall man with a badge who told him to shut up. The gunman was speechless for a moment, then cursed the marshal until rage and lack of breath overcame him.

"We don't want your sort of people in our town," the lawman said, "and I give you an hour to get beyond the city limits."

The drunk was insulted; no "pretty" marshal could tell him what to do; he was going nowhere except into the bar for more whisky.

"That is a question for you to settle as you see fit," the marshal said, "but if you are determined not to go, just leave with the barkeeper what disposition you want made of your horse and outfit."

The drunk looked at the officer incredulously for a moment, then went into the saloon and asked the bartender, "Who is that bluffer?"

"That is Old Rip Ford, our mayor," the bartender said. "He is a doctor and if I wanted to enjoy long life I would rather take his advice than that of any man I know."

There was a long silence.

"Pardner, you please tell your mayor I wouldn't stay in his d——d town if he made me a present of the whole she-bang. Adios."[22]

When his term as mayor ended, Ford went back to editing his paper, whose name he had changed to the *Texas State Times*, took on a partner named Joe Walker, an old ranger friend, and with open glee resumed

---

[21] H. P. N. Gammel (comp.), *The Laws of Texas: 1822–1897*, III, 151–152; *Texas State Times* (Austin), April 21, 1854.

[22] Captain W. C. Walsh, "Austin in the Making," Austin *Statesman*, February 24, 1924.

his war with "that pop-gun of democracy across the street"—the *State Gazette*.[23]

Perhaps influenced by a marked rise in the number of radical, anti-slavery Europeans in Texas, Ford's politics now underwent a sudden and drastic change. Democracy for him no longer meant freedom of thought and equal opportunity. He became a Know Nothing, accepting the tenet that a truly loyal American was an extreme conservative who fanatically defended the old and sacred institutions like slavery and states' rights, who advocated as a universal truth the inherent supremacy of free, white, American-born Protestants whose main purpose in life was to combat the "alien menace" and harass Catholics. In becoming a Know Nothing, Ford joined a nation-wide movement in which suspicion and opportunism replaced reason and morality.

He advanced rapidly in the party: served as chairman of two major committees, one to discourage the use of Mexican labor and the other to prevent Negroes from "hiring their own time"—working for others for pay when their masters had nothing for them to do. In the 1855 election for mayor, rightist Ford campaigned rigorously for J. T. Cleveland, an avowed Know Nothing. Cleveland won an astonishing victory, receiving all but two votes cast, something that Ford would not let his critics at the *State Gazette* forget.[24]

In 1856 the Know Nothings came under galling fire. Intelligent people charged that the party was run by bigots, that it was a danger to American democracy because of its veil of secrecy. Indignant, Ford replied: "The greatest moral reforms of the age have been accomplished through the aid of secret associations."

Slipping further and further to the right, he joined the Order of the Lone Star of the West. In months he was one of its leaders, telling outsiders that the purpose of the movement was to liberate Cuba, while in privacy he discussed with members the fastest means of establishing a slave empire in Cuba and Mexico. There was a rumor that he had also joined the Knights of the Golden Circle, another secret society of the radical right whose object, like that of the Lone Star of the West, was to set up a gigantic slave empire with Havana as its capital.[25]

---

[23] *Texas State Times* (Austin), March 1, April 28, 1855; Brown, "Annals of Travis County and of the City of Austin," ms., Chapter XI, p. 46.

[24] *Texas State Times* (Austin), October 14, 1854, January 6, August 25, 1855; Brown, "Annals of Travis County and of the City of Austin," ms., Chapter XVI, p. 35.

[25] Brown, "Annals of Travis County and of the City of Austin," ms., Chapter XVII, p. 43; Dallas *Herald,* May 20, 1860; C. A. Bridges, "The Knights of the Golden Circle: A Filibustering Fantasy," *Southwestern Historical Quarterly*, XLIV, 287, 294; Earl W. Fornell, "Texans and Filibusters in the 1850's," *ibid.*, LIX, 411–428.

That summer Ford endorsed archconservative Millard Fillmore for president. "Is any man North or South fairer on the record?" He "stands radically and uncompromisingly opposed to the miserable foreign love, instincts, and policy" of the Democratic party whose platform was "a fit example of the thousand and one reckless base declarations of men who are strangers to all principle excepting that of public plunder."[26]

The Democratic victory that November killed the Know Nothing movement in Texas; and Ford, perhaps because he had had a change of heart, suddenly stopped writing invective editorials. Evidently he was tired of radical nativism; his personal religion wasn't anti-Catholic anyway, for he had always believed strongly in the right of a man to have his own opinion in religious matters. He had decided also that not all foreigners were evil. There were Germans, Poles, and Mexicans living in Austin who had proved themselves loyal Americans. He was a little ashamed, told himself later that his Know Nothing affiliation was "one of those inconsiderate things men do sometimes."

In January, 1857, he went to San Antonio for a vacation. While there he took in all the cultural entertainments the city had to offer. He started seeing women too, for the first time since his wife had died. His friends in Austin heard one day that Rip was "about to migrate to the *State of Matrimony*" and wrote the San Antonio *Herald* asking if it were true. "For the information of all inquiring friends," the *Herald* replied, "we would state that he has been making his sojourn among us for several weeks past, and that we had the satisfaction of seeing him no later than yesterday in our sanctum, looking in fine health and exuberant spirits.— As to his taking to himself a fair one, we are ignorant, but he has been dashing about here pretty extensively with 'em." The editor of the *Southern Intelligencer* of Austin was "glad to hear it is no worse as yet" for while matrimony was "elegant" in its way, it lessened public interest in "handsome men" like Rip Ford.[27]

He returned to Austin in early May, relaxed and rested. In a public gathering later in the week he announced that a wayward son had returned to the Democratic party. He had become a Know Nothing, he said regretfully, because of a "firm conviction" of the need to protect America and preserve "inviolate" the sacred institutions of the South. But from this day on, he promised the Democrats, "Your country is my country, and your God is my God."[28]

---

[26] *Texas State Times* (Austin), August 2, August 16, 1856.

[27] *Southern Intelligencer* (Austin), February 4, 1857.

[28] *Texas State Gazette* (Austin), May 16, 1857; *Texas State Times* (Austin), May 23, 1857.

In August, 1857, Ford sold his newspaper, vowing that he was through with journalism, at least for the time being. As a man of leisure, he traveled about the state visiting old friends and listening to irate frontiersmen tell frightful tales of Indian massacres out in west Texas. There was no protection in the region; almost every day newspapers carried stories about Comanche depredations. Ford wondered why the governor had not called for volunteers to fight the Indians as he had done before. The settlers did not know why. All they knew was that the Comanches were going to take over the frontier if things followed their present course.

When Ford returned to Austin in January, 1858, he went to see Governor H. R. Runnels about the Indian menace. After a lively talk in which they covered the whole area of frontier defense, Ford walked out of the capitol as senior captain of all state troops with orders to get up a company and strike at the Comanche heartland out on the Canadian River.

By April 23 the captain was on the march with 101 rangers; two days later Indian Agent Shapley Prince Ross and his 113 Brazos Reserve Indians joined them; and the force rode almost day and night to reach the Comanche nation on May 12. In a frantic ten-hour battle that followed Captain Ford won a decisive victory, scattering the Comanches and burning their villages.

Ford's rangers returned to civilization military heroes. Governor Runnels congratulated them for their "successful" effort, then disbanded the company and nobody was happy because a few months later the Comanches were at it again. On November 28, 1858, Ford and Runnels had another conference, in which Rip talked at great length on the need for a permanent ranger force to police the frontier. The governor agreed that something like that should be done, but the state couldn't afford it; besides, frontier protection was supposed to be the responsibility of Albert Sidney Johnston's Second United States Cavalry, which in turn insisted that it couldn't possibly do the job alone.[29]

Again Ford left the capitol with a six-month commission. He took a second company into the west where he fought the Comanches in a number of running fights, accomplishing little. Then he offered to ride alongside Earl Van Dorn's United States troops in a joint operation, but the regulars would have nothing to do with a bunch of raw volunteers.

---

[29] Ford to H. R. Runnels, April 7, May 22, May 27, 1858, Governors' Letters, ms.; W. J. Hughes, " 'Rip' Ford's Indian Fight on the Canadian," *Panhandle-Plains Historical Review*, XXX, 1–26; Webb, *Texas Rangers*, pp. 151–161; *Southern Intelligencer* (Austin), June 2, 1858; *Texas Sentinel* (Austin), July 11, 1858.

When his commission expired, Ford returned to Austin pretty well fed up with the whole business. If Runnels and company were too stubborn to take his advice about a standing ranger service, then the government would have to suffer the consequences.

But the settlers were the ones who suffered. Across the frontier that summer swept a wave of horse stealing, cattle rustling, saloon shootings, and Indian massacres. The only law was the law of the wild: kill or be killed.[30]

While captain of the second ranger company, Ford was involved in one of the most unfortunate crimes of the decade—Peter Garland's massacre of a group of peaceful Indians on December 27, 1858. Since Ford in Chapter XXI of the memoirs defends his action in the Garland affair but fails to give the details, it might be well to give them here.

The captain was in San Antonio during the Christmas holidays when news of the massacre reached him. According to reports about twenty rowdies from Erath County under Peter Garland, a known gunman, had ambushed a party of Brazos Reserve Indians, including women and children, who had been hunting on Keechi Creek. The whites had killed seven Indians, three of them women, and scattered the rest.

Supervising Indian Agent Robert Simpson Neighbors, when he heard what had happened, snapped angrily that it was a barbaric, cold-blooded crime, worse than any the Comanches had ever committed; and if the law did not punish the "perpetrators of this most foul murder," the reserve Indians "will disband and seek satisfaction."[31]

But the law was amazingly silent. Only when Chief José María's braves painted for war did Governor Runnels call on all civil authorities and peace officers to assist Neighbors in apprehending the killers.

Meanwhile Ford had joined his company at Camp Leon. It seems that he had already promised to help capture Garland, but when Judge N. W. Battle of Waco sent the captain a writ of arrest, he flatly refused to act, contending that no civil officer on earth had the power to give soldier Ford an order. This pronouncement stunned Neighbors, for it appeared that his old friend was siding with the murderers. He sent Ford a letter pointing out that his force was the only one in the area strong enough to bring Garland to justice. The captain did not answer.

Then Governor Runnels himself ordered Ford to arrest Garland. But the ranger remained adamant, replying that he would "help" the civil au-

---

[30] Ford to Runnels, November 2, 1858, Governors' Letters, ms.; Dallas *Herald*, October 10, 1858.

[31] Neighbors to Denver, January 30, 1859, *U.S. Senate Exec. Docs.*, 36th Cong., 1st Sess., vol. I, Doc. 2, pp. 588–592.

thorities but that he wasn't going after the killers alone. At that Judge
Battle, E. J. Gurley, counsel for the Indians, and Neighbors all three accused Ford of being downright irresponsible. Somewhat shaken, Ford told
them that if he tried to make the arrest, a civil war would inevitably break
out between his troops and the Garland mob. And that was that. Nobody
ever tried to arrest the offenders; and when a grand jury assembled in
Palo Pinto County, it disregarded the Garland case and indicted Chief
José María for horse stealing.[32]

Neither Neighbors, Battle, nor Gurley ever really forgave Ford for
his "excessive prudence" that allowed a gang of murderers to go free.
Neighbors said later that "the contemptible pandering of that individual
. . . to the prejudice of a band of lawless men, against the very Indians
who had led him to victory last spring over the hostile Comanches,
should, in my judgment, forever preclude him from" any position "where
firmness or honesty of purpose is required."[33]

At forty-four he had made mistakes; he was not perfect, nor did he
claim to be, for no man knew and embraced his own faults better than
Rip Ford: the impatience, the compulsive discipline, the strict adherence
to principle (even at the expense of administering justice), and the
restless spirit that would not let him remain very long in any one capacity.
But all in all Ford was a fair and reasonable man and no one ever accused him of hurting others to help himself. He was known for being
generous and dependable.

Malaria was bothering him again in the fall of 1859, so he stayed in
his Austin home reading and resting. One thing he read with a compelling
interest was the newspaper accounts of a Mexican outlaw named Juan
"Cheno" Cortina, whose army of gunmen during the past month had
raided nearly every settlement along the Río Grande from Brownsville
to Laredo.

Since Ford had experience in leading Texas Rangers, the governor
asked him to organize a ranger company and go after Cortina. In October
Captain Ford with a small command of six-month volunteers was on his
way to the Río Grande, where he joined force with a company of United
States regulars under Major Sam Heintzelman. In a wild, running campaign lasting nearly sixty days, the combined forces whipped Cortina in
three straight battles, at Río Grande City (or Davis Ranch), La Bolsa,

[32] *U.S. Senate Exec. Docs.*, 36th Cong., 1st Sess., vol. I, Doc. 2, pp. 588–604; Runnels
to Ford, February 11, 1859, Governors' Letters, ms.; *Texas State Gazette* (Austin), April
30, May 21, 1859; Neighbours, "Robert S. Neighbors in Texas," ms., pp. 563–579.
[33] Neighbors to Denver, February 14, 1859, *U.S. Sen. Exec. Docs.*, 36th Cong., 1st
Sess., vol. I, Doc. 2, p. 604.

thirty-six miles above Matamoros, and La Mesa, about four miles from Agua Negra, Mexico. When Lieutenant Colonel Robert E. Lee's United States cavalry reinforced the Americans, Cortina's band gave up the war and rode away from the border. The Cortina War had cost the United States 95 lives and a half million dollars in destroyed property.[34]

With peace restored to the lower Río Grande country, Ford went to Austin to settle his accounts, then set out for Brownsville, certain that he would "catch hell" for his "non-performance of promise" to meet a "friend" there the week before. Her name was Miss Addie Smith, and she was the daughter of a wealthy border merchant named Elihu Smith. Rip had met her last November when his command had bivouacked in Brownsville a few days before going after Cortina. She was a pretty woman, strong and young—going on twenty-two, she was less than half his age—and as he rode toward Brownsville, thoughts of marriage consumed him.[35]

Ford dated her steadily through the summer and fall of 1860. Then word came of trouble to the north: Austin was in a turmoil over the 1860 presidential elections. Both Republicans and Democrats were holding freedom rallies. A group of fire-eaters headed by Oran M. Roberts, John A. Green, and C. R. Johns were warning that if Lincoln and his sectional party won the election, Texas would secede from the Union. Ford, asking Addie to wait for him, left for Austin at once.

Rip found the capital a scene of feverish activity, for Abraham Lincoln had just been elected President by a largely sectional vote. Up and down the streets marched groups of secessionists waving torches and carrying signs condemning Lincoln and his "abolitionist" government. Ford became immediately an active agitator. With other secessionists he broke up small Unionist meetings and denounced anyone who spoke for moderation. "Me and Old Rip had like to got to fighting the other night," Unionist Aaron Burleson told his cousin on November 19, "and dam him I will whip him if he does attempt to stop me from speaking my sentiments at any place or time in these States God dam him."[36]

"Damn the Union and Lincoln's Black Republicans," chanted hundreds at a secession rally. On the platform Rip Ford spoke wildly in favor

---

[34] *U.S. House Exec. Docs.*, 36th Cong., 1st Sess., Vol. VII, Doc. 52, and Vol. XII, Doc. 81; *U.S. Senate Exec. Docs.*, 36th Cong., 1st Sess., vol. IX, Doc. 21; *Reports of the Committee of Investigation Sent by the Mexican Government to the Frontier of Texas,* pp. 196–197; Webb, *Texas Rangers,* pp. 175–193; J. Fred Rippy, "Border Troubles along the Rio Grande, 1848–1860," *Southwestern Historical Quarterly,* XXIII, 91–111.

[35] Ford to Burleson, Burleson Papers, ms.

[36] A. B. Burleson to Ed Burleson, November 19, 1860, Burleson Papers, ms.

of another Texas Republic, followed by others advocating similar dreams. But over in the capitol, Governor Houston, in the face of state-wide sentiment for secession, still refused to call a convention to consider it, still argued that as loyal Americans who believed in the democratic process, they must all submit to Lincoln's victory at the polls. So secessionists Ford, Roberts, and George Flournoy ignoring law and constitution issued their own call for a convention to assemble at Austin on January 28. Delegates were to be chosen in a special election on January 8.

When word came that towns around the state were flying the Lone Star flag and holding torchlight demonstrations, Ford and friends planned a huge parade in Austin for January 5. At mid-morning it moved off from the capitol, with parade marshal Ford in front on a white stallion, followed by a blaring band, then a long line of carriages full of screeching ladies who waved Lone Star flags, and finally a mass of yipping political leaders and agitators on horseback. Down Congress Avenue went the blatant mob, swinging around the corner to Eighth Street and stopping at last at the intersection of Eighth and Colorado. There, while everyone shouted as loud as they could for a full ten minutes, a color guard ran the Lone Star flag up a 130-foot flagpole especially erected for the occasion.[37]

A few days later, when things had quieted a little, Ford learned from a friend that Cameron County voters had elected him over Judge E. J. Davis as their delegate to the secession convention. The sudden responsibility sobered him. Were he and his friends doing the right thing? He had never really believed in the constitutionality of secession, but he still believed in the right of revolution; and that, he decided, was how Texas must finally justify her course.

When the secession convention assembled, Ford helped get Oran M. Roberts elected president, then made a speech calling for immediate separation but warning in grave tones that war would be the inevitable result. On the convention floor Rip worked with his typical relentless zeal, helped draw up the document that Texans claimed took their state out of the Union. Whatever reservations he had about their action he dismissed when Texas voters overwhelmingly approved the secession ordinance on February 23, when days later Texas became a state in the newly formed Confederacy whose constitutional government guaranteed state supremacy and human bondage.[38]

---

[37] Brown, "Annals of Travis County and of the City of Austin," ms., Chapter XXI, pp. 4–5.

[38] *Ibid.*, Chapter XIII, p. 39; for a detailed description of secessionist activities in

Because of Ford's extensive military experience, Oran Roberts had appointed him to the Committee of Public Safety whose task was to raise an army. Rip had told Roberts that while he appreciated the appointment, it was a desk job: Ford was a soldier and his place was in the field. Presently he had a colonel's commission with orders to raise a cavalry regiment and capture Union forts in the Río Grande valley.

Quickly he raised a command of nearly 500 untrained volunteers and sailed down the coast to land at Brazos de Santiago. After some difficulty, the colonel reached an understanding with the Union commander at Fort Brown who then surrendered all his forts from Brownsville out to El Paso. Ford had just congratulated his men for their bloodless victory when news of Fort Sumter arrived.

War, however, was not Rip's only concern. While in Brownsville, he resumed his courtship of Addie Smith and married her in the Brownsville Presbyterian Church on May 31, 1861. They saw little of each other in the hard war years that followed. With the exception of a brief tour of duty as state conscript commander, Ford spent most of his time in the field fighting Yankees, renegade Comanches, and Mexican outlaws led by his old enemy, "Cheno" Cortina. The colonel also supervised the construction of coastal defenses in the Brownsville area and in the spring of 1862 negotiated a trade agreement with the Mexicans. This agreement was extremely important to the Confederacy, since Matamoros furnished a medium for Confederate-European trade as well as a good market for the sale of cotton and the acquisition of arms and war matériel. If it had not been for Ford's ability to deal with the Mexicans and for the cavalry patrols he detailed to guard the wagon trains that rolled back and forth across the border, the Confederate Trans-Mississippi might have collapsed early in the war.[39]

While Ford was kept incredibly busy, he never forgot his "boys." Whenever he could he took time off from his vortex of paper work and visited the cavalry outposts along the lower Río Grande. Around flickering campfires he sat with lonely pickets sipping coffee and gossiping about a variety of subjects from horses and women to the course of the war. One young picket, Lieutenant Charles L. Martin, recalled that the

---

Austin, see Roberts' notes and journal in the O. M. Roberts Papers; Hughes, "Rip Ford, Texan," ms., pp. 227–263; Anne Irene Sandbo, "The First Session of the Secession Convention of Texas," *Southwestern Historical Quarterly*, XVIII, 162–194; E. W. Winkler (ed.), *Journal of the Secession Convention of Texas, 1861.*

[39] The passages on Rip Ford's activities in the Civil War are based in the main on my article, "John S. Ford: Prudent Cavalryman, C.S.A.," *Southwestern Historical Quarterly,* LXIV, 289–314, which is heavily documented.

colonel treated him "as a father would a son." Several times when Martin had picket duty, Ford spent the night with him in the guard's quarters, thrilling the youth with tales of wild Indian fights. In recounting his military experiences, Old Rip said little about his own ability, gave the credit for victories to the men who served with him. "I never knew a more modest, retiring man," Martin said. Yet "he was a plain, blunt man always speaking what he thought."[40]

Physically, he was the ideal officer, another soldier remembered. He was hard and muscular; his determined walk, his flashing blue eyes, his loud voice personified authority. Beneath his black felt cavalry hat was a face of sober features, with a stubby gray beard that framed his wide chin. He had a smile that radiated strength; this, his optimism, his energy, his gusto and exhilaration aroused in others not envy but a self-confidence that made them aware of their own possibilities. "Ford was idolized by his men," said Captain W. H. D. Carrington. "They knew his bravery and unsleeping vigilance . . . his unyielding perseverance in accomplishing purposes."[41] They loved and respected him too because he made it a point to know the name of every man in his command, he helped them with their personal problems, and he treated a soldier as an individual, a human being, rather than as a military designation without care or feeling.

This was the outer man. Underneath was a tough and calculating soldier, with an almost inhuman drive and endurance, a person even more complex and profound than the polygonal public servant.

Colonel Ford's reward for good work in the Río Grande country was a new assignment. On June 2, 1862, General H. P. Bee appointed him superintendent of conscripts with headquarters at Austin. Ford had little taste for his new job, regarding the draft law as "an unfortunate enactment"; but he suppressed a recurrent desire to resign his post and for over a year discharged his duties faithfully.

He returned to the field in the winter of 1864 to lead a regiment of voluntary cavalry against United States forces that had captured Brownsville, cutting off the all important trade with Mexico, and had pushed deep into the Texas interior. From March 18 to July 30, 1864, Rip Ford's "Cavalry of the West" defeated Federal horsemen and their Mexican allies in a series of skirmishes, driving them from Laredo through Ringgold Barracks, Rancho Las Rucias, Brownsville, Palmito Ranch, and

[40] Charles L. Martin, "The Last of the Ranger Chieftains," *The Texas Magazine*, IV, 38–39.
[41] Carrington's statement in John Henry Brown, *History of Texas From 1685 to 1892*, II, 432–435.

onto Brazos Island. To the war-weary people of that region Ford became a "demi-god, the very incarnation of the war."[42] In token of their appreciation for gallant work, a group of Brownsville ladies presented the colonel with a silk flag. Admiring the symbolic gift, he assured them that it would be "upheld by the expeditionary forces as long as human endurance can allow a stout arm to wield a keen blade."[43]

That evening Ford collapsed, wasted and emaciated from a burning fever that had plagued him since the opening of the campaign. It was malaria again. Somehow his wife found out he was sick and with their baby daughter (who had been born on August 15, 1862) came to Brownsville to take care of him. In the weeks that followed Ford under Addie's care gradually recovered; but what probably helped more than anything to restore him was the unexpected announcement that his wife was pregnant (in a few months she would have another girl whom they named Addie, thus increasing Rip's family to three daughters—including the one by his first wife, Fannie, who the year before had married a Mr. Thomas in Austin). The last of August, 1864, Ford declared himself fit for duty and, in a flurry, was off to negotiate with Emperor Maximilian's French army that had landed at the mouth of the Río Grande a few days before.

The French and the colonel were quite soon on cordial terms, although he knew they were in Mexico for reasons other than to collect old debts. At the same time the Federals, never forgetting the Monroe Doctrine, sided with Benito Juárez' Republican government and, as rumor had it, even offered Cheno Cortina (now one of Juárez' respectable generals) a brigadier general's commission in the United States Army.

Ford returned to Brownsville a harried man. His district, once an area of bush league skirmishing, had now become a strategic theater in which a war involving four armies was a real possibility. Yet, except for a brief engagement south of the border in which the French defeated Cortina and captured Matamoros (September 29, 1864), the armies in the lower Río Grande country lived in peaceful coexistence until May 13, 1865, when the last land battle in the Confederacy was fought at Palmito Ranch several miles down the river from Brownsville. Colonel Ford's Confederate force of some 1,300 engaged a Federal column of about the same number in the thickets above the ranch, driving them back to Brazos Island in wild, running fight. From a prisoner Ford learned the next day that General Lee had surrendered over a month before at Ap-

---

42 *Ibid.*
43 Ford to H. P. Bee, September 21, 1864, John S. Ford, Letter Books, III, 81.

pomattox. Rip said the news struck him like a phsyical blow. Lee's surrender forced him to face something he'd known for many months but could not bring himself to acknowledge: the South was not indomitable, the cause was not eternal, the Confederacy was dead. Yet to John Salmon Ford and thousands of other loyal Southerners the Confederacy never really died for it was something more than a government or an army: it symbolized a way of life that must continue even though the machinery that made it tangible had been destroyed.

A few days after Palmito Ranch, Ford and his Texans, looking forward to civilian life with soft beds, good cooking, and honest work, rode north across the brush toward Brownsville.

Ford was sick again. This time it was pneumonia, brought on by the privation, fatigue, and exposure endured in the field during the past few years. He had no money for medicine or for food. And Addie was pregnant again.

Fearing that the Federals might persecute them, the Fords crossed the Río Grande and purchased a small shack on the edge of Matamoros. In a few days a Federal officer came to visit Ford. The officer, assuring Rip that President Johnson had no intention of persecuting loyal Confederates, asked him to help persuade ex-Confederates in Matamoros to accept amnesty pardons and return home. Ford said he bore the United States no malice and agreed to help. A few days later General Frederick Steele heard about Ford's promise and made him a parole commissioner. While gravely ill Rip Ford did more than any other man to get the Texas Río Grande country started on the long road to recovery.[44]

In the spring of 1866 Ford felt well enough to help his old friend José M. J. Carbajal drive Maximilian's French troops from Matamoros. Carbajal then proclaimed himself military governor under authority of Benito Juárez and made Ford a brigadier general. Rip stayed in Matamoros for several months until malaria compelled him to go to Brownsville, where his family, including a new baby boy, John William, was now living.

Sick as he was, Ford refused to go to bed and went out looking for a job. His friends helped all they could. Somers Kinney made him assistant editor of the Brownsville *Ranchero*, but Rip had so little energy, so little desire to write anymore that he quit, knowing he was more a hindrance than a help. The need for money, however, forced him into journalism again, this time as a writer for the Brownsville *Courier*. Ignoring the

---

[44] Hughes, "Rip Ford, Texan," ms., pp. 343–350; Lea, *The King Ranch*, I, pp. 175–236.

fever, he then took on the added burden of serving on the 1867–1868 grand jury. He kept up this pace for several months before collapsing again. Still he would not go to bed. He slouched around the *Courier* office only a shadow of the former man of causes, and the paper finally had to dismiss him. Only then did he agree to go to bed. For the Fords the outlook had never been gloomier, for they had no money at all, not even for the rent.

Though Ford was too proud to ask them, his friends helped again. One day the banker called to tell the invalid colonel that a handsome sum of money had been deposited in the bank for him. Ford never found out who the benefactor was, never knew that a rancher of means, Richard King, had not forgotten the kindness his old commander had showed him during the late war.[45]

By the fall of 1868 Rip felt strong enough to organize with J. E. Dougherty a pro-Democratic paper called the Brownsville *Sentinel*. Ford's editorials in it were simple and provocative, but gone was the vigor of old.

By 1869 he had fully recovered. To prove it he served as guide for a cavalry force that rode up the Río Grande to apprehend a gang of cattle rustlers. When he returned home, he found a man in the living room who introduced himself as Mr. Champini, a goat rancher. During the past five years, Champini complained, Mexican outlaws had robbed him of 150 goats, and he wanted Ford to present his case before a congressional committee that had come to Brownsville to review indemnification claims for stolen property. Ford agreed to help. At the hearing the next day, Rip, according to Champini's instructions, sought payment not only for the stolen goats but also for what might have been their natural increase over the past five years. The committeemen were aghast. No one knew how fast goats reproduced. But Ford, loyal to his new friend, got some ranchers to help him derive a formula that would measure the reproduction expectancy of goats. After explaining the formula to the amazed committeemen, Ford began his calculations. He figured and figured, paused to scratch his head, then figured some more. "Damn the goats!" he cried. "They seem to me to multiply in the most unreasonable way. Let me see. A goat has three kids in March and two in September. Then the March kids have young when they are eighteen months old, and by that time—well, in short, I make it two million five hundred and twenty-one thousand and eighteen goats. The Lord help us!" he said looking helplessly at the committee chairman. "If figures don't lie, and

[45] San Antonio *Express*, April 15, 1885.

the goat business ain't stopped, in ten years, sir, Texas won't hold her goats."

Outside the door an old German farmer, who an hour before had collected for five stolen mules, listened intently to what Ford had to say, then burst into the room, pointing a gnarled finger at the committee. "Schentlemens, I vants natural ingresse on mine mooles, by tam! It vas not fair to giff ingresse on der goats, and not on der mooles. I vants dot schentlemans vot gounted der goats to poot some of dot figuring on mine mooles."

At that, the committee gave Champini credit for exactly 150 goats and quit for the day.[46]

In the spring of 1872 Ford became increasingly interested in politics, spent more time writing anti-Republican editorials for the *Sentinel*. As a reward for his efforts, south Texas Democrats chose him as a delegate to the Democratic National Convention that assembled in Baltimore on July 9. Ford returned to Brownsville highly irritated at the hard-put Democrats for endorsing Liberal Republican Horace Greeley; the more he thought about it the madder he became; and vowing he was through with politics, he took a position as cattle and hide inspector for Cameron County. In Rip's opinion, the party of democracy was dead.

The state party, however, proved to be more alive than ever. Although Grant won the presidency that November, the well-oiled Democratic machine in Texas carried the state solidly for Greeley and elected most of the members to the Thirteenth Legislature. Then moving at top speed the Democrats entered Richard Coke as their candidate for the crucial 1873 governor's race and started campaigning. They must defeat incumbent E. J. Davis or Texas might be doomed to the Republican-military coalition that had governed the state since the end of the war. The Republicans campaigned fiercely for their candidate, Davis, but they were so unpopular that Coke won in December by a majority of two to one.

Davis, however, wasn't giving up that easily. He promptly entrenched Negro militia units outside the statehouse and, insisting that the election was illegal because the polls had remained open for only three days instead of the four required by the constitution of 1869, called on President Grant to invalidate the election returns. Grant refused but Davis still wouldn't quit.

Sensing a fight, Ford, who had supported Coke editorially in the Brownsville *Sentinel*, left for Austin at once. There he found a crisis

---

[46] Alex E. Sweet and J. Armoy Knox, *On A Mexican Mustang through Texas: From the Gulf to the Rio Grande*, pp. 550–551.

almost as foreboding as the secession movement of a decade before. Talk of civil war between Coke and Davis was in the air. When Ford volunteered his services for the Democrats, speaker of the house Guy M. Bryan promptly appointed him, along with several others, sergeant-at-arms to protect Coke and his government. Ford then joined Henry E. McCulloch and William P. Hardeman in calling out the Travis Rifles, a white militia outfit that had the best marksmen in the county. The organization had been formed back in 1852 and Ford had been its first commander. Singing the "Yellow Rose of Texas," the Rifles with Old Rip in front marched up to the statehouse and, to the Republicans' horror, offered their services to Coke, who then warned Davis that while the Democrats wanted to settle this thing peacefully they would not hesitate to meet force with force.

Meanwhile Ford was having trouble. His men, recalling the humiliating years they had been without political rights, were spoiling for a fight. But they quieted when Ford threatened personally to thrash the first man who stepped out of line. Twice he prevented his men from firing on the Negro militia. Governor Coke remarked later that Old Rip's control over the Rifles had probably prevented another civil war. Until January 23, when Davis finally gave up the governorship and went home, Ford never left the capitol, spending the nights on a straw couch in the executive office.[47]

After San Jacinto Day celebrations on April 21, 1874, Ford went back to Brownsville. He soon discovered that he was one of the most popular men in the town. Without campaigning, he was elected mayor almost by acclamation. The year term passed with speed although without incident. After that Ford made some extra money as official translator of Spanish documents for the eastern district court. At the same time he investigated the state of border crime for the Legislature and made reports suggesting various ways of coping with frontier violence—a much larger ranger service for one thing.

At length Cameron and neighboring counties chose Ford to represent them in the Constitutional Convention of 1875. After the constitution was finished and adopted, he went back to Brownsville and campaigned for senator. He won with one of the largest majorities in the history of

---

[47] O. M. Roberts, "The Political, Legislative, and Judicial History of Texas for Its Fifty Years of Statehood, 1845–1895," in Dudley G. Wooten (ed.), *A Comprehensive History of Texas*, II, 201–209; Hughes, "Rip Ford, Texan," ms., pp. 349–357; T. B. Wheeler, "Reminiscences of Reconstruction in Texas," *Quarterly of the Texas State Historical Association*, XI, 56–65; George W. Paschal, *A Digest of the Laws of Texas*, II, 1393i–1393k.

the Twenty-Ninth District. As senator, Rip Ford worked hard for a more efficient police force and for more and better public schools.

When his senate term was over, Rip accepted an appointment as super-intendent of the Deaf and Dumb Institute in Austin. Managing it from September 1879 to December 1883, he made it a school rather than an asylum for illiterate handicaps. He revised the curriculum, introduced the teaching of trade skills such as shoemaking and bookbinding. In time he conducted a crack typography course and this led to the institute's own newspaper, the *Texas Mute Ranger*, for which Ford wrote a num-ber of historical articles and lively editorials on current political issues. He came to love his work at the institute more than anything he had ever done, taking great pride in the rapid progress his pupils were making.

One day he collapsed with fever. It was an ominous sign. Ford himself diagnosed it as the old malaria. Soon he was so sick that he had to resign his position at the institute. It was, he declared, the last public office he would ever hold.[48]

During the Christmas season 1883 Ford realized, perhaps for the first time, that he was an old man, going on sixty-nine now, and what was worse, he was an old man without money and without land: the two most important things in life to an American in the 1880's. "Improvidence, and the want of a proper appreciation of the value of land acquired by toil," Ford wrote in 1886, "were the prime causes of [my] failure to become, eventually, the possessor of a moderate fortune."

In January 1884 Rip, feeling considerably better, moved his family to San Antonio. In those days the Alamo city was full of prominent Texans who had come there to retire. Ford, however, did not go there to retire: he went there to promote Texas history and in a few years he became one of the leading historians in the state. He joined the Alamo Associa-tion and in 1894 wrote an excellent little study entitled *The Origin and Fall of the Alamo*; for newspapers over the state he wrote a number of historical articles covering topics from the feats of Texas Rangers to the battle of Palmito Ranch; he spent countless hours in local coffee houses talking "shop" with other history buffs.

Since he had been involved, in one way or another, in every historical event in Texas since 1836, a number of writers prevailed on him for information and contribution. One of the first was young James De Shields who was preparing a book on Indian warfare in Texas. He and Ford corresponded for many years, exchanging notes and points of view,

---

[48] Hughes, "Rip Ford, Texan," ms., pp. 357–367; John S. Ford, *Annual Reports of the Superintendent of the Texas Institution for the Deaf and Dumb, 1879–1883*.

and Ford wrote for De Shield's book a short account of the Taylor Indian fight of 1831.[49]

In 1894 Colonel W. H. King sought Rip's help in writing a section on the Texas Rangers for Dudley G. Wooten's projected comprehensive history of Texas. After Ford had related his ranger experiences, King noted that the old soldier at seventy-nine still had "an active mind and a fair share of physical vigor; and though lacking worldly wealth and official station, he is held in deserved esteem by those who value life-long devotion and able service to the State, and who appreciate modesty, manliness, and uprightness in public and private life."[50]

One day Oran Roberts who was also promoting Texas history came to see Ford. As the two old friends sipped coffee and reminisced together, Roberts told how he was engaged in half a dozen different enterprises; the most difficult ones were a section on Texas during the Civil War and another on Texas judicial development for Wooten's history, and a comprehensive study of Texas in the Civil War for Clement Evans' multivolume Confederate military history. Ford told Roberts all he knew about these topics, then opened his massive note files for his friend to look through. Ford also wrote an account of the battle of Palmito Ranch which Roberts included in his study for Evans' history.[51]

In 1896 author-painter Frederic Remington, out collecting information on the Texas Rangers for *Harper's New Monthly Magazine*, came to interview Ford as "one of the old originals." Remington found Rip "a very old man, with a wealth of snow-white hair and beard—bent, but not withered."

For hours Ford captivated his visitor with harrowing tales about Indian fights, the Mexican War, and frontier gun battles.

"I suppose, Colonel," Remington interrupted at one point, "you have been charged by a Mexican lancer?"

"Oh yes, many times," Ford replied.

"What did you generally do?"

"Well—you see," Ford said with a wink, "I reckoned to be able to hit a man every time with a six-shooter at one hundred and twenty-five yards."

And that, Remington reflected, no doubt meant many dead lancers.

---

[49] W. T. Davidson to Ford, March 2, 1887, John S. Ford Papers, ms.; James T. De Shields, *Border Wars of Texas*, pp. 141–143.

[50] W. H. King, "The Texas Ranger Service and History of the Rangers, with Observations on Their Value as a Police Protection," in Wooten (ed.), *Comprehensive History of Texas*, II, 338.

[51] O. M. Roberts, "Texas," *Confederate Military History*, XI, 126–129.

"Then you do not think much of a lance as a weapon," he continued.

"No; there is but one weapon. The six-shooter when properly handled is the only weapon—mind you sir, I say *properly*."

Then Ford with great excitement related the details of the 1858 Canadian River campaign; and when the interview was over, Remington went away assured that old Ford could "tell you stories that will make your eyes hang out on your shirt front."[52]

For nearly forty years Ford had been interested in a state historical association. Back in 1856 he had tried but failed to organize a historical group that would "preserve records that otherwise may be lost";[53] again in 1874 Rip and a number of "Old Texians" founded an association but it collapsed in a few months because of the lack of funds; and with that most everybody agreed that Texas simply wasn't "history minded."

Then in February 1897 Ford received an invitation to attend a meeting in Austin whose purpose was to organize a state historical association. With some reservations about the success of the project, Ford went to the meeting. Soon he was laughing with everyone else at Roberts' ludicrous anecdotes about Thomas J. Rusk and, in general, was having a great time talking history until the Constitutional Committee announced that it planned to make no distinction between members and lady members in the constitution.

Ford stood up and shouted that there had better be a distinction. Refusal to do so was disgraceful—another victory for that abortive campaign to secure the female equality with the male. The committee, however, was recalcitrant. So Ford, banging his cane on the floor, told the committee what it could do and stalked out of the meeting. The next day Dudley Wooten and University of Texas Professor George P. Garrison went up to Ford's hotel room and told Rip that his support was vital to the success of the association. Wooten and Garrison left with no idea whether Ford would cooperate and told the executive council as much.

Several days later Roberts received a note:

I anticipate remaining with the "Texas Historical Society" as long as I can do anything to promote the interests of Texas history.

John S. Ford

The executive council promptly elected Rip an honorary life member; and a few days later Ford submitted to George Garrison a short article entitled "Fight on the Frio, July 4, 1865," which was later published in

---

[52] Frederic Remington, "How the Law Got into the Chaparral," *Harper's New Monthly Magazine*, XCIV, 60–65.

[53] *Texas State Times* (Austin), September 20, 1856.

the second issue of the *Quarterly of the Texas State Historical Association.*[54]

Back in 1856 Ford had written that "it is very important that a contemporary historian take up his pen and record things known by living participants that future historians would not know about."[55] In 1885 Ford took up his pen to write an ambitious history of Texas covering everything of importance that happened between 1836 and 1886. He asked a number of prominent Texans to send him information on their personal and public lives; he traveled around the state collecting records and conducting interviews; he even wrote Washington for duplicates of United States Army reports and correspondence during the Mexican War, the Cortina War, and the Civil War; and then, integrating these with his own personal notes and reminiscences, Ford began writing a sweeping, eyewitness account of a most exciting span of Texas history. Having completed nearly 600 pages by April, 1887, he started looking for a publisher and called on potential readers to subscribe for advance copies of what he called: "Memoirs of John S. Ford, and Reminiscences of Texas History, Civil, Military and Personal, Ranging from 1836 to 1886." For some reason he found no publisher, but he apparently got enough money from loyal backers to keep on writing. By the late summer of 1897 he had brought the story down through the Civil War and Reconstruction periods and had written an account of the King and Kenedy enterprises in South Texas. It appears that most of the latter information he dictated to an adopted daughter, Lily, whom Rip and Addie had gotten through common-law adoption and had raised as their own.

Ford got no further with his story. That October he suffered a severe stroke. For weeks he was in a coma and then, late in the evening on November 3, 1897, he died. In a brief ceremony attended by his wife and daughters and a few old friends, Ford was buried beside the San Antonio River.

Staring at the fresh grave, a ranger friend thought: "He rests by the bright waters of the San Antonio in the bosom of his loved Texas, and 'after life's fitful fever' he sleeps well, the perfect ending of the good man."[56]

Gone now, said the Austin *Daily Statesman*, was "the last of the ranger

---

54 Ford to Roberts, March 20, 1897, Roberts Papers, ms., Scrapbook I; "The Organization and Objectives of the Texas State Historical Association," *Quarterly of the Texas State Historical Association,* I, 1–17; Bride Neill Taylor, "The Beginnings of the State Historical Association," *Southwestern Historical Quarterly,* XXXIII, 1–17.

55 *Texas State Times* (Austin), September 20, 1856.

56 Martin, "Last of the Ranger Chieftains," *The Texas Magazine,* IV, 41.

chieftains whose name for nearly half a century has been a household word in Texas."[57]

Just before he died, Ford wrote Oran M. Roberts:

The proper history of Texas is yet unpublished. The men who enacted the great deeds, rendering the Lone Star Republic famous, have generally died without writing what they aided in doing. . . . Where is the historian who lived in those days of trouble and danger? . . .

The Texians have proved themselves good soldiers. If we look at their utter neglect to record what they have done in war, and in the matter of legislation, we must conclude they are not willing writers.[58]

Here, in the pages that follow, are the memoirs of a historian who lived in those times of trouble and danger—a willing writer, an able journalist whose narrative is distinguished for its simplicity of style and dignity of purpose; a story often sad, often ludicrous, always glowing with warmth and humanity; a history that provides a graphic sweep of virtually every significant military and political event in Texas for a full half century.

---

[57] Austin *Daily Statesman*, November 4, November 7, 1897.
[58] Ford to Roberts, March 20, 1897, Roberts Papers, ms.

MEMOIRS OF JOHN S. FORD, FROM 1836 TO 1886.

The undersigned, with the view of assisting in the collection and preservation of data to be used in writing a correct and comprehensive history of Texas, has prepared a manuscript, at considerable labor and some cost, with the intention of publishing a work to be entitled:

"MEMOIRS OF JOHN S. FORD, AND REMINISCENCES OF TEXAS HISTORY, CIVIL, MILITARY AND PERSONAL, RANGING FROM 1836 TO 1886."

The style is unpretentious; the design being only to state facts, and to contribute to the truth of history without being biased by prejudice, malice, partisan or personal enmity. The writer has aimed to do justice to every person mentioned, to describe the situation, and let the reader draw his own conclusions, and to steer clear of unseemly egotism inducing many to write themselves down as heroes. Incidents are presented to illustrate the traits of character of distinguished persons in connection with important events.

Campaigns against Indians and Mexicans, scouts, battles, peace-talks, sketches of pioneer life, have been introduced to give an idea of the toils, privations and loss of life incurred to place Texas in the proud position she occupies now. Notices of leading Texians have been made. Political affairs have received attention, particularly the causes and action culminating in the annexation of Texas to the United States. Mexico was a valueless cipher. We feared England and France.

In short, the writer has been actuated by the laudable ambition to get up a book which every Texian can read with pleasure and profit. He has not confined himself to the insipid details of the every-day life and doings of an ordinary individual, but has left them to the "snapper-up of unconsidered trifles."

The part ready for publication comes down to the year 1860 It will make a volume of more than five hundred octavo pages, according to the calculation of printers. The purpose is to use good paper and leather binding. The price is five dollars.

The undersigned asks the indulgence and the confidence of his friends and the public in the matter of subscribing for the first volume, and paying in advance, in order to enable him to pay for printing the same. He feels sure he will give each subscriber the worth of his money.

The following gentlemen have spoken in commendation of the work:

EX-GOV. O. M. ROBERTS, Austin.　　　　GEN. W. H. YOUNG, San Antonio.
HON, THOMAS J. DEVINE, San Antonio.　　MAJ. JOHN A. GREEN, San Antonio.
COL. H. C. KING, San Antonio.　　　　　GEN. W. H. KING, Austin.
CHARLES W. OGDEN, ESQ., San Antonio.　　DR. R M. SWEARINGEN, Austin.
COL. H. F. YOUNG, San Antonio.　　　　REV. DR. R. K. SMOOT, Austin.
GEN. H. P. BEE, San Antonio.

JOHN S. FORD.

SAN ANTONIO, APRIL, 1887.

SUBSCRIPTION.

NAME	POST OFFICE	AMOUNT

PROSPECTUS FOR FORD'S MEMOIRS
Courtesy of Texas State Library, Archives Division

RIP FORD'S TEXAS

Prologue

I

>>>

MY FIGHTING STOCK

The Fords came to the new world at a rather early date. They settled in Virginia, New Jersey, and Maryland, if reports be true. John Ford, the writer's grandfather, emigrated to South Carolina from Virginia during the days of British rule. He was a major in the service of the United States during the Revolutionary War. He was in many battles, and escaped without any serious hurt. At the siege of Savannah, Georgia, by the Americans under General [Benjamin] Lincoln, he was much exposed. Ford visited home shortly afterward, and his wife said he had more than twenty bullet holes in his clothing. Some balls had grazed and discolored the skin, but not one had entered the flesh. The French and Americans assaulted the British works on October 9, 1779, and were repulsed. The French loss was six hundred —the Americans lost four hundred. At the battle of Camden on August 16, 1780, John Ford is said to have made many narrow escapes.

George Salmon, the father of the writer's mother, was attached to the commissary department during the Revolutionary War. He had the small-pox in 1780, and was sent out of camp. On his return he was captured by the British and was in [Major Patrick] Ferguson's camp on King's Mountain when the Americans attacked it on October 7, 1780. Salmon described the battle very vividly. When the fire became hot the British soldiers sought shelter wherever they could. So many got behind wagons that they overturned them. He said wagons had wooden covers in those days. The firing had grown terrific. Confusion prevailed generally. He approached the officer in charge of the guard and asked: "Am I to stand here, and be killed by my own people?"

The officer replied, adding an oath: "Every man must take care of himself now."

Salmon ran down the mountain. The first man he met was an American captain, an old acquaintance. His salutation was: "My God, Salmon, have you turned Tory?"

"No, I am just escaping from the British," was the reply.

George Salmon's wife, Elizabeth Young, was then a young girl of about sixteen. She was staying with an uncle. The British came and encamped on the plantation. The ladies retired into a room, and closed the door. Major Ferguson occupied a room across a hall.

He came to our door [Elizabeth Young recalled] and said: "Ladies, you may open your door. I am a gentleman, and will see you are not molested." We opened the door. The major came in and was seated. He entered into conversation, and asked me: "My daughter, where is your uncle?"

"In the Whigs' camp, sir."

"If he had as much sense as you have he would not be there, would he?"

"I think he would, sir."

He then began telling us that he was in the habit of fooling the rebels, that in action he wore a short coat and acted with his sword in his left hand. "They have wounded me eleven times, but can't kill me." I was told that it was the method our officers adopted to distinguish them from the enemy while in battle. Soon after the British left, an American scouting party came along. They were informed of the boasts of Major Ferguson. I was told that our troops made it a point to fire at the British officer carrying his sword in his left hand.

The major's ruse failed that time: he was killed—almost his whole army killed or captured. One thousand one hundred and ninety-eight constituted the British loss—American loss, eighty-eight.

Major John Ford had his plantation and house robbed by a band of Tories. They carried off the clothing of an infant child. One of his neighbors, whose name will not be repeated, headed the infamous expedition. Ford swore vengeance. He obtained a furlough, learned the Tory was at his house, armed himself, and was in the Tory's room before he took the alarm. The leader of robbers was taking his supper with his gun across his lap. It was now useless. An attempt to raise it would have invited instant death. Ford told him of his crime, perpetrated upon innocent women and children, and that he had come to kill him. Ford struck him on the head with his sword. The Tory's wife was aroused. She screamed, and begged so piteously for her husband's life that Ford relented, telling the cowardly thief he could go.

The reader will say: "What do you mean by introducing these old things?" Simply this: when one comes of fighting stock, he has a right to be proud of it.

2

The writer's great grandfather, by the mother's side, was in the employ of Lord Fairfax of Virginia at the same time Washington was. Our grandmother saw the great man on many occasions. She said he was tall, and had a commanding presence. "He was the finest looking man I ever saw," were her words. She was also acquainted with General [Francis] Marion. She described him as a rather small man, with a French cast of features. He was simple in his manners, blessed with good sense and a sound judgment. She heard him relate, long before it appeared in print, the incident of asking the British officer to dine with him and having nothing but sweet potatoes to set before the military representative of Great Britain.

She spoke of Colonel [Peter] Horry, one of General Marion's favorite officers. The colonel stuttered, and this sometimes led to ludicrous scenes. He furnished data to write the life of General Marion, and confided the execution of the work to Reverend Mason L. Weems, a Baptist preacher. Horry is said not to have liked the rather grandiloquent and sensational style of the reverend gentleman, and charged him with having made a "Noh-noh-novel of muh-muh my buh-buh-book."

In 1781 or 1782 the Indians and Tories made a descent upon the country adjacent to Greenville Courthouse, South Carolina. They killed the writer's great grandmother by the father's side. They were very old. Their cold-blooded slayers placed the muzzles of their guns against their heads, and blew their brains out. The holes were reported to have been as large as one's fist.

A Tory named Bates, a leader in these sanguinary operations, went to the house of a gentleman named Motlow, and murdered his wife and children, Motlow not being at home. The Tories afterwards managed to capture him. He was undaunted and ready to meet the fate seemingly in store for him. Bates began plundering his person. He was stooping down taking the buckles of his prisoner's shoes. Motlow said: "Bates, can't you wait until after you have killed me before you rob me?" Just at that moment a gun was fired. The ball passed through Motlow's body; he fell upon Bates. The latter raised himself up, and placed Motlow on his feet again. Motlow ran, and was pursued some distance. The blood was gushing from his wound. He held his arms over his breast and endeavored to staunch the flow. He reached a precipice on a stream, made a leap, alighted unhurt, and escaped. His bloodthirsty pursuers did not dare to make the effort he had; they halted. Motlow recovered from his wound.

Some years after the close of the war, a man was put in jail at Greenville Courthouse for horse stealing. Someone told Motlow the description suited that of Bates. Motlow armed himself, went to the jail, demanded the keys, and obtained them. Finding the prisoner to be Bates, Motlow carried him out on the public square and shot him. Such was the infamous reputation of Bates, the red-handed assassin, and such the state of feeling in the community that no one dared to interfere with Motlow while enacting the tragedy or to call him to account for it. They felt that a just retribution had overtaken a bloody fiend.

It was during one of these raids of Indians and Tories that our grandfather, George Salmon, piloted a party of men to a store which the Indians had robbed. They were on a big spree, and could have been whipped easily. The men did not wish to attack. While Salmon was endeavoring to persuade them to fight, an Indian shot him through the body. He said that to cleanse the wound a silk handkerchief was passed through it from side to side several times. He lived to do good service afterward.

3

After the close of the war, John Ford was engaged in the practice of law in Greenville and was elevated to the bench. He died at forty-five years of age from a disease of the lungs brought on by a severe cold contracted during the war. Ford left several children. His son, William, born in 1785, was an honest man, always candid in his expressions of opinion, and fearless of consequences. He married Harriet Salmon, by whom he had children, all of whom died in early life, except Elizabeth and the writer, John Salmon Ford. The latter was born in Greenville District, South Carolina, May 26, 1815. William Ford immigrated to Lincoln

County, Tennessee, in 1817. He went to Texas after annexation, where he died at the age of eighty-two in Travis County in 1867.

John Salmon Ford, at an early period of existence, exhibited some marked and rather positive traits of character. He possessed the capacity to get into fights with the boys, to fall in love with the girls, and to take a hand in the deviltry set on foot by his playmates. The old ladies of his neighborhood looked upon him as a sort of prodigy, and predicted he would be killed for his general "cussedness" before reaching the age of maturity, or hanged for some infernal mischief he might commit.

In 1834, while reading medicine under Dr. James G. Barksdale of Shelbyville, Bedford County, Tennessee, Ford volunteered to wait upon his friend, Wilkins Blanton, who had contracted smallpox in a virulent form. He was eventually sent outside of town to a small house. One of the attendants, an old darky, died of the disease. Blanton recovered. The young pill peddler got his name in the newspapers.

4

The war of Texas independence commenced in the fall of 1835. The capture of San Antonio gave to the Texians a fame for gallantry, and caused many men in the United States to turn longing eyes towards the new land of promise. Many young men aspired to take part in a struggle which appeared to involve all the principles for which our forefathers fought in the revolution of 1776. During the early part of 1836, Ford penned an address to the public which was distributed in handbills and otherwise. The result of this address was that a number of men volunteered to go to Texas.

In those days a journey to Texas seemed to be a perilous undertaking. It was bidding adieu to the rest of the world and, under existing circumstances, volunteering in a war of desperate chances. All knew less than 100,000 people had thrown down the gauntlet to a nation of 8,000,000 souls. The fall of the Alamo on March 6, 1836, the surrender of [James W.] Fannin a few days after, and the inhuman butchery of prisoners of war, occurring by order of General Santa Anna at Goliad on March 27, 1836, left no doubt of the character of the warfare waged upon the Texians by the government of Mexico. These events shocked the civilized world, and deterred many from joining the Texas revolutionists. Others felt differently; they conceived it a bounded duty to aid those who were battling for the cause of constitutional government, for the rights of man, for liberty. They stepped to the front, determined to avenge their slaughtered brethren, to accept the alternative of victory or death. For such it literally was. The black flag of Santa Anna—the insignia of no quarter—told the tale. None but stout-hearted men were likely to take service in a cause surrounded by so many fatal risks.

Preparations were being made to complete the organization and equipment of the company. The day of starting was under discussion when the whole country was electrified by the news of the victory of San Jacinto on April 21, 1836. Ford gave up his intention of running for captain under the impression that the fighting was over, and left for Texas, where he arrived in June, 1836, [and settled in San Augustine]. A gentleman named [George W.] Jewell was elected captain. The company reached Texas and served on the Trinity River against the Indians.

1 *The Wilderness*

II

>>

OLD TEXIANS

San Augustine, a town in the county of the same name, stands in the "Redlands"—so called from the color of the soil. Around San Augustine many former residents of the state of Tennessee had settled. They were men of respectability and influence, and had taken an active part in the war against Mexico. Captain William Kimbro commanded a company at the battle of San Jacinto. Dr. Joseph Rowe was a prominent actor in affairs. The Holmans were men of intelligence, and had much to do in the shaping of public opinion. The Burdetts, the Paynes, and last though not least, the Greers, were among the leading men of that section. The list might be extended, and would include many others of equal worth.

General Sam Houston stopped on the "Redlands." His home had been at San Augustine. Houston was on his way from New Orleans whither he had gone to have the wound received at San Jacinto treated. His wound was on the ankle. It was still unhealed. It was dressed while he was at Natchitoches by Dr. [Robert Anderson] Irion, who was later General Houston's secretary of state during his first presidency.

Houston was then a splendid specimen of manhood. A form and features which would have adorned the walks of royalty, a fund of conversational powers almost unequalled, the matchless gift of oratory, a vast grasp of intellect—all marked him a great man.

General Houston accepted the hospitality of Elisha Roberts and of his son-in-law, Colonel Philip Sublett. The latter commanded the Texians at the "Grass Fight," which came off near San Antonio in 1835 and was one of the hardest contested affairs of the war.

It was arranged to have General Houston meet his friends at San Augustine on the fourth of July, 1836. It was a joyous reunion. The fearless pioneers, who had left home and kindred and all their attendant attractions to aid in reclaiming a vast and fertile empire from the predominance of Indians, came together to salute their friend, the successful leader of a revolution, with the laurels of San Jacinto fresh upon his brow. Honest and stout hands were clasped, and true hearts thrilled in response to the promptings of sincere friendship. It was a scene one could never forget.

The gentleman chosen to welcome the general was Colonel Jonas Harrison, long and familiarly called "Old Jonas Harrison, the Hunter." Memory paints him now as he stood in his brown, home-spun clothes, slouched hat, and coarse boots, to receive the Washington of Texas. The mental question was "Old chap, what can you say worthy of this memorable occasion?" He drew himself up to his full height, and in a short address combined eloquence and logic so deftly and ably that all were assured a master stood before them.

General Houston replied in his happiest manner. The two held the audience entranced, unconscious of aught save the enthusiasm engendered by their burning words. At this moment when more than fifty years have been measured upon the sundial of time, the grand Old Hunter looms up before the mind's eye as the equal, if not the superior, of General Houston in oratory. A few months thereafter a mighty mind was eclipsed, a gifted tongue silenced in death; the man of the people was gathered to his fathers. Few of this day know of him.

In the assembly which greeted General Houston were men of note. Colonel James Bullock who commanded the Texians in 1832, when they expelled the Mexican troops under Colonel [José de las] Piedras from Nacogdoches, and Colonel Alexander Horton, one of General Houston's aides at San Jacinto, were there. One splendid old soldier must not be omitted: Donald McDonald was captain of a company, on the British side, at the battle of Lundy's Lane [during the War of 1812]. He went into the fight with eighty odd men and came out with fifteen. Colonel S. W. Blount, a signer of the Texas Declaration of Independence, was also present, if memory is not at fault.

These gentlemen of eastern Texas are mentioned to show the kind of men constituting the class since called "Old Texians." A more candid, friendly, and hospitable population never occupied any country. A stranger was not allowed to pass a house without being invited to stop. No difference how long a guest remained, provided he minded his own business, he was entertained free of cost. If he asked for his bill, he was told a repetition of the inquiry would be taken as an insult. The coffee pot was on the fire at nearly every house in the country from daylight till bedtime. A visitor was invited to take a cup—a refusal was not taken in good part.

Energy, bravery, a practical view of all matters, self-reliance, moderation, and a disposition to act in concert with their fellow citizens were the characteristics of the early settlers. Danger menaced them unceasingly, rendered them cautious, and moulded them into soldiers. Having to take care of themselves gave them an idea of what their far-off neighbors needed to make them comfortable and to protect them. Thus they acquired correct ideas of what was necessary to preserve order and give adequate protection to person and property. Many of those common-sense men rose to the full height of soldiers, legislators, and statesmen.

2

In the winter of 1836 or the spring of 1837, a Sunday School was instituted at San Augustine. The writer was one of the teachers. The wife of Christopher Dast was one of the principal agents in setting the school on foot.

During the fall of 1838 a Thespian Corps was organized in San Augustine. It included members who would have sustained a good reputation as actors upon any stage. W. W. Parker, the editor of the Red-Lander, the pioneer newspaper of the place, was a gentleman of fine appearance. He was said to resemble the actor Edwin Forrest. Parker had a fine voice, and his conception of a character was usually just. His forte was in tragedy and melodrama. He possessed ability as a writer, was a genial companion. His views were liberal and comprehensive. He died young, in 1841, if memory is not amiss.

Harry Richardson was good in tragedy and genteel comedy. He was good looking, generous, and manly. His delivery was excellent and earnest in manner. He never failed to interest an audience. He was a poet of no mean capacity. His pieces were much admired. He wrote under the assumed title of "Nerva."[1] He died in the prime of life.

Charley Sossaman did well in comedy. John P. Border was a first-class low comedian. He is dead. Frank Sexton was then a mere boy. He was cast to represent the heroine in the play of any sort—tragic or comic—and never failed. He has now achieved considerable eminence as a lawyer and statesman. Dr. Lycurgus E. Griffith acted well. He is a gentleman of fine attainments. Captain Duncan Carrington was a member of some prominence. William R. Scurry was versatile. He represented heroes, and sorrowful ladies in scenes where death cast a mantle of gloom. Judge William B. Ochiltree was a gentleman of great ability, possessing the gift of eloquence and an enthusiasm almost unequalled. He has "passed the river."

The writer composed a three-act comedy, which was played with success. General W. R. Scurry wrote and recited a prologue. His brother, Judge Richardson Scurry, wrote some humorous verses in which he ascribed to Ford's comedy a position somewhat more elevated than the works of Shakespeare, and rather sharply criticized the prologue. The young authors considered this poetic effusion an outrage upon their literary merits and fame. The public enjoyed the fun and laugh. This effort bore the title of "The Stranger in Texas." It was based on facts which had fallen under the author's view. A gentleman of rather dubious character came to Texas with the intention of acquiring headright certificates and of becoming the owner of a princely domain. He had bags full of "wild cat" paper money. His Texas customers were equal to the emergency. They gave quit claim titles to spurious headright certificates, and practiced some tricks on the "Stranger" not known to Lord Chesterfield or any other writer on etiquette. One of these was known as the "Spanish Burying," which ended in administering a first-class paddling to the gentleman in search of landed estate. When carried into practical opera-

---

[1]   *The Victim of Jealousy*

He rests beneath the clay—
   The deed of darkness done,
His soul has passed away,
   Its hour of trial gone.
His eye is glazed and dim,
   And where his relics lie,
There flows no requiem,
   There echoes not a sigh.
                              NERVA
        (San Augustine *Red-Lander*, May 19, 1840)

tion, off the stage, the victim for several days would prefer standing to a seat on a cushioned chair.

The next effort in the dramatic line was "The Loafer's Courtship." It drew a large house, and increased the writer's vanity to an alarming extent. He imagined the lightning had striken him and developed in him a genius of sublime proportions. Young simpletons often enjoy their juvenile follies more than old fools do their worn crotchets, and fancied achievements.

3

General Houston married his second wife, Miss Margaret Moffette Lea, at Marion, Alabama, on May 9, 1840. Some months after their arrival in Texas, they visited the eastern part of the Republic. While at Nacogdoches many of the general's old friends called upon them. Among these was N. D. Walling of Shelby County. A story gained circulation, as follows.

General and Mrs. Houston were taking breakfast. Walling was at the table. He inquired: "Mrs. Houston, have you ever been in Shelby County?"

The reply was in the negative.

"You ought to go there, madam. General Houston has forty children in Shelby County."

At this announcement the lady looked rather confused.

"That is, named after him," Walling added.

"Friend Walling," General Houston remarked, "you would oblige me very much by connecting your sentences more closely."

At that time Nacogdoches boasted of excellent society. Colonel Frost Thorn and lady were esteemed among the leaders of those who dispensed princely hospitality. Their entertainments were graced by the presence of youth, beauty, and talent. Nacogdoches was the home of General Thomas J. Rusk, of Colonel James Reily, General James S. Mayfield, Dr. James H. Starr, Colonel [John] Forbes, General Hayden Edwards, Colonel Thomas J. Jennings, Colonel Adolphus Sterne, Colonel J. S. Roberts, the [Henry] Raguet family, and many others of celebrity and note. These gentlemen exercised great influence in the Republic.

General Rusk stood first among them. He was an acknowledged power in the land—a ruler in Israel. The lawyer, the statesman, the general, the patriotic citizen, the steadfast friend had the heart-felt esteem of all who knew him. He was the only man in Texas who could show the shadow of a claim as the peer of General Houston in the esteem, admiration, and love of the people. He was simple in his manners, republican in his tastes, candid and outspoken in the expression of his sentiments, fair and honest in everything. He had a giant intellect, mastered questions as if by intuition, and was great without ambition and pride.

He and General Houston were personal friends. They differed sometimes on matters of policy, and on a few occasions the difference involved principle. It was understood that General Houston favored the cultivation of peaceable relations with the Indians; General Rusk wanted to cut that Gordian Knot with the sword. He placed no reliance in the good faith of the red man, and lent a deaf ear to his protestations of friendship. He did a great deal towards bringing about the Indian war of 1839, and the expulsion of the Cherokees and their confederates from Texas. On many political issues he and General Houston accorded. It might be justly said that the infant Republic of Texas, like a beautiful and innocent girl, had two friends on whom she could lean with equal trust and confidence. The impression of a large majority of the people of Texas was that these two great men placed country before self, and it appears that those who have come after them, and now fill their places, are willing to endorse the opinions of their predecessors with hearty good will. These noble co-laborers in the cause of liberty and constitutional government deserve a warm place in the hearts of Texians for all time to come.

4

Eighteen forty was signalized by the exhibition of considerable party spirit, which sometimes, where excitable persons were involved, degenerated into personal animosity. General Houston came in for a large share of abuse. He was never behind hand on such occasions. His sarcasms were bitter and galling. He was in the habit of acquiring the history of men of prominence, especially of anyone opposed to him. If a black spot could be found the general was sure to put it into circulation and claim to be acting on the defensive. He and Burnet were enemies. It appeared that designing persons could make either of them believe anything bad about the other. In some instances these tales would scarcely bear any investigation, yet they would be repeated with great gusto and a flourish of trumpets by either of the distinguished gentlemen. Judge Burnet was ornate in his contemptuous denunciations; Houston was less choice in his maledictions, but they were intensely provoking. Grog-shop bullies, cross-road politicians, and self-inflated shysters aped their respective favorites. The artificers of bad blood, the Jerry Sneaks, and the Rausig Sniffles of that day had a glorious time in blustering and making faces at each other. Duels were frequently talked of, but never came off. It was understood at one time that an agreement had been made among the enemies of General Houston to keep calling him out until some lucky fellow put a ball through him. This rumor obtained more credence than it was entitled to perhaps. Allison A. Lewis of San Augustine County published a card proposing to do all of General Houston's fighting, and inviting bloodthirsty gentlemen to "pitch in." No one seemed to be spoiling for a fight.

The county of San Augustine was entitled to two representatives in the lower house. There were four candidates in the field: General Sam Houston, Colonel S. S. Davis, William Duffield, and John S. Ford.[2]

The latter would have been elected but for having repeated what was told him, or what he is yet confident a gentleman said to him: "General Houston is on a spree in Nashville, Tennessee, and will not be here on the day of election." The gentleman denied having used the word "spree." The supposed declaration was not repeated with a malicious intent. It was done without thought and without reflecting as to consequences. It was repeated in a spirit of exultation under the belief that the speaker's election was sure. General Houston's friends became very much excited over the matter and electioneered and voted against the writer. He was defeated by seventeen votes.

All political parties in Texas were soon merged into two—Houston and Anti-Houston. The strife between the advocates of the two was at times very bitter. Notwithstanding the heated election contests there were few hostile collisions of individuals. Had Texas been the paradise of scoundrels and the refuge of cutthroats, as some continued to asseverate, the campaigns for president of the Republic would have been signalized by numerous murders and a fearful reduction of our population.

5

For a number of years San Augustine had been acquiring residents of talent, worth, and influence. One of those arriving about this time was General James Pinckney Henderson, late minister of Texas to the French court. It would be impossible to do him justice in a short notice. He was a lawyer of eminent ability, a statesman of extended and liberal views, and a diplomat of acknowledged capacity. He entered into every measure calculated to advance the welfare of the people with earnestness and persistency. He was a dauntless defender of what he conceived to be the right. To these qualifications he added those of candor, uprightness,

---

[2] H. W. Augustine instead of William Duffield was in the race for San Augustine's two representative seats. Augustine and Houston won.

sound common sense, and moderation. He was a warm, consistent friend and an enemy to none. He was not an office seeker, but served the people when an expression of public opinion demanded of him to do so, even at the sacrifice of his own individual interests.

Next to Henderson in point of ability but his superior in oratory was Colonel Kenneth L. Anderson. The son of humble Scotch parents, he arose from the position of shoemaker to be one of the first men in Texas. He was the artificer of his own fortunes; as the First Napoleon expressed it, the Rudolph of his own house. He remained in Texas two or three years, and his friends placed his name before the voters of his district as a candidate for Congress. To the surprise and delight of his supporters, and to the disappointment of his political opponents, he displayed the powers of a champion speaker. He was the equal of General Houston on the stump. He played upon the feelings and the passions of an audience as a master would upon the strings of a harp, and the responses given to his appeals were as sure, as pronounced, as were the cadenced, melodious notes answering to the deft fingering of the harpist. He was elected to Congress, chosen speaker of the House of Representatives. He was nominated for vice president on the Houston ticket, which was headed by Anson Jones, who was President Houston's secretary of state. The election was held on the first Monday in September, 1844, and was a vindication of the policy of General Houston. Colonel Anderson presided over the Senate, and won friends from all sections of the Republic by his urbanity and fair rulings. It was understood by many, after the terms of annexation had been accepted by the Texas Congress, that Anderson would be the first governor of the new state. All the preliminary steps had been taken to render annexation an accomplished fact, the last Congress which ever met in the Republic had adjourned, the delegates to the constitutional convention were on their way to Austin to commence their session on the fourth of July, 1845, when the mournful news of Vice President Anderson's death of congestion on July 3 saddened every heart in Texas. He was taken off in the full tide of a successful career, before he had an opportunity to exhibit to the world the full extent of his intellectual powers, his rare gift of eloquence and energy, and his capacity as a statesman.

There was Royal T. Wheeler, the accomplished gentleman, the profound lawyer, the learned and the just judge. Though his lot was cast in a new country, where the sparse population was clustered in distant settlements, dotting the bosom of a vast territory whose residents were almost strangers to each other, he acquired a wide-spread reputation for incorruptible integrity, a high-toned sense of honor, and all those qualities which can adorn humanity. The ermine he wore for near a quarter of a century was the unspotted reflex of a pure heart, honest motives, and noble purposes; its unsullied white seemed to be emblematic of the glorious vesture of those who have gone through the ordeals of this world unscathed, and have passed the golden gates between Time and Eternity.

Among the men who played conspicuous parts in forming public opinion on a proper basis, during the days of the Republic, was Dr. Joseph Rowe. He was twice a member of Congress, and was elected speaker of the House of Representatives of the Second Congress. He was a forcible writer and a sensible and pointed speaker. He was very kind to immigrants, especially to young men. This class usually found in him a safe counsellor, and a good friend. The writer has a lively remembrance of his obligations to that kind-hearted gentleman.

Judge John G. Love was on the bench in San Augustine district during the existence of the provisional government. He was a gentleman of sterling worth. He never permitted selfish considerations to stand in the way of a faithful performance of duty. He was one of those patriots who live without ambition and die without reproach. He left behind him the odor of a useful and well-spent life.

Colonel Sam Davis and his brother, Judge A. M. Davis, were great factors in promoting the general welfare, and in preserving order.[3] O. M. Roberts, very soon after his arrival in Texas, was recognized as a man of mark, one of the coming leaders of the people. A. W. Canfield, the editor of the *Red-Lander* after the death of W. W. Parker, exercised great influence throughout the Republic. Richardson Scurry stood high as a gentleman of remarkable talent and ability. He was a judge of unblemished reputation, a prominent member of Congress—speaker of the House —a hero of San Jacinto, yet he never claimed anything for having discharged his public duties with fidelity. His brother, William R. Scurry, the lawyer, the orator, the poet, was a leader in the Texas House of Representatives in 1844–1845, a prominent candidate for the United States Senate against [John] Hemphill, a general in the Confederate service who yielded up his life in the "lost cause" at the battle of the Saline in 1864. William B. Ochiltree, the readiest and most eloquent off-hand speaker in the Republic, was impartial as a judge, and discharged his duties regardless of threats. He was a confirmed Whig, and that always stood in the way of his advancement in a state so intensely Democratic as Texas.

---

[3] Sam Davis was San Augustine's second sheriff. His brother A. M. Davis served as chief justice of the county from 1840 until his death in 1845.

General Travis G. Broocks, General John G. Berry, General N. H. Darnell, Colonel Alexander Horton, [Henry W.] and Philip A. Sublett, Colonel B. Rush Wallace, the Polks—[Judge Alfred and his father "Civil Charley"]—and others, some of whom have been mentioned and others might be, were efficient laborers in every work the public good demanded.

San Augustine aimed to become the Athens of Texas. The able and true men aforementioned were the consistent advocates of schools. They were aware that education, enlightenment, constituted the safeguard of free institutions.

Not far from this period two schools were established at San Augustine. One was the San Augustine University, under the presidency of Reverend M. A. Montrose, a native of Scotland, and a Presbyterian. He was a gentleman of undoubted talent, and varied acquirements. In a copy of the *Red-Lander* of 1843 can be found an advertisement signed by Matthew Cartwright and Iredell D. Thomas, on the part of the trustees of the institution. They were two of the principal merchants of the place, and influential in the community.

The members of the Methodist Episcopal Church, under the lead of Elders Francis Wilson and Littleton Fowler, established the Wesleyan College. Captain H. W. Augustine, Major [James] Perkins, and other prominent citizens were trustees. Reverend L. James, the first president, was a gentleman of much capacity, an impressive speaker, and he proved to be a valuable acquisition to society.

The two schools had in attendance for several sessions more than three hundred pupils. More on this subject under the topic of annexation.

These remarks concerning the men of early times have been made to show the kind of people constituting the bulk of the population occupying Texas. Old Texians, when tried by the rigid rule of "by their fruits ye shall know them," had nothing to fear. Success vindicates their acts. Ingratitude may endeavor to throw the dark pall of indifference and forgetfulness over their labors, their achievements, and their memory, but the light of history will penetrate the envious obstruction, and cause justice to be done to them.

III

>>>

PAGAN UPRISINGS

During the summer of 1836, a Lieutenant Bonnell of the United States Army conveyed the intelligence to San Augustine that the Cherokee and other Indians in Texas contemplated attacking the settlements. Volunteers were called for. Captain William Kimbro, who had commanded a company on the field of San Jacinto, had charge of a company raised in San Augustine County—the writer belonged to it. We marched to Nacogdoches. On the way, at Mr. Moss's farm, a stalk of corn was on exhibition. It was twenty-one feet in height, according to the say-so of William Garrett, corroborated by Mr. Polley. They both saw it.

Troops from some of the eastern counties were concentrated at Nacogdoches, General Houston in command. We passed the encampment of the United States troops, and Houston received the honors due to a major general. We spent several days in camp.

Messengers were sent to Bowles and Big Mush, two distinguished Cherokee Indian chiefs, inviting them to come in and have a talk. They acceded, and matters were amicably adjusted for the time being. The Texians were disbanded, and returned to their homes.

The writer made the acquaintance of Colonel [William] Whistler, Surgeon [Leonard C.] McPhail, and other Federal officers. The friendship between the military representatives of the United States and the less-disciplined soldiery of Texas was frank and cordial.

The presence in Texas of a portion of the regular army of the United States gave rise to many surmises. It was received by all as an evidence of an intent to befriend the revolutionists and to interfere in their behalf should they be forced by dint of numbers to abandon their homes and fall back east of the Trinity River.

The latter opinion was entertained by Francis T. Daffau, a gentleman of good intelligence and a well-to-do druggist at Austin for many years. He came to Texas in April, 1836, as a member of Captain John A. Quitman's [Mississippi] company. He was Quitman's clerk, and possessed his confidence. He stated on various occasions that he was the custodian of papers which his captain averred contained important secrets of state. He was enjoined to preserve them at all hazards. Daffau's opinion was that he had in his keeping assurances from General Andrew Jackson, then president of the United States, to General Houston, that, in the event Santa Anna forced the Texas army east of the Trinity River, the Americans would take a part in the war. It was believed our government would claim the Trinity as the southern boundary of Louisiana and declare the passage of that stream in pursuit of Houston's army an invasion of the territory of the United States and a cause of war. The presence of Colonel Whistler's command at Nacogdoches gave Daffau's theory a tincture resembling truth.[1]

It is presumable that when Captain Quitman began his march to Texas, it was generally thought Houston would not be able to make a successful stand with his handful of men against the vastly more numerous army of Mexico. The stampede of families and noncombatants from southern, western, and central Texas created the impression that

---

[1] According to Henderson Yoakum, Daffau's "theory" was true. Yoakum says that General Edmund P. Gaines, under orders from Jackson, sent Colonel Whistler's United States regulars to a post near Nacogdoches for the purpose of carrying out the Thirty-Third Article of the treaty between the United States and Mexico ratified back in 1822. Whistler had orders to keep the Indians in line, which would leave the Texans free to meet the Mexicans.

(Yoakum, *History of Texas from Its First Settlement in 1685 to Its Annexation to the United States in 1846*, II, 405.)

all was quite lost. A large majority of the early settlers in Texas were from the United States. Santa Anna was waging upon them an inhuman and merciless war. No quarter was given even to prisoners under the protecting shield of a surrender made under the most solemn pledges of treatment in accordance with the rules of war as practiced by civilized governments. It would have been very natural for President Jackson to have felt a yearning desire to protect his countrymen against a power setting at naught observances consecrated by time and the sanction of illustrious names. He could have intervened as the friend of humanity. Had he done so it is very probable his action would have been endorsed by a verdict of approval by the jury of mankind. The crowned heads of Europe were not allowed to enter their protest against a move calculated to strengthen the United States, and to extend the area of freedom based upon constitutional government—liberty defined by law and protected by law. A few years sufficed to develop the opportunity so ardently wished for, and to evince to the world that a struggle was going on between the advocates and upholders of monarchy and the supporters of republicanism.

For a great part of 1836 there was little trouble on account of Indian depredations. General Houston, even before he was inaugurated president, was the recognized head of Texas. He was known to be favorable to peace with the red man, and they seemed willing, to a certain extent, to adopt his sentiments in relation to their transactions with the whites.

2

In February, 1838, the Land Office of the Republic of Texas was opened for the location of land claim—head-right certificates, land scrip, and so on. Richard Hooper of Shelby County appointed the writer deputy surveyor. His district was in Harrison County. The country was full of Indians. Captain Jack Graves, a very clever and hospitable gentleman from Alabama, had settled on Eight Mile Creek. The surveying party had moved on foot from San Augustine through a sparsely settled country. They swam a creek or two while snow was falling and encountered a good many hardships. It was a real pleasure to accept the kind attentions and hospitalities of Captain Graves and his family of eleven. He had a certificate for a league of land which he wished to have located on the land surrounding the Big Spring Village.

This point was inhabited by Caddo Indians. They were leaving home for the up country, as they said, to hunt. Ford, out of sheer greenness, set his compass and explained to them the object of his mission into their hunting grounds and villages.

The surveying party built large fires, put on no guard, and acted like other inexperienced simpletons would. Within a radius of twenty miles there were three or four Indian towns.

All went merry as a marriage ball—nobody fell sick and no one got too lame to work. The locality where Post Caddo was afterwards laid off was reached. A few settlers were nestled around it. They obtained supplies by hauling on wagons from Shreveport and by flat boats which navigated Lake Caddo.

This body of water was at that time full of fish. In half an hour one could hook enough fine trout or bass for a meal. Alligators were plentiful, and mainly of large size. We killed a good many.

The next stopping place was Wray's Bluff, a small town not far from the head of the lake. Dr. Sanderson kept a boarding house which he called a hotel. At this place the writer made the acquaintance of Robert Potter, formerly a member of the United States House of Representatives from the state of North Carolina. He was the secretary of the navy in the Provisional Government of Texas. He was a gentleman of fine address and persuasive eloquence. He was much opposed to the occupation of any portion of the territory of Texas by Indians who had emigrated from the United States. Not far from Colonel Potter's residence the Muscogees had a settlement between Lake Caddo and the Red River, including a large part of what was afterward erected into Bowie County. He managed to disseminate his sentiments very generally among the settlers. A public meeting was called. A speech from Potter caused great excitement. He charged General Houston with being the friend and ally of the very Indians who were depredating upon the frontier settlements. His picture of the hero of San Jacinto, luxuriating in a breech-clout and spreeing on "bust-head," was extremely ludicrous.

To a person in the habit of looking into things without prejudice, it was evident some unstated project was behind this outpouring of indignation. It was developed: the Caddos had gone down to Shreveport to receive their annuity and presents from the United States. Potter wanted the settlers to attack the Indians on their way up country.

The meeting resolved to raise and organize a company. An old gentleman named [Isaac] Ferguson was elected captain. John S. Ford, without any knowledge of the move, was elected first lieutenant. It was deemed inexpedient to enter a protest against the contemplated expedition. A day or two was allowed for preparation, a time and place of rendezvous named. Ford was on hand. He represented to Captain Ferguson and others the dangers likely to arise from the attempt. In the first place we were not apprised of the number of the Indians, and not sure we could whip them. Secondly, should we be defeated we would ensure measures of retaliation. A cruel war of inexpressible horrors would be waged upon a defenceless frontier, and we had no assurance of help from any quarter. The government and the people of Texas might view the enterprise in the light of an attempt to plunder. In those days there was hardly a settler from near Sabine to the Sulphur Fork of Red River.

The men agreed, disbanded, and went to their respective homes. If memory is not greatly at fault, Colonel Potter was not at the place of rendezvous. The writer was then quite young, but he had an idea that fire-eating orators are not often found in the front of battle. He is now willing to take an affidavit that these gentry are photographed by Shakespeare: "At the beginning of a feast and the end of a fray suits a keen guest, and a dull fighter."

Ford surveyed the tract of land on which the town of Marshall was laid off. It was then the property of Mr. Peter Whetstone of Shelby County. Pete Whetstone was a man of great originality. He was witty, advanced many peculiar ideas, and was the life of a camp, though he was an almost uneducated man.

During our peregrinations, a portion of the surveying party encountered a family living on the road from Nacogdoches to Jonesborough on Red River. The hope of his fond parents was Ike, a youth of 17 or 18 years. Ike seemed to be the fabricator of his own fortunes, and his own wardrobe. The latter consisted of a coffee sack, with a hole cut for his head, and two holes for his arms. He strutted around, conscious of his own dignity and importance. What a pity Ike could not be presented to-day, in his habiliments of 1838, to be studied by the belles who delight in being the most undressed female at the last ball.

The country now constituting Harrison County was a beautiful one in 1838. The uplands were timbered; the trunks of the trees were straight, usually. Very little undergrowth was met with to impede the progress of the passer-by and to obstruct his view. The creeks were fringed by thickets, sometimes dense. There were some prairies, not large but pretty.

Improvidence, and the want of a proper appreciation of the value of land acquired by toil, were the prime causes of the writer's failure to become, eventually, the possessor of a moderate fortune.

In the scattered settlements were found ladies and gentlemen of culture and refinement. The rude cabin was no indication of the class of inhabiters.

The only loss sustained from the Indians was the theft of one of our horses from the settlement on Morris Creek. We did not see an Indian after meeting those near the Big Spring Village, except the widow of McIntosh, her family and servants.

3

The happenings just referred to begot a spirit of distrust and hostility between the Texians and the Indians. Previous to the campaign of 1838, troops were called out to defend the advanced settlements, and fighting occurred between them and the red men.

Some very atrocious and cruel murders were committed, at different times, upon settlers living adjacent to the Cherokee country of Texas. Women and children were killed and scalped in the most barbarous manner. It was generally believed that the Cherokees assisted in the perpetration of these outrages.

Another cause of bitter feeling was the clashing claims to lands between the Texians and the Cherokees. The latter set up a title professedly derived from the Supreme Government of Mexico and strengthened by a *quasi* confirmation by the authorities of the Republic of Texas in 1835. The Indians pleaded as a consideration their neutrality during the campaign of 1836. There was a strong shadowing of truth as to the effects of this neutrality in the spring of 1836. Had the startling war whoop been sounded while the stream of women and children, [in flight before Santa Anna's columns], was pouring upon the Sabine from eastern and central Texas, there is no guessing what might have been the result.

Our people were troubled by a continual sense of insecurity arising from their proximity to a race who had been the enemy of the white man for three centuries, and with strong coloring of proper reason. The American proclivity to acquire land played a part in the matter, very probably.

One effective agent of disturbance and bad blood was the fact that emissaries from Mexico were known to visit the Cherokees and stir them up against the Texians. One of these was an officer of the Mexican army. He was killed in the northeastern part of Texas while passing from the Cherokee country to the Indian Territory. His diary shed light upon the secret workings of the Mexican authorities. He had seen Chief Bowles and, no doubt, arranged matters with him to the disadvantage and danger of Texas. General Rusk used his influence with the people, by public addresses and otherwise, to prejudice them against the Cherokees. He was of opinion they were bad and dangerous neighbors. He knew they exercised an undoubted ascendency over their confederates, the Kickapoos, Wacos, and other Indians. The Wacos were the avowed perpetrators of horrible murders of men, women, and children. General Rusk felt sure that should a proper opportunity present itself the Cherokees would make open war upon the Texians. The declared intention of the Supreme Government of Mexico to reconquer Texas was known to all the world. Had a large Mexican army invaded Texas, the able-bodied young men of the eastern section would have been drawn to the "West" to meet the advancing foe. In that event the Cherokees could attack the "East" and almost depopulate many counties, and thus endanger the very existence of the Republic. In those days all the country west and south of the Brazos River was called the "West." The "East" included all the area east and north of the Brazos.

General Mirabeau B. Lamar, then president of Texas, was in favor of expelling the Cherokees from the country. He and General Rusk had some experience in Indian affairs in their native states of Georgia and South Carolina respectively.

It cannot be presumed that Bowles was ignorant of the feeling prevalent in eastern Texas and of the probable course our government would pursue. He prepared, no doubt, for the emergency. Many of his people had built houses, opened fields, and had means to render them comfortable. It was no hard matter to induce them to defend their homes.

In the summer of 1839 the regular army of Texas, under the command of Colonel Edward Burleson, was marched into the "East." Volunteer companies were raised and organized in various counties of that section; they were commanded by General K. H. Douglass of the militia. General Rusk was colonel of a regiment; he was, in fact, the ruling spirit controlling the volunteers.

Vice President David G. Burnet, General Albert Sidney Johnston, Hugh McLeod, adjutant general or inspector general of the army, accompanied the command of General Burleson. Efforts were made to treat without effect. Bowles had determined to risk an appeal to the sword. He incautiously assembled his forces in close proximity to the Texians.

On July 15 a fight occurred which was not decisive. Bowles fell back about a mile, took another position, and awaited the onset of the Texians. A fierce conflict ensued in which the Indians were defeated and Bowles killed.

The writer joined Captain William Kimbro's company. It was sent to disarm the Shawnee Indians. The locks of their rifles were taken off and carried away. It was said they only showed their ordinary pieces, and kept the best concealed. There was no positive proof of the fact.

From what was then known as the Big Spring Village, the headquarters of the Shawnee Chief, Linney, our company marched to the battleground [where the Cherokees and the Texans were engaged]. A Shawnee war captain, Spy Buck, joined us. He said he was a looker-on while the fight was progressing. We rather suspected he took a hand. The tracks of his pony led to the scene of the last combat.

The defeat was already complete. The enemy had broken and dispersed. Tracks of vehicles leading up the country were visible along our line of march to the main army, indicating that families had fled in terror from their houses to avoid coming into the presence of a civilized foe.

On arriving at the battlefield of the sixteenth, we saw many evidences of the collision. A house on a small hill, it was pointed out, was where Bowles had addressed his warriors. He had remained there until quite all his followers had gone. His horse was either killed or ridden off by another. The victorious Texians pressed upon the resolute chieftain. He was the last to leave the field—on foot and wounded. He was overtaken and killed in a small cornfield.

We gazed silently upon his body as it lay unburied. He was dressed rather in the American style, had a red silk velvet vest said to have been a present from General Houston. It was not difficult to accord to him the deed of bravery and to believe he sacrificed himself to save many of his people. Under other circumstances history would have classed him among heroes and martyrs.

In one of the deserted houses the writer found a Bible. It contained a register of the births of an American family. This was a significant fact: it spoke of bloodshed and robbery.

4

In 1845 the capitol building at Austin was surrounded by a palisade intended to give protection to those assembled there to transact public business against Indian forays. The palisade included the crest of the hill to the street west of Mr. Firebaugh's residence.

While the convention on annexation was in session, on a Sunday, an Indian alarm occurred. A stalwart darky came galloping into town on a mule. He had been bathing and felt the want of time to make his toilet. His clothes were before him, between his body and the horn of his saddle. Every jump the mule made, the gentleman from Africa raised his arm high in the air, and vociferated: "Ingens!" "Ingens!" When he came in front of the old Treasury Department—Crow & McKean's store—the mule shied, and he tumbled off. He clung to his toggery, pursued the fleeing animal, and at the same time shouted "Ingens!" in a kind of "hark from the tombs" intonation of voice, calculated to disturb the nerves of weak-kneed gents, and hysterical old ladies.

There was a gathering of the clans: a motley crowd it was, numbering about one hundred. With bold front and manly strides they moved upon the foe at the mouth of Shoal Creek. A few had guns; some flourished pistols; others had no visible means of shedding blood. Ex-President Lamar was one of the warriors bold.

He was asked: "General, where are your arms?"

"In my pocket," was the prompt reply.

We meant business, diabolical, bloodthirsty business. When we pranced up to the ford of the Colorado, in real warhorse style, not a single red devil dared to show his dirty face. We felt sure they had seen our terrible array and had stampeded like so many mustangs. We solaced our disappointment by telling what we would have done had they audaciously remained to be annihilated by our ruthless and irresistible onslaught.

A party of fishermen were sighted on the opposite bank, just above the ford. They excited no little contempt and disgust in our martial breasts by asserting that some Negro and white boys had been bathing in the river and the darky had mistaken the laughter of their crowd for the Indian war whoop, hence the alarm.

This story lowered our enthusiasm down below the bragging point, and we sauntered back to town in no enviable mood. The chance of going home and relating how we had slaughtered Indians was gone.

Not long previous to the meeting of the Constitutional Convention a boy and girl of Mrs. Simpson were captured by the Indians from a point just above where Pecan Street crosses Shoal Creek. The girl was killed near the present residence of John Hancock. It seemed the poor creature knew the fate in store for her and bravely courted death to avoid outrage and dishonor. The boy was released by purchase, if memory serves.[2]

In those days travelling near the frontier settlements of Texas was attended by danger. Persons travelled in squads in order to protect themselves against attacks of Indians. Peril was everywhere, generally unseen, but none the less imminent. The sudden charge, the blood-curdling war whoop, the kiss of the arrow, the thrust of the lance, and the closing work of the scalping knife usually occupied minutes, if not seconds; the white man was dead and mutilated. Thousands were thus taken off. With a full knowledge of the terrible risks the early settlers had the daring and the fortitude to do their duty. The members of Congress and other public

---

[2] The Indians captured the Simpson children in the late summer of 1842. The girl was brutally murdered at Spicewood Springs, about six miles outside of Austin; the boy was kept prisoner for eighteen months and then traded to a party of Indian traders who returned him to Austin.

(J. W. Wilbarger, *Indian Depredations in Texas*, pp. 139–140.)

officers residing in the counties adjacent to Red River and having to visit the seat of government made it a practice to go to San Augustine or Nacogdoches in eastern Texas, and to pass through the then more densely settled regions of the country. The reader must remember that Texas is larger than France, and was then inhabited by less than 150,000 souls.

5

While the writer was attending Congress he corresponded with the *Red-Lander* of San Augustine almost daily. The paper quotes his speech in regard to the frontier on January 25, 1845, as follows:

A bill has passed both Houses for the protection of the whole frontier, with the exception of some amendments of no great moment, which will be adjusted by a Committee of Conference. The amount appropriated for carrying out the provisions of the act, was for the frontier from Fannin to Bexar, $30,000; for Corpus Christi and vicinity, $15,000. I am in favor of protecting the frontier, for reasons both obvious, and to mind, cognate. Let me call your attention to the situation of seven frontier counties. They were areas once possessing a population of hardy, industrious, brave citizens, surrounded by all the comforts which could be acquired in a newly settled country, bound to the soil by all the endearments and the fond associations which will ever cling to the heart of a man after he has undergone the privations and fatigues incidental to a frontier life, and has reared in the solitude of the wilderness, *a home*, around which have clustered friends and neighbors. What are they now? The inhabitants have fallen or fled—the fields are a waste, a desolation; the houses, ruins, beneath many of which lie the bones of their once happy females, who lived not to tell the tale of their misfortunes, but perished amid the flames of the domiciles, which were lighted up to be, as it were, their funereal pyres! This is no fancy sketch; truth places her indelible impress upon it in characters too legible to be misunderstood.

It is beyond the powers of calculation to compute the losses of life and property which have thus occurred. It remains *our duty to protect* those who are left, to throw a shield between them and their ruthless destroyers, and prevent a recurrence of those bloody tragedies. Suppose, for instance, we should fail to give adequate protection to the frontier on the western border, the Colorado would soon be its limit; the next recess would bring us to the Brazos; the third would not stop short of the Trinity. Thus would we be driven—step by step, from one portion to another, until we could not make *a single foot print upon the soil of Texas without incurring molestation*. By protecting the frontier we of the East *would protect ourselves* indirectly; we would keep danger at a distance; we would give an impetus to immigration; we would develop the resources of the country, and would reap a rich harvest by an increase of revenue derived from the great accession of population and wealth which would be induced to flow into the country.

I voted for appropriating $15,000 to Corpus Christi, and the country adjacent thereto, because we have no other possession of the country west of the Nueces River. Politicians of the United States have denied our right to this portion of country, and have accompanied that denial by asserting that we did not occupy it. This is not the fact; a company was on duty, ranging the region between the Nueces and Rio Grande last year, officered and paid by this Government. The Custom House at Corpus Christi yielded a considerable revenue, and which found its way to the Treasury. The Senator from San Patricio, Refugio and Goliad, is a resident of Corpus Christi. The Representative from San Patricio County resides at the same place. To protect this post, which is one of great importance in a national point of view, to encourage a trade with Mexico, and divert it from its present channel, is a matter of economy, because it will save to the country more than twice the amount appropriated, by its tariff and imposts. Protection and allegiance are reciprocal terms. I care not if a man were placed upon the banks of the Rio Grande, and the sands were crumbling from beneath his feet, if he claimed to be a citizen of Texas, and demeaned himself as such, I would go for protecting him.

The writer is proud of having said this, and still prouder of having acted upon it through a rather long life. It should be the motto of every American. Wherever a citizen of the United States goes he should be protected.

IV

>>>

THE CONTINUING WAR

A goodly number of Mexicans remained in the town and county of Nacogdoches after the battle of San Jacinto. It would be difficult to assume that these people always received fair and honorable treatment at the hands of Texians without an infraction of truth. On the other hand it would be hard to prove these citizens of Mexican origin demeaned themselves blamelessly.

[One certainly did not. In the summer of 1838 Vicente Córdova, who had a bitter hatred of Anglo-Americans, issued a *pronunciamiento* calling for Mexican and Indian volunteers to fight the Texas government. Córdova, who was a man of some means and considerable influence among his countrymen, soon had an army of 600 men—200 Mexicans and 400 Cherokees. They assembled on an island in the Angelina River and then marched into Nacogdoches.]

The news spread fast. In a few days militia companies were marching from many counties of eastern Texas to meet Córdova. It was the custom in those days for men able to do military duty to outfit themselves with arms, ammunition, and provisions. It was usual to meet at the county seat and organize. Elections were primitive affairs. For instance, when two candidates were in the field for captain, they were placed some distance apart. At the word "march" the friends of the respective candidates fell into line by the side of their favorites. A count was made and the result declared. The captain of the San Augustine company, to which the writer belonged, was H. W. Augustine.

The different commands were concentrated between Nacogdoches and the Angelina River. General Thomas J. Rusk commanded the whole force. Some field officers were on duty by virtue of their commissions in the militia. Our major was Dr. Alexander G. Hale.

We remained in camp about two days. More good feeling and hilarity never prevailed among the citizen soldiers of any country. Everything was given and taken in good humor. The "greenies" suffered as usual. A sentinel named Purse one night mistook the noise made by a rat while packing sticks to complete a nest for the furtive tramp of a savage, and fired. The line of battle was speedily formed, an investigation set on foot, and the truth ascertained. Every once in a while someone would bawl out: "Who shot the rat?" A multitude of voices would respond: "Purse!" He grew tired of the fun and swore a goodly lot of extra oaths, but the cry ceased not.

Captain Augustine's company was ordered to make a reconnaissance between the Angelina and the Neches rivers. The duty was performed without any incident occurring of moment. A night alarm caused the command to be placed in line. The officer of the guard sported a brigadier general's uniform. He reported: "Something approached a sentinel—he hailed—receiving no answer, he fired. He is sure it was not a woman." The latter assertion set every one to laughing; and thus the affair ended.

2

The line of march was up river to form a junction with the main body. We halted at Lacy's Ranch, a large farm on the road from Nacogdoches to Washington-on-the-Brazos. The house was on an elevated spot over-looking a considerable extent of territory. It is on or near the town of Alto, as the writer has been informed. We remained here about two days. In the evening of the second day news was received that a body of four hundred Mexicans and Indians were not far off. That night we moved back on the Nacogdoches road and encamped in a mat of timber surrounded by prairie on every side. The position was good for defence, but lacked water. It was a matter to attract notice to the regularity, order, and silence observed as we marched along by fours. Not many hours before the road was not sufficiently large to prevent men from falling out of a column of twos. All was quiet during the night.

The next morning we resumed our march by twos. Very soon a large body of men was seen coming across the prairie in our direction. They were supposed to be enemies. The order was given: "Front into Line!" We moved at a gallop. An elderly gentleman, Mr. Shofner, seemed to feel the necessity of going into battle with a full stomach. He detached a piece of dried beef from the cantle of his saddle, made a vigorous effort to fill his mouth. The ground was "sidling," his horse began stumbling, was unable to recover, and fell a long distance, leaving the rider on the ground behind him. The prostrate man made a desperate effort to finish his meal. It did not take long to learn the force in sight was General Rusk's main command.

That day or the next the trail of the enemy was followed. The command passed by the house of Bowles, the celebrated Cherokee chief. He was standing at a short distance from his house, a comfortable appearing log cabin, conversing with some of our officers, perhaps General Rusk. An interpreter was present. Bowles' face had somewhat the contour of a Caucasian. The nose was rather on the aquiline order. He impressed one with the idea that he possessed force of character and great firmness. He denied all connection with the movement set on foot by Córdova and his Indian allies. As far as his people were concerned, we were induced to form a different opinion very soon thereafter.

The enemy moved up country, not far from the valley of the Neches. In time they divided. The Mexicans headed more to the westward. The army followed the trail trending to the right. It grew smaller as we advanced. Men reported Indians travelling on foot to their homes. On reaching the Neches Saline there was scarcely anything visible to follow. The general impression was that the Cherokees, at least, had abandoned the cause of the *pronunciados*, yet the evidences of their hostility were undoubted by us. This caused many a prudent man to consider the danger of having a people about half civilized, possessing property, arms, and munitions of war and harboring a hereditary enmity to us, living as our near neighbors, really in our midst. It seemed to many very like a situation destined to culminate in bloodshed and disaster, when a fair opportunity to inflict them upon us presented itself. What was most dreaded was the terrible fate in store for the families exposed to the operations of savage men who would make slaves of their sons and mistresses of their daughters. [The war that ensued between the Texans and the Cherokees has already been noticed.]

The army disbanded at the Neches Saline. The men turned their faces homewards, with strong presentiments that the enterprise they had undertaken was not abandoned but suspended, and would be completed ere long as an act of necessity, of self-protection dictated by imminent, impending dangers.

V

>>>

STAR LIGHT, STAR BRIGHT

The question of annexation to the United States was presented to the people of Texas in the election of 1836, and decided in the affirmative by a large majority. In 1837, under the auspices of President Houston, through Stephen F. Austin, the minister of Texas, the proposition was formally presented to the government of the United States. President Van Buren was not in favor of the measure, and its consummation was not considered probable by the Texas government and its friends. The proposition of annexation being deemed hopeless during the administration of President Van Buren, it was formally withdrawn by Mr. James Reily, the Texas *Chargé d'Affaires* at Washington, on October 12, 1838.

On December 9, 1838, General Mirabeau B. Lamar was inaugurated president of Texas. He opposed annexation. But he later changed his mind.[1] On December 13, 1841, General Houston entered upon his second presidential term. The question of annexation was cautiously broached to President [John] Tyler by Mr. Reily in 1842. It was again withdrawn in July of 1843. In September President Tyler moved in the matter. On October 16, 1843, Mr. [Abel P.] Upshur formally presented the subject for the action of the two governments.

Meanwhile the intention of England and France to interfere in the affairs of Texas began to assume a practical shape. M. [Alphonse de] Saligny, the French minister to Texas, inspired, if he did not write, a bill known as the "Franco-Texienne Bill" providing for the settlement of a colony of Frenchmen on our western frontier. The colonists would have retained their own language, customs, and sympathies. The introduction of foreigners in the manner proposed was fraught with some danger to a weak people occupying an immense territory. They would have been introduced under the auspices of the French government. In case of trouble they would have appealed to France to redress any real or imaginary wrong sustained from the action of the Texas authorities. The pretext would have afforded an opportunity to France for intermeddling in our affairs. The bill failed to pass the Texas Congress much to the disappointment of M. Saligny.

The statesmen and the people of the United States now became apprised of the motives actuating the British government in their conduct relating to the Republic of Texas. It was not a part of the Texans' plan to give England control of Texas and Mexico, and to cramp the United States in the acquisition of territory deemed necessary to advance her interest and prosperity. Above all they would not have consented to injure and circumscribe the commercial relations of their own country to augment those of England.

The issue was defined; both governments understood and appreciated it. They prepared for the struggle for supremacy accordingly.

---

[1] Lamar said in his inaugural address on December 9, 1838, that "a long train of consequences, of the most appalling character and magnitude, have never failed to present themselves whenever I have entertained the subject [of annexation], and forced upon my mind the unwelcome conviction that the step, once taken, would produce a lasting regret, and ultimately prove as disastrous to our liberty and hopes as the triumph sword of the enemy." Lamar, however, was a shrewd politician, and, when the people began to clamor for annexation, he changed his position radically. Annexation, he said with all sincerity in August, 1844, was "the most effectual means of enabling" Texas "to protect her rights and to save herself from the ruin which her foes are preparing for her."

(Lamar, *Letter of Gen. Mirabeau B. Lamar, Ex-President of Texas, on the Subject of Annexation, Addressed to Several Citizens of Macon, Geo.*, p. 8; Henderson Yoakum, *History of Texas*, II, 253.)

2

The stake for which England and the United States were playing was immense. Could England have gained control of Texas, and established a state south and west of the Colorado River to be populated by manumitted slaves, she would have dealt the institution of slavery in the United States a terrible blow, if not a fatal one. In this England would not have been actuated by a sense of humanity, but a lust for commercial expansion and a thirst for more power. The Asiento Treaty with Spain providing for the introduction of 144,000 Africans per year into the Spanish colonies of America had not faded from the memory of mankind.

The accomplishment of this object regarding Texas could have set a limit to the acquisition of territory by the United States in the direction of Mexico and possibly in the direction of the Pacific. England would have monopolized the trade of Texas. She already controlled the trade of Mexico to a great extent, which, together with control of Texas, would have given England quite a commercial empire in North America.

It was British influence which induced the Mexican government to agree to acknowledge the independence of the Republic of Texas, with a proviso—a pledge that she would not be annexed to the United States. Had the people of Texas accepted the proposition the war between Mexico and the United States would not have occurred or, if it had, the circumstances would have been different; Mexico might have had England and France as her backers.

Had the efforts of England and France proved successful they would have become arbiters, controllers, in the political affairs of America. They intended to gain this position without incurring hostilities with any power. The condition of Europe, the danger of causing a European war, and the uncertain results of such a contest would, no doubt, have induced these powers to carefully abstain from declaring war. The United States would have been actuated by no such considerations, and it is almost certain that government would have thrown down the gauge of battle. The infraction of the Monroe Doctrine, the interference in the affairs of governments on this side of the Atlantic, would have been too palpable and too pronounced to be passed over without action on the part of the United States.

In the event Texas had acceded to the demands of the two great European powers, she would have placed herself in antagonism with the United States. This action would have been in opposition to the teachings of the people of Texas, a departure from the great principles taught by American statesmen, and in favor of monarchy. In that event, in case of war with a foreign power, and in case her welfare required it, the United

States could not have used Texian territory upon which to move her armies. She might not have acquired California and a port open to the commerce of the East. As it happened she has secured a highway for the transmission of the commerce of the East which has enriched every nation which has had the good fortune to secure and enjoy it.

With England in alliance with Texas, and controlling her almost as a province of the great empire and absorbing her trade, with English influence paramount in Mexico and Central America, her navies riding upon the Gulf of Mexico, the sails of her merchant vessels whitening her water, her flag floating on every port from the mouth of the Sabine River to the capes of Yucatán, what would have been the condition of the United States? The control of the cotton and the sugar markets of the world would have been lost; the Gulf of Mexico would have been little better than a closed sea, dominated by England; the Monroe Doctrine would have been a thing of the past, a dead letter. There could have been but one way to avert these happenings—war. At that period the monarchies of Great Britain and France were in close alliance, and a struggle between the three great powers would have been terrific—almost a calamity to the civilized world, certainly entailing untold miseries upon the people of the belligerents.

The ordeal was passed, and not a hostile gun fired by any one of the powers against another. The leading men of Texas who thought, and had the hardihood to act upon their convictions, furnished the means by which an escape from impending evils was effected. They appreciated the motives of Great Britain and France, and saw plainly that the question of annexation involved a struggle between two monarchies and the Republic of the United States, and they determined to throw their weight, though small it might be, in the scale of republicanism. They rejected the advances of Great Britain, spurned the acknowledgment of their independence, and were true to the principles they had been taught to revere and to the people with whom they were allied by blood. They never for a moment doubted their ability to maintain themselves against the combinations and the arms of Mexico. They were governed by love, by those memories of home and childhood which cluster around the heart of the wanderer in every land and every clime, and not by fear. They met the advances of the United States in a spirit of candor and fairness. They removed every obstacle in the way of success and presented to the Union an empire larger than France, without money and without price. It was an unselfish offering, made to extend the area of freedom and constitutional government. The work was engineered by men who understood its scope, its importance, and whatever of sacrifice it might cost to merge their nationality, and be almost lost sight of as an integer in a confederacy of great States, yet they faltered not. A nobler work was never performed by men who were governed by nobler impulses. It stands as a monument to the wisdom of the old Texians. May God preserve it.

3

In 1844 the Democratic party nominated James K. Polk of Tennessee for President and George M. Dallas of Pennsylvania for Vice President; the Whigs nominated Henry Clay and Theodore Freelinghuysen for the same offices. The annexation of Texas became a political question. It was favored by President Jackson, who in retirement at the Hermitage and on the verge of dissolution, was able apparently to name his successor. He was apprised of the action of France and England in opposition to annexation and used all his influence to thwart the schemes of the European monarchs. They had gone so far as to draw up a joint protest against the acquisition of Texas by the United States. It was withheld for fear of producing excitement in the United States and precipitating the consummation of the measure.

The Whigs held antiannexation meetings in various parts of the Union, and, in some of the proceedings, the people of Texas were vilified in the most shameful manner, particularly at a public meeting at Milford, Massachusetts. To their resolutions the writer responded, and takes the liberty of reproducing his reply, with the following letter of transmittal, which was published in the Dallas *Morning News*, December 28, 1892:

San Antonio, Tex., Dec. 23.—To The *News:* A great many people of Texas, if they ever knew, have lost sight of the presidential contest of 1844 in the United States, when the annexation of Texas became a political question of much importance. General Jackson was at that time almost dying. He was the untiring, zealous advocate of annexation. He did not support Mr. Van Buren for the presidency because he opposed the measure. He used his influence to secure the nomination of James K. Polk of Tennessee. This was the last great public act of the hero of New Orleans. He died soon after, full of years and clothed with honors. . . .

General William R. Scurry was then a member of the Texas congress. He visited Ohio during the electioneering campaign for president. The Whigs had a big meeting, a grand blow-out. He noticed among the transparencies one that attracted his attention particularly. It was a representation of the five-pointed star of Texas. It was being rolled into the union by a number of unnamable black bugs. The Whigs of Milford, Mass., held a meeting, and they let fall language in relation to Texas which the undersigned considered disrespectful to say the least, and which he answered. The reply he made is submitted to your judgment for publication.

John S. Ford

Col. Ford's Ringing Reply
to the Defamatory Resolutions Passed by the Whigs of
Milford Mass., Against Texas

To Gen. Brison Underwood—Sir: A Texan takes the liberty of addressing you as chairman of a meeting held at Milford, Massachusetts, for the purpose of taking into consideration the proposed annexation of Texas to the United States; and in so doing he wishes to be as calm, respectful, and dispassionate as the meeting over which you presided was boisterous, violent, and defamatory. As it is not intended to take up the resolutions of said meeting and discuss them seriatim, indulgence will be claimed if the following remarks should be desultory. In the outset, any unfriendly feeling toward the people of Massachusetts is disclaimed; for every Texan views that state as a part of that mighty confederacy into whose bosom we wish to be admitted. The greater portion of our citizens are natives of the United States, and have brought with them into the bright and sunny land of their adoption, a love for its inhabitants, its institutions and laws, which will survive in their breasts so long as there remains a tender chord to thrill in response to the endearing remembrance of the land that gave them birth, the home of happy childhood. Neither will it be attempted to answer your abusive by recrimination, as that is not argument, no more than scurrility is truth. We have been unfortunate in having the judgment of the world passed upon us, when it had only the evidence of rumor, of false, interested accusers, and the traductions of an enemy who first tried to enslave, them to conquer, and finally to ruin us by foul aspersions upon our national character, upon which to find a verdict. We have never had a fair and impartial trial at the bar of public opinion—the necessary means have not been used to acquire correct information concerning our population, our laws and institutions, or if they were, they have been received with a distrust amounting almost to incredulity, or viewed through the jaundiced glass of prejudice. Upon what evidence yourself and compeers have pronounced our government "infamous" is unknown to ourselves. That our government is weak, yet in the feebleness of infancy, it is not denied; that we are unable to redeem our outstanding liabilities; that our credit is almost destroyed abroad; that our government is not able to afford as much protection to the property and lives of its citizens as they might enjoy under other states that have acquired strength by time, are also facts. But, sir, does this, do all these render us "infamous?" If so, we can throw the charge back, not only upon the United States, but many of the greatest nations upon the earth. Trace the history of every people, of every nation, go back to those times when years had not conferred power in arms, when experience and matured wisdom beamed not upon their councils, compare them to Texas, and we shall suffer nothing from the arbitrament if rendered in the spirit of justice and candor.

If by the term "infamous" reference was had to our military operations, you did us more than injustice—you slandered the reputation of the living and the fame of the dead. At no time, whether victorious or beaten, whether conquerors or in chains, have our people failed to display a coolness and courage worthy of themselves and the noble cause in which they were embarked. They have marched out with the decision and the firmness of veterans to meet death, certain, inhuman and glorious. And often while their fellow prisoners were being massacred around them, have they shouted the vengeful war cry that animated them in the strife of battle, and died with the name of "Texas" quivering upon their lips. Never have we retaliated upon our enemies the bloody murders they have inflicted on our people, nor have we made victory a degradation by inflicting cruelty upon the vanquished. Let it be understood by all the world that since the firing of the first gun in '35 up to the present moment, we have never engaged our enemy without worsting him, if numerical force be considered. Are these, sir, indications of an "infamous" people acting under the orders of an "infamous" government?

In another resolution you say "the territory of Texas of right belongs to Mexico." We look on our title as incontestable. We were invited by the Mexican authorities to settle in Texas, under the assurance of enjoying the rights and immunities guaranteed to every citizen of that republic by the constitution of 1824, with certain other stipulations, which assumed the character and sacredness of a contract by an acceptance from us of their conditions. We emigrated to the country—after incalculable fatigue, many hardships, the loss of much property and many valuable lives, we succeeded in converting a country from a savage wildness to a state of civilization; from a forest waste into a state of cultivation. Upon our uplands, upon our streams, in the seclusion of our lovely valley, were seen numerous plantations teeming with a profusion of the necessaries of life. In the forest the strokes of the woodman's ax were heard to follow each other in rapid succession, making way for the admission of families. Upon the bosom of our broad and verdant prairies were seen hundreds and thousands of cattle and horses—where once the Indian roamed —where stalked the stately buffalo, and proudly neighed and wildly curveted the mustang, and bounded the timid deer. In short, every sight that met the eye, every sound that pierced the ear, were convincing that a hardy, industrious population had seated themselves in a country which Mexican enterprise and Mexican bravery had considered irreclaimable and untenable. After these changes had been wrought, the government of Mexico was altered from a republic to a central, military despotism, without the knowledge or consent of the Texians. We remonstrated—our agent was imprisoned. We petitioned— our petition was spurned. We adjured the Mexican government and people to desist their mad career, and listen to the voice of reason and justice. An army was sent into our country to deprive us of all the means of defence. We resisted—and we conquered.

This, sir, is a correct history of the robbery you pretend we have committed upon the territory of Mexico. If you call this robbery, every people, every nation beneath the broad canopy of the heavens, are robbers likewise. It was use-less to observe that we have held an uninterrupted possession of the country since the battle of San Jacinto. Our enemy has not dared to send again a respect-able force within our limits. True, we have been harassed by predatory incur-sions, whose force was never large, who came upon our borders in haste, and retreated from them in precipitancy. Allow me, sir, to ask if the United States can show a better title to her territory? Royal grants, papal bulls, and Indian treaties, to the contrary notwithstanding?

Should we concede that we acquired the territory of Texas unjustly (which we do not), how many examples could we bring forward to attest it as a custom long in use among all nations, in all ages, to acquire territory by revolution? And, sir, to travel beyond the limit of your own government to adduce instances of forcible, fraudulent occupations of territory, and a detention of the same by no other title save the mockery of a treaty imposed upon a weak, defence-less, timid nation, or the arrogant dictations of haughty conquerors to a de-feated, injured people, would be a useless expenditure of time. When, sir, did the Indians invite the ancestors of the present population of your own state to come and settle at Plymouth? Did they treat the Indians as friends or foe, as brothers, as human beings, or as brutes?

How does your title look by the side of ours? Does it not bring a tinge of shame upon your cheek when you reflect by what means you acquired pos-session of the territory of Massachusetts? It well becomes those who stigmatize a people as plunderers of the soil they claim to take a retrospect of their own history, lest it furnish precedents for the commission of deeds far more im-moral, lest it be pleaded in justification of acts that are criminal and flagitious. The history of the settlement of Massachusetts will serve for every State in the Union, with but few exceptions—Pennsylvania is one. But our title to the Texian soil stands upon other and better grounds.

"Texas with her population of lawless renegade ruffian adventurers, her mock republican constitution, decreeing eternal slavery to the colored race, and her desperate insolvency, is a sheer burlesque upon the name Republic." To be amenable to the charge of 'lawless' is, of course, to exist without any municipal regulations whatever. I for one, cannot think, sir, that you flatter yourself with the hope that the assertion of our being "lawless" will be believed by any reasonable person, nor do I even imagine that you hold that opinion your-self. That we have a constitution, which is the foundation of all laws, you admit; that we obey those laws made in accordance with it, a little inquiry would have convinced you, else why the electing of officers, the holding of courts, to carry them into effect? All of which is done with regularity and precision; any of which facts would have been evident had you taken up a Texian newspaper and read it. That the law has not, will not, nor cannot, yet be administered with as much certainty and severity as in some other govern-ments that have acquired ability by time and order by practice, we are free to admit. We have a population estimated at 200,000 souls, scattered over a space of country nearly forty times as large as the state of Massachusetts. They were

born in, brought up, and emigrated from all parts of the world—these hetero-
geneous materials have not had time nor opportunity to accommodate themselves to the habits, customs, of each other. They are just emerging from a state
of revolution. From the distance at which they generally live apart, they do not
feel that social dependence upon each other which is usually the result in a
firmly established community; each man, having to depend on his own energy
and resources in cases of emergency, eventually considers himself competent
to the task of protecting himself under ordinary circumstances. He feels little
need of law, because he feels little need of protection afforded by the governing power; hence, as a general rule in a government weak and situated as ours,
the laws would, as a matter of course, be executed feebly, timidly, and with
uncertainty; but such is not the case in Texas. Our courts are held regularly,
debts collected, fines imposed, punishment inflicted, without evasion by force
or fraud. Let me ask you sir—eight years from the declaration of her independence could the United States say as much? When the state of Massachusetts
contained a people of but 500 souls, had they been scattered over the whole
state, would you pretend to say the laws would have been executed more fully?
They were not. And in one respect a comparison cannot be instituted, because
Massachusetts had an effective and powerful arm upon which to lean, that
could at any time carry her laws into effect by force—she was a British province.
Texas has had to rely upon her own resources; nevertheless we will challenge
comparison.

You are pleased in the excess of your politeness and modesty to call us
"ruffian adventurers." We came mostly from your own country—how can *you*
refuse to take back your own coin? Do you view Texas as an asylum to those
who have fled from the law's vengeance? Why then, in the name of God, let
her remain so; deny not to your contemporaries a convenience similar to the
one that saved the necks of numbers of your ancestors—allow them a city of
refuge also. But, sir, in the language of sober seriousness you are not certainly
so badly misinformed as to really believe we are the set of miscreants you
represent us to be. You must be well aware that Texas, as all other new countries, has been settled by all sorts of characters, good and bad—enterprising
men who came to better their conditions in life without spot or blemish upon
their fame—men who fled from justice—the pious, meek bearer of the cross,
who came to preach salvation—and the greedy speculators, who came to make
a fortune by any means, foul or fair. Note our progress—look at the number
of preachers we have within our limits; go to our churches, view our people
assembled there in silence and decorum to worship the only true living God.
Go out among our farmers, they will treat you with kindness and friendly
hospitality. Walk with us to our schools, refresh your eyes by looking upon
the smiling, happy countenances of our children engaged in the acquisition of
useful information. Then, sir, if you will, if you can, pronounce us "renegade
ruffian adventurers." The very village from which I write contains a population
of about 1500 souls; has two churches and a university founded by government, with liberal, magnificent donations of land; a college built by individual

enterprise—these institutions have under pupilage nearly 300 children and youths. Similar establishments devoted to the cause of education are numerous throughout the Republic. These, sir, are not surely the works of "ruffian adventurers"; they bespeak a people of enlightened views and high toned moral character. Our "mock republican constitution" is nearly a parody upon that of the United States. Some of your great statesmen have spoken of it in the language of approbation and eulogy; and it could not more effectually "decree eternal slavery to the colored race" in theory than does your own in tolerance and *practice*.

You must assuredly deem our "desperate insolvency" most damning, from the grave manner in which you prefer the charge. Were we alone in this respect, we might perhaps have cause for shame, but we do not stand solitary in this respect; we may, indeed, with propriety, be said to have reached almost the last stage of national humiliation. There is scarcely anything that can wound the pride, or degrade the character, of an independent people, which we do not experience. Are there engagements to the performance of which we are held by every tie respectable among men? These are the subjects of constant and unblushing violation. Do we owe debts to foreigners and to our citizens, contracted in a time of imminent peril, for the preservation of our political existence? These remain without any proper or satisfactory provision for their discharge. Is public credit an indispensable resource in time of public danger? We seem to have abandoned its cause as desperate and irretrievable.

These remarks have become a portion of your history; any person can recollect to have heard of your continental currency and the legislative enactments of your government with regard to it. In the face of all these facts you urge insolvency as an argument against our admission into the Union. Our government cannot at present redeem her liabilities, not from a disposition to violate her pledged faith but because she is unable to command and develop her resources. Your attention is respectfully requested to the following facts:

First. We owe not a dollar, but that we can, and will, pay, by means of our public domain.

Second. We have never repudiated any just and equitable contract.

Third. We never will.

Here, sir, I shall drop the Milford resolutions, but not the subject of annexation. You appear not to have asked yourself whether Texas can *lose* anything by being annexed to the United States? The mere supposition of such a case may perhaps excite derision or contempt in your breast, yet numbers of thinking men in this Republic espouse the affirmative of this question. We have a consolidated form of government; laws that accommodate themselves to the condition and wants of our population which we feel confident will be bettered by future amendments, so as to keep pace with the march of moral and intellectual improvement that is going forward in our land. Our institutions are adapted to the genius of our people—in the course of twelve months we can amend, alter, or entirely abolish any legislative enactment that may bear unequally. Were we annexed to your government, when could we hope to obtain even the most trivial relief? Never: or perhaps when we did not need it. Shall we alienate our immense public domain, yield up our sovereignty, and even forget that we have been a nation, for the purpose of becoming a *speck* in a powerful government, confederate in its form, vast in its extent, and cursed and divided by the most virulent political factions that ever disgraced any country, that ever cheated and duped and caterwauled any people, a portion of whom oppose our admission into the Union from a desire to thwart the measure merely because it chanced to emanate from their opponents, from an overweening disposition to advance their own factious insolent intrigues, an itching to hold the reins of power in their own selfish hands, and not from a conviction of the impropriety and danger of the measure? I ask again: shall we surrender the sovereignty for which the heart's blood of our chivalry flowed in torrents, which we won by our valor, and have sustained by losses and privations and want, and every sacrifice that a generous, brave people could make, for the purpose of obtaining a part and parcel of these *inestimable blessings* and for a *protection* which we at this period but little require? Our citizens, with one voice, have said "Yes—let us give up all, to have again the proud banner of the brave and the free to wave its omnipotent folds over our heads, and to assure us that we are once more the fellow citizens of the people who are bone of our bone and flesh of our flesh, and who should receive us with joy and gladness, because we come not empty handed, not in poverty, not in fear, but as free, independent people, the germ of a mighty nation, the scion of a puissant republic—take us as friends, as brothers, as your children." How did, how does a portion of your citizens respond to this appeal? By abuse, by unmitigated, base, foul slander, degrading defamation, and malevolent maledictions. What, sir, will the United States lose by refusing to take us? She will lose a territory as large as that of France. By means of the commercial treaty we are about to set on foot with Great Britain, she will lose the cotton trade, she will lose a market for her cotton fabrics, she will render her Southern States bankrupt, her manufacturing ones she will impoverish. She will lose a river, a desert for a boundary. She will lose command of the Gulf of Mexico, and she will sever the Union. By annexation she will save all these losses, and acquire a public domain worth more than all of her public lands, completely shut out British influence and British domination from a point from which it would cripple all her relations, political, commercial, and social. These are considerations, sir, which you as a public man, or as a private citizen, should weigh well. They should over-balance all minor considerations of party, all sectional feelings and prejudices. They are of vital and solemn import to every citizen of your government. Perhaps, sir, you may expect an apology due for having troubled you with so long a communication. I, sir, have none to make.

As chairman of the Milford meeting, you have appeared before the world as the calumniator of my country and its people. I, sir, have addressed you in the language of vindication, in the tone of a free man, and have only to regret that the task devolved not upon abler hands. But, sir, when I conceive my country needs any services, such as they are, my motto has ever been "ready, aye, ready."

I am, with due respect,
Your obedient, humble servant,
John S. Ford
San Augustine, Texas

4

The Ninth Congress of Texas adjourned February 3, 1845. The writer remained at Washington-on-the-Brazos several weeks after adjournment. He used every honorable effort to ascertain the action of Captain Elliott, the British Minister, and of M. Saligny, the French Minister, in reference to annexation. Major Andrew J. Donelson, the United States Minister, was at Washington. The writer had conferences with him and imparted such information in his possession, as he deemed useful to promote the measure of annexation. He was in correspondence with the vice president of the Republic of Texas, Kenneth L. Anderson, and kept him advised of passing events, as far as he was able. The vice president and other friends of annexation felt assured the best interests of Texas would be subserved by going into the Union. They feared England and France.

President Jones called an extra session of the Ninth Congress to meet at Washington-on-the-Brazos on June 16, 1845. On the seventeenth "Mr. Ford, by leave, introduced a joint resolution accepting the propositions of the U. States Congress, for the annexation of Texas . . ."

The representatives of the people came together with a determination to annex Texas to the United States, if the same could be accomplished by their action. There were able and influential men in both Houses who could not have been satisfied by anything short of a full acceptance of the terms offered. R. M. Williamson, W. R. Scurry, James W. Henderson, Tod Robinson, General [William Leslie] Cazneau, General McLeod, George B. Erath, M. T. Johnson, and others were in control of the House. Senators [John A.] Green, [John] Caldwell, [Jesse] Grimes, [David S.] Kaufman, [Richard] Roman, and others stood as sponsors for the affirmative action of their body. The chances of defeating the acceptance of the terms proposed were desperate.

It would be unwise, perhaps unjust to the memory of the dead, to assert positively that President Anson Jones and a large part of his cabinet were opposed to annexation, yet candor demands the allegation that in the opinion of the writer they would have defeated its consummation if they could. It would be difficult to point out acts and array facts to support this opinion at this date of forty-one years after the events preserved.

[While Ford's motion was pending the Congress concerned itself with a treaty with Mexico, mediated by France and England, that would recognize Texas independence, provided Texas would promise not to annex herself to another power. President Jones came before the Congress to say:]

The Executive has the pleasure, in addition to presenting Congress the propositions concerning Annexation, to inform them that certain conditions preliminary to a [definite] peace, upon the basis of a recognition of the Independence of Texas by Mexico, were signed on the part of the latter at the City of Mexico on the nineteenth of May last, and were transmitted to this Government on the second instant by the Baron Alley de Cyprey, Minister Plenipotentiary of his Majesty the King of the French, at that Court, by the hands of Captain Elliott, Her Britanic Majesty's Charge d'Affaires near this Government. In consequence of the signing of these preliminaries the Executive believed it to be his duty, in the recess of Congress, to make the fact known to the people of Texas, and to declare and proclaim a cessation of hostilities between Texas and Mexico, until the same could be communicated to and acted upon by Congress and the Convention, about to assemble. A proclamation for this purpose was consequently issued on the fourth instant, a copy of which is herewith transmitted. These preliminaries being in the nature of a treaty will ... be forthwith communicated to the Honorable Senate for its constitutional advice, and such action as in its wisdom the same shall seem to require.

These were the conditions preliminary to a treaty of peace between Mexico and Texas:

1. Mexico consents to acknowledge the Independence of Texas.
2. Texas engages that she will stipulate in the treaty not to annex herself or become subject to any country whatever.
3. Limits and other conditions to be a matter of arrangement in the final treaty.
4. Texas will be willing to remit disputed points respecting territory and other matters to the arbitration of umpires.

The Senate of Texas took a vote on the treaty on June 21, 1845. It was referred to a committee of the whole. They reported unanimously in favor of rejecting the treaty. Thus ended the effort of crowned heads to acquire control of Texas, and gain a foothold in the southern part of North America.

The conditions of the treaty opened the floodgates of discussion and claim concerning boundary and many other questions. Its adoption would have left Texas at the mercy of England and France. They would have been the arbiters of our destiny. Captain Elliott had the credit of engineering that treaty. He was said to have visited the City of Mexico. He was the man of the "White Hat" about whom a great deal was written. No wonder that the Senate of Texas and the people of Texas indignantly rejected and spurned propositions embodying so many chances to injure and dishonor them and to cripple the United States.

It may be suggested that the nature of the preliminary conditions were of such a character as to render the assent of Mexico to them a positive acknowledgment of the independence of Texas. The very fact of presenting alternatives and allowing Texas to exercise her discretion in choosing was, in fact, a recognition of Texas as a sovereign state.

President Jones and his cabinet now fairly and honestly carried out the wishes of the people. The president told the Senate,

The state of public opinion and the great anxiety of the people to act definitely on the subject of annexation by a Convention of Delegates induced the Executive to issue his proclamation, on the fifth of May [1845], recommending an election throughout the Republic on the fourth of the present month, and to assemble in Convention, at the city of Austin, on the fourth of July next. This recommendation has met the sanction of the citizens of Texas generally, and the deputies in the several counties, so far as heard from, having been elected on the basis proposed, it is confidently expected the Convention will assemble at the time and place fixed upon. To this Convention the question of Annexation, and the adoption of a State Constitution, will properly belong; and they will determine the great question as to the nationality of Texas, as to them shall seem most conducive to the interest, happiness, and prosperity of the people whom they will represent.

The consent of both houses of Congress was obtained to the terms of annexation. They endorsed the action of President Jones in calling a convention, provided for the paying of the delegates, granted them the franking privilege, and did whatever they conceived necessary to expedite annexation.

5

When the members of the Ninth Congress separated there was considerable feeling evinced. Many of them entertained the belief that another Congress never would convene in Texas. In their estimation the proud Republic they had aided to establish and maintain was about to surrender its nationality, and the gallant and unselfish patriots who had shared their labors and privations were, many of them, about to pass from their view forever. Alas, how prophetic the foreboding.

All who answered at roll in December, 1844, have "passed beyond the river," save two or three. Until the history of Texas shall have been correctly written the world will know little of the actors in the stirring dramas enacted therein in the days of its infancy. It seemed as if Providence furnished them for these momentous occasions. Had they failed to perform the grand mission assigned them, what might have been the results God alone can tell. Had the men who guided affairs in 1844–1845 been allured by the promises of England and France, and refused to accept the proffered terms of annexation, what would have been the effect upon the United States, upon Texas, and Europe? Imagination cannot portray them. To go further back, had the statesmen, the soldiers, and the sages, who established the Republic of Texas, proved unequal to the task, what a change would have been wrought upon the history of the world. How pleasant should be the labor of the historian who lends his time and talents to redeem their memory from the dark thraldom of oblivion.

The writer can say this without incurring the charge of selfish egotism. He was not one of the first: he came as a volunteer to aid them in noble work. He now stands as a link between two generations; one has almost disappeared, to them he pays the tribute of love and hallowed recollections; the other now fills the places of the mighty dead, to them he owes affection, duty, and unwavering allegiance to the principles which promote their happiness and prosperity.

6

In pursuance of the recommendation of President Anson Jones contained in his proclamation of May 5, 1845, the delegates of the people of Texas met in convention at Austin on the following fourth of July. The object was to form a constitution preparatory to the admission of the State into the Union of the United States.

General Thomas J. Rusk was elected president of the convention. The other officers were as follows: James H. Raymond, secretary; Thomas J. Green, assistant secretary; John M. Swisher, second assistant secretary; Mr. Neely, sergeant-at-arms; Mr. Cockburn, doorkeeper; Rev. John Haynie, chaplain; José A. Navarro used Mr. George Fisher of Houston as an interpreter. Fisher was a native of one of the Dunabian provinces of the Turkish Empire.

The following are extracts from President Rusk's address:

The object for which we have assembled, deeply interests the people of Texas. We have the hopes of our present population, as well as the millions who may come after us, in our hands; the eyes of the civilized world are upon us; we present this day a bright spectacle to all lovers of freedom and republican government. The history of the world may be searched in vain for a parallel to the present instance of two Governments amalgamating themselves into one, from a pure devotion to that great principle, that man, by enlightening his intellect, and cultivating those moral sentiments with which God has impressed him, is capable of self government.

The terms of annexation are alike honorable to the United States and to Texas, and as a Texian, acting for myself and my posterity, I would not, were it practicable without in the slightest degree endangering the great question involved, seek to alter the terms proposed to us by the Government of the United States. Texas, animated by the same spirit, and following the bright examples of the fathers of the American Revolution, has acquired at the cost of blood, her freedom and independence from those who would have enslaved her people. She now, with a unanimity unparalleled, enters that great confederacy to whose keeping the bright jewel of human liberty is confided, content to bear the burthens and share the benefits which republican government carries in her train.

President Jones communicated to the convention all the papers he had laid before Congress at the extra session. They acted on the resolutions providing for the annexation of Texas to the United States on the first day of the session, and accepted them with one dissenting vote, Mr. R. Bache.

On the eighth of July the convention passed resolutions gratefully thanking President Tyler and the members of his cabinet for the active part they had taken to promote the cause of annexation.

The Constitution of 1845 speaks for itself. Its provisions indicate that it was the work of statesmen. The convention was impressed with the importance of educating the masses. They required the Legislature to appropriate one-tenth of the funds raised by taxation to establish and maintain a system of free schools, donated four leagues of land in each county for educational purposes, and provided for leasing lands granted to public schools. The delegates were chosen from among the pioneers who had aided to make Texas free and independent, and they kept in view the idea advanced in the Texas Declaration of Independence concerning the public domain and free schools. They passed an ordinance declaring colonization contracts unconstitutional and prohibiting the Legislature from entering into such contracts. That ordinance was submitted to the people with the Constitution.

The writer [was not a delegate to the convention, but he was present and] reported proceedings for the *National Register* of Washington-on-the-Brazos. He wrote one communication that opposed the election of judges by the people, which he has since doubted as to its correctness.

On one occasion Judge Ochiltree offered an amendment to a clause in the Constitution and supported the same in a speech. He said the constitutions of some of the States of the Union had a similar provision, particularly the constitution of North Carolina, one of the best, if not the very best, of the old States.

"Order! Order!" Colonel Young called out. "Mr. President!"

"The gentleman from Red River will state his point of order," General Rusk said.

"The gentleman from Nacogdoches was in disrespect of the balance of the old States," Colonel Young said, with assumed gravity.

Judge Ochiltree took his seat, and a general titter was heard over the house. Judge Ochiltree was a native of North Carolina, and Colonel Young was poking fun at him.

A body of men more devoted to their country had never assembled. They were remarkable for talent, and that practical knowledge acquired by experience. A great many of them had been elevated to positions of great trust and responsibility.

Not only were the members of the convention known to fame; the men they placed in office were some of the leading politicians in the State. No deliberative assembly ever labored with more zeal and fidelity to accomplish a work than those delegates. They were well advised on matters coming before them for action, investigated them thoroughly, and conducted affairs with a prudent discreetness tempered by public spirit and love of country. They adjourned on August 28, 1845.

The delegates turned their faces homeward as lighthearted and hopeful as if no danger lurked on their paths. They had discharged the trust confided to them, and they looked to Providence to shape their future destinies. A body of men better qualified to perform their duties, actuated by purer motives, and a more exalted patriotism never met and never separated.

7

After returning to Washington from Austin after the close of the convention, the writer and Michael Cronican, a practical printer, purchased the printing establishment of the *National Register*. The conductors of the *Register* had opposed annexation, and their journal was unpopular at that time. The new firm was styled Ford & Cronican. The press and material were transported to Austin and the name of the paper was changed to the *Texas Democrat*. The appearance of a weekly sheet conducted by friends of General Houston was not palatable to many of the residents of the "City of the Hills" because of the recent "Archive War" which had engendered much bitter feeling. A proposition was made to throw the press and type into the Colorado River—it met with no encouragement. Luckily, the editor indicated great partiality for the place and made all right with the citizens. He acted on the line of conciliation that he had advocated in Congress.

There were no exciting scenes enacted during the latter part of the year. A political campaign was progressing. The issues which had stirred the people were decided—dead. There was nothing to cause the bitter feeling that had prevailed before; hence, many voters did not attend the polls. General James Pinckney Henderson was elected governor, Colonel A. C. Horton, lieutenant governor.

The Legislature met. They elected General Sam Houston and General Thomas J. Rusk to the Senate of the United States. The election took place previous to the action of Congress upon the Constitution of 1845 and the final admission of Texas into the Union.

The news of final admission, anxiously expected, came. It was the cause of general congratulation. To many the idea of our infant Republic being stricken from the roll of nations brought sadness. People came to Austin from many portions of the State to witness the solemn ceremony—the funeral of a nation, as it were.

On the nineteenth day of February, 1846, the seats were taken out of the Representative Hall and Senate Chamber and placed on the long gallery east of the capitol building, which was located where the Austin Market House now stands. Both houses of the Legislature were seated. Hundreds of citizens were in attendance. Many were standing grouped around the point to be occupied by the speakers. There was little conversation—a hush seemingly induced by an effort to stifle emotions difficult to master was prevailing, and noticeable. Many gazed with evident affection at the Lone Star flag which floated from the southern gable of the capitol. President Jones arose and read his valedictory in a clear and serious tone of voice from which the following are extracts:

The great measure of annexation, so earnestly desired by the people of Texas is happily consummated. The present occasion, so full of interest to us and to all the people of this country, is an earnest of that consummation, and I am happy to greet you as their chosen representative, and tender to you my cordial congratulations on an event the most extraordinary in the annals of the world, and one which makes a bright triumph in the history of republican institutions. A government is changed both in its officers and in its organic law—not by violence and disorder, but by the deliberate and free consent of its citizens, and amid the most perfect and universal peace and tranquility, the sovereignty of the nation is surrendered, and incorporated with that of another.

The Lone Star of Texas, which ten years since arose amid clouds, over fields of carnage, and obscurely shone for a while, has culminated, and, following an inscrutable destiny, has passed on and become fixed forever in that glorious constellation which all freemen and lovers of freedom in the world must reverence and adore—the American Union. Blending its rays with its sister Stars, long may it continue to shine, and may generous Heaven smile upon this consummation of the wishes of the two Republics now joined in one. "May the Union be perpetual, and may it be the means of conferring benefits and blessings upon the people of all the States," is my ardent prayer.

The final act in this great drama is now performed. The republic of Texas is no more.

When the last sentence fell from the lips of the earnest speaker, the beloved flag of Texas was unfurled and was lowered, seemingly into the silent shades of the grave. The boom of artillery announced the fact. The glorious banner of our fathers ascended in its stead. All were ready to welcome it, to make a mental vow to stand by it to the death; yet there were feelings none could express. They came as do the pangs which rive the heart when loved ones are snatched from our embrace. A flood of thought like a torrent rushed upon the memory. The scenes of years passed by in review: stricken fields, murdered relatives, toils, privations, victory, came before the mind's eye apparently in palpable reality. To be severed from these, to bid adieu to the past, to pay the last tribute to the national flag they adored and almost worshipped, was too much to be borne by human nature. Many old pioneers, who had done duty on the skirmish line of civilization for years and had never flinched in the face of danger and death, were overcome, and tears coursed down sunburnt cheeks where they were almost total strangers. The writer will never forget that scene. It was too impressive to be eradicated from the tablets of memory. It was a blending of sorrow for the past, joy for the present, and radiant hope for the future. May God forever bless and perpetuate the union then effected, and which called forth those mingled emotions.

BOOK 2 *The Valley*

VI

>>>

WAR BEGINS

The events leading to a war between Mexico and the United States are known, more or less, through the medium of history. That struggle between the Spanish-American and the Anglo-American races was a consequence of the Texas Revolution of 1835–1836. It was one of the results, the fruits, of the victory of San Jacinto. The expansion of the United States was in the direction of the South and West. Her acquisitions were peaceful, the returns arising from diplomacy and the outlay of treasure. She had thus obtained possession of an immense area bounded on the south by the Sabine and the Red River. On their banks stood the proud hidalgos of Spanish descent, jealous of their reputation, ready to defend the honor of their country, and suspicious of the intentions of their grasping neighbors. It was plain there existed in the very nature of the situation elements calculated to produce heart burnings, disputes, and ruptures.

The settlement of Americans in Texas was the cause of a collision. The annexation of Texas to the Federal Union brought on a war. Mexico claimed that the northern boundary of the State of Tamaulipas was the Nueces River which was also formerly the southern boundary of the State of Texas—Mexico had forgotten the broad distinction between the Republic of Texas and Texas as an integral part of Mexico. Texas claimed that, by the treaty with Santa Anna in 1836, the southern boundary was the Río Grande.

The troops of the United States, led by General Zachary Taylor, advanced to the northern bank of the Río Grande and received the baptism of fire from the soldiers of Mexico in the battles of Palo Alto and Resaca de la Palma.

The Congress of the United States solemnly declared that "war exists between Mexico and the United States by the act of Mexico," or words equivalent in meaning. This declaration was based on the claim of Texas to all the territory between the Nueces River and the Río Grande. If the claim of Texas was null, then the United States was an aggressor, and her Congress, in accusing Mexico of opening the hostilities, had stated a falsehood.

2

When the Congress declared war, the people of Texas were prompt in organizing commands and offering their services to the President of the United States. Captain Sam Walker, with an efficient company, was with General Taylor on the Río Grande, previous to the battles of Palo Alto and Resaca de la Palma. These affairs caused great and intense excitement in the United States.

This history of much which happened during the war has been written and needs no comment. The part played by Colonel Jack Hays' second regiment of Texas Rangers has not received due notice.[1]

The first act of Colonel Hays on assuming command of the northern and western frontier of Texas was to report the condition of affairs there. After consulting with officers who had seen service on the frontier, he established a line just above the edge of the outer tier of settlements and stationed the companies of [Middleton T.] Johnson, [Shapley P.] Ross, [Samuel] Highsmith, [James S.] Gillett, and [Henry W.] Baylor upon it. The intention was to have these company commanders send patrols be-

---

[1] Hays' First Regiment had been discharged after the battle of Monterrey and Hays had been appointed to command the Texas frontier. He later received permission to recruit a second ranger outfit, which is the one Ford writes about.

tween their respective stations almost daily and to take the steps necessary to give protection to life and property.

Lieutenant Colonel [Peter H.] Bell was left in charge of the companies designated for service in Texas. He was an officer experienced in frontier affairs and managed matters carefully. Several of the commanders of companies were men of ability and well qualified to do good duty. The operations of this frontier battalion inspired confidence in the people. The settlements were pushed outward rapidly.

Having arranged matters on the frontier, Colonel Hays made his headquarters at San Antonio [and called for volunteers for his second ranger regiment]. Major Reeves was his quartermaster, Lieutenant [Joseph] Pancoast his commissary of subsistence. Dr. [A.] Parker was assigned to his regiment as surgeon. Reverend Samuel H. Corley, a Presbyterian minister, performed the double duty of soldier and chaplain. He was a man combining the rare qualities of a gentleman, a Christian, and a soldier. He will be spoken of again. Frank "Buffalo Hump" Harris held a position in the quartermaster's department.

The command was composed of men of good character. The officers were generally very kind to the men, and were courteous to each other. Captain [Isaac] Ferguson had served in three wars—that of 1812 with England and two Indian wars. He was seventy years of age, prompt in the performance of duty, gallant and generous in his dealings with friend or foe; he was a favorite of the regiment.

On August 12, 1847, the rangers left for the Río Grande. Our march to Laredo was attended by nothing sensational. It developed a good deal of rawness on the part of some of the command, especially in reference to guard duty. The countersign was a mystery to many.

At Laredo the company of Captain [Mirabeau B.] Lamar was stationed. He had been president of the Republic of Texas, yet with the spirit of true patriotism he accepted service where he supposed he could be instrumental in promoting the public good. Hamilton P. Bee was one of his lieutenants.

We crossed the Río Grande and marched down the stream toward Matamoros. When we reached Mier our entrance caused some excitement among the Mexicans. A good looking young lady was credited with having said: "I had rather see every relative I have, dead, here, before my eyes, than to see the Texians enter Mier unresisted." The fight at that place between the Texians and Mexicans, back in 1842, had caused bitter recollections.[2]

---

[2] Despite the hostility of many Mexican citizens, the rangers while encamped in the

We camped near the Río Grande a short distance below Matamoros. It was now understood that we were to embark at Brazos Santiago for Vera Cruz, and report for duty to General Winfield Scott. In a week or so we were moved down the river to a place called Ranchita. From this point Frank Harris was sent to Texas in charge of quartermaster property.

Mier vicinity attended *fiestas* and *fandangos,* drinking and dancing with the "bright-eyed Señoras" and entering the jousts and riding tournaments which they always won with their fast horses. The Mexicans were highly respectful of the Texans' ability with horse and pistol, and somewhat resentful of their way with women. "Many a lady stood behind and cried" when the tall *gringos* mounted and resumed their march toward Matamoros. "Either in fighting or in love," reflected a Mexican correspondent, "these Texans are hard to beat." *Texas Democrat* (Austin), September 16, 1847.

VII

>>>

TO THE VALLEY OF MEXICO

To a majority of us — and a large majority — the idea of proceeding to Vera Cruz was exceedingly palatable; others felt differently. The discontents were busy in presenting their side of the question. They represented the dangers of campaigning in the interior of Mexico as very numerous; the valleys of Mexico were little better than graveyards; they played "Home, Sweet Home" on a harp of a thousand strings, and they had listeners. They descanted on the pains of absence from loved ones for twelve long months, and much more of that sort of "rigmarole." These appeals were addressed to the heart, the affections, and caused some tender-hearted boobies to blubber. The next appeal was to the stomach; they insisted the United States ration of subsistence was not enough to keep off the pinching pangs of hunger. They professed to be starving—slowly dying a lingering and torturous death.

Captain Truitt talked plainly to the malcontents. He accused them of hypocrisy, falsehood, and hinted strongly that cowardice was a factor in the mutinous movement. He promised the ringleaders a quick, short journey to Hades by the court-martial and rifle line, which annoyed them greatly.

John Glanton, who afterwards figured on both sides of the Sierra Madre,[1] managed to get a drink or two, called the boys together and began speaking to them. The officers discovered the drift of his speech, and let him proceed.

"I understand you fellows have been preaching all sorts of stuff to the men. You talk about the distance to the valley of Mexico, and what you will suffer in being absent from your families a whole year, as if no one with a heart as big as a pin's head could not stand all that. From my acquaintance with some men I am certain their families would be better off without them than with them, and many of you ought to leave home. You have run around camp and tried to look like starved wolves, poor dogs, whipped away from a pile of offal, and you succeeded. You have turned your backs upon the truth and said that the United States ration was not enough to keep soul and body together. This sounds nice, coming from your sort. D——n you, I know the most of you grumblers; when compelled to stay at home, you don't get a meal of greasy victuals once in two weeks; now you are putting on airs, and turning up your snouts at better living than you ever had in your lives."

The wind up of Glanton's impromptu speech was less complimentary to the "strikers for better grub" than the above quotations. They slunk away. They had done enough to have the ringleaders spotted and sent home. It was the safest procedure. According to memory there were not as many as five of them. Captain Truitt gave them one of his comforting addresses before they departed. Order reigned at Ranchita.

Justice to the memory of Colonel John C. Hays requires the declaration that no officer ever possessed more completely the esteem, the confi-

---

[1] Only 26 when he joined the United States Army in January, 1847, John Joel Glanton got into trouble for shooting a Mexican civilian—Glanton claimed he did it in self-defense, eyewitnesses said he did it in cold blood. When army police sought to put him in irons, he borrowed food and ammunition from his friend, Walter P. Lane, and rode for Texas.

Later he re-enlisted in Jack Hays' second regiment and saw action throughout the Mexico City Expedition. In 1849 Glanton, attracted by the stories of gold in California, left his wife and two children in San Antonio and headed for the Pacific Coast. He paid his way by killing Apaches and selling the scalps at fifty dollars apiece to Mexican authorities. Some said the scalps were not always Apache. He was killed in an Indian fight at Yuma, Arizona, early in 1850.

(*Handbook of Texas*, I, 693–694.)

dence, and the love of his men. The complaints of the discontented involved no charge against him. No combination could have been made in that command to antagonize him. A move in that direction would have brought trouble and danger to the instigators. The "home-sick" squad were jeered and laughed at by most of the boys.

Flem Bardley, the son of a very respectable widow of San Antonio, accompanied the command. He was about fourteen years of age—a noble and brave youth. He was very useful about headquarters in many ways. He was very much liked by all of us. Gilbert A. Brush was sergeant-major of the command. He will be spoken of hereafter.

Major [Michael H.] Chevaille, one of Colonel Hays' old rangers, resigned the command of a battalion on General [J. E.] Wool's line in order to join his old commander and friend. Chevaille was an officer of more than ordinary qualifications. He was a good clerk and accountant, and could make out quartermaster papers, and almost any other papers pertaining to the service. He was a gentleman of chivalrous impulses, of a high order of courage, a good rider, a fine shot, and was seldom thrown off his balance. He had seen much service. He eventually became one of the contractors to furnish supplies of subsistence and forage to our command. He possessed the good opinion of officers and men. He had been crossed in love and, in moments of despondency, had recourse to the inebriating bowl.

To mention a quadruped may seem out of place, and must be pardoned: the adjutant rode a noted horse, "Ball Higgins." He had been entered in races in eastern Texas and had won considerable money for his owners. He carried a man in the campaign of Monterey, and was noted for his extraordinary powers of endurance, his sagacity, and his rascality. More of Higgins by and by.

2

The necessary transportation was furnished to carry the command by water to Vera Cruz. Colonel Hays directed the adjutant to go in advance with Truitt's company and locate a campsite for the regiment. On board the officers were assigned staterooms. An Irishman, acting as watchman, or in some such capacity, made two efforts to turn the adjutant out of his stateroom. The second one ended in trouble. The Hibernian did not come out winner. The next trouble was to get him away from the men who came pouring up from below.

The adjutant soon succumbed to seasickness. One day while he was on deck a terrific outcry was heard below, followed by exulting shouts.

"What happened?"

One of the men came up, and made the following answer: "You remember the old Irishman who tried to turn you out? Well, he had been annoying us about drinking water, and in various other ways. Today he was meddling with the horses. He came in reach of Old Higgins, and the old scoundrel pitched at him, open-mouthed. He took Paddy's ear off clean as it could have been done by a pair of shears; then chewed it up, and swallowed it. He looked all the time like the devilment pleased him. We boys couldn't help laughing."

3

In due time the Castle of San Juan de Ulúa and the city of Vera Cruz loomed up, and they gladdened our hearts. Landsmen do not enjoy being cooped up on a sea-going craft. There was rejoicing when our feet touched the land.

Captain Ferguson and Captain Truitt were about the first to reach Vera Cruz. The rangers were directed to encamp at Vergara, three miles from Vera Cruz on the road to Jalapa. There were a few small houses on the ground. It was a sandy locality and quite unpleasant during high winds. About two hundred yards to our right, on a small height, on the coast of the Gulf of Mexico, lay the Massachusetts regiment, raised and organized by General [Caleb] Cushing, of whose brigade the Texans formed a part.

In a short time tents were erected and camp scenes began to be enacted. We were anxious to sustain the reputation of Texas Rangers and not lie around in idleness. Camp was laid off, company messes located in proper form, and everything done to prevent surprise by the enemy. The bane of nothing to do was not allowed to enervate and dissatisfy the men.

4

During the fall of 1847 the Mexican guerrilla bands were giving considerable trouble outside the walls of Vera Cruz. Their activities were known to General [Robert] Patterson who had been on leave and had returned a few days before to report for duty at General Scott's headquarters. Scott was in command at Vera Cruz and was organizing a force to proceed to the City of Mexico. Captain Truitt, Captain Ferguson, and the writer waited on General Patterson and paid their respects. In the course of the conversation, Patterson referred to the guerrillas, and asked if the rangers could be used against them successfully. We replied in the affirmative. He mentioned Colonel Zenobia as particularly troublesome. He spoke of the hacienda of San Juan, about thirty miles away, as a place of resort for the irregular forces of Mexico, who were fighting more for plunder than for their government. He intimated a doubt of the rangers being able to penetrate the country and do effective service. We assured him that we would willingly make the effort, but suggested the propriety of having a guide. He had one called in. He described the country we were to pass over, mentioning a ruined cabin on the right hand side of the Jalapa road and a "blind path" leading off.

"When can you start?"

"At any hour the general designates day or night."

"Say four o'clock in the morning."

"All right. Have your guide on hand or we shall leave him."

The general treated the latter remark as an idle boast, but furnished all the supplies demanded.

At four o'clock the next morning our bugle sounded the advance. The guide had not arrived. The command consisted of parts of several companies—as well as is remembered, those of Ferguson, Truitt, and Roberts. We marched at the trot. The "blind path" was found and followed. It led through a country of great fertility, a dense jungle walled in the dim trail. We made about twenty-five miles and struck a more heavily-timbered country where the parasitical vines rendered the field of vision quite circumscribed. The adjutant was at the head of the column. Without notice he spurred his horse, drew his revolver, and dashed off at a gallop. In advance of him was discovered a small party of guerrillas. He levelled his revolver; his horse tumbled over, turning a somerset, Ford falling over the animal. The men had followed. One of them fired, and it was supposed he had killed Ford and his horse. Some threats were uttered concerning the soldier's rash act. The adjutant, covered with mud, was soon on his feet. His horse had stepped one foot into a small hole in the ground and had fallen.

The mishap caused a delay of seconds only, but it gave the fleeing guerrillas a better chance to escape. A ranch was reached in a few minutes. The guerrillas and rangers entered it at a run. Two or three of the guerrillas were killed. The balance escaped. One was hard pressed by Ford. He snapped his pistol at the Mexican several times: the caps were wet and the weapon did not explode. Ford drew his sword, rushed at the *guerrillero*; the latter abandoned his horse and jumped into a cabin. Ford followed on foot, sword in hand. It was a small hut; a good looking woman was standing in the middle of it, on a dirt floor; no man could be seen. The excited ranger ran around the house a time or two but discovered no man into whose vitals he could plunge his sword. He sheathed the unblooded weapon, mounted Old Higgins, and looked very like a fellow who had peeped through a crack and had seen his rival playing yum-yum with the gal of his heart.

A short march brought us in sight of an hacienda. We sent a detachment to the left to gain that side and the rear of the buildings. The main body moved briskly on, encountered and fired on some men, killed one or two, advanced on the hacienda. There we met with no resistance. The detachment moving to the left had to fall in our rear; they encountered a small stream they were unable to pass. Captain Truitt commanded that detachment.

The main building was large and fine and was richly furnished. It had a tessellated marble floor. Upon the premises were found American-made shirts with ball holes in them and blood upon them. American corn sacks and many other things, taken from our people without a doubt, were discovered. This was the home of Colonel Zenobia and the headquarters of the guerrilla bands. Upon consultation it was resolved to burn it. The family was advised to leave. The men had a minute or two to pick up valuables. The torch was applied and the splendid edifice was consumed. It was an unpleasant scene, one a man may hope never to witness again.

Some nice things were taken from Colonel Zenobia's house. One chap had placed behind his saddle an old fashioned clock with a long pendulum and long cords to the weights. He was ordered to drop it, and did so.

Someone carried us over to the road leading from Orizaba to Vera Cruz. On the march to camp several other little affairs occurred. In one of these a Mexican officer, said to be a general, was killed. His uniform and chapeau were donned by a ranger.

Just before sundown we passed General Patterson as he was reviewing some troops. We had the credit of having marched sixty miles that day. Everything was reported to General Patterson, who told us we might have trouble over the house burning, but promised to stand by us. The owner had a safe conduct from General Scott. Nothing was ever done in the matter. It was presumed that the commander-in-chief recognized the act as legitimate under circumstances.

5

The landing of Colonel Hays after the scout gave the command great pleasure. He was very popular.[2] He was employed most of his time. He

---

[2] John C. Hays was a deceptive man. He was small, standing just under five feet eight and carrying barely 150 pounds on his wiry frame. He couldn't grow a beard or a mustache; he wore modest clothes, usually a black leather cap, a blue roundabout, and black pants; he spoke little and ate little; he was nervous and walked slightly stooped; his cheeks were gaunt and his hands were thin and pale; beside his bewhiskered rangers

was frequently in the saddle heading scouts. During his absences, his tent was in charge of his permanent orderly, John Buchanan. The writer was made the acquaintance of this specimen of humanity.

Colonel [J. M.] Withers had presented Colonel Hays with a half barrel of fine whiskey. While Colonel Hays was off scouting, his orderly was keeping open house, doing the amiable and the hospitable. It is due to the truth of history to say that many of the members of Colonel Cushing's late regiment were not perfect. If some of them had been in Egypt in the time of Moses, they would not have left the flesh pots if said pots had contained a supply of "Monongahela." These gentlemen were strong friends of "Buck." High old times were had on the sly.

One day a Massachusetts semiofficial called on his Irish companion. He saw something he liked, picked it up, and started out. A little man was sitting there, plainly dressed—rated by the Massachusetts worthy as a camp follower. He had the impudence to tell a free-handed representative of Massachusetts chivalry: "Put that down, sir!" Perhaps indignation, contempt, and scorn were never so strikingly personified as on this occasion. Massachusetts first beat the long roll of profanity, and then he spoke: "You don't know who I am, sir! I am sergeant of the guard, sir! I'll have you put in the guardhouse, sir!"

Up to this moment we of Texas had been enjoying the joke. The scene was so ludicrous we had to laugh. When the sergeant stepped out of the tent and called for his guard, and they were on the eve of coming, the feeling changed.

---

in their huge, wide-brimmed hats and loud garbs, most of them over six feet and solidly built, Hays looked "more like a boy than a man." (One officer of the regular army, seeing Hays for the first time, asked who that little fellow was at the head of the Texas regiment, stared incredulously when someone said it was Jack Hays, "the world renowned" ranger and Indian fighter.) At first the colonel was as much an enigma to Adjutant Ford as he was to those who did not know him. How could this boyish soldier control an outfit of hardened frontiersmen, killers by necessity, who had come to Mexico to settle a score and who were not going to be bothered by rules and regulations in going about it? Why did they worship him, idolize him? After a few months of fighting, Ford would know the answer: because Jack Hays, quick and well-coordinated, could use his Bowie knife, his Colts, and his fists better than any man in his command, could swear longer and yell louder, when he wanted to, than any other ranger, could ride harder and longer than anybody Ford ever saw, and because Hays possessed those qualities that made a man an excellent officer: he mixed kindness and strictness in such a way as to command respect and obedience, he knew the potential of his men both collectively and individually, and he well understood that a leader at bottom must be decisive, aggressive, and highly confident. Old Texans agreed to a man that Jack Hays was among the more distinguished soldiers in Texas during its formative years.

(James Kimmins Greer, *Colonel Jack Hays: Texas Frontier Leader and California Builder;* John S. Ford, "John C. Hays in Texas," ms.; *Jack Hays, the Intrepid Texas Ranger;* Albert G. Brackett, *General Lane's Brigade in Central Mexico,* pp. 194–195.)

"What!" Ford thundered. "Put our colonel in the guardhouse? Don't you try it!"

Colonel Hays was terribly mad. "Ford, order a file of men here."

The ranger guard was already on the way. The indignant sergeant was rudely placed in "durance file." When he learned he had been talking to Colonel Hays his countenance fell. He saw a court-martial in the near future, punishment, reduction to the ranks, and all that. He remained cooped up 48 hours and then was released. No charge was made against him. He quit calling on Buchanan.

While at Vergara, we drew six-shooters, the old fashioned long-barreled arm. It carried a ball as near the mark, and to a greater distance, than the Mississippi rifle. Many of the men had not used revolvers. Some of them put the small end of the conical ball down first. A single fire usually burst the cylinder. Some let the loose powder trail around the cylinder; six shots would be fired at once. One day a "greeny" was in his tent cleaning his pistol. The adjutant advised him to remove the caps. He said he would. In a minute or two a pistol shot was heard. Greeny had shot his own horse in the head and put himself afoot.

6

Joe Sanders was a good humored soldier, jovial, full of anecdotes, never grumbling; he was the life of the camp. A scout was going out to Santa Anna's hacienda of Mango de Clavo. The night before they started Joe dreamed that he borrowed John Glanton's short rifle, went along, and while dismounting, the rifle went off, the ball striking him near the left nipple and mortally wounding him. The next morning he borrowed the rifle, and got permission to accompany the scout. He rode with the muzzle of the rifle to the left side of the horse. When in the act of alighting, his leg came in contact with the hammer, the gun was discharged, and Joe wounded near the left nipple. He exclaimed: "My dream has come to pass." And he died.

These presentiments defy the depth and grasp of our philosophy. They may be the workings of what we call "special providences"—the warning directed to the intellect, the mind, of the person interested. Had Joe Sanders heeded the dream and remained in camp, he might be living yet.

7

Colonel Hays was the only field officer in the command. An order was obtained allowing the election of a major—Captain A. M. Truitt, Captain Gabriel M. Armstrong, and Sergeant Major Gilbert Brush were candidates.

Brush had been a Mier prisoner. He was brave, generous, and aimed to do right. He was a soldier when he should have been a school boy. His faults were those usual to a man of ardent temperament and limited education. He was wounded at the battle of Monterey.

A. M. Truitt became our major. He was a gentleman of ordinary education. He had a vigorous intellect, a clear head, and was actuated by pure motives. He was firm, immovable in resolution, but just and generous. He could be moved by an appeal to reason and equity, and was intractable under threats and menaces. He possessed a high order of physical and moral courage and never shirked any legitimate responsibility. The men of Hays' regiment loved and feared him. On more than one occasion, when taunted by the false accusation that his official position protected him, he waived rank and invited his accuser to settle the matter in his own way. The swaggerers were careful not to accept the invitation, and changed base instanter.

8

A sail vessel having on board men of our command encountered contrary winds. The danger grew so imminent that the horses were thrown overboard. After the men landed at Vera Cruz steps were taken to assist them to procure remounts.

Brush came one day and informed the adjutant that he had obtained permission to go out with a party to hunt for beef and capture horses for the men. He was advised not to go. "You have no official rank, having resigned"—he had resigned his captaincy to run for major. "The men may not obey you. Things may go wrong, and you may get into trouble."

The raiders went. About 3 P.M. runners came post haste, bringing intelligence that the men had been attacked by guerrillas and scattered; its seeming definiteness caused a force to go to the rescue promptly, Colonel Hays in command. At about seven miles from the camp, a ranger or two were met. One of them had a man behind him; he was desirous to unhorse, but had not succeeded. We will call the rear rider Gutterbury. He had been in the reputed fight. He professed to have had his horse killed from under him, to have hid in a thicket from the bloodthirsty Mexicans, and to have made a narrow escape. He expressed thanks to the man who had picked him up, and said much about that sort of thing. The front rider repudiated thanks, swore the other had jumped up behind him against his will and to his peculiar discomfort. The fact is, Gutterbury was not in a condition to be either ornamental or useful in a parlor, a boudoir, or even in a barber shop.

No dead were found on the battlefield. Gutterbury's horse had resurrected and gone. In process of time it leaked out through Van Walling that the raiders had divided; one detachment charged the other out of pure "cussedness." Gutterbury's horse did good service during the campaign; he never rode him on a scout, being afflicted by a chronic colic. When an expedition was about to be sent out the attacks became terribly acute.

9

A messenger came into camp in great haste with official information that the guerrillas had killed four men of an Ohio command outside the city of Vera Cruz. Colonel Hays was directed to send out rangers to pursue and chastize the enemy. The company of Captain Jacob Roberts was detailed. The trail led in the direction of Medellín. A skirmish ensued. The next day Captain Roberts returned, and, at his request, the adjutant wrote his report. He claimed a victory and set down the loss of the enemy at five killed.

A confidential conversation came off.

"Look here Jake, I want the truth, how many did you kill?"

"Not more than twenty-five."

The command had men in it who had suffered loss of relatives by the Mexicans massacring prisoners of war. There were men who had been Santa Fé prisoners, Mier prisoners, and prisoners made at San Antonio by Vásquez and Woll. Young Lewin Rogers was in Mexico on a mission of revenge. Mexicans had cut the throats of his family: Mr. and Mrs. Rogers, their daughter, and their son William, who lived as if by a miracle. This affair had happened on the Arroyo Colorado, thirty miles north of Brownsville. Was it a wonder that it was sometimes difficult to restrain these men, whose feelings had been lacerated by domestic bereavements and who were standing face to face with the people whose troops had committed these bloody deeds? They never made war upon any but armed men, when the field was open and the lists free. They scorned the role of the assassin and loathed petty thieving. If in need of a horse they would take one. Their rule was to pay for anything to eat or wear. They waged hostilities upon a scale they deemed legitimate, and calculated not to wound the honor and injure the reputation of Texas soldiers. The men of Hays' regiment loved Texas, and they would do nothing to bring dishonor upon their State or themselves. Visitors at a ranger camp frequently expressed astonishment when they heard expressions of men, ordinary in appearance, indicating a high grade of patriotism for Texas. It was that feeling which enabled a few men, a mere handful, to maintain a government against great odds in numbers and to place a rich and immense country in the Union. That feeling of devotion to the Lone Star State has made them good citizens and meritorious soldiers.

10

Antigua is a small town on the Antigua River about twenty or twenty-five miles from Vera Cruz in a northerly direction. The river is broad and deep, and enters the Gulf of Mexico about eight miles from the little town.

By permission of Colonel Hays and the commanders of companies, a spy company was organized. It was intended to include only good men and good horses, to do duty on emergencies, to be ready to march on short notice, to be the eyes and ears of the ranger corps. The men and horses were selected with care to the number of fifty. John S. Ford was made captain and John Glanton lieutenant.

Information was received that a force of guerrillas had been concentrated near Antigua. Colonel Hays was sent against them. The spy company was placed in advance. When the sun arose we were marching along the coast. The peak of Orizaba, more than sixty miles distant, appeared to be within half a mile. The optical illusion was complete and beautiful. Near the mouth of the Antigua River the spy company drove in a picket of the enemy, and the matter was reported to Colonel Hays immediately. Ford suggested to the colonel to try the bar at the mouth of the river and, should it be impracticable, seize the fishing smacks lying there, swim the horses over by the vessels' sides, and then move along the beach. He insisted that a Mexican could be captured and forced to guide the rangers to the guerrilla camp. In this way the rear of the enemy could be gained and a surprise inflicted upon him. Ford argued that the picket had by now apprised the commander of the guerrillas of our approach, and they would be watching the main road for our coming. Colonel Hays was of opinion that his orders required him to move by the road and to return that day, which would be impossible should we cross the Antigua at the mouth. The adjutant dissented, saying: "If you get a fight, General Patterson will not care for your being out a day, or a week, longer than he anticipated." This conference was friendly and good humored. The march was resumed. The spy company halted in front of Antigua. A Mexican lancer was sitting on his horse, looking at the Texians. The river was too wide for our guns to reach him.

The main body came up. Colonel Hays ordered Ford to take a detachment and pass the stream. The skiff held eight men. Sixteen rangers crossed. They made a reconnaissance of the place. The expectation was an attack from an overwhelming force of guerrillas; the determination was to hold our position.

A Negro was encountered. He could not speak a word of English. The rangers accused him of "throwing off"—they spoke of killing him. The adjutant interfered, telling the men he had been raised there and probably had never heard a word of our language spoken in his life.

Antigua was a rather enchanting place. Tropical fruits, flowers, and birds of brilliant plumage, everything greeting the eye and the ear were beautiful and pleasant. A ripe pineapple attracted the writer's attention. He plucked it and had a luxurious feast. While awaiting a recall he laid down and unconsciously fell asleep. He was sick, and had been broken of his rest. When he awoke the Negro was standing by him. He told the African in Spanish that he wished to cross to the other bank. The black man ordered a Mexican to carry the American across. It was done promptly. The writer believes to this day that the Negro saved his life, and he has more than once endeavored to repay the debt.

VIII

>>

LOS DIABLOS TEJANOS!

We had long since tired of our encampment when the note of preparation to march was sounding in earnest tones. As we construed the order to Colonel Hays, he was directed to report for duty to General Winfield Scott. Several of our officers advised Colonel Hays to show his order to the ranking quartermaster at Vera Cruz and ask for transportation. In the event of a compliance with this request, Hays should then call for pack mules, and light wagons, and a good supply of ammunition. Our idea was to go as light as possible and march by ourselves. We insisted we could make the march in spite of all opposition. We had about 580 effective men. With the improved revolvers we felt confident we could beat any number the enemy could bring to bear upon us. We thought no body of Americans as small as our command had marched from Vera Cruz to the City of Mexico—we predicted the feat would place Colonel Hays in the front rank of distinguished commanders. He considered it prudent to go with General Patterson's column and incur no unnecessary risks. We submitted at once, and let our ideas give no trouble to our superior.

Our men were beginning to use their six-shooters effectively. They were defective in drill, and not well up in the ordinary discipline of armies, though there was a moral discipline based on a sense of duty, a love of country, and a pride of character, serving as a good substitute. Men thought of what would be said of them at home, of relatives, wives, sweethearts, and all that helped to make them good soldiers.

We made the acquaintance of several officers of the United States Navy. Commodore [M. C.] Perry was an admirer of Colonel Hays. He paid him visits. At a military review the Commodore accompanied General Patterson; the Texians cheered both these officers, who made graceful acknowledgments.

Complaints were made that the spy company interfered with the company duties of its members. The officer instigating this was said to be Captain Armstrong. The spy company was broken up, and no bad feeling engendered.

Captain Armstrong began to evince a contrary and insubordinate spirit, and he availed himself of opportunities to make trouble. The other officers and the men of his company behaved in a proper and laudable manner.

The guerrilla bands annoyed the troops less than previous to our arrival. Their operations had caused many of them to come to grief, and they grew more circumspect.

2

To our intense delight a forward movement was made in November, 1847. The day we reached the *Puente Nacional*—the National Bridge— Colonel Hays suggested, rather than commanded, that Major Truitt and the writer remain in the rear of the marching column. Hays was anxious to have as little straggling as possible, anticipating trouble from guerrillas. We had little difficulty, except with Captain Armstrong. He was often too far in the rear to have received protection had the enemy attacked us. The adjutant conveyed the order of Colonel Hays in a respectful manner, and Captain Armstrong should have obeyed. He made a weak effort at evasion by averring that Lieutenant [Alfred] Evans was in command of the company that day and orders should be delivered to him. By what authority was Captain Armstrong absent from his company? Owing to his failure to be elected major he was not ordered under arrest. Early in the afternoon the column was halted to allow the men a breathing spell and time to close up. Armstrong was more than a hundred yards in the extreme rear, an officer or two with him. They were not of our command. Major Truitt and the writer were each sick and out of humor. They let fall some ugly words, and expressed a hope that the guerrillas would make a descent on Armstrong and his companions. The uncharitable words had scarcely been uttered when "bang," "bang" went the Mexican *escopetas*, and here came Armstrong's crowd in unceremonious haste. The enemy scampered off in another direction. A reconnaissance developed no guerrilla band in the vicinity.

That night Colonel Hays slept under the National Bridge. No tent was spread. Late in the evening Ford was endeavoring to cool a fever, which succeeded a chill, by bathing in the small stream. All at once he discovered a man sitting on his horse in the midst of the cooking utensils. The stranger was inquisitive; not receiving an answer to suit his taste he administered a string of maledictions to the adjutant, assuring him: "I am a wagon master and if you get sick I'll see you in hell before you shall ride in one of my wagons!" Not liking the motions of the other party, he inquired in a mocking tone of voice: "Whose camp is this anyhow?" When the reply reached his ear—"It is Colonel Hays' "—the little man used whip and spur to get out of it. The two met afterwards; the adjutant always laughed, and the wagon master never spoke. He acted like one who had pressing business somewhere else.

3

We reached Jalapa and encamped two miles beyond. Colonel Hays went to Puebla, taking with him the companies of Roberts and Armstrong. Major Truitt remained with the balance of the command; the adjutant also. They were not well, but neither reported sick. Major Chevaille remained with them.

The march to Puebla was without any event worthy of note.[1] General

---

[1] Puebla citizens thronged in the streets to see and touch the rangers as they rode through, some on horses, some on mules, some on jackasses. Then, to the astonishment of the swelling crowd, the rangers alternately trotted and galloped around the main plaza jumping off and back on their mounts and picking handkerchiefs and sticks off the ground, and the amazed onlookers suddenly gasped and pointed at one Texan who came galloping by standing upright in his saddle and waving his six-shooters wildly about. One of General Lane's junior officers watching the performance thought that they certainly were an odd-looking set of fellows, and it seems to be their aim to dress as outlandishly as possible. Bobtailed coats and "long-tailed blues," low and high-crowned hats, some slouched and others Panama, with a sprinkling of black leather caps, constituting their uniforms; and a thorough coating of dust over all, and covering their huge beards gave them a savage appearance. . . . Each man carried a rifle, a pair of . . . Colt's revolvers; a hundred of them could discharge a

Joe Lane was there on his way to the City of Mexico. He and Colonel Hays became quite attached. They received information of a body of Mexican troops in the country to the left of the road to the City of Mexico at a place called Izúcar de Matamoros.

A heavy forced march carried them upon the enemy at daylight. A fight came off, and the Americans were victorious. They killed a good many Mexicans, captured artillery, small arms, and ammunition. They recaptured fifteen American prisoners.

The skirmish having taken place in a town, it involved the capture of horses belonging to noncombatants. Colonel Hays issued an order directing men to return to pacific citizens any property they had taken, upon proper proof of ownership. A Mexican claimed the celebrated black horse of Reverend Samuel H. Corley. He was one of the most noted animals in the regiment, in fact, in Texas. He had been in service on General Taylor's line. He had the habit of running away whenever it suited his whims. He had the credit of having run off with Captain Robert H. Taylor, while on General Taylor's line. The horse carried his unwilling rider into a funeral procession, jumped the hearse, and did many ugly things. He sometimes stampeded with our reverend friend and acted in a very unbecoming manner for a parson's Rosinante. The Mexican claimant came forward with immense confidence and declared he had raised that black imp of horse flesh from a colt. What was more, he proved his allegations by a couple of his countrymen whose character for veracity had never been impeached before any court. Our preacher friend refused to believe it and spoke somewhat of fighting before he would surrender the black colt to the truthful claimant. It was one of the best jokes of the season.

Our troops remained in Izúcar de Matamoros until the next morning. General Lane had impressed teams to transport the captured ordnance and ordnance stores. He took up the line of march for Puebla by way of Atlixco. One of the Mexican spies, Miguel, was in advance, watching carefully against ambuscades and surprises. A small force preceded the head of the column commanded by Second Lieutenant James G. Gaither, of Roberts' company.

After having proceeded four or five miles, Miguel came running at full

---

thousand shots in two minutes, and with what precision the Mexican alone could tell.

(Albert G. Brackett, *General Lane's Brigade in Central Mexico*, pp. 173–174; Lieutenant Colonel Ebenezer Dumont's Letters, published in the *Indiana Register* and quoted in the *Democratic Telegraph and Texas Register* [Columbia], February 24, 1848.)

speed, closely pursued by about two hundred lancers. They attacked the advance. Colonel Hays moved to the sound of the firing and assumed command. He ordered a charge, which was obeyed by all of Captain Roberts' company who heard the order. About forty rangers rushed upon the enemy, drove them in confusion, and pursued them nearly a mile. On passing the crest of a hill they found themselves in presence of a line of about fifteen hundred troops. The precipitation of the retreating lancers upon the line caused it to waver. It was the opinion of many present on that occasion that a dash upon the main body of the enemy would have broken his line. Colonel Hays thought differently and directed the rangers to fall back to the main body. As soon as they wheeled to execute the order they received the fire of the whole Mexican line. This they followed up by a charge. Lieutenant [Henderson] Ridgely of the United States regulars was killed, so was a Private Malpass; Captain Roberts' horse was killed. Several of his men wheeled to assist him, among them James A. Carr. The captain gathered hold of George White's stirrup and ran by his side, and, assisted by the momentum of the horse, finally jumped up behind him, and was carried along with the retiring rangers. On reaching the head of General Lane's column some confusion ensued. General Lane and Colonel Hays rallied the men. They poured in a galling fire from their revolvers, charged the enemy to the teeth and, despite their superior numbers, forced them off the field. Officers spoke of this as one of the most brilliant affairs of the war. The fighting covered two days— November 23 and 24, 1847.

A few years ago a correspondence sprung up in reference to the officer in command of the Texas Rangers in this affair which will be noticed further on. The writer received letters from James G. Gaither and one from Captain Alfred Evans. An extract from Evans giving details of a rather amusing character was published in the Austin *Mute Ranger* and is reproduced:

You doubtless recollect that we had several wagons loaded with Mexican *escopetas* [or muskets] taken at Matamoros and we were deluged with rain that evening. The wagons were in rear of the command, and protected by a guard. A report was sent to the front that the wagons were bogging and the horses stalling. A halt was ordered. General Lane gave directions to unload the muskets, pile, and burn them. They were throwing out, piling, and burning muskets for a distance of half a mile. The guns were loaded. The first pile got heated and began to go off. The rear guard thought the Mexicans were firing at them, and came running up. By that time several piles were adding to the fusilade. You remember, no doubt, that our company was dismounted in water ankle deep, caused by the rain, and sent to the rear to repel the attack. We soon found out what was the matter, and reported all. We resumed our march and reached Atlixco at midnight, where we remained the balance of the night.

There was an incident connected with the night march worthy of record. Bill Hicklin, of Captain Witt's company, fell asleep during a halt. When he awoke he felt rather desolate. He wandered about in the mountainous surroundings, not knowing which way the Americans had gone. Impelled by hunger, he went to a Mexican residence. He was treated with extreme kindness, secreted from other Mexicans, and finally sent into Puebla, where he joined his company. Bill was a great wag, and recounted the adventure with much humor. Until his unexpected arrival it was supposed he had been killed. He was extremely fortunate in having fallen in with a kind-hearted and humane Mexican gentleman.

Four or five years ago, the writer wrote and published a notice of the affair which took place near Izúcar de Matamoros. The report was made up from the statements of officers and men who took part in it. In that article Colonel John C. Hays was credited with the control of the Texas Rangers who did most of the fighting. James G. Gaither denied the allegation, and affirmed that he was in charge of the rangers on that occasion. It was difficult for the writer to understand how a lieutenant could command in an engagement when the colonel of his regiment was present on the field. Mr. Gaither replied that Colonel Hays was not in the fight; and his assertion was backed by the evidence of Captain Alfred Evans. In order to decide the disputed point, the writer endeavored to procure a copy of General Joe Lane's official report of the battle. He was unable to do so in Texas. He applied to Major General David S. Stanley, who had the kindness to refer the application to Brigadier General R. C. Drum, adjutant general of the United States Army. The latter official had the generosity to respond promptly and forwarded the reports of General Lane and other officers.

General Lane's report is dated December 1, 1847, at Puebla. He said he had in his command "one piece of artillery and twenty-five men, under the command of Lieutenant B. Field of the Third Artillery, and one hundred and thirty-five men, consisting of Colonel Hays' Texas Mounted Riflemen and of the Louisiana Dragoons under Captain Lewis." [Lane goes on to describe the fighting in great detail and tells how he personally ordered Colonel Hays to make particular movements.] "Never did any officer act with more gallantry than Colonel Hays in this affair of the twenty-fourth. When he found it necessary to retire for the purpose of reloading, his men having no sabres, he halted in their rear and, as the enemy advanced, deliberately shot two of them dead, and covered his [own] retreat until the arrival of reinforcements."

The official report of General Lane decides the question as to the person commanding in the fight of Galaxa Pass. It must not be supposed that James G. Gaither would set up a claim without any foundation in truth. He commanded the small detachment of observation, hence the descrepancy concerning commanders.

4

Our entrance into the City of Mexico on December 6, 1847, produced a sensation among the inhabitants. They thronged the streets along which we passed. The greatest curiosity prevailed to get a sight at *Los Diablos Tejanos*—"the Texas Devils."[2] The streets of the city are paved mostly with smooth, round pebbles. One of the men let his pistol fall from his belt by accident. One of the chambers was discharged; the ball struck a Mexican on the leg. He had the credit of an attempt to murder. The column was halted for the purpose of having quarters assigned. The center of the column was about opposite the Grand Cathedral, which stands on the Grand Plaza. The following incident was related by Captain Parry W. Humphreys, an eyewitness:

While the rangers were sitting on their horses a Mexican passed with a *cesto*—basket—of candies on his head. A ranger beckoned to him. He came near and the Texian took a handful of candy and ate it. He did so a second and a third time. The Mexican supposing he was being robbed, stooped down, got hold of a pebble, and threw it at the ranger with great force. The latter lowered

---

[2] An American watching the wild Texans enter Mexico City said they "excited as much lively interest as if President Polk and the American Congress had suddenly set themselves down in front of the Palace. . . . Crowds of men flocked to see them . . . and women, affrighted, rushed from the balconies into the houses." The rangers, yipping and hooting, then began to demonstrate their peerless horsemanship, as they'd done at Puebla—much to the despair and mortification of a group of regular officers who had come up to see what all the commotion was about. Lieutenant Colonel Ebenezer Dumont of the Fourth Regiment, Indiana Volunteers, told them not to worry:

A nobler set of fellows than these same Texian tatterdemalions never unsheathed a sword in their country's cause or offered up their lives on their country's altar. Young and vigorous, kind, generous, and brave, they have purposely dressed themselves in such a garb, as to prove to the world at a glance that they are neither regulars nor volunteers, but Texas Rangers—as free and unrestrained as the air they breathe, or the deer in their own native wildwood.

(*Jack Hays: the Intrepid Texas Ranger*, p. 21; Dumont's Letters, published in the *Indiana Register* and quoted in the *Democratic Telegraph and Texas Register*, February 24, 1848.)

his hand towards his holster—a pistol shot rang on the air—the Mexican fell dead. There must have been ten thousand people on the Grand Plaza. They were desperately frightened; a stampede occurred. Men ran over each other. Some were knocked into the filthy sewers, all were frantically endeavoring to increase the distance between themselves and *Los Tejanos Sangrientes*—the bloody Texians. Those lucky enough not to be trampled under foot were imminently successful.

The ranger would have paid for the candy. Thieving was not tolerated. The troops were paid as regularly as circumstances permitted. A thief was not respected by Colonel Hays's men.

A company was marching to the quarters assigned; one of its members, a mere boy, became enraged at his horse, and struck him on the head with the butt of his gun. It fired and the ball wounded a Mexican in the abdomen.

During the evening some rangers were about to enter a theatre. A Mexican sneak thief stole one of their handkerchiefs. The theft was detected. The thief was ordered to stop in Spanish; he ran faster. A six-shooter was levelled upon him and discharged. The Mexican dropped lifeless to the pavement. The ranger recovered his handkerchief and went his way as if nothing had happened.

These reports obtained so much currency that a deputation of Mexicans waited upon General Scott and supplicated him to order the Texians out of the city, else no one would be left alive soon. This was never authenticated, but generally reported and believed.[3]

Some Texas officers engaged board at the Inn of the National Theatre. They were ushered into the dining room. A Mexican waiter eyed them inquisitively. He was at a loss to make out their rank. All of them were dressed in garbs indicating a respectable position in the world, but none wore uniforms. He began questioning as to State residence. He had almost finished the roll of States when someone spoke up: "*Somos Tejanos*"—"we are Texians." He glared fearfully at us for an instant, dropped a tray, and rushed from the room. In a few minutes another Mexican came in laughing. He was asked: "Where is the other waiter?"

"Gone! You will see him no more. If you are Texians, you are my countrymen." He remained. It was almost a self-evident truth that a very slight menace from one of his "countrymen" would have sent him off at full speed.

---

[3] The war correspondent to the New Orleans *Picayune* said that a number of frantic businessmen had come to army headquarters and begged the officers not to let the rangers go into the streets without a strong guard over them.
(New Orleans *Picayune*, December 29, 1847.)

The next day we began taking observations. On some occasions two or three Mexicans would pretend to be passing an American officer at the same moment. In the melee the *gringo* frequently landed in the sewer. They usually found business on the other side of the street when a Texian passed along, however.

It was a hard matter to keep a handkerchief in the street. We adopted the plan of pinning them in our pockets. The unlucky rogue clutching at one thus secured generally received a good beating.

At the date of our arrival from three to five Americans were found dead in the streets of a morning; some *gringo* lost his life every night. These things were not officially reported. There were police and an American patrol or police guards on duty, yet the assassin's knife did its work with great regularity. How these murders were checked will be related in due time.

5

Early during the year 1848 a ranger of Captain Jacob Roberts' company named Adam Allsens was alone in a part of the city inhabited by artisans, mechanics, and people of the lower orders. It was known among the rangers as "cutthroat." It was in the afternoon. He was assailed by a murderous crowd and almost literally cut to pieces. Those who saw him said his heart was visible, and its pulsations were plainly perceptible. His horse brought him out. He lived eight hours in that dreadful condition. His explanations gave an idea of who had been instrumental in perpetrating the atrocious assassination. He was buried the next day with military honors. He was a good and a brave man, and had the esteem and the confidence of the whole command.

An ominous silence reigned among the rangers. Not one of them appeared to speak of their murdered comrade, unless in answer to a question, and then no more was said than was absolutely necessary to convey a definite and respectful answer. The writer felt sure there was trouble ahead. How to avert its coming was the problem to solve. Colonel Hays was not aware of what nature it might be, or what agency might be brought into requisition to render it practical and formidable. Who could he employ to nip in the bud any scheme to wreak a bloody vengeance on the assassins? The sequel will show he was powerless to checkmate what he could not foresee.

The day wore away without an incident of moment. Night came; ten o'clock sounded. Colonel Hays was in his quarters, No. 26 Doncella Street, conversing with Captain P. W. Humphreys and the writer; shots were heard. Humphreys inquired: "Were not these shots from six-shooters?" Colonel Hays deprecated the idea. Ere long firing was heard again. This time it resembled platoon firing. Humphreys declared these were six-shooter shots. The colonel insisted it was firing done by a company of horse marines who had been outside the walls drilling. "They are always making a noise," he said. The firing increased in frequency, spread over more ground, yet had the sound as if proceeding from a body of skirmishers occupying an irregular line. The character of the shots were unmistakable. The ear soon becomes educated in the matter.

This state of things continued until about twelve o'clock. Captain Humphreys observed: "I wonder what the commanding general's orderly is coming for?" For once in his life Colonel Hays seemed intimidated. He sprang to his feet and started for the rear of the building, remarking as he went: "Ford, if he comes tell him I am not in." Humphreys had seen no orderly: he was testing the opinion of Colonel Hays of the men firing. We all knew they were Texians.

Captain Humphreys and the writer listened until after one o'clock. The former left for his quarters. The adjutant bethought himself of the colonel. He began searching for him. He found him, but do not ask where: you will never be told. This was a night of serious disquietude to many.

The next day Captain Humphreys was again on hand about 10 A.M. The writer asked: "Captain, what news do you bring?"

"I am told the Military Patrol heard the firing and went to it. They inquired of our boys what it meant and were informed. Instead of trying to stop it they joined in. In going to my meals I past by the headquarters of the Mexican police. They have a kind of wooden litter, quite covered over, on which they carry anyone found sick or dead in the streets. At breakfast time they had brought in fifty-three corpses, so they reported."

In the evening the captain reported more than eighty bodies lying in the morgue. These were parties who had no relatives or friends to care for them. They had been shot in the streets and left lying. It was a fearful outburst of revenge. It had been brought on by a number of attacks upon the rangers. In a later affair six Mexicans were killed. It was said a complaint of this incident reached General Scott. He sent for Colonel Hays and put the question: "Colonel, is it so that your men have killed six Mexicans in the city?"[4]

"Yes, general, the Mexicans piled rocks on a house and began stoning my men, and they used arms in self-defense."

---

[4] Colonel Dumont said that Scott was "extremely wrathy" about the slayings. When Hays came into the general's tent, he burst out: "I have been informed, Sir, that since the arrival of your command in this city, two Mexicans have been killed. I hold you

The general said it was right, and the matter ended. On another occasion, Pete Gass, one of our interpreters, and Van Walling, if memory is correct, were in the street. They had six-shooters under their clothing. Without any provocation the Mexicans attacked them with rocks and then ran on them with knives. According to accounts then given, they killed and wounded four or five before they could get away. The affair in revenge for Allsens and Van Walling's and Gass' incident broke up the murder of Americans almost entirely.

---

responsible, Sir, for the acts of your men. I will not be disgraced, nor shall the army of my country be, by such outrages." Hays quickly replied: "The Texas Rangers are not in the habit of being insulted without resenting it." He paused for a moment. "They did kill two Mexicans as I entered the city, and I, Sir, am willing to be held responsible for it." Said Colonel Dumont: "The manner in which this was said, and the whole bearing and deportment of Colonel Hays, was so sincere, frank and manly, that none could have doubted his own belief that his men had done right." To Hays' great relief, the general's anger soon abated, the two men talked pleasantly over coffee, then the Texas Ranger returned to his command to tell his boys that they must watch their step from now on.

(Dumont's Letters, published in the *Indiana Register* and quoted in the *Democratic Telegraph and Texas Register*, February 24, 1848.)

IX

>>

HUNTING *GUERRILLEROS*

There was an American living in the City of Mexico, apparently fifty years of age. He was lame, having been wounded by a cannon shot while making a reconnaissance with a United States officer, in front of Churubusco, according to memory. This gentleman looked older than he was and had a sickly appearance. He was known among the Mexicans as *Juan el Diablo*—John the Devil. They stood in great awe of him. They seemed to think he bore a charmed life. A menace from Juan was sufficient to start an ordinary Mexican at a brisk gait. He had been a stage driver in the Valley of Mexico, and knew the surrounding regions quite well.

The guerrillas had been giving trouble, particularly a band under the command of the celebrated priest-leader, Padre [Celedonia de] Jarauta. He was reported to be in the neighborhood of Otumba. Colonel Hays at the head of about sixty-five Texians marched from the City of Mexico about the Christmas holidays of 1847, or perhaps early in January, 1848. He had Juan el Diablo as guide. In the first night's march we became bothered concerning the road from some misinformation given to our guide. We returned to the road to Vera Cruz leading out from the Piñon Gate. We laid by our horses till daylight. We encamped in a large ranch during the next day, and used precautions to avoid being seen by anyone outside the plantation.

The second night we marched to Otumba, said to be sixty miles distant. While on the march an unfortunate incident occurred. About two o'clock in the morning we passed near a town. The white houses could be seen. Suddenly firing commenced in the village. We were unable to account for it. Colonel Hays halted us ten or fifteen minutes. Someone suggested sending a man down the column to ascertain whether Julius Roach were present. He was not. A detachment was sent in the direction of the firing. They found that Roach and a man or two had made an attempt to rob the place, and had been fired on. Roach was not a Texian by birth.

We reached Otumba at daylight. We were told Padre Jarauta was at San Juan Teotihuacán, twelve miles away, but nearer the City of Mexico. The march occupied about three hours. The plaza of that town is very large and is built up quite all around; the houses are generally of stone. A large stone building occupied the principal part of one side of the square. It had lots and stables attached, which we occupied.

We had then passed two nights without rest. A large majority of us fed our horses and went to sleep very soon afterward. The writer was sick and scarcely able to lift his saddle. His repose was profound. It was disturbed in a short while. Shots were heard in quick succession; a sickly yell arose, and the sleepers slowly awoke to discover they were attacked by Mexicans. Infantry, posted on the tops of houses, were keeping a lively din by firing their *escopetas* at us, with no effect.[1] The cavalry,

---

[1] Throughout the Mexico City operations the Americans found the enemy soldier to be an extremely poor shot, even at close range. A look at his ammunition revealed why this was so: a Mexican cartridge contained twice as much powder as was necessary. This caused the *escopetas* to kick bruisingly, which in turn spoiled the Mexican aim. Some feared the recoil of their weapons so much that they closed their eyes and flinched while firing. Poor Mexican marksmanship was a major factor in the American ability to win victories at relatively light cost. Another important factor, said Captain Ephraim M. Daggett, "was the holy awe and superstition entertained by the untutored greaser in regard to the 'revolver.' They understood the term to mean a turning around and about— a circulator; and were led to believe the ball would revolve in all directions after its victims, run around trees and turn corners, go into houses and climb stairs, and hunt up folks generally."

(Daggett, "Adventure with Guerrillas," in Isaac George, *Heroes and Incidents of the Mexican War*, pp. 210–213.)

probably seventy-five strong, charged across the plaza upon our quarters. Captain Ephraim M. Daggett and about five men placed themselves in the large door of the building and repulsed the first charge. Jarauta rallied his men, and returned to the attack without delay. This time twelve or fifteen Texians were on hand. They advanced into the square to meet the foe. Some saddles were emptied, and the *guerrilleros* began to evince respect for the six-shooter. They halted before reaching us, and held their lances to the front as if they expected us to run upon them. One of them, supposed to be an officer, came at a brisk gallop into our line, was wounded by Major Chevaille, and went over his horse's head against a stone wall.

By this time Colonel Hays had awakened and ordered men to occupy the top of the building. Those already in the fight had all they could do to hold the door. We saw the priest-general marshal his mounted men, and come at us again. He led his followers, sword in hand, and made a good appearance. Our fire was heavier than previously. Several of the enemy fell. The Padre had passed our position about a hundred yards, was struck by a ball, and tumbled to the ground. Some of his men endeavored to carry him into a house, and got hurt. He was finally placed under cover. This ended the fight.

During the effort to repulse the second charge of Jarauta, a Mexican officer made himself conspicuous. Captain Daggett fired at him, and he made no sign of having been struck. The writer fired; at the crack of his pistol the officer dropped from his horse.

Captain Daggett exclaimed: "There now I killed him."

"No you didn't. He did not fall till I fired."

This altercation was ended by the officer. He arose and ran across the square at almost railroad speed.

A Mexican was killed from the top of the house. It was a long shot. Two men claimed to have killed him. They got into a quarrel, and were about to fight. This was just before the last charge was made. Ford advised them to wait until we had beaten the enemy before deciding the question.

"If I struck him, it was in the head," one said.

"If he is not shot in the breast," the other affirmed, "I do not claim him."

After we had driven the enemy from the town, the dead man was examined: he had a ball in his head, and another had penetrated his breast.

In making our march the night before we had passed near the Padre's camp without discovering it. He had followed and attacked us in the morning. He made a blunder; had he dismounted his cavalry, concentrated his whole force and made a descent upon our quarters, he would have effected an entrance before one-half of us would have been awakened. We were almost exhausted for want of sleep; some had not closed their eyes for three nights, and were greatly fatigued. As it was we owed our getting through all right to Captain Daggett and a few men. It was asserted the Mexicans had 400 infantry on the tops of the houses. According to memory the loss of the enemy was fifteen or twenty killed and wounded. We had no one injured.

The writer is of opinion this encounter with the Padre was not reported officially. It was mentioned in Jesse Barnard's paper published in the capital of Mexico.

Our spies, Miguel and Vicente, reported about two o'clock P.M. that within five or six miles the Mexicans had another force of 500 or 600 men. We discussed the feasibility of attacking them. Upon inspection we ascertained we had not a sufficient number of cartridges on hand to fight another battle. Who ought to have been blamed for the shortage was never ascertained. We determined to return to the City of Mexico. The march was made by ten o'clock P.M. Our estimate was that in less than thirty hours we had marched one hundred and seven miles, and beaten a force at least five times superior to our own.

In the afternoon we took up the line of march for the City of Mexico. A detachment of mounted Mexicans marched parallel to us for an hour or two. They declined to fight when we sent out detachments to attack them.

We carried a wounded officer probably fifteen miles. We thought he had been drinking. His language became incoherent. On examination it was discovered his skull was fractured. His condition was commiserated, and he was left at the first house we reached.

None of our horses were rendered unserviceable by this toilsome march. They were fed on barley, one of the best articles for horse feed ever used. Not one foundered horse can be brought to mind during our operations on General Scott's line in which the founder could be fairly attributed to barley. Our men were generally careful with their horses. They were well groomed and well fed. No one fancied losing his American horse, and then being mounted on a Mexican *caballo*. He was an animal of great endurance, but was not as fleet as his American brother. Two things are considered uncomfortable by mounted men of pluck—to be in the rear in a charge, and behind in a retreat.

2

The expedition of Tehuacán started from the City of Mexico; as the writer understood, it was under General Joe Lane from the beginning. At the time of leaving Adjutant Ford was sick, confined to his room, and cannot speak now of his own personal knowledge.

Some amusing incidents occurred on the expedition. If memory is not at fault, while at Cordoba Major Chevaille and an Englishman were on a trade about a saddle. A misunderstanding ensued. The Englishman waited on General Lane, and the following colloquy took place:

Englishman: "General, Major Chevaille has been beating me."

General: "Did he beat you badly?"

Englishman: "Yes, quite badly."

General: "Keep a sharp look out or he will beat you again."

The matter ended with no further trouble.

Hardy Stockman, one of our interpreters, while passing around in a town, saw a large number of chickens in a yard. About nightfall he conducted some of the men to the place. The owner was told that the Texas boys had come to buy some chickens. The Aztec asseverated he had none.

"Where are those I saw here to-day?"

"The soldiers stole them."

This was recognized as a case of "elongated veracity."

"Then, sir, if there are any chickens on your premises they do not belong to you?"

"No sir, they do not."

This proved to be a very damaging admission. Stockman went into the backyard, gathered a handful of gravel, and made what the Irishman called a "slinging shot." Some of the gravel struck a large bake-oven, and, very unluckily for his master and himself, a rooster told where he was. The boys went for him and his whole family. The hidalgo was terribly exercised. He told a tale of poverty, and declared he would be ruined unless he got pay for his chickens.

"Your chickens!" Stockman exploded. "You lying old rascal, you have no chickens. Should we pay you for them, you would swindle the rightful owner out of the money. Come, none of your tricks, Old Sharpey."

The old simpleton saw his last darling pullet as she squalled a final adieu to him and his.

At the risk of being put down as an old taleteller, a secondhand vendor of Joe Miller jokes, another incident will be related. Press Polly gave no evidence of having descended from Goliath. He weighed one hundred pounds, that is, if a man is not particular in his statement of details. He filled the bill of a man "Old Rip" hunted for forty years. He could stand flat-footed, strike overhanded, and hit a gander in the breast. A *claco* is a Mexican coin worth one-eighth and a half cents. Press rushed up to a crowd of rangers in a towering passion. He claimed to have been swindled by a Mexican.

"How, Press?"

"He only gave me one hat full of oranges for a *claco.*"

Press wanted blood, but the boys controlled him.

This indicated the abundance of oranges grown in that section, and their cheapness. They were delicious. Mexico, beyond the Sierra Madre, is a land of fruits of many kinds and qualities. They are so luscious that many of our troops overgorged themselves, and saved the seeds of disease and death.

3

[The Treaty of Guadalupe Hidalgo which ended the Mexican War was signed on February 2, 1848.] This, however, did not abate the zeal and activity of the guerrilla captains, Padre Celedonia de Jarauta and General Mariano Paredes, late president of Mexico. They were soon in charge of guerrilla forces, and giving trouble.[2] We heard that Jarauta was in the mountains northeast of the City of Mexico and that General Paredes was at Tulancingo.

An expedition was set on foot, on February 17, 1848, to make a thorough reconnaissance of the country dominated by the Padre. The command consisted of 250 Texas Rangers under Colonel Hays, 130 of the Third Dragoons under Major William H. Polk, brother of the presi-

---

[2] *Guerrilleros* were lawless bands including many ex-soldiers who refused to follow the surrender of the central government. They robbed American supply trains; when these were not available, they plundered their own countrymen. They lived freely among the *peons* and *leperos* in the villages, gorging themselves and dancing in luxurious *fiestas* lasting for days. They made the law and the law was the bullet; they fancied themselves indomitable warriors and dressed in picturesque costumes that kept in awe the pauper youths who worshiped them, who lied and stole for them. To the youths he was a kind of god, this *guerrillero*, in his great sombrero, his velvet jacket elaborately embroidered by his special señorita, his skin-tight trousers, slit open at the sides and fastened by dazzling gold buttons, and the tiny silver bells on his green boots that tinkled as he walked, and those monstrous spurs, and his sword, carried under the left leg, and the *escopet* in his hand, and his lasso, slung over his shoulder, which he could use with amazing dexterity in close-quarter combat. They knew, the poor knew: he was ruler in this poverty-striken land. The Americans might defeat him, might scatter him, but when they left, he would come back to reclaim his crown through bloodshed and intimidation, and the Mexican national government, rife with dissension and intrigue, would not be able to stop him. This *guerrillero* would rule them for two and a half generations, until the death of the most infamous *guerrillero* of all time: Francisco "Pancho" Villa.

(Albert G. Brackett, *History of the United States Cavalry, from the Formation of the Federal Government to the 1st of June, 1863*, pp. 91–92; Daggett, "Adventure with Guerrillas," in George, *Heroes and Incidents of the Mexican War*, pp. 210–213.)

dent of the United States, and the Mexican Lancer Regiment of Colonel [Manuel] Domínguez, now in the service of the United States—the whole under the command of General Joe Lane of Indiana. We had more than a thousand mounted men all told. There were some officers of other corps accompanying us; among them Lieutenant Colonel [Jesse] Leftwich, Major [Perrin L.] Solomons, and Lieutenant [William B.] Bate, all of Tennessee. The latter has since been elected governor of his State, and is now a senator in the Congress of the United States. The march was made in great part at night. Several mountain ridges were crossed, and the cold was felt severely by the Texians. For several days nothing of interest happened.

One evening after eight o'clock we moved out. The pace was quite brisk—trot out and gallop. An hour or two before daylight we were going at a fast gallop, almost half-speed. The writer was sent to the rear to deliver orders. He saw dragoons with their saddles under their horses' bellies, and the dismounted men were swearing at a terrible rate. Some horses gave out; others were reported to have died under the saddle. The men thus set on foot managed to mount themselves at the haciendas we passed. It was a no good section in which to be left in the rear; none were reported lost.

At daybreak Tulancingo was sighted. It lay in a long valley, said to be nine miles distant from the eminence where we were. This stretch was made almost at a run. Major Polk had the front that day. Lieutenant Bate and the writer rode near the head of the column. At an early hour in the morning the Americans dashed into Tulancingo, and were directed to the house of Paredes. Major Polk ordered a prison to be opened, and the inmates poured into the street. Bate and Ford questioned a Mexican. We promised to pay him to show us General Paredes. He told us to follow him. We were moving after him.

"I've got General Paredes!" Major Polk yelled out to us.

We joined him, supposing he had anticipated us. We were taken up stairs in a large stone building, and introduced to "General Paredes." There was a twinkle about the gentleman's eye not in keeping with the status of a prisoner to an invading foe. It was explained. Major Polk had bagged General Paredes' brother. When Major Polk asked his name he replied "Paredes." It was reported that at the time the Mexican was conducting Bate and Ford to General Paredes, that distinguished individual was at the place indicated putting on his pants. The laugh was on Major Polk.

Colonel Domínguez stated positively that in getting to Tulancingo we marched over ninety Mexican miles in about fourteen hours. He knew the country thoroughly. We rested ourselves and horses that day and part of the next. The mounted man has an affection for his charger, and treats him kindly.

A loud hurrah and shouting was heard. The adjutant left his pallet, and hurried to the spot.

"What is the matter?"

"We drove up a beef the contractor had bought, and were going to shoot it. A Mexican woman came up, and asked us to let her kill the animal as the bull fighters do. She took a sword, and aimed to plunge it into the creature's neck just behind his horns. She missed her aim, and the bovine tossed her about twenty feet into the air, and she didn't go up head first."

"Where is the woman?"

"I reckon she has not stopped running yet."

The men found time to have a boisterous laugh on that occasion.

Our spies obtained information of the whereabouts of Padre Jarauta. We started to find him. The second night on that trip, if recollection is correct, we camped in a narrow valley between two mountains. There was an hacienda there. The owner was said to be wealthy. He had houses, a church, and many *peons* on his place. A nameless individual was prying around, and found a barrel of wine in a room attached to the church. General Lane, Colonel Hays, Captain Alex Hays, the general's adjutant, and some more were advised of the momentous discovery. A consultation was had. Mr. [G. M.] Swope was sent for. He was nicknamed the "Frazzler." It meant little more than "bummer" did during our Civil War.[3] The "Old Frazzler" was not long in putting himself in communication with the contents of that barrel. It was pronounced a superior article of Madeira wine. It was sipped with keen relish. While the liquid feast was progressing harmoniously and pleasantly, the master of the house came in, greatly excited. He informed us he was a poor man, and if we drank that wine it would bankrupt him. Alex Hays was our spokesman.

He rejoined: "But my friend we will pay you for the wine we drink."

Our host changed tactics: "Oh, do not drink that wine, it belongs to the priest."

"We will pay the priest."

The Mexican was full of resource: "I implore you not to drink that wine, it is consecrated!"

---

[3] During Sherman's march through Georgia in 1864, bummers were armed riffraff who, following in the wake of the army, pillaged farms and plantations and looted towns.

Alex came back with a clincher: "Then we will drink it for the love of God."

The discomfited Don left in deep disgust. Nobody drank too much. The barrel and lessened contents were left in good order.

About midnight the march was resumed. The mountain road was chosen, it being the shortest and most difficult. The other road was longer, more travelled, and more likely guarded. Our information was considered positive that Jarauta was in Zacualtipán at the head of 450 or 500 men. It should have been stated that the Lancer Regiment of Colonel Domínguez had been detached, and sent in another direction, consequently our force was greatly reduced in number.

The night march was toilsome and without any untoward incident. We had great faith in Miguel and Vicente, our spies and guides. Just as the sun was casting a golden tinge upon the mountain peaks behind us on that morning of February 25, we entered the outskirts of Zacualtipán. A Mexican officer emerged from a house, and was made a prisoner. He was utterly ignorant of our presence. This was positive proof of the proximity of the enemy. The command moved on at a fast trot, our regiment in advance. General Lane announced no plan of battle. We were to find where the guerrilla bands were located and fight them.

The firing began at buildings inside of a large lot. The sentinel on duty attempted to close a large gate but was too late. We ran our horses against it and knocked it wide open. Colonel Hays now ordered the adjutant and Major Truitt with 15 or 18 men to stop and engage this force while the Colonel and General Lane proceeded forward to the main plaza. We rushed into the large lot and began a hand-to-hand combat with the guerrillas, and drove them with loss. About thirty or forty yards in front of us was a large wooden house, and to the right of it a kitchen and a stone house. They occupied a separate inclosure and had a heavy fence in their front. From these a heavy fire was opened upon us by the enemy. We were protected by a stone wall running parallel with the palisade fence for some distance. We had just over a dozen men to engage two companies of guerrillas. The enemy fired much oftener than we, but not with as good effect. A Mexican exposing his person was quite certain to be hit.

This unequal contest lasted for some time, and the Mexicans began to exhibit signs of demoralization. Soldiers would load their pieces under the cover afforded by the houses, go to the front, fire, drop their guns, and scale the outer wall. To prevent these escapes, Ford suggested covering the point of egress. He and Jacob Horne did so. They were partially covered by the heavy palisade fence. Meantime Major Chevaille came to our aid. He was on his horse, in full view of the enemy, and they fired many shots at him, without damage. Horne was not so fortunate: a ball penetrated his chest, wounding the upper portion of the left lung. He turned to Ford in perfect coolness and said: "I am killed."

"No you are not; the wound is too high to be necessarily mortal."

The next small reinforcement came under Lieutenant Dan Grady. It consisted of Jim Carr and another man or so. Here a rather ludicrous scene was enacted, which will be referred to further on. The cross fire annoyed the Mexicans greatly. Their left flank was turned in effect, and they were losing men almost constantly.

In the rear of their right was a large gate, well barred. A few men forced that, and opened fire upon the Mexicans from the right of their position. In addition they set fire to the large building. This squad was led by "Old Frazzler" Swope. It was now quite lucky for a *guerrillero* to come out of the house, and get a shot at us without being terribly hurt. Several of them had an eye shot out. The enemy hung out a white flag, and the firing ceased. They surrendered. Their loss was about fourteen killed, as many wounded, and about forty prisoners. Our loss: Jacob Horne mortally wounded, Tom Greer badly, Pete Gass slightly wounded, and a few others scratched. We captured a large number of horses—if memory serves, more than a hundred.

In the meantime, Colonel Hays, General Lane and Major Polk were engaging the enemy in the main plaza. [What happened there will be told by Colonel Hays himself:]

I advanced rapidly to the plaza, from whence I discovered in a street to the left thereof, a strong detachment of the enemy, lancers and infantry, coming forth from a large barrack.

I instantly divided my force, taking the principal part with me in the direction of these barracks, and at the same moment, General Lane, with some 15 or 16 men, charged straight forward to attack another detachment of the force of the enemy, which General Lane discovered in a cuartel [barrack] in another street.

With my immediate force I attacked those of the enemy which had shown themselves on the left after firing at us from within and without the walls, a running and mixed fight took place, which was continued so long as the enemy was visible and over a space of road equal to half a mile.

The result of this conflict was a loss to the enemy of about thirty killed.

With all possible dispatch I returned to the plaza and was there met by Adjutant General Alex Hays, who informed me that General Lane with his small force was hotly engaged with superior numbers of the enemy. Hearing also the rapid firing in the direction of General Lane, I with all haste dispatched Captain Daggett, with a small command, to that point, where they arrived in time to assist in completing a total rout of the party of the enemy thus engaged.

At this point the enemy fought with determination and bravery, taking every advantage of their position and firing from behind every object that seemed to afford him concealment and protection, but the unflinching material of that command was invincible, and about thirty of the enemy were here killed.

While in pursuit of some scattered and fugitive Mexicans toward the western angle of the town, I was met by Major Polk and a portion of his command, who had been previously engaged in another part of the town, and were now occupied in the interception of those of the enemy who came in their way, or were to be found.

Near this we took a Mexican prisoner, from whom we learned that the quarters of Padre Jarauta were in the large church which fronted the main plaza. We immediately directed our course to the church and, when we arrived there, found that a portion of Major Polk's command had already been there; but that Jarauta had a very few minutes before their arrival effected his precipitate escape, thereby for the present saving his person from the treatment he so wisely dreaded.

Every officer and man of my command is entitled to the utmost praise for the manner in which they endured and performed a most fatiguing journey by day and by night, and for the unflinching courage displayed during the several conflicts of the day.

Major Truitt and Adjutant Ford deserve great credit for the manner in which they defeated so unequal a force, with so small a number, in the chosen stronghold of the enemy.

It may be proper to say we had not an average of twelve men in our fight at one time at the first *cuartel*, but six during most of the affair. The enemy were quartered in many parts of the town, and our men, if left to themselves, went to the heaviest firing; hence our paucity in number. Our total loss was one probably killed and five wounded. According to General Lane the enemy lost "not less than one hundred and fifty" killed including second in command Padre Martínez and "in wounded his loss is considerable, including Colonel Montaña, mortally, with fifty prisoners, three commissioned officers and three Americans, believed to be deserters." (A letter written by a Mexican from Zacualtipán placed the loss of the guerrillas at one hundred and twenty-six. A wag used his pencil and went from place to place; he put the boys on the stand, took an account of the number each man had killed, and reported that eighteen hundred Mexicans had ceased to feast on *tortillas*.)

As soon as the enemy surrendered at the first *cuartel*, Ford directed some of the men to extinguish the fire on the wooden building. It was reported in camp that the order was not promptly executed. Colonel Hays, the members of his staff, and some others were quartered nearly opposite the wooden building after the fight. They unsaddled their horses, and were strolling about town. A man came in haste, and informed the writer that the town was on fire and that the house he was in was about to be burned. Here was a dilemma: eight horses to saddle and no one to help! The flames were already in contact with the roof of one of the buildings occupied. If ever a man did hard and fast work it was done on that occasion. Six of the animals had been caparisoned and led forth. The coming of a man or two was a streak of good luck. The adjutant had been so weakened by overexertion that he was barely able to mount his horse. He left in good time; the fire was roaring close behind him.

Other quarters were found. Some of the party had lost things by the fire. They were mostly trophies. John Collins, our cook, appeared inconsolable; when pressed he claimed to have been bereft of a flour sifter he had realized at a deserted storehouse.

The fire did not consume a great many buildings. The town was situated on hills; a creek ran through it. The houses were not close together, and a general conflagration did not occur.

A good many horses of the command were tenderfooted; remounts were furnished from the captured animals.

Horne was carefully attended to. A litter was made to carry him on. The prisoners transported him by turns. A Mexican sergeant had charge; he ran down men at the towns and ranches we passed on the return march and forced them to help. Our wounded comrade was left in the hospital at Pachuca, about forty miles north of the City of Mexico. He died, but probably would not have, had the ball been extracted.

Major Chevaille had, at some previous time, made General Lane a present of a fine Mexican pony. A Mexican had followed us many miles to present his grievance. He told his story to the general, about in this way: "I am a peaceable man and have taken no part in the war. My two daughters went to Tulancingo on a visit. The Texians stole their horses."

"Well, sir, if you will point out your horses they shall be returned to you," the general informed him blandly.

He escorted the horse hunter to a balcony of the second story overlooking the main encampment.

The Mexican pointed at General Lane's pony and said: "There is one of them."

"Old Gritter Face," as the men called General Lane, lost his temper and shouted: "Get out of here, you infernal liar, or I will have you hung in fifteen minutes."

It should be mentioned that the owner of the hacienda in the mountain valley had the pleasure of our company for a night on our return march. The men were accused of making free with his shoats and chickens. Bill Hicklin became involved in trouble about a hen. One chap threw a rock at a pig; it bounced, and struck the general on the shin. He used ugly expressions and actually avowed his willingness to see the landlord, the hens, and the pigs settled where the thermometer never reached zero. He stopped the foraging.

Our line of march led us by Real del Monte, a great mining district. A very intelligent English gentleman, in conversation with Colonel Hays, pointed to a hill and affirmed there was more silver in it than in all Europe.

Padre Jarauta did not recover from his defeat at Zacualtipán sufficiently to give the Americans much trouble during the continuance of hostilities. He was brave and energetic. Being implicated in an unsuccessful revolution he was executed by order of the Mexican authorities some years after the conclusion of the peace between Mexico and the United States. He is said to have been born in Spain. It was not publicly known why he doffed the cowl and assumed the sword.

X

>>>

THE MAGNANIMITY OF TEXIANS

Colonel Hays received an order to proceed down the country in the direction of Vera Cruz, and it was expected he would send out detachments to operate against robbing parties.

When the elevation between Ayotla and Río Frío was reached, many halted and gazed upon the Valley of Mexico. The City of Mexico, about twenty miles distant, seemed like a white spot. Many recollections crowded upon the gazer. Some felt the full fruition of success had rewarded their labors. Others had the consoling reflection of having done their duty. Not a few were goaded by regrets, arising from a sense of unimproved opportunities. To many the devil-may-care feeling of letting tomorrow take care of itself came to their relief, and they wended their way without a thought of the past, or any solicitude for the future.

There were two individuals in a bad humor—Adjutant Ford and Major Chevaille. Colonel Hays had a young man taking care of his horses. The hostler was well apprised that the horse of Major Chevaille, if excited, would fret all day and that Old Higgins would act worse, if possible. He managed to pass Chevaille and Ford several times with a lead horse, and at a gallop. They both remonstrated, and finally used bad language. Chevaille made a wish that the guerrillas would catch the young man and kill him. It was communicated to him in very forcible language.

That night we slept at Río Frío. A German gentleman kept a wayside inn there. For a wonder, Colonel Hays did not have his horses brought up, and no one spoke of the young man, or thought of him, probably. He was supposed to be camped with the quartermaster's men. The next morning we broke camp tolerably early; Chevaille and Ford were riding at the head of the column. After having gone about two miles they came to an abrupt halt. The unfortunate young man was lying in the road dead—done to death by guerrillas. Ford dismounted to see if anything could be done. Poor fellow, he was beyond human help. Chevaille gazed abstractly at the corpse.

"Mike, what are you thinking of?" Ford asked.

"I'll be damned if I ever make such a wish about a man while I live," he answered.

His countenance had been the index of his thoughts.

While this was going on some persons on foot were seen approaching on the road. Then the clatter of horses' hooves was heard—"bang!" "bang!" went pistols, fired at short range. The two rangers vaulted into their saddles, and charged the assailants, followed by others who raised the Texas yell. The locality was heavily timbered and the robbers escaped. The parties on foot averred that the robbers were after them; and so intent were they upon plunder that they ran upon the rangers before they saw them.

Colonel Hays lost two good horses by the affair. According to memory, Major Truitt was left in this section with Daggett's and Handley's companies. They did good service. One noted robber was pursued, fired at, and had his arm broken. He entered a ranch, and could not be found. After long, repeated, and unsuccessful searches, a small boy was approached, and money promised him to tell the robber's hiding place. He maintained a sullen silence, went to a well, looked down it, and ran away from it. The well was a rather deep one. The rangers began talking as if they knew a man was at the bottom. They intimated an intention to fire at the individual down there. He spoke agreeing to come up. A rope was lowered, and he came up, hanging to it with one hand. He was a man of wonderful strength.

The operations of the rangers extended to various localities. A skirmish ensued at a little place called San Carlos; Sergeant Major William Hewitt stood in one place and killed three Mexicans with a six-shooter. After the firing ceased the rangers measured the distance, and reported it over one hundred and twenty yards. Hewitt was one of the best shots with a pistol the writer ever saw.

2

As we moved down towards Vera Cruz, we went into camp for a day or two at Tepetiualco. The place is called Tepejahuilco on a late map. While there, information was received that a band of guerrillas was at San Juan de los Llanos, six miles off. The adjutant was instructed to take a detachment, proceed to the place, and ascertain the facts. He had fourteen men, including Miguel and Vicente, the two guides. The ride was sixteen miles instead of six. It was almost dusk when we rode into the plaza. There we discovered four thousand people at least. They were celebrating a Saint's day. Ropes were stretched at the corners of the plaza to prevent horsemen from entering. We were not apprised of the motive for placing them there, but being inside we were determined not to retrace our steps. It was evident that we were surrounded by a hostile population.

On inquiry the adjutant learned the head man of the place was a prefect of police. He made a demand on him for quarters, fuel, and rations for man and horse. An official was sent who conducted us to a large stone building, near the corner of the plaza. It had a large inner court where we put our horses. Rooms surrounded the court.

The officer informed Ford that the prefect declined to furnish rations. He went with Pete Gass, the interpreter, and inquired of the prefect what was the cause of refusal. The prefect told of having been imposed upon by deserters from the United States Army. Ford gave his name, rank, and assured him the supplies would be paid for when he presented the bill at regimental headquarters, taking care to impress the official with an idea of the great strength and courage of Hays' regiment. The rations were furnished instanter. The adjutant and any friends he chose to bring were invited to sup with the prefect at 9 o'clock. The invitation was accepted. The game had to be played boldly. Any faltering would have invited attack. They had men enough to knock us on the head with stones.

The adjutant returned to quarters, and put everything in a position for defense. Each man was assigned to defend a specified point. The men were told what to do should they hear firing in the direction of the prefect's residence. He took Gass and Miguel with him. Each man was armed and ready for emergency.

The prefect received the party cordially. The supper was a grand affair; sixteen courses, served on silver. Miguel made an excuse for not pulling off his cloak. He sat down with a six-shooter in his lap, Gass in quite the same way. The adjutant retained his sword, and pulled his revolvers to the front. The motions of master and servants were closely watched. We intended to fight, if attacked.

One of the men at the quarters became demoralized. He knew the prefect had slaughtered his guests. He claimed to have heard their groans. He formulated a plan of retreat, and would have tried it on, had the others agreed. When we returned he got a terrible tongue-lashing from all parties. He richly deserved arrest and punishment; the war being virtually at an end, the adjutant concluded to let the matter pass, and now withholds the man's name.

Vicente had been moving about town, seeing what could be found out. At last he met an old comrade, from whom he learned they had but four guns in the place, and were afraid to attack us. He told us there were four large churches in the city and several thousand inhabitants. In spite of the reassuring news, we spent an almost sleepless night.

One of the guides told the adjutant his wife and family were only a short distance from San Juan. He received written permission to visit them.

The march to camp occupied about three hours. The whole command was much concerned about our long stay. The adjutant's report set all right.

The guide was absent about ten days. Some of the knowing ones knew, of course, that he had deserted. The adjutant insisted he was faithful, and would come back. He said the guerrillas had gotten after him probably. The guide did return and that is exactly what happened. He had eluded the guerrillas by exchanging clothes with a vendor of charcoal and by driving his donkey, loaded with coal, into town and visiting his family. Subsequently, he had to flee to the mountains; eventually, he threw his pursuers off their guard and made his way to our headquarters. No two men connected with our command did more efficient service than Miguel and Vicente. The Mexicans may say what they please; these men were faithful to the United States.

Colonel Hays made his camp two miles above Jalapa, near the road to the City of Mexico.

3

The writer published an account, in 1882, of an incident which occurred at this camp. The following is based on that account.

One day news came that General Santa Anna was on his way out of the country, and would stop for dinner at General Bernard's, about four miles above us in the direction of the City of Mexico. This intelligence produced considerable excitement. Colonel Hays and a few other officers left camp with the view to meet General Santa Anna and pay their respects to him. Major Alfred Truitt and the writer concluded they would ride into Jalapa and witness the demonstrations of the Mexicans in honor of their great general. We had not been in the city very long before a couple of rangers came in with a request for us to return to camp.

"The men say they are going to kill General Santa Anna when he reaches there."

We mounted and rode in haste.

On reaching camp we discovered everything at a white heat, if that expression can be applied to anger. Revenge was the ruling passion of the hour. We knew the men we had to deal with. No attempts to exercise the authority of officers were made; no threats of punishment were let fall. We appealed to reason and to honor. What was said may be summed up in this wise. The men said General Santa Anna had waged an inhuman and un-Christian war upon the people of Texas, had murdered prisoners of war in cold blood. We knew many in the crowd around us had lost relatives in the Alamo, Goliad, and elsewhere.

This is what Ford told them: "Yes, that is admitted, but did not the world condemn General Santa Anna for this cruel butchery of prisoners? That was a stain upon his reputation as a soldier. Now, was it not considered an act of magnanimity on the part of the government of the Republic of Texas when its officials liberated General Santa Anna after what had happened? Reflect a moment. General Santa Anna dishonored himself by murdering prisoners of war; will you not dishonor Texas and ourselves by killing him?"

"General Santa Anna is not a prisoner of war," the men said.

"He is virtually a prisoner of war. He is in his own country and is travelling under a safe-conduct granted by our commanding general; to take his life would be an act the civilized world would brand as an assassination. You would be doing the very thing you charge to him as a crime. You would dishonor Texas."

"Then we will not do it," they answered.

The determination to murder was thus abandoned. Not one of the rough pioneers and frontiersmen was willing to play the role of an assassin, to cast a blemish upon the fame of Texas. They insisted upon having a talk with their ancient enemy.

"No boys, not a word. We will align you on the road, and enable you to see the general as he passes, but you must observe profound silence while he is in hearing."

Of course other officers assisted in allaying the wrathful indignation of the rangers.

The line was formed on each side of the road. A courier came down it at a brisk gallop and informed us that General Santa Anna was near by. Every eye was in the direction of the anticipated passer. He, his wife, and daughter were in a carriage, which appeared to be an open one. All had a fair view. The writer was of opinion that the old warrior's face blanched a little at the sight of his enemies of long standing. He might have thought of the bitter recollections these bronze and fearless men had garnered up from the past, and how easy it would be for them to strike for vengeance and for retribution. He sat erect, not a muscle of his face moved; if his hour had come he seemed resolved to meet it as a soldier should. His wife was very pretty. She bowed frequently, and a smile played upon her countenance. Miss Donna Santa Anna resembled her father—had a rather long nose, and was undemonstrative.

The "uniformed" representatives of Texas stood motionless, and silent; not even a whisper disturbed the air. They had made up their minds to let the president-general, who had prosecuted a war of extermination, of rapine and plunder upon them in by-gone days, who had reaped the benefits of a leniency and a mercy he did not merit by his antecedent actions and examples, again trust to the magnanimity of Texians and go his way unharmed.

The carriage passed on; the Mexican guard of honor marched by in good order. There were no salutations, no ungraceful remarks, indulged in between the soldiery of the belligerent republics. The mute tokens of respect glanced from eye to eye. It is probable those composing the Mexican column felt relief after having played a prominent part in that review. The Texians broke ranks and returned to camp. Not a murmur of disappointed feeling at the failure to wreak a bloody revenge was uttered; not an unseemly bravado was heard. The memories of the bloody past were buried, and no one cared to disturb their repose. General Santa Anna halted at his hacienda of Encerro, twelve or fourteen miles below Jalapa on the road to Vera Cruz. He was visited by American officers.

It is difficult to be exact after a lapse of almost thirty-four years, but the writer is confident that when General Santa Anna left for the coast he was escorted by a company of Texas Rangers. He remembers to have heard Hardy Stockman or Pete Gass tell of seeing a Mexican soldier of General Santa Anna's bodyguard bet 100 *doubloons*—$1600—on a single card in a game called *monte*. This was at a place called Antigua, on a river of the same name, fifteen or twenty miles northward from Vera Cruz. The point where General Santa Anna embarked is not remembered. He bade adieu to Mexico, and remained in voluntary exile until 1853, when he returned and assumed authority as dictator. He was expelled in 1855, but eventually returned, and died, old and poor, in 1879.

4

Our next encampment was at Encerro, General Santa Anna's hacienda fourteen miles below Jalapa on the road to Vera Cruz. The surrounding country reminded us of the hilly country in Gonzales County, Texas.

We bought beef from General Santa Anna's major-domo. It soon degenerated in quality. Commissary Pancoast complained. The Mexican protested it was the best he could do. Of course the men grumbled. They had little duty to perform and this generally makes good soldiers energetic grumblers. The adjutant asked Lieutenant Pancoast to let him know when the major-domo came into camp. He did so. A detachment of men saddled up. The adjutant informed the major-domo he knew he had great trouble in procuring good beef, and he proposed assisting him. The party visited small ranches in the vicinity and "rounded up" cattle wherever found. A fat animal would be "cut out." The adjutant would ask the owner: "What is the price of that beef?" On being informed he would turn to the major-domo and say: "Pay for it." The Texas boys would take it in charge. All purchased were driven to camp. There was not a poorer herd in Mexico. The major-domo lost money on the transactions of that morning. The Americans were paying for supplies they might have taken free of charge, and Santa Anna's representative was swindling them: a sample of what was done throughout the war.

While we were at Encerro, Dr. Dane, afterwards so distinguished as an Arctic explorer, called, in passing by. He had a Mexican game chicken with a spur on the end of his comb. The doctor considered him a great curiosity. Whether the spur had grown there naturally, or there had been tricking in the matter, this deponent sayeth not.

While at this camp the men made a trial between the Mississippi rifle and the six-shooter of Colt's last pattern. The six-shooter threw a ball greater distance than the rifle.

We were in daily expectation of orders to proceed to Vera Cruz, to be mustered out of service and embark for Texas. There were men in the command who had never been in that state. They had been recruited after we landed in Mexico.

Strong attachments had been formed during the campaign. The entire command entertained a high regard—a feeling amounting almost to affection—for the Reverend Sam Corley. He had been our friend, our good Samaritan, in every vicissitude. No difference what sort of trouble came, he was prompt to give good and wise counsel. He was ever on the side of right, order, and duty. He preached to the troops wherever he went, and they heard him gladly. His reproofs were so kind, so full of charitable impulsion, that they never gave offense.

When the roar of battle struck upon the ear and the charge sounded, he was on hand and in the front; when the stricken soldier needed a nurse, he was present; when the pangs of sickness created despondency in the heart of a lonely patient, he was at his humble couch; when sad tidings came from the loved ones at home and sorrow shadowed the soul, he was the ministering agent to dispel the gloom by words of cheer and comfort. He was a wonderful man. When the day of parting came, officers and soldiers, without any intimation or knowledge on his part, presented him a souvenir—a memento of respect and love. It was five hundred dollars in gold. He accepted it in the sincere and grateful spirit in which it was offered. Some months afterward, in a letter to the adjutant, he remarked: "God bless Hays' regiment; but for them I could never have paid my debts." During the fall of 1848 the Reverend Samuel H. Corley visited Austin and preached several sermons. Our reunion was pleasant. A nobler man never lived. To the day of his death he continued to call on God to bless Hays' regiment. The faithful follower of the cross, the gentleman, and the gallant soldier, has gone to receive the reward of a well-spent life.

Of Major Truitt a record has been made already. He maintained his popularity to the end of the campaign. Captain Armstrong resigned while the command was in the City of Mexico. The noble old patriot, Captain Ferguson, died on January 1, 1848, mourned by all. Captain Handley came out all right. He suffered terribly of erysipelas in the head. Captain Daggett was well liked by all. He had shown himself cool and courageous at San Juan Teotihuacán. He and five or six others saved us from a fight at great disadvantage, perhaps from defeat. Many of us felt grateful for the service he rendered. Captain Roberts retained the good will of his company; Captain Evans also.

In this condition of harmony between officers and men and of fraternal regard existing between all, regardless of rank, the regiment marched into Vera Cruz and were mustered out of service, except Colonel Hays and the adjutant, who returned to Texas as officers of the battalion on duty there. Miguel and Vicente parted company with us at Vera Cruz. Let it offend no one to remark that Old Higgins, the renowned, was taken back to Austin.

The leave-taking was sad. In many instances the adieus exchanged were the last on this earth. Scores and scores of that gallant band have taken the eternal furlough of death. May God have been merciful to them.

There remains a duty unperformed, that is, to give a more extended notice of Colonel John C. Hays.

5

The valuable services rendered by this gentleman in defending the pioneer settlers of Texas should have passed into history and been made familiar to children in school. It is a wrong and a shame that a trustworthy history of one of the most meritorious sons of Texas has not been written.[1] It would be an injustice to his memory to suppose that a proper idea of his heroic labors could be conveyed by such a cursory notice as the annexed.

The fame of Colonel Hays rested on a substantial basis: it was acquired by hard fighting, by suffering privations, and by the exhibition of the high qualities adorning a citizen and soldier. His campaigns against the Indians and Mexicans making descents upon Texas, and the success of his operations rendered him one of the most famous rangers in the world. His exploits during the early days of the war between Mexico and the United States won him additional laurels. He became one of the most popular leaders of men in the United States. At Vera Cruz all the distinguished personages of our army and navy sought his acquaintance and prized his friendship. In passing by the troops of other States of the Union, they would rush from their tents and "Hurrah for Colonel Hays!" It was amusing to witness the mistakes made on such occasions. Colonel Hays was a rather small man, and wore no uniform. Some large, good-looking ranger would be taken for him. One man humored the notion, and gave it encouragement. Major Chevaille saw him, and registered a vow of vengeance. Not long afterwards Chevaille gave the fraudulent colonel a terrible drubbing. He never repeated the act.

General Joe Lane and Colonel Hays were kindred spirits. They made

---

[1] So passionately did Ford believe Jack Hays to merit a biography that in the early 1890's he set aside work on the memoirs to do the task himself. But like the memoirs, the biography was never published. A typescript copy of Ford's "John C. Hays in Texas" is in the Archives Division of the University of Texas Library. Here is another work worthy of publication if someone cares to edit it.

campaigns together. It was currently reported in certain circles in the City of Mexico that in this matter Colonel Hays displayed an unselfish magnanimity highly creditable.

He expressed no feeling of jealousy towards his subordinate officers. He gave them opportunities to distinguish themselves, and was outspoken in his commendations of good conduct. He was lenient to the erring, unless the offense had involved a taint of dishonesty; then he was immovably rigid. He was almost idolized by many. He was modest and retiring; an expression of admiration of his acts would cause him to blush like a woman.

As a commander he trusted a great deal to the good faith of his officers. He went among his men and patiently heard their complaints and redressed abuses. He knew how to conduct marches requiring toilsome endurance and to prevent his men from becoming despondent. On the battlefield he saw everything, and readily took advantage of the errors of the enemy. He was cool, self-possessed, brave, and a good shot. The man who singled him out in a fight came to grief.

Had the Mexican War lasted longer, another brigadier general would have been appointed. It was understood in the City of Mexico that Colonel Hays had an excellent chance to receive the appointment.

Among the old settlers his memory is revered. They cannot forget he once stood upon the frontier as a tower of strength. They trusted him in the dark days of weakness, danger, and peril, and he responded with efficient fidelity and a full measure of success.

Colonel Hays, according to his sister-in-law, Mrs. Johnston of Seguin, married Miss Susan Calvert of the same place on April 27, 1844. They had six children. Four died young, leaving only a son and a daughter. Miss Hays married Mr. John McMullen, the son of a Texian of note. Mrs. Hays and children reside in California. That lady is remarkable for her good sense, amiability, and kindly disposition.

In 1848 and 1849 the people of Texas were zealous to show the public they possessed a route for a practical railroad from her eastern limit to the neighborhood of El Paso and from that point to the seacoast of California. From San Antonio to El Paso, a distance of about 600 miles, the country was unknown to a great extent. For the purpose of showing that Texas possessed facilities for such a road, Colonel Hays assumed control of an expedition destined to reach El Paso and to exhibit to the world that the most direct and the best railroad route to California was to be found across the territory of Texas. The expedition was deficient in not having an able and efficient guide. They struck the Río Grande some distance below El Paso, and failed to accomplish the object aimed at. This failure did not lose the good opinion of the friends of Colonel Hays.

Colonel Hays started to California in 1849. He left a people who loved him because he served them long and well; he had never led them in defeat. As an evidence of their estimation of the man and his services to Texas in the hour of infancy and need, the Legislature named Hays County for him.

Colonel Hays died in Oakland, California, on April 21, 1883. His works live after him. The people of southern and western Texas can truthfully say that but for the watchfulness of Colonel Hays and his eminent and illustrious acts in their behalf, there is no telling when their regions would have been settled.

6

During the writer's absence in Mexico, he corresponded with the *Texas Democrat*, giving an account of events and the praiseworthy acts of his companions in arms. Copies were kept of these and of the reports and orders of Colonel Hays. They were deposited in a trunk. When we landed at Port La Vaca they were left on the steamship. Colonel Hays supposed the writer carried them ashore, and the adjutant thought Colonel Hays had done so; they were left and never heard of.

On arriving at Austin, Ford asked Michael Cronican about his communications and was told they were too long for publication, and had been thrown into the waste basket. Truth requires the admission that this information caused an uncommon emission of profanity.

Shortly after Ford returned to Austin, a relative called him to account for his reckless bearing, averring that he was verging towards "desperadoism." Ford, [who had lost his young wife before going to war,] made this answer: "When a man has had the bosom of destruction to pass over his domestic hearth, and feels he has little to live for, he may appear reckless; yet, if he has a proper sense of duty to restrain him he will be true to himself, and kind to his fellow men. A belief in the existence of God and the reality of religion may not prevent a man from appearing reckless and even feeling a disregard for life, but such a one can never make a desperado—the cowardly elements are wanting."

BOOK 3 *The Trail*

XI

>>

WEST TO EL PASO

The discovery of gold in California produced intense excitement in the other states of the Union. Reference to the map indicated that an overland route to the new El Dorado would, for people of the middle and Southern States, pass through Texas, and not very far from Austin. Early in 1849 public meetings were held at the state capital for the purpose of ascertaining whether a practicable route could be had between Austin and El Paso. Dr. Joseph K. Barnes, afterwards surgeon general, United States Army, participated actively in the proceedings. Finally, it was decided to send John S. Ford to accompany Major Robert S. Neighbors, supervising Indian agent in Texas, on an expedition to El Paso. Neighbors had obtained the concurrence of General [William Jenkins] Worth, then commanding the Military Department of Texas, in the proposed enterprise.[1] On his way from

San Antonio, General Worth's headquarters, to Barnard's Trading House, Neighbors stopped at Austin. He and the writer had a conference. The major anticipated starting on the second day of March, 1849.

Ford left Austin, in company with Thomas M. Woolridge, a young frontiersman who was to go as far as the trading house, and carry Old Higgins back to Austin. It was understood that none but mules would stand the journey. The settlements between Austin and the site of Waco were not numerous, and they were sparsely populated. The town of Belton was not established. There was a settler at the crossing of Little River. He told us there was scarcely a house on the road until near the Brazos River. We took the left hand when the roads forked, rode all day, and at night found ourselves at the station recently occupied by the ranger company of Captain Shapley P. Ross on the Bosque River. Luckily we struck the house occupied by a Delaware woman, the mother of John Harry. Our horses were fed. John Harry guided us to the trading house, which we reached next morning at daylight. The ride was very long and extremely laborious. Several days were spent in making preparations. Major Neighbors depended on the Comanches to furnish guides, and their coming had been delayed.

The trading house was a few miles north of the site of Waco. It was under the control of George and Charles Barnard, and David and John Torrey. Friendly Indians traded animals, buffalo robes, deerskins, and such things as they manufactured for provisions, clothing, and cutlery. Very few Comanches and other wild Indians of Texas had firearms. Some of the more civilized and friendlier tribes had guns.

Captain Ross lived on the Brazos, opposite where Waco was afterwards built. He had a few neighbors. At this house we found D. C.— "Doc"—Sullivan. He was what people call a "character." He was of medium height, compactly built, and weighed about 135 pounds. His hair was white, his eyebrows and eyes likewise. The latter were in constant motion, as if under the influence of a current of galvanism, yet they produced no unpleasant impression upon the beholder. His countenance was pleasant, his impulses generous, his intercourse with his fellow men

---

[1] Worth decided to send two parties to El Paso. One from San Antonio under Lieutenant W. H. C. Whiting took a more southerly trail (later named the lower route) while Neighbors' party traveled over what was called the upper route. After both parties completed their missions, military and civilian authorities studied their reports and decided that Neighbors' upper route was the more practicable. Hundreds of emigrants were soon on it heading west.

(A. B. Bender, "Opening Routes across West Texas," *Southwestern Historical Quarterly*, XXXVII, 116–135; Kenneth F. Neighbours, "The Expedition of Major Robert S. Neighbors to El Paso in 1849," *ibid.*, LVIII, 36–59.)

gave evidence of manliness and frankness. He was insensible to the feeling of fear, brave to a fault, a kind and accommodating friend, and a bitter and dangerous enemy. He had an inseparable companion, Alpheus D. Neal, of about the same height, but more robust. Neal had all the manly qualities of his friend. They agreed to accompany the expedition. Mrs. Ross had known them from childhood. Before the day of starting she photographed the two young men to the writer, in order to let him know who were to be his companions. She gave a graphic account of two devil-may-care chaps, who were never still when there was any mischief they could set on foot. They never stopped for an impending danger but went straight ahead in anything they understood. The chance of getting shot did not deter them from playing a practical joke. Sullivan was made a prisoner at Mier, when a mere lad. He indignantly refused to be bribed. He was intractable and incorrigible. The Mexicans could not control the boy prisoner. They gave him tools and put him to work; he threw the tools into a water closet, and took a long rest in spite of the guards. They placed him in the kitchen to assist the Mexican cooks; in a little while one of them rushed out with a broken head. A good-hearted old priest tried his hand on him. After a short probation he brought him back saying he was *muy vicioso*—a spoiled child. After his release, and while in Captain Ross' command, he pretended to be eating buck eyes. The members of a company, from further east than the Colorado River, inquired what they were.

"Spanish chestnuts," Sullivan replied. "You can find plenty of them down on the branch."

His were too precious to be given away. The "chestnuts" were gathered and eaten; and there was a grand cascading, and a terrible swearing, heard in that camp for hours. To cut short, Mrs. Ross closed her account thus: "They can starve like wolves, and when they get food, they can eat like wolves."

Full of fun, Sullivan was the life of a camp; he could sing for hours, and not repeat a song. He was a terror to pretenders and windbags.

2

Preliminaries were arranged without trouble. The expedition set out before the middle of March. It was a motley crowd. The Americans were Major Neighbors, Doc Sullivan, A. D. Neal, and the writer. Captain Jim Shaw, a Delaware, was interpreter. The other Indians were: Joe Ellis and Tom Coshattee, Shawnees; Patrick Goin, a Choctaw, and John Harry, a Delaware. A band of Comanches travelled with us too.

We crossed the Brazos, and got on the waters of Little River. About the third morning out, the Comanche war chief—Porchanaquaheap, or, Buffalo Hump—regaled us with a medicine song. It was a grand thing, no doubt, to an appreciative audience. It stirred up recollections of boyhood—the calling of hogs, the plaintive notes of a solitary bull frog, the bellowing of a small bull, and all that sort of noises. Anon, the awful melody of the sonorous song was reproduced; the next moment the mournful howl of a hungry wolf saluted the ear, which gradually softened into something like the gobble of a turkey. It might have been a choice assortment of Comanche airs gotten up to amuse and do honor to the supervising agent, but it failed to solace his white companions. The performance commenced about an hour before daylight and did little to soothe the slumbers of the morning.

We reached the main encampment of Mopochocupee on the fourth day. The camp was located near the headwaters of the Leon. In it there were forty or fifty children bathing. As soon as they discovered the whites, they hurried to the bank and ran for the wigwams, crying "pavotivo!" "pavotivo!"—white man! white man!—as loud as they could. The excitement soon subsided. We encamped near the Indians; numerous delegations of children came to look at us and our trappings. The squaws also evinced curiosity; many of them had never seen an American. We had time to examine the wigwams and to learn something of every day life among the Comanches—of this more hereafter. A deaf and dumb woman attracted our attention. She was the only person we saw laboring under these defects among several thousands of Indians. A very old woman was frequently in our camp. The Comanches said she had seen more than a hundred summers. She appeared to have things her own way: found fault, lectured, and scolded like other old feminines. She had the appearance of a skeleton moving around with skin on it.

The writer wore long boots—à la Napoleon. He had found out that a snake will recoil when anything is descending upon it suddenly. A nimble person may jump with both feet on a snake, and leap off instanter, and not be bitten. It is a dangerous and foolhardy thing to do, yet Ford did it to the great astonishment of the Comanches. We reached the "Cross Timbers"—[two parallel strips of timber region that ran down the middle of Texas]. The Indians found a large diamond rattlesnake, and waited for the snakeman. He came up. There was the reptile in a huge coil, his head about three feet from the ground, eyes brilliant and scintillating with anger. His rattles were sounding the alarm of danger, and seemed to be capable of being heard at the distance of a hundred yards. The spots on his body were diamond shaped, and of a bright yellow color. He was about ten feet long. A more beautiful serpent is seldom seen, and one more able to inflict a fatal sting. The writer was cautioned by Jim Shaw:

"Don't go any nearer, that snake can bite a man a little further from him than his length—about ten feet. He can strike you on your mule. He jumps as he strikes."

These snakes were reputed to be remarkably active and very strong. The force exerted in delivering a blow or bite was sufficient to move the whole body. The snakeman gazed at the serpent for a few minutes, rode away, and has not jumped on even a garter snake from that day to this blessed moment.

3

It was decided that Buffalo Hump should be our guide.[2] He managed to get most of his pay in advance. Mopochocupee separated from us. Buffalo Hump's band was travelling south of west and rather down the country. We were having a good time, moving along leisurely, with a long cavalcade, putting on no guard, having no care for our animals, sleeping in quietude too nice to last long. One day, while on the march, a squaw came riding by at almost full speed. She was followed by a brave, with a gunstick in his hand. She straddled the fleetest horse, but would get off her guard occasionally, when the warrior would dash at her and give her a rousing whack with the gunstick, and away she would go. Meantime Neal came up.

"What is the matter Alf?"

"Oh, it's some of Doc's deviltry. The squaws were anxious to learn something of white men. Doc was delivering a lecture, and promised them a matinee tomorrow. The warrior came along, discovered that his wife constituted one of Sullivan's audience, and the row commenced."

We encamped, and were not dreaming of danger. Not long after dark, Jim Shaw returned from Buffalo Hump's wigwam. He was a badly-scared Indian, and communicated to quite all of us his feeling of alarm and the cause of it. Jim thought it probable we might all be killed before morning. He lectured and swore at Sullivan considerably. Every time a stick

---

[2] Ferdinand Roemer, a German scientist who had gone with Neighbors to visit the Comanches back in 1847, thought that "Buffalo Hump was the genuine picture of a North American Indian. Unlike the most of his tribe, he scorned European clothes; his upper body naked, a buffalo robe fastened around his hips, with brass rings on his arms, and a string of beads around his neck; his black, straight hair hanging down long." To the European, Buffalo Hump's countenance was the epitome of "the serious . . . apathetic, facial expression of the North American savage. He drew one's attention especially, since formerly he had shown great daring and bravery in leading raids against the Texans."

(Roemer, *Texas: With Particular Reference to German Immigration and the Physical Appearance of the Country*, p. 324.)

was broken during that night the writer awoke. Sullivan slept "like a log," as the saying is. The next morning the women and children were sent away before daylight.We were kept in camp until the sun was two hours high. Buffalo Hump's main band was sent in a different direction from the one we travelled. He retained one of his wives and her children. The cause: one of Buffalo Hump's wives attended Sullivan's exhibition.

On our marches the Comanche children would beat the thickets for rabbits, birds, and rattlesnakes. When they encountered one of the latter there would be a general shouting, and a grand rally. The serpent would coil, strike into the air, and do all he could to punish his foes. The children would encircle him at a safe distance, and fire arrows into him until he gave up the ghost. Then notes of triumph would go up. The young warriors would gallop to the front to impart the news. The women would shout, whip up the pack animals; all would be going at half speed. The long poles of the wigwams, with ends dragging on the ground, would make a clattering noise you could hear two miles away. The whole band would join in the din. The whites would catch the excitement, and yell as lustily as their savage companions—it does not take a civilized man a great while to lapse into semisavagery. To roam amid the unchanging scenes of Nature, where the foot of civilized man never trod before, perhaps to view the works of God in their primeval grandeur, and to realize that you constitute a part of these, conspire to produce a buoyancy of spirits, pleasant sensations, a rapture earth seldom affords to men: these are the charms which allure the woodsman to a life apart from other men. The picture above is the bright side of savage life. Turn to the other: ignorance of God and the world, hunger, thirst, cold, filth, the deprivation of the comforts, the amenities, and the social pleasures of civilized life, and then choose for yourself. If savagery is right, civilization is wrong. There can be no middle ground.

4

The writer kept the journal, and carefully noted the events of each day. It was lost at the same time with a number of his other papers during the late Civil War.[3] As far as the writer knows there is not a member of the El Paso Expedition living now, except himself.

---

[3] Throughout the memoirs, Ford refers to the loss of private and state papers in the Civil War and in the great capitol fire in 1881, thus giving the impression that he was writing almost entirely from memory. This he did to some extent, but he relied quite heavily on remaining documents, notes, and reminiscences in his possession which may now be found in the Ford Papers in the Archives Division of the Texas State Library, Austin.

We reached the Colorado River at a point above Austin, probably one hundred and forty miles. There Buffalo Hump was trying to drive up some horses. His dogs were in full cry after the horses, the horses were showing symptoms of panic and a stampede, and the angered chief was pursuing the dogs, with bow strung and arrows in hand. The canines seemed to understand what was up, and managed to dodge arrows with great adroitness; yet, those left kept up the chase. They were considerably reduced in numbers when they quit the field.

At a camp near the mouth of Spring Creek we found the bands of Shanaco and Yellow Wolf, and a part of Buffalo Hump's band—about ten thousand Indians, as we supposed.

Shanaco was a plain, matter of fact man. He was very kind to us, sending us venison and doing us other favors. When he talked to a man he looked him in the face. He said at one time he thought he would never make peace with the Texians.

"They killed my father. I did all I could to avenge him. I have buried the hatchet."

Major Neighbors said Shanaco's father was killed in the affair at San Antonio [in 1840 where Hugh McLeod and the Indians met to exchange prisoners] but the Comanches saw some troops near the council chamber and believed the Texians meant treachery, and opened the fight.

While in Shanaco's camp, the writer was placed almost face to face with a white woman who was a prisoner to the Comanches. She had sandy hair, rather inclining to red. Her eyes were blue, her face rather fair, but disfigured by long cuts made by a knife on her cheeks. This was supposed by Jim Shaw, and other Indians along with us, to be an indication that she had lost a husband or some very near relative, and the gashes on the cheeks were made as indications of grief. Luckily, Jim Shaw was near the writer, and told him not to speak to the poor captive as it might cost him his life. There was no expressed penalty for gazing at the unfortunate creature.

She was mounted. Her face seemed the personification of despair. It filled the beholder with the idea of unutterable woe. The mind naturally reverted to her probable former condition. The loved daughter of affectionate parents, the bright sister of noble brothers and lovely sisters, the wife of a gentle and chivalrous husband, was now rendered forever desolate and disconsolate by being made a captive by savage Indians, and forced to become the wife of a barbarian—not only his wife but his menial, his slave, to be the humble servitor of his shams and caprices, to be punished for a seeming disposition to disobey his behests, to be beaten, lassoed, and pulled through prickly pear, with a rope around the middle, and filled full of thorns to gratify the vengeance of one possessing less pity than a brute.

Then what a sting was a retrospect of her once happy life. Where were the loved ones who made her young life a scene of joy and gladness? Could she meet them, would they recognize and love her? Would they take to their bosoms the wife of a savage, the mother of young savages, though she was made so by force and by cruelty? What a pang would the meeting bring! What a terrible ordeal would the presence of those loved ones produce! The husband, what of him? Let us shut out the harrowing thoughts which must have taken possession of her soul.

The writer has since that period done some rather rough Indian fighting. When he led a charge against the red men, the woman with auburn hair, slashed cheeks, and countenance of extreme sorrow appeared to lead him. She was before his mind's eye, and he struck for her and for vengeance.

5

Sullivan had by this time established a reputation among the Indians: they considered him crazy, and not responsible for his acts. He took advantage of the supposition, and was seldom out of devilment. He stuck pins in warriors, and made them cut capers very unusual for braves to perform. He notified the Indian public that he would give a performance, free of charge, and invited a general attendance. He had a good audience. He played the buzzard, performing feats imitative of those customary to that melancholy bird, in near proximity to a dead horse. He next illustrated the antics of a lizard. He went off on all fours at a brisk gait, ensconced himself behind a log. He would peep over the log, and drop out of sight in the twinkling of an eye. The sight of his contorted face and his white eyes as they danced in his head produced shouts of laughter. Anything more ludicrous has seldom been witnessed. He sang a lisping song: "Miss Julia was very peculiar" was the course, if memory serves. The Comanches did not understand a word, yet they applauded and laughed immoderately. One young warrior laughed himself almost into convulsions. His friends carried him off, fearing he would make himself sick. To use a worn-out phrase of the day, the performance was a complete success.

While here a big council was held by the Comanches. They protested against the employment of Buffalo Hump as a guide. They reminded him that the Mexicans in the vicinity of El Paso had formed a conspiracy to take his life by treachery, and expressed a strong belief that it would be unsafe to trust himself among them again. Jim Shaw was at the council and reported the proceedings to Major Neighbors. Anyway, Buffalo Hump backed down, yet he did not proffer to return the articles received as an advance payment. Another guide was hired, Tall Tree (also known as Guadalupe) who was a captain of one of the Comanche bands from the Panhandle. He had acquired some fame as a warrior.

Our guide was a bachelor. He had a married sister who obtained permission from her husband to accompany her brother, and a female friend went as her companion.

In travelling across an elevated plateau almost covered by rock we had the misfortune to lose the services of Neal. He went hunting, and was unable to discover our trail which was almost imperceptible. He wandered around for a day or two and was picked up by the Comanches. He made his way to the settlements.

On Brady's Creek we camped near a war party of Comanches who were on their way to Mexico. They spent most of the night singing and yelling.

In this section prairie dogs were numerous. They lived in towns which covered a considerable area. There, as at other points, the dogs, rattlesnakes, and small owls entered the same hole. It is impossible to tell the character of this strange communal arrangement. It existed, notwithstanding gentlemen claiming to be learned in natural history who have advanced theories to prove the contrary. Theories are nice things in their way when based upon ascertained truth, but when they stand in direct antagonism to well-attested facts, they do not amount to much. The rattlesnakes were not very large; they were shorter and thicker than the diamond species and more sluggish. The ground owls were rather peculiar in appearance. Some of them had tufts of feathers on their heads, and they looked as if they wore spectacles. When disturbed they emitted a shrill cry, and kept bowing their heads. The rangers dubbed them "French Dancing Masters."

Our half-civilized Indians were skilful hunters, particularly John Harry. They killed turkeys daily, and we fared well. A large party of Kickapoos had been hunting on the Colorado and its tributaries. They had killed many deer and antelope and made what they left very shy.

The streams we crossed were named in accordance with their Comanche designations, or from incidents. Antelope Creek was so called because Captain Jim Shaw missed an antelope at about forty yards. We struck the main Concho about ten miles below the mouth of the North Fork, and moved up the valley to its head.

The camp at the Mustang Water Hole was distinguished by an incident which came near ending the trip. About daylight in the morning

a gang of mustangs stampeded nearly all our mules. Our Indians secured a few; these they mounted and pursued the fleeing animals. It was
after twelve o'clock before they returned. They brought back all we had
given up as lost. The pursuing party heaped many maledictions upon
the writer's mule, Tantrybogus. He was accused of leading the stampede,
notwithstanding he had on hobbles and had been noted for his laziness.
He exhibited one very uncommon habit: he managed to fall down going
up hill as often as he accomplished that difficult feat upon level ground.
After the stampede he had not a single friend in camp.

On the fifteenth day of April, 1849, a terrific wet norther struck us
on the bare and almost sterile plain between the head of the Concho and
the Castle Mountain. The cold was intense. It sleeted and snowed for
hours. We had to move on as fast as possible. There was nothing visible
for miles but bushes. At last we reached some stunted hackberries and
managed to make a fire. It was no easy matter to bear up under the be-
numbing influence of the norther blast. Sullivan was in his shirt sleeves,
having packed up his coat with the blankets. None but a person of iron
will and great endurance could have passed through such an ordeal. The
packs were not disturbed for fear of wetting all the blankets.

We reached the Castle Mountain, so called because there were boulders
on it resembling castles in appearance, and then entered what the Comanches called *week pah*—a gap with water in it; the writer, contrary to
his custom, was ahead. He discovered a man riding towards him who
made a sign, and an Indian galloped up to within thirty yards of him,
with a lance in rest. Ford reined Tantrybogus to the right and went up
the mountain a few yards to break the force of the Indian's charge, if he
made one. He drew a six-shooter and made ready for action. The Indian
halted. The writer raised his hands to indicate peace. The Comanche construed it to mean: "I have ten men at my back." He became very respectful. Things remained in this condition until Tall Tree came up. There
was a mutual recognition, and we camped together. We were now on the
main war trail from the Comanche hunting grounds into Chihuahua.[4]
Our friend was on his way home with animals and other spoils. He had
with him his squaw and a Mexican prisoner, or slave, for the terms are
equivalent.

Tall Tree informed his friend we were short of rations, and he gen-

---

[4] To inhabitants of the Staked Plains region the Comanche war trail seemed like "a
great chalk line on the map of West Texas from the Llano Estacado to the Rio Grande."
From the Llano Estacado the trail ran southwesterly through Big Spring to the Horsehead
crossing of the Pecos, then forked southward to the Comanche Springs where it divided,
one part of the trail crossing the great river near Boquillas and the other at Presidio.

erously slaughtered a fat mule. There was a feast all enjoyed with great gusto. Mule meat is almost as palatable as beef, if that feast is an average test. The next day we ate our last piece of bacon, and had the unpleasant prospect of suffering from hunger. We camped at the Horsehead Crossing of the Pecos, so named on account of the large number of skeletons of horse heads lying on both sides of the river. The Indian explanation was simple and plausible. The crossing, being on the main trail to and from Chihuahua, was a favorite camping place, both going and coming. The first water hole southwest of the crossing was sixty miles distant. Indians returning from Mexico, with stolen horses, would drive them hard to reach water. The loose animals, on reaching the Pecos would plunge into the stream to quench their thirst, and would drink until they became sick and died.

We moved up the Pecos one day, and then crossed over and struck the Toyah River, not far from what was said to be an old military station. We camped near an immense boulder, close to which a spring of good water was boiling up. Not far from us, corn had been planted by Mescalero Indians, as our Indians said.

6

For several days our guide and Sullivan had been cross to each other. Sullivan persisted in dubbing the great Comanche war captain "Blunk," which incensed him, and got him laughed at.

We were satisfied a company of emigrants had been there ahead of us. They were evidently moving at random without a guide. That day we picked up a poor horse, which had been broken down and abandoned. We managed to get him to camp, and we decided to kill and eat him. Horse flesh is considered a delicacy by the Comanches. Tall Tree roasted a bountiful portion, enough to feed about ten hungry men. He announced his intention to "come mucho"—eat a great deal. He ordered Sullivan to bring water from the spring, about ten feet off. A large-sized row commenced then and there. Sullivan gesticulated, and swore in English, Spanish, Soc, and a sprinkling of Caddo. Tall Tree called down anathemas upon Sullivan in pure Comanche, bad Spanish, English, and in tongues unknown to all of us. The quarrel progressed until a resort to arms was purposed, when Major Neighbors and others interfered. The muss did not take off the keen edge of Tall Tree's appetite. He stowed away meat enough to feed a family of buzzards.

Our next camp was at Joe Ellis' Water Hole. Near it was a small hill, at the base of which cropped out a beautiful stonewhite, with red streaks running through it. Someone afterwards decided it to be porphyry. *Quién*

Sabe? Here we gathered the heads growing in the middle of the mescal plant. This had the color and almost the shape of a white cabbage head. A hole was dug, a fire built in it, and, after the whole cavity had been heated, the coals and ashes removed. The bottom was lined with cactus leaves, from which the thorns had been burned. The mescal was deposited and covered by cactus leaves; a layer of dirt was placed over them, and a fire built on top of all. It should have been kept burning all night. We judged it had been allowed to wane; the mescal was not properly cooked the next morning. We ate it nearly half raw. The writer was in possession of a first-class appetite. He could not eat horse meat. It tasted like a sweaty saddle blanket smells at the end of a day's ride. The liver had an offensive smell; by holding his nose he forced down some of that strong-scented viand. He made a hearty breakfast on mescal and, as a result, suffered from colic.

We were anxious to find the Indians inhabiting that section, and failed. Not a Mescalero Apache could we see. We hoped to get something to eat from them. Major Neighbors had a supply of goods and trinkets suitable for the Indian market. We could see very few deer and antelope, and they ran long before we could get in shooting distance. We were in what old frontiersmen called a starving man's luck. A species of maguey had a long stalk running up from the center. We gathered, roasted, and ate it. The taste was not savory by any means. A man would sally out of camp, and return bringing a load of green stalks. Sullivan said it reminded him of "feeding horses on green corn stalks." In addition, we had a cup of coffee, and a quart of mush made of *pinole*—the meal of parched corn and divided into thirteen parts. No one contracted gout.

Going through the "Dead Man's Pass" we passed what we called the Carrizo Mountains. We emerged into a valley. The Puerto del Cola del Aguila—now called "Eagle Springs"—was visible to our right. The writer called the attention of Major Neighbors to it and suggested the propriety of going through it. The major thought it better to follow the guide. He was leading us directly towards a mountain. We began ascending ridges. The sides were not far from perpendicular; the tops were only a few yards across; it was up and down; the evolutions of Barry Cornewall's "Stormy Petrel" was a small thing by the side of ours. That night we slept without food or water. To make the matter worse, the writer fell sick: the green maguey stalks were too much for him.

The next morning we started, blindly following the infernal Comanche. The country became rougher, more rocky, and the ridges more precipitous. Sullivan and the writer were on the rear. Major Neighbors called out that those in front had gotten into a place where an advance was impossible, and a retrograde about as bad. The rear men turned more to the south. They discovered not far ahead an open valley, and made for it, followed by one of the squaws. A trail was reached with horse tracks on it. We expressed a determination to die on that path. The squaw began yelling. The others came up soon. In about a mile the Río Grande was reached.

To give an idea of the demoralized condition of the writer, it is only necessary to state that Sullivan remarked: "I am glad we are on the Río Grande."

"The Río Grande, where is it?"

"You confounded fool you have been riding on its banks for more than two miles."

"Is that so? I thought it was a pond."

A deer was killed that evening; the hide was on hand next morning. We felt certain we would make a human habitation by following up the river, provided we did not die of starvation. We had no idea of our whereabouts, or of the distance to El Paso. Captain Tall Tree was not held in high esteem as a guide. He had managed to render himself un-popular with the other Indians. He was a lazy fellow. One day he let fire get out from his camp. The wind carried it away from him, and he seemed little to care who might be scorched. A sudden squall came from the opposite direction. The flames went with speed in the dry grass and soon reached the pallet of the Comanche, who was enjoying a siesta. The other red men were watching their progress with indifference. When Tall Tree's blankets were singed and some small articles ruined, the semi-civilized men cried out "*cha-ta!*" "*cha-ta!*"—good! good!

Tall Tree had done an extra amount of grumbling at the leanness of our larder. He said so much that his sister and the other squaw called him to account. Jim Shaw interpreted the lecture about this wise:

"You ought to be ashamed of yourself to complain. You seem to for-get you are a Comanche war captain. Look at the other Indians, look at the white men. They are not murmuring."

The Comanche brave did not bear fatigue and hunger with the forti-tude we supposed he would exhibit. The Delawares, Shawnees, and the other more-civilized Indians, showed themselves superior to the nomads of the prairies during the whole trip.

A council was held. It was decided to send two men ahead, who were mounted on the best mules. Major Neighbors and Sullivan were selected. The object was to reach a settlement, procure a supply of provisions, and send them back to us in the rear. The writer and Jim Shaw were left in charge. We travelled at a good pace: starving men are not apt to make unnecessary delays. At one camp we were annoyed by huge swarms of the most voracious mosquitoes that ever drew blood from man. They were accused of crawling under blankets, and thrusting their bills an inch or so into the bodies of sleepless knights.

On one occasion our way was barred by a bluff bank, too high and too steep for us to ascend. The writer managed to get Tantrybogus to the top at one point. He called Jim Shaw, who made the ascent. The point of land on which we stood was about six feet wide; on either side was a deep gully. Our way was blocked by a large rattlesnake. Jim Shaw attracted his snakeship's attention; the writer struck him hard with a small stick, knocked out an eye, and stunned him. Shaw got off a loud guffaw to celebrate the victory. Just then a huge six-footer began rattling almost under Shaw's feet. He gave a tremendous yell, and leaped high in the air. The crippled snake managed to precipitate himself into the gully, and the well one followed suit. Such a din of hissing and rattling scarcely ever arose from one gulch. There must have been hundreds. We hurried away from a den so full of angry foes, cautioning those in the rear to move carefully to avoid being bitten.

Cart tracks became visible; we were greatly rejoiced. We saw a Mexican driving a cart. The writer approached him, with a view to learn something of our surroundings. He sighted the Indians, abandoned his vehicle, and made a frantic rush for the neighboring chaparral. He disappeared in a bunch of cactus, and could neither be seen nor induced to speak.

At the old bed of the Río Grande we were met by a Mexican carrying supplies for our relief. It was four or five miles to San Elizario, the nearest town. We could not resist the temptation to eat at once. The pangs of hunger were too acute and pressing to be borne longer. The writer ate sparingly, and advised his companions to do likewise. It was not a propitious time to lecture on moderation. Several of the company made themselves sick for a few days.

At San Elizario the people treated us very kindly. We learned that Tall Tree had taken us to a point opposite an old fort on the Río Grande called Fort El Paso.

We recruited a day or two; then several of us accompanied Major Neighbors to El Paso. On our side an American woman known as the Great Western kept a hotel. She was very tall, large, and well made. She had the reputation of being something of the roughest fighter on the Río Grande, and was approached in a polite, if not humble, manner by all of us, the writer in particular.

We visited El Paso del Norte, and were received and treated courteously. The story of our starving was soon known to all. We received many invitations to lunch which were warmly accepted. The quantity of victuals Sullivan and the writer stowed away that day would be considered incredible. In addition to three regular meals, they counted up forty-two eggs they had eaten, besides other things.

7

We returned to San Elizario, and made preparations for our homeward march. An old Mexican gentleman was hired to guide us. His name was Zambrano. We moved by the way of the Waco Tanks, the Alamo Springs, the Cornudos de la Alamo, and the peak of the Guadalupe Mountains. We followed the base of the mountain for some distance, and then the valleys of two streams running into the Pecos. When we reached that river, our guide returned home.

No incidents worth noting occurred up to this point. We killed a panther, and ate him. The meat was not very good. It had a peculiar fresh taste, very difficult to get rid of.

Our route was down the valley of the Pecos to the Horsehead Crossing. Before reaching the crossing we met Captain Duval's party of emigrants bound for California. An old Texian named Johnson had joined us at El Paso; he hired to the company as guide as far as El Paso.

Our guide, Captain Tall Tree, was spending his spare time in fitting for use a new shield. He indulged in some very peculiar orgies. The most of those affairs were gotten off before daylight in the morning. Sometimes they caused some of our party to lose sleep. One morning we were awakened by what we at first supposed was a Mexican hog—peccary—in a very violent passion. There was a "chomping" and a "gritting" of teeth, and a great deal of grunting, and other hoggish capers which caused some horrid oaths to be sworn.

Tall Tree had a nice mule, but seeing a shot-bag and a velvet vest in the writer's possession, he honed after them. He got John Harry to propose a swap with the writer. He offered to give his mule for Tantrybogus, the shot-bag, and the velvet vest. After due consultation, had in a pompous and solemn manner, the trade was made. On our way to the settlements Tantrybogus, according to his custom, fell down, going up hill, in chase of a panther. Tall Tree came back with a "big mad" on. He affirmed he would have his mule back. John Harry told him: "No you won't. You knew the mule. Knew he would fall down whenever he took the notion. You offered to make the trade. You have got the mule, and you must keep him. None of your sharp tricks will be played on this trip." Tall Tree concluded to take the advice, but he felt hard about it.

On the tableland, between the Castle Mountains and the head of the Concho, we rode into a large camp of California emigrants, under the control of Captain B. O. Tong of Seguin.[5] John Harry was employed to guide them to El Paso. This meeting was a streak of good luck to both parties. We were about out of rations, and they did not know how to go.

We followed their trail. They had come from Fredericksburg, which was on our line of travel to San Antonio, whither Major Neighbors wished to go to report to General Worth. Not far from the head of the San Saba we encountered quite an old gentleman leading a pack animal. We began interrogating him, and he fought shy, feeling convinced he had fallen into the clutches of bloodthirsty savages, who were going to murder, scalp, and rob him.[6] We came to the conclusion that the antique wayfarer would have been willing to let us do pretty much as we pleased with his person, provided we spared his worldly goods.

A ride of a few miles carried us, on May 29, to the noon camp of a party of emigrants at Old San Saba Fort.[7] Sam Whiting, formerly the editor of the Austin *Daily Bulletin,* was of the party. He was an acquaintance of Major Neighbors. Sullivan was employed to guide them to El Paso.

8

We reached San Antonio without accident or any unpleasant happening. We had previously learned of the death of General Worth. When the writer presented himself on the main plaza, his appearance was quite uncouth. If memory is not at fault, he had on a pair of old drawers and a breech clout, no coat, and a shirt chock-full of the free-soil element. One saloon and restaurant keeper entered a protest against Ford's entering his dining room. The boys played a confidence game on him by reciting the number of murders "Old Rip" had committed. To purchase silence the unfortunate victim set out the drinks.

---

[5] Ford said in the memoirs that a Colonel Thorn led the train, but according to his reports in the *Texas Democrat* (Austin), June 16 and August 4, 1849, and to Major Neighbors' report, the man was Captain B. O. Tong of Seguin.

(Robert S. Neighbors [ed. by Kenneth F. Neighbours], "The Report of the Expedition of Major Robert S. Neighbors to El Paso in 1849," *Southwestern Historical Quarterly,* LX, 531.)

[6] The man whom Ford and his Indian friends were interrogating suddenly jumped back. "Oh!" he yelled, "gentlemen, you certainly wouldn't hurt a poor lone man—there are seventy men just behind: go take them." This, Ford told the editors of the *Texas Democrat,* "was addressed to five hungry chaps, who had hardly strength to have committed *petit larceny* on a henroost!"

(*Texas Democrat* [Austin], June 16, 1849.)

[7] The party Ford and Neighbors met at San Saba Fort was the P. F. Smith Association from San Antonio.

Major Neighbors made his report, and was assisted by the writer. His accounts for expenditures made on the expedition were settled in a satisfactory manner.

On reaching Austin, the writer made a report to the citizens whom he represented. He contended that a railroad on or near the parallel of thirty-two degrees north latitude could be constructed at a moderate cost per mile. He wrote articles for an Austin newspaper setting forth the fertility of the soil of the valley of the Río Grande in the vicinity of El Paso.[8] Major Neighbors accorded in opinion, in fact had briefly called attention to the natural resources of that region in his official report.

Previous to the expedition of Lieutenant [W. H. C.] Whiting and the expedition of Major Neighbors, the country between San Antonio and El Paso was esteemed almost a desert. The public were now placed in possession of proofs to the reverse. At the next meeting of the Texas Legislature, Major Neighbors was sent to El Paso as the agent of the state. He organized the county of El Paso, and proceeded to Santa Fé. President Taylor claimed that the territory belonged to the United States, and issued a proclamation and designated "one Robert S. Neighbors" as a trespasser. The contest between the general government and the State of Texas concerning the ownership of this territory became a political question, and engendered bad blood. [Henry] Clay introduced a bill known as "The Compromise Measure"—the "Compromise of 1850," as it is also called—which became law and probably prevented serious trouble to the people of the United States. According to this compromise, the United States gave Texas ten million dollars for relinquishing her claim to New Mexico. With this money Texas was able to settle her revolutionary war debt. It is no strain upon truth to assume that the expedition of Major Neighbors was a factor in these important events. It certainly precipitated action in the matter.[9]

---

[8] These reports are reproduced in C. L. Greenwood (comp.), "Opening Routes to El Paso, 1849," *Southwestern Historical Quarterly*, XLVIII, 262–272.

[9] Actually, the debate over whether California should be admitted into the Union as a free state did more than the New Mexico trouble to necessitate the 1850 compromise between the North and the South.

XII

>>>

THE SAVAGE

At this period of time the Comanches were a large tribe or nation. They wielded great influence over the other Indians of Texas. They were divided into five bands. At the lowest estimate each band could furnish from 300 to 500 warriors. Major Neighbors placed the number considerably higher.[1] He said that when all the bands assembled in council, and stretched out in encampment along a stream, it took a whole day to ride from one end of the camp to the other.

---

[1] *Comanchería*—Comanche land—in those days included all the vast South Plains area bounded on the east by the Cross Timbers, on the southeast by the frontier settlements near Austin, Fredericksburg, and San Antonio, on the southwest by the Pecos River, on the west by a line that extended from the Mexican settlements of Santa Fé and Taos northward to the headwaters of the Arkansas River, which then formed the northern boundary as it wound and twisted through the northern portion of the Louisiana Territory.

The names of the different bands were distinct—the Nakoni, the Penateka, the Kotsoteka, the Quahadi, and the Yamparika. The Comanches are generally tall and well formed. Many of them have well-developed heads.

The chief of a band of Comanches usually makes a talk to his people very early in the morning, imparting the news and discussing its purport; this is succeeded by his orders.[2] When a change of camp is contemplated, the women gather the animals, saddle and pack them. The lodges are taken down and placed on animals. The men and women ride after the same fashion. Very young children are on horseback at an age when they would not be suffered to manage a horse with us. The point of destination is known to all. The families leave as they get ready, except on some extraordinary occasion, or when danger is apprehended. In any event they have a number of warriors as lookouts on every side. It is almost impossible to approach a Comanche camp without being discovered.

When moving with their women and children, a party of Comanches exhibits scenes of liveliness—the women talking, laughing, and running pack animals to keep them in place; children with bow and arrows in hand, beating thickets for small game, shooting snakes, shouting for pastime, running helter-skelter in every direction; mules going at half speed over rocky places, with long lodge poles trailing on either side, making a noise louder than many empty wagons; young warriors, with gaudy trappings, frolicking and gibing. When all these things are jumbled together into a discordant mass, it must be rather exciting to be travelling with the red children of the forest. Sometimes a stampede occurs, to give additional variety to the scene.

A halt being made, the women arrange everything—take care of the horses, set up the lodges, pack the wood and the water, and cook. The warriors lounge about, gather in groups, and talk over matters and things in general. In things they cannot properly comprehend and account for in some way, they possess considerable incredulity. They deny the tales they hear of the speed of a railway locomotive. When some of them were in-

---

[2] A young Comanche brave usually arose before the chief and awakened the rest of the village with a song. This act, said Noah Smithwick, who lived with the Comanches for several years, "seemed rather a spontaneous outpouring akin to that of the feathered songsters than a religious rite; the song itself resembling the lay of the birds in that it was wordless save for the syllables, ha ah ha, which furnished the vehicle on which the carol rode forth to the world; the performance ending in a keen yell," as others, sleepy eyed, joined in the yelling while the chief emerged from his tepee, stretched, and prepared to deliver his morning talk.
(Smithwick, *The Evolution of a State: or, Recollections of Old Texas Days,* p. 181.)

formed that a steam car could run from Colorado to Chihuahua, Mexico, in less than a day, they declared it impossible: "A horse could not run that far in a day."

They have a game which may be called "hide-the-bullet." The players sit down in a circle and sing a curious kind of song. One takes a bullet, changes it from hand to hand, throwing his arms in every possible direction; when he thinks his manipulations have sufficiently mystified the man appointed for that purpose, he holds out both hands and lets him guess which one the bullet is in. Every guess counts on one side or the other. The number constituting the game is, the writer believes, a matter of agreement; the tallies are kept with arrows. In this way a great many articles change hands. There is one garment and one only an Indian never parts with: it stands betwixt him and nudity.

They play another game with painted sticks counted by the way they fall, so many sticks or spots falling in a certain way counting so much. The writer never could understand the game.

While all this is going forward, the women get a resting spell. They are talkative, are great laughers, and seem to enjoy a bit of scandal with as much gusto as their more civilized neighbors. One of their peculiar amusements would not be much relished in polite circles. A Comanche woman never seems more happy than when "verminizing." The luckless little insects are eaten by those upon whom they had feasted; they get the full benefit of the *lex talionis*. Meantime, the children are roaming about, examining every thicket and every hole, bathing, shooting arrows, and making all those interesting noises incidental to promising juvenility.

2

The Comanches formerly owned large droves of horses. They have thinned them greatly within the last few years, by being compelled to kill them for food. Being shut out from the mustang range between the Nueces and the Río Grande was the cause. Horse meat, with them, is preferred to any other. The neck immediately beneath the mane is considered a rare delicacy. The meat has a coarse fiber, is glutinous, smells badly, and has a peculiar sweetish taste, which remains in the mouth for nearly a day. The writer never liked it, and will say so every time he has the chance. The liver does a little better. Never commit the indiscretion of applying a piece to your nose. A sudden rebellion of the stomach often follows such an act of imprudence.

Mule meat resembles beef in flavor, as was said. To the Comanche a fat mule makes very palatable eating. Young fauns are fine too. Terrapins, rattlesnakes, prairie dogs, and pole cats are very good.

The Mescalero Apache takes his name from the mescal plant. It belongs to the order of plants usually called "beargrass," which has a white head like cabbage and is cooked by digging a hole in the ground, building a fire in it, removing the coals and ashes, and lining the bottom and sides with prickly pear leaves—deprived of thorns—then by burning them, putting in the mescal, covering with cactus, and building a fire upon the same, which must be kept up for twelve or fourteen hours. The edible part is soft, and tastes a little like an Irish potato. It is covered by thin fibrous substance. When on an expedition between the Pecos and the Río Grande, the Comanches use this and a species of the maguey for food. The latter is cooked by simply roasting. It has an unpleasant taste. These plants will grow upon sterile uplands. A Comanche will eat liver, young fauns, and many other things while raw. In Shanaco's camp during the expedition to El Paso, we saw an old rascal who offered to bet he could eat anything. For a plug of tobacco, he proposed making a breakfast upon a substance banished the furthest possible distance from our tables. He was the nastiest-looking thing in human shape we ever saw.

The Comanches live, as our phrase is, "from hand to mouth." They have little providence, and, when provisions are plenty, they consume enormous quantities. They do not bear the pangs of hunger with the stoical resignation one would suppose. In this particular, as in almost every other, the Delawares are infinitely superior to them.

3

Among the Comanches, war parties are formed by volunteers. In many instances the commander has only temporary authority, which ceases with the campaign; in others an acknowledged chief takes the lead. It is not unusual for a party to remain absent, while operating in Mexico, for the space of twelve months.[3]

A young warrior will make any sort of sacrifice to equip and mount himself for an expedition. The officer second in command always places himself at the head of the column; the superior officer is in the extreme

---

[3] The Comanches got their horses by raiding ranches in Mexico when the moon was full in September—the time of the Mexico moon, when the summer rains were over and cool winds began to blow across the prairies of wild, succulent grasses. After a ceremony of songs and dances and tales of war, Comanche warriors took the war trail into Mexico. The Indians must return with large herds, for horses were their most valuable possessions; they represented wealth and prestige and were essential to the locomotion of a nomadic and warlike people.

(Ernest Wallace and E. Adamson Hoebel, *The Comanches: Lords of the South Plains*.)

rear where he is presumed to be in a position to have everything under his immediate inspection and can superintend the movements and rectify errors. A front guard usually precedes the main body from a quarter of a mile to two miles in advance. They keep a strict lookout, ride to the top of eminences, scan the surrounding country in every direction. When an enemy is supposed to be near, they approach the apex of a hill with great caution. They will crawl on the ground, carrying before their faces a bunch of green branches or grass, to prevent suspicion, if discovered. Unless one is well acquainted with Indian contrivances, the moving or disappearance of a bunch of leaves would be attributed to the agency of the wind.

Discoveries made by the vanguard are speedily communicated to the officer in command. There is a rear guard whose duty it is to prevent surprises from that direction. Flankers are often thrown out. When a large body is moving and are approximating a point of supposed danger, pickets are sent out in every direction, which operation is on a more extended scale than the above mentioned guards.

There is a place of rendezvous appointed, at which everything in relation to the expedition is decided upon. For instance, if a foray upon the country adjacent to Laredo is contemplated, time, manner, and second place of rendezvous are all arranged. Formerly they used to make the Raices, a creek in Webb County, the point where they formed their camp preparatory to active operations. From here they would send out scouts to ascertain the conditions of the country and the presence of troops. Upon the information thus acquired, they would act. Sometimes they would move down in a body, fall upon ranches boldly during the daytime, kill, plunder, and carry off women and children prisoners; at others, when secure from danger, they would divide into squads, and make a simultaneous descent upon different ranches. After having made prisoners, collected horses and other booty, they would, if unpursued, move for the Raices and remain in camp several days recruiting animals, feasting, and preparing for a quick march to their own camps.

In the event of being pursued, immediately after the preparation of depredations, the Comanches move day and night, very often not breaking a gallop except to exchange horses (which they do several times) and to water the caballada, until they deem themselves safe. Under these circumstances they will travel at least 70 miles a day, which is a long distance with the incumbrance of loose animals. A party of warriors dressed in their trappings—embellished shields, fancy moccasins, long pig tails, bedecked with silver shoulder belts worked with beads and adorned with shells, fine leggings, ornamented cases for bows and arrows—mounted upon spirited horses, singing a war song, and sweeping over a prairie is a beautiful spectacle to a man with plenty of brave fellows to back him. Their motions are easy and graceful. They sit a horse admirably, and manage one with a master hand. Charge them and they will retreat from you with double your numbers. But beware when pursuing them; keep your men together, well in hand, with at least half their arms loaded, else you will find when it is too late, the flying Comanches will turn upon you and charge you to the very teeth. A Comanche can draw a bow when on horseback, standing or running, with remarkable strength and accuracy. They have been known to kill horses running at full speed over one hundred yards away.

In the commencement of a fight, the yell of defiance is borne to you loud, long, and startling. The war whoop has no romance in it. It thrills even a stout heart with an indescribable sensation. The excitement of battle is quite as evident among these people as among others. Let the tide turn against them, send lead messengers through some of their warriors, and then the mournful wail is heard: its lugubrious notes are borne back to you with uncouth cadences, betokening sorrow, anger, and a determination to revenge.

Never ride upon a bowman's left; if you do, ten to one that he will pop an arrow through you. When mounted, an Indian cannot use his bow against an object behind and to his right.

The dead are usually borne from the field. Nothing but the most imminent danger prevents them from performing the incumbent duty of not leaving the body of a comrade in the hands of an enemy. Over a fallen chief they will make a desperate stand. Their caution seems merged in the determination to risk everything to bear him from the field. To attain this object, they will fight furiously, bravely, and often. If they abandon him, it is in despair. Flight is no longer methodical and menacing to the pursuer. Retreat degenerates into rout. After this they have seldom if ever been known to resume the offensive. They will hide themselves in the first chaparral affording security against discovery, remain during the day, visit the dead at night, and if not able to remove them will spread blankets or some covering over them.

The bow is placed horizontally in shooting; a number of arrows are held in the left hand; the bow operates as a rest to the arrows. The distance—the curve the missile has to describe in reaching the object—is determined by the eye without taking aim. Arrows are sped after each other in rapid succession. At the distance of 60 yards and over, arrows can be dodged, if but one Indian shoots at you at one time. Under forty yards the six-shooter has little advantage over the bow. At long distances the angle of elevation is considerable. It requires a quick eye to see the arrow and judge the whereabouts of its descent, a good dodger to move out of the way, and a good rider withal to keep in the saddle. A man is required to keep both eyes engaged in an Indian fight.

Comanches treat prisoners with extreme cruelty. They are beaten, starved, made slaves of, and subjected to many torturing indignities. This rigor is relaxed when a man or youth evinces a design to become one of the tribe. The man is suffered to marry and the boy is educated to become an Indian in his habits. An expert rogue is held in great esteem.

A war party, when returning to the encampment where their wives and children are, generally impart the news in advance from elevated points, provided the arrival is during daylight. If any of the raiders have been killed, an unearthly wail goes up from men, women, and children —a lamentation for the dead. The wife is required to keep this up for many moons, some say twelve. The mourning song is sung after nightfall. It is not wanting in melody and is one of the most melancholic strains which greets the ear of a civilized man.

A woman who has lost her husband is known by the marks left upon her face or arms from cuts inflicted by herself in the agony of grief. In some cases these amount to disfiguration. (A woman may be badly cut or defaced for another reason: if she has been untrue to her liege lord, the end of her nose is cut off. This is a punishment for infidelity, as well as an indelible evidence of the crime.)

The writer based the above discussion on an article he wrote for the October, 1883, issue of the *Texas Mute Ranger*.

4

The writer found in the Dallas *Herald* an excellent article on how the plains Indians made use of sign language, which he deems worthy of reproduction here.

There are seventy-six different vocal languages used by the American Indian, which are as distinct in pronunciation as are the English, German, French, or any other language known to civilized man. Hence, the migratory Indian from the north must have some mode of communication when he followed the buffalo to warmer climate late in autumn, and in turn the fellows who escaped from the scorching sun of the south to enjoy the cool breezes of the north found that they must co-operate with their brethren in order to make their visit endurable. Thus, these children of nature, for they are nothing more nor less, have by common necessity organized a system of sign language, which, though unworthy of being dignified by being termed a complete code, is sufficiently intelligible to permit of a pretty general use of it among the most intelligent men and women of the various tribes.

The plains Indians are credited with perfecting the sign language to a greater extent than any other. To such an extent is the sign language used that there are those who can converse as rapidly in this manner as by vocal speech, and although two seldom used the same sign, the general outline of the pantomime is so easily comprehended that frequently a description of some great event is imparted by one Indian to another, whose homes are separated by hundreds of miles and no possible means of communications ever existed between their respective tribes. In other words, there are certain general signs that are thoroughly understood by tribes of the British Possessions and of the Malbipais district of Arizona.

The signal of a horseman riding rapidly in a circuitous route is well known to be one of danger, and before the aborigines had a Great Father to provide them with ponies, this sign was given by one of the Indians running backward and forward as rapidly as his legs would carry him. Just before departing on any enterprise of murder and a separation is to occur, certain signs are agreed upon. As an illustration, the old Biblical term of "a cloud of smoke by day and a pillar of fire by night" was never more strikingly exemplified than when mounted Indians climb a hill and, after building a fire of damp or green wood, cover the same with a blanket. As soon as sufficient smoke has accumulated for the purpose, the blanket is quickly lifted so that a ball of smoke arises steadily into the air and finally disappears among the clouds. This is a day signal and is supposed to be witnessed by allies in another section of the country. The night signal for disclosing a retreat of friends is made by a wisp of dry grass or hay, which is lighted at one end and whirled around in the air so that a perfect circle of fire is visible. In their native simplicity, these children of the forest have adopted the modes of the days of Moses and Aaron to communicate with each other.

Suppose that two Indians of different tribes meet. They have met before and formed a mutual admiration, and their families may be particularly interested in each other. The visitor is welcomed by the host, and a conversation by signs commences. The new arrival will, in a short space of time, relate how a friend had suddenly come in contact with an enemy; what weapons were used; who drew the first blood; where either was wounded; the length of time consumed in the battle; the position of each at different times of the combat; the courage displayed and the stoical indifference assumed. In fact, every detail will be told almost as quickly as if related by the tongue, and yet not a word will pass between the parties, because they could not understand each other.

Since civilization has encroached upon the privileges of these savages, and they have learned the art of chewing tobacco and loafing around on store boxes like white people, they have not been slow to utilize many of the articles used for domestic purposes. They will take a medium size mirror, and from the top of a lofty mountain flash the movements of an enemy to their friends far in the distance. A blanket is considered an excellent medium for communicating intelligence. It is taken by the corners and waved back and forth to show that an engagement is anticipated, and after a battle it is laid flat upon the ground, which indicates that the party is anxious to surrender. A sign for after night is the firing of a lighted arrow in a certain direction, which may represent various things. . . . The rude figures of various animals and birds that are so common to the heathenish . . . arts, all have their significance, and are read with ease by those who understand them. A moving band can, by leaving pictures of birds and inanimate objects scattered along their route, inform a party of friends following as to what occurrences have taken place so accurately that the second band will know just what to do to guard against danger or lend assistance. An illustration of a steep mountain with a goat in the act of climbing, while a horse appears in a position where the soles of his hoofs are liable to get sunburnt, indicated that though a goat can climb up the rocky trail, a horse may stumble, and hence it is unsafe for the Indians to attempt the ascent.

The Comanches have in addition to signs, as indicated in the article quoted, a kind of picture writing representing events. These include a species of hieroglyphics and symbolic characters which convey ideas. When they wish to inform their friends of the death of a warrior, it is done by drawing an Indian without a head. If wounded only, the figure is complete, with a streak of red at the part wounded. Upon a tree on the Nueces River, some thirty or forty miles above the Laredo and San Antonio Crossing, at a place known as the Comanche Crossing, are a number of these symbolic representations. One of them is descriptive of a combat between a Comanche with a lance and a Mexican with a sword. The sword is woefully deficient in length. The rough painting conveys a rather ludicrous idea of the matter, evincing very clearly the contempt in which the Indian held Mexican prowess, and the almost inevitable conclusion that the fight resulted in the Don's overthrow and death.

Comanches make other uses of signs and picture writings. When a party is on a raid, they have a man or two who ascends any high grounds near which they pass in order to discover any party in pursuit. He is sometimes several miles in the rear. Should another band of Indians be raiding at the same time, the man in the rear leaves on the top of a hill or in a mat of timber in a prairie a statement of the situation. A long mark is made on the ground. On one side of it there are short marks indicating the number of Indians in the party, another set of short marks tells the number of captives, another set represents the number of stolen horses. In some instances the casualties are set forth. A small branch of a tree, a stick or something else, is struck in the ground, leaning in the direction the detachment is moving. Should the other band of raiders pass near the same point, their flankers, or rear guard, will be sure to hunt for these signals, and communicate the information they convey to the captain in command.

5

The Comanches have a religion; they practice incantations and believe in removing disease by charms and observances. The Comanche enjoys a modicum of real pleasure. His roving devil-may-care life has attractions to him. There is buoyancy of spirit in roaming over a vast expanse of country, unreclaimed by the hand of civilization; there is a pleasure in traversing a prairie upon whose broad bosom the foot of Christian man has never before left its impress; there is a chastened emotion, not without pleasantness, stealing over the mind when threading the mountain pass, gazing upon the summit of a mighty pile and losing almost the very impressions of individuality, by merging them in the thought, the comparison of our utter insignificance, when contrasted with those gigantic monuments of His creative power before us. Are we to suppose the untutored mind, which has only been able to read leaves from the book of nature, does not enjoy these things with a zest we know not? Are not the winds, the waters, the mountains, in short, the whole gorgeous sheen of Nature, when enrobed in primeval resplendancy, but so many chapters in the magnificent book of creation, teaching him there is a God? He too has a creed. He adores the Great Spirit. He abhors the treason that would place him at the foot of any other shrine but that consecrated by the devotions of his fathers. Fortified by his own system in ethics, his own sense of freedom, notwithstanding all he may admit to the contrary, the Comanche imagines he covers as much space in the life of the world, in the estimation of the Great Father, as any man living. These feelings, this spirit of independence, or nationality, if you will, enable him to enjoy life with an avidity, a keen relish that many a cultivated mind can never feel or appreciate.

In the arts, the mechanical trades, and the various matters incident to civilized life, the Comanche feels his inferiority. Sound him upon the estimate he places upon one of his tribe, confronted with an American in a wilderness, with like equipments and equal arms and he will give the palm of superiority to his countryman.

The love of country, the spirit of nationality, is as strongly developed in the Indian as in any man on earth. An Indian loves his own mode of life, venerates the great braves that have gone before him, detests the people whose steady advance forces him to abandon the hunting grounds of his ancestors. It is no wonder that a people thus cultivated, thus believing and thus living, should enjoy much of that repose of mind which is nearly allied to happiness.

With plenty to eat, no enemy near, the Comanche is not disturbed by a single care for the present, or thought for the future.

XIII

>>>

THEY DID RIGHT
BECAUSE IT WAS RIGHT

In 1848 Indian alarms were not infrequent in Travis County, and even in the city of Austin, the capital of Texas. In those days a gentleman seldom rode into the country any distance without carrying arms. It was not safe to ramble in the suburbs of the town unarmed. Mr. Horst lived within the corporate limits of Austin. He was attacked by Indians on his way to market. Early in 1846 the writer noted hearing the "check" of billiard balls, the howling of wolves, and the yelling of Indians whilst he was standing on Congress Avenue. Austin was a bona fide frontier town. The Indians had killed a goodly number of people within the city and nearby. The citizens would get together and make a reconnaissance in the adjacent country, usually with little effect.

Early in 1849 depredations were committed in various localities south and west of Austin. It was known that the Indians often passed down the valley of the Colorado River, which was almost unsettled above the capital. It was a known habit of theirs to go out by the same route by which they came in. A suggestion was made to raise a company of citizens, move up the Colorado, and endeavor to intercept the murdering marauders. John S. Ford was elected captain of a detachment of a little more than twenty men.

After having ascended the river about twenty-five miles, we found a fresh Indian trail. It was followed two days with a good prospect of overtaking the savages. The second day, in the evening, small fires were built and coffee made—a very indiscreet proceeding. At night a heavy rain fell. It was probable the Indians and whites were camped near each other. The redskins discovered us and left in a hurry. The trail could not be followed the next morning. The scout was not a success.

2

During the summer of 1849, General George Mercer Brooke, commanding the Department of Texas, urged Governor [George T.] Wood to call out three companies of volunteer rangers to operate against the Indians, who were committing fearful outrages upon the frontier settlers of Texas.

Governor Wood absented himself from Austin without designating the men who were to raise and organize these companies. Colonel John D. Pitts was then adjutant general of the State of Texas. He gave John S. Ford authority to enlist one company. The work was done quickly. Ford issued an address explaining why he was going out against the Indians:

The defense of our frontier is entitled to a prominent place in the public mind. I have long believed, and acted on the belief when I could, that an aggressive policy is the only one which will force the Indians to sue for peace. They should be made to feel the iron hand of war upon their hunting-grounds, and within their lodges. Whip them and then talk of treaties. Cost what it may the pioneer settlers must be protected. It is the imperative duty of the State to do so. It matters not what motive carried them to the frontier. They had a right to go, and they are entitled to the fostering care of the Government.

Ford's volunteer command was organized on August 23, 1849, and mustered into the service of the United States for six months by Lieutenant T. J. Wood. The next day, or the day after, the line of march was taken up for San Antonio. Governor Wood had a favorite—whether worthy or not it is needless to discuss—whom he wished to substitute in Ford's place. He failed. General Brooke, upon the legal advice of Volney E. Howard, decided that Ford could be ousted only by the action of a court-martial or by expiration of term of service.

The command was marched, in obedience to orders, to Corpus Christi to receive their arms. The route was over a region infested by Indians. Andy Walker, a noted frontiersman, had headed a body of citizens recently, and defeated a band of Comanches not far from the road leading from San Antonio to Corpus Christi. A few of our men had six-shooters. A dozen determined Indians could have defeated the whole command with heavy loss.

The company was stationed for a while at the Ozo, a ranch of Colonel H. L. Kinney's, about eight miles from Corpus Christi. News was received of an Indian raid on the Nueces above San Patricio. A scout under the captain went out without delay. [Thomas M.] Woolridge and [Jeremiah W.] Robertson remained in camp.

The valley of the Nueces was followed for several days. The rain fell in torrents. Dry creeks were converted into rivers; their waters were deep and their currents impetuous. We waded, and swam, and splashed through mud and bogs. The march was slow and laborious. For many days no one had dry clothes. The horses became jaded, and lost flesh daily. The road from San Antonio to Laredo was reached, and we rejoiced at the sight of land that was apparently dry. No fresh sign of Indians was discovered.

Fort McIntosh was made to obtain supplies for man and horse. We remained a few days in Laredo, and marched over a district, covered by water holes and lakes, to our camp.

3

In the country between Laredo and Corpus Christi we encountered countless droves of mustangs and herds of deer. In many places wild cattle were numerous. These were the increase of the animals abandoned by Mexicans when they were ordered to evacuate the country between the Nueces and the Río Grande by General [Valentín] Canalizo, the *commandante* of the line of the Bravo and the representative of the Supreme Government of Mexico. The penalty to any Mexican found three leagues north of the Río Grande was arrest and trial as a spy. It must be remembered that the Nueces was formerly the northern boundary line of the Mexican state of Tamaulipas, but this line was given up by President Santa Anna in the treaty of 1836 and the Republic of Texas extended to the Río Grande.

The horses and cattle abandoned invited the raids the Texians made upon this territory during the period of the Republic. The men thus engaged acquired the name of "cow-boys." It was not meant as a term of reproach. War existed between Mexico and Texas at that time, and the operations of the "cow-boys" were considered legitimate. The debatable land was the scene of many hostile meetings between the Mexicans and Texians.

In process of time the Comanches put in an appearance. They made no claim to the territory. Their intent was confined to the procuring of horses to ride and to eat. Horse flesh is a dainty to the Comanche. In order to obtain it he did not scruple to invade, murder, and rob.

At the period of which we are writing there were hundreds of mustang pens between the Nueces and the Río Grande. The Mexicans engaged in catching wild horses were rather uncouth in their habits. Many of them paid no regard to the laws governing the rights to property. A wayfaring man was about as secure in meeting a band of Comanches as in encountering a company of "mustangers"; in either case he was not likely to be treated as an honored guest.

In order to open up the country to settlers, to enable the owners of the soil to occupy it, and to give protection to person and property, the rangers had been called into requisition to aid the Federal forces in ridding that section of the intruders who were preying upon it. These objects being in view rendered the location of a camp a matter of some importance. Reconnaissances were made with care of the region watered by the Agua Dulce, the San Fernando, and the Santa Gertrudis. An encampment was made on the latter stream, about a half mile above where the house of Captain Richard King now stands.

4

After placing the command in comfortable quarters and providing supplies, Ford made a scout in the direction of Río Grande City. He moved up the valley of the Bravo and made the acquaintance of the inhabitants. He ascertained that many families owning lands in Texas were afraid even to go upon them on account of the insecurity to life. The Indians were in the habit of raiding ranches between Laredo and Río Grande City; laborers were intimidated from pursuing their vocations; the laws were seldom observed and feebly administered; smuggling was done on a rather large scale. He visited Mier, Mexico, for the purpose of procuring information concerning the Seminole Indians who were attracting attention on account of their reputed raids upon the people of Texas. The Mexicans reported some of them to be residing in their country at Laguna Leche, and seemed to fear them. He reported fully to General Brooke. It was fortunate for him he did.

The night he slept at Mier some Americans recaptured some goods which had been seized by the Mexican customhouse officials as smuggled.

The military commander at Mier sent a complaint to the City of Mexico implicating Ford in the transaction, which was forwarded to the Minister of Mexico at Washington. The Secretary of War, without inquiring into the facts, ordered General Brooke to have Ford arrested on the charge. The general denied the allegations, quoted Ford's report, and saved him twice from a position which could have been painful. He could have proved his innocence. The night in question he slept in the same bed with his guide, Andrew J. Walker, at the house of Margarita García, known to the Americans as "the Pearl of Mier." There were several other ladies there; they played on the guitar and sang, and all retired at a late hour.

This reconnaissance was extended to Laredo, thence to the Nueces River, thence partly down that stream to Camp Santa Gertrudis. These scouts gave Ford a general knowledge of the country he was endeavoring to defend.[1] The last one involved a march of about four hundred miles.

5

The writer never subscribed to the theory that Texas Rangers needed no drilling. He had seen enough service to convince him it was necessary for men to know how to perform simple evolutions to render them efficient in the presence of an enemy. He exercised the men in the manual of arms, wheeling, changing front, and other maneuvers.

The discipline had little that savored of that enforced in the regular army. It appealed to the pride and to the sense of honor of the men. The guard for the next twenty-four hours was detailed at roll call in the morning. When on a scout two noncommissioned officers were usually placed in charge. Each sentinel was required to stand two hours; he was trusted as to time and permitted to wake up his relief. Only a few instances of shirking occurred. The offender was brought to light in every case and punished. Men distinguished for neglect of duty, disregard of their word, and want of courage were not allowed to go on a scout, to be

---

[1] Ford reported to Governor Wood that so extensive were the Indian raids that "a general dread prevailed everywhere" in the lower Río Grande region. It was "impossible to procure Mexican laborers to work in the fields on the east bank of the Río Grande." Moreover, a "large number of Texas citizens, of Mexican origin, and paying State taxes upon their lands, were living on the west bank of the Río Grande in consequence of the inadequate protection given them." The captain found that not all the raids were made by Comanches. One night, by the full of the moon, Ramón Falcón's band of Mexican outlaws raided Brownsville, killing a few civil and military officials. One of them was Colonel Trueman Cross of the United States Army who was a good friend of Ford's. "Should the villain who bathed his hands in the blood of one of the best officers in the army, fall into my hands," Ford said angrily, "I shall hang him to the first convenient tree, as an act of retributive justice for his crimes."

(*Texas State Gazette* [Austin], December 12, 1857.)

detailed as an escort, or to enjoy the privileges accorded to honorable soldiers. They were on duty as camp guards, or in other services which are generally distasteful to men of energy and enterprise. This punishment was dreaded. It carried with it a loss of the respect and the confidence of the whole command. It caused fellows, apparently hardened to the ordinary ideas of propriety, to beg, and even cry, when told they could not leave camp. Should the captain place a man under ban, his example would be followed by all down to the fourth corporal. It required no order to bring about such a result.

6

On a scout the guards detailed in the morning were used as front and flank guards while on the march. The next day they constituted the rear guard, and had charge of the pack mules and the wagons, when we moved with any, which was very seldom. The mustangs frequently gave the rear guard something to do. It was wonderful to witness the evolutions of those animals. Sometimes they would bear down upon us in column. The leader would usually halt his followers, advance and reconnoitre. Should he dislike the appearance of things, he would retire, neigh in a peculiar manner, and all would wheel about, and retreat. A lagger would catch a biting. At times the wild horses would advance upon us almost at full speed, with an evident determination to run over us. This, on many occasions, demanded prompt measures of defense. A hollow square would be formed around the pack mules; when the mustangs came in reach of our guns, we opened fire. It was the practice to aim at the leader; when he was brought down, the herd would run off in wild disorder.

Our horses were not allowed to be hoppled or to be turned loose. Disobedience to this standing order was sure to incur punishment. A few ventured to do so, and in most cases they lost their horses. A ranger on foot was considered "a poor thing."

We had tents at permanent encampments—never on scouts. Any move in the direction of effeminacy or dandyism was put down by the boys. Once on a scout between the Nueces and Río Grande, and above the road from San Antonio to Laredo, an unlucky ranger, troubled with sunburnt and blistered nose and lips, hoisted an umbrella. Nothing was said or done the first day. The second day the captain took two men and went hunting. When they had gone quite a mile, a brisk fusillade was heard in camp. The two men were much excited: "Let us run back—the Indians have attacked the camp!"

The captain listened attentively for a while, and remarked: "No such thing—the boys are shooting Henderson Miller's umbrella."

It was shattered and torn into hundreds of pieces. The captain, for once, let the matter pass unnoticed. He did not see how he could remedy the affair, and thought that silence was wisdom.

A large proportion of the command were unmarried. A few of them drank intoxicating liquors. Still, it was a company of sober and brave men. They knew their duty and they did it. While in a town they made no braggadocio demonstration. They did not gallop through the streets, shoot, and yell. They had a specie of moral discipline which developed moral courage. They did right because it was right. You might kill them but you could not conquer them. Napoleon's Old Guard never met danger and death with more fearless heroism. It might as well be said here as anywhere else that the men of "Ford's Old Company" made effective, splendid soldiers. When mustered out of the service they made excellent citizens, good neighbors, and faithful husbands. No dishonor could be attached to any of them. A man who would not feel proud of having commanded such noble men would be dead to the finest feeling which elevates humanity. Years have elapsed since we separated. Death has done its work upon us, but nothing can efface the ties which bound us together: they are stronger than the love of woman. They defy the work of time and of change. Gallant defenders of the hearthstones of the helpless and loved, pioneers who stood in bold relief at the skirmish line of civilization and aided gloriously in opening up an immense territory to settlers who carried with them the gospel of Christ and the arts of peace, may God protect you and bless you, here and hereafter.

7

The operations of 1849 yielded nothing hoped for. A rain fell to put out a trail, or some unseen and unexpected event happened to prevent our getting a fight.

Captain John J. Grumbles had another company of rangers which was stationed on the Nueces River about seventy-five miles above Corpus Christi. Captain Henry E. McCulloch with a third company was posted between Goliad and Corpus Christi. It was thought advisable for Ford to take post nearer the Río Grande. He was allowed to choose his own camp. But of this more hereafter.

Early in 1850 a young man named James Doyle was killed by Indians beyond the "reef" seven or eight miles from Corpus Christi. Captain Ford was, at the time, in town on business. He gathered a few of Captain

Grumbles' men and a few of his own, and made an effort to follow the murderers. It was found impossible to discover the trail. If the act had been committed by Indians, they were on foot and left no visible tracks.

A rather ludicrous affair occurred. The mail rider from Goliad sighted the rangers and mistook them for Indians. He and his companion struck across the prairie at a run. The rangers supposed they were Indians and pursued vigorously. The chase continued for several miles. The rangers were gaining perceptibly. The pursued were obstructed by a lagoon. They dismounted, and managed to get their horses over just as the rangers came up. The mail bags were left behind, and told all. The two parties were not more than fifty yards apart. The captain bawled out: "Come —get your mail bags, we are not Indians." He was unheeded. The flying men plied the whip and spur as far as they could be seen. It was reported that when the mail rider reached Goliad he told how closely the Indians pressed him, and boasted of his smartness in evading the trick the red rascals tried to play on him: "They couldn't fool me with their English!"

XIV

>>

READY, AYE, READY

A reorganization of the company occurred late in February, 1850. Andrew J. Walker was made first lieutenant and Malcijah B. Highsmith second lieutenant and acting quartermaster and commissary; David M. Level was orderly sergeant. Dr. Philip N. Luckett had been our surgeon from the first. He was afterwards a colonel in the Confederate service. We had a guide, Roque Maugricio. He was a Mexican crossed with Indian. He had been captured at an early age by the Comanches. They made him a war captain. He spoke their language fluently, knew all the country above the upper line of white settlements, also west and south of the Colorado River. He was an expert trailer. His sense of smell was wonderful. He was indefatigable, never appeared to flag, never complained of being tired or hungry. He was in the habit of reporting the truth, and had nothing sensational about him.

The point chosen by the captain for his camp was forty-five miles from
Ringgold Barracks, on the road leading from Río Grande City to Laredo
—distant from the latter place about seventy miles. It was known as San
Antonio Viejo—Old San Antonio. It was at the southern edge of the
sand belt.[1] It had been the seat of a large stock raiser who had been
driven off by the Indians. There were several large wells of excellent
water, with watering troughs of stone. From these we obtained our supplies of water for man and horse. We had a wagon and barrels and
hauled water for drinking and cooking to the camp, a half mile to the
southward of the wells. Our tents were pitched in a mat of oaks. They
occupied three sides of a square; a rude building for storing supplies of
all kinds stretched quite across the western side of the square. These details are given to make what will be stated further on more easily understood.

2

Our pistols were unserviceable. Early in May the captain organized a
scout of about forty men. His object was to scour the country above Laredo, then move across country in the direction of San Antonio, turn to
the right, make Corpus Christi, draw better pistols, and return to San
Antonio Viejo. He felt certain he would find Indians should any be down
in the regions indicated.

A halt of a few days was made at Fort McIntosh to complete the outfit. We moved up the Río Grande thirty miles or more. We proceeded
cautiously, keeping our men out of sight as well as we could. Roque and
a few prudent and trusty men—one of which was Sergeant Level—were
kept well to the front. No certain signs bespoke the proximity of Indians,

---

[1] The sand belt was a desert 65 miles wide and 100 miles long which must be crossed
to get from Corpus Christi to Brownsville. To travelers it was a nightmare of drouth
and searing heat, for there were no trees and no water fit to drink.

Entering the sands from the north, you felt, suddenly, a blast of hot air—the winds
coming off the Gulf—and your first impulse was to turn back, but you pushed on because
you must get to Brownsville. After a mile or so you were nauseated from the pelting sun,
and your lips were cracked, and your throat parched. Wiping your soaked forehead and
drinking deeply from your gum-elastic water sack, you noticed for the first time the
brooding loneliness of the land about you, and you gazed out across it: everywhere you
looked there was the same sun-baked earth with occasional sand dunes and without a
sign of life beneath moving clouds of dust; and you began to worry about your water,
because you knew that there were no water holes for a hundred miles or more. But you
were determined. Pulling your hat down over your eyes and adjusting the scarf protecting
your nose and face, you spurred your horse southward across this God-forsaken country.
What was it the Mexicans called it? *El Desierto de los Muertos*—the Desert of the Dead.

An English traveler, Arthur James Lyon Fremantle, crossed over the sands in 1863.
He thought that compared to the "terrible" sands, the prairie and chaparral further
inland were "luxurious." (*The Fremantle Diary*, p. 29.)

yet it was believed from the indications they were not far off. An arrow taken out of the body of a deer, killed recently, removed all doubt. We marched slowly, silently, and with great circumspection through timbered sections.

The captain directed Lieutenant Walker to take one half the men and move down the country, feeling assured the Indians would discover one detachment, and in trying to avoid them would run foul of the other. Ford marched towards the Nueces, inclining to the left, and rather up that stream. He halted a day on the San Roque Creek, a tributary of the Nueces, and kept Roque and others scouting and on the alert. An incident may be noted. Sergeant Level and a man named Jack Sharpe were out of camp watching for Indians. They heard wolves barking, as if they were baying something. They approached them stealthily and discovered a gang of prairie wolves—coyotes—had forced a leopard to take a tree. They killed and skinned the leopard, which was hardly discreet.

That day one of Walker's musketeers went out of camp, and was chased by Indians almost within gunshot of the rangers. The command were in the saddle promptly and in pursuit. The Indians circled, doubled, and did all they could to throw their pursuers off their track. Walker was a good trailer and a practiced Indian fighter. The red men saw they could not fool him; towards the afternoon they concluded to make an effort to outrun him. They pointed up country and towards the Nueces. Walker strained every muscle to overtake the foe. They had relays of horses; when one evinced fatigue they mounted another. Late in the evening Walker drew off his men. He had made a terribly hard run and could do no more. He could not have followed the trail at night: the attempt would have been futile.

On the morning of May 12, 1850, Captain Ford broke camp. He moved down the country in order to make the Nueces at a point known as the Comanche Crossing. A few miles therefrom a fresh Indian trail came into view. It had been made by the rascals Walker had chased the day before.

Every ranger's heart beat high with hope; there was a chance to get a fight. Every precaution was observed to approach the enemy unseen. When the head of our column entered the narrow valley of the Nueces the shrill neigh of a horse was heard on the opposite bank; luckily none of our animals answered it. A reconnoitering party was thrown forward. They reported the Indians gone. A man or two, with jaded horses, was detailed to remain with the muleteers and pack mules. The river had to be swum; drift wood furnished means of passage for the men. A few minutes sufficed to accomplish the object, and for all to saddle and mount.

The Indians, presuming all the rangers had left, were moving at their leisure. They were using whips on the prickly-pear leaves, cutting and slashing them. They were evidently enjoying themselves.

The rangers followed, marching as much as possible over low grounds, galloping when practicable, doing all they could to force a fight. About eight miles from the crossing the Indians emerged from the timber and entered an extensive prairie. The captain saw their heads as they were descending the other side of an elevation. "Here they are!" he yelled, and galloped up within fifty yards of them. They did not see him until he hallooed at them. The men thought he had directed them to stay where they were. Roque and another, probably Sergeant Level, joined the captain. The Comanche chief told his warriors they could easily whip three men. They began to prepare for action. By this time the rangers came up and formed. Here was a fair chance to test the fighting capacity of the rangers and the Comanches: each commander had sixteen men. The Indian had his bow, his arrows, and his lance. The rangers were armed with Mississippi rifles—muzzle loaders. The captain and Sergeant Level alone had revolvers. The preliminaries consumed very little time.

The captain, having passed some time in the Comanche camps, had a good idea of their mode of warfare. He cautioned his men to fire alternately and to keep well together. While he was giving these instructions the Comanche chief rode down the rear of his warriors, then out and down the front of the rangers not more than thirty yards from our line.

"Be steady boys!" the captain exclaimed. "He wants to draw your fire and then charge you with the lance!"

When the chief was passing Sergeant Level, the sharp crack of a revolver was heard: blood spurted from the chief's arm. He wheeled his horse.

"Charge!" fell from the captain's lips. The rangers raised the Texas yell. The fight had opened.

The Comanches, in obedience to the orders of their chief conveyed by means of a whistle, made some maneuvers. They formed two sides of a square, refusing their right wing, forming their left in column at an angle with their right wing. This disposition gave the rangers the chance of attacking the left wing in flank, which was done gallantly and effectively. It was not long before the notes of mourning were borne upon the breeze. Some of the rangers mistook it for a sullen shout of defiance, but they were told that it meant the loss of distinguished warriors. The left being hard pressed, the right would face about, and let fly volleys of arrows. It was a fight almost hand to hand—fifteen feet lay between the combatants. The captain ordered: "Ride up to the right and the rear of an Indian, and he cannot use his arrows." This proved a safe procedure, especially in close quarters.

The captain led in the charge; he had the best horse. The Comanches made several attempts to cut him off; he foiled them. He made a dash at a warrior, approached within a few yards of him. The savage made strenuous efforts to put his bow and arrows into requisition. In endeavoring to turn in his saddle, he broke the girth and fell. He sprang to his feet instantly, bent his bow to the fullest extent, and was in the act of firing. A pistol shot was heard: the warrior fell dead. A ball had pierced his head. Meantime five or six of the enemy faced about apparently to assist their comrade. About as many rangers were within short range of the Indians. Not a shot was fired by either side; they seemed absorbed in watching the result of the duello. When it was obvious the Indian lay dead, the rangers pushed on shouting in triumph; the death wail went up mournfully from the retreating foe. Arrows hurtled through the air. They could be seen, the point of descent measured by the eye, and the field of danger abandoned. The arrows "lofted in the air"—those sent up at an angle to cause them to light upon our heads—were difficult to avoid. One of these struck private David Steele; another penetrated the captain's horse.

Just about a year before, the captain, Doc Sullivan, and Alpheus D. Neal had been in the camp of these same Indians and were recognized. One of them asked Sullivan: "Are you going to kill your companions?" Sullivan answered by sending a ball through the body of a brave.

The Indians, seeing the day was going against them, being demoralized by the fierce onset and the damage they had suffered, left the prairie, entered a wooded country, and managed to outrun their inveterate and dreaded foes. The skirmish covered a line of four or five miles.

The rangers were elated by their victory, and felt chagrined because they could not make it more complete and disastrous to the enemy. They had done remarkably well. A running fight has seldom been made by men armed with muzzle-loading guns and no pistols, inflicting such heavy loss upon their opponents. The Comanches had four men killed and seven wounded. One of the killed they were unable to carry off the field, which was their practice. The rangers captured eleven or twelve horses, bows, arrows, and other trophies.

One man of ours and one horse were wounded; the horse died. The captain had a scratch, as it appeared, on the back of his right hand. For days his arm was very painful. He thought nothing of the matter. Five or six years afterward, his right arm was almost completely paralyzed. An eruption has made its appearance on his hand once every year since. He formed the opinion that the abrasion was made by an arrow poisoned by the venom of a rattlesnake.

On the twenty-ninth of May we captured a young Comanche brave who informed us of the loss sustained by the Comanches. After the skirmish the rangers marched back to the Comanche Crossing, passed the Nueces, encamped, and placed a picket on the river. General Brooke, commanding the Department of Texas, issued a general order complimenting Captain Ford and his men for their efficiency and gallantry.

3

The captain had a servant who rejoiced in the euphonious name of Don Francisco de la Garza Falcón. The rangers substituted a shorter title —"Monkey." The Don was in the habit of regaling the men by recounting his war exploits, particularly the feats he performed at the battle of Monterey.

On the twelfth of May he was within gunshot of us when the skirmish commenced. He seemed to forget his bloody record of 1846 and began a retreat, by no means orderly. He encountered Mat Nolan, the bugler, whose rope had been dragging. Mat was a brave boy. He informed the Don he was moving in the wrong direction and would come to grief should he persist. The Don changed front, and went well until he came in sight of the combatants and in hearing of shouts and yells. The promise of being shot instantly did not deter him. He went to the rear at full speed. He continued to advance and retire until the fighting ceased. Not many days thereafter the Don was giving a very graphic account of the fight to one of the men.

"Notwithstanding the *capitán* was on a fine horse and I on a pony, we were side by side—*parejitos*—all the time. I fired all my cartridges, and went into them with my knife."

"What?" said the ranger. "With nothing but your knife?"

"*Con nada solo mi puro belduque*"—with nothing but my naked knife.

4

On the morning of May thirteenth, two of our horses were missing. It was ascertained the owners had turned them loose during the night. Men scoured the bottom in every direction, but did not find them. Roque was directed to go back on the trail of the day before. He returned soon, and reported the animals had taken the back trail and had not gone far before they met a party of nine—evidently Indians—and were captured. The order to saddle was obeyed with alacrity. The captain borrowed the horse of Captain Ashmore Edwards. Between nine and ten the fresh trail was definitely located. It led down the Nueces through a timbered region. It was followed at a brisk gallop. At times the rear of the Indians was visible; then our horses were put at almost full speed. The horses of the red men were fresher than ours; they got out of the way every time we tried to force them into a fight. These spurts lasted till a while before sunset. In the pursuit, we had described a large circle, and now found ourselves on our trail of the twelfth, and not a mile from where we began the pursuit that morning. We had made the horses do all they could. The command proceeded to the camp not far distant. The guard and muleteers had been instructed to make a certain water hole and remain there until further orders.

The next morning we discovered a large party of Indians quite close to camp. The timber was thick, and there was a great deal of undergrowth intermixed with it.

A turkey gobbled about a hundred and fifty yards from camp. Doc Sullivan shouldered his gun, but hesitated some time.

"I would go and shoot that turkey but I am afraid it might be an Indian," he said.

The captain was watching his movements, intending to check him if necessary.

We were in rather a predicament. From some cause, not now remembered, our rations of meat had given out. We had to depend upon our hunters for a supply of venison. They did not dare to leave the command more than a hundred yards or so.

A prisoner, taken later, explained the situation. The band defeated on the twelfth ran into a camp of about seventy-five Comanches. They were very mad when they learned the extent of the loss sustained by their brethren. They moved that night with a view to surprise our camp. On finding a picket at the Comanche Crossing they deferred the attack. The operations next day prevented them from ascertaining where we were. On the night of the thirteenth they formed a junction with the nine Indians we had chased. On the fourteenth they were hovering around us in the hope of gaining some advantage and attacking. During that day the line of battle was formed more than once, and efforts made to force an engagement. The Comanches backed down. They would not meet a force about five times less than their own. They had scouts moving parallel with our line of march. They were so near our flankers that sometimes they could hear the prowling savages as they forced their way through the chaparral. One day two of the captured horses got a few yards away from the rear guard, and were taken by the Comanches.

At night we camped in a circle. Each man was directed where to sleep and what to do in case of an alarm. The horses, mules, packs were inside the ring of pallets, the guard outside. No alarm was made: a false alarm would have subjected the maker to punishment and to the loss of the privilege to go on a scout.

We made short marches. Every foot of the way had to be scanned thoroughly. One false step meant defeat and death. For more than three days and nights the Comanches tried to deceive us—to use a common expression "to get in their work on us."

The men were out of coffee. Every mess had some sugar. The captain had both coffee and sugar. The heads of messes were directed to bring their coffee pots to the captain.

The Don, in great trepidation, inquired: "Is it possible you are going to divide *our* coffee among the men?"

"Yes, sir, that is just what I am going to do."

"My God! Who can expect me to fight Indians the way I have been doing without coffee."

We moved down the Nueces in the direction of Corpus Christi. A tea, which was then palatable, was made by boiling the dark wood of the mesquite tree in water and adding sugar. Without any incident occurring worth noting, we made Fort Merrill, where rations were obtained for man and horse. The fort was then commanded by Captain [J. B.] Plummer.

Captain Ford proceeded to Corpus Christi on his mountain pony in order to procure a horse, if possible. He did not succeed, and returned on the evening of May twenty-fifth. Captain Edwards had been on guard the night before, and was telling of having heard owls.

"Did one hoot on one side of the camp, and did an answer come from the other side?" Ford asked him.

"Yes sir."

"Captain, your supposed owls were Indians. These people say there is no echo from the voice of a beast. You probably didn't pay any attention to that. Anyway we must be on the alert, and not suffer a surprise."

We were encamped in the valley of the Nueces, half a mile below Fort Merrill. The moon was full and sent a flood of silver light upon a beautiful landscape. A more romantic scene has seldom been presented to the human eye. Hill and dale, clumps of live oak dotting the adjacent prairie, forest trees casting shades here and there upon the river bottom, a balmy breeze wafted from the broad bosom of the Mexican Gulf, all combined to lend a sort of enchantment to the spot. We enjoyed it only as the lovers of Nature can. The indications, however, were of a character not to allay apprehension; the officer in charge was not in the habit of trusting to luck. It was his rule to prepare for the worst and hope for the best. He endeavored as a leader of rangers to be true to his motto: "Ready, Aye, Ready." The guard was carefully stationed and well instructed, the horses brought close in, tied short, near to their respective owners. Arms were inspected and properly loaded. Every ranger slept with his gun under his blankets. The whole guard remained awake, ready for any emergency.

At three o'clock in the morning of May twenty-sixth the reports of four or five rifles broke upon the weird silence of the hour. Every man grasped his gun and sprang to his feet. There was no undue excitement. Orders were distinctly given and unhesitatingly obeyed. The firing receded, showing our boys were driving the enemy. The captain directed men having gentle horses to mount barebacked, and move to the assistance of the guard. He feared an ambuscade. A detail was made to hold and defend the camp. The firing had been brisk for a short while. The voice of a man arose above the various sounds. It was recognized as that of an Indian. Roque said he was asking not to be shot. He was not understood by the boys. He fell mortally wounded. Roque inquired his name. "Piyute" was the answer. He acknowledged the near presence of a band of savage marauders. He was in the agonizing throes of death. His horse and rigging, lance and bow, were in our hands.

Mat Nolan had rushed barefooted through prickly pear to get a shot at the retreating foe. Others had evinced coolness and presence of mind.

In spite of our vigilance the Indians had cut loose several horses and intended to stampede the camp. Our timely discovery of them prevented the execution of their plan. We lost no one killed or wounded. We did not learn whether the Indians lost more than one. We were convinced they did.

A reconnaissance assured us the Indians had gone. By this time it was daylight, and we went in pursuit of the Comanches. We rode several miles, but the wily red men had scattered so much they could not be trailed. We returned to camp with reluctance, though we had done all we could.

On examination we discovered a fine mare missing; she belonged to Milt May. All considered her disappearance to be a rather mysterious occurrence. It was whispered there was a white agent in the case.

After the skirmish ended, the captain sent a message to Captain Plummer stating what had occurred. He was reported to have exclaimed: "What! Indians so near my post! I thought it was you Texians fighting among yourselves." Captain Plummer was a disbeliever in Comanche raids. The bearer of the message was young Ed Burleson, the son of General Ed Burleson, who was vice president of the Republic of Texas during General Houston's second presidential term. More will be said of young Burleson after a while.

A regular soldier, whom his comrades represented as "luny," went to the corpse of the Indian and cut off his head. The rangers, on seeing him pass in sight, ordered him to drop it, which he did just in time to escape something more than their expression of indignation.

One of the rangers got off a homily upon the subject of blasted expectations.

"Now, boys, that Indian sneaked into camp expecting to steal our horses and to whip us, no doubt. He got himself killed, lost his horse, saddle and bridle, his bow and arrows, and his lance. Finally, the regular soldier served him like David did Goliath: he chopped his head off with a butcher knife. That Indian was the 'worst broken up' man in the world."

We broke camp on the twenty-seventh, moved leisurely in the direction of Camp San Antonio Viejo. The next day a half-broken mustang got away from one of the men, carrying with him all the ranger's rigging. He had mounted the mustang to give his own animal a little rest.

Great circumspection was observed in order to take note of everything visible from our lines, and to get the advantage of any robbing party by sighting them first.

5

On the morning of the twenty-ninth we were in the saddle as soon as our horses had finished grazing. This is indicated by their standing still, and apparently taking short naps. To start a grass-fed horse at an earlier hour subjects him to the danger of breaking down, if required to perform hard service.

In order to give the reader a correct understanding of things, which will be mentioned soon, the following explanations are made now.

A squad of four or five men had been sent to Corpus Christi, with pack mules, to receive and transport one hundred dragoon pistols—old fashioned, one-barreled weapons—and cartridges for the same. These men had orders to remain in the vicinity of Corpus Christi until the arrival of the scout, or of further orders. They joined us at Fort Merrill. Among them was William Gillespie, a cousin of Captain [Richard Addison] Gillespie, of Colonel Jack Hays' regiment, who fell at Monterey, Mexico, at the taking of the Bishop's Palace. Young Gillespie was a good soldier and a splendid shot, particularly with a Colt's revolver. He was mounted on a noted horse—Higgins. The horse was under saddle at the capture of Monterey. Captain Ford rode him from Austin in 1847, when he was adjutant of Colonel Hays' last regiment, carried him by water from Brazos Santiago to Vera Cruz, rode him to the City of Mexico, to many places in the surrounding country, and took him back to Austin. He was an ill-natured beast, guilty of many ugly and vicious tricks.

Another of our men was Andrew Hayhurst, an orphan who was determined to make money. He washed clothes for the men, and received the nickname of "Nance."

About ten o'clock in the morning a fresh trail was struck. The rear guard was strengthened and ordered to follow the main body as closely as possible. Preparations were made to pursue and to fight.

Roque and another man or two were thrown to the front as spies. The command was ordered to "Trot Out." A march of four or five miles brought us within sight of the Indians. They were encamped on an elevation in a mat of mesquite trees. As we were advancing to the attack, Gillespie rode up near the captain, who cautioned him:

"Bill, look out for that rascally horse or he will get you killed. I know him."

The Comanches did not stand to receive our charge. They galloped out of camp. Very soon we were going at almost full speed and firing at the flying foe. Several Indians were hurt. One warrior fell from his horse. He was shot twice through the body and once through the neck. He was supposed to be dead. Gillespie was in the act of passing him; he saw him move, aimed at him with his revolver. Just as he touched the trigger the horse jumped to one side, and the ball struck the ground. In the twinking of an eye the wounded savage let fly an arrow, struck Gillespie in the side, penetrating the left lung. He knew he was mortally wounded. The man or two with him assisted him to a mesquite tree and laid him down.

The Comanches made signals when passing over high ground. The captain inquired of Roque what they meant. He told him the Indians had men not far off, and were making signs for them to come up. He suggested possible danger to the rear guard.

Gillespie was in the rear when he was wounded; the captain did not know it. He saw an attempt on the part of the Comanche to gain his rear. Ford intended to prevent it by a headlong charge. Putting himself in front he called on his men to follow. After having proceeded about thirty yards he turned in his saddle and saw the men standing still. They were bawling out something, but the din they created was unintelligible. The captain turned his back to the enemy, and swore at the men, calling them cowards and other bad names. He thought his boys had "gone back on him" and made up his mind to avoid the sense of disgraceful defeat by plunging into the Comanche ranks and ending his career. Just then Roque rode up and reported:

"Gillespie is mortally wounded and is lying under a tree behind the men. They think the Indians are trying to flank us to scalp him and get his horse."

An order was at once given to place Gillespie in safety.

Roque was dispatched to order the rear guard to move up as briskly as possible. The Comanches, supposing we were demoralized, kept their ground. Both parties were playing for time. The rangers galled the Indians by killing their horses and wounding the red rascals. We drove them before us slowly, wishing to continue near the spot where Roque left us to effect a junction with our rear guard.

The redskins tried a ruse by sending out two warriors to pass our left flank. It was too thin. Hayhurst took it into his head to immortalize himself by cutting off the flankers. He asked the captain's permission; it was not given. Hayhurst misunderstood, and started to effect his object. The captain moved to his support to save him from being killed. Hayhurst's horse fell and threw him into a puddle of dirty water. The command passed him.

"Boys," Ed Burleson cried out, "all your wash bills are paid now, there lies Nance."

We were crowding the enemy. They evinced signs of being crippled. The rear guard came up and struck the Comanches in the flank. They were troubled to get their dead and wounded off the field. The chief and a young warrior dismounted, and gave their horses to the wounded. The Indians attempted to make a stand, but we routed them in a furious charge.

Robert Adams and a warrior had a fight almost hand-to-hand. The object of the Comanches was to hold us in check and enable their footmen to reach the Agua Dulce about a mile off, and take advantage of the timber to effect their escape. They abandoned their men and fled in disorder. They whipped their horses like men who were riding for life. Their horses were fresher than ours, and they gained on us steadily.

The captain caught sight of the chief as he wended his way over the prairie. He pursued. At one hundred and twenty-five yards distance he fired his revolver at the Indians. One of the rangers, David Steele, was by his side. He ordered him to dismount and held his horse. Steele fired and struck the chief behind the ear as he looked back. The captain's ball had passed through his left arm. The name of the chief was Otto Cuero.

Steele was permitted to appropriate his arms and rigging. He sent them to Governor P. Hansboro Bell of Texas.

The other Comanches were now almost to the Agua Dulce. Further pursuit was useless. They out ran us.

There had been firing in the rear. A young warrior was wounded in two or three places and secreted himself in a clump of small trees. Roque spoke to him in his own language, assured him his life would be spared. He surrendered. When Ford came back from the pursuit the wounded brave was sitting down, looking quite unconcerned. He saluted, calling out "Captain!" "Captain!" The young captive was named *Carne Muerto* —the Spanish for dead meat.

During the fight the captain noticed Sergeant Level; he appeared very angry.

"Level, what is the matter?"

"Damn them," he replied with clenched teeth, "they've shot my horse."

"Oh, is that all?"

"No, they've shot me too."

An Indian, armed with a Swiss Yager, had fired a ball that had struck the shoulder of Level's horse, passed through the fleshy part, and entered the rider's leg just above the ankle. When this brave levelled his gun, the men seemed to hold their breath, expecting someone to be hit. Rangers could see an arrow and dodge; not so with a ball.

The loss of the Comanches was about five times as great as ours. If memory is correct, it was reported four killed and seven wounded. They carried everyone off except the corpse of the chief and the prisoner. The number engaged on each side was nearly equal until after the arrival of the rear guard.

A litter was improvised for Gillespie. We marched late in the evening for the camp of a detachment of Captain Grumbles' company, stationed ten or twelve miles lower down on the Agua Dulce. Gillespie became very weak. A halt was made. He died eight hours after being wounded. He received all the attention and consolation his sorrowing companions could extend. The next morning his body was conveyed on a mule to the encampment mentioned above.

A grave was dug; the men of both commands were formed in line, and permitted to fire over Gillespie's grave. They asked this privilege of paying their respects to the memory of a gallant ranger. It was a sad, though simple, ceremony.

Our prisoner watched the proceedings keenly. He imagined the preparations being made referred to his execution. It was said he shed tears. It may have been so. Full of life and vigor, he was about eighteen years of age, the reputed son of the celebrated Comanche war chief, Santana. To be buoyed with the hope of kindly treatment one day and to believe he was going to be shot the next, was an ordeal few men could have passed through without evincing melancholic emotions.

The march to our camp was without incidents of interest. Roque treated the wounded prisoner. A ball had passed through his groin, yet he rode on horseback and seemed to get better every day. The Comanche methods and remedies for treating gunshot wounds must possess great merits.

On receiving the reports of operations during our scout, General Brooke had his adjutant issue the following statement on June 15, 1850:

Captain: The General commanding the Department has received the intelligence of your second encounter with the Indians with great satisfaction, and I am instructed by him to convey to you and the Company under your command, his decided commendation for the activity, zeal, and success which have characterized your operations since you have been under his orders. A continuance of such efficient service, exerting, as it naturally does, a proper emulation on the part of others, will have a most happy effect in carrying out the objects for which Texas volunteers were called into the field. The names of Sergeant Level, and privates Gillespie and Adams, are noticed as being particularly distinguished for good conduct in your affair with the Indians on the twenty-ninth ultimo.

Yours very respectfully,
George Deas
Asst. Adjt. General

6

Early in June the Comanches were depredating upon the inhabitants of Webb County; many of the settlers left their homes and took refuge in Laredo. Captain Ford directed Lieutenant Walker to proceed, with twenty men, to a proper point to intercept parties of marauders and give protection to Laredo and its vicinage. Walker stationed his detachment near Laredo, in order to avail himself of the information which would reach that point from persons remaining on their ranches, sheep herders, *vaqueros* (cow herders), and others.

About the middle of June, 1850, Indians were reported in the neighborhood of Laredo. To saddle, mount, and march required a short space of time. The trail was found. It led down the Río Grande. The Indians had gone to Don Basilio Benavides' ranch, twenty miles below Laredo.

When the rangers reached the ranch the "noble red men" were just below, in a bend of the river, rounding up horses. He intended to move upon them by a shorter route than they could travel. Being sure they would spend some time in getting horses together, he concluded to unsaddle and rest his horses, they being fatigued by the rapid gait they had been forced to travel.

The Comanches, having finished the round-up sooner than was anticipated, came up driving a large number of horses. Their intention was to drive the animals into Benavides' corral and to select remounts. They were riding ponies on which they had started from their hunting grounds. They were of inferior quality and in bad condition, as was discovered.

A few shots were fired while the rangers were on foot. They were soon in the saddle and in pursuit. A run of a mile and a half brought the ranger advance into collision with the Comanches. Ed Stevens, late sheriff of Bexar County, and José Morales, a citizen of San Antonio, rushed up to two Indians. One of them put an arrow into Stevens' head. It entered at the edge of his hair, followed the rounding skull bone, and bulged the skin at the top of his head. He placed his rifle almost against the temple of his antagonist, fired, and scattered the Indian's brains into the face and one eye of Morales' horse.

Morales was paying attention to a warrior whom he had dismounted. This savage made an effort to shoot Stevens. Before he could do so, Morales spurred his horse and ran over the Indian. This Morales did two or three times. He then shot the brave dead in his tracks. Meantime Stevens had dismounted and pulled the arrow out of his head; the blood gushed from the wound. Morales wound up the wound with his handkerchief. These matters consumed but little time.

The men soon came up. The pursuit was continued with renewed energy, and resulted in the killing of seven Indians—the whole party. Stevens brought two to the ground, Morales one. These factors are noted because of Stevens getting hurt, and Morales having had a brother killed by the Comanches exactly one year previously. José was highly delighted at the idea of having avenged his relative. The others did their full duty. The loss of numerous reports, rolls, and other military papers during the war of secession does not allow the writer to mention the names of other rangers who acted gallantly.

Here was another proof of the efficiency of Ford's rangers: twelve men, armed with muzzle loaders and one-barreled pistols, had attacked seven Comanches and killed them all—more than half their own number.

One Comanche was left behind wounded. It was determined to save his life, if possible. He was taken to Benavides' home. On examination it was ascertained that both his hips were broken, the bones badly shattered, and he was injured otherwise. The chance of recovery was deemed hopeless. It was decided to kill him as an act of mercy to save him from fruitless suffering. Not one of the rangers would agree to do the deed. A Mexican muleteer named Lorenzo performed the sanguinary part of an executioneer. It was afterwards developed that this young Indian was a cousin to Carne Muerto.

This victory gave Lieutenant Walker additional reputation as an Indian fighter and a leader of frontiersmen. It was also another proof of the capacity of the men to perform effective service.

A number of trophies were left in the hands of the victors. The most valuable and valued result of the affair was the recapture of Benavides' horses. It restored confidence to the citizens of Mexican origin. A day or two after the fight a party of them visited the battleground and their ranches.

7

The Comanche prisoner informed us that a large band of hostile Indians would make a descent upon the Río Grande frontier at an early date. This information was conveyed to General Brooke in order that the troops serving on the upper line of the frontier[2] would be put on their guard. The captivity of Carne Muerto was considered a reason for a movement to be made with a view of recapturing the young brave. In any event, it was known that the Comanches and their allies were very mad because their grounds for hunting mustangs, killing white people, and robbing had been occupied by men in the service of the United States.

Here it may not be out of place to refer to Don Francisco de la Garza Falcón. He had not pitched into the enemy at the Amargosa fight, but had thrown away the captain's gum-elastic sack, full of water, and had cast other things overboard to lighten up for "tall running." He served a notice on the captain that he could not think of risking his life and fighting Indians, as he had been doing, for the paltry sum of ten dollars a month. He demanded ranger wages—$23.50 per month—or he would strike. He struck. The feats of the Don will be dealt on hereafter.

Captain Ford concluded to move up the country in June with the intention of forming a junction with Lieutenant Walker and making an effort to intercept and fight the enemy when he advanced. Walker, as

---

[2] In 1850 the "upper" line of the frontier extended from Fort Worth down through six cavalry outposts to Fort Duncan at Eagle Pass on the Río Grande.

has been stated, had been sent to cover and protect Laredo and ranches in that area. When Ford's scout joined Walker, there would be a total force in Laredo of not quite sixty men, all well mounted and tolerably well armed for that period. Before leaving San Antonio Viejo, Ford directed Lieutenant Highsmith to keep his command as much concentrated as possible, to send out no detachments, if he could avoid it—in short, to protect the camp with every precaution while Ford was gone. Highsmith's force consisted of twenty-six men, rank and file (including the rascally Falcón). Ford impressed upon Highsmith the necessity of keeping a sharp lookout for the Comanches, and even left his spyglass to be used by a sentry posted on a hill near the camp during the daylight hours.

When Ford took up the line of march for Laredo, he carried Carne Muerto and turned him over to Captain Sidney Burbank, commander of Fort McIntosh.

Upon reaching Laredo, the command was deeply incensed to find that an order had been issued by the commanding general for the inspection of our horses. It was issued before the reports of the captain's and Lieutenant Walker's encounters with the Indians had reached headquarters. It was based, as we were informed, upon the allegations of Captain Gabe Armstrong, of unenviable fame acquired during the Mexican War. The charges were that the men had been permitted to exchange their American horses for Mexican ponies; and, consequently, "Ford's men were incapable of doing efficient service." Captain Burbank made the inspection in a polite and soldierly manner. His report refuted the slander upon the company. It was difficult to restrain the boys from expressing their indignation.

These incidents consumed much time. One day a messenger, coming up on the Mexican side of the Río Grande, brought intelligence that our camp at San Antonio Viejo had been attacked by a large body of Indians and all the men killed. The Mexican said that a Carrizo Indian (who had been employed as our guide) had carried the news to Río Grande City, and the Mexican had then brought it to us.

We were beside ourselves with apprehension. Here was mounting and riding in hot haste. The command made seventy miles in quick time. The Indians, however, had all gone before we arrived. We discovered to our great relief that the savages had only blockaded Highsmith's little garrison for more than two days and, other than that, no great damage had been inflicted.

According to Highsmith, here is what had happened: The Don had heard bellowing up near the wells; he had gone in that direction to kill a bull for the marrow bones. Very soon a dust was seen approaching the

camp. The Don bolted in quite breathless. He reported many people at
the wells. The war whoop told its own tale. More than two hundred
dusky warriors formed a circle around the camp. The men seized their
arms and showed fight. A few went out to save the horses. The Comanches opposed them. The first shot from our side—fired by Mr. Hardy
—struck an Indian. The redskins did not relish their reception and
formed out of range of the ranger guns. There were but ten rangers, a
few hired men, and some camp followers inside the garrison. Luckily,
they had hauled up, that day, a large supply of water, enough for the
whole company; they had a good supply of food, provisions, and ammunition, and could have stood a blockade of many days.

Various efforts had been made to entice the Indians within gunshot,
but without effect. The red robbers got several horses, among them the
old rascal, Higgins. He had a chance to do all the prancing and pitching
he wished. The wagon mules were fat. One of them was killed at once
and feasted upon. Our driver, August Harmuth, was greatly incensed.
He cursed the Indians vehemently, pulled off his coat, and bantered them
to come and fight him fisticuff. The Don allowed his angry passions to
rise immeasurably. He menaced the enemy. Pistol in hand, he shut his
eyes, turned his head aside, and banged away. The balls hit the ground
within ten feet of his noble self. At each discharge he would ask: "Did
I kill one?" A negative reply caused his weapon to get a terrible cursing.

The cooped-up rangers, disregarding the danger, amused themselves
at the above recited demonstrations.

Regular troops, under the command of Captain [J. J.] LaMotte—this
was the First United States Infantry Regiment—marched to the relief of
the beleaguered rangers. No Indians were in sight when they arrived.
Just after the regulars left, Captain Ford reached camp at a gallop.

Much praise is due to Lieutenant Highsmith and his men for the coolness and bravery displayed in a situation surrounded by so many perils.
Nothing but their undaunted bearing saved them from a death of torture
and the camp supplies from utter destruction.

Scouts were sent out into the sand belt and along the river. It was
known that the Comanches had broken into squads and were moving in
different directions. It was supposed they would raid the ranches on the
river and break up the camps of the "mustangers." One trail led towards
the settlements above Roma.

The signs induced us to believe we were close to the enemy; we halted
and were preparing for action. The captain carried a double-barrel shotgun, contrary to his usual course. He was recapping. His thumb slipped
off the hammer; it fell and exploded the fulminate left on the nipple:

one barrel was discharged. A heavy noise was heard on the Mexican side of the Río Grande; a dust arose, and a party of Indians came into view at a full run. It was a trying ordeal, not to be able to chase them, but the captain had been ordered not to cross into Mexico, and he obeyed. The Comanches could have been overtaken. The scouts produced no fighting results.

8

After the attack upon Camp San Antonio Viejo, which might have had for its object the rescue of Carne Muerto (now a prisoner at Fort McIntosh), the region we were endeavoring to cover and protect was almost unmolested by Indians. We believed the fear of his being put to death by way of revenge for outrages committed by them acted as a restraint.

In the latter part of the summer, the camp at San Antonio Viejo was abandoned. It was the opinion that the settlers in Webb County were in more danger from Indian incursions than those lower down the valley of the Río Grande. The points below Laredo could be better protected by a force stationed above the town and near the line of travel followed by depredating bands.

There was considerable trade between Corpus Christi and Laredo and adjacent points. Merchandise was transported upon Mexican carts. They moved slowly, were easily overtaken, and captured. The freight carried on these vehicles were frequently very valuable. To say nothing of the loss of life always incurred, the capture of a loaded cart inflicted a heavy pecuniary loss upon the owner of the freight. In those days, insurance was a process almost unknown in that part of Texas. The protection of this commerce was a matter of importance. It involved, to a great extent, the occupation and the development of the country between the Nueces and the Río Grande.

On the march from San Antonio to Laredo, we found the Río Frío too full to be forded. We had wagons loaded with rations, arms, and ammunition. The wagons were unloaded and pulled through the water by ropes. Then we passed a strong rope through a stirrup and stretched the rope across the stream, fastening it to a tree on each side. To the stirrup were attached short ropes that swung above the water. We tied the packages to these ropes. Then two longer ropes, both as many yards long as the river was in width, were attached to the stirrup. Grasping the two long ropes we then slid the stirrup along the stretched rope, carrying the packages of provisions from one side of the river to the other. These operations were commenced early in the day and completed just before dark. A stiff norther was blowing. The captain and some of the men were in the water nearly all day. It was quite cold. The persons in the water suffered considerably. Captain Ford shortly after reaching Laredo was confined by sickness. As will be seen the company was kept in active operations by Lieutenant Walker and Burleson.

In order to select a proper locality for a permanent encampment and to accomplish the objects designated above, the company scouted the area around Laredo. Finally Los Ojuelos—the Little Springs—was selected. It was nearly forty miles from Laredo, in an easterly direction, and was on the main road from Laredo to Corpus Christi. Los Ojuelos had been a great resort for Indians, and was situated between and near two other of their travelled routes. The camp had a great advantage: an abundance of good water, wood, and grass.

XV

>>

SAVORING OF THE SUPERHUMAN

While encamped at Los Ojuelos, Ford's company on September 24, 1850, was sworn in for another six months enlistment. Shortly after this, we were quite surprised to be honored by a visit from two ladies. One was the mother of Carne Muerto, the Comanche prisoner, and the other, the mother of the young brave whom we had been forced to kill at Benavides' ranch. They had come to learn the fate of their children. How they managed to make the trip, to pass between the different military stations of regulars and rangers, no one could guess. But here they were, speaking for their children and for themselves.

They found an able interpreter in Roque and also in Warren Lyons, who had recently joined the company. Everything was explained to them, and they started, accompanied by Roque, to find *Taiaistes Chemohecut*

—Bad Finger.[1] They met Captain Ford at the gate leading out from Fort McIntosh. Carne Muerto's mother took his hand and gazed into his face imploringly; the tears coursed down her cheeks. There was an earnest sadness in her mute appeal possessing a force, an eloquence, which went to the heart of everyone present. This scene lasted three or four minutes. The captain instructed Roque to say that her son was safe and would be taken care of as long as he remained in the hands of the Americans. Roque was also to suggest that she report to her people the good treatment Carne Muerto had received at the hands of the white men, to say to them they owed us the life of one warrior, at least, and in the event any of our people fell into the hands of the Comanches, to beg them to treat the unfortunates as we had her son. He expressed regret that the wounds of Carne Muerto's cousin were so serious, so certainly fatal, that his life could not have been saved by an human agency. He pointed out that the whites had killed the Indian out of mercy.

These women remained at Laredo for some time. They were rationed by order of Captain Burbank. They received many presents from all classes, and finally departed.

These incidents developed facts. The power of parental love is strong in the bosom of the Indian; even to them war has its sorrows, sacrifices, and bereavements.

We decided to make a scout in the vicinity of our old camp site. The march to San Antonio Viejo, the efforts by Captain Larkin Smith to get additional recruits, require only a passing notice. Second Lieutenant Highsmith retired and was superseded by Ed Burleson.

2

A notice of three rangers—Doc Sullivan, Alpheus D. Neal, and [John] Wilbarger—in point of time should have been made several pages back. As their acts were not immediately connected with the company, they can be related here just as well.

After the scout of May reached Fort Merrill, the three rangers mentioned asked permission to visit their respective homes, not on a plea of pleasure, but in obedience to subpoenas directed to them as witnesses in suits of some importance. Captain Ford granted them leaves of absence. When they were ready to start, he enjoined on them the danger of passing over the country between the Nueces and the Río Grande and directed them to join some other party to assure them of a better chance to make the trip in safety. It was estimated that the distance from Fort

---

[1] Rip had lost a finger in an earlier Indian fight.

Merrill to Camp San Antonio Viejo was one hundred and fifty miles.

After their furloughs expired, the three men arrived at San Antonio Viejo on their way to rejoin the company, which was by this time encamped near Laredo. Had they waited a few days longer than they did they could have travelled with a surveying party. They insisted that they had already overstayed the time they had been furloughed, that the captain might not like their being absent so long, and left.

They went by way of San Patricio and Santa Gertrudis. They nooned at a water hole twenty miles beyond Santa Gertrudis where the late Captain Richard King's ranch is located. The locality at that time was almost destitute of trees. One mesquite stood near the water hole. They mounted their horses and were in the act of leaving camp when they discovered thirty Indians not far off. Their actions left no doubt of their intention to attack. The rangers had good horses and might have escaped by retreating in the direction of the Nueces.

They decided to fight. The Indians advanced upon them. One of the enemy had a long-range gun; he fired and the ball passed through Sullivan's body. He was lifted from his horse; the animal was tied to the lone tree. Sullivan told the boys not to stay with him.

"I am killed . . . you can do me no good . . . make your escape."

Another shot took effect in his head, and he died instantly.

Wilbarger ran in the direction of our camp. Judging by the pools of blood and other signs, he killed two or three Indians before he fell.

Neal had inadvertently attached his arms to the pommel of his saddle. He mounted; his horse ran under the rope of Sullivan's horse, and Neal was dragged off. The Indians soon caught the animal, possessed themselves of the arms, and began firing at Neal. He walked along unable to defend himself. He received eight wounds, according to memory; several of them would generally be considered fatal. He fainted from loss of blood.

Neal was not aware of how long he remained insensible. He revived, but was prudent enough not to open his eyes fully. He peeped out the corner of one eye and saw the Indians packing up to leave. He was conscious of the near approach of one warrior and of his scrutiny to ascertain whether the white man was dead. Neal was careful not to exhibit any evidence of life. He remained at the water hole more than an hour after the savages had gone. He managed to extract several arrows from his body and, in his efforts, broke two or three. He was naked. In this condition, with a nearly tropical August sun pouring its rays upon him, he began to drag himself in the direction of San Patricio. The heat of the sun blistered him from head to foot; the winds, so refreshing to others, chilled him at night; his festering wounds agonized him; hunger tormented him; the anguish of unquenched thirst rendered him quite frantic; yet the dauntless, indomitable ranger wended his way, with a will nothing but death could overcome. Sustained by a courageous determination savoring of the superhuman, he pursued his weary and painful way for sixty-five miles, when his eyes were gladdened by the humble edifices of San Patricio. His appearance created excitement. He was supposed to be an Indian. Here another trial had to be undergone. After having suffered what few human beings had ever borne and reaching the goal of his hopes and of his safety, he was in danger of being slaughtered by his own countrymen as an enemy. The bitter cup of despair was again at his lips, and he seemed destined to drain it.

He managed to make them understand he was a white man, though his blistered mouth, and parched, lacerated, swollen tongue rendered utterance a torture, almost an impossibility. When it was ascertained that the spectral being who had staggered into their presence was the mutilated ranger Alpheus D. Neal, the good people tried to excel each other in their attention to his wants and comfort. A messenger was sent post haste for a doctor. Much to the surprise of all, Neal began to grow better, and in the course of time he was able to walk and ride, though troubled by an arrow spike in one lung.

A party of men left San Patricio and buried the bodies of Sullivan and Wilbarger. Their murderers must have been Comanches who knew Sullivan personally. They had attached a rope to his body and had dragged it over the prairie; bunches of his blonde hair were scattered around where he fell.

It is said that Harvey Wilbarger removed the remains of his brother John, and of Sullivan, to a resting place on the Colorado River below Austin. Of this the writer is not sure.

The fathers of these men were also killed by Indians. They fought fairly and gallantly for revenge, and fell victims to their own fearless contempt of danger. The scalping of Wilbarger's father, about fifty years ago, will, when properly described, form one of the most remarkable chapters in the history of Texas.[2]

---

[2] The Wilbargers had come to Texas from Missouri in 1828 and settled on a tract of land on the Colorado River some ten miles above present-day Bastrop. In August, 1833, Wilbarger, a neighbor Reuben Hornsby, and four other men rode into the country northwest of the Wilbarger settlement to find suitable homesteads for a couple of immigrants. While riding up Walnut Creek a few miles northwest of present-day Austin, the party met an Indian painted for war, chased him across prairies and through forests, only to find themselves suddenly ambushed. Arrows flew. Comanches screamed. Every white fell from his horse, dead, except Wilbarger who with arrows in his leg and hip

When the hosts of the South began mustering to meet any emergency the move of secession might bring, the writer was sent by the Secession Convention of Texas to the lower Río Grande as their military representative. His force consisted of about fifteen hundred men—among them was Alpheus D. Neal. One day in Brownsville, Ford was relating to some gentleman the wonderful sufferings and escape of Neal, when who should come in but the identical man.

"Colonel," Neal said, "here is that arrow spike which has been in my lung eleven years."

He had it in his hand. It appeared somewhat corroded.

Neal passed through the Civil War alive and vigorous for one who had suffered so greatly, only to be killed by a Negro soldier after peace was brought about.

3

Near the first of January, 1851, an order was received to send Carne Muerto to San Antonio. Captain Burbank forwarded it to Captain Ford. He detailed Lieutenant Ed Burleson to execute the order. His detachment consisted of nearly twenty men. He proceeded by way of Fort Merrill.

Carne Muerto, before he left, made a solemn promise never to fight the Americans again. He had expressed himself to the same effect previously.

One day in Laredo a Mexican had asked him: "What would you do with me should you be free and meet me in the chaparral?"

"Kill you, damn you!"

The Mexican talked of killing the Comanche then and there. He was

---

and a bullet wound in his neck tried to crawl into the brush. The Indians laughed and whooped delightedly while the man pulled himself along the ground; then tiring of the game they grabbed him, stripped him naked except for one sock, and proceeded to rip the scalp from his head. Only semi-conscious, Wilbarger stared dumbly at the mat of skin and hair dangling before him, recalling how the scalping had "sounded like distant thunder." After the Indians had gone, Wilbarger began to crawl through the forest . . . one day . . . two days . . . he crawled on in spite of the profuse bleeding and the army of maggots now eating away at his festered skull. A relief party finally found him lying face down beneath a tree, but he was so covered with dried blood that one man mistook him for an Indian, crying: "Here they are boys!"

Somehow Wilbarger raised a bloody arm and whimpered, "Don't shoot, it is Wilbarger."

The man lived miraculously. But the scalp never healed. The bone became diseased and exfoliated, decaying finally and exposing the brain. Wilbarger died in a coma sometime in 1844.

(J. W. Wilbarger, *Indian Depredations in Texas*, pp. 7–14.)

advised to wait: perhaps he could capture another Indian (who was not the son of a chieftain) and kill him.

The captive had many opportunities to escape. He rode horses to water, knocked about camp and around town, and was true to his word. He had acquired some knowledge of English and Spanish. He entertained great contempt for Mexicans as soldiers and brave men. He was good natured, and was easily controlled by those he considered his superiors. He was always ready to resent the exercise of an assumed authority. When mad he swore in plain and forcible English. We heard of him once after he was released, but never learned what became of him.

Captain Ford was sick for more than a month and was at Laredo for convenience, being able to procure medicines not at hand at camp and to avail himself of comforts not obtainable at Los Ojuelos.

About the middle of January, 1851, news came that the Indians had killed a Mexican, while out hunting on the Chacon, a small creek about two miles from town. The captain was scarcely able to ride, but he got together a few rangers and citizens and proceeded to the Chacon. From appearances the Mexican had made no resistance, but had run when the Indians went at him. The race had continued for a hundred and fifty yards perhaps. The tracks were perfectly visible. The Indians had caught the Mexican, who then had thrown down his gun. It appeared that an Indian had killed the Mexican with the latter's own gun.

About eleven days after this affair, the news reached Laredo that a scout under Lieutenant Walker had fought the Indians out on Cat Creek. The captain returned immediately to Camp Los Ojuelos. Very soon thereafter a courier conveyed the intelligence of another Indian fight: this one involved a scout under Lieutenant Burleson. The courier was under the impression that our loss in that affair was very great. His report induced the belief that it was necessary to have more men on the San Antonio Viejo-Laredo road. Captain Ford marched all night with all his available force. He had to be lifted from his horse on reaching Laredo. He found Walker and Burleson both at that point. Walker had gone there to turn over captured property to the United States quartermaster. These details are given in advance. They will aid to make the matters following more easily understood.

First Walker's Gato fight. On the nineteenth of January, 1851, Lieutenant Walker made a reconnaissance on the Arroyo Gato—Cat Creek —about thirty miles from Camp Los Ojuelos and about fifty miles east of north from Laredo. He discovered where the Comanches had been encamped recently, and had left horses and mules hoppled and other things. He divined, at once, what it meant. He knew they had slipped by our camp and had gone into Mexico on a raid. He directed the men not to ride on the trail that the Indians made leading down the country. He was sure they would return to their cache. As a general rule, they went back on the trail by which they came in.

He formed a plan to surprise and defeat them as they moved up the country. He encamped on a high, well-covered spot about two miles from their cache. His position afforded a good view of the country, particularly of the route he expected the Indians to travel. He stationed videttes about two miles from his camp, and another detail at half the distance. When the Indians approached, the outer station would signal the inner station which would then signal the camp to prepare for battle. The horses were grazed on the low grounds in the rear of the camp. No smokes were made during the day and little fire was permitted at night.

Day after day these requirements and orders were rigidly enforced and faithfully executed. Some of the men grew impatient, some predicted a failure, suggesting that the Comanches would pass out some other way. Walker did not falter; he had an abiding confidence that success would smile on his efforts.

On the sixth day of the vigil, about four o'clock in the evening, the long wished-for signal was given. Every ranger's eyes glistened with pleasure, every heart thrilled with hope, and every countenance was lighted with the animation the expectation of battle imparts to the brave soldier who is defending those dearer to him than life.

The Indians were moving on their former trail. They had two warriors thrown to the front to scan the country and guard against surprise. These Walker allowed to pass unmolested. Everything was kept out of their sight. The main body followed, driving about 150 mules and about fifty horses. They numbered seventeen.

All at once they heard the roar of horses' feet, and were astounded on seeing nineteen rangers charging on the head of their column. The furious onset caused the braves in front to recoil. They fell back on the rear, and came near to being rolled up in utter confusion. The chief's whistle sounded, and, responding gallantly, they formed and faced the pursuers. The rangers coming at almost full speed struck the Comanches and killed one and wounded others. They broke the Indian lines and drove everything before them. The fleeing red men again rallied at the call of their chief. They vainly attempted to check the furious attack of the rangers. The chief fell; ball and arrow sped through the air; the combatants formed a struggling mass of men and horses; the defiant shout of the rangers was answered by the vengeful war whoop of the Comanche, but the latter lost its full tone and degenerated into a funereal wail. There was no longer a dauntless chief to inspirit the dusky warriors. They fell back, closely pressed by the Texians. The whistle of the chieftain, however, had gone into worthy hands; its notes rose above the din of battle, and were again heeded by the fearless freebooters of the prairies.

By this time Walker's men were somewhat scattered. He was in front and followed closely by Sergeant David M. Level, Alfred Wheeler, Wallace McNeill, and John E. Wilson. Numbers, at the moment, favored the Comanches; they charged the rangers. Three attacked Walker; he sent a ball through the body of a red assailant. The Indian, maddened to desperation, ran upon Walker, clutching a long knife; before he could use it, Wheeler sent a ball crashing through his head. The two others were driven back. Wallace McNeill killed a warrior and captured his rigging.

Two or three warriors engaged Sergeant Level. The arrows fell fast and thick. Level dropped behind his horse, holding to the horn of his saddle. An arrow fastened his hand to the saddle bow. He was unable to release it. An arrow passed through Level's horse. The animal fell dead. Level was entangled in his own rigging. In this dilemma he saw a Comanche bearing down on him, lance in rest.

"Boys," he called out, "don't you see that infernal Indian coming to lance me?"

Wilson put a ball into the Indian's side, and he ran.

[Volney] Rountree had occasion to throw himself on one side of his horse to avoid being struck by an arrow. This caused all the weight of his body to fall on one stirrup—it broke and he fell head-foremost to the ground. His horse ran off and carried his arms. Rountree followed the rangers. There was an Indian lying on the ground, dead, as all the Texians supposed. Rountree found a mule and mounted him. He cantered gaily by the "dead" Comanche. To his astonishment the savage rose to his feet, made the arrows fly at Rountree, who had to abandon the mule. The resurrected barbarian mounted it himself, and went his way rejoicing. It is said that the long-nosed ranger used very intemperate language in commenting on being forced to part company with his long-eared companion.

The Comanches had a prisoner, a Mexican boy twelve or fourteen years of age. An Indian claimed him as his slave, that being their custom. While the fighting was progressing, the boy evinced a determination to escape. His savage master kept by his side and plied the whip to the horse he was riding, at the same time jabbing the boy with an arrow. The boy held back all he could. The rangers pressed the redskins and made it dangerous to the master. He found his safety depended on an instant and precipitate retreat. He made it, leaving the boy behind. As the rangers past him he raised in his stirrups, and exclaimed: *"Estan buenos Americanos!"* As much as to say, "Hurrah for the good Americans!" The boy was sent to his parents in Mexico.

These happenings covered a very small space of time. The main body of the rangers was arriving rapidly. They rushed the copper-colored soldiers, who quickly dispersed, taking advantage of a heavy chaparral. To follow them was impossible.

A hard fight had ended. Our loss was one man wounded and one killed, also one horse missing. The Comanches left four men dead on the field, and had six or seven wounded. These escaped. They lost all the horses and mules they had stolen in Mexico and a number of riding animals.

The captured animals were turned over to the United States quartermaster at Fort McIntosh (at Laredo), and many of them restored to the owners who were principally citizens of the Mexican Republic.

A month or so after this affair of the Gato, a lawyer waited on Captain Ford at Los Ojuelos and inquired concerning the mules captured in the Gato fight.

"I know nothing about them," Ford replied. "They were never in my possession. Walker turned them over to the U.S. quartermaster."

"What I desire to say is that my client lost thirty-five head of mules, and got back only twenty-eight. He has instructed me to bring suit for seven mules."

"I consider your client a very lucky man," the captain responded. "If I were in Lieutenant Walker's place, and you were to bring any such suit against me, I would cut off your ears."

The suit was not brought. The gentleman's client was understood to be a citizen of Mexico.

4

The subjoined description of Burleson's fight is based on an account by the writer published in the Brownsville *Sentinel* not long after the close of the Civil War.

During the month of January, 1851, Lieutenant Ed Burleson was ordered to San Antonio to deliver to an officer of the United States a Comanche prisoner [Carne Muerto] taken in a fight at Amargosa, May 29, 1850. The captive was returned to his people.

Burleson was on his return to Camp Los Ojuelos on the 27th of January, when just this side of the Nueces, on the road from San Antonio to Laredo, he saw three Indians on horseback. He took eight men and pursued them, directing the balance of his party to keep to the road and move on.

After a vigorous pursuit for two or three miles, the Indians halted, and prepared for battle. In addition to three mounted, there were eleven red devils on foot. The rangers promptly opened the fight, moving up to within fifty or sixty yards of the Comanche line. By some mistake the men dismounted, as they improperly thought, by order of Burleson. The Indians charged them immediately and a terrible hand-to-hand fight ensued. Shots were delivered at the distance of a foot or two.

They fought under the bellies of the horses and over the saddles; there was a general melee of red men and whites. Colt's six-shooters, carbines, bow and arrows, repeating pistols and lances were blended in a confused and struggling mass. There was no time for shouting, for maneuver; each man fought for life and taxed his energies to the utmost.

The field was an open prairie devoid of even bushes. There could be no cover. It was a trial of skill, strength, and courage. A few minutes decided it. Victory trembled in the balance. Baker Barton, a gallant soldier, received three mortal wounds and died on his feet, holding to the horn of his saddle. He knew not how to yield. William Lackey received two or three wounds—one of them mortal. Jim Carr, brave and cool, received three or four severe wounds.

"It was like clock work," he said later. "Every time I raised my Colt's carbine, they stuck an arrow in me."

A warrior singled him out and charged him. The brave still advanced, discharging arrows; they came with less and less force, until at last they scarcely left the bow. Jim, however, had ceased to fire at him, knowing there were others demanding his attention.

Jim's last wound was inflicted when he had his carbine at his face and ready to fire; an arrow passed through the last joint of his right forefinger and penetrated the breech of his gun; luckily, the wood splintered and his hand was released.

Burleson himself had an encounter with a stalwart savage. He received an arrow wound in his head before he sent his antagonist to "Kingdom Come." Burleson has been for many years a peaceful and thrifty farmer. He lives near the town of San Marcos in Hays County.

Alf Tom was wounded, but fought nobly. Jim Wilkinson was wounded severely, and continued fighting. Warren Lyons, the guide and interpreter, had been raised among the Comanches. He came at his old *compañeros* in true Indian style—jumping, stooping down, and changing position in various ways. He wished his "boots off"; they were too heavy. He told Burleson what the Indians were saying.

Leech did his duty well. He was perfectly self possessed. Burleson saw an Indian aiming at him with a pistol. He immediately presented his six shooter.

"Don't shoot at him lieutenant," Leech called out, "he's only bluffing."

Jack Spencer had had two or three Indians to deal with at one time. He was wounded, yet there was no time for surgery. He was using his horse for a covering and fighting as best he could. The chances were rather against him. At other points the charge of the savages had been repulsed. Spencer received help, and the Comanches left the field. They had been consulting in a hurried manner about retreating. They did not see their way clear. They had gotten into a tight place and feared they could not make their way out without great damage. Lyons told Burleson this and said the Indians were whipped. They left four dead on the field, and had eight wounded. The defeat was complete, else they would have carried off their dead in defiance of the rangers.

This was one of the most closely contested Indian fights that ever occurred in Texas. Thirty days after it came off, the writer was on the battlefield. It was literally covered with arrows. Over two hundred were picked up on a space of less than one-fourth of an acre. All the evidences of a desperate struggle were apparent. Both parties were exhausted. The wounded rangers were unable to pursue the discomfited and flying Comanches.

A number of Mexican carts had been travelling the road to San Antonio. The Comanche gentlemen had been so busy watching them that they failed to discover the near approach of the rangers. They had set a trap and were caught themselves. What a difference there was between murdering and scalping unarmed cartmen and meeting rangers in deadly conflict. There was no plunder for them to divide, no captives for them to beat and drag through prickly pear at the end of a rope. There were deaths, and wounds, and effort to escape from danger to contemplate instead. It was to the cartmen an escape savoring of providential interposition. They expressed their gratitude to the victors.

About the time the fight closed, Sam Duncan came upon the field. Burleson immediately sent him to a water hole twenty miles to the front. The water gourds had been exhausted, and the wounded were suffering terribly from thirst. After caring for the wounded as well as circumstances permitted, Barton was packed on a mule and buried on a hill some miles from where he fell.

Burleson made a forward movement about nine o'clock A.M. At one o'clock P.M. he met Duncan returning with water. The water hole was reached that evening and a courier dispatched to Laredo for ambulances to carry the wounded. Several of them were unable to ride on horseback. They reached Fort McIntosh the next day. Captain Sidney Burbank was in command. He saw that the transportation was sent out for the wounded and a doctor also. He extended every aid and every kindness the circumstances demanded.

The writer takes this opportunity to testify to the generosity of his old, immediate commander, Captain Burbank. He understood perfectly the difference between a regular and a volunteer command. He was mild, yet firm, in his method of governing. He never interfered unnecessarily in the manner of conducting the affairs of the company. Ford does not remember a single instance in which Captain Burbank expressed displeasure at his action in any case. Captain Burbank possessed, and he merited, the esteem and the confidence of the officers and men of the company. More than forty years have elapsed since Ford's company was in service. The feelings of respect and gratitude for Captain Burbank are unabated: time, chance, and change cannot abate or dim them.

A similar feeling exists towards General Brooke, Captain Deas, General [John Spotswood] Garland, Captain [James] Longstreet, Captain [William J.] Hardee, and other officers, then of the regular army. Ford served with them and cannot remember a single instance in which any one of them treated him wrongfully or with discourtesy. Now, in his advanced age, Ford remembers the officers of the old army with pleasure and, in many instances, with sincere regret. Death has thinned them, but time has wrought no change in the writer's estimation of the men who did service in Texas in days gone by.

5

Not long after the affairs of Walker and Burleson, Captain Ford made a scout and, as has been mentioned, visited Burleson's battleground. Ford scoured the country between the Nueces and the Frio, but found no Indians. He passed the Nueces at the Comanche Crossing, and had time to inspect the pictorial scenes on a tree made by gunpowder partially dissolved by water (which the writer discussed in the chapter on the savage). The first picture represents a combat between an Indian, armed with a lance, and a Mexican, armed with a sword. The second exhibits a Mexican with his head severed from his body, and the blood running from his neck, thus leaving no doubt that the Aztec gentleman came to grief and establishing the claim of the Comanche to superiority, that is, as far as Comanche authority could do so.

Despite all the care which could be taken on the march, the horses of the scout were failing in flesh and in energy. San Antonio was visited on a matter of business connected with the quartermaster and commissary departments. The camp was fixed near the city, where the means of subsisting man and horse were easily made available. In spite of our efforts to recuperate them, the horses did not improve. This induced the return march to be made on the regular road.

Not far from the Nueces, a large trail was discovered, which Roque and Lyons both pronounced as Indian. It was two or three days old, perhaps more. When we crossed the Nueces in the evening, we expected to find water a few miles beyond, but failed. It was concluded to make a night march and reach a water hole in a dry creek, having high banks, in order to secure good shelter against the stiff norther then blowing.

We proceeded several miles, and discovered a light in our front which illuminated the sky. It was evidently caused by a large fire. It appeared to be at the point to which we were moving.

A consultation was held. The opinion was unanimous that the light was an Indian camp. It was thought to be fifty miles from Camp Los Ojuelos, consequently the savages felt safe in making rousing fires and keeping themselves comfortable. The march was resumed and silence ordered in the ranks. A small guard was kept a proper distance in advance. We moved cautiously, almost noiselessly. Notwithstanding the numbing cold, every heart beat high at the prospect of a fight, a surprise of our wily foe at night.

When two miles from the water hole, Roque, Lyons, and Rountree rode ahead to reconnoitre. The command moved slowly, and halted half a mile from the supposed enemy. Preparations were made for battle. We had seventeen effective men. They could deliver one hundred and five shots without reloading—a large number for those times. Our spies reported the campers were Indians, but could not say as to the tribe.

Every man was instructed in regard to plan of action: charge them boldly and to the teeth and watch the captain who would give the signal to retire should the Indians be too strong for us. We formed in line and proceeded steadily to within thirty yards of the ravine sheltering the Indians. Just as the word "charge" was about to be uttered, Roque asked permission to hail, saying it might be a party of our rangers scouting or hunting. If not, the campers could not escape. Permission was given.

Roque hailed; at the same instant one of our men let a pistol go off accidentally. In a moment a voice was heard saying:

"Don't shoot, you will make these Indians run off. They are friends."

The voice was recognized to be that of Lieutenant S. B. Holabird, United States Army.

The captain and a few men dismounted and descended the bank of the ravine. The first Indian Ford saw, he pointed out to the men as one he had seen and fired at in the affair of May 12, 1850. The Indian was white, had a belt of polished sea shells hanging from his shoulder. The leader of the Comanches was also an acquaintance made in 1849. Roque interpreted his name into Spanish: Fusil Recortado—we called him Short Shotgun. Roque and Lyons were directed to pump our red friends and find out what was in the wind. We were convinced there was rascality at the bottom of the strange move. Captain Short Shotgun expressed himself as hugely in favor of peace between the red men and the white men. With this laudable and humane sentiment thrilling his bosom, he had travelled hundreds of miles to hold a peace talk with the commander of Fort McIntosh. He dispatched a few squaws, if memory serves, to announce the object of his mission. Lieutenant Holabird had been directed to take charge of a detachment of regulars and escort the august diplomat and his motley attachés to Fort McIntosh.

The next day the mongrel crowd marched into Laredo. Captain Ford remained in Laredo with his men. He kept Roque and Lyons and others on the watch day and night. Little passed in the Comanche camp which was not reported. He managed to get a private interview with Captain Short Shotgun. Ford told that dignitary:

"You are aware that I am acquainted with your people and know their tricks. You have come here pretendedly to talk peace; at the same time you have a party of warriors on the Nueces to kill and murder the Americans. I saw their trail and was unable to follow it. You cannot deceive me. It might be bad for you to try it."

The old fraud made a clean breast: "Yes, some of our young men did go down the Nueces. We told them not to go near your camp, that you were our friends and that we did not want you molested."

This development was true, and did not add greatly to the good understanding of the parties concerned.

The captain made an acquisition to his family circle. Mr. Pinohiachman—Mr. Saddle Blanket, by interpretation—was famishing for another brother upon which to lavish his pent-up affections. He conferred that distinguished honor on the ranger captain, and they became a modern edition of Jonathan and David, with the stone "Ezel" left out. When too late, Warren Lyons notified his superior officer that the assumed relationship might give him trouble in the future. It meant a sort of alliance which obligated the parties not to fight each other, to render mutual assistance in case of peril. To the honor of the Comanche let it be stated that in 1858 and 1859, when Ford was again in the field, chasing Indians, Mr. Saddle Blanket remained true to his pledge.

One night Warren Lyons came at a run and reported: "The man with the shell belt is drunk. He says he lost a brother in the fight of May twelfth, 1850, and he thinks Roque had a hand in killing him. He is loading his gun to kill Roque."

Every man was ready in a minute. We marched quietly and cautiously to the cabins the Comanches occupied, to find they had flown noiselessly. They left everything they could not carry on their persons. It was impossible to trail them. We received no orders to do so. They had come as messengers of peace. They had departed when the mask fell from their faces. Let them go, as we will show our respect for even a false envoy of peace. We moved up country soon, and ascertained they had formed a junction with their brethren who had been on the war path.

The account above given is not intended as a reflection upon the action of Captain Burbank. He was not well acquainted with the Comanche character and supposed Captain Short Shotgun was telling the truth when he represented himself as so very much in favor of peace with the white people. The Comanche was more wicked and insincere than he imagined. After the lapse of more than forty-one years the writer cannot conscientiously assert he would have detected the old Comanche scoundrel had he not first seen the trail of the war party. That sight placed Ford pretty much in the position of "forewarned, forearmed."

It is said that General [William S.] Harney, then in command of the Department of Texas, swore lustily when he received a report of the mission of Captain Short Shotgun. Harney was mad because the Comanche envoy extraordinary was not beaten.

No account was received of any troops stationed on the Nueces, or anywhere on the coast, having seen and pursued the war party just mentioned.

There was a cessation in the matter of Indian scouts in the region between the Nueces and the Río Grande. This region, as has been stated previously, was a favorite resort of the Comanches. Their late visits had been unfortunate for them. They had lost some of their distinguished leaders in attempting to retain control of the territory where wild horses were plentiful. Their aim was to rob and to make war, without the loss of a man, if possible. Their measures in peace, and their efforts during hostilities, were based on these principles.

6

About this period, Captain Ford had ordered that the running and killing of wild cattle should cease, unless by his permission. Horses were jaded and men sometimes hurt by these wild operations. Some of the men in camp felt that they would be better off could they have broiled beef ribs to eat. Roque seemed to feel similarly. He was deputed to slip out and capture fresh meat. In the heat of the pursuit Roque's horse fell and threw him into a big batch of prickly pear. Of all the mishaps of that character, this appeared to be the worst. Roque was full of thorns from head to foot. The men were engaged two or three days in picking them out. The captain never mentioned the matter. He thought Roque sufficiently punished. This ended clandestine hunting for beef ribs.

The events detailed covered a space of some months of time. Occasionally a band of Comanches would penetrate the region between Camp Los Ojuelos and the Laguna Madre. They would manage to cross the Nueces between stations and revisit the section where they formerly hunted mustangs, mustangers, and small parties of Americans. By reference to a map, it will be seen the country bounded by the Río Grande on the south, the Nueces on the north, the Laguna Madre on the east, and a line from Laredo to the San Antonio Crossing of the Nueces on the west, includes a large area of territory. It was impossible to keep out Indians entirely. When their presence was discovered, they were pursued, and driven out. In some instances they managed to sneak past our camp and reach the Nueces.

It may be observed here that a pursuit commenced after the committing of a depredation generally failed of success. The Indians moved with celerity. They usually had loose horses, driven along for remounts. They travel day and night. Pursuers could seldom follow a trail after nightfall. This involved an advantage of about twelve hours in favor of the pursued. The Comanches kept a man or two in their rear to advise them if pursued. Major [Earl] Van Dorn affirmed that he followed a party of Comanches four hundred miles, and they made but three fires in the whole distance. A party delaying two or three days, taking the trail, moving at a moderate gait, was more apt to overtake marauding savages than those who pursued at nearly full speed. The Indians, feeling secure, would stop to rest, eat, and sleep, and would be overtaken, surprised, and beaten.

XVI

>>>

THE TIE THAT BINDS

O n March 23, 1851, Ford's company was enlisted for another six-months tour of duty. Not long afterward, the outfit trotted out of Camp Los Ojuelos to seek out renegade Indian bands operating below Laredo. A trail was discovered leading down country between our camp and Laredo. We were on the alert, sent out scouts to follow and intercept them on their way out. The captain commanded one of the scouts and operated in the direction of Laredo and above the road leading from that place to Corpus Christi. The water holes were examined and the country scoured to discover trails and to find out whether any party intending to do mischief was lurking in the chaparral. None were discovered. The scout turned to the northward, struck the trail passing down country, and halted at a water hole to noon. Roque took a little scout, and came back speedily, reporting a party of Indians encamped nearby. A few minutes sufficed for the men to be in the saddle. The Comanche camp was charged. There were nearly a dozen horses staked, but no Indians. The enemy had entered an immense thicket of cactus and chaparral growth. They left little sign. We made strenuous efforts to find and dislodge them—all to no purpose. We were chagrined at the idea of returning to camp with nothing to show but Indian ponies. Several days of active work developed no enemy. We returned to camp not one whit elated. According to recollection, that scout was not reported.

In August of that year, Lieutenant Burleson, in charge of a detachment, proceeded to Redmond's Ranch, opposite Guerrero, Mexico. News came that a band of Indians was at a ranch a mile or two below. It was "mount and away" almost instanter. The cunning savages were on the lookout and beat a hasty retreat. The rangers followed rapidly. It was a run over a rough country. Rocky spurs of hills were crossed, deep ravines passed, and jaggy thickets penetrated. To the Comanches it was emphatically a ride for life. The copper-colored braves did their utmost; they had tested the courage, the endurance, and the untiring persistence of their pursuers, and were conscious of the danger threatening them. The hope of a battle, of success, fired the heart of every ranger, and he spurred his foaming charger to the full bent of his speed. The flying foe would seem to be in easy reach of the rough riders, but, by some unlooked-for turn, they escaped. This race lasted for more than twenty miles. Burleson's horses evinced fatigue, and he called off the men with deep regret.

The Indians had crossed from Mexico, no doubt. It is probable they returned there; no sign of them could be found on the American side of the Río Grande, except the trail made by the run from Burleson.

The passes on the Río Grande were watched. Detachments of rangers were stationed near the Paso de la Mujeres—the Women's Pass—and above Laredo. Scouts traversed the section between the Nueces and the Bravo. All was performed which propriety could suggest and unsleeping vigilance effect.

2

Late in August the captain visited Redmond's Ranch. A courier from Guerrero conveyed the news that a fight was progressing between Indians and Mexicans beyond the river. Next came intelligence that the leader of the Mexicans, Colonel Zapata,[1] had been killed and that the

---

[1] Ford states that the Colonel Zapata killed in Mexico in 1851 was the man after whom Zapata County, Texas was named. As far as is known, Colonel Antonio Zapata who was killed in the Federation War in 1840 was actually the county's namesake.

Indians had crossed into Texas. The rangers moved at once. They discovered an Indian sign, but experienced trailers failed to trace it from the point where the Indians appeared to have buried two or three persons. They had scattered and returned to the Mexican side. The evidences favored their being Seminoles. It was reported that they were armed with rifles and were not dressed like Comanches. In other words, they wore some clothes. Of course nothing could be done in the premises. The scout returned to Camp Los Ojuelos.

We came to the conclusion that the Comanches had given up the idea of raiding the section we were guarding, at least for the time being. The property owners and residents of the valley of the Río Grande had acquired confidence, and were making preparations to occupy their lands in Texas. They believed the United States government was earnestly endeavoring to give adequate protection to person and property throughout the broad expanse of the Union. Trade was established between the people of Texas and Mexico. Droves of mules and horses were being taken into our State almost daily. Commerce was brisker than heretofore, the roads less dangerous to travel; in fact, a good time seemed to be dawning upon the denizens of southern and southwestern Texas.

3

It was understood that the ranging companies would be mustered out of the service of the United States. Captain Ford had notified the commanding general of the Department of Texas that he did not care to remuster. This notice was the result partly of the desire to return to the walks of private life, and partly of a determination not to wait and be discharged summarily. Many of the men had not seen home for more than two years and wanted to disband, while others would have remained in the ranging service willingly for life.

The order came. We marched to Laredo to be discharged. A feeling of sadness prevailed. We knew many of us would separate, never to meet again in this world. We had lived more like a band of brothers than as a military company.

On the twenty-third of September, 1851, the command was mustered out. We formed for the last time on the plaza at Laredo. Captain Ford delivered a short address:

"If there is anything that endears one man to another more than having stood shoulder to shoulder in the moment of danger—I am not apprised of its existence. The Tie binding soldier-comrades has its origin in the deepest recesses of the heart. But these ties, hard as it may seem, have to be broken. We must make ourselves familiar with other scenes than those transpiring in the camp and the field. We must form other associations.

"In the transition from Rangers to citizens, we should strive to render ourselves as useful in the one sphere as, I hope we have been bold and efficient in the other. Ours has been a wild life. We have had the utmost latitude of conduct that could be allowed within the pale of law and propriety. Let us remember that we are about to return to our places of abode, where we shall mingle with relatives and friends, who have a right to circumscribe our actions within the bounds of civil life.

"We must not forget our responsibility to the laws and usages of society. A brave man generally makes a good, peaceable citizen.—When the test is applied to us, it is to be hoped that we will not be found wanting.

"It may not, perhaps, be considered an infraction of modesty to say, we have done some hard fighting; and have served our Government with zeal, if not with ability. The reputation we have acquired, should be valued beyond price. I trust there is not one of us who will so act as to tarnish our good name, but that each one of us will, on the contrary, use every exertion to sustain it here and elsewhere.

"Nothing more remains, but to pronounce that bitter word—farewell."

When those gallant and successful defenders of the frontier broke rank, there were aching hearts and tearful eyes; there were clasping of hands and the exchanging of fraternal adieus, but not an unmanly expression. For forty-one long years, through dangers, vicissitudes of fortune, and temptations to do unlawful deeds they have kept their faith, plighted on the plaza of Laredo, and if one of "Ford's Old Company" has ever dishonored himself this writer has not heard of it. They belonged to that class of men who lived without fear and died without reproach.

4

[Many South-Texas citizens were extremely upset over the leaving of Ford's rangers.]

Now that the company is disbanded, [said the editors of the San Antonio *Ledger*] the Indians, who have so much dreaded its presence as to abandon their visits altogether to the country through which it ranged, can again carry devastation and death, with little dread of molestation, from the Nueces to the Rio Grande. Again they can resume their cattle stealing and scalping forays along the whole line of settlements from the farms and ranches above Laredo, to Davis's ranch, and from thence across the country to Corpus Christi. The property and lives of the citizens of Laredo, in particular, fell a daily prey to marauding bands of Indians until Capt. Ford's company of Rangers was stationed within striking distance of the town, and a short period afterwards—a very brief one indeed, as a rapid succession of bloody and victorious encounters with the Indians, soon taught them that Rangers could ride, shoot and manoeuvre rather differently from mounted infantry. It is to be hoped that Governor Bell will redeem his promise to give the frontier protection. The ranging companies have done the State good service; the abandoned farms and ranches have been re-settled during their service, and the roads have been freed from danger to the traveler and merchant. We hope Governor Bell will recall them immediately to protect the frontier, or it will be again devastated and destroyed.

The above quote from the San Antonio *Ledger* was copied into the *Texas State Gazette* of October 11, 1851.

BOOK

4 *Between Two Rivers*

XVII

>>

EL PLAN DE LA LOBA

The existence of a revolutionary spirit in Mexico has been long known to the world. It had its origin in the great variance between the principles controlling the methods of government in Spain and those the English-speaking people introduced into North America and formulated in the Constitution of the United States and all laws passed in pursuance thereof. The principles underlying the Constitution and the government of the United States were introduced into Mexico, and had a direct agency in bringing about the revolution which ended in establishing the republican institutions of that country. These institutions, recognizing the people as the source of all legitimate power, were antagonistic to the theory and practice in vogue in the administration of governmental affairs in Spain. For centuries the king of Spain was the arbiter of the fortunes of the Spanish nation. A wise, honest, and fair-minded monarch would secure prosperity to his people while the contrary would be obtained when a weak-minded monarch ascended to the throne. The king of Spain was esteemed the most zealous advocate of the Roman Catholic faith in all Christendom. He was carefully educated in that religion, and taught to pay a respect to its ministers amounting almost to servile reverence. Many of the prime ministers and statesmen of Spain were dignitaries of the Roman Catholic Church and wielded great influence and power. State and church were united; the king and the clergy were absolute; they ruled Spain. One thing was rather remarkable: notwithstanding the sway of the clergy and the attachment of the king to the doctrines of the Holy Roman Catholic Church, on many occasions when the Pope interfered in the affairs of the kingdom in a manner conceived unauthorized, he met with determined opposition.

Under the viceroys of Spain, who governed Mexico for about three centuries, a similar state of affairs was reproduced, except that many Mexican-born officers of the church were attached to their native country and were always ready to aid in advancing its interests in preference to those of the mother country. When the standard of revolt was raised, there were among the people of Mexico two distinct parties: the Reactionary Party, advocating stronger political power for the Catholic clergy and more centralization, and the Republican Party—the "Party of Progress"—favoring the ideas of a free government as prevailed in the United States. In process of time the Republicans triumphed, but the leaven of the one-man power and the union of church and state remained.

A long struggle ensued between the parties. Revolutions were fomented, battles fought, governments established and overthrown; in the end there were men in Mexico who were revolutionists by profession and practice. Their names figured, on one side or the other, in every popular outbreak. The patriotism of the masses—and no people love their country more devotedly than the Mexicans—was skilfully manipulated to produce internal dissensions and bloodshed. They were misled by the cry of "reform" and seduced into thrusting daggers into the bosom of their beloved Mexico, in unconscious ignorance of the crimes they were perpetrating.

In many of these fratricidal contests, the branch of the Roman Catholic Church in Mexico furnished the money to make war upon men who were endeavoring to administer the government upon republican principles. The clergy was not amenable to trial by the civil courts. Ecclesiastical courts alone had jurisdiction over offenses committed by ecclesiastics. Practically, this immunity grew into an incentive to violate civil law with impunity. Wrong, robbery, and kindred offenses were often perpetrated by men who professed to have the care of men's souls and who claimed the right to hear others confess their sins and to be instrumental in getting them absolved and pardoned. These abuses were not brought about by the creed they professed, or by the rules and discipline of the church and state, but by the intermeddling of the clergy in political issues.

The clergy became an important factor in revolutions. Clergymen had amassed capital by the usual methods as well as by the acquisition of real estate as mortmain property. Many zealous Catholics made wills giving their estates to the Church, in the event the heirs became extinct or incapable of holding them. To illustrate, the case of Vicente Olmos, formerly a member of the United States Lancer Regiment of Colonel Manuel Domínguez, is stated. On being requested to state how it was that he became a soldier of the United States to serve against his own country, he answered substantially as follows:

"My father was one of the richest men in the City of Mexico. He made a will by which the Catholic Church was to succeed to his estate in the event his heirs all died or could not inherit. The priests took charge of the children, and superintended their education. My sisters were induced to become nuns; two of my brothers were made priests, and I was treading in their footsteps. Nuns and priests were politically dead—nullities— outside the pale of civil law, and not capable of inheriting property. As soon as the last one of us passed this political and legal dead line my father's estate would be vested in the Church. I escaped from the hands of my ghostly guardians twice. The soldiers of the Mexican regular army captured me each time and returned me to the priests. I swore, with uplifted hand, that I would be an enemy for life to a government which assisted in the perpetration of such robberies and oppressions. I escaped the third time, joined the robbers in the mountains, and fought against the tyrannical government which helped to wrong and rob orphans."

These mortmain holdings increased almost daily. They amounted to many millions of dollars. The real estate was rented and produced a large revenue. The ambitious dignitaries of the Church had money to loan to any chieftain who promised to favor a restoration of the one-man power and of their former exclusive privileges. One of the watchwords of the Reactionary Party was *Religion y Fueros*—literally translated, Religion and Forums. The meaning, however, was accepted as a pledge to restore to the clergy thier former exemption from trial by civil courts.

2

Among the advocates of American principles in Mexico was José María Jesús Carbajal.[1] He was born in San Antonio, Texas, and was edu-

---

[1] Carbajal is also spelled Carabajal, Carvajal, or Caravajal. Emmanuel Domenech

cated by Alexander Campbell, the celebrated theologian. He was educated at Bethany College, Virginia. He spoke, read, and wrote English.
His great ambition was to free his country from the domination of military chieftains and to set on foot institutions similar to those of the
United States. He resided at Camargo, and in 1851 he led a revolution
which culminated in a plan—El Plan de la Loba—[that, among other
things, advocated a great many constitutional reforms, demanded that the
national army be withdrawn from northern Mexico, and insisted on a
marked reduction in tariffs]. It was promulgated by the towns of northeastern Mexico, and General Carbajal was entrusted with the chief command of the forces raised to uphold it. One of the articles in the plan
favored the sale of the mortmain property of the Catholic Church in
Mexico and the appropriation of the proceeds to defray the governmental expenses and to pay the public debt. The other objects expressed
were quite in keeping with what has been since reduced to practice by the
leaders of the liberal party.

During those days slaves held in Texas, induced to run away from
their masters by Mexicans, found refuge beyond the Río Grande. It was
calculated that there were, at that date, three thousand colored men north
of the Sierra Madre who were owned by men living in Texas. General
Carbajal acceded to a proposition to have them surrendered to their
masters and, if in his power, to secure the passage of a law making it a
felony for a person in involuntary servitude to escape therefrom and
take refuge upon Mexican territory.

The knowledge that the people of Mexico were oppressed by a centralized government administered by military despots was prevalent in
Texas. The liberal views expressed in the plan of la Loba—and the hope
of strengthening the institution of slavery in Texas and in the South, as
stated by Carbajal—caused Texians to sympathize with a people struggling for liberty.

General Carbajal captured Camargo in September, 1851, and was
organizing a force of *pronunciados*—anti-*Centralistas*—to make a descent upon Matamoros. He appealed to Americans for assistance in men.
On September 23, 1851, Captain Ford's company of rangers was disbanded. Ford had agreed to join General Carbajal, and did so early in
October, carrying with him about thirty of his trained Indian fighters

---

described him as a "brave and enterprising" Mexican, "more a distinguished soldier . . .
than a good leader. . . . He was of middle size, symmetrically formed, and had regular
features; his lively eyes bespoke at once address and energy."

(Domenech, *Missionary Adventures in Texas and Mexico: A Personal Narrative of
Six Years Sojourn in Those Regions*, p. 328.)

with their own arms and equipment and pack mules. The accouterments were paid for out of Ford's pocket. He formed a junction with Carbajal at Camargo, and was placed in command of the auxiliary troops with the rank of colonel. Americans at Brownsville had organized, and were ready to cross and join in the neighborhood of Matamoros.

Colonel McMicken occupied a position on General Carbajal's staff. Major Robert Wheat commanded the artillery.[2] Major James Taylor was a line officer of the auxiliary corps. Andy Walker, late lieutenant of Ford's company, commanded the old rangers. Another of General Carbajal's officers was a Captain Howell, a brother-in-law of Jefferson Davis.

Carbajal's *pronunciados* moved from Camargo in October. The march was made without molestations from the *Centralistas*, as the adherents of President [Mariano] Arista's administration were called.

On nearing Matamoros the garrison under General [Francisco] Avalos was summoned to surrender. It was told on trustworthy authority that responsible parties made a proposition to General Carbajal that if he would dismiss the Americans in his service, these parties would join him and advance $50,000 towards defraying the expenses of the war. The offer came in a shape leading the general to believe the intention was to act in bad faith towards the Americans or to place him in a position to cause the world to believe he contemplated perfidy towards his auxiliaries. He indignantly rejected the proposition.

The liberal troops camped a day or so at the Guadalupe Ranch, about two leagues above Matamoros. In the auxiliary corps there was a tall Hungarian. He was placed as a sentinel over the artillery. When the relief reached his post, an effort was made to inform him of the purpose for which they had come. John, the Hungarian, refused to be interviewed, and gave unmistakable evidences of an intention to "charge bayonet." The sergeant of the guard reported to the officer of the guard. He endeavored to relieve John, but was repulsed by a bayonet thrust. The officer of the guard reported to the officer of the day, who "pooh-poohed" the whole transaction and proceeded to relieve the valiant Hungarian.

---

[2] In Ford's opinion Roberdeau Chatham Wheat was one of the best fighters in Carbajal's army. Wheat, a Virginian whose father was an Episcopal clergyman, began his spectacular career as a soldier of fortune at the age of twenty. Built powerfully, over six feet tall, "and with manners that bespoke his upbringing," he had been a captain of cavalry in the Mexican War before becoming a major of artillery in Carbajal's revolutionary army; Wheat later served under William Walker in Nicaragua, under General Juan Alvarez in Mexico, under Garibaldi in Italy, and finally under Stonewall Jackson in the American Civil War. Wheat died leading his battalion of Louisiana Zouaves—"The Tigers"—in the battle of Gaines' Mill in 1862.
(Douglas Southall Freeman, *Lee's Lieutenants: A Study in Command*, I, 87–88, 525.)

The officer of the day approached in a persuasive manner and informed John in good English that his watch of two hours had expired, and he could go to the guard fire and go to sleep. John pointed his bayonet and rushed furiously at the officer of the day, who then went at full speed around the piece of artillery. It was an exciting race: the official proved winner by a length. After waiting a few minutes to get his breath, the officer went to Colonel Ford and reported the matter. The officer was of opinion no man in camp could guard the artillery more faithfully than John; therefore, "let him remain." The next morning John was indignant at being left on guard all night. A man was found who could speak the Magyar language. He explained the situation to John, who spoke no English.

We moved on Matamoros and got possession of an earthwork on the river at the upper part of the city. It was called Fort Paredes. There was a jubilation. Our "youthful general," as Bob Wheat styled General Carbajal, called for music, and the band responded harmoniously.

After some preparation, the Americans made an attack. They penetrated to the northwest corner of the main plaza, got possession of the customhouse, and opened fire on the enemy occupying the church. Late in the evening the *Centralistas* got some pieces in position and cannonaded the buildings on the corner of the plaza, with little effect, except on the houses.

During the cannon firing Captain Andy Walker was in the upper story of a brick building. A cannon ball crashed through the wall above his head, and dislodged a cart load of brick. Walker was covered. He scrambled out, looked at his wool hat, and exclaimed: "Damn them, they have mashed my new hat." It had cost him $1.25.

A young Mexican officer, under a heavy fire of artillery and musketry, sat and played the piano with perfect composure.

At dusk Ford directed his officers to withdraw to a position on the street just west of the customhouse, where the artillery could not reach. The movement was made in perfectly good order. Captain Edward Hord of the Brownsville Company conducted the advance. Our loss was one killed and two or three wounded; that of the enemy was reported to be heavy.

From this position detachments were sent in various directions to annoy the enemy by firing upon his reconnoitering parties and patrols. This was done well. When challenged, our men answered in Spanish and managed to get the first fire. The *Centralistas'* loss in this way was considerable; ours, nothing.

Colonel Ford's intention was to remain where he was for the night, to renew the attack in the morning, and meantime to request General Carbajal to advance with his whole force and hold the places taken by the Americans. Ford deemed it hazardous for a few hundred men to advance upon a force five or six times greater than their own, and having the advantage of fighting under cover. It was natural to expect the enemy to turn his flanks and take possession of houses in his rear. General Carbajal's main body had been spectators of the day's fighting, though Mexican troops were on duty in Ford's rear. This is stated as a fact, and not censoriously. General Carbajal had sent two orders to Colonel Ford directing him to withdraw. One, if memory serves, was brought by Colonel John L. Haynes. Both were delivered in an undertone of voice and not heard by the men. To each of these Ford replied that he wanted to remain where he was. A third order came. It was communicated in a loud tone of voice. The officers and men protested against giving up what they had fought for and won during the day and against having to do the same tomorrow. To this Ford replied:

"Gentlemen, if we were in the service of a regularly organized government, I would disobey and be court-martialed. Inasmuch as we are aiding in a revolution, and as yet without a government, I shall obey because obedience is the only tie which can hold this army together."

The Texian auxiliary troops and some companies of Mexicans sent to support them late in the day were marched back to Fort Paredes. General Carbajal quoted the precedent of General Taylor at Monterey to justify his course.[3] Ford said he thought the cases very dissimilar. The matter ended there.

3

When we reached Fort Paredes we were fatigued and made out beds on the outside of the fortification. A rain fell before daylight and many of us awoke covered by water. Our blankets and clothes were wet and, what was worse, our cartridges were spoiled. In those days the waterproof cartridge was not in use. Had the *Centralistas* attacked us we would have been in a woeful plight for defense.

No attack was made which would have brought into action all the

---

[3] The Taylor precedent to which Carbajal referred was briefly this: on the third day of the battle for Monterrey (September 23, 1846), Taylor sent Alfred M. Truitt's Texas Rangers into the lower part of the city while the main army concentrated on the plaza and elsewhere. The rangers drove everything before them, only to receive another order from Taylor that they must withdraw so that his artillery could shell the city. The rangers, having already carried the lower part of the city, refused to budge, and the bombardment commenced with the Texans still in the target area. The beleaguered Mexicans soon surrendered, however, and no Texans were hurt.

revolutionary troops at the same time. The auxiliaries were frequently
under fire; so was the Mexican contingent. Concert, however, was wanting.

The auxiliaries attacked the corner of the main plaza. Under a heavy
but ineffective fire, they moved through the houses on both sides of the
street leading to that point. They advanced to within thirty steps of the
plaza. At the corner thereof was a barricade from behind which the *Centralistas* were firing. Ford went to the door to make a reconnaissance; a
ball struck him on the head, cutting his hat band and passing out at the
top of the hat. There was a copious flow of blood. He remained at his
post until he discovered the wound affected his mind, creating a temporary forgetfulness of words. He remarked that no man ought to have
charge of men and be responsible for their lives unless his intellectual
faculties were in full operation, clear and unclouded. For these reasons he
withdrew, and the command of the Texian auxiliaries devolved upon
Major Taylor.

The fighting continued quite all night. A fire was kindled near the
customhouse. Many thousands of dollars worth of goods were stored in
that building. Hundreds of soldiers and citizens were engaged in removing the merchandise to a place of safety. The *pronunciados* fired on
them. The United States Consul, Mr. J. F. Waddell, received a buckshot
in the cheek. Jo Mason said he fired that shot. There was a great uproar:
cannon boomed, musketry rattled, men shouted, and no great amount of
damage done. Ford could hear all distinctly. With a wound about three
inches in length, beginning close to the edge of his hair, he was in no
condition to take a hand in the melée. He was treated by Surgeon Jarvis
of the United States Army and was pleasantly located in Judge D. Dunlap's house in Brownsville. Under the excitement and quasi-delirium
arising from the situation, want of sleep, and so on, Ford penned an address to the auxiliaries *à la Napoleon*, which Edward Hord had the
"cussedness" to preserve.

Soon after these occurrences, a night attack was made on the quarters
said to be occupied by General Avalos. There was a fierce struggle at
quite close quarters, and the *pronunciados* withdrew. The same management prevailing, there was no concentration of men upon the point assailed. The *Centralistas* had the advantage in position and numbers, and
they fought under cover.

The combats were frequent. The numbers engaged were too small to
affect general results. They wasted the strength and lessened the enthusiasm of the *pronunciados*.

John E. Wilson—"Black Tan," as the rangers called him—was reported to have taken charge of a detachment of Mexicans, whom he had palavered into making a dash upon the *Centralistas*. He carried them to where the enemy discovered them. Wilson mounted on top of a cabin to reconnoitre. A cannon ball came hurtling through. Wilson descended quickly. The boys said that he claimed to have been struck in the side by the six-pound ball, further, that he had angered his comrades by telling them he had been badly wounded, and was lame. He advised a retreat should the firing become hotter, but as he was disabled he would start at once.

At Cerralvo one of the "Old Rangers," Plas McCurly, had a dream that he would be killed the next day by a ball passing through his neck. The men tried to keep him from going to the front. He went anyway. The rangers were pitted against a band of Seminole Indians fighting with the enemy. A small hole was made in a brick or stone wall. Each man took his turn to fire through it; McCurly went, fired, and stepped back; a ball entered, struck him on the neck, and killed him.

This exasperated the Texians; McCurly was a good soldier and very popular. They began fighting in earnest. A goodly number of Seminoles were soon sent to the "happy hunting grounds." In less than twenty-four hours their commander had bad dreams and marched his dusky warriors home.

While the revolution was progressing, two Americans were made prisoners and carried into Matamoros. A suggestion was made to shoot them, to which General Avalos was reported to have replied:

"It will not do. Shoot these two Texians and a thousand will come to their funeral."

4

One morning all were astonished to hear that General Carbajal had withdrawn from Matamoros. The opinion of his friends was that he was practicing a ruse to get the *Centralistas* outside the city. In view of this being the state of the case, Ford, though advised to the contrary on account of his uncured wound, proceeded up the Río Grande, intending to cross and rejoin his command. He would have passed to the Mexican bank at the Ranch of Guadalupe had there been facilities. Had he succeeded he would have fallen into the hands of the *Centralistas*. A ride of ten or twelve miles did not secure a sight of the *pronunciados*. They were leaving in earnest. A halt was made at Reynosa, sixty miles from Matamoros.

The "old rangers"—twenty-eight in number—were in charge of Captain Andy Walker. They constituted the rear guard of Carbajal's army.

Walker moved at his leisure, supposing General Carbajal was maneuvering to get a fight in an open field. Seven or eight miles from Matamoros he halted at a ranch to get breakfast. He placed a picket on the road.

Shots were heard. A courier galloped up and reported to Walker that a large force of Mexicans had attacked the picket, and they were struggling manfully to hold their ground. The matchless riders of the West sprang upon their horses and went as if impelled by the force of a resistless cyclone. They spurred for their companions. Walker scanned the field for a moment, saw four hundred men, with artillery, pressing his heroic picket; pointing his revolver ahead, he cried,

"CHARGE!"

The Texas yell arose fierce and menacing; the rifle and the revolver began their deadly work; the impetuous horsemen rode at full speed upon the astounded enemy. They broke their line, attacked the several portions in flank, rolled them up, and forced them from the field as they would a drove of mustangs. They lost two men, and killed more than their own number of the enemy. It was the last charge of these invincible rangers. It was worthy of them; it was in keeping with their former deeds of daring gallantry; and it was an evidence of the unconquerable spirit animating them in the face of dangers appalling to men of ordinary mould.

On learning that General Carbajal was retreating, they felt much disappointed. Faithful to their pledge, they moved on to effect a junction with the main body the next day. They continued in the service as long as the revolution continued. In every encounter with the *Centralistas* they evinced indomitable courage.

This force of *Centralistas* was commanded by General [José Nicolás de la] Portillo. After his defeat he returned to Matamoros and made a vaunting report to General Avalos. Verbally he told Avalos,

"General, your enemies have gone like dogs with their tails between their legs."

Some of the citizens of Texas living in the valley of the Río Grande returned to the American side. Detachments of them were seen encamped near the river.

General Ovid F. Johnson was editing a paper in Brownsville. He called the retreat: "General Caravajal's pale-faced flight." The reasons for the move will be stated soon. General Carbajal still retained the respect of his American friends, with few exceptions. Many of them doubted the wisdom of his measures and movements, yet they accorded to him honesty of purpose and a patriotic desire to redeem his countrymen from the thralldom of military despotism.

5

Ford engaged passage on one of King & Kenedy's steamers. On reaching Reynosa he had an interview with General Carbajal, who explained the cause of his retreat. General Antonio Canales had received orders to reinforce General Avalos. Canales was a personal friend of Carbajal. On various pretexts Canales delayed the execution of the orders. He had sent messages to General Carbajal to hurry his march into Matamoros. To avoid complications with his old companion in arms, General Carbajal withdrew from Matamoros. Had he moved slowly and reinforced the "Old Rangers" he could have beaten General Portilla and captured his whole command and returned to Matamoros with the morale of victory in his favor. The probabilities were in favor of General Canales joining him. Up to that date the Texians entertained a strong dislike of Canales. They had not learned he was innocent of the treachery attempted on the Texians under Colonel Jordan during the Federation War in 1840. It is now known Colonel Molano was the Judas on that occasion. These sentiments existing on our part would have made it unpleasant, if not dangerous, to place us on duty with General Canales. Such a procedure might have led to bad results. General Canales' son, Servando Canales, was with General Carbajal. Servando was at that date a mere youth. He later showed ability as a general and a statesman. He did Americans many favors while he was governor of Tamaulipas, and they regretted his death very sincerely.

General Carbajal stated to the writer the substance of a proposition made to him by Captain M. Kenedy, of the firm of King & Kenedy, to organize a provisional government with Carbajal as the head of government as well as commander-in-chief of the army. The control of the army in its field operations, however, would rest upon another. The acceptance of the proposition was to be attended by an advance of supplies of ordnance and other war materials. The general declined.

"I told him my ambition was to be the Washington of my country."

The matter of forming a provisional government had been presented to the consideration of General Carbajal previously; but the earlier proposal did not suggest that another man command the troops in the field. The reasons favoring the measure, and the advantages likely to result, are too obvious to be repeated here.

John S. Ford was promoted to the command of a brigade for "gallant" conduct and "meritorious" services in the Matamoros campaign. General Carbajal insisted on sending the writer to the interior of Texas on recruiting service. Carbajal furnished an escort of three men to accompany Ford and advanced sixty-four dollars to defray expenses. He proceeded to Austin and took steps to induce men to proceed to Mexico, and there organize. He endeavored to avoid an infraction of the neutrality laws of the United States. He was apprised that the class of men likely to engage in such a service were seldom blessed with a superfluity of the good things of this world, particularly soul-endangering gold and silver. Recruits would have been numerous had there been funds on hand to purchase outfits in advance. As matters stood, there were few who could furnish means to purchase the articles needed.

6

General Carbajal had an affair at Cerralvo, also one at Camargo early in 1852. He then withdrew to Texas, where he was arrested for violating our neutrality laws. He was not found guilty.

Colonel H. L. Kinney and others got up a fair at Corpus Christi in May, 1852. It was supposed that the fair would promote the cause of the Carbajal revolution. The general attended and delivered an address. He was a pleasant speaker and handled the English language well.

A number of distinguished Texians gathered at the Corpus Christi fair —Ashbel Smith, [Benjamin Franklin] Terry, General Hugh McLeod, General H. Clay Davis, Major James H. Durst, Captain Bill Maltby, Major W. M. Mann, and others of note. There was an interchange of ideas on the subject of Mexico and her methods of administering affairs of government. It was a rather general belief that she constituted a dangerous neighbor. A great many were willing to assist General Carbajal in the much needed work of reform, inasmuch as he made the government of the United States his model. The want of money was the great drawback. As a general rule, war, without a well-filled military chest, degenerates into robbery. Many of us who had spent considerable money in the revolutionary service and had drawn almost no pay now felt unable to do anything more. Fate seemed against General Carbajal. The revolution was virtually at an end.

7

General Carbajal's want of success depended on various causes. One was the employment of Americans. If there is any one thing which will fill an average Mexican full to the brim of intense wrath it is the sight of an American. Juan N. Cortina, whom we will deal with further on, once said: "The sight of an American makes me feel like eating little kids." Of course they had to be killed first. In 1851 the feeling of hostility was more implacable than it has been since. The telling charge against Carbajal was: *El esta muy Agringado*—he is very much Americanized. This was sufficient to crystallize Mexican opinion against him. They hated Texians horribly, yet feared them. They had a lively remembrance of the fight at Saltillo in 1840.

The writer's connection with the Carbajal movement did him injury in the estimation of his fellow citizens. Many of them were not informed of the motives actuating him. They did not know he was endeavoring to give an additional support to an institution of the South, namely, slavery. They overlooked the fact that a man has a right to assist a people who are resisting tyranny and battling for the exercise of their privileges as free men. They judged the whole transaction by the rigid rule of success and, because it failed, condemned it. An over-cautious man might have felt himself justified in passing by the matter in silence. It seems more proper just to tell the truth about the writer's actions and shoulder the responsibilities arising from such a course.

XVIII

>>

THE ERA OF SUSPICION

General Edward Burleson, the senator of the district including Austin, the seat of government, fell sick and died on December 26, 1851. He was a man who had rendered many eminent services to Texas. He had been the leading spirit in driving the Indians back from the infant settlements on the Colorado River and its tributaries. He succeeded Stephen F. Austin in command of the army in front of San Antonio. He was its commander-in-chief when the storming column under Milam and, after his fall, under Colonel Frank W. Johnston forced General Cós to surrender. Burleson commanded a regiment at San Jacinto, was a colonel in the regular army of Texas, and participated in the engagements with the Cherokee Indians and their allies in eastern Texas in 1839. He was vice president of the Republic of Texas and, finally, a senator in the State Legislature.

Death had indeed chosen a shining mark. A ruler in Israel had fallen.

An unambitious patriot had ceased to respond to the call of his country-men. A leader of nerve, brain, and dash had taken his eternal furlough. The place once filled by a hero, one of Nature's noblemen, one who re-ceived the gifts of wisdom, prudence, and a high sense of honor from the hand of God, was vacated. Who could fill it? Alas! No one in the sena-torial district could advance the claims he did. The analogy might be adduced of the matchless bow of Achilles whom none could draw after he made his abode in the garden of the Hesperides. In the scrutiny, the writer was selected by his fellow citizens. He accepted the proffered trust, fully sensible of the disparity of the claims General Burleson justly had upon the people and those Ford's most partial friends could set up in his behalf. He was opposed by Major Clement R. Johns and Josiah Fisk and was elected by the vote of Travis County on January 12, 1852.

ELECTION RETURNS

Travis		*Hays*		*Gillespie*		*Total Votes*	
Ford	179	Ford	0	Ford	11	Ford	190
Johns	43	Johns	30	Johns	68	Johns	141
Fisk	42	Fisk	0	Fisk	18	Fisk	60[1]

Ford took his seat in January, 1852. He favored every measure tending in the direction of paying the public debt of Texas, paying particularly such men as Fred Dawson who had almost ruined himself in furnishing vessels for a Texas navy when we were weak, penniless, and bidding fair to go to pieces for the want of funds to sustain our governmental exist-ence.

The writer advocated every measure necessary to give defense to the frontier. He was the steady friend of the pioneer, and always voted to protect the settler against any and all opposing parties.

After the adjournment of the Legislature Ford returned to the Río Grande and reported to General Carbajal, who was living at Río Grande City in Starr County, Texas.

2

In the fall of 1852 the writer purchased from Phineas de Cordova the printing establishment from which the newspaper called the *South-Western American* (Austin) was issued.[2]

---

[1] The editor has added the election returns. See the *Texas State Gazette* (Austin), January 17, 1852.

[2] When Ford took over the *South-Western American*, he dropped the hyphen from southwestern. He told his readers that the *American* was "a Democratic Newspaper— Devoted to Agriculture, News, Politics and Texan Interests."

At this time the building of a railroad to a harbor on the Pacific coast was a matter much discussed. An editorial appeared in the *American* on the subject which attracted notice in Texas. At the next meeting of the Legislature, the editors reproduced the article by request, and a number of legislators mailed copies to their constituents.

Early in 1853 Captain Joe Walker and the writer established the *State Times* in Austin. It was the largest weekly in the State, except the Galveston *News*, and contained quite as much reading matter as the *News*. The *State Gazette* of Austin was owned and conducted by Major William R. Scurry and Wade Hampton. Of course the usual rivalry sprang up between the *Gazette* and the *Times*. Two newspaper firms seldom preserve harmonious relations when divided by a street only, and it is hard for either of the editors to do anything the other does not find out about.

The great question then agitating the people of Texas was whether donations of the public domain should be made to companies to encourage them to build railroads in the State. The *States Times* advocated the policy of state aid dwelling on the advantages arising from having railroads to promote commerce and intercommunication with the other States of the Union. Railroads would act as agents to appreciate the price of land and other property, increase taxable values, and become mediums for the introduction of immigrants. The *Gazette* remained silent on the question.

It was understood that General Rusk and General Houston both expressed opposition to the idea of donating money or land to railroad companies to induce them to build railroads in Texas. They both appeared afterwards to entertain different views, General Rusk particularly. As a United States Senator, he seemed very much interested in the construction of a railroad to the Pacific coast and seemed confident the most direct route was over Texas territory.

The Legislature of Texas passed a bill to provide for the building of a railroad through Texas to constitute a part of a line to the Pacific Ocean; it was approved by the governor on December 31, 1853. The annexed was the only bid which complied with the requirements of the law:

City of Austin
July 29th, 1854.

To His Excellency, E. M. Pease, Governor of the State of Texas.

Sir.—We hereby propose to enter into a contract with your Excellency, by which we will obligate ourselves to construct the Mississippi and Pacific Railroad from a point on the eastern boundary line of the State of Texas, not north of the town of Fulton, in the State of Arkansas, to a suitable point on the Rio Grande, at or near the town of El Paso; to cross the rivers Trinity, Brazos, and Colorado as near the 32d degree of North latitude as practicable. This we will undertake to do on the terms and conditions and for the consideration expressed in the act of the Legislature of the State of Texas, passed for that purpose, and approved December 21st, 1853.

We will agree and bind ourselves to commence the work within thirty days after the execution of the contract, in case it will be awarded to us. We will undertake to finish and place in running order, fifty miles of said road, within eighteen months from the date of said contract; and to finish and place in like order, one hundred miles of said road each and every year thereafter, until the whole shall be completed. And we will undertake that this shall be of the first class of railroads. We further propose to deposit in the Treasury of the State of Texas, par stocks to the amount of three hundred thousand dollars, to be forfeited to said State, in case fifty miles of said road shall not be completed within eighteen months from this date of the contract proposed.

(Signed) R. J. Walker	G. W. Hancock	H. P. Bee
T. Butler King	John Hancock	John W. Harris
M. T. Johnson	James H. Raymond	Matt Ward
J. A. Green	James B. Shaw	Leonard Randal
W. C. Lacy	Wm. H. Bourland	J. Pinckney Henderson
S. A. Maverick		E. B. Nichols

The bonus offered by the State for the construction of the road was sixteen sections of land—10,240 acres—per mile.

The terms were agreed upon; and the deposit of three hundred thousand dollars in stock was made. The stock, however, was pronounced below par by Governor Pease and his advisors. A contest arose over the value of the stocks. The conductors of the *Times* advocated the cause of the company, while the *State Gazette* and nearly every other newspaper in the State sustained the action of Governor Pease.

It was charged that the company entering into the contract did not intend to build the road, but to sell the right to build. To this the *Times* replied that there was no evidence of an intention to sell, and should they do so, what difference would it make with the State whether she deeded the land to the original company or to another? That should there be a failure to comply with the terms of the contract the State would part with no land, hence no loss could accrue to Texas, happen what might. The cry of bogus stocks, speculation, and the like, created excitement, and Governor Pease was looked upon as a sort of financial savior.[3] It was

---

[3] As if in answer to the attacks against the Mississippi Pacific Railroad, Thomas J. Green proclaimed that

this road is emphatically the Southern—yea, what the abolitionist truly calls the "*great slavery road.*" Its five principal connections with the Mississippi from New

useless to dwell upon the high standing, integrity, and unimpeachable honesty of the company. None of the Texas members of the company were attacked, if memory is correct. A. J. Hamilton expressed the opinion that the Mississippi and Pacific Railroad matter re-elected E. M. Pease governor in 1855. It is probable so much was seldom written about railroads by men who knew so little about them.

3

The *Times* editorialized on a number of other issues. It recommended the payment of the public debt of Texas, but it was not satisfied with the "scaling system," urging that this system had the twang of repudiation about it and that no state could afford to repudiate an equitable claim. It would cost her more in the end than dollars and cents could purchase: her reputation for honesty and fair dealings. The scaling system of paying off the public debt had been introduced by James B. Shaw,[4] comptroller of public accounts, and adopted by the Texas Legislature after the 1850 Compromise. Briefly, this was the way it worked: Shaw collected data by which he could tell the rate at which Texas paper money was paid out, so many dollars in paper rating as a dollar in current money. The decrease in the market value of a Texas paper dollar was gradual, yet sure. When our paper currency went at about sixteen for one, we were supposed to abandon it. Notes of the government bearing interest calculated in current money were then to have paid the holder in one year the principal invested. For instance, a ten-dollar bill would have been worth about sixty-three cents in market; the interest for one year at ten per cent would have been one dollar, at eight per cent, eighty cents. The holders

Orleans to St. Louis, uniting in Eastern Texas, and thence on a common Trunk to El Paso, with its two great branches to the two bays of Texas, is entirely in slave territory; and if the people of Texas and the South be true to themselves, they will see that the remaining five hundred miles to the junction of the Gila and Colorado will, under the privileges of the Nebraska bill, be also a slave State. This is due to Texas, to the South, and to the Union; which we will endeavor to show.

The effort to build a transcontinental railroad through Texas failed and with it went the hopes of making the state rich and prosperous. Over a decade later, two large corporations with Federal government support began building such a road westward from Omaha, Nebraska, and eastward from California.

(*Texas State Gazette* [Austin], July 29, 1854.)

[4] Ford says that James B. Shaw "was the ruling spirit in the Treasury Department in the days of the Republic. He knew more about the financial affairs of Texas than any other man." In his work as state comptroller, Shaw had an able assistant in Auditor John M. Swisher, who in the "prime of life" was "endowed with native talent, quick perception, and wonderful memory . . . and the genial qualities which conspire to render a man influential and popular." John M. Swisher was the son of Captain James G. Swisher, whom Ford mentions further on in his story.

of our liabilities made immense profits on their outlays. They were paid in proportion to the value of our currency at the time they invested and at the rate of interest agreed upon.

Even though the holders of Texas liabilities received good returns for the respective amounts invested, Texas was not exonerated from paying a dollar worth 100 cents when she promised to pay a dollar. It is useless, however, to moralize now, since the creditors acquiesced in the settlement reached through the scaling system.

The *Times* insisted on educating Texas children in Texas; consequently the paper favored building first-class schools in the State. The Scriptural injunction of training a child in the way he should go and training him to know the people with whom he would go was extended. Educate a child at home, with those who are to be his companions for life, and he will acquire no foreign habits, no aristocratic airs, and will stoop to ape no brainless fop because he is a nobleman.

During 1853–1854 the editor of the *Times* had a number of able correspondents: Robert Green, Charles S. West, John Duval (a survivor of the massacre at Goliad), Joseph Smith (formerly a paymaster's clerk under Albert Sidney Johnston), George Simcox, John Ireland (later governor of Texas), Major James H. Durst, Judge George W. Paschal, General H. Clay Davis, the Reverend Edward Fontaine, and many other gentlemen of distinction.

James A. Beveridge was assistant editor for a length of time. He was a forcible writer, a poet of some ability, and a strong partisan of the old American Party. He was the author of quite all the tirades against the Roman Catholic Church which appeared in the *Times*.

4

In 1854 the writer became a member of the Know Nothing Order. The act of joining was one of those inconsiderate things men do sometimes. The Know Nothing or American Party did not take well in Texas. General Houston was its great high priest in the Lone Star State. He made many eloquent speeches in advocacy of its principles. The Democratic Party made war upon its doctrines and finally crushed the party out.

When the writer became acquainted with the principles of the order, he was not in accord with them, especially the anti-Catholic plank in the platform. He enunciated his own opinions. They were briefly these: a voter when he deposits his ballot performs an act of sovereignty as complete as can be performed by the Emperor of Russia. A republican government is maintained by the intelligence of its citizens. A citizen who votes in ignorance of his rights under the Constitution and the laws endangers the perpetuity of our free institutions in a direct ratio with the extent of that ignorance. A residence of twenty-one years is not conclusive evidence of a proper acquaintance with our institutions and laws to enable a foreign-born person to vote understandingly; time is not a proper test of qualification. A man twenty-one years of age who cannot speak, read, and write the English language should not be permitted to vote, unless laboring under a disabling affection. His place of birth should make no difference.

John C. Calhoun held that no foreign-born person should be allowed to vote in any election in any State until he had become a naturalized citizen of the United States.

Many patriotic men in the Union during the Know Nothing excitement believed some safeguard should be thrown around the process of naturalization so as to prevent citizenship from becoming too easy of an attainment to command due respect. They thought a residence of twenty-one years before acquiring the privilege to vote would be a hardship as time decides nothing. The test of speaking, reading, and writing the English language would decide a great deal. Add citizenship in the United States to this statement and the remedy would be quite effective.

No man who scans the signs of the times can conscientiously say nothing of men whose principles and practices endanger the peace, good order, and the very existence of society. There must be a brake put on somewhere. The bidding of different states for immigrants by conferring the privilege of voting on a foreign-born person within a few months after his entering their territory needs looking after. We are reaping the fruits of this cheapening of the exercise of privileges of inestimable value to free men. The native-born American has to live in the country twenty-one years before he can vote; the immigrant from Turkey, Siberia, or Persia can step up to the ballot box and cast in his vote after a residence of one year in many of the States of this Union. There must be some inquiry into the antecedents and character of immigrants.

5

General Rusk, one of our senators in the Congress of the United States, visited Austin in the winter of 1852 and 1853. He made a speech in the rear of the old capitol, at a barbecue, in which he discussed public questions. At that period he considered the Kansas-Nebraska bill of Mr. [Stephen A.] Douglas a sell upon the South. Rusk afterwards voted for it, no doubt under party pressure. He had no concealments, was outspoken, and superior to the shifts and evasions of little minds. His declarations at Austin portrayed his individual opinion of the bill.

A week or two later General Houston came to Austin. His removal of a portion of the public archives from that point had caused much bitter feeling against him among the people of that vicinity, and it had not altogether died out. Captain James G. Swisher had intimated an intention, perhaps a mere disposition, to do General Houston a personal injury should he come to the state capital. Swisher was a bold and fearless gentleman, and one very likely to put an intention into execution. Thomas Ward had expressed similar sentiments.[5] These old gentlemen were watched, without their knowing it.

General Houston appointed a day to speak at the old capitol, where the Market House now stands. A great many old settlers were present to hear him. He stood on the passage between the senate chamber and the representative hall, facing to the east, and addressed his audience.

He spoke of his official career, explained things which he claimed had not been understood by the people. He said friends had asserted he had made mistakes in his acts in reference to Austin; if he had, happy results had been accomplished anyhow. He complimented the city on her location, the beauty of the surrounding scenery, the progress made in population and wealth, and the flattering prospects before her. He reverted to Texas, her magnificent domain, her glorious history, to his identification with the land of his adoption; yet with all his love he had nothing to leave to her people but his children, and no legacy to bequeath to them but an unsullied name.

Here the tears streamed down his cheeks, and he looked like a prophet inspired by a vision unfolding the events of a thousand years to come. In glowing language he painted the magnificent destiny within the reach of Texas, the giant state of the Union: first in natural resources, first in arms, first in diplomacy, and first in the arts of peace. Her sons would achieve renown in every walk of life, and her daughters would command the homage of chivalrous men.

In the audience were old pioneers who had passed through every ordeal incident to frontier life, who had seen loved ones slaughtered and

---

[5] Ford notes that

Colonel Thomas Ward was one of the New Orleans Greys. He lost a leg at the taking of San Antonio, where he displayed unflinching courage. He afterwards lost an arm by the accidental discharge of a cannon in firing a salute on the fourth of July. He was commissioner of the general land office for a time. Maimed as he was, he was a dead shot with rifle or pistol. He had a quarrel in the streets of Austin with a gentleman; hard words passed; Colonel Ward left. In a short time he returned, followed by a colored man with a basket on his arm. The colonel approached his antagonist and removed a large napkin from the basket, bringing into view a pair of loaded pistols. He politely invited the gentleman to take his choice. The gentleman left in a hurry. Ward was a warm friend of General Houston.

scalped, and who while mourning their dead had taken the trail in an implacable mission of revenge. These stern sentinels on the outposts of civilization wept when they saw the grand patriot and hero permit his feelings to overmaster his resolution. After his close, General Houston started down the hill; Captain Swisher had one of his arms and Thomas Ward the other.

No shorthand writer was on the ground to take down that burst of impassioned eloquence; and had the attempt been made, it would have proved a failure. It would have been difficult for any man to have controlled his feelings sufficiently to render a correct version of a speech stirring the recesses of the hearts of the auditors.

6

The possession of slaves in western Texas in 1854 was rendered insecure, owing to the contiguity of Mexico and to the efforts of Mexicans to induce them to run away. They assisted them in every way they could. When once on Mexican soil, slaves were safe from pursuit—free and very popular. The Mexicans expressed horror at the idea of slavery as it existed in the United States and seemed to forget that they made their own countrymen slaves—*peons*—for the inability to pay a debt. When the head of a family became a *peon*—pronounced pay-own—he was allowed about twenty-five cents a day to support himself and family. The owner of a ranch usually kept a small store to supply his slaves. The articles most in demand were corn, beans, and pepper. Of course coffee, sugar, and stuff for coarse cotton clothing were obtainable. Meat was a luxury a *peon* enjoyed on only rare occasions. At the end of each month the *peon* became deeper in debt. The result usually reached was that his wife and children became slaves in process of time. There was little prospect of release.

At the time war commenced between Mexico and the United States, the lower Río Grande was a cotton growing country. Between Matamoros and Reynosa there were six cotton gins. Cotton could be cultivated at a considerable profit. *Peon* labor was cheap, more so than that of the African slave in the United States. Cotton was sold at a high price, sometimes at fifty cents a pound. After the occupation of the valley of the Río Grande from the mouth of that stream to Laredo by American troops, Mexican slaves commenced leaving their masters; many were hired by our quartermaster at thirty dollars a month. The writer knows of no instance in which a fugitive *peon* was delivered to his master on demand; such things may have happened. This did much towards destroying the labor system prevailing on the lower Río Grande. After the conclusion of the war in 1848, the culture of cotton ceased almost entirely, and has been resumed only partially. Agricultural pursuits were abandoned to a great extent. Stock raising was substituted for almost any other business or calling.

It will not be difficult for the reader to draw conclusions relative to these two systems of slavery practiced by two peoples, in many respects the antipodes of each other in customs, modes of living, and methods of thought, especially when the embittered feelings arising from a war were lively and vigorous.

The writer called attention, in the *State Times*, to the continuous exodus of slaves into Mexico and to the remedy once within reach during the Carbajal revolution.

In 1854 General [Santiago] Vidauri was in a state of quasi revolution against the Supreme Government of Mexico. He gained control of the state of Nuevo León.

In 1855 a public meeting was held at Bastrop to consider what was best to be done to prevent the exodus of slaves into Mexico and to reclaim those already there and within the territory dominated by General Vidauri. It was decided to send two agents into Mexico to confer with Vidauri and offer to aid him with men and money.

On his part he was to assist in surrendering fugitive slaves to their masters and to place obstacles in the way of their finding refuge in Nuevo León. Colonel B. Riddle and John S. Ford were appointed agents.

On arriving at San Antonio, Ford heard that Captain [James H.] Callahan had crossed the Río Grande in pursuit of Indians who had committed depredations in Texas. Knowing how easily the suspicions of the Mexicans could be aroused and how strong the feeling of hostility to Americans existed among the masses in Mexico, Ford declined to visit General Vidauri at Monterey, not deeming it safe. Colonel Riddle was a resident of Chihuahua, had married a Mexican lady, and was merchandising in that city; he could execute the mission in safety. He proceeded, but found everything blocked because all Mexico was crying out in protest against Captain Callahan's entrance upon Mexican territory.

Captain Callahan, in pursuing Indians on the Mexican side, suddenly found himself confronted by a force of Mexicans and Indians more than five times greater than his own. A fight opened; the place was in a mat of timber on Escondido Creek near Piedras Negras. The enemy drew up in Callahan's front, throwing both wings forward and refusing their center. Instead of attacking one of the wings in flank, rolling it up, and getting a flanking movement on the center, Callahan made the attack on the center in a furious charge. He received flanking fire on both his wings and direct fire from the enemy's center; he broke and drove the center and gained the day. Indications were too palpable of a general rising of the people and an attack from an overwhelming force, so he moved to the Río Grande. He occupied Piedras Negras, set the town on fire, and while it was burning, he crossed into Texas. It was understood that the commandant of Fort Duncan and his officers helped Captain Callahan cross over to the Texas side.

Men were collecting at San Antonio to reinforce Callahan. Among those in camp were Captain Henry E. McCulloch and other old soldiers who had seen service. The withdrawal of Callahan left them no opportunity again to cross swords with the *hidalgos* of the magnanimous nation.

The Callahan invasion was the cause of large claims being preferred by pretended citizens of Piedras Negras against the United States. One of these calling for several thousand dollars was presented by a Mexican who, at the time of the burning, was a citizen of Cameron County, Texas. He did not have the credit of those well acquainted with him of having ever owned many hundreds of dollars.

Major Anderson of the United States Army was despatched to the Río Grande to examine the merits of claims against the United States, made by Mexican citizens, which had been placed before the mixed Mexican and American commission for their action. Out of many thousands of dollars claimed, there was only a single claim that was apparently genuine. In reference to that claim no evidence of any character could be found. Most of the complainants based their claims on matters happening during the war between Mexico and the United States, and these claims were not properly considered by the commission.

7

A number of communications appeared in the *State Times* criticizing the manner in which General Persifor F. Smith conducted the affairs of the Military Department of Texas. Captain Givens was the reputed author of the articles. At this date it is difficult for the writer to say whether Captain Givens or Colonel Thomas F. McKinney was responsible for what was published. The allegations produced excitement and comment in military circles.

General Smith caused charges to be preferred against Captain Givens. Captain McLean was judge advocate of the court-martial; he addressed a subpoena to John S. Ford, Austin, Texas. When that document reached its destination, Ford was in San Antonio. It was taken to the *Times* office and burned by Mr. Beveridge. Ford did not see the subpoena, nor did he know of its issuance and disposition until after the court adjourned. He remained in Austin during the sitting of the court, and it did not occur to Captain McLean to summon him, believing Ford was disobeying a subpoena already served.

Captain Givens was acquitted for want of evidence. Captain McLean informed Ford of his intention to report Ford's refusal to obey a summons to appear before a court-martial and testify. McLean's object was to test the power of a court-martial to compel a citizen to appear before it as a witness. When he learned that Ford had not been subpoenaed, or had not received the subpoena, McLean dropped the matter. Between these gentlemen there was no ill feeling. It was understood that the writer would have been invited to the miscalled field of honor had he been subpoenaed.

General John A. Quitman, Mr. Thrasher, and others were making efforts to revolutionize Cuba between 1857 and 1859. The writer visited New Orleans to consult with them on the subject. The move ended in effecting nothing. The risk of landing in Cuba, of being left without the means of withdrawing, and of being garroted might have had an influence.

During the period between 1853 and 1860, an order known as the Lone Star of the West was very popular in Texas and received many initiates. It was ostensibly connected with Cuban affairs, though nothing in the shape of a tangible benefit to the oppressed islanders ever grew out of it. There was one thing the novitiate never ceased to remember—the ceremony of initiation. It was impressive and intensely unique. Its cabalistic passwords were indelibly impressed on the mind.

8

General Houston's opposition to the passage of the Kansas-Nebraska Bill had made him temporarily unpopular, at least with the politicians of our State. He refused to be a candidate for re-election to the Senate of the United States. It was believed he was preparing to run for governor. It was considered doubtful whether he could be beaten easily. The party of democracy banked on the unpopularity of the tenets of the American party to defeat Houston. At the convention at Waco in the spring of 1857, the Democrats nominated Hardin R. Runnels as Democratic candidate for governor. He had differed in sentiment with them on a few questions.

The campaign was a warm one. General Houston stumped the State. His oratorical powers were unimpaired. He was answered in central and western Texas by Judge Williamson S. Oldham. The hero of San Jacinto proved himself a master of invective. He was defeated.

Governor Runnels was conservative in his official course. An opinion gained currency that he had imbibed an idea that Captain Ford might become a candidate for the office of governor in 1859. The opinion attained so much the semblance of truth that the writer addressed Governor Runnels on the subject, assuring him that Ford had no intention of running for the position. He had received no invitations to do so.

Governor Runnels and all Texas then became convinced that General Houston would be a candidate again. They were right. In 1859 Houston announced himself at Nacogdoches in a splendid effort, in which he paid a glowing tribute to woman. He stayed at home and was elected by a good majority. The people loved him and were not ready to give him up; hence his election.

The writer had a number of letters from General Houston, also autographs of many of the distinguished men of the first half of the nineteenth century. They were lost during the Civil War.

During 1857 Colonel John Marshall, formerly of Mississippi, was the principal editor of the *State Gazette*. It was the organ of the Democratic party. Ford sold the *State Times*. It took another name, and finally was merged in the *Intelligencer*, which was edited with ability by Judge George W. Paschal. A paper war ensued. It was bitter and personal. Duels were often threatened and spoken of as in the near future; yet, no blood was spilt. Paschal and Marshall did not meet on the bloody field. They were both brave. It is not generally known why they failed to duel.[6]

---

[6] Perhaps Marshall and Paschal failed to duel because, as Traveler Thomas North discovered, the code of honor "was a good deal demoralized in Texas, in comparison with its status in the older Southern States—if such a thing can be demoralized. It assumes more the form of open and secret assassination—shooting a man down behind his back, or in the dark, or on sight with the simple warning, 'Take care of yourself.' " Consequently, in Texas "a man is a little nearer death . . . all the while than in any country we know of."

(North, *Five Years in Texas: or, What You Did Not Hear during The War from January 1861 to January 1866*, pp. 71, 72).

XIX

>>

ON TO THE CANADIAN

The Indian tribes residing in Texas between 1852 and 1857 became very troublesome and committed many depredations. The state at various times called out troops to protect particular localities. In 1853 several companies were mustered into service. These were attached to a Federal force; an expedition was made upon our northwestern frontier, with some beneficial results, but no fighting. Minute men were raised also. There was no cessation of hostilities.

The Legislature of Texas passed an act on February 6, 1854, setting apart four leagues of land on the Clear Fork of the Brazos and four leagues on the main Brazos to be used as agencies for the collection, settlement, and control of Texas Indians. In 1858 Major Robert Simpson Neighbors, the supervising Indian agent of Texas, stated the whole number of Indians in his charge, on these two agencies, at 1,398—386 at the

Comanche Agency and 1,012 at the Brazos Agency. At that period Captain Shapley P. Ross was the agent in charge of the Brazos Agency and John R. Baylor was in charge of the Comanche Agency.

Major Neighbors defended the Agency Indians against oft-repeated accusations of being active parties in the commission of outrages upon border settlers by seven bands of marauding Comanches which roamed unrestrained across West Texas.[1] Neighbors averred that his Indians were not off the agency grounds unless by permission of the agent, and were amenable to civil processes—to arrest and punishment as others guilty of criminal offenses. A select committee of both houses of the Seventh Legislature, to whom was referred the matter of Indian depredations, rather questioned the feasibility of the mode of procedure recommended by Major Neighbors. They dwelt on the fact that Indians on the warpath were generally almost nude and painted in the most grotesque manner; consequently, an Agency Indian, if he had been on one of the plundering expeditions, could not be recognized by a witness when dressed in the rather full garbs worn at the agencies. The report was therefore against giving the Indians civil rights. It was made on January 13, 1858.

Previous to this action on the part of the Legislature, an effort was made in Congress at the suggestion of General [David E.] Twiggs, commanding the Department of Texas, to provide for raising a regiment of mounted men—rangers—for service on the Texas frontier against the hostile Comanches. John S. Ford was highly recommended for the position of colonel. The failure of the movement induced our leading men

---

[1] Ford joined Neighbors in defending the Agency Indians against accusations of barbarism.

They have cut loose from the wild Indians for good, [Rip told Governor Runnels on April 7, 1858], and have, so far as they can, identified themselves with the whites, in every way. They say they wish to become Americans. The strides they are making in the way of becoming civilized are great, and, I might even say, astonishing. They are trying to imitate the whites in manners, in dress, in agriculture, and in all essential particulars. They have large fields of wheat and corn, which they have planted themselves, and are now cultivating. Waggons drawn by oxen and driven by Indians; women and children dropping corn; all give the scenes at the different villages quite an American appearance. There is no disorder, no discontent, and no disposition to give trouble to the Agent or the Government. They are endeavoring to fulfill the treaty stipulations and to give satisfaction to the Americans. I speak of what I have seen and heard, and believe it is true. I should view any combinations of circumstances which tended towards the breaking up of this Reserve, as a serious misfortune to the State of Texas, and a calamity over which the philanthropist might mourn.

(Governors' Letters, 1846–1860, ms.)

to adopt a line of policy calculated to give adequate protection to person and property in the border settlements.

2

[The United States regulars then stationed in Texas must assume much of the blame for the increasing violence on the frontier. They had not done a proper job of policing the area.] It has never been the habit of the writer to cast obloquy upon the officers and men of the regular army. It was just that they did not understand and appreciate the Indians' mode of fighting, did not know that savages could be such experts with crude weapons like the bow and arrows and the lance. The red men had their peculiar tactics. They fought in open order generally; their line of battle was similar to our line of skirmishes; a conflict with them was something approaching a series of single combats. Their retreats were feints to deceive their enemies. At a proper time, when the white men had discharged quite all their firearms, the Indians would face about and resume the offensive with vigor and courage. Good men, drilled and disciplined, but without some knowledge of the Indian mode of warfare, could not always be handled effectively by officers who had not seen service against the skilful riders of the prairies.[2]

---

[2] Procrastination on the part of regular officers—quite aside from their practical inexperience in Indian fighting—was a chief reason why the United States Army had failed to keep peace on the Texas frontier. In 1858 one of the agency Indians, Chief Ketumse, offered to lead a force of regulars into the Wichita Mountain region where Indian renegades had hidden stolen horses. His offer was appreciated, he was told, but it must be discussed and analyzed and of course the problem of logistics must be considered before any definite plans could be made. . . . Angrily Chief Ketumse told them to forget it and rode back to the reservation certain that all the white soldiers wanted to do was to sit and drink coffee and "talk and talk, and write and write," but never fight.

As Ford pointed out, the Second United States Cavalry was a marked exception. Soon after its arrival in Texas in 1855, it earned the coveted title of a "fightin' outfit" and its Texan commander, Colonel Albert Sidney Johnston, was considered an example of the military's finest. Aiding him was a staff of brilliant officers—men like Lieutenant Colonel Robert E. Lee, Lieutenant Colonel W. J. Hardee, and Major George H. Thomas. Secretary of War Jefferson Davis sent to the regiment such a galaxy of precocious officers, many of them known for their pro-Southern sentiments, that persons who knew later accused him of anticipating the Civil War. He probably was. What better place than Texas to send a promising officer to get experience in the handling of commands and the construction of military roads? Seventeen Civil War generals had served in the Second Cavalry, twelve of them Confederate. Besides Johnston, Lee, and Hardee, some other Southern officers were Earl Van Dorn, E. Kirby Smith, John B. Hood, Charles W. Phifer, William P. Chambliss, Charles W. Field, and N. G. Evans—sounds like a roll call of Confederate stars. Noted Union generals were George W. Thomas, I. N. Palmer, George Stoneman, R. W. Johnson, and Kenner Garrad.

(Kenneth Franklin Neighbours, "Robert S. Neighbors in Texas, 1836–1859: A Quarter

It was rather an unfortunate experiment to mount infantry soldiers, many of whom had never been on a horse in their lives, to operate against the best horsemen in the United States—the Comanche.[3] Yet the United States Army tried it.

A sergeant of the regular army related an occurrence he professed to have witnessed. One day news came to Fort Duncan, near Eagle Pass, that a party of Indians was on the Río Grande about twenty miles below. Lieutenant Brewerton was sent out very promptly, at the head of a detachment of mounted infantry, to find and chastise the savages. He moved at a good pace. After having marched eight or ten miles, he passed a deep ravine. The lieutenant halted to verify. He found all the horses in their proper places, but about nine of the men were missing. A squad was sent back to the ravine; they found the bold riders right where they had tumbled from their horses. This is repeated as told by the sergeant.

In 1850, when Captain Ford was preparing to make a scout up the Nueces, he camped a few days just below Fort McIntosh. The lieutenant in temporary command of the post asked Ford when he expected to start. These inquiries became rather too frequent to promote pleasant intercourse. One day, just after the water call had been sounded, the captain was surprised to hear hooting, yelling, and uproarious laughing in his camp. He ascertained that all the din had been raised to excite the horses into a trot and to see the mounted infantrymen go to the ground like so many bags of sand. It was reported that some of those embryonic Indian fighters had been sent to the hospital for repairs. The anxiety of the lieutenant was explained.

As usual on such occasions, all the failures to do effective service were published and had in remembrance. The good fighting done by Captain Oakes, [John B.] Hood, Hazen, and others did not redeem the regular

---

Century of Frontier Problems," ms., II, 476; Thomas B. Van Horne, *The Life of Major-General George H. Thomas*, pp. 12 ff; Carl Coke Rister, *Robert E. Lee in Texas*, p. 23; Douglas Southall Freeman, *Robert E. Lee: A Biography*, I, 360 ff.)

[3] Dismounted, the Comanche was awkward and sluggish, but when he was on a horse he moved with remarkable ease and grace, as if he "took lordship from the animal who was lord of the prairies." War chiefs owned great herds of stallions—no mares, since maleness meant superiority—and each stallion carried his master's essence: when the Comanche broke a wild mustang, he roped and threw it and, covering its nostrils with his mouth, exhaled his breath and his controlling spirit into them. On horseback the Comanches were a formidable foe and few were the white riders who could match their peerless horsemanship.

(Paul Horgan, *Great River: The Rio Grande in North American History*, II, 848–849.)

army in the opinion of the people of Texas. [Major Earl] Van Dorn did a great deal to reverse the verdict of the Texians.

3

In the winter of 1857–1858 murders and robberies were regular occurrences on the whole line of the frontier from the Red River to El Paso and from El Paso to the mouth of the Río Grande. The sinuous line of settlements, here advanced and there drawn in, represented a distance of two thousand miles. The mounted troops serving in Texas were totally unable to cover and defend so long a line. It must be borne in mind that the pursuit of a band of marauding Indians was an undertaking requiring prudence, endurance, and fortitude in undergoing privations.

The Legislature of Texas determined to put citizens of the state into service. On January 26, 1858, the Legislature passed a bill authorizing Governor Runnels to call out 100 rangers and appropriating $70,000 for this purpose. The Austin *State Gazette* of January 30, 1858, had the annexed paragraphs:

The . . . one hundred and ninety additional men . . . together with those already in the field, are to be placed under the command of a Senior Captain . . . and Col. John S. Ford has received the appointment of Senior Captain.

We congratulate the people of the frontier upon the assurance this bill gives them of efficient protection against the hostile incursions of the Indians. To the untiring exertions of Senator Erath, whose sympathies were warmly interested in the measure, are they more indebted than to any one else for procuring the passage of this much needed act. Others gave efficient aid but with him it was a labor of love.

In another article the editor, in speaking of Ford's appointment, said:

It is an excellent appointment. The Captain had previously been recommended to the President, by members of both branches of the Legislature, by the Supreme and Federal Courts, and by many private citizens, for a field officer in the new regiment expected to be created at the present Congress. He is an old Indian fighter, and we predict that he will rid the frontier of all annoyance in the first campaign. All the State troops on the frontier will be in the field at the earliest moment. Enlistments will be made for six months. It is in the power of the Governor to extend the term if the exigency demands it.

Thus Texas, with little or no Federal patronage, is left by the Federal Government to protect herself from the savage foe, or to heedlessly stand by and witness the daily and brutal murder of our people.

These expressions were complimentary, but were calculated to lead the public to expect a great deal, perhaps too much, from the officer mentioned. It had the good effect of spurring him up in an effort to merit the encomiums lavished upon him.[4]

Governor Runnels' orders were simple and direct. "I impress upon you the necessity of action and energy. Follow any trail and all trails of hostile or suspected hostile Indians you may discover, and if possible, overtake and chastise them, if unfriendly."[5]

The recruiting was done as rapidly as was consistent with the good of the service. The intention was to get good men. When as many had joined as would authorize a company, an election was held. John S. Ford received a unanimous vote for captain, though he held a commission from Governor Runnels; Edward Burleson, Jr., was elected first lieutenant and William A. Pitts second lieutenant. He was also ex-officio paymaster.

About the first order issued was to secure payment to citizens aiding recruits in procuring outfits. Notes given for horses were privileged debts. Any amount in that connection placed on the payrolls by consent of the maker of the note was to operate as a stoppage against him; indebtedness for intoxicating spirits was not recognized as a proper cause of stoppage. The men of the company were prohibited from galloping their horses in the streets and doing things calculated to demean themselves as rangers.

There were state troops already in the field. Captain John H. Conner had a command on Pecan Bayou, near where the town of Brentwood now stands. Lieutenant T. C. Frost had charge of a detachment on duty in the same section of the country. Captain [Allison] Nelson had a detachment in Bosque County. Lieutenant [James H.] Tankersly was stationed in Comanche County. These were to be continued in the service, or not, at the discretion of the senior captain. A conference was had with Captain Henry E. McCulloch, and he agreed to raise a company for Ford's command. Among old Texas rangers there was little rivalry. Jealousy and envy were supplanted by a noble feeling of patriotism.

---

[4] The Dallas *Herald* was even more laudatory than the *Gazette* in speaking of Ford's appointment as senior captain.

> He is an old Indian fighter, familiar with their mode of warfare, and is never more at home, than when leading his gallant Rangers in a headlong charge against them. —We make no calculations for his defeat. Such a thing we regard as out of the question. The only fear is that the bird will have flown, and that he will find an empty camp. We await intelligence of the result of the expedition, with intense anxiety. If fully successful, it could be a fatal blow to the hostile Indians, and will effectually drive them from the Northern frontier.

[5] The editor has added Governor Runnels' orders to Captain Ford. A copy of Ford's commission (dated January 28, 1858) and the orders from Governor Runnels (dated January 28 and February 13, 1858) are in the Governors' Letters file.

It was decided before leaving Austin not to continue Captain Conner's company in the service for reasons satisfactory to the captain commanding. Whatever they were, it is useless to say. Captain Conner has since paid the debt of Nature, and a repetition of the causes for disbanding his company might be unjust to his memory. The detachment of Lieutenant Frost was also mustered out. The senior captain felt he might have done an injustice in the latter case, and in after years asked General McCulloch as a personal favor to do something for Frost. He was made a lieutenant colonel in McCulloch's regiment in 1861.

A very minute estimate was made of the probable cost of the campaign. The intention was, from the beginning, to carry the war into the hunting grounds of the Comanches and their confederate tribes, to let their families hear the crack of Texas rifles and feel the disagreeable effects of hostile operations in their own camps. No one advocated any but a civilized mode of warfare. As far as the braves were concerned—the savages who had visited our frontier and slaughtered our people, regardless of age and sex—with them it was war to the knife.

The supplies were purchased as fast as possible. The arms were the best procurable at the time upon short notice; the ammunition was good. The field transportation comprised sixteen pack mules with leathern cayaques—a kind of pannier of tanned leather, so constructed as to be waterproof. The cayaques, the girths, cruppers, and saddles were so well arranged that a mule might fall and roll over without displacing anything. It was a great point in those days to transport cartridges free from the effects of falling rain. It was a great comfort to have dry blankets at the end of a hard day's march. All these advantages were secured through the use of cayaques.

4

In February the command left Austin for the frontier. Lieutenant Burleson went by way of San Antonio to buy some articles not to be had in Austin. The captain and Lieutenant Pitts moved up the valley of the Colorado and Pecan Bayou and halted in the Chandler settlement. Here they were joined by Burleson.

At the solicitation of citizens on Pecan Bayou, a small detachment of six or seven men, in charge of a noncommissioned officer, was left to protect the families of that locality. This was done contrary to Captain Ford's conviction that men are not as apt to do as effective service in the neighborhood of their homes as when removed to some distance. This is the case where the soldier is in easy striking distance of members of his family. He is apt to become too much absorbed in his own affairs to be a vigilant observer of what is going on in camp and in its vicinity and is apt to spend time at home which should be devoted to scouting and other military duties. In order to test the matter, Ford left the detachment. No very active or efficient service was reported as done by them. On the contrary, it was asserted—and no proof to the contrary ever produced—that the Indians stole the pack mule turned over to them.

Lieutenant Burleson was directed to take the main body of the command and proceed to the mouth of Hubbard's Creek and to make a permanent camp near that point. It was about twenty miles from either the Comanche or the Brazos Indian Agencies, and nearly the same from Fort Belknap, and was but a little way from the main Brazos. The motive for the location was to give facilities for watching the Indians residing on the agency lands and learn whether they were implicated in the depredations being committed on the border settlers. In the event guilt had been conclusively proven on them, measures would have been taken to drive them away.

In order not to leave an enemy in our rear, Captain Ford and Lieutenant Pitts took charge of a detachment and scoured the valleys of the Pecan Bayou, the Jim Ned, and the Colorado River. They passed up the country following a range of hills running nearly parallel with the Pecan Bayou and a little to the north of it. They felt assured no savages were left lurking in that region .

An incident occurred at a camp between the Jim Ned and the Colorado River, which the rangers could not account for. When the twilight had about faded into darkness, a noise was heard resembling brisk firing, of apparently twenty men on a side. It seemed to be within less than half a mile of our camp. We mounted in hot haste, going at a gallop. The mimic firing ceased. We fired pistols a time or two and yelled without receiving an answer in any shape. We have never satisfied ourselves concerning the matter. On returning to camp, we took every precaution to prevent a surprise, and to give any party attempting to steal up on us a prodigal supply of lead. The remainder of the night passed off quietly.

On reaching our destination, we discovered that Lieutenant Burleson had misconstrued his orders and made the camp on the Clear Fork of the Brazos instead of on Hubbard's Creek. It was just above the confluence of the two streams. Wood, grass, and water were plentiful; the latter, however, proved to be unpalatable in hot weather. We named the place Camp Runnels, in honor of the governor of Texas.

We had been in camp but a short time when a party of hostile Indians made a descent on the Clear Fork. They were discovered by Lieutenant Burleson, who was returning to Fort Belknap, accompanied by two or three men. He galloped on to camp. A short while was spent in preparation; two detachments were soon in the saddle—one commanded by Burleson, the other by Pitts. They followed different trails—the Indians having divided, the better to throw the rangers off the track and to insure the escape of one party or the other. The pursuit was vigorous. There was a generous rivalry as to who should draw the first Indian blood. The rangers rode furiously, determined to overtake the foe and make him fight. It was a long and hard run. When the Comanche knew he was pursued, nothing but an inferior pony against a first-class horse ever caused him to be overrun. Pitts was starved in. He had nothing for rider or horse; the Indians were going faster than he was. He drew rein with reluctance.

Burleson was a little better prepared to remain out. He went further and stayed longer. There is a limit to human endurance. He thought he was gaining ground, made a desperate dash, failed to overtake, and turned for camp. In speaking of his last effort, he told of a creek, evidently more than twenty feet wide, which the Comanches passed at full speed; every horse of theirs had cleared it without breaking his gait. Burleson felt convinced his horses could not come up with animals able to make such leaps at such speed. The commands were much disappointed at not outmarching the "red devils." They felt that all had been done that could be done. The senior captain was at the Brazos Agency while these things were going on.

Captain Nelson and Lieutenant Tankersly joined us at Camp Runnels. Drilling was done daily. The Indian drill was not neglected. Firing at targets on horseback at all gaits was practiced. An espionage was kept up on the Indians of the agencies, particularly on the Comanches.

It was now growing late in March. Nothing had been heard of or from McCulloch in regard to his raising a company. From a private source Ford learned that Governor Runnels had gone to his plantation in northern Texas without giving McCulloch the requisite authority to raise and organize a company. Without this reinforcement, our force was not sufficiently strong to make a forward movement in the direction of the Comanche camps. Authority was given to Captain William Preston to raise a detachment of 25 or 30 men. He did so without delay.

The Brazos Agency people were doing a great deal to aid in getting up the expedition. Captain S. P. Ross was recruiting among the friendly Indians at his agency. It was decided that he should take the field in person. He discovered the Caddo chief, José Casa María, was holding back. He was an able Indian leader, brave, a hard fighter, but not cruel. It was his boast that in all the wars he had had with the whites, he had not killed or sanctioned the killing of a woman or a child or the burning of a house. The burning of Taylor's house back in 1831 was referred to. He denied he had had anything to do with it and brought witnesses to prove that it was done by renegade Kickapoos—refugees from the Indian Territory. He explained to Captain Ross that he had made a treaty with the Creeks and the Comanches and that the contracting parties had passed white wampum. The agreement was that one party should not make war upon the other without notice to the third party. He stated how the notice was to be given, saying:

"If I make war upon the Comanches without returning the white wampum to the Creeks, then I shall have Comanches and Creeks both to fight; it will be a violation of my promise."

Captain Ross told him he was right, but assured him he could, if he chose, send a messenger to the Creeks bearing back the white wampum. He started a trusty warrior on the mission. It was not many days before José Casa María waited on Ross and remarked: "I am ready now." The old man had gotten a message from the head of the Creek nation acknowledging the receipt of the white wampum. He began inducing his people to join the expedition.

Captain Ross suggested to the leading Indians of his agency the propriety of getting up a "war dance." It was cheerfully seconded. The momentous day came, to the definite delight of the copper-colored denizens of the reservation. The senior captain and some of the command went down to witness the performance. Preparations had been made on a proper scale to feast the dancers and the spectators. It was a scene well worth seeing, especially to those not conversant with Indian pastimes. The senior captain described the appearance of the gay warriors to T. Scott Anderson, secretary of state of Texas, in a letter, in substance as follows:

The war-dance was "grand, gloomy, and peculiar." Every participant had his own way in the matter; some sounded the fear-inspiring warwhoop; others crept along, cat-like, to pounce upon their astonished and demoralized foes; a squad would move up and attack an imaginary band of Comanches, and a shout of triumph would go up, loud enough to set a donkey's ears to ringing. Many sang in a style which would have crazed an old maiden music teacher. Every face had a daubing of rueful colors, intended to strike terror into the beholder. The sight of one was enough to stampede a regiment of dudes, and a battalion of school-marms. The impression made upon a civilized spectator may be illustrated thusly: an immense paint pot, hundreds of miles in depth and circumference, filled with colors of every conceivable hue and shade has been overturned, the contents have deluged the infernal regions; hell has taken an emetic, and cast up devils upon the earth, and here they are.

5

The note of preparation was sounding in Camp Runnels. Powder, caps, and cartridges were put up in a manner to assure easy transportation and quick distribution in case of emergency. Dr. Powhatan Jordan, our surgeon, got together a supply of instruments and medicines, adequate to meet all anticipated demands. A light wagon, drawn by four animals, was secured. Captain William Ford had arrived in camp with a light but strong ambulance; it was obtained for the use of the sick and wounded. A strong stake rope was provided for every animal in the command. A coil of rope was purchased to aid in patching gearing.

It was known our animals would have to live on grass. For the men there were quantities of bacon, flour, sugar, and coffee. We had an unusually plentiful supply of coffee and sugar for the number of men we had and for the probable length of time we were to be out. It was expected that buffalo meat would be substituted for bacon. It is a poor soldier who cannot get along on meat and no bread.

Lieutenant Burleson had business demanding his presence in the settlements and was reluctantly granted leave of absence. Captain William Ford was anxious to accompany us. He was 73 years of age, possessed of strong will, a good rider, and capable of enduring considerable fatigue.[6]

The command was in good spirits and eager. We moved on April 22, 1858. We numbered 102. After the junction with Captain Ross and his 113 Indians at the Cottonwood Springs, the command had a rather motley appearance. A number of Tonkawa Indians were on foot. They marched well.

At an encampment on the Little Wichita the Tonkawas went "a snaking." They were successful. Our friend, Don Francisco de la Garza Falcón, alias "Monkey," took it upon himself to add a black snake to the pile raised by the Tonks. It made them very mad. It appeared probable from the demonstrations of the incensed snake eaters that under other circumstances, the Don would have come to grief.

The locality where we crossed the Big Wichita was a dreary one. The sand, the apparent sterility of the soil, the abhorrent taste of the salty water combined to produce a gloomy feeling. Some of us spoke of the Dead Sea and Sodom and Gomorrah.

When we reached Red River on April 29, the prospect of crossing was not encouraging. The stream was a succession of rivulets running be-

---

[6] Captain William Ford was Rip's father, who had moved to Texas after annexation and had settled in Travis County.

tween long beds of sand, dry in the middle. The wetted portion, not under water, was quicksand; in places it would quiver under the feet of the horses. The Indians told us a halt of a few minutes on one of these unstable spots would bog a horse almost irretrievably and endanger the safety of a man. Captain Ford seemed to lose heart. He thought of being unable to cross, of failure, and of its disagreeable attendants.

A camp was pitched on the north bank of the river, at what looked like the mouth of a creek. The water was fresh and tasted quite good. Lieutenant Tankersly was officer of the guard and was in charge of the two wagons, the ambulance, and the 15 pack mules. To the surprise and joy of every one the cry was heard—"here comes the wagons." Tankersly had unloaded the vehicles and transported the loading across on horseback. The packs of heavily-laden mules were divided and partly carried over by horsemen. It was well done.

We had no trouble in passing creeks and ravines having one bluff and one shelving bank. We had picks, spades, and grubbing hoes; it took but a little while to dig a trench in a bank wide enough for a horse to pass down. The team would be taken out, the wagon unloaded and let down by ropes, and all would be passed over in a short space of time.

The march from Red River to Otter Creek was begun on May 7. This rather pretty little stream runs for several miles at the base of the Wichita Mountains and empties into Red River. We camped near the mouth, remaining two nights and a day, according to recollection. Our Indian advance guard, flankers, and spies were often twenty miles ahead or a like distance on either side of us. We had to march so as to enable them to reach us at the different encampments and report. The work they were doing was hard on horse and man. We were now at a point where it was necessary to ascertain who might be within fifteen or twenty miles of us in any direction. We had the desired information before breaking camp.

There was a considerable stir among the Indians. They attributed the excitement to the fact that they had found an Indian of a new tribe. They were directed to bring him to headquarters. A mulatto man was marched up. He had been riding a fine mare, pretended he was lost, and had been travelling down Red River instead of up it. He had run away from his owner, and had been trying to find the Comanches. He had cut steaks from the mare he was riding and ate them. He was secured and eventually sent back to his owner, a farmer residing on Red River.

We were in the buffalo region. We ascended hills and became spectators of a buffalo chase on the broad plains around. It was grand to hear the cry: "Ton-ne-hah!" "Ton-ne-hah!"—the Caddo word for buffalo—see the Indians sally forth, get the wind of a large herd and charge into them. There were whooping, firing, a mingling of horses and buffalo, bending of bows, putting of lances in rest, the full, rumbling, thunder-like sound of a mighty host rushing to the combat, all saluting the ear at once. The cunning and practiced Indian would force his horse up to the side of a buffalo, with his gun across his lap; he would fire at the distance of a few feet. Then his nimble-footed horse had to be turned aside to avoid the thrust of the wounded and maddened animal. The feat was not so easy; a buffalo in good trim can run nearly as fast as an ordinary horse for about two miles. To be caught and lifted, horse and all, upon the horns of so huge a beast, tossed like a feather many feet in the air, to fall all mixed up with your four-footed companion, perhaps "with the bottom rail on top," to almost feel the short black horns goring you, to disentangle yourself from your rigging and bury yourself in the grass and dwarf your precious body behind a clump of small bushes, to watch the red-eyed brute as he beats a retreat, or falls to the earth: these, all these, constitute the incidents of a run after buffalo.

The successful hunt brings its pleasurable results: the juicy tongue, the fat "round" from the hump, and other favorite pieces, roasting slowly and steadily; but beyond all, the marrow bones browning and simmering would tempt the appetite of confirmed vegetarians. Bring to the feast the sauce of work and hunger, and you may talk yourself hoarse of Parisian cooks and epicurean dainties: they would have had no charms for the woodsman.

6

In various councils with our Indian chiefs and captains, they invariably marked out maps on the ground, sometimes on paper, and in no instance did they fail to designate the North Fork of Red River as the main fork. They called it Red River. Most of them were beyond middle age, and for many years had hunted and campaigned in the region watered by Red River. Some of them had lived on its banks.

The Indian commanders were: Jim Pockmark, captain of the Caddos and Anadarkos, and his second in command, José Casa María; Placido, chief of the Tonkawas, and his second in command, O'Quinn; Ah-qua-quash—Shot Arm—captain of the Wacos; Jim Linney, captain of the Shawnees and Delawares; and Nid-e-wats, captain of the Tahuacanos. In addition to these were Caddo John, Chul-e-quah, Jem Logan, and others, many of whom spoke English. Then there was Keechi, our spy, who had camped and hunted with the Comanches for a long while and who spoke their language fluently. He was quite noted as an Indian linguist.

These Indians were men of more than ordinary intellect who possessed minute information concerning the geography and topography of that country—of all of Texas, most of Mexico, and all of the Indian Territory and adjacent regions.

We marched up Red River several days after leaving our Otter Creek encampment, passing a marker known as Marcy's Corner.[7] Captain Ross examined it. He is of opinion that the names of Marcy, Neighbors, and others were on it.

On reaching the gypsum region we had an opportunity to test its nauseous waters. We made a deflection to the right and struck the waters of the False Washita. Our scouts reported a large trail, no doubt made by Comanches. Our Indians counted their camp fires and asserted the party must have four hundred warriors. The trail was three or four days old. We proceeded to follow it, using great caution and circumspection. Our march was down the False Washita. The Indian scouts and spies made reconnaissances in every direction. On the evening of May 10 the spies brought in a couple of Comanche arrow heads, extracted from a buffalo found wounded, which they killed.[8]

We became convinced that we were now in the vicinity of a large body of the enemy. Every precaution was taken to avoid being discovered and every possible execution made to find their camps. The next day, May 11, the spies reported having seen Comanches running buffalo, and they likewise had gotten a correct notion of the course to their camp by watching pack animals as they transported buffalo meat to it. The captain prepared his force to move upon the enemy without delay. He left a small guard of rangers and muleteers under Captain William Ford at the make-shift camp, and at 2 o'clock P.M. marched with one hundred Americans and Captain Ross' command of one hundred and thirteen friendly Indians. When we reached the Fort Smith and Santa Fé road we saw Comanches moving about in the valley beyond the "divide," apparently unconscious of our proximity. When they had gone we resumed our march, confining ourselves to the low grounds and ravines to keep out of sight. We halted at dusk, camped and sent forward some Indians to overtake Keechi, our spy, who was trailing the Comanches. Unfortunately they missed him, and he remained outside of camp until daylight on the morning of May 12, when he joined us on the march.

Our plan had been to approach the enemy camp under the cover of

---

[7] Marcy's Corner had been made by Captain R. B. Marcy and Captain G. B. McClellan who had explored the Red River region in 1852.

[8] The memoirs account of the Canadian River Campaign, from the point where Ford started down the False Washita, is disconnected and in places wholly obscure; therefore the editor has integrated with it Ford's lucidly-written report to Governor Runnels, dated May 22, 1858, and located in the Governors' Letters file.

darkness and, just before daylight, to send in a party of our Indians to stampede the horses, the rest of the command then to attack the enemy in a surprise charge. Our plan was now frustrated, since the sun was coming up: we were compelled to march upon the foe in open day. At 7 o'clock A.M. a small camp of five lodges was discovered and taken. The Tonks remained, demolished the camp, took some prisoners, and mounted their footmen. Two Comanches fled towards the Canadian; we followed at full gallop, knowing that they were hurrying to inform their people of our approach.

After a run of three miles at nearly full speed, a large encampment was visible from a hill top, about three miles distant, on the Cherokee side of the Canadian River. We saw the two Comanches crossing it and followed at a run. We fortunately came to a good crossing on the river. The stream was notoriously boggy. We passed through it nearly at a gallop. Sergeant Bob Cotter's famous charger, Old Wooly, struck his forefeet against a rock, nearly turned a somerset, and plunged with Bob, weapons, and all into the water. Bob quickly recovered his arms, mounted Wooly, and was at his post before the white troops had formed line of battle.

The friendly Indians were on our right and in front. They were put there to make the Comanches believe they had only Indians and bows and arrows to contend against. The head Comanche chief, Po-bish-e-quash-o —Iron Jacket—sallied out to meet our Indians. He was a great medicine man, professed to blow arrows aside from their aim. He would move forward a short distance, describe a circle, and expel his breath from his mouth with great force. He was followed by warriors who trusted their safety in his armor. He was destined to fail: our Indians were armed mostly with Mississippi rifles and six-shooters; only a few had bows and arrows. The mail-clad and gorgeously-caparisoned Comanche chieftain moved in, seeming confident of being invulnerable. About six rifle shots rang on the air: the chief's horse jumped about six feet straight up and fell. Another barrage followed, and the Comanche medicine man was no more.

Meantime Captain Ford's rangers had charged a body of Comanches at the main camp. They intended to make a stand at this point, but the rangers pressed them gallantly. The Indians fled in every direction. Our right wing, in charge of the writer and Lieutenant William A. Pitts, moved straight through the camp and poured in a galling fire upon the retreating enemy. Lieutenant Allison Nelson in command of our left wing, assisted by Lieutenant William G. Preston, charged to the left and pursued the flying Comanches with vigor and effect.

The fight was now general and extended, very soon, over a circuit of six miles in length and more than three in breadth. It was, in fact, almost a series of single combats. Squads of rangers and Indians were pursuing the enemy in every direction. The Comanches would occasionally halt and endeavor to make a stand; however, their efforts were unavailing. They were forced to yield the ground to our men in every instance. The din of the battle had rolled back from the river—the groans of the dying and the cries of frightened women and children mingled with the reports of firearms and the shouts of the men as they rose from hill top, from thicket, and from ravine.

It was not an easy matter to distinguish Indian warriors from squaws. The dress of the male and female does not differ greatly. The woman has a short buckskin tunic, wears her hair shorter, and her moccasins are somewhat different.

Will Howard encountered a young brave about 17 or 18 years old. He was mounted on a good horse, and had three or four children with him. Howard fired, killed the youth and the horse. We annoyed him by telling that he killed a whole family. Some said it was a woman.

The second in command of the Comanches had now rushed into the conflict with the friendly Indians. A shot from the Shawnee captain, Chul-le-quah, closed the Comanche's career. The Comanches between the camp and the river were all killed or driven from the field, and our red allies sent up a wild shout of triumph. By direction of Captain Ross, a portion of them held the camp of the enemy.

The rangers and the friendly Indians still pressed the Comanches, nor did they stop pursuing until their failing horses admonished them that they could do no more. Between twelve and one o'clock the firing had almost ceased; and squad after squad of the troops were returning to the Comanche camp, bringing with them horses, prisoners, and other trophies of victory. Captain Ross had very properly suggested to Lieutenant Nelson the propriety of keeping the men well together, and when Ford returned from the pursuit he found a large proportion of the men drawn up in order of battle.

The Comanches had another large encampment three or four miles above on the Canadian. They had heard the firing, embodied, and were coming on the run.

Two of our rangers—Oliver Searcy and Robert Nickles—who had pursued the retreating Indians alone, suddenly ran headlong into this mass of new Comanches, turned and hightailed it for their own lines. Searcy told Nickles not to gallop, but to halt occasionally, try to kill some Indians, menace them, hold them in check, and they might finally reach a detachment of rangers and safety. When Nickles got to running he could not be stopped. The charging Indians lanced him. Searcy continued his tactics: fired, reloaded, eventually abandoned his horse, kept in ravines, gradually nearing the river. The friendly Indians heard the firing and went to the rescue. Searcy acted with prudence, coolness, and gallantry.

Lieutenant Nelson was sent out with his detachment to bury Nickles. He returned and reported that a heavy body of Indians threatened to attack him. He deemed it dangerous to attempt the burial, as the probable sacrifice of life resulting would be a useless waste of human blood.

The new body of Comanches now came into view; they were evidently playing for an advantage and their maneuvers induced our Indians to believe them very strong. Our allies proposed to draw them out, and requested Ford to keep his rangers in line to support them, if necessary.

One of our Indians rode out and told the Comanches:

"We have nothing up there to fight for. We have some of your women and children captives, also your wigwams, your buffalo meat, and your horses. You come down. You have something here to fight for."

The Comanches descended from the hill to accept their proffered invitation. With yells and menaces and every species of insulting gesture and language, they tried to excite the reserve Indians into some act of rashness by which they could profit. A scene was now enacted beggaring description. It reminded one of the rude and chivalrous days of knight-errantry. Shields and lances and bows and head dresses, prancing steeds and many minutias were not wanting to compile the resemblance. And when the combatants rushed at each other with defiant shouts, nothing save the piercing report of the rifle varied the affair from a battlefield of the middle ages. Half an hour was spent in this without much damage to either party. A detachment of rangers was advanced to reinforce the friendly Indians, and the Comanches quitted the field, and the imposing pageant vanished from the view like a mimic battle upon the stage.

It was determined to leave the Indians in possession of the prisoners and captured horses and to hurl the rangers upon the Comanches. Ford's men made a forward movement, if not with the precision of practiced veterans, yet with as much coolness and bravery. The enemy instantly began the retreat. Ford directed Lieutenant Pitts to show himself and his detachment upon the hill with the intention to steal upon them. Lieutenant Nelson anticipated me and passed around the base of the eminence at a run. The untimely arrival of the Tonkawa Indians upon our left flank prevented the complete success of the maneuver.

The Comanches broke and fled in various directions. We pursued as fast as our jaded horses could carry us. After a run of two and a half or three miles Ford saw that he could effect no more and called off his men. In this second conflict the enemy lost seven killed and left on the ground, and a number were wounded. Our loss was one Waco Indian killed and one ranger wounded—George W. Paschal, Jr.

It was now 2 o'clock P.M. and we had been running our horses much of the time since 7 o'clock that morning. The senior captain determined to march to his camp that night, fearing the Indians might ascertain its locality and overpower the weak guard left to protect it. We learned from a captured woman that Buffalo Hump was twelve miles below us with a considerable body of warriors, and we knew fugitives had reached his camp and notified him of our presence.

As we moved back through the Comanche camp, we saw the fine buffalo robes, the eatables, and the goods. The dead were lying around. Some of them were minus hands or feet. When we looked at the empty Tonk saddles we knew where they had gone. They had a feast soon after the fight.

The march back to camp finished the toilsome labors of the day. Our total loss in the fight was 2 killed and 3 wounded; the Comanches lost about 76 killed and a great many wounded.

Captain Ross expressed the opinion that the friendly Indians were satisfied with what they had done and with the number of horses captured. Ross thought, perhaps, it would be wise to let well enough alone. In the division of the captured horses our Indian allies secured the lion's share. No one cognizant of the number of warriors the seven bands of the Comanches could bring into the field and of the accessions they would receive from other tribes was of the opinion that our small force could maintain itself very long in this dangerous country. Moreover, our horses were worn down by service, our rations of meat had been exhausted, and there appeared but little prospect of effecting anything by remaining longer; therefore, it was decided to leave on the morning of May 13 for Camp Runnels, which we reached on the 21st of May, after an absence of thirty days.

7

When the rangers and friendly Indians were returning, someone asked O'Quinn, the Tonk war captain, a question.

"O'Quinn, you have eaten all sorts of people, what nationality do you think makes the best eating?"

He replied promptly, giving the preference to "a big fat Dutchman" he and his men killed on the Guadalupe River in 1849. This answer got O'Quinn into trouble. Billy Holzinger rushed at him, six-shooter in hand, wanting to know if O'Quinn was "making fun of his countrymen?" It took force to curb the irate German. To pacify him was not an easy task. His rotund form might have created a suspicion that he carried the drum so often reported missing. He resented any allusion to that possibility. It, however, dawned upon Holzinger's mind that O'Quinn had told the truth about a crime which came near getting his own scalp lifted in that same raid.

Captain Ford had picked up a young boy while returning from the pursuit of the foe routed early in the morning of May twelfth. He was reputed to be the son of the chief, Iron Jacket. He was four or five years old at the time of capture. It was not long until he expressed a preference for the American mode of living.

"Me go back to Comanches? They got no sugar, no coffee, nothing but buffalo meat and pecans. No go."

When in the presence of the agency Comanches, he was sullen and silent. One night he hid out, fearing they would carry him to his tribe. He did not show himself the next day until after his countrymen had gone. When last heard of, he was in Harrison County with the relatives of Mrs. Calhoun, by whom he was raised.

8

Before setting out on the campaign, Captain Ross requested the Reverend Mr. Tackitt, an old frontiersman, to visit the Brazos Agency and preach to the Indians. He did so, Jim Shaw acting as interpreter. The Reverend prayed for the success of the expedition and for the safe return of those about to engage in it.

After we returned safe and victorious, a Tahuacano captain was loud in his praises of the efficacy of the American man's "medicine."

"It must have been mighty strong," the Indian said. "We killed seventy-six men; some were not counted. We took sixty prisoners, 400 horses, many fine buffalo robes, and other nice things. We lost two men killed, and four or five wounded. He is a wonderful medicine man."

The night before Ross and his many-colored force reached the Brazos Agency, a messenger was sent ahead to herald their coming. When the imposing pageant of men in grotesque apparel, bearing trophies of victory—lances and shields, bows and arrows, hundreds of horses, and sixty prisoners (half grown boys, women, and children, since it was seldom a Comanche warrior surrendered)—reached the agency buildings, shout after shout went up. The women, in their finest dresses, met the dusky warriors with songs and dances. It was indeed a day of rejoicing, reminding one of the reception of Saul and David from the field of Schocoh. The prisoners were taken to the store, dressed, and told to go where they pleased. It was reported that a Comanche woman had been whipped by the Tonks. She was taken away from them by the other Indians, as a rebuke for mistreating a prisoner. The Comanche captives were distributed among the other tribes; many of them married and seemed contented.

One feature of the day's doings was the presentation to Mrs. Ross, by a warrior, of a fine pony which had but one gait, a pace. The brave said Mrs. Ross had acted as agent during the captain's absence, had distributed rations, kept the women and children from suffering hunger, and as a recognition of her valuable services, he, in the name of his comrades, presented her the pony. She accepted the present.

That evening Captain Ross was waited upon by the Indian rain king. Ross inquired how it was he had failed to bring rain during his absence, as the Indian had promised. The rain king said he had done all he could to cause copious showers to fall. He succeeded in procuring an auspicious cloud and brought it over the agency and all hearts were gladdened. The infernal Tonks, always bent on mischief, had stronger medicine than his and turned the cloud away. The Tonks were the black beasts of the agency and were made responsible for many such happenings.

[In his official report to Governor Runnels, written at Camp Runnels on May 22, 1858, Ford said:]

The conduct of the men of my command was characterized by obedience, patience, and perseverance. They behaved, while under fire, in a gallant and soldier like manner and I think that they have fully vindicated their right to be recognized as Texas Rangers of the old stamp. . . . In justice to our Indian allies I beg leave to say they behaved most excellently on the field of battle. They deserve well of Texas and are entitled to the gratitude of the frontier people.

[Ford then told the governor that this expedition had decided several questions:] Indians can be pursued and caught in the Buffalo region,—the country beyond Red river can be penetrated and held by white men, and the Comanches can be followed, overtaken, and beaten, provided the pursuers will be laborious, vigilant, and are willing to undergo privations.

The troops were mustered out at the end of six months. The cost of the expedition was $35,000. Nelson and his men had a barbecue given for them at Stephensville, Erath County. The company raised at Austin moved down the country to Lampasas Springs. This company was in charge of Captain Ford, Lieutenant Burleson and Lieutenant Pitts. The citizens of Austin gave them a barbecue too.

Twenty-eight years have passed since this campaign was made. The writer has lived to mourn the loss of many of those he led. They were men of gallantry, fortitude, and untiring energy. They were excellent shots, and seldom missed their aim. The loss sustained by the Comanches proves the fact.

It may be proper to say that the cordial relations existing between Lieutenant Allison Nelson and Captain Ford were interrupted. At the present period the writer cannot positively state the causes leading to the temporary estrangement. He is willing to shoulder his part of the wrongs which may have been committed. Nelson died during the Confederate War, leaving a good record as an officer. The writer has long since buried every unpleasant feeling in that connection in the deep sea of forgetfulness.[9]

---

[9] The trouble between Ford and Nelson came about when Ford, in a council with his officers, decided to break up the Comanche Reserve if he could catch the Comanches in the act of depredating. He planned to send out patrols to watch them, but he told the officers to swear that they would keep the operations a secret. As they did so one remarked that a trail found from a scene of plunder to the reserve would be proof enough.

"That thing can be managed," Lieutenant Nelson said, "the trail can be made."

Ford grabbed him by the collar and exploded: "No, Sir, that will not do, I am responsible to the state, and to public opinion, and I will take no step in the matter, unless I am backed by facts, and of such a character as to justify me before the public. I am willing to punish the Comanches, if they are found guilty; but I am not disposed to do so unjustly and improperly."

At that Nelson shrugged his shoulders and walked off. Ford and his officers continued the discussion but reached no conclusions as to what should be done with the Comanche Reserve.

Sometime later, Indian Agent John R. Baylor, who hated Neighbors, collaborated with Nelson in an attempt to remove "the Major" as supervising Indian agent and to put Nelson in his place—"I want Nelson in the place of Neighbors," Baylor declared, "and will do all in my power to aid him."

Captain Ford warned Nelson to stay out of Neighbors' and Baylor's feud, but the lieutenant, with dreams of name and position, remarked that he would do what he pleased and then broke his promise to keep quiet about Ford's secret observation of the Comanches.

So Baylor and Nelson continued their reckless campaign to ruin Neighbors. They charged that under his direction the agency Indians were scalping and raping white women and murdering their husbands and sons. If only Neighbors would die a premature death, Baylor would personally erect a tombstone with the epithet, "Vive la humbug!" and then would personally lead a citizen posse to the reservation and teach the bloody savages a lesson they would never forget.

Meanwhile Neighbors had gone to Washington to warn the Secretary of the Interior that if a brutal Indian war was to be averted, the government must stop these outrageous charges and take positive steps to maintain a peaceful coexistence between white and red.

At this point, Nelson, like a true conspirator who figured he had gained all he could from his allies, suddenly disparaged both sides in an attempt to portray himself as a chaste and moral servant caught in the middle of two battling extremists. The lieutenant wrote President Buchanan that while Neighbors was an obnoxious fool and utterly incompetent, Nelson had nothing to do with that vile movement, directed by untrustworthy

Captain Ford wrote a communication to Governor Runnels on May 23 urging him to call out a regiment of rangers to end the Indian war. Ford put forward many reasons, supported by facts, favoring the move. Then and only then would the Comanches sue for peace and agree to be put on a reservation. It was an appeal for the protection of the frontier by aggressive action and was sanctioned by humanity, good policy, and all the great principles which govern statesmen and patriots and Christians. Self-protection is the first law of Nature. The blood of our murdered citizens cried from the ground for revenge. The privations of our captured sons, the slaves of savage masters, the shrieks of our outraged sisters and daughters, the concubines of barbarians by force, and the tortures of the lash, the lasso, and the inhuman punishment of being dragged at the gallop through prickly pear: all these spoke to us with trumpet tongues and called for vengeance.

---

citizens with "sinister" motives, to get himself appointed supervising Indian agent.

When Captain Ford heard about this, he condemned Nelson as "a man who had and is endeavoring to subserve his own ends, and thought it necessary to play a double part to effect his object."

Everything was now so confusing that Washington sent out a special investigator to ascertain the truth about Neighbors' conduct and that of his enemies. In a court of inquiry, the investigator found that Baylor's and Nelson's charges were nothing less than false and malicious intimidation and concluded that although the agency system on the whole was sound and effectual, it would be wise to move the Comanches to the western Choctaw Country in the Indian Territory (present-day Oklahoma)—a move that Neighbors had recommended long before. Said Captain Ford of these happenings: "The ordeal through which Major Neighbors has passed endorses him. He needs no commendation from any quarter."

(Ford's affidavit to Thomas T. Hawkins, Austin, November 22, 1858, Indian Affairs Office, Letters Received, ms.; Dallas *Herald*, April 1, 1858; Neighbours, "Neighbors," ms., II, 505–556.)

XX

>>

SLEEPLESS VIGILANCE

While Captain Ford was still at Camp Runnels, he mustered into service a detachment of men, twenty-five if memory is correct, commanded by Lieutenant William Marlin, an old frontiersman and Indian fighter. They were stationed in a position calculated to cover and protect the settlements between the two Indian agencies. These people, as was said earlier, had been induced to believe the agency Indians were implicated in depredating on the frontier by hostile Indians, and it excited some settlers so much that they "forted up" or left their homes. Their position was by no means enviable. It is true there were regular troops at Fort Belknap, yet the distances from where each settler lived to that post was so great that the Indians might kill and scalp them all before the news of their being in the country could reach the commander at the fort.

By the time winter of 1858 had set in, news—authentic news—had reached the governor that murders and robberies had been committed along the western and northwestern frontier. Colonel James Bourland received orders to raise a company, which he did promptly. He was stationed between the Trinity and Red rivers.

Delegations of citizens from frontier counties and those contiguous to them waited on Governor Runnels and asked for protection. The governor favored frontier protection, but he was beset by a desire to spend as little money as possible. He had been bitten by the economic bug.

Believing the emergency demanded a larger force, the governor authorized John S. Ford to raise a company of volunteers on November 2, 1858. The Austin *State Gazette* of November 27, 1858, is quoted:

On Tuesday and Wednesday last, Captain Ford's Rangers, in two detachments, broke camp near this place, and started for the frontier. We believe the material of the company is good. The youthful ages of many of them will not disqualify them for the duties of good soldiers. The boys are all good riders and expert marksmen. We are confident they will sustain the high character for chivalry, courage, fiery energy, daring enterprise, and obedience to orders, which in times past on many a bloody field, have distinguished the conduct of the young men of Texas. Their captain, John S. Ford, knows how to unite the prudence and system of the regular officer, with the zeal, activity, and bravery of the high-spirited volunteer—while his sleepless vigilance will always guard against surprise; his rapid movements, enterprising and energetic spirit, and impetuous charges, will destroy or scatter his savage enemies. The first lieutenant, [John] Gibbon, is unknown to us, but he has a fine reputation as a soldier. The second lieutenant, Aaron Burleson, is a very young man, a citizen of this county. He is a nephew of the late celebrated Gen. Ed. Burleson, and a son of the late Jacob Burleson, who fell, gallantly fighting, and refusing to retreat, in the well-known disastrous Brush Fight with Indians. Aaron is a brave young fellow, and distinguished himself in the Piedras Negras expedition, by killing an Indian chief in the battle. We know this young officer well, and believe that he will prove worthy of his brave and distinguished family.

A high encomium.

2

The command moved in the direction of Mercer's Creek in Comanche County, and remained in camp there a day or two. A permanent encampment was pitched a few miles west of that point and was called Camp Leon. After the completion of a stockade enclosure, a commissary building, and a guardhouse, the work of drilling commenced. Previous to that an Indian alarm was sounded and an effort made to strike the trail, which failed. The hostiles made their way to Cora, in Comanche County, where they stole horses. Captain Ford thought the Indians would go out west-wardly, so he moved in that direction and scoured the country. They went nearly in the direction of the mouth of the Pecan. Captain Williams, commanding a company of minute men, overtook and defeated them.

Scouts were made in various directions and no Indians discovered. A letter from the Brazos Agency induced Captain Ford to march to that point. The first intent was to pass through what was called Buchanan County (since named Stephens County). The sand encountered caused a deflection to be made to the left to the "Old Mercer Road." The march was made upon this road.

On arriving at the Brazos Agency, we learned that the Comanches had recently stolen horses from the friendly Indians. An expedition was organized to follow the robbers. The command consisted of rangers and agency Indians. The Indians had serviceable arms. The rangers were armed with Minnie rifles, which carried an oblong ball at a range of over half a mile; and they carried a ball close to the mark, when well directed. They were muzzle loaders, very long and heavy for service on horseback.

3

Before leaving the agency, the rangers heard that Major Van Dorn of the regular army, stationed at Camp Radziminski on Otter Creek, had expressed a wish to have the assistance of troops other than his own in making a campaign against hostile Indians.

This rumor was particularly interesting to Ford, because a force of agency Indians had gone on the trail of the horse-stealers, and the captain entertained a doubt of his ability to handle the Indians properly. He concluded to march to Camp Radziminski and get up an expedition jointly with Major Van Dorn. A communication to that effect was for-warded to the major. While on the march, Captain Ford learned to his surprise that Major Van Dorn had left his camp to make a scout against the hostiles.[1] Ford saw that he had made a blunder. It was then too late

---

[1] After the Canadian River Expedition, Van Dorn and other regular officers accused Shapley Ross of favoring volunteers over the regular army—Ross' Indians had after all never helped the regulars fight the Comanches. Ross was irate. He had offered his help many times before, but always had been turned down. Any time the regulars were ready to undertake a campaign like Captain Ford's, Ross would certainly help them. Thus when Van Dorn announced that his company—without the help of Ford's menagerie of undisciplined volunteers—would invade the Comanche homeland, Ross joined him with 125 warriors from the Brazos Reserve. Ross, however, relinquished field command of the Indians in favor of his son Sullivan, who had only recently returned from school.

Van Dorn's mixed command moved from Camp Radziminski in September, 1858, and engaged a band of Comanches some ninety miles out. In the fight—a victory for the United States Army—Van Dorn and Sul Ross were both severely wounded, and the

to find the trail of the Comanche horse thieves. The command kept the road to Radziminski.

Just before reaching that point the captain with a few men went ahead in order to procure some needed supplies. He reached the fort about March 1, 1859. That night a terrible snow storm occurred. The cold was intense. Two of the rangers' horses froze to death, or were so reported. The rangers were encamped eight or ten miles from Radziminski.

The cold forced Van Dorn to return to the fort. He did not speak encouragingly of a joint campaign. Nevertheless, we decided to move to another camp on Otter Creek, this time only four or five miles above Radziminski. The Wichita Mountains were in close proximity. A level prairie, covered with grass at least a foot high, led off from them. The moon was full. The view at night was grand and picturesque.

One night, all except the sentinels had gone to bed. Not far from the captain's pallet two rangers were bunked. One of them was Tom Bowles, who from boyhood was fonder of devilment than his books, and was not a whit improved by attaining stalwart manhood. His bedfellow was blessed with a fruitful imagination and a flow of words. He descanted on the clearness of the night, the brightness of the stars, the beauty of the landscape, and much of that sort of thing. Bowles would occasionally drawl a drowsy-sounding assent. The speaker launched out on a rather new but kindred theme.

"I wonder why it is that lovers are so fond of such scenes, why they delight to walk arm in arm in the balmy light of the glorious moon?"

"O, I don't know," Bowles mumbled out. "I suppose it is because they are damn fools and don't love good sleep."

The romantic ranger subsided.

Nothing of moment happened while we remained on Otter Creek. We had a buffalo hunt on several occasions and consequently had a supply of good meat. One day an unfortunate ranger, [G. T.] Waugh, set fire to the grass by accident. It required hard work to prevent the entire destruction of everything we had. It was rather amusing to hear our Indians yell out "Yahoo!" "Yahoo!" the instant they discovered the flames mounting into the air. Waugh got the nickname of "Yahoo." It stuck.

---

expeditionary forces had to return to the fort. This successful expedition restored the Brazos Indians in the eyes of the critical white public and, according to Van Dorn, proved that whatever volunteers could do, regulars could do better. Ford discusses this expedition in Appendix I.

(Van Dorn's report, October 5, 1858, in Dallas *Herald*, October 10, 1858.)

4

The idea of a joint campaign was abandoned as hopeless. Captain
Ford adhered to his resolution to hunt up a fight. He moved from Camp
Radziminski with more than fifty men, nearly half of them Indians. His
stay had been pleasant. He made the acquaintance of Lieutenant Fitzhugh
Lee, Lieutenant [Manning M.] Kimmel, and other regular officers who
were polite and agreeable.

Our march was in a westerly direction. We crossed Red River a few
miles above the point where the Radziminski road crossed that stream.
We moved up the river some distance, left it, and struck the Pease River.
We followed it a day or two and then turned to the left. These marches
were made over an open country having little timber except on the banks
of streams. The plains were almost level in many places and were covered
with young grass. Large herds of buffalo were visible in every direction.
When standing on an elevation affording a view over ten or twelve miles
in every direction, the men estimated they could see 30,000 buffalo—
perhaps an exaggeration. They appeared, however, to be grazing close
together. The number was immense.

This led to a conclusion that the public was a long time in admitting
as true. If that section, and the Staked Plains above it, afforded grass to
sustain so many thousands of buffalo, would it not afford sustenance for
many more domestic animals? The soil upon which such grass grew
would produce wheat and other products to subsist men. If the Indians
occupied these areas all the summer hunting buffalo, there must have
been water, and wood, or substitutes for wood, available for themselves
and families. On these facts and deductions Captain Ford expressed a
firm conviction that the territory in question would in time become the
great wheat-growing region of Texas. He has always insisted that an
American is equal to an Indian in any good work and can live wherever
the Indian can. In fact, he claims that an enlightened, civilized, and
Christianized man is superior to a savage.

5

We proceeded cautiously; every foot of ground over which we passed
was examined carefully. Chul-e-quah had charge of the front scout, or
spies. He was never too far ahead to convey or receive a signal. Jim Linney
was with the advance guard. The main body regulated their movements
by Chul-e-quah. We were where the Comanches were known to be in
force, where the buffalo were feeding, the season not being sufficiently

advanced for them to go upon the Staked Plains. Our lives depended upon our vigilance. One false step, one failure to be watchful on guard, might have proved fatal to all. A trusty ranger or two always accompanied Chul-e-quah.

We were beginning to hope for success. We were traversing an open prairie country south of the Pease River and saw no indications of a scarcity of water. Jim Linney stopped, and was evidently receiving communications from Chul-e-quah in the sign language of the Indians. All at once Linney changed the course of marching almost at an angle of ninety degrees. This astonished the captain.

"Hallo, Jim," Ford called out. "What does this mean?"

"Chul-e-quah say, no water up there."

It was not believed, but what could be done? Here was what was tantamount to a declaration that our allies were not going to move in that direction any further. It meant "To your tents, O red men." Without them we were too few to effect anything good. The hunt was reluctantly abandoned.

One of the rangers with Chul-e-quah was [George W.] Morris, who rejoiced in the aristocratic soubriquet of "Chicken." About a year after this expedition the captain questioned Chicken and got the truth:

"The signs we saw convinced us we were near a large band of Comanches. Chul-e-quah said it was too big for us to whip, but if we told you of it, you would fight anyhow. So we turned down Beaver Creek."

We would have whipped them; the captain was sure of it; the Comanches had never fought against long-range guns and would have been demoralized by them. Chul-e-quah was right in his conclusions. The captain had gone to hunt a fight: he could be satisfied with nothing else. He had no intention to count noses. He meant to "pitch in," satisfied that the pluck of his men and the superiority of his arms would insure success.

Chicken was one of Nature's noblemen. He needed a little more education to fit him to fill high positions. He was a friend whom nothing could swerve from the strictest adherence to those he esteemed. He was brave as a lion, self-possessed under all circumstances, and of sound judgment. He was an unerring shot who aimed at a man as he would at a deer, and he was always ready to meet an emergency. His integrity was undoubted. He never betrayed a trust, nor divulged a secret confided to his keeping.

6

The march to the Comanche Agency was without an incident of interest. At the agency we were treated very kindly by Agent Leper. The captain received a visit from his Comanche brother, Pinohiachman, Mr. Saddle Blanket.

At the Brazos Agency, Lieutenant Marlin's men were paid off. So were our Indians who had remained with us to the end of the scout. The captain had carried funds for that purpose. One account for supplies furnished Marlin's command of between $2000 and $3000 was not settled. The State of Texas still owes the debt to the estate of Charley Barnard.

Our march to Camp Leon was through Palo Pinto County. Our appearance created great excitement. It was supposed we had come to arrest Peter Garland and his aiders and abetters who had been charged with the killing of seven Indians of the Brazos Agency. Judge N. W. Battle had tried to deputize Captain Ford to make the arrests, but the captain had declined, for reasons stated quite fully in the chapter immediately following. It was no doubt a fortunate thing for Ford, and perhaps for the State too, that he did not accept the deputation and attempt to make the arrests: it would have caused a civil war on the frontier.

7

On arriving at Camp Leon, we were mortified to learn that one or two horses had been stolen from the corral during our absence. Lieutenant Gibbon explained it in this way: one night a sentinel left his post and ran to the tents, affirming there was an Indian in the corral. If the simpleton had fired on him, all would have been all right. Gibbon turned out a detachment and scoured the country, finding neither horse nor Indian. He could keep on a guard, be on the alert day and night, but it was beyond his power to put brains into the thick skull of a natural born booby.

We were mustered out of service on the expiration of our time. A large number of the men retained their arms, and they were charged to them on the rolls. No appropriation had been made to pay the company. The $70,000 dollars had been exhausted. The arms not retained by the rangers were turned in to Captain Bird Holland, who was authorized to receive them. The writer was to blame for not exacting a receipt at the date they were turned in. After General Houston became governor, a controversy arose between him and Major Clement R. Johns, comptroller of the State of Texas. Governor Houston charged that Comptroller Johns had settled with a military officer and paid him when he exhibited a receipt for "some arms" only. The facts of the case were these. There was considerable trouble on our Indian frontier. Citizens had organized and asked for arms and ammunition with which to defend themselves. Captain Holland very properly issued them. Among those thus given out were the guns turned in by Captain Ford. In 1860, when Ford was settling his accounts with the comptroller for the campaign against the Indians in 1859 and the later campaigns against the Mexican outlaw, Cortina, in 1859–1860, Ford called on Captain Holland for a receipt, and it was given for "some arms," for Holland appeared not to have counted them. The identical arms had again gone back into the service of the State. Major Johns, with a full knowledge of all the circumstances, decided the receipt sufficient to relieve Ford of all liability and paid him. This was the last incident connected with the last campaign against the Comanches.

The results of that campaign did not satisfy Captain Ford. His conscience did not accuse him of a failure of having done all he could to achieve success. But a still voice yet whispers: "You blundered when you went to Camp Radziminski."

XXI

>>

THE REASON WHY

Ford's defense in the Peter Garland affair was first published in the *State Gazette* in April and May, 1859.[1] This defense is republished here as a matter of history, also as an evidence of the writer's opinion concerning the points involved in the controversy. In truth these happenings left no trace of animosity in the captain's breast. He regrets their occurrence, but no unkind and bitter

---

[1] It should be remembered that Ford's defense in the Peter Garland affair was purposely one-sided. E. J. Gurley's argument in the *State Gazette* which outlined in great detail why Ford should have arrested Garland was equally provocative and equally persuasive. As I pointed out in the introduction, it is recorded fact that almost everybody involved, including Ford's close friends, considered the captain to be in the wrong. Ford's argument may be eloquent, but it is prejudicial (as it was meant to be), misleading,

recollections are connected with them; let them sleep in the broad tomb of the past.

I

Mr. E. J. Gurley has published a statement of the judicial proceedings had in the case of the *State of Texas* vs. *Peter Garland and others,* charged with the killing of certain Caddo Indians. Gurley pretends to be actuated by a desire to vindicate the official conduct of Judge Battle, but his article degenerates into an attack upon myself for refusing to accept the proffered deputation of Judge Battle to act as a special constable in the case. Some persons not well-versed in the art of reasoning might not be able to discover how my refusal to accept the deputation could in any manner affect Judge Battle. He must stand or fall upon his own acts, and any attempt to shield him from censure upon the ground that I had failed to do my duty is absurd coming even from a legal luminary. In my reply to Mr. Gurley I stated my reasons for declining to accept the deputation. The learned lawyer has not attempted an answer to any of them. He condemns me upon his mere dictum.

---

and in some cases incorrect, indicating that Rip, rather than Gurley and Battle, was not in full possession of the facts. First, for two years the settlers had accused the agency Indians of committing the depredations so rampant on the frontier; consequently, Palo Pinto County citizens would never have sanctioned the arrest of gunmen like Garland for killing a few of the "red robbers," even if the "robbers" happened to be squaws and papooses. The prevailing philosophy was still, "The best Indian is a dead Indian." Second, the murderers had openly declared their intent to fight anyone who tried to arrest them—civil officers as well as military. A good fight would have occurred no matter who tried to enforce the law. Third, civil authorities more than anyone else had the right to call on the Texas Rangers, who were less a military force than a civil law enforcement agency, to administer justice on the frontier. In other words, Ford was a lawman and not a soldier in the true sense of the term. Fourth, Rip, in making such a careful distinction between assisting the civil authorities and doing the job himself, was belaboring a point so fine and technical as to be wholly irrelevant. Clearly, this was not the man of action who the year before had successfully executed a most daring expedition against the renegade Comanches. Ford's stand is all the more interesting when considered in the light of what he said later, in the Civil War: "It is always the duty of the military to aid the civil authorities, when called upon, in any legal way. I should have no hesitancy in using the whole force of this military District to sustain a civil officer, and to aid him in the discharge of his duties. The laws must be enforced. Whoever sets them at defiance is an enemy to the State, and deserves to be treated as such." (See Chapter XXVI.) Finally, it does not seem unfair to ask what Ford would have done had the murdered been white and the murderers been Indian.

The documents, including the statements of men involved, for the Peter Garland affair are in the *U.S. Senate Exec. Docs.,* 36th Cong., 1st Sess., Vol. I, Doc. 2, pp. 588–604. Ford's and Gurley's lively debate is carried in the issues of the *Texas State Gazette* from April 30 through May 21, 1858, when Gurley said that he was weary of such "barbarous" correspondence and quit. An objective and well-documented account of these events is in Kenneth Franklin Neighbours, "Robert S. Neighbors in Texas, 1836–1859: A Quarter Century of Frontier Problems," ms., II, 563–579.

The following extract will place the reader in possession of Gurley's conclusions, but he leaves us to infer how he arrived at them:

The writs were directed to Captn Ford, who was at that time upon the frontier and in command of a company of Rangers. Here again the Judicial action has been questioned, and it is contended that it would have been more proper to have directed the writs to the civil officers. Now this plan was entirely precluded by the Affidavit of Major Neighbors to the effect that the offenders were armed and organized and could not be arrested by the Sheriff of the county, and subsequent events have proved this to be true, for the alias writs directed to the sheriff have been returned unexecuted. Judge Battle was induced to direct the writs to Captn Ford, not only because he was thought to be the most suitable person to execute them, but because he was assured by Major Neighbors and others, that he (Captn Ford) had expressed a willingness to do so. Notwithstanding, however, the voluntary assurances of Captn Ford, Judge Battle accompanied his writs with the Governor's proclamation calling upon all officers and good citizens to arrest the offenders and I, as a counsel for the prosecution, wrote to Captn Ford that prompt and efficient action on his part was the only way to avert the pending difficulty upon the frontier—vindicate the supremacy of the law, and restore good order and quiet. In the face of all this, Captn Ford declined making the arrests, and the present fermenting condition of the frontier is to some extent at least, the result of his "excessive prudence."

2

Early in the month of January, I went to Austin on official business. While there Major Neighbors frequently spoke to me in regard to the unfortunate affair on the frontier. In every instance I expressed a willingness to aid the authorities in making the arrests, provided all other means were resorted to and found inadequate, and then I proposed only to help them under the direction of a civil officer. The proposition to accept a deputation myself and to execute the processes was not made to me, or if it was, I did not understand it in the light it assumed when presented afterwards. Suppose I had promised, and upon examination I should have discovered a compliance with my promise would have involved a violation of the law. Then would any sensible man contend the promise was binding? Any jack-leg lawyer knows it would have been null and void, and, if reduced to writing and a penalty annexed for nonperformance, the penalty could not have been recovered by law.

The annexed document—the second warrant issued by the authorities —will show what Judge Battle and his advisers called upon me to do. The first warrant was incomplete and was superseded by this one, which is addressed to me as a military officer.

The State of Texas
McLennan County
The State of Texas to John S. Ford, Captain Commanding the Texas Rangers, Greeting:

Whereas, it appearing to the undersigned Judge of the 19th Judicial District, upon the affidavit of Joshua T. Carmack, that E. Friash, Robert Duval, Peter Garland, Daniel Thornton, W. E. Motherill, W. Fitzgerald, R. Dupuy, W. Wood, W. Highshaw, Dalton J. Hightower, T. Wilie, W. W. McNeil, J. P. Harris, A. L. Braw, W. J. F. Lowden, J. Barnes, J. R. Waller, George Harden, did on or about the 27th day of December, A.D. 1858, in the county of Palo Pinto, State of Texas, kill and murder the following named persons, to wit, Cheatis Chouta, Choctaw Tom's wife, and other women and children amounting to seven in all. And it further appearing to the undersigned Judge as aforesaid, that said persons committing said murder were an organized body, and since committment of said murder have caused or procured other persons to organize with them so that it is not possible for the legally constituted officers of Palo Pinto or any other county to arrest them, in case resistance should be made,

You are therefore commanded, in the name and by the authority of the State of Texas aforesaid, that you forthwith arrest, and for this purpose you are authorized to use and command as much assistance as is or may be necessary, the bodies of said E. Friash, Robert Duval, Peter Garland, Daniel Thornton, W. E. Motherill, C. W. Fitzgerald, R. Dupuy, W. Wood, W. Highshaw, Dalton J. Hightower, T. Wilie, W. W. McNeil, J. P. Harris, A. L. Braw, W. J. F. Lowden, J. Barnes, J. R. Waller, and George Harden, who are accused of the crime of murder aforesaid, and bring them severally before me at the Court House in the town of Waco, and county of McLennan, aforesaid, then and there to be dealt with as the law directs.

Given under my hand and official signature this the 17th day of January, A.D. 1859.

> N. W. Battle,
> Judge 19th Jud'l District,
> State of Texas

Now, how did Judge Battle expect an organized body of men to be arrested except by force? Was his warrant anything more or less than a command to me to take my company and attack a body of American citizens? The sheriff had the power to call out the force of the county, and, backed by such numbers, could he not have been more effective than a company of 80 men?

Admit the principle that a district judge has the power to deputize a military officer to arrest citizens for offenses, merely because some man may take it upon himself to swear that the sheriff or other civil officers cannot execute the process, and where would be the liberty of the citizen?

A man might at any time be arrested by force of arms and carried to any point and for any purpose the judge might indicate. A district judge would be a military officer, his orders would be supreme, and no military man would dare to disobey them. He would in fact be clothed with more power than the constitution vests in any other officer, and he could, were he so minded, play the tyrant on an extended scale. I may be mistaken, but in my humble opinion Judge Battle possesses no such powers, and his command to me, as the captain of a company of rangers, to arrest Garland and others was illegal, and my duty was to disobey it and to refuse to act except in strict subservience to law.

Mr. Gurley and his associates cannot deny but that they anticipated a collision between my company and the citizens. They knew it would be a sure result—a civil war might have been the consequence; yet they were willing to involve the country in trouble, disaster, and bloodshed in order to accomplish their ends. They knew that the offenders had published a card detailing their version of the killing, that they would offer no resistance to a civil officer, but that they denied the right or power of a military officer to arrest them. In the face of these facts Gurley and associates madly persisted in the attempt to send me upon a bloody errand.

3

To show that Major Neighbors himself did not claim to have received a promise from me to act as the arresting officer, his letter on the subject will be laid before the public. He may claim that I have violated propriety by publishing a letter marked "private," but his friends and associates should have thought of that before attacking me. I use it in self-defense. The reader will please pay particular attention to the italicized portions, but they were not italicized by the major.

> January 16th, 1859
> Waco, Texas

To Capt'n J. S. Ford, near Cora, Comanche County, Texas

Dear Capt: By this express . . . I send you a writ from Judge Battle for the arrest of the parties engaged in the late murder of the Indians near the reserve.

You will see that only seven names appear on the writ, from the fact, that at Waco we could not find out the names of the others. It is confidently believed that by the time you arrive at Stevensville, and arrest those named you will have a writ for the balance of the party who was with Capt. Garland. *I had the writ directed directly to you under the proclamation of the Governor, because I did not wish to embarrass you with a go between, and your friends expect that you will use all due diligence in bringing the parties before the legal tribunals. This has been decided upon by your best friends and we all confidently expect that you will take decisive and prompt action in the whole affair.*

*Public opinion is decidedly in our favor, and I have employed the best legal
authority in Waco for the prosecution, and will see that the parties are properly
prosecuted as soon as they are arrested.*

In this matter it brings on the direct issue that we want with Capt. Nelson,
as he is now with the men who are threatening the reserve.

There is sufficient force of U.S. cavalry and citizens now with Ross, to
defend the reserve and protect the Indians.

I send you copies of the Governor's proclamation for your information, and
shall meet you here when you come down, and hope that our action in the
premises will be satisfactory.

With respects to all of my old friends in your company,
I am very truly
Your friend,
R. S. Neighbors

If I had promised Major Neighbors to act as a special constable to
arrest Captain Garland and company, why was it necessary for him to
explain his reasons for having the deputation made to me directly? If I
had promised, is it not probable that he would have mentioned the fact?
I leave it to Mr. Gurley to reconcile the discrepancy between what he
avers Major Neighbors said and what he wrote. They don't agree.

4

The letter of Mr. Gurley, given below, squints at the employment of
force, and assigns reasons for my appointment to a constabulary office
somewhat on the score of availability. It is a very good specimen of what
the learned call "self-soaping."

Jan. 15th, 1859
Waco, Texas

Capt. John S. Ford

Dear Sir: I send you most of the news yet received about the troubles at the
agency by the express who carries your official deputation. The course to be
pursued has been fully discussed by attorneys, judges, and State officials, and it
is settled that the matter rests with the judicial authorities here. And it is
believed that you are the only proper person to execute process, and the citizens
are therefore looking to you, and believe that by your prompt action, jurisdiction will be obtained over the offense and a quietus had to be the present
excitement. *It is not believed that resistance will be made to the arrests.* Should
there be, and it should be necessary, I have no hesitation in saying that you
will be sustained by the lawabiding citizens, and that the Governor will go to
the extent of declaring martial law. I have no hesitancy in saying further, that
unless the Civil Authority proves equal to the emergency, the reserve Indians
will disband and desolate the frontier. I state this from the settled convictions

of Major Neighbors and Charles Barnard, and others whose opinions are to be relied upon. For these and other reasons the country looks to you as the only person who can at once, by prompt action under the authority herewith sent, give peace and quiet and satisfy the law and the people, both whites and Indians. I deem it proper to state that I am at present associated with the District Attorney for the prosecution of the persons you are authorized to arrest, and in that capacity will be glad to receive any communication you may wish to make and will do my duty under all circumstances.

Very respectfully,
Your obed't serv't,
E. J. Gurley

How does the italicized portion of Mr. Gurley's letter accord with his other assertions quoted at the opening of the chapter and with the affidavits of Major Neighbors and with the acts of Judge Battle?

Notwithstanding, however, [Gurley says] these voluntary assurances of Captn Ford, Judge Battle accompanied his writs with the Governor's proclamation calling upon all officers and good citizens to arrest the offenders and I, as a counsel for the prosecution, wrote to Captn Ford that prompt and efficient action on his part was the only way to avert the pending difficulty upon the frontier—vindicate the supremacy of the law, and restore good order and quiet. In the face of all this, Captn Ford declined making the arrests, and the present fermenting condition of the frontier is to some extent at least, the result of his "excessive prudence."

To decline making war upon American citizens, under the imposing array of inducements presented by Mr. Gurley, was indeed a grave offense! Wasn't it terribly aggravating to Judge Battle, his legal advisers and associates, that the aforesaid Ford refused to recognize the judge's right to command the captain to imbrue his hands in the blood of his countrymen? And then to do so after having been written to by E. J. Gurley. What impudence!

Mr. Gurley, no doubt, considers himself included in the term "good citizens." Now let me inquire where he was all this time, what part he intended to take in the sanguinary drama he was getting up to be enacted in Palo Pinto County? Did he offer his services to aid in the matter? He doubtless intended to remain quietly in his office at Waco and await the result. Does this smack of "excessive prudence?" It was a very easy matter for you, sir, to counsel others, to turn them loose with arms in their hands upon citizens, with the manifest knowledge that the parties in question would resist the execution of an illegal order, and that blood would flow and life be lost, while at the same time, "good citizen" and public spirited man as you are, you proposed remaining at a safe distance from the scene of strife; yet you have the effrontery to talk to others of "excessive prudence." Because I did not see proper to execute the unlawful and bloody mandates of your chief, you endeavor to hold me up to the public as a fit subject of odium and punishment. I could justly say to you, in the language of the Scripture:

"God shall smite thee, thou whited wall: for sittest thou to judge me after the law, and commandest me to be smitten contrary to the law?"

Mr. Gurley says the writs were not directed to the civil officers because Major Neighbors had sworn to the effect that the offenders were armed and organized and could not be arrested by the sheriff of the county. How did Major Neighbors know that? By hearsay. He had not been in Palo Pinto and his affidavit could not justify Judge Battle for having issued a warrant contrary to law. The organization was, no doubt, effected to a great extent after the issuance of the writ, because the people of Palo Pinto County expected they would be visited by an armed force, acting under illegal orders, and consequently invaders of the soil and violators of the law; and it is probable they would have resisted to the death. The fact that the alias writs have been returned unexecuted does not prove the truth of Major Neighbors' supposition. There is no evidence that any resistance was made to their execution; there was no organized band of citizens to be found at that time in Palo Pinto County; and the sheriff did not execute process because the parties avoided him. This is the statement made to me by a respectable citizen of the county, while I passed through it a few weeks since.

The attempt to arrest the offenders by an armed force would not have restored peace and quiet in that region, as before stated; it would only have increased the excitement.

5

The following admission of Mr. Gurley is very complimentary to the "excessive prudence" of Judge Battle:

After the legality of the order was settled by Judge Battle, he, knowing the intensity of the excitement that pervaded unanimously throughout the frontier amongst both white people and Indians, very wisely concluded not only that it would be hazardous to bring together these inflamable elements at any point upon the frontier where this excitement prevailed, but that a court of inquiry under such a state of affairs would add fuel to the flames and be at best a mockery of justice. Hence from motives of policy it was ordered that the investigation be had at a point free from the prevailing excitement and where law and order would maintain the ascendency, and give dignity and decorum to the proceedings.

A committing trial is conducted by a judicial officer without a jury. Will Mr. Gurley state in what manner the "excitement" was expected to influence Judge Battle so as to reduce his "court of inquiry" to the awful extremity of being "at best but a mockery of justice?" If outside influences were to exert such control upon a man who claims to be clothed with the ermine and to wield the sword too, what effect would they have upon twelve ordinary jurymen? The final trial has to take place in Palo Pinto County, and if Mr. Gurley has not misrepresented the facts, where is the use of an arrest and of the farcical forms of a trial being observed? According to his own showing, if I had made the arrests no good would have resulted from them.

I shall pursue a different course from Mr. Gurley. He says I am guilty of an offense of great magnitude, but in the hurry of the moment, no doubt, forgets to show how and why. Judge Battle and his advisers were wrong, and to prove them so, it is only necessary to refer to the law bearing upon the question. For the information of Mr. Gurley and his military judicial chieftain, I will give them the law, with such references as will enable them, if they can read, to examine for themselves.

1. Any officer authorized to execute process, when resisted, or if he has sufficient reason to believe he will be resisted, may call on the citizens of his county, or any military company of the same to aid him. See *Code of Criminal Procedures*, Sec. 96.

2. If it be represented to the governor in such manner as to satisfy him that the power of the county is not sufficient to enable the sheriff to execute process, he may, on application, order any military company of volunteers from another county to aid in overcoming such resistance. See *Code of Criminal Procedures*, Sec. 98.

(There is no provision in the Code or in any statute which provides that the capias or warrant of arrest shall be directed to the commander of a military company, or which authorizes him to execute or return the same. All that he can do is to *aid* in the arrest.)

3. A private person may be appointed to make an arrest when it is proven to the magistrate that a peace officer cannot be found or so much delay will be occasioned in finding one as will probably enable the accused to escape, but the appointment must be with the consent of the person appointed. See *Code of Criminal Procedures*, Sec. 224.

Judge Battle thus had a right to issue the warrant, and it might be executed by any lawful officer in any part of the State where the accused could be found. But while Judge Battle may have had the right to issue a warrant of arrest in this case, he violated the law, if he directed that warrant to any other person than a peace officer. (See *Code of Criminal Procedures*, Sec. 221.)

The law requires writs to be issued:

First, to the sheriff,

Second, in case there is no sheriff, or he is disqualified, then to the constable or coroner,

Third, in case of no officer, any person who will agree to execute the writ may be officially appointed.

The officer charged with the execution of process may call upon the *posse comitatus* to aid him.

If the resistance is so great that the officer and his *posse* are unable to execute the writ, the fact being properly made known to the governor, it will be his duty "to see the laws faithfully executed" and he may put any military force, subject to his command, under the authority of the civil officer to enable him to execute the process.

It is apparent that Judge Battle did violate the law when he directed the warrant to myself; that the warrant was thereby vitiated and conferred no right or power upon one to make the arrests; that the accused had the right to resist, and, had they killed any of my party, it would not have been murder—they would have been held harmless.

These facts are incontestably proven by the law, and they fix upon Judge Battle the indelible stain of having ignorantly, but perhaps innocently, issued a process, the execution of which, or the attempt to execute, would have been the cause of life being taken and the cause of a state of things approaching civil war. They show his utter incapacity to discharge the duties of his office; and he stands before the world as a ripe subject for impeachment. He is probably the first judge in the United States who has attempted to elevate the military power over the civil. He is one of the few judicial officers who has violated a plain principle of freedom— he has attempted to deprive citizens of their liberty without due course of law, and his acts in the premises would have led to the subversion of the rights of the people and would have conferred upon district judges powers destructive to freedom. This judicial chieftain, whose misconduct has threatened these results, should be arraigned and made to answer for his official sins.

6

After my refusal to attempt to execute the warrant, I addressed a communication to the Hon. T. S. Anderson, secretary of state; he fully approved and endorsed my course. Governor H. R. Runnels at a subsequent period addressed me an order from which I make the annexed extracts:

"Should there be application made to the command from the civil authorities, to assist in the arrest of Garland and his men for the alleged murder of the friendly Indians in Palo Pinto County, in December, you will give your assistance promptly, as heretofore instructed, to the authorities for the execution of the warrant . . ."

The reader will notice, that the governor ordered me to *assist* the civil authorities, which I have been, and am yet, ready and willing to do.

In this whole affair I endeavored to act in accordance with the law. I believe my declining to accept the deputation saved the State of Texas from being the theatre of scenes of violence and homicide. My course meets with the approval of my own conscience. I thank God that my hands are not red with the blood of my fellow citizens, shed under the orders of Judge Battle and at the instigation and advice of the Ciceronian E. J. Gurley.

I have written to repel an unjust attack, and if things I have said grate harshly upon the ears and feelings of those concerned, theirs is the fault —I am acting within the pale of the inalienable right of self-defense, and am not aiming to injure the reputation of any man from feelings of hostility. My object is to place myself right before the public, to shield myself from detraction and misrepresentation, and not to gratify a spirit of revenge. I give to malice and those kindred passions no abiding place in my bosom.

John S. Ford

XXII

>>

THE RISE OF CHENO CORTINA

I n 1859 an order was is-
sued to remove the gar-
risons from the posts on
the lower Río Grande.
As a result, from Laredo to the mouth of the Río Grande, about two
hundred and fifty miles, there were no soldiers of the United States Army.
Lieutenant Lomis L. Langdon of the United States Artillery was left to
take care of the public property on the lower Río Grande, probably
another officer also. Langdon made his headquarters at Ringgold Barracks, but soon changed to Fort Brown.

In September, without warning, Cheno Cortina and his bandits attacked
Río Grande City, killing military custodians and looting the town. As
was the case at Río Grande City, so it was all along the valley of the Río
Grande from Laredo to the Gulf of Mexico. Cortina soon had undisputed
possession. This gave an invitation to the desperadoes, cutthroats, and
robbers of that region to kill and plunder the unfortunate residents of

the valley of the lower Río Grande. How promptly and cordially the invitation was accepted will be seen in the succeeding pages.

I

In order to let readers know something of the history of the great marauding chief who led the sanguinary cohorts of Mexico in these predatory operations, a notice of the early life of General Cortina is given.

Juan Nepomuceno Cortina is reputed to have been born at Camargo, Mexico. His mother's name was María Estéfana Goceascochea Cavazos de Cortina. She first married a Mexican gentleman named Cavazos. After his death she was married to Señor Cortina. He died, leaving her a widow the second time. According to Mexican usage a woman retains her first name and adds that of her husband. During the life of Señor Cavazos, then, she was known as María Estéfana Goceascochea de Cavazos. After her second widowhood she signed documents thus: María Estéfana Goceascochea Cavazos de Cortina—pronounced, Mar-e-a Es-tay-fan-ah Go-say-as-co-chi-a Cav-a-zos day Cor-te-nah. Nearly sufficient to break an ordinary sheriff's jaw to call.

Señora Cortina owned a large body of land on the Río Grande, not far above Brownsville. There were other claimants. Suit was instituted, but the Texas courts decided the case in favor of the lady.

Juan Cortina's half brother, Don Savas Cavazos, amassed valuable property and was a peaceful and law-abiding citizen of the United States. In process of time his brother José María Cortina became collector of taxes in Cameron County.

"Cheno," as Juan Cortina was familiarly called, was considered the black sheep of the family. He was bad in school. He never remained many days under a teacher without beating some boy terribly and getting himself expelled. He attained manhood without being able to read or write. While a youth he kept company with stock herders—men of wild, and in many instances, of dissolute habits. He acquired an ascendancy over this class of men. They roamed over prairies, threaded their ways through chaparrals, and occasionally figured in towns. They were often in attendance at fandangos, and the man who crossed Cortina courted trouble and danger. He was of medium size, with regular features, and a rather pleasing countenance. He was rather fairer than most men of his nationality. He was fearless, self-possessed, and cunning. In some cases he has acted towards personal and political enemies with a clemency worthy of imitation. When he thought he was being pushed to the wall and in hazard of his life, he acted decisively and promptly. It is related that in 1863, when [José María] Cobos started Cortina out to be shot in

Matamoros, Cheno turned and said to the guard: *"Tu hermano"*—"You brother." The guard was immediately won over, seized Cobos, and shot him instead. This was during some of the revolutionary commotions happening in Mexico.

In native intellect Cortina ranked high. No uneducated man could have played the part he did otherwise. He understood his countrymen of the lower classes almost thoroughly. Mr. Nesmith told an anecdote in illustration. Cortina was approached by one of his men, who asked him for money to buy a suit of clothes. The general told him to wait a few minutes. He finished his business with Nesmith and handed the soldier twenty-five cents, saying:

"Here, my man, take this money and go buy a suit of clothes."

"General, why do you fool that poor fellow," Nesmith remarked. "You know two bits will not purchase a suit of clothes."

"Yes, sir, I do, and so does he. I knew he only wanted money to get drunk on, and now he has it."

This knowledge enabled Cortina to get backing from the common people of Mexico in any enterprise he undertook.

Cortina did not seem to have a very well-defined idea of the rights of property. He and his lawless companions feasted upon fat calves and anything they liked, regardless of ownership. They were indicted. It was asserted that the records in Cameron County show about twenty indictments against Juan N. Cortina for all sorts of crimes—from murder down to grand larceny. He was never tried and might have been innocent. He was the enemy of the United States, however, and had his own statements to indicate the fact.

A story has been told of Cortina. It may need confirmation. In 1846 a young Kentuckian bought mules on the Río Grande. He hired Mexicans to assist in driving. Juan de la Luna was their leader. He was a bad man. It is said he induced the Mexican hirelings to murder the young man and seize his property. La Luna sold it to the American quartermaster at Point Isabel. Cortina was said to be of la Luna's party. His return, it is stated, gave his mother much trouble. This story came from those not friendly to the general. It is said to have happened on the Alto Prieto.

2

At the close of the Mexican War a great deal of public property of the United States was in Mexico. Many thousands of dollars worth were sacrificed on General Scott's line. On this side of the Sierra Madre an immense quantity of public property was brought out by land. In July,

1848, a train of seventy-five wagons was made up at Matamoros, each wagon having a train of six mules (there was also a herd of 1,000 horses and mules). The train was in charge of Captain [Thomas B.] Ives of the quartermaster department. John J. Dix superintended the management of the loose animals. He had under him about thirty Mexicans. They were divided into two detachments—one under the immediate control of Captain Dix, the other in charge of Cortina. He then figured as a United States quartermaster man. The Mexicans were paid twenty-five dollars a month.

Captain Dix remembers giving Cortina leave to go to Brownsville to make a bond for his appearance at the next term of the district court, to answer to the charge of murder.

Dix had his appointment and orders direct from Major [William W.] Chapman of the United States Army, then assistant quartermaster on duty on the lower Río Grande. He was responsible, or supposed himself so, for the animals under his control. He informed wagonmasters and teamsters that they must not take mules or horses from the herd without the knowledge and consent of the person in charge of the herders.

The train made Goliad without anything of moment having happened. Cortina was on duty. A wagonmaster went to the herd, and was in the act of replacing some of the fatigued mules by fresh ones. Cortina objected. Angry words were spoken. The wagonmaster struck at Cortina. The fight began at once, and was soon in the favor of Cortina. A Mexican ran and told Dix what was going on. Luckily he was near by. When he reached the place of combat, Cortina was astride the wagonmaster, and was choking him. The American's face was black; his tongue was protruding from his mouth; he was incapable of making any resistance; he was almost dead. Dix thinks a little while would have sufficed to end his earthly career. Dix released the wagonmaster. This incident caused ill feeling between the Mexican herders and the Americans.

At La Grange, Captain Dix went ahead to visit his father's family in Washington County, leaving Cortina in charge of the loose animals. Another effort was made to take mules, without the order of Captain Ives or the consent of Cortina. Angrily, Cheno told the captain to take care of the mules himself. He and nearly all the Mexicans left camp, and followed Dix to his father's place. Dix carried them back to the train, which had moved forward from La Grange.

A day was spent in discussing the matter. Captain Dix insisted that his position was independent of Captain Ives, as he derived his orders from Ives' superior in rank. Dix disclaimed any authority except over the loose animals. Captain Ives demanded the return of all the Mexicans to duty. Cortina and about five others declined to serve any longer. At first Captain Ives refused to pay Cortina or to give him a pay voucher. He finally consented to deliver him a voucher. Cortina and his companions returned to Fort Brown, and were paid by Major Chapman.

Captain Dix gives Cortina credit for strict obedience to orders and for faithful and effective discharge of his duties. Thus ended Juan Nepomuceno Cortina's career as a quartermaster's man.

Cortina soon acquired great influence over the lower class of Mexicans in Cameron County. In an election he was good for forty or fifty votes. Hence he became a political factor of some importance. It was said in the heated discussions of those days that there was a culpable negligence in not arresting him for the criminal offenses charged to his account. This was attributed to a fear of exciting his hostility. However, this is not among the things designated as fixed facts.

In 1859 Juan Cortina obtained authority from a Mexican source to raise troops for the Mexican service in the neighborhood of Tampico. He enlisted a great many men, crossed the river, and entered Brownsville on the night of September 28. The hostile descent was not anticipated by the Texas citizens. Many of them were in Matamoros aiding the Mexicans to celebrate a day connected with the independence of Mexico. When they returned to the American side of the river, they were astonished to find the city in the possession of Cortina, who was more celebrated for lawlessness than for anything else. Everything was at his mercy.[1] He and his followers killed whomever they wished, robbed whomever they pleased. They intended to finish their diabolical work by burning the city. General José M. J. Carbajal and Don Miguel, a kinsman of Cortina, had the credit of having induced the robber chieftain to evacuate the place.

When the marauders retired, the note of preparation was sounded inside Brownsville. Captain Mifflin Kenedy was elected to be chief commander. Francisco Ytúrria was elected to command the company com-

---

[1] On the evening of September 28, 1859, someone sighted riders approaching Brownsville on the road from Río Grande City; but before the alarm could be sounded, Cortina's bandits entered the city at a gallop, firing their pistols at windows and cowing storekeepers and shouting: "Death to the Gringoes!" "Death to all Americans!" After they had looted the city and ridden away, a newspaperman wrote fearfully that while "there is no respectful Mexican on our side of the river openly in his favor," we "have every fear that the mere hatred of the Gringoes—as all Americans are called by them—will unite them in the common design of blotting out our unfortunate city and its whole population."

(Correspondent for the New Orleans *Picayune* as quoted in "Difficulties on the Southwestern Frontier," *U.S. House Exec. Docs.*, 36th Cong., 1st Sess., Vol. VII, Doc. 52, p. 40.)

posed of men of Mexican origin. Brownsville was converted into a military encampment; guards were set at proper points, scouting parties were sent out, and all the incidents of war were visible. Cortina made efforts to surprise the town, but a sleepless vigilance was exhibited, and Cortina's efforts were gallantly repulsed.

The Mexican commander issued proclamations. His programme was to drive the Americans out of Texas. This was a popular move in Mexico. It gave Cortina the sympathy of the Mexican people. He was backed by Mexican officials and citizens, from whom he received men and supplies. It must be borne in mind that General Carbajal, then in command of the State of Tamaulipas, was not in accord with Cortina.

Several affairs occurred that were disastrous to the Texians. An expedition under Captain Thompson, sent out to engage Cortina, was defeated and lost two small pieces of artillery. This mishap inspirited the Mexicans greatly. The arrival of a volunteer company under Captain Tobin gave confidence to the Americans. This disappeared when the Texians attacked General Cortina in his camp about ten miles above Brownsville, but he rode away without giving fight. In truth we lost in all the fights with that desperado until Major Samuel P. Heintzelman's regular troops appeared on the theatre of action. The legislature of Texas convened in November. A rumor reached Austin that Cortina had taken and burned Corpus Christi. The writer went in search of General Forbes Britton and found him on Congress Avenue, near where the Raymond House now stands. General Britton lived in Corpus Christi, and the rumor was calculated to make him extremely uneasy, if nothing more. Ford endeavored to convince him the report was unfounded, and thought he had succeeded. Meantime Governor H. R. Runnels passed along. General Britton accosted him, portrayed the condition of things at Corpus Christi: the town sacked by a dissolute crowd of barbarous marauders, the houses burned to the ground, his family depending for the necessities of life upon the charities of a cold world. The general's eyes danced wildly in their sockets, his chin trembled, and his voice quivered with emotion.

Governor Runnels was deeply moved, and exclaimed: "Ford you must go; you must start tonight, and move swiftly." The governor was assured his order would be obeyed as soon as a horse could be obtained to ride. The question presenting itself in regard to General Britton's impromptu speech was that he either felt very intensely on the subject, or he was a first-class actor. Opinion leaned rather in the latter direction. There was, however, grave cause for disquietude and for prompt action.

Work began at once. Authority was directed to S. B. Highsmith, one of Ford's old lieutenants, to raise a company. He was written to, begging him in the name of old companionship to enlist his men and move at once without waiting for further orders.

An order was made conferring on John S. Ford the rank of lieutenant colonel, vesting him with authority to command all the State troops and to purchase supplies of every kind for the troops and mules. Strangely enough, the word horse was omitted, which was manipulated afterwards with a view to give Ford trouble. An order was subsequently issued modifying the original order by reducing the rank of Ford to major and directing an election to be held for that office. Ford had no objection to the latter proposition. He foresaw quite clearly that the results arising therefrom might unavoidably mar the effectiveness of the state troops. He aspired simply to do his duty, and let consequences take their own shape.

The next day, late in the evening, Ford with eight men crossed the ferry at Austin and moved south. There were a gun or two and a few pistols in the crowd, but not one dollar of public money.

A few men joined us on the road to Goliad. There arrangements were made to procure some funds through the kindness of Judge [William] Dunlap. The next point where a halt was made was Banquete, twenty-four miles west of Corpus Christi. Ere this it was ascertained that Highsmith would not be in the field.

At Banquete, arrangements were made with [George] Byington for supplies of various kinds. The force amounted to fifty-three men. They were quite well armed, mounted on serviceable horses, and gave evidence of possessing good fighting qualities. The first encampment was on the Pintos, six miles from Banquete. Ford remained at Banquete. The boys incautiously pitched camp on the north side of the timber. A fiercer norther, accompanied by sleet, has seldom frozen the marrow in a Texas man's bones.

About the first of December, 1859, camp was broken, and we made the ranch of Captain Richard King, the baron of modern times. There a note was received from General H. Clay Davis inviting us to go by way of Río Grande City, where Captain Harmon of Seguin would stop with his volunteers and would join us. The invitation was declined, because Brownsville was almost as near as Río Grande City; the distance to Brownsville by Río Grande City was nearly twice as great.

The march to the Ranch of Los Indios was made without any events of importance. We could see smokes going up ahead of us, and felt assured we were closely watched by Cortina's spies.

When in camp near the Los Indios, we were convinced an enemy was in close proximity to our line. That night we camped in a circle. The animals were tied inside and the sentinels placed outside the pallets of the men which formed a ring. It is needless to remark that we had attempted to extricate a bogged wagon at the Indios. There an election was held for company officers. The company elected Joseph Wheeler captain, William H. Fry, first lieutenant, William Howard, second lieutenant.

Captain W. R. Henry, a grandson of Patrick Henry, the celebrated orator, was indignant at not receiving the captaincy instead of Walker. He had been a sergeant in the regular army and a captain of rangers. He had rather exalted notions, and was difficult to control. He was brave, and possessed merit, but had the credit of interfering with his superior officers. He was not always in the wrong.

The march was resumed at 8 or 9 o'clock in the morning. We discovered that the enemy had slept at the house of the nearest rancho. After marching an hour perhaps, the booming of cannon was plainly audible. A fight was in progress above and to our right. The only man of our command acquainted with the section was ahead with Captain [S. K.] Dawson of the United States Army. We rode at full gallop, expecting to overtake the man and have him lead us to the firing. The church steeple in Brownsville loomed up when we passed Captain Dawson. It appears probable that faster time was never made by a road wagon and ambulance than on that memorable occasion.

We galloped into the city, and our advent produced some commotion, the citizens supposing we were a detachment of Cortina's men. Captain M. Kenedy formed his citizen company across the street in our front. They had seen us from the church steeple. When they discovered who we were, they gave us three cheers, and we loped out of town. We reached Major Heintzelman's regulars shortly after they had driven Cortina from the field.

The two commands went into camp a short distance above the battlefield. That night a heavy rain fell, and ruined quite all our cartridges. The next morning we heard Cortina's bugles, and could have found him. On examination it was made evident our ammunition was too short to risk an attack upon an enemy fully prepared and occupying a position chosen by himself. We tried to lure him into attacking us, but he refused. We returned to Fort Brown during the day.

It was said that Cortina was not in his camp at the Ebonal Ranch on the morning of December 6, 1859, when Major Heintzelman attacked. He was understood to have been near the Los Indios, intending to cut off the reinforcement column under Ford. Cortina probably hurried back to the Ebonal when he heard the artillery duel between his cannon and

Heintzelman's commence. Cheno's trail was reported to Ford; he deemed it safer to go to the firing than to risk an encounter with a force sent probably to hold him in check.

3

After the operations already detailed Major Heintzelman and Major Ford had an interview, in which they interchanged instructions, ideas, and suggestions. They decided to cooperate. A similar agreement existed between Major Heintzelman and Captain [William G.] Tobin, who commanded a volunteer force independent of Ford's command. The following order was issued:

> Headquarters Brownsville Expedition
> Fort Brown, Texas
> December 17, 1859

Orders No. 4

Major Ford and Captain Tobin of the Texas Rangers having expressed a desire to co-operate with the U.S. troops in the operations against the marauders under Cortinas[2] the following arrangements will go into effect.

Captain Tobin will proceed with Sixty men towards Point Isabel, and attack and disperse any men he may meet in a hostile attitude.

Major Ford will take Sixty men and proceed to the Fresnos, and there intercept any who attempt to escape in that direction.

Captain Stoneman 2nd Cavalry with his Company will proceed to Las Norias, and there watch the roads for the same purpose.

Captain Tobin will take five days' rations and Major Ford and Captain Stoneman each four days' rations. The three parties will each be furnished with a guide.

The first detachment will leave to day at one o'clock p.m.; the second to day at dark, and Captain Stoneman at daylight tomorrow.

> By order of Major Heintzelman
> C. W. Thomas, Adjutant
> 2nd Lieut. 1st Infantry

The rumors of Cortina's movements were contradictory. One account represented a party of the enemy marching upon Port Isabel. At that time the United States customhouse was at that point and a sum of money, variously estimated, was in the government safe. The population of the place was then larger than it has been since, if reports are correct. Brazos Santiago, four miles away by water, had a depot for ordnance and ordnance stores and had residences and business establishments on it. It is yet the sea harbor to Brownsville. At the period of which we are writing,

---

[2] In the documents one often finds Cortina erroneously spelled Cortinas.

the merchandise entering Brazos Santiago and passing up the Río Grande and into Mexico amounted usually to as much as $10,000,000 a year. King & Kenedy had a fleet of steamboats plying between Brownsville and Brazos Santiago. The steamships of the Morgan Line were at anchor at the Brazos Wharf every eight or ten days. A successful raid upon Point Isabel and Brazos Santiago would have placed Cortina in possession of a considerable sum of money, goods, and several steamers. The latter would have been almost worthless to him. He had a strong propensity to destroy American property. He would certainly have burned everything he could not have carried away with him.

Ford moved at the hour designated by General Orders No. 4. We marched quite all night, circling through the chaparral, scrambling over prickly pear, and encountering thorns at every step. A short while before daylight, the guide was interrogated as to our whereabouts. His answers were not satisfactory. Not knowing where we were, we simply laid down until day dawned. Suddenly, the church bells of Matamoros were heard distinctly, indicating that we were near that city and therefore only seven miles from Brownsville. This development caused the boys to get off a good many frontier oaths and some threats against our circumlocutory guide.

We made the Fresnos Ranch that day and encamped there during the night. Every disposition was made to prevent a surprise and to receive the enemy in a proper manner in case of an attack. The Fresnos is not quite three miles from San José, a cattle ranch then owned by Cortina. The Fresnos is on the road leading from Corpus Christi to Brownsville, and about twenty-three miles from the latter place. We returned to Fort Brown and reported.

These operations were attended by no incidents of moment, and produced no visible results beneficial to the work on hand. We could only report that Cortina was not at any point visited by our columns.

It became known that Cortina had proceeded up the Río Grande at the head of 400 or 500 men. Major Heintzelman worked assiduously to get the troops in readiness to follow the marauding chief. Everything was done which could be done to place the troops in fighting trim.

About the twentieth of December a forward movement was made. The main body consisted of regular infantry, cavalry, and artillery. Tobin's and [Peter] Tomlinson's companies followed the road leading from Brownsville to Río Grande City. The second encampment was at the Carricitos Ranch, twenty-two miles above Fort Brown. Ford and Captain Hampton were directed to move to the right and nearly parallel with the main body in order to make a thorough reconnaissance of the country and to cover Major Heintzelman's right flank. The guide began to zigzag. He carried us into immense and dense groves of *huisache* and ebony trees and evinced an intention to do anything but go in the direction desired. These exhibitions of indecision exasperated the men. Late in the evening Ford rode up to the guide and, in a low tone of voice, assured him of the danger he was incurring, pointing out that nothing had saved him from being shot but Ford's influence over the men—it was the fact. Ford advised him to take the course necessary to carry the command into the main road and prevent a tragedy. He appreciated the advice and the situation.

We were in a rough country without a road, and guided by a man we doubted. The march was difficult and laborious. During the night we passed a camp Cortina had occupied recently. This accounted for conduct of the guide. He had supposed Cortina still there, and was afraid to lead us to him. When we reached the main road, the guide was so badly demoralized that he wanted to take the route leading to Brownsville.

A short while before daybreak Ford reported to Major Heintzelman. Little time for rest. The third day's march brought to light many acts of vandalism. Houses had been robbed and fired, fences burned, property destroyed or carried into Mexico. Settlements were broken up for the time being; the inhabitants had fled for their lives. Cortina had committed these outrages upon citizens of the United States regardless of race and upon Mexicans suspected of being friendly to Americans.

On the evening of December twenty-sixth we encamped at Las Cuevas Ranch, eighteen miles below Río Grande City. A council was held, at which Ford was present, and a plan of operations determined upon. Major Ford, with his old company (under the field command of Captain Joe Walker), and with the companies of Captain Hampton and Captain Harmon, was to make a night march and, if possible, pass around Cortina's flank and get on the road from Río Grande City to Roma. To use Major Heintzelman's exact words: "You must be extremely cautious; do not stir Cortina up tonight." The main body was to move at midnight. The intention was to attack at daylight. We had information that Cortina was in Río Grande City.

With Ford's detachment went General H. Clay Davis, an old veteran of fame who was minutely acquainted with the whole region, and [James B.] McClusky, the sutler for Ringgold Barracks. In the command were some of Ford's old rangers, and others who had seen service. Ford had every confidence in the courage and staying qualities of his ninety men, and was willing to risk them in an encounter with Cortina, even though he outnumbered the Texians more than six to one.

Just after nightfall we broke camp. After having marched a little more than an hour at a slow gait, we encountered a party of men. Our guide hailed: *"Quién Viva?"*—the Mexican for, "Who comes there?" A shot answered. It was promptly returned by the guide. A charge was ordered and the enemy was forced into the chaparral. General Davis affirmed that the chaparral was so thick that the scout of Cortina could not make Río Grande City at night, except by the road. This ensured the chance to surprise Cortina.

When within a few miles of Ringgold Barracks, General Davis suggested making a deflection to the left in order to reach the house of a Mexican friend of his, from whom he could get reliable information. In making the movement we passed several houses of Mexicans. Some of our men spoke to the inmates. We were taken to be a reinforcement for Cortina—a mistake we encouraged. We made the ranch designated. It was about a mile and a half below Ringgold Barracks. The Mexican gentleman said he had left Río Grande City at three P.M. that day. At that time Cortina was encamped in the main street, his right resting on the Río Grande and his left on a little hill overlooking the town. The Mexican assured us that we could not pass around Cortina's left flank; the only practicable route was over an open flat to the right of Ringgold Barracks. This flat was occupied by a heavy picket. In addition there was a picket on the road a few hundred yards from us. This intelligence made it impossible to persist in the attempt to make the flanking movement without arousing Cortina and giving him time to get out of the way. We were firmly resolved to force him to fight.

A picket was placed on the road. It was less than two hundred yards from Cortina's men, who were at the crossing of a creek. Every Texian held his bridle in his hand, and got what sleep he could on the bare ground. We were apprised that Cortina had a heavier force than had been represented. Our position was not one calculated to increase happiness, though not one of us felt the least alarm. Just before daylight, the rumble of the artillery carriages announced the approach of Major Heintzelman. We moved out to the road. Major Ford made a hurried verbal report to Major Heintzelman, which the Texian afterwards found out was not understood by the commanding officer. Ford detailed Cortina's position and proposed to continue the effort to turn his left flank, which was assented to.

Major Ford assumed command of the whole ranger force, threw out an advance guard, and moved to the front at once. We marched by the road and drove in the enemy's picket. It was hardly daylight. Cortina sent out a reconnoitering party. We met it at Ringgold Barracks, fired into it, and forced it back. We moved to the right, under an ineffective fire from Mexicans on the tops of houses, gained the crest of the hill, and found no enemy in the town. No one seemed willing to tell us where Cortina was. An American, [John S.] Phelps, pointed to some large ebony trees above town, and said: "He is there." Ford directed Captain Tobin to move upon Cortina's left wing resting upon the cemetery, attack, and hold it there. Tobin moved by the Roma road with a view to strike Cortina's left flank, and engage his artillery. These dispositions were made under the belief that Major Heintzelman would soon come up and occupy the center, and thus have sufficient scope to use his artillery. It was extremely foggy, and the artillery firing was heard only a short distance.

Cortina's right flank rested on the Río Grande; his artillery was at the corner of a fence on the Roma road. It was supported by two or three companies, reported to be infantry. Ford was within a hundred and fifty or two hundred yards of the two pieces before he knew their exact location. They opened fire with little effect upon the head of our column.

For some inexplicable reason Captain Tobin did not attack Cortina's left flank resting on the cemetery. The number of Texians actually engaged at any time was not much higher than ninety. The fire of the enemy was terrific for a while. Every time they discharged a piece of artillery those near by in our front felt as if struck by handfuls of gravel. Captain Ford was not more than thirty steps from the pieces; he averred he was struck almost a hundred times. After the capture of the cannon, we found the intervals or spaces between the grape and canister had been filled by buckshot. These would strike at a short distance and sting, but not penetrate. They had cannon cartridges with slugs of iron in them.

Lieutenant James H. Fry, at the head of a small detachment on foot and armed with old fashioned Minnie rifles, was directed to move up a string of fence and to pay his respects entirely to the artillerymen. Our mounted men advanced at a brisk gallop, and left the road by an inclination to the right at less than a hundred yards from the enemy artillery. Cavalry halted, dismounted about forty yards from the cannon, and opened fire. Ford now instructed them to advance under cover of the chaparral and take the pieces in flank. The enemy advanced in force and attempted to repel our attack. They opened a heavy fire of small arms. The artillery was discharged briskly. In a few minutes sixteen troops fell wounded in close proximity to Ford, who was sitting on his horse encouraging the men. The opposing forces were within a few yards of each other. The very heavy fog rendered it difficult to distinguish a Mexican from an American at the distance of twenty yards. Our men fought with gallantry. Colonel [Samuel A.] Lockridge, who was in the forefront, complimented them highly, saying:

"Those boys of yours fight like old veterans."

Lieutenant Fry's galling fire and the flanking movement silenced the artillery. Preparations were being made to charge and capture it. At this juncture the Mexican buglers sounded the charge, which Ford recognized. He directed the men to lead their horses into the thick chaparral, take post in front of them, and receive the charge. The order was executed promptly and with indomitable courage. Many a charger galloped off, carrying an empty saddle; Cortina's bold riders were left on the ground.

Colonel Lockridge, of Nicaragua fame, was on foot while we were endeavoring to flank the artillery. The two lines were very near each other. Lockridge went to the extreme front and emptied his revolver. He saw a Mexican about ten yards from him take deliberate aim at him. The Mexican missed, loaded again, took a second pop at the tall *gringo,* but failed again to bring him down. As he began loading a third time, Lockridge had a presentiment of a fatal result from the next shot. At this critical moment George W. Morris walked up. The colonel saluted him blandly.

"Good morning, Mr. Morris. Will you please kill that Mexican," and pointed at his opponent.

Quick as thought, Morris' Sharpe carbine exploded: the Mexican fell dead.

Lockridge bowed politely. "Very much obliged to you Mr. Morris." Morris smiled calmly and walked off.

A short while before the charge was made by Cortina, his dismounted men were firing into us from front, right flank, and rear. One of the rangers announced the fact in a loud tone of voice.

"All right boys," Ford said, "we can whip them just as easy in that shape as in any other."

About this time Captain Tobin with a few men appeared in our rear. Captain Tomlinson had gone to the front and had used his rifle effectively. A larger portion of Captain Tobin's unit then came up.

The repulse of the charge demoralized the enemy. While we were repelling it, the artillery was moved off the field. The Mexicans were obviously retreating. The rangers pursued a short distance on foot. Ford ordered them to fall back to their horses, mount, and resume the pursuit.

Major Heintzelman came up. Ford reported to him what had happened. Heintzelman said he had not heard the firing. Two couriers had been sent to find him and to inform him we had attacked Cortina and would endeavor to hold him till the regulars arrived. These messengers never reported.

After hearing Ford's report, Major Heintzelman approved the pursuit. Major Ford said to Captain Stoneman, one of Heintzelman's junior officers:

"There are three companies of infantry under the river bank. Had you not better compliment them with a notice?"

Stoneman did so, and out of all congregated there only ten or twelve were ever heard of again. The Sharpe's rifles reached the Mexican bank with fatal effect. Many Mexicans were killed in the river. None of them proposed to surrender. Captain Stoneman told of one Mexican who crossed the river, jumped into the air in glee, and fell dead, pierced by a rifle ball.

The rangers pursued the defeated Mexicans. They were endeavoring to get off with their artillery. They made efforts to fire their guns at their American pursuers, but were too hard pressed to do so with effect. Four or five miles above Río Grande City, the Roma road crossed a ravine. On the western bank Cortina halted his bodyguard, rallied what men he could, and tried to make a stand.

Ford's rangers pelted up to the opposite bank. The Mexicans invited us in no polite terms to dismount and fight them on foot. At the same instant they fired on us. Lieutenant [John] Littleton was in the act of cocking his gun; a ball struck the barrel, and the rifle was discharged in the air. The matter of nationality was decided then and there. A furious charge scattered Cortina's bodyguard and left one of his pieces in our possession. It was loaded. Captain W. R. Henry—"Big Henry"—mounted the piece and fired a salute. The enemy attempted no further resistance. They seemed panic-stricken and, abandoning the other cannon, fled.

A large number of the Mexicans still followed the Roma road. Ford feared Cortina might enter Roma and rob it. The Texians pushed on with a strong detachment of rangers. About five miles from Roma, Cortina left the road, turning away from the river valley. "Red-Head" Thomas and a few other rangers saw Cheno's trail and followed it. They came in sight of the marauding chief, but were not strong enough to attack his escort. Ford did not learn this till the next day.

The main body of rangers marched to Roma and gave the inhabitants assurance of protection. The riders returned to Ringgold Barracks, fifteen miles distant, that night. It was claimed that the mounted men had marched seventy miles in thirty-six hours and had won a fight.

The loss of the enemy was officially reported at sixty killed. We afterwards ascertained it was much greater. A half-breed Mexican, said to have been raised at San Antonio, was wounded in the fight and taken prisoner. He was removed to Reynosa and lived three months. One ball had penetrated his stomach. He spoke Spanish and English fluently. He represented Cortina's loss at two hundred in killed alone. In addition we had captured both of Cortina's loaded cannon, many of his papers, some small arms, and some horses. Judge Sam Stewart had been made a prisoner by Cortina. When we entered Roma he told us that the Mexicans had had about seven hundred effective men. While still a prisoner, he had been informed by his Mexican captors:

"Tomorrow we are going to kill you, rob, and burn the town."

"Just after daylight on the twenty-seventh," Stewart continued, "I heard Major Ford shout out these words: 'O yes, you yellow sons-of-guns, we've got you.' I thought his was the sweetest voice I ever heard."

Colonel Lockridge wrote a graphic description of the engagement at Río Grande City on December 27, 1859. It was published in the New Orleans *Picayune*. Not long afterwards, an effort was made to have him change some statements, which some pretended to think did them injustice. He sternly refused to change anything, told his interviewers that he was at their service in any way and that he was always ready to stand by his averments with arms or without arms in Texas or on the Mexican side. Without intending to impugn the courage of anyone concerned, let it suffice to say that there was no fighting on that occasion.

This indomitable soldier yielded up his life at the battle of Valverde during the Civil War; a nobler, more undaunted spirit never winged its way to the realms of immortality. A generous foe, a true friend, a heart of sympathy, and pure impulses made him the peer of any gentleman lending his services to the Southern Cross.

4

After the defeat and dispersion of Cortina's forces at Río Grande City, the bandit crossed into Mexico, near Guerrero. A large detachment of his men were driven across just below Mier. They were well received by the Mexican people.

Major Heintzelman moved up the Río Grande to Roma and endeavored to learn as much as possible of Cortina's whereabouts and intentions and at the same time to give protection to the frontier. On January 1, 1860, Heintzelman wrote Ford:

Sir: It is now 11½ A.M. I have just conversed with a man from the Mexican town of Mier. He reports that last night Cortinas with 30 men demanded permission from the Alcalde of Mier to march his men through the Plaza of the town on his way to Monterey. The Alcalde refused permission.

This morning, a party of some 20 or 30 men, were met about three hours ago, a few miles from Mier on the road to Camargo. These no doubt were Cortinas and his men. They were well mounted and well armed and I presume are what he calls his body-guard.

You will no doubt by sending out several persons, learn of their whereabouts, and the direction they are travelling and perhaps succeed in cutting him off. His capture I consider of the utmost importance. If you can dispose of your men in small parties through the country you will pick up all stragglers and prevent their entering in force.

The troops from above must now be this side of Laredo. I have ordered those directed to rendezvous at Fort Brown to advance up the river.

If we continue active here I don't see how his small parties can escape.

I expect to day to hear from Guerrero, but now consider it of little importance, as no doubt these are the 32 men said to have crossed over from this side of Guerrero.

The fact that Cortina was publicly rallying and recruiting his broken forces in Mexico was patent to all in that section. Nothing but the knowledge that the Mexican authorities were knowingly permitting their soil to be used for the setting on foot of a hostile invasion of the territory of the United States could have justified the measure first proposed by Major Heintzelman. One of Cortina's projects, set forth in some of his proclamations, was the reconquest of Texas. This had been for years a dream in which many Mexicans had fondly indulged. In the beginning of his career Cortina was so successful that many of his countrymen were led to believe him to be the instrument, in the hands of the Almighty, destined to chastise the insolent North Americans and restore Texas to the Mexican Union. In the enthusiasm of the moment they seemed to overlook the atrocious means by which Cortina purposed attaining his end. His defeat at Río Grande City had not caused his admirers to lose confidence in him. They supposed he would retrieve his fortune and fame by some happy stroke, and woo Fortune to his side once more.

5

During these operations the efficiency of the Texas Rangers was materially lessened by the order for an election for major. Captain Tobin was a candidate, and, as was usually the case on such occasions, he at times appeared amenable to the charge of working more to secure his election than to assure success to the operations. Lieutenant John Littleton was a candidate for captain. The election of Tobin was the only chance to make a vacancy for Littleton. His manipulations were not always marked by fairness. Captain Tomlinson—"Old Uncle Pete"—labored under the impression that a Texas Ranger was a nondescript creature who needed no discipline, and the less restraint imposed on him the better he would fight.

Ford wanted discipline—not the rigid discipline of the regular army, but that moral discipline and drill which had made his old company invincible. He required men to move in line, and when they galloped off without permission to visit a ranch, he ordered them back. He objected to charging through the streets, yelling, and firing pistols into the air, and to all those displays savoring more of the blackguard than of the soldier. He spoke but one way: "I will do my duty, and you will do yours." He well knew what would be the verdict of the men who wanted an easy time under a good easy fellow. They would become shirkers, military dudes, incapable of performing the duties necessary to be performed.

After Ford had prepared his official report of the recent operations, he ordered the election for major to be held, but made no effort to succeed his rank. He made a proposition to Captain Tobin that they both resign and that the unsuccessful party then serve as a private. Tobin declined. In the election he was declared elected by six votes.

The day after the election Ford requested the command to come to his quarters in the hay lot at Ringgold Barracks. He read his official report to them. He had tried to do justice to all, mentioning them in friendly terms and finding no fault with any man. After Ford had read it, many of the rangers asked him:

"Why did you not read that yesterday morning? Had you done so you would have been elected major."

Inasmuch as Major Tobin had declined to accept the terms proffered by Ford, he did not conceive himself bound to remain in the service. Ford announced his intention to retire. Captain Walker and his men did likewise. They had been mustered for no specific time, and claimed the right to leave when they chose, more particularly since Cortina had been routed and his followers driven into Mexico.

In his determination to return to Brownsville, Ford was governed by other considerations than those expressed above. He was convinced Cortina had proceeded down the Río Grande, and was gathering men as he moved. It was almost certain he would resume hostile operations. Ford wished to be at the point of danger, feeling assured that were there anything to be done he would be called upon. He knew Walker's men could be depended on and would stand by him, commission or no commission. Ford expected fighting on the way down.

The march to Brownsville was attended by no startling event. We were confident that Cortina was moving down the opposite bank, almost at the same time. We slept at Edinburg, and had every reason to believe Cortina slept at Reynosa on the other bank. About 25 miles lower down, some shots were fired across the river. We camped a short distance above the Bend of La Bolsa; that night Cortina's men crossed stock at the bend.

When we reached Brownsville, citizens irrespective of race treated us with great courtesy. Our greeting from the state commissioners, Angel Navarro and Robert H. Taylor, who had been sent down to investigate the Cortina trouble, was warm and cordial. They soon announced their intention of reorganizing the ranger command and of retaining two companies in the service. The command at Ringgold Barracks under Major Tobin was to be discharged as soon as possible.[3] These arrangements had been decided upon before Captain Ford's arrival; hence he had nothing to do in the matter.

Captain Walker concluded to return to Austin. Some of his men went home. This left a small nucleus around which to form a company. A camp was pitched at Ramireno, a short distance above Brownsville. The ordnance and ordnance stores, the camp and garrison equipage, the public animals, were all retained.

Cortina was known to be heading a considerable force on the Mexican side. He was depredating on the property of United States citizens. We were anxious to meet him again in battle.

---

[3] The Río Grande Commissioners, Navarro and Taylor, discharged Tobin because he was "utterly incompetent to command in the field." The commissioners told Governor Houston that Tobin's command, lacking discipline and morale, had hanged an innocent man during the fighting the preceding November, had proven themselves completely unreliable in the battle at Río Grande City, and then had harassed and plundered peaceful citizens in the surrounding country. One rancher said that when Tobin's men encamped on his land, "they burnt up my pens and fences for firewood, and one horse by accident. They also used a few hogs and goats and fifty barrels of sweet potatoes, and for which their commander refuses to pay me." Such men did not belong in the Texas Rangers, who carried with them the reputation of a proud country; therefore, "we have ordered 'Major' Tobin from Rio Grande City to this place for discharge."

(Taylor to Houston, Brownsville, January 16, 1860, Governors' Letters, 1846–1860, ms.)

XXIII

>>>

THAT VENGEFUL WAR CRY

When Robert H. Taylor and Angel Navarro, upon an investigation of all the facts connected with the campaign, ordered a reorganization of the state troops and authorized John S. Ford to superintend the same, they were, in effect, endorsing Ford's official acts and nominating him as senior officer in command of all state troops in that section.

Captain John Littleton, for some reason not positively known to the writer, left Ringgold Barracks and went into camp near Fort Brown. It was reported that Major Tobin and Captain Littleton failed to agree. Tobin owed his election to Littleton, and the latter may have attached too much importance to the reputed obligations thus imposed upon his superior in rank. In any event they separated. Both the gentlemen have passed away. The writer's personal relations with them were amicable, and no official misunderstandings had occurred; consequently these remarks are free from any coloring caused by ill will, envy, or prejudice. They are made to account for the presence of Captain Littleton's company, as explained at the time. It soon became well known that Captain Littleton had broken with Tobin and had determined to take his chances with the new organization under Ford.

Recruits came in from counties on the Nueces, and even beyond. The muster was made on January 20, 1860. The term of service was for twelve months, or "unless sooner discharged by order of the Governor." The rolls were signed: "Angel Navarro and Robt. H. Taylor, Mustering Officer, Commissioners of State." They authorized "Captain John S. Ford to receive recruits into the service so as to fill up his company to eighty-three men rank and file."

This authority was made a part of the roll. The privates at the date of muster numbered thirty. The commissioned officers were John S. Ford, captain, and Matthew Nolan, first lieutenant. The muster roll of Company B has not been found. John Littleton was captain, John H. Paschal, lieutenant, and Arthur Pugh and Bennett Jordan, second lieutenants. This statement is made from memory.

On February 2, 1860, Taylor and Navarro wrote Ford: "Sir: From and after this date your movements and the troops under your command will be directed by Major Heintzelman, or other comdg officer of U.S.A. on this frontier. You will, therefore, obey all orders emanating from such officer."

This was given in order to show who was the over-all commander of the State troops on the Río Grande under the new order of things.

It was a matter of some difficulty to procure supplies. There was no money on hand, and some felt unwilling, and others unable, to await legislative action to provide an appropriation to pay the claims. There was difficulty in procuring the adequate number of mules for wagons and for packs. Captain Ford ordered Lieutenant [William] Howard, acting quartermaster, to purchase mules at any price. He bought a few at reasonable prices; but the most of them cost one hundred dollars apiece—an extortion.

The steamer *Ranchero* of the King & Kenedy Line was at Río Grande City awaiting an opportunity to sail for Brownsville without hazarding $300,000 in coin and a large and valuable freightage, to say nothing of the passengers and crew whose lives would have been sacrificed in the event the steamer should be captured by Cortina. This adventurer was known to have recruited another force of 300 men in Mexico. He had taken post at the Bolsa Bend of the Río Grande, about thirty-six miles above Matamoros. Cortina and his officers visited Matamoros almost daily. It was a fact no one disputed on the lower Río Grande that these marauders drew supplies from Matamoros, with the full knowledge and implied consent of the authorities of Mexico, all the while they were depredating upon the property of citizens of the United States. No one doubted the intention of Cortina to capture the *Ranchero*. His force was distributed along the banks of the river in such a manner as to throw a murderous fire on the steamer every foot of the way from the moment she got abreast of the upper end of the bend until she cleared it.

This condition of things continued for about a month. Every effort was made to place the ranger companies in a position to make a forward movement, clear the country of robbing bands, and dislodge Cortina, also to protect the *Ranchero*.

About February 1, 1860, the command broke camp. It consisted of the companies of Captain George Stoneman and Lieutenant [Manning M.] Kimmel of the United States Cavalry, and the two companies of state troops. The cavalry took the road, accompanied by the wagons and pack mules. The rangers scoured the bends of the Río Grande. The place of encampment was named in the morning and reached at night by both commands. It was up above Brownsville on the Río Grande.

2

The next day Ford was on the way back to camp, after a short patrol with a small body of rangers and Don Savas Cavazos, a half brother of Cheno Cortina by a previous marriage of their mother. When they arrived at Mrs. Cortina's ranch, about seven miles above Brownsville, Cavazos invited the officers of the party to go into the house. After doing so, they were introduced to Mrs. Cortina. She was a small woman, not weighing more than one hundred pounds, being at the time over seventy years of age. She was very good looking, had a pretty face, bright, black eyes, and very white skin. She was a lady of culture, and indicated as much in her actions, and had all the politeness of a well-bred Mexican. She was held in high esteem by both her Mexican and American acquaintances. She had taken refuge in Matamoros when Cortina commenced to make war upon the people of the United States, and had recently returned to her home. When introduced to Ford, she took his hand and looked appealingly into his face for several minutes. By and by tears were visible in her eyes; finally they wet her cheeks. All this was an appeal for her wayward son. It was as much as to say:

"I know my son has violated the laws of war. He has trampled upon right, and in some instances, I am afraid, he has forgotten the rights of humanity. He has attacked and killed Americans and their friends without provocation. You have defeated him, you are sent again to make war upon him. Should he fall into your power remember to be merciful to him, as you expect to obtain mercy from our Great Creator."

The writer vividly remembers this meeting. He has never attempted to describe his feelings during the interview. He gave the lady an assurance of protection, as far as lay in his power. His men obeyed his orders, and did not molest the lady. As long as she lived, when danger of any kind seemed to threaten her, she would go to Brownsville and appeal to Ford to aid her. If it were possible, he extended assistance to her. She was never troubled by American troops. They respected her and her property. They knew the mother was not to blame for the acts of her son.

While all this was going forward, her daughter went into a small Catholic Church on the premises. There she began crying and finally went into a spasm. The surgeon of the command, Dr. John T. Eldridge, was present and went to help the lady.

To those who knew Juan N. Cortina as an enemy of the Americans, it was not presumed this occurrence would make any difference in his estimation and treatment of Americans, but in later years he actually demonstrated a regard for his mother and esteemed those who treated her well.[1]

3

The rangers in their operations in the immediate valley of the river came upon squads of Cortina's men in the act of committing robberies. A number of them were killed.

On the fourth day of February, Captain Ford directed his guard, under Corporal Milton A. Duty, to halt the wagons and pack mules at a small ranch called Zacatal near the Bolsa Bend. The guard reached that point about 1 P.M. They discovered a party of armed Mexicans, thirty in number, in the act of crossing the Río Grande, fired on them, and drove them from their horses and other stolen plunder. Fifty or sixty horses had already crossed. The guard moved back to the wagons, without receiving any damage from the fusillade opened upon them from the Mexican side. At this juncture the head of Major Tobin's command came up. The firing commenced again. The major went with Duty's guard and found a detachment of his men under Bennett Musgrave engaged with Mexicans. Duty and his men approached near the river bank at the Bolsa Crossing. A heavy fire opened from the other bank; [Fountain B.] Woodruff was

---

[1] As Ford points out later in his story, his wife Addie went to Matamoros in 1864, and Cortina, then governor of Tamaulipas during the Benito Juarez administration, treated her kindly. Ford thought Cortina was returning the courtesy Rip had extended to Mrs. Cortina in 1860.

mortally wounded. He was perfectly cool, handed his revolver to a comrade, saying:

"Take it. I shall never be able to use it again."

About that time the steamer *Ranchero* arrived at the convex end of the bend. The steamer was fired upon by Cortina's men. Lieutenant Lomis L. Langdon was on board, with a small detachment of regular troops. He had two field pieces taken from Cortina at the fight near Río Grande City on December 27, 1859. He opened up on the Mexicans and saved the boat from capture. She had to run the gauntlet again. There was no way out of the bend, except to pass by Cortina's force. It was a self-evident truth that these desperadoes were bent on spilling American blood and plundering American property. Mrs. Langdon, Mrs. Downey, and several other ladies were on the *Ranchero,* Judge Downey and other gentlemen also. The throat of the bend was narrow, only about 150 yards from bank to bank. Occupying it, sheltered by houses, fences, and timber, with undergrowth, were Cortina and his 300 bloodthirsty followers.

There was a lull. Tobin's men halted near the boat. Cortina concentrated his men to attack the steamer as she was leaving the bend. A courier was despatched to advise Captain Ford of what had happened. About three P.M. he galloped into camp. Lieutenant Langdon met him and inquired:

"Captain are you going to cross into Mexico?"

"Certainly, sir."

The two ranger companies were not full, not numbering more than a hundred men. Many of the men had not yet come up. Captain A. C. Hill, commanding a detachment styled the "Spy Company," was not expected to arrive until that night. Captain Stoneman's command was some distance off, and was not looked for till morning. He was making a scout inland from the river. It was understood that a large number of Major Tobin's men pointedly declined to pass the Río Grande. [They were on their way to Brownsville to be mustered out of service. Tobin, although he claimed no command, offered to help us personally.]

Ford ordered ammunition to be distributed, had a guard detailed to hold camp and protect property. The men had made coffee. Major Tobin and Captain Peter Tomlinson with a detachment of about ten men crossed the Río Grande and made a reconnaissance. Soon after, Captain Ford passed to the other bank with about thirty-five men. He moved in the direction of Cortina's supposed position, intending to make him develop, if possible. Major Tobin was returning to the steamer. When they met, Tobin remarked:

"We found nobody; they have gone."

Cortina, supposing an attack was meditated on his center and left flank, began massing his men on these points.

"I do not think they have gone," Captain Ford observed. "I see a large number near the houses and behind the fence."

At that time the rangers were advancing in line. Captain Ford ordered a "Right Face" and moved the command toward the upper side of the bend. Cortina's right flank was covered by about 60 mounted men. They failed to charge, and thus gave the rangers time to reach the river bank and form under it. The line of attack was at a right angle with the line of defense.

The right of the rangers was about thirty yards from the Mexican left. The bank furnished excellent shelter. By kneeling, the rangers could load and fire without exposing but the tops of their heads.

The Mexicans opened fire while our men were moving under the bank. It was soon returned. The rangers were ordered to fire slowly, to take deliberate aim, and to throw away no ammunition foolishly. Major Tobin and Captain Tomlinson both used firearms and delivered no orders. Captain Ford remained standing, exposed to the fire of the enemy. He remembers to have been lectured by Captain Tomlinson for being on the field without a gun. Captain Tomlinson was a brave old frontiersman, had seen much service, and was not much concerned about questions of military import.

Captain Littleton was placed on the right, with orders to move slowly in the direction of Cortina's left, with a view to turn his flank. Twelve rangers were directed to keep up a brisk and well-directed fire on the mounted men.

The struggle had now become earnest. The Mexicans poured in a heavy fire, taking numbers into consideration. The rangers shot to kill: it was victory or death with them. Someone called Captain Ford's attention to the terrific firing of the Mexicans.

"Don't mind that," he replied. "They will soon need the ammunition they are wasting."

Cortina encouraged his men, assuring them of victory.

Captain Ford passed along the ranger line speaking inspiring words to the boys. He told them that there was plenty of cartridges for all, that the fight would be won, and that any effort at a foot race would end in shooting the delinquent.

There was a commotion. Ford trotted around to the rear where one or two men had become demoralized. One fellow made for the steamer at race horse speed. Ford discovered that the demoralization in the rear was caused by a volunteer from the steamer calling for "cartridges" in an

obstreperous manner, and creating the impression that we were in want
of ammunition. Some pointed remarks, couched in rather incisive language, from Captain Ford silenced the loud-mouthed *hombre.*

A goodly number of Tobin's men were still on the American side,
mere spectators of the combat. Some of them predicted "another Dawson scrape."[2] It looked a little doubtful to those on the boat as to the
result of the skirmish. Captain Ford sent an order to Captain [John]
Martin of the *Ranchero* to steam up, and allow Lieutenant Langdon to
use the two field pieces. Lieutenant Pugh, assisted by Lance Corporal
Hubbard, collected a few men, marched up on the American side, and
fired across the river at the Mexicans on Cortina's extreme left.

The Mexican mounted men had already abandoned the field. Captain
Ford now ordered an advance of his command. With Ford in the lead,
the column moved steadily, delivering a galling fire as they marched. The
Mexicans began to waver. The head of the ranger column passed beyond
the palisade fence, wheeled to the left, and encountered the left flank
of Cortina; a few yards separated the combatants. Captain Littleton, Lieutenant Howard, and Captain Ford ascended the second bank of the river,
and were exposed to a heavy fire. Ford ordered the other two officers
down from the bank. As soon as the fire of the Mexicans had been
drawn, Ford shouted,

"CHARGE!"

The rangers came at a run, firing rapidly. With six-shooters in hand,
they rushed upon the Mexicans, drove them, rolled them up on the center, and routed them. The fleeing enemy were hotly pursued.

Cortina was the last to leave the field. He faced his pursuers, emptied
his revolver, and tried to halt his panic-stricken men. Lieutenants Dix and
Howard and Private George Morris were near Captain Ford. He ordered
them to fire at Cortina. They did so. One shot struck the cantle of his
saddle, one cut out a lock of hair from his head, a third cut his bridle

---

[2] The Dawson Massacre occurred in September, 1842, when a Mexican invasionary
force under Adrian Woll captured San Antonio. From Gonzales came a body of militia
under Matthew Caldwell, all boiling for a fight, to engage the Mexicans. Badly outnumbered, the Texans fought with knives and muskets in the mesquite and prickly pear,
but they soon were calling for reinforcements. Colonel Nicholas Mosby Dawson managed
to gather 52 volunteers and rode to help Caldwell, who was entrenched near the Salado
River some six miles east of San Antonio. Somewhere behind the Texan lines a Mexican
force lay in wait; making not a sound, they let Dawson's men pass along the trail, then
opened a murderous fire on them from three directions. The Texans tried to surrender,
but the ambushers kept on firing until 35 *gringos* lay dead. The remaining seventeen were
marched barefoot and starving to Perote Castle deep in Old Mexico.

(L. V. Spellman [ed.], "Letters of the 'Dawson Men' From Perote Prison, Mexico,
1842–1843," *Southwestern Historical Quarterly*, XXXVIII, 246–269.

rein, a fourth passed through his horse's ear, and a fifth struck his belt. He galloped off unhurt. But for the obscurity, it being almost dark, the frontier pirate would have been killed.

About that time the *Ranchero* arrived—too late for Lieutenant Langdon to use his field pieces.

The victory was won. The troops were shouting and whooping in their victory. Someone, without orders, set fire to the houses and some of the corrals from which Cortina had fought. Our loss was one killed—Private Woodruff—and three or four slightly wounded, none of them so seriously as to require treatment, out of a total engaged of 48 rangers. The Mexican loss was twenty-nine killed and forty wounded. This information and the matters connected with the firing at Cortina, we acquired from Mexican eye-witnesses, one of whom was in the fight.

The skirmish covered an hour and a quarter of time. The firing was brisk. The Mexicans shouted frequently. Once in a while the Texas yell arose, clear and distinct above the din of battle.

At one point in the battle, one of the ladies on the *Ranchero* had expressed uneasiness, asking:

"Is that the Mexicans shouting?"

"No, madam, it is Texians. Mexican lungs cannot produce such a sound as that vengeful war cry."

It was an hour and a quarter of deep suspense and solicitude to those on the steamer. They knew what victory for the Mexicans meant. They also knew the Texians were fighting against great odds—more than six to one. It is needless to say they had an abiding confidence in their countrymen, and assurance that they would do all that brave men could.

After the pursuit ceased, the command moved back to the convex part of the bend, where the *Ranchero* was anchored, and were assisted by Captain Martin in recrossing to the American side.

In the early part of the night Major Tobin and his men left for Brownsville. A report came to light, with his name attached, claiming that he had commanded during the fight at La Bolsa. He avowed to the contrary on various occasions, in the presence of witnesses. (For instance, in the presence of Major James A. Carr and the writer, in San Antonio, not a great while before his death, Tobin distinctly denied having claimed to command at La Bolsa.) Major Heintzelman was in command of all the troops operating against General Cortina, and Heintzelman recognized Ford as commander of the State troops, in view of the order of the commissioners of the State of Texas.

Let it be said here that the relations between Major Tobin and Captain Ford were always friendly and agreeable, and were never otherwise.

On the arrival of Captain Stoneman and Lieutenant Kimmel, a conference was held. It was decided that Captain Ford should pass the Río Grande the next morning, for the purpose of protecting the *Ranchero* from hostile attack from the Mexican side. The regulars were to keep abreast of the steamboat. In the event of a collision with a force of Mexicans, Captain Stoneman pledged himself to cross both his companies to Ford's assistance. The wagons, pack mules, and accoutrements were to remain on the American side.

During the night a reconnaissance was made on the Mexican side, and no troops discovered in the vicinity of La Bolsa. Everything was quiet. Preparations were made for an early move in the morning. Lieutenant Langdon was quite efficient in action and advice during the passage of the *Ranchero* from La Bolsa towards Brownsville. He did good service with the artillery.

4

The affair of La Bolsa produced salutary effects. It emboldened Mexican-born citizens of the United States to return to their ranches on the American side of the Río Grande. One of the first to take this step was Don Juan Miguel Longoria of Santa María Ranch, about thirty miles above Brownsville. He was adequately protected.

Scouts were made in various directions. The chances for Cortina's men to pass to the American side, steal stock, and cross them into Mexico were greatly reduced. These enterprises became dangerous.

An encampment was made at Agua Negra, a deserted ranch about 45 miles above Brownsville. The *Ranchero* afforded facilities for the rangers to pass into Mexico. The horses were taken. The force numbered forty-eight. On February 5, 1860, they moved with precaution in order to avoid surprises and ambuscades. Not far below La Bolsa was the large ranch Las Palmas. When we approached it, signs of commotion were visible. On nearing one of the principal houses, people of both sexes were seen leaving it, carrying moveables. Captain Ford assured them there was no necessity for such a course. He wrote a note which was translated into Spanish, and sent out unsealed. He stated the passage of the Río Grande by American troops was not with a view to invade the territory of Mexico, but to wage war against Cortina and his followers, and he pleaded authority for so doing from General [Guadalupe] García, commanding the line of the Bravo. Ford urged that the attack on the *Ranchero* from the Mexican side justified the act as a measure in defense of the persons and the property of citizens of the United States.

A norther blew up. The *Ranchero* got aground opposite Las Palmas.

A Mexican official made his appearance about 10 A.M. He was a prefect of police from Matamoros. A conference was had and explanations made by Captain Ford in accordance with the allegations above set forth. The prefect asked for time to communicate with the Mexican authorities at Matamoros and to receive their orders.

Notice of the prefect's proposition was conveyed to Captain Stoneman. He had no objection to Ford's accepting it. The two men then met on the *Ranchero* and consulted. The steamer, it was believed, could not be gotten off that day. The delay gave time for preparation to engage the Mexican troops near Las Palmas, in the event the Mexican authorities refused to permit our troops to protect the *Ranchero* from their side of the Río Grande.

The prefect received from us an affirmative answer to his proposal to become communicative. When asked to what corps a force of about 600 men we had seen in our front belonged, he responded promptly that they were Mexican, stating the corps. In regard to a body of about 200 in our rear, we asked:

"To what corps do the 200 belong drawn up on our right and rear?"

He shrugged his shoulders and answered: *"Quién sabe?"*—who knows —the Mexican mode of evading a proper answer.

They were Cortina's marauders. The situation might have been more inviting—forty-eight Texians holding a ranch in the immediate presence of 600 to 800 Mexicans. No mistakes were made. All were convinced that a contest with one detachment involved a contest with all the Mexican forces. No one backed down by weighing the consequences or doubting a successful result.

Captain A. C. Hill had charge of our picket guard. He reported in person that a small detachment of the men on our right had approached the picket and menaced an attack.

"Why in the devil's name didn't you fire on them?" Captain Ford inquired rather sharply.

Captain Hill retired with a full conception of what was expected of him.

Our right rested on Las Palmas, strengthened by some houses, and our left on the Río Grande, strengthened by Lieutenant Langdon's pieces and the troops of Stoneman.

Here is food for reflection: Cortina had been at La Bolsa for a month; his aims were patent to the world. During all those days no effort was made by the Mexican authorities to cause him to abandon his position and to prevent him from recruiting men on Mexican soil to make war upon the persons and the property of American citizens. Within less than twenty-four hours after he had made a hostile assault on the *Ranchero* and within twelve hours after he had been attacked and driven from his position by Texas Rangers, almost a thousand of his Mexicans were again on the ground ready to make common cause with their lawless leader, who had violated international law as well as the terms of the treaty between Mexico and the United States. In the opinion of the regulars and rangers on the ground these things spoke for themselves and called for redress.

The night was passed in rather feverish anxiety. No sensational alarm disturbed our slumbers. The norther abated during the night. Our bivouac was not uncommonly pleasant. The sentinels were vigilant. Had one gun been fired, Captain Stoneman would have crossed over to join us and nothing could have averted a battle.

On the morning of the sixth the Mexican officials were on hand at an early hour. Stoneman and Ford acted in concert. Ford did most of the talking. He explained the object of the crossing as heretofore given. Then he pointed out that General García had had quite a month to remove Cortina from the Bolsa. He knew perfectly the object Cortina had in view in placing a force at La Bolsa. The intended attack on the steamboat *Ranchero* was a fact discussed in Matamoros. In no uncertain terms Ford cautioned the Mexican officials against permitting expeditions being fitted out on the territory of the Republic of Mexico to wage a depredatory war upon the soil and the citizens of the United States, told them should a war be set on foot in this manner it would be a war in fact, one in which the United States would fight to the end.

The final enunciation was that the American troops could march down the Río Grande on either bank in order to protect the *Ranchero*. The Mexican authorities gave an assurance that, in the event the rangers returned to the American side, the Mexicans would see that the *Ranchero* received no hostile assault from their side of the river. In answer to this liberal suggestion, Captain Ford said that he would return to the American bank, confiding the steamer to the care of the Mexican authorities. He crossed without delay. Ere this, the *Ranchero* had gotten off the obstacle and had steamed down the river a short distance. She had tied up to await the result of the interview and to conform to whatever might be agreed upon.

The *Ranchero* reached Brownsville without molestation on the eighth of February. She was escorted immediately by the rangers who followed the sinuous Río Grande, scanning the horizon for trouble with great circumspection.

XXIV

>>>

HIGH CARNIVAL IN THE VALLEY

La Mesa is a ranch on the Mexican side of the Río Grande, situated on one of the roads leading from Camargo to Matamoros. It is about forty-five miles above Matamoros, and four miles in a southerly direction from Agua Negra, where we were encamped.

During the month of March, 1860, Major Heintzelman received a communication from General Guadalupe García, commanding the line of the Bravo, stating that Cortina was at La Mesa. Our spies had informed us he was near that place in a heavy chaparral, having but one channel of ingress and egress. A copy of the note in question was forwarded to Captain Ford. He showed it in confidence to one of his officers, who asked:

"Aren't you going to cross and engage Cortina?"

"No, sir, I am not. The note is not sent in sincerity. General García is not a good friend of Americans. The order allowing us to enter Mexican territory in pursuit of Cortina and his followers originated from General José Carbajal, who is our friend and the superior in rank of General García. The latter makes a show of obeying the order. This pretended information is a bait thrown out to get us into trouble. Should we pass the Río Grande and march upon La Mesa we shall find a Mexican force there large enough to defeat our two companies. Provided you can honorably avoid doing so, it is a good rule never to fight an enemy on his own ground, when the topography of the surroundings is not known to you. Let us await developments."

The next day we were drilling; a noise was heard, which proved to be the approach of Captain Stoneman at the head of his company and the company of Lieutenant Kimmel.

"What, you here!" Captain Stoneman exclaimed. "I expected to find you over in Mexico."

"I concluded to wait for an order to cross this time," Ford said.

Stoneman assured him the order had arrived. Preparations were made to pass the river. Several weeks before this, Captain Ford had been hurt in an accident, and, on this account, he requested Captain Stoneman to superintend the crossing. What had happened to Ford was this. He was drilling the men on horseback. He ordered a charge in the direction of a chaparral to test the horsemanship of the rangers. His horse stepped into a hole, fell, and sent the rider into the air. Just as the captain struck the ground, he saw his horse standing on his head in the act of turning a somerset. Ford made an effort to crawl away from the descending animal, but it was unsuccessful. The equine's hinder parts struck Ford between the shoulders and flattened him out considerably. One of the rangers called out as he passed by: "Boys, look at Uncle Rip!" The blow had come with terrific force. For more than a month after the captain "spit blood."

Captain Stoneman did a good job of directing the crossing. An excavation was made in the bank to force horses into the river. It was too narrow for two animals to go abreast. By whipping the horses in the rear, we compelled the ones in the front to take the water. It was about three o'clock the next morning before the four companies were transferred to the other bank.

The first thing Captain Ford did after setting foot on Mexican soil was to place a skirmishing party in his front. In this detachment were some of his old and tried rangers. Dan Givens was among them. He spoke Spanish fluently, was self-possessed, and fearless, and consequently in charge. It was not long before Givens reported men in his front. He was instructed to be silent and watchful and to hold his ground if fired upon. After a short lapse of time, Givens reported that he had reconnoitred and ascertained that a detachment of Mexicans were in our front. He was enjoined to avoid discovery, if possible.

When Captain Stoneman reached the Mexican side, he was informed of the situation. Not being acquainted with the country, he asked Ford's opinion. He replied in substance:

"A Mexican force has intended to ambuscade the main road. In order to avoid falling into it, I suggest the propriety of taking a path leading down the river to an adjacent ranch, going through it, and following the road leading from there to La Mesa."

Captain Stoneman adopted the suggestion. The command moved at once. The small ranch was passed without incident. Our picket on the road from there to La Mesa would have intercepted any courier sent to give notice of our movements.

When within half a mile of La Mesa, we saw a light off to our right. Lieutenant Nolan was ordered to ascertain what it was. He reported that it was a Mexican picket. On his approach the guard retired at a brisk gallop. It was concluded to follow the picket, thus giving the enemy as little chance to get ready as possible. Very soon the long roll was beaten at La Mesa; all of us expected a fight. Ford asked Captain Stoneman which position he would take with the regulars. Stoneman replied: "You are on the right. Remain there."

We were moving in column by twos.

"Halt!" "Front into line!"

One of Ford's platoons took the wrong direction. He reprimanded the erring officer quite sharply. The Mexican officers and men knew perfectly well we were Americans. They did not hail us. We pushed to the front, and the firing began about the same time on both sides. We kept advancing. In less than ten minutes the Mexican infantry began to recoil. Their right was composed of cavalry. They were rolled up and routed; many of them dropped their guns and ran into the houses. Our men were busy dragging them out. They carried prisoners and arms to a large house which was lighted up.

A Mexican officer fired at Captain Stoneman at the distance of a few yards, then rushed into a house. A Mexican woman sprang to the door and shut it. Several men fired at the door and unintentionally wounded the woman. She was reported to have died of the wound.

A rather exciting commotion arose. A Mexican was vociferating at the top of his voice. Both regulars and rangers took a fancy to kick him. He blurted an obstreperous call for *el Coronel Ford*. That gentleman came forward, and inquired what was wanting. The response was:

"I am Major So and So, commanding these troops. It is a lucky thing for you I slept out of my quarters last night, otherwise you would have been badly whipped."

Here the men chimed in: "We saw his feet sticking out from under a bed, and dragged him out." He professed to have been robbed of money, his sword, and valuables.

It was demanded of him to state to what command he belonged.

"The Mexican National Guard."

"If you belong to the National Guard, what the devil are you doing here?" Ford asked, quite perplexed. "Your general told us Cortina was here."

At this juncture Stoneman rode up. Ford said to him: "Well, captain, we have played Old Scratch. We've whipped the Guardia Nacional, wounded a woman, and killed a mule."

The fact was we had killed four or five Mexicans, wounded others, and made many prisoners. Lieutenant Nolan killed the mule. He averred it was quite dark, and he mistook the animal for a Mexican. The major who stationed himself under the bed was later tried by a court-martial, and suspended or cashiered for unofficerlike conduct.

Our men were ordered to restore arms and other captured property, which was done. That unfortunate sword of the major's was an exception. It was restored to him three times. The news in camp was that when last seen, one of our Mexican guides was wearing it.

A Mexican came up wringing his hands and told a tearful tale in a funereal tone. He claimed to be a peddler, travelling in company with the Mexican troops and selling them supplies. He accused the rangers of having appropriated a large lot of *piloncillos*, which means a small loaf. It is a way the Mexicans put up sugar. Captain Ford told him he was sorry for him, but Ford could not promise to return his sugar. About this time a ranger answering to the sobriquet of "Dutch John" was on his horse, with a large sack full of *piloncillos* tied to his saddle. He wanted them for his mess and refused to give away even one. While the conversation was going on someone applied a sharp blade to one end of John's sack: the *piloncillos* came pouring out. Such a scramble as occurred has seldom been witnessed. John begged hard for "just one." Rumor had it that the plundering rascals did not leave liberal John a single one to glad his eyes.

It was now full daylight. There were wells a short distance away. The command went to them to make coffee. A sharp lookout was kept up for the troops left behind us on the main road. Captain Stoneman's companies were further from the well than the rangers. All at once the cavalry was seen mounting in haste. The rangers were in the saddle quickly. A force of about six hundred men became visible. A horseman rode towards the rangers. He was permitted to approach. He inquired for Captain Ford. When in the presence of the captain, he announced himself as the adjutant of a Mexican colonel, whom he named, saying his colonel wished to have an interview with "Colonel Ford."

Ford pointed to the regulars and said: "Yonder is Captain Stoneman of the United States Army. He ranks me. Had you not better see him?"

"No, sir," the adjutant replied. "The colonel holds you responsible for all that has happened."

The adjutant was assured the Mexican colonel could enter our lines with perfect safety.

In a few minutes the Mexican colonel arrived, accompanied by his adjutant, who was raised at San Antonio and spoke English. The colonel depended on him as a correct interpreter. Lieutenant Dix acted for Ford, if memory is not at fault. Previous to this Captain Stoneman had expressed a desire not to be present, and authorized Captain Ford to say what he thought right, and Stoneman would stand by it.

The Mexican official led off by a long string of questions: "Why have American troops invaded Mexico? Why did they attack the National Guard? Why did the Americans fire on the Mexican troops at La Mesa without notice? Did not the American authorities expect to be held accountable for the acts of the regulars and rangers? To pay damages, and so on?"

The speaker held up to rest his lungs. Captain Ford proposed to answer a few questions: "We were authorized to pass to the Mexican side in pursuit of Cortina and his band by a general order of the officer commanding the line of the Bravo. He informed us Cortina was at La Mesa. Now, sir, I desire you to answer why and how your command occupied La Mesa? Why your officers in camp failed to hail our troops, instead of beating the long roll on drums and engaging us? Why did you place an ambuscade in our front?"

"I went to the point of crossing to interview you," the Mexican colonel said.

"Why did you bring 600 men along with you to interview me?" Captain Ford asked.

The colonel evaded answering, but dwelt upon what would have happened had he and his whole command been at La Mesa. He intimated that few of us would have been left to answer at roll call.

"Since you place matters on this ground," Ford said, "I will make this proposition: I have two companies of Texas Rangers under my immediate command; you have several hundred men; I am ready and willing to fight it out here, at once. I will request Captain Stoneman not to take part in the engagement."

The colonel declined acceptance.

"Then, sir, you will please change your tone as to the probable results of a collision, or prepare to decide matters on the instant."

Assurances were given that our troops did not occupy Mexican territory with a view to make war upon that government. No cross-questioning drew out the reason why Mexican forces were found at La Mesa. It was understood that the mounted force Captain Stoneman struck and drove from the field was composed of Cortina and his ruffians. Our conclusions were that the Mexican troops were acting in concert with Cortina.

The movement down the river and through the neighboring ranch was unobserved by the Mexicans. We passed between the point where Cortina was reported to be lying in wait and the National Guard was occupying La Mesa. Two or three of our men got separated from the command, fell into Cortina's ambuscade, and were made prisoners, and afterwards released. From all we learned, the Mexican officers did some extra swearing when they heard the firing at La Mesa.

Our troops remained on Mexican soil a day or so after the affair at La Mesa. The official report of this affair is dated March 18, 1860, and signed by Stoneman and Ford. A report obtained currency that the people of Reynosa, Mexico, proposed to give a reward of $30,000 in the event American troops dared to enter their town as they had La Mesa.

2

Major Heintzelman's investigations had convinced him that the soil of Mexico had been used to fit out hostile and predatory expeditions against the territory and the people of the United States. Cortina, carrying property robbed from United States citizens into Mexico, always found a place of deposit and a ready market for it. The authorities of Mexico, on duty on the lower Río Grande, appeared to be parties to this highhanded mode of plundering a neighboring state. The recent experiences at La Mesa and others bore the impress of bad faith so palpably that a denial from Mexican sources was deemed untruthful.

The question of making armed reprisals was frequently discussed by regular and ranger officers and was decided affirmatively. Our understanding was that Major Heintzelman coincided. News was received reporting Cortina not far from La Bolsa. Captain Stoneman and Lieutenant Kimmel went with the rangers into Mexico. The command consisted of four companies. We scoured the valley of the Río Grande, but could not find Cortina. We reached the ranch of La Bolsa; it was populated. An old Mexican Indian who had killed six Americans near the Texas Salt Lake—*Sal del Rey*, the King's Salt—and had been a pest on the frontier, was captured at the ranch. One of the guides, "Red-Head" Thomas, came and reported:

"Captain, we have taken the Indian Faustino."

"I do not wish to see him."

A shot was heard. The scene closed.

We felt sure we would march upon Matamoros. All was going merrily; here would be a chance to pay Mexico back in some of her own coin. We saw the smoke of a steamer, concluded we could get a supply of forage, and got her to touch at the bank. The corn was found. Captain Ricketts of the United States Artillery was on board. Mrs. Ricketts and another lady or two made their appearance. These incidents might have delayed getting off the forage. A ranger rode up, and was assisted aboard.

"Is Captain Ford on board?" he asked.

"Yes, what will you have?"

The ranger gave a despatch to the captain. "I saw the smoke and thought I would find you here," the ranger said.

"I wish the devil had found you first. Why didn't you go to camp?"

The envelope contained an order to Stoneman and Ford to return to the American side with their commands. At this length of time there is a recollection of many unsanctified expressions floating around in the air. The man who delivered that despatch had lost an eye. To this blessed moment the writer feels a sort of resentment towards a one-eyed letter carrier. The feeling of disappointment originated from a strong desire to punish the Mexicans who had made atrocious attacks upon life and property in Texas, and not from hostility to the whole Mexican people. This matter will be referred to again.

Sometime during the day, it was ascertained that Cortina was at his ranch of Maguey, twenty-four miles southerly from Matamoros, and, by the route we would have to march, about sixty miles from our camp. The way was over a rough country abounding in chaparral and other impediments. The march was in silence and at a brisk gait. When within eight or ten miles of Maguey, we saw a Mexican mount a horse and start off at a run. We knew this meant advice of our approach in order to give Cortina time to prepare for a fight or to get out of the way. Lieutenant Kimmel with a few men made a vigorous pursuit, but failed to overtake the fleeing messenger of approaching danger.

Our speed was increased. When within about a mile of the ranch, we heard gun reports which we supposed were Kimmel's troops engaged with Cortina. We rode at a gallop, passed some houses, and saw the head of a column emerging from a grove of mesquite, which proved to be a religious procession, it being Saint Joseph's day. The officers endeavored to halt the galloping rangers. It was almost impossible, those in the rear not hearing the order distinctly and pressing upon those in front. The procession was much disturbed. A man who had been watching the ceremony suddenly broke and ran; we requested that he stop, assuring him that we would not molest him. He ran on, reached the chaparral, and opened fire on the rangers. For a time bullets flew. The angry rangers charged into the thicket. Soon the man was dead. We suffered no casualties. It was now about 12 noon.

The command was dismounted, but held together sufficiently to form a line of battle promptly. No enemy presented himself, however, and we relaxed somewhat. Our ride had given us sharp appetites. A beef was contracted for and bread purchased. Captain Ford sent for the beef, then approached a house, and saw three women. One was a rather pretty girl, and she was crying. Lieutenant Dix and "Red-Head" Thomas whispered into the captain's ear:

"This elderly woman is Cortina's wife. The one shedding tears is his favorite child."

Ford told the rangers to say nothing to the men and to keep an eye on the women and prevent anyone from molesting them. The captain remained near their house until all was ready to move out a short distance to water and grass. Such a zest for roasted beef was never known in refined circles, where nature is overwhelmed by fashion and fettered by conventionalities. It was a feast to which men who had ridden sixty miles, hardly breaking fast or drawing rein, could do justice.

Our sudden march beyond Matamoros had produced intense excitement, especially in that city. Couriers were galloping in at short intervals, reporting where the *gringos apestosos*—the stinking gringos—were last seen. After eating, we marched a few miles, then stopped to graze our horses on a grassy plain. We remained there until after eight o'clock. Mexican spies who had been following us rode off to tell the Mexican officials in the area that they had us located for the night—the Dons slept soundly. We had news that Cortina had gone up the Monterey road. We started after him, expecting to pounce on him about daylight next morning. We made another forced march of forty miles or more. At sunrise we were knocking at the doors of affrighted rancheros and learning from them that Cortina was not in that locality. Rumor had it that on receiving the news of our being about sixty miles away and moving towards Monterey, our Aztec dignitaries lost patience and "swore terribly."

There was a company of the National Guards, or some other local organization, commanded by Captain Benavides, a clever gentleman, camped near by. It was understood that he had particular orders to keep the *gringo* force in sight. If so, he did some hard marching.

Our failure to find Cortina is reputed to have been because of the warning given by the solitary horseman. We came so near striking Cortina that he felt very uncomfortable, as will be developed soon. It was difficult to procure correct information of his whereabouts, because he was extremely popular among his countrymen, especially the lower classes. Nothing but money would break the spell of silence prevailing like an epidemic on the Río Grande where Mexican residents predominated. Captain Ford had Mexicans employed as spies. Their real names were not borne on any roll or attached to any receipt. Such a procedure would have been equivalent to a death warrant; hundreds of Mexicans would have gloried in killing them. On the present occasion, we had no trustworthy spy to furnish the information desired. We had to request Lieutenant Dix to act as guide. The head of our column was directed towards Agua Negra. We moved at a full trot. During the day we struck the camp of Captain Benavides at the Ratamites, some twelve miles south of the river. We stopped long enough to speak a few words to him, and none but courteous expressions were used. The captain looked somewhat surprised when we rode into his camp. He claimed to be hunting Cortina. We thanked him and rode on. A long march carried us to the Río Grande opposite Agua Negra. We calculated that in something more than forty-eight hours we had marched nearly one hundred and forty miles.

This expedition had a beneficial effect. Cortina was impressed with a lively sense of insecurity while remaining adjacent to the Río Grande. Reports located him at Burgos on the edge of the mountains. Our recent operations had caused a sensation among the Mexicans. Americans entering upon the territory of the "magnanimous nation," fighting, making forced marches, and acting pretty much like a foreign enemy, constituted a combination of events rather unpleasant for a proud people to contemplate. They seemed disposed to put an end to our neighborly calls by inducing their notorious champion to seek for rest and a recuperation of his energies, by a resort to a watering place in the spurs of the Sierra Madre. He was satisfied, no doubt, that his health and personal comfort demanded the change. The official report of the expedition is dated March 24, 1860.

3

Reynosa is situated on the south side of the Río Grande, about sixty miles above Matamoros. The place is not remarkable for many things, except rocky streets, stone houses, and a rather strong anti-American feeling. It was stated as a fact susceptible of proof that this pueblo furnished a company to Cortina's brigade while it was on the march to Río Grande City in 1859. So exact was the information that they were represented as armed with Mississippi rifles, with German silver mounting. A number of these men were known to be living in Reynosa, also in Old Reynosa about twelve miles above. The sheriff of Hidalgo County, Don Sixto Domínguez, knew the names of a great many of these adherents of Cortina, and was ready to point out the men, provided he had proper backing. At a public gathering on that side, attended by residents of Reynosa, the cry of "*vive* Cortina"—live Cortina—was raised. These and many other things conspired in us to create a bitter feeling against Reynosa and to bring back memories of how we had acted against Las Palmas and La Mesa. Stoneman and Ford maturely considered the matter. They kept the fact in view that the men who aided Cortina to lay waste to one hundred and twenty miles of our frontier were criminals—men who fought under no flag—and we had the permission of the Mexican military authorities to follow them into the territory of Mexico.

These discussions culminated in an agreement to set on foot an expedition to capture these members of Cortina's marauding band, or drive them from the valley of the Río Grande, or kill them.

The troops were to move up the country by unfrequented routes or during the night and to camp during daylight in out-of-the-way places. Ford, with eighty-five men, was to march to the Tobasco Ranch, about thirty miles below Río Grande City, cross under cover of the darkness, move down the river, and surround Old Reynosa. Seventeen of Cortina's followers were known to be taking refuge there. The rangers reached Tobasco late in the evening. No one had a correct idea of the intended destination of our force. The venerable owner of the ranch, Señor Francisco Garza, was drawn into a conversation concerning Old Reynosa. The old gentleman admitted it was a place of *muy mala fama*—of very bad fame.

At eight o'clock in the evening, the rangers were marched to the bank of the Río Grande. The arms, saddles, and "kits" of the men were passed over in a skiff. The horses swam to the other bank. The practice heretofore had rendered the operation an easy one. By ten o'clock we were in the saddle, and moving upon Old Reynosa. It was necessary to observe great precaution. About twelve o'clock the line of circumvolution was completed, or supposed to be. It was discovered that one detachment did not get into line as promptly as anticipated, and our friends escaped through the gap. They knew what the descent of the *gringos* foreboded, and went in a hurry. We had men with us who could identify the parties we wanted. We passed a night without sleep.

The inhabitants were treated with civility and informed of our object in paying them so unceremonious a visit. Some supplies were purchased, music was furnished, a *fandango* started, and the time passed rather pleasantly.

The next morning we moved for Reynosa. We marched with care, knowing that word had been conveyed to Reynosa of our presence on Mexican soil. Aware of the general unfriendly feeling towards Americans, we expected trouble at Reynosa, although we were determined to avoid the commission of any act calculated to cause a hostile rupture. We continued to avoid any aggressive action toward a citizen of Mexico.

It was supposed the Reynosa people would resent our coming and fire on us. This was to be the signal for the companies of Captain Stoneman and Lieutenant Kimmel to cross into Mexico and come to our support. Stoneman was secreted in a bend of the river, thickly overgrown by cane, and not far from Edinburg, a small town in front of Reynosa. Kimmel was at a laguna surrounded by heavy chaparral in back of Edinburg. In addition, a force of rangers was in hiding near Edinburg. Should an engagement have occurred, Ford's rangers felt sure of being reinforced.

By means of an American, the Mexicans learned there was something in the wind. They imagined trouble was coming in the shape of a robbing expedition. The able-bodied men of the town were armed and organized. Recruits poured in from the neighboring ranches. A force of more than four hundred was stationed around the main plaza. Colonel Juan Treviño was the *commandante* of the city. His brother, Don Manuel Treviño, had charge of the artillery—a one-pounder mounted on a water cart. This formidable array was on the lookout for land pirates. Between ten and eleven o'clock in the morning, a Mexican discovered a column approaching the town from up the river. Treviño sent out scouts who came back to report that they got no reply when hailing the approaching riders —the reason they got no reply was that they retired so fast upon seeing and hailing us that we had no chance to give notice of who we were and what our reasons were for being there. We decided against trying to catch them and explain our purpose—probably an error. We had a vivid remembrance of what the Mexicans had done to our people without provocation or warning—many of these Mexicans were now in Reynosa—and we marched on in silence. The appearances indicated a fight, and we were willing to accept the issue.

We entered the town in three detachments, one under control of Captain Ford, a second commanded by Captain Littleton, and a third led by Lieutenants Nolan and Dix. These detachments were conducted along three different streets.

As the rangers approached the plaza, they were menaced by armed men occupying houses on both sides of the street. Guns were leveled and were ready to be discharged. The Texians taunted the Mexicans, saying in Spanish: "Fire on us if you dare." Sharpe's rifles were dropped in the street, as if by accident, hoping one would fire, and thus bring on an engagement.

When Captain Ford entered the plaza the Mexicans recognized him, and one called out: "It is Old Ford. He has not come to rob us."

A parley ensued. A message was received from the *ayuntamiento*—city council—requesting a conference with Captain Ford. That august body was in session. He went to the *juzgadeo*—courthouse—accompanied by Captain Littleton and followed by Surgeon John T. Eldridge. Dr. Eldridge carried a Sharpe's rifle. The Mexican sentinel on post at the courthouse door demanded him to give up his gun. Eldridge brought his piece to a present arms position and remarked:

"I won't give you my gun, but I will give you its contents."

The sentinel shut up.

Dix was our interpreter. He recalled later that when the presiding officer of the council inquired the object for which we had come, Ford answered:

"To get the thirty thousand dollars you promised us if we would come into your town and run things as we did at Las Palmas and La Mesa."

The motive inducing our entrance into Mexico was candidly explained and a demand made for the followers of Cortina living in Reynosa to be surrendered to us, in order that our courts could try them for high crimes committed in the State of Texas. We claimed they had waged an inhuman and predatory war upon the territory and citizens of the United States. It was assumed that a refusal to surrender them was an endorsement of their acts rendering the Mexican authorities and government responsible for their acts. It was agreed that Captain Ford should make the demand in writing.

It is time to speak of the activities of Lieutenant Nolan's detachment while Ford was negotiating. When Nolan neared the plaza, he was confronted by a much superior force having a small piece of artillery in advance of them. Their commander, Don Manuel Treviño, ordered Nolan to halt.

"I don't receive orders from you," Nolan said.

"Halt, or I shall fire on you with my cannon."

"Fire, and be blasted!" Nolan thundered. "If you do I'll take the confounded thing away from you."

The Texians heard no more from the belligerents.

About this juncture news came that there was to be no fighting. The two commands began grouping together. The conversation had been carried on in Spanish, and not understood by some of the rangers. One of them, an old sailor known as "English Tom," asked permission to kill Treviño, because "he has two six-shooters and a gold watch."

"No, no, don't kill him," another ranger expostulated. "We can make him prisoner, carry him to Texas, and sell him for $1500."

At that, Treviño, who spoke English, became very mad.

After having heard the reasons for our crossing into Mexico, the *ayuntamiento* inquired if there was any way in which they could serve Captain Ford.

"I should be obliged to you for any facilities afforded me to pass to the other bank. I have rations in Edinburg; we have had little to eat for two days."

The request was acceded to. Don Juan Treviño accompanied the ranger column to the ferry. He and the captain were conversing in a friendly manner.

"Had a fight come off this morning, we would have whipped you," Treviño remarked.

Ford stared at the Mexican coldly. "Very well, Don Juan, about half my men have crossed the river. I can order them back, and we can test the matter."

Treviño deprecated anything of the kind.

"All right, sir, but you must stop that sort of talk or fight."

The conversation took a different turn.

The rangers were camped in a field, a short distance above Edinburg, opposite Reynosa. Notes passed between the Mexican authorities and Captain Ford. The Mexicans denied that any of Cortina's followers resided in Reynosa. They knew Ford was apprised of the contrary, and expected trouble. They were receiving reinforcements and getting ready to repel any attempt we might make to take the Cortina men by force.

An old gentleman of Reynosa—one of Ford's old friends—came into the ranger camp and agreed to furnish information of the numbers and intentions of the Mexican forces. The price demanded for acting as a spy upon his countrymen was that, in the event we attacked Reynosa, his property was to be respected. He gave the exact location of his homestead. The captain was not deceived; he was satisfied the real object of his old friend's coming was to find out all he could about the ranger force. The old Don was treated kindly and courteously. He was assured that in case of hostilities being commenced, notice would be given in order to allow the women and children to be taken out of Reynosa. He was told that in case of hostilities, no woman, or any residence in Reynosa, would be interfered with under ordinary circumstances.

If memory is not at fault the second night of our stay near Edinburg was marked by an incident. Captain Littleton and some other officers asked leave to have a "little fun." It was given, provided no wrong should be committed or harm done to anyone. These conditions were assented to.

The party proceeded to Edinburg and got possession of some brick with which they built a short wall, leaving an open space in the center to represent an embrasure. They ordered the artillery to be brought up. It consisted of a stick of wood mounted on an ox cart. The ammunition was a huge cow's horn, filled two-thirds with tar and grease and one third with powder. Then the men made a hole in the ground, poured powder into it, and proceeded to pack the powder as best they could. After that they placed the big horn on top of the powder and pointed the thing so that it would fire across the Río Grande. They backed away and someone applied a slow match: a dull sound boomed on the air, a stream of light shot across the river, and the men cheered. The Mexican guard on the other bank was heard galloping towards the plaza, a commotion was heard in Reynosa, and the notion was prevalent that something extraordinary had happened.

The next morning the captain was in Edinburg; his old friend waited on him. He was indignant.

"You have told me a lie," was his salutation.

"How so?"

"You promised me you would not attack our town without giving notice."

"The town has not been attacked," Ford said.

"Do you think me a fool! How about the artillery fire of last night?"

"But we have no artillery."

Captain Littleton asked the *hidalgo* to take a walk. Others followed. Littleton exhibited the cart and the log, fragments of the horn and spots of tar and grease upon the ground. The old gentleman's indignation was intense, his face paled and flushed alternately, the sweat stood on his forehead. Silence was oppressive and impossible.

"I am more than sixty years of age. I have travelled and have seen iniquity in many shapes, but you Texians are the most consummate rascals I have ever seen. Last night no one in Reynosa slept a wink. We had a heavy guard on the river bank, above and below the town, to ascertain where you would cross. The women packed rocks in their laps with which to barricade the streets. All, all, on account of this infernal deviltry of you Texians."

About this date both Mexicans and rangers exchanged some shots across the river. One or two Mexicans were wounded. Correspondence ensued. The aggressive acts were charged upon each. It was difficult to ascertain from which side the first shot came.

A day was set apart from these events for the Mexicans to celebrate a Saint. The fiesta was held with great éclat. Mass was said and salutes were fired in conjunction. It was customary to use blank cartridges on such occasions. This time was an exception. The firing was brisk for some time. Balls fell in the ranger camp where the men were eating their noon meal. They became very excited and evinced a strong desire to send a few shots in reply, which Ford forbade.

Lieutenant Kimmel heard the fusillade. He supposed a fight was progressing, placed himself at the head of his company, and galloped to the ferry between Edinburg and Reynosa. The Mexicans saw the blue coats, and were astonished. They had banked on the supposition that eighty-five rangers were all the force engaged in the effort to capture the Cortina criminals they were harboring and protecting. The appearance of United States cavalry added a new and important feature to the matter: "The Texas Devils" had an unexpected and a strong backing.

It may be asked, why was this demonstration made? Major Heintzelman, Captain Stoneman, and the writer were thoroughly convinced of the complicity of the Mexican authorities on the Río Grande in the war prosecuted by Cortina against the United States. They had permitted him to enlist men on Mexican soil and to procure supplies in Mexico. It was believed to be susceptible of proof that supplies had been furnished him by Mexican officials. Mexican troops had been handled in a manner to render him aid by their presence and, no doubt, by their active cooperation if required by circumstances. In order to put an end to this quasi war, or to cause it to expand into actual and open hostilities between the two governments, we descended upon Reynosa. An armed collision was, in our opinion, sure to cause the prompt inauguration of hostilities or a settlement of the matter and ultimate peace. We deemed that our action was in the direction of protection to life and property, and of the vindication of the rights and the honor of our government, and that it would be sanctioned by a patriotic people.

Had a war between Mexico and the United States ensued, it is possible that the sectional quarrel then splitting the Union might have been stilled for a season at least, wise counsels might have prevailed, and the fratricidal contest might have been averted. However, this is only supposing what might have been and lessens none of the terrible realities which came to pass.

4

News had been received of the coming of Lieutenant Colonel Robert E. Lee with full authority to settle all controverted points between Mexico and the United States relating to the Cortina war and to end the same. Lee was moving down the Río Grande. As he was to relieve Major Heintzelman of his command and was not presumed to be cognizant of matters connected with that frontier trouble, we thought it prudent to suspend action until his arrival.

Lieutenant Colonel Lee arrived and pitched his camp a mile or so above Edinburg. The writer rode over to pay his respects. Colonel Lee met him where he alighted from his horse, extended him great courtesy, and invited him to take supper. In the course of conversation the only suggestion made, which indicated a reproof or a difference of opinion, was in the matter of entering Reynosa.

"You should have sent a courier to inform them who you were," Lee said.

Colonel Lee's appearance was dignified without hauteur, grand without pride, and in keeping with the noble simplicity characterizing a true republican. He evinced an imperturbable self-possession, and a complete control of his passions. To approach him was to feel yourself in the presence of a man of superior intellect, possessing the capacity to accomplish great ends and the gift of controlling and leading men.

One of the officers accompanying Lee was Captain [Albert G.] Brackett who had seen service in Texas and had a good knowledge of Mexican character and some acquaintance with the Spanish language. Lieutenant Dix, however, was the trusted translator of Mexican official documents.

The correspondence between Lee and the Mexicans occupied a few days. Colonel Lee's notes were pointed. In the opinion of the Mexican authorities, they presented the alternative of restraining their citizens from making predatory descents upon the territory and people of Texas or a war with the United States. The warning came at a time when the Mexicans were prepared to heed it. Satisfactory assurances were given to guarantee security for the future. Colonel Lee marched in the direction of Fort Brown. All the troops moved down the country.

This was the last active operation of the Cortina War. Scouting parties were sent out to protect property and escorts were furnished parties travelling up the valley of the Río Grande. It was a period of comparative repose. The war was considered at an end. In view of an early disbandment, Ford allowed his men the opportunity to put their horses in good order.

5

For many years there was a Mexican on the lower Río Grande known far and wide as Don Sixto. He was a fiddler of rare merit, and the leader of a musical band. He was indispensable at public balls, private parties, and all places where dancing constituted a part of the amusement.

During the period that Cortina was holding high carnival in the valley of the Río Grande, Sixto and his associates were going up the Brownsville and Laredo road to play at a contemplated merrymaking. Someone of Cortina's detachment of scouts pounced upon the band and marched them to Cortina's headquarters. The leader of the scout did not fail to claim a large amount of credit due him for his extraordinary vigilance and skill in discovering and capturing the prisoners. He dwelt on their dangerous appearance and the amount of damage they might have done had they been suffered to run at large. Cortina was impressed with the enormity of the case. He had the dangerous parties ushered into his august presence, and proceeded to examine them in the most rigid manner. Sixto, the spokesman, answered the questions with much solemnity. It is sufficient to say that the result of the examination angered Cortina. He delivered a caustic lecture to his officer.

"What in the name of the devil induced you to bring such men as these before me? Musicians! Fandango sharps! Turn them loose instantly!"

Much to the surprise of every one Don Sixto was highly indignant at the treatment received from Cortina. "Musicians indeed. Send them away indeed. Why could he not have treated us like men and had us shot?" To the day of his death, Don Sixto was a mortal enemy of Cortina's. He always reported ready to join any command to fight the "Red Robber of the Río Grande."

A story went the rounds that Cortina's favorite daughter married a trifling fellow who fiddled at fandangos for a precarious livelihood. It was understood that the father was savagely incensed and refused to forgive his child. In the event this report was based on truth, Don Sixto had his revenge.

6

A gentleman arrived in Brownsville who announced himself the agent of Governor Houston. George McKnight was known by many of us and was received and treated with courtesy and kindness. By some means the report obtained circulation that he had been sent by Governor Houston to keep the command from stealing. This caused some unpleasant feeling, but did not prevent the agent from receiving considerate attention.

When it was known the rangers were going to be mustered out soon, the citizens of Brownsville tendered Captain Ford a supper and ball. Colonel Lee was in attendance. A toast was offered "to the men who could always find a 'ford' to the Río Grande." The captain was called upon to respond. He did so, and expressed sentiments in favor of preserving the Union.

The rangers took up the line of march for Goliad, where they were to be mustered out of service. The captain remained in Brownsville a day or two after the command left. Colonel Lee and Major Heintzelman started for San Antonio. Their guide took the Point Isabel road seven miles out from Brownsville, and they lost some time. Captain Ford overtook them at a watering place in the sand belt called *Las Mujeres*—The Women. They separated at Banquete, where Major Heintzelman and the writer were the guests of Colonel Lee. Lee had made a great impression on the writer. In the troublous times that followed, we closely scanned the public prints to see what part was being played by the accomplished soldier who had given a finishing touch to the Cortina War (although Major Heintzelman had performed the main part of the work). It inspired confidence when we saw Robert E. Lee announced as the commander of the Army of Northern Virginia. Once in his life the writer's estimate of a man was realized to the full extent.

Agent McKnight was to be our mustering officer. An ambulance belonging to the quartermaster department was placed at his disposal. The acting quartermaster, Howard, and the military clerk, Frank L'Estrange, left Brownsville together with the agent. The mustering officer sported a stovepipe hat; it was missed soon after starting. They stopped for dinner. The hat was found: Lieutenant Howard had been sitting on it during the half-day's drive. It was mashed beyond the chance of restoration and, at the time the party arrived at Goliad, was one of the most uncouth-looking objects a white man ever placed on his head. This mishap, and some other little affairs reported in connection with the trip, produced the impression on our minds that the mustering officer had been victimized by his companions.

For the last time the Río Grande Squadron was formed in line. The officers offered to assist Colonel McKnight in making the muster out. He declined to accept their services. He called the roll; each man moved to the front when his name was pronounced, delivered his arms drawn from the State of Texas to the mustering officer, and moved off. The mustering officer handed the arms to a man in the front part of a large covered wagon. The command was discharged early in the afternoon; they bade each other good-by—in many cases for the last time on this earth—and dispersed to many points of the compass. Captain Ford left for Austin, accompanied by Dr. Charles B. Combe, of Brownsville, and John Ingram, one of his old ranging company. On the road to Gonzales Ford passed several squads of the boys. Some of them had arms. Ford was astonished to see it. One communicative chap explained it all:

"That man McKnight thought he was mighty smart, coming all the way down to the Río Grande to keep the rangers from stealing. We just thought we would put up a job on him. He had a man in the forepart of the wagon receiving the arms, and we had a man in the hindpart handing them out. Oh, no, he didn't want you officers to help him."

The writer cannot vouch for the truth of the man's statement; he certainly saw guns in the hands of the discharged rangers. How they got them Ford does not know positively. Had any such game come to the knowledge of the officers, they would have blocked it.

The writer returned to Brownsville in July, 1860, and remained there until November. During that brief period peace, order, and security prevailed on the Río Grande. Cortina was not on the war path. The relations between the inhabitants of both sides were amicable.

7

Thus ended the Cortina War, but not its evil consequences. Mexicans ambitious to acquire riches without work saw a man make a predatory war upon a neighboring state and people, commit murder, perpetrate robberies, carry his feloniously-gotten property into Mexico, devastate a frontier, burn houses—in short, write his name in blood and fire. They saw that man, clothed with official authority, a brigadier general in the Army of Mexico, become the idol of the Mexican masses.[1] Under these

---

[1] All along the Río Grande, beneath the façade of tranquility there were undercurrents of anti-Americanism. Although the killing and looting had stopped, Cortina and his *guerrilleros* were still there, riding from settlement to settlement, talking and handing out circulars on street corners and in saloons. Sometimes Cortina would make a speech

circumstances it was very natural for him to have imitators. They came to the front at all seasonable periods. The Civil War that followed filled the valley of the Río Grande with armed men, sent there to defend the new nation and to protect a commerce of vast importance to the Confederate States. The time to begin the work was not auspicious. When the Confederacy went to pieces, and the armed hosts dispersed, then the depredations were renewed: murder again bared his red arm, violence prevailed, and robbers held high carnival in the region between the Nueces and the Río Grande. These atrocious deeds were the legitimate fruits of Juan Nepomuceno Cortina's infernal labors. The way was opened for him when the Federal troops were removed from the lower Río Grande. This unfortunate move was interpreted by him as an invitation to kill, to plunder, and to amass wealth at the expense of peaceful Texian frontiersmen.

---

in the market place and the poor would listen intently to what he had to say. He would not harm the innocent, but would fight for the emancipation of the hungry *peons* along the border. He told them to love nature, for "Nature will always grant us sufficient means to support our frames." They must love the land, for land was all they had. Yet their "*personal enemies*"—the land hungry imperialists to the north—were out to take the land from them. But if the Mexicans followed Cortina, the *gringos* would not have it without "*fattening it with their own gore!*"

He blamed the *gringos* for their misery and poverty. "Many of you have been robbed of your property, incarcerated, chased, murdered, and hunted like wild beasts, because your labor was fruitful, and because your industry excited the vile avarice which led" the *gringos apestosos* who were "criminals covered with frightful crimes." Yet "to these monsters indulgence is shown, because they are not of our race, which is unworthy, as they say, to belong to the human species." What was it the Americans called them? "Greasers, Yellow greasers."

"Mexicans! Is there no remedy for you?"

The same question revolutionists like Antonio Canales and Carbajal had asked many times before as they saw their people dying from starvation and disease.

"Mexicans! My part is taken; the voice of revelation whispers to me that to me is intrusted the breaking of the chains of your slavery"—he talked on about a Río Grande Republic with Cortina as its benevolent ruler—"and that the Lord will enable me, with a powerful arm, to fight against our enemies, in compliance with the requirements of that Sovereign Majesty, who, from this day forward, will hold us under his protection."

"On my part, I am ready to offer myself as a sacrifice for your happiness. . . ."

To the poor who heard him, Cortina was a sign of hope in a land where hope heretofore had had no meaning. "Vive Cheno Cortina!" "Mueran los Gringos!" "Vive Cheno Cortina!"

"Mexicans peace be with you."

After Cortina and his bodyguard rode away, the *peons*, seething with hatred for Americans, returned to their baked fields and mud huts to await his signal for them to follow.

As Ford shows later in his story, that signal came in the summer of 1861, when Cortina again crossed into Texas to terrorize and plunder. He would continue his bellicose activities until his death in 1894.

(Juan N. Cortina, Miscellaneous Papers, ms.; "Difficulties on the Southwestern Frontier," *U.S. House Exec. Docs.*, 36th Cong., 1st Sess., Vol. VII, Doc. 52, pp. 79–82; Walter Prescott Webb, *The Texas Rangers*, 179–193.)

BOOK 5 *Distant Horizons*

XXV

>>>

MY SECTION IS MY COUNTRY

The causes leading to the secession movement originated from a difference of opinion on the slavery question. Slavery came to the Southern man authorized by the Supreme Law of the Land. It came to him authorized by time, and custom, and law. The assumption in the Declaration of Independence that "all men are created equal" was not intended to include the African race, or was a falsehood on its face. It was an institution sanctioned by the Bible, and it had all the authority of time to uphold it. The Northern states where it had been abolished were actuated, as we believed, by a sense that climate rendered it unprofitable. In all the contests in Congress upon slavery there was no preparation made to pay the Southern owners for their loss of property.

When the Virginia Convention was in session in 1831 and 1832 and some of the great men that state had furnished were members thereof, a plan was under consideration to abolish slavery gradually. A deputation waited upon them from Pennsylvania to discuss the question of slavery. The Pennsylvanians were informed of the intended action of the convention. They replied that the plan was too slow; they wanted slavery abolished immediately. They offered no consideration for the Negroes. The Pennsylvanians seemed to forget that when slavery ceased in the Northern states it had been the result of a gradual process. Many of them had gotten rid of their slaves by selling them to Southerners and then had turned around to demand their release. The Pennsylvania delegation left rather disgusted. The Virginia Convention—containing such men as [James] Madison, Chief Justice [John] Marshall, Alexander Campbell, and others of high national reputation—suspended its work of gradual abolition. The delegates could not view the proposition of Pennsylvania in any other light than as an effort to rob the South of what the Constitution of the United States recognized as property, and they stopped short in their work. In the three decades that followed, Southerners defended themselves against what they considered to be an unjust effort to deprive them of their property. The only proposition was to take it for nothing, and it was finally taken in that way. Some gentlemen contend that a moneyed consideration was offered for the slaves after the war commenced. Be that as it may, if you have an offer to make to your adversary, do it before you attempt to knock him down. Enough of this.[1]

---

[1] Rip Ford always took a strong and unequivocal stand on the slavery issue. His views were typically Southern. "The Savior erected his standard in the very midst of thousands of bondsmen," Ford wrote in the *Texas State Times*, "and while rebuking every species of sin, never raised his voice against the legitimacy of the institution." Abolitionists, Ford said in another issue, search the Bible "to find something to favor" their "fanatical doctrines." They make

irreverent and profane allusions to the Deity. The South has the Bible on their side. If there is any one institution by the Word of God, it is that of slavery. From Genesis to Revelations there is not one word against it, and thousands in favor of it. The Abolitionists have become convinced of this, and many of them war upon the Sacred Scriptures, as well as upon slavery. They wish to remove the prop, the foundation stone of the institution in order to tumble it to ruins.

When the Kansas-Nebraska Bill was passed in 1854, Ford declared that "Southern men need not look to" it "for relief—it has no balm for them. Its squatter sovereignty and alien suffrage provisions are not panaceas to Southern ills—they are remedies for Northern diseases." Throughout the fifties Ford waged a persistent war against squatter sovereignty which would allow the voters of each territory to decide for themselves whether or not to have slavery. Such a procedure, he contended, would give territorial legislatures equal status with the existing state legislatures.

He decried Congressional "meddling" in the slavery issue. "Congress has no power to legislate upon the subject of slavery, in the States where it exists," or "to exclude any State from admission into the Union, because its constitution does, or does not recognize the institution of slavery," or "to abolish slavery in the District of Columbia," or to pass any "law or regulation . . . touching the question of slavery in the territories."

2

The summer of 1860 was remarkable for the political campaign which caused a split in the Democratic party and ensured its defeat. None of the excitement over who would win the presidency that prevailed in some of the states extended into Texas. There was no possible chance to defeat the Democratic nominees in our state; [John C.] Breckinridge and [Joseph] Lane were strongly advocated and supported.[2] There was, however, a great deal of excitement over the possibility of a rupture, and many minds were filled with disquietude.

The writer was on the Río Grande until after the presidential election. When he returned to Austin, he found everything in a state of turmoil. The community was divided. A large proportion of Travis County favored the government of Mr. Lincoln. They wished to wait for an overt act on his part. They insisted on waiting until he did something to justify opposition and resistance. The secessionists were for getting ready at once, for not giving Mr. Lincoln time to make ready to force them into measures. Governor Houston was known to be in favor of calling a convention of the Southern states and letting them decide upon what measures to take—more of this later. Houston had a strong following, though not nearly a majority of the states.[3] To this mode or procedure, it was sug-

Congress must, on the other hand, maintain and "vigorously enforce" the fugitive slave law.

When the Supreme Court ruled in the Dred Scott Decision that Congress could not prohibit slavery in the territories, Ford wrote with joy that "it is a fatal stab to the anti-slavery agitators." The decision was indeed a mighty victory for the South and demonstrated to the world that "the perpetuation of constitutional rights and justice is our object and not the overthrow of a nation, whose greatness, wealth and prosperity is the wonder and admiration of civilized Christendom."

The election of Lincoln and his "Black" Republicans, he pointed out, reversed this decision and proved beyond all doubt that the aggressive Yankees intended to destroy the South's most cherished institution for their own economic gain.

Abolitionism wasn't the only reason Ford thought Texas must secede. The lackadaisical attitude of the United States government in protecting the state's frontier was, "in my opinion," ample "cause to sever . . . connection with the Union on this very head." Thousands of Texans agreed with him. And in their secession ordinance, they insisted that inadequate frontier protection as much as abolitionism and economic coercion justified Texas in leaving the Union.

(*Texas State Times* [Austin], June 7, August 2, 1856, February 28, April 11, May 2, 1857; Neighbours, "Robert S. Neighbors in Texas, 1836–1859: A Quarter Century of Frontier Problems," ms., II, 514–515.)

[2] Not a Texan voted for Lincoln in the 1860 election. Only 410 votes went to Stephen A. Douglas, whom Texans considered "the bitterest pill a State Rights democrat could be made to swallow." (Houston *Tri-Weekly Telegraph,* April 3, 1860.) John C. Breckinridge carried the state with 47,548 votes. John Bell received 15,463 votes.

[3] Governor Houston continued to oppose the secession convention. As a result secessionists declared his office vacant and gave Lieutenant Governor Edward Clark the governorship. Humiliated and disillusioned, Houston retired from the political scene, fearing

gested that by the time such a convention could be held, Mr. Lincoln could have his measures perfected and could be prepared for any emergency. It was argued that he could easily put down what he had time to prepare for.

A majority of the people of Texas favored opposition to Mr. Lincoln's assuming control of the United States government. The Lone Star Flag had been hoisted in almost every town and village; the people, without distinction of party, were avowing their determination not to submit to Black Republican rule. Hence the clamor for the calling of a secession convention.

3

Thus the contest brought about by the secession movement was sharp, though not necessarily bitter. Men of different opinion remained friendly. There was a settled disposition not to get up a civil war. All parties considered such a thing a calamity of the most perilous and destructive character, and most of those who thought of its horrible details labored to save the people of Texas from its terrible effects. There was a disposition to pass by things of a disagreeable nature which would have armed neighbor against neighbor under ordinary circumstances. The people of Texas deserve credit for their moderation in this respect.

A great many affected to believe there would be no war. They pretended to think the Yankees too prudent to venture upon a fight with the blood-and-thunder men of the South. The opinions were various. One man declined to attend a meeting because he did not think there was "much of a crisis." One of our speakers was going to set an immense trotline, bait the fish hooks with postage stamps, and "catch all the Yankees." There were a great many men amongst us who considered Yankees cowards.

The writer took a different view of the matter. He had stood in dan-

---

that "the time has come when a man's section is his country." When war broke out, he said that while he was still a confirmed unionist he would not fight against the Confederacy. "All my hopes, my fortunes, are centered in the South. When I see the land for whose defence my blood has been spilt, and the people whose fortunes have been mine through a quarter of a century of toil, threatened with invasion, I can but cast my lot with theirs and await the issue." In the remaining years of his life the old general remained loyal to Texas but not to the Confederacy. Fremantle, the English traveler, saw him at Galveston in May, 1863—only two months before his death—and recorded that "though evidently a remarkable and clever man, he is extremely egotistical and vain and much disappointed at having to subside from his former grandeur. . . . In appearance he is a tall, handsome old man, much given to chewing tobacco, and blowing his nose with his fingers."

(Llerena Friend, *Sam Houston: The Great Designer*, p. 349; Arthur James Lyon Fremantle, *The Fremantle Diary*, pp. 53–54.)

gerous places with all sorts of men. He had discovered no very great difference in them. He was of opinion that an attempt to secede from the Union would produce a terrible war. He did not believe in the right or the possibility of peaceable secession. The right of revolution to resist oppression and wrong he acknowledged. In the event the people of the Southern states decided they ought to secede from the Union, in other words, to inaugurate a revolution, he determined to go with them. He thought, as General Houston expressed it after the war commenced: "The time has come when a man's section is his country." Ford acted on that principle throughout the contest.

4

The writer remained in Austin during the agitation of the question of secession. Believing only in the right of revolution, he sided with the friends of secession. Without his being consulted his name was placed before the people of Cameron County as a delegate to the convention. He was elected, though not a resident of the county. He considered the compliment a high one, and accepted. Judge E. J. Davis was a candidate but was not given a certificate of election. It is very probable if he had come to Austin he would have been seated. The ruling members of that body were very likely to accept the services of anyone possessing popularity. They were entering into a contest of great risk, and they naturally accepted the services of anyone who had acquired influence with his fellow citizens. This Judge Davis possessed. He was then assuredly an ultra-Southern man in his views. He changed.

There was a general disposition on the part of the members of the secession convention to make Judge O. M. Roberts president. Roberts was then associate justice of the Supreme Court of Texas. He was a man of undoubted ability and a leader in the cause of secession. For a long time he declined to accept the position on account of his want of experience in presiding over a deliberative body. All his pleas of want of experience were set aside by the members, and, when the convention met on January 28, he was made president.

After Texas left the Union, Roberts raised an infantry regiment and served in the Confederate Army until declining health induced him to resign and accept the position of chief justice of the Supreme Court of Texas. He served as governor of Texas from 1878 to 1883. In every position he proved himself of extraordinary talents, of great industry, and of integrity. He examined a matter well, and when he formed an opinion, it was difficult to cause him to abandon it. He has grown old in the service of Texas in various capacities and has always shown himself to be a man firm in the advocacy of right and a fearless opponent of wrong.

The writer assumed the duties of a delegate in the secession convention. He spoke in favor of submitting the question of separation from the government of the United States to a vote of the people of Texas. It was carried by a majority of the voting population.

On February 1, 1861, O. M. Roberts appointed the writer to the Committee of Public Safety.

I called him to my assistance in selecting the members of that committee from the extreme west, [Roberts said] because, first, of his general acquaintance there, and, secondly, on account of his knowledge of military men upon the frontier.

He was of very great advantage to that committee on account of his information of military matters within the State, as well as his general military knowledge. By these he was called to take a leading part in devising the measures for taking possession of the public property, and especially in dictating the necessary orders to commissioners, officers, and agents of that committee who were employed in that bold and hazardous enterprise.

Ford was named by that committee as the commander of an expedition to visit the lower Río Grande and demand the surrender of the post of Fort Brown and the public property belonging to the same. After having received the order, the author proceeded by stage to the Houston railroad at Hempstead, and proceeded thence to Houston. Previous to leaving Austin he gave authority to Captain Mat Nolan to raise and organize a company and join Ford on the lower Río Grande. Similar orders were delivered to Captain John Littleton and John Donelson, if memory is correct.

At Houston the colonel accepted the services of a company commanded by Captain [Frederick] Odlum. They were all Irish, and the same men later won distinction in defense of a fort at the mouth of the Sabine River.

Ford picked up men hurriedly, and on the twenty-third of February, 1861, reached Brazos Santiago. There a lieutenant of the United States and a small body of soldiers were on duty. The place was surrendered to the State of Texas. This was the first time the writer ever saw the flag of the United States lowered to an opposing force. His ancestors had fought to create and sustain it, and he had marched beneath its victorious folds. Now to see it lowered, even to men who were born beneath it, was a trial of no ordinary character.

General E. B. Nichols represented the State of Texas. He was charged with furnishing the funds to defray the daily and ordinary expenses of the command. He charged the vessels to carry the troops from Galveston to Brazos Santiago. Lieutenant Colonel [Hugh] McLeod of Galveston was made second in command of the military, by the influence of Colonel Ford. McLeod commanded the Texas troops which had surrendered near Santa Fé during the existence of the Republic of Texas.

It is useless to refer to the various measures adopted to ensure success in procuring the abandonment of the country by the Federals and the accession by the State of Texas to all that pertained to the United States within the limits of the Lone Star State. Captain [B. H.] Hill, the commander of the Fort Brown troops, seemed determined at first to fight and not to yield to the demands of the men representing the State of Texas. Captain George Stoneman, commanding the Federal cavalry, was in favor of maintaining peace, believing that the unfortunate matter could be settled without a war. Stoneman's course prevented the commencement of hostile operations on the lower Río Grande. The order of General [David E.] Twiggs, yielding up the State of Texas to the secessionists, settled the question of war for the time being.

The troops occupying posts on the Río Grande, at least below El Paso, moved out of Texas by way of the mouth of the Río Grande. A large number of them were at Fort Brown. If memory is correct, they had twenty-eight pieces of artillery on the parade grounds at that place, and men to serve them.

Nichols went to Galveston for more men. He reached Brazos Santiago on March 22, 1861. B. F. Terry was appointed major of the new forces. He afterwards commanded the celebrated Terry Rangers.

Texas now had at Brazos Santiago a force of 1,500 men. They knew little of each other; many of them were not secessionists by belief; yet they were Texians, true to the interests and the welfare of the state, and could be depended on in any emergency.[4]

---

[4] Fremantle, who visited Brownsville during the war, agreed with Ford that his Confederates were indeed a fearless body of horsemen. One day while riding below Fort Brown Fremantle found some of them "seated round a fire contemplating a tin of potatoes. . . . Their dress consisted simply of flannel shirts, very ancient trousers, jack boots with enormous spurs, and black felt hats ornamented with the 'Lone Star of Texas.' They looked rough and dirty, but were extremely civil to me."

Those enormous spurs in the end attracted more attention than the rest of the Texans' motley garbs.

The masses of them wore spurs on their heels, [Thomas North noted] generally the immense wheel-spur, and though they were not born with them on, yet they might as well have been, for they not only rode in them, but walked in them, ate in them, and slept in them. Their clanking as they walked was like a man in chains. They wore belts around the waist, suspending one or two revolvers and a bowie knife; were experts in the saddle, had a reckless dare-devil look and were always ready

5

On the fourth day of March, 1861, Captain [Edward R.] Platt of the United States Army was out drilling his artillerymen at Fort Brown (a thing which happened almost every day). Someone reported at Brazos Santiago that he had fired salutes in commemoration and honor of Mr. Lincoln's inauguration as President of the United States. This report reached Brazos Santiago. Lieutenant Colonel McLeod and others held a meeting on the subject. They addressed a communication to Colonel Ford expressing their determination to march up to Brownsville and avenge the insult offered to Texas. In reply, Ford stated the fact that if Captain Platt's men had fired cannon on March 4, no one in Brownsville had noticed it. Ford advised the officers that, in his opinion, there was no insult intended or offered the State of Texas. He directed them to cause any troops which might have marched off Brazos Island to return. He had understandings with an officer of the United States that, if the Texas troops remained on Brazos Island, Union troops would not be marched there to attack them, but if the Texians marched off the island to attack the United States soldiers, he would be compelled to fight. Ford hoped for a peaceful solution of the disagreement. In addition to these reasons, the colonel had a secret fund which he was using to induce Southern men of the United States Army to quit it in the event of hostilities. A camp had been formed and quite a number of men had already gone to it. Captain Mat Nolan commanded it.

6

On March 3, 1861, Major Fitz-John Porter of General [Winfield] Scott's staff arrived at Brazos Santiago. He had come to superintend the embarkment of the United States troops. There was talk of an intention on the part of the United States to concentrate at a point not far from Indianola and make an effort to hold the State of Texas by force. The matter, if ever contemplated, was not probably practicable after the capture of a number of companies marching in the direction of San Antonio. In regard to the opinion of Federal military officers as to their ability to retain possession of Texas, in spite of its opposition, I will refer to an incident. While yet at Brownsville, Captain Stoneman asserted that

---

for whisky and a big chew of tobacco, and the hand-writing of passion and appetite was all over them. They were cow-boys from the wild woods and prairies, and sons of the low class planters, with a strong sprinkling of "low white trash" and "clayeaters."

(Fremantle, *The Fremantle Diary*, p. 7; Thomas North, *Five Years in Texas: or, What You Did Not Hear during the War from January 1861 to January 1866*, p. 104.)

with his two companies of cavalry he could march all over Texas. The writer heard this boast, but treated it with derision.

About the twentieth of March the last of the Federal officers bade farewell to Texas, and took passage on a river steamer for Brazos Santiago. It was a sad parting. Colonel Ford bid adieu to men with whom he had served, whom he respected, and with whom he had faced danger. The future was full of uncertainty, dark, and lowering. Each one of us felt a dread of what might befall us. A terrible foreboding of civil war warned us that we might meet as foes and, under a sense of duty, might take the life of a valued friend. Having been companions in former conflicts, having stood by each other as only warrior-comrades can stand, we were extremely depressed; it was a dreadful feeling to reflect that these recollections of the past, these memories of honorable deeds, were to be swallowed up, embittered by the rancorous and hellish hostility of civil war, in which the ties of friendship, the relations of life, the regard between father and son, brother and brother, were to be swamped, strangled, and obliterated by the demoniac passions of the combatants.

The officials who left last when all felt that no more could be done except with the sword left many sincere friends behind them, who noted their actions. Lieutenant [James Boneparte] Witherell stepped overboard, and was drowned in the Río Grande. Captain Stoneman became a general in the Federal service and, after the war, served as governor of California; Lieutenant Kimmel became a colonel in the Confederate service. Lieutenant Ramsay, when he called for the purpose of saying good-by to the family of Major Smith, wrote on a piece of music "do you really think he is dead?" He then remarked: "That is what you will say when you hear of the first battle."

When the news of the opening fight at Manassas reached Brownsville, with it came the unwelcome intelligence of the killing of Lieutenant [Douglas] Ramsay. It is said he died with his resignation as a United States officer in his jacket pocket. Of Major Platt, United States Artillery, we heard that he had died, and nothing more. Major Porter had previously departed, also [Alex N.] Shipley, later a colonel in the United States Army. The writer and Colonel Shipley have known each other for forty years. They exchanged mementos of friendship in 1861. Colonel Shipley is a citizen of Texas. He served long and faithfully.

When the Río Grande country was finally in Confederate hands, O. M. Roberts said of Ford: "I do believe that, but for his prudence and masterly management of the troops, and his address with the United States officers, the war would have opened there, before we had finally seceded, and very probably to our disadvantage greatly."

XXVI

>>>

REBEL BORDER

The withdrawal of the forces of the United States imposed a great responsibility upon the officers who assumed their places. Our nearest neighbors, the Mexicans, we well knew had an old question of revolutionary import they would be glad to reverse and settle in their own favor. The war between Mexico and the United States had increased the feeling of antagonism and almost hatred entertained for *Los Americanos*. The intended division of the country of Washington into two independent governments, if effected, was not calculated to allay the animosity of a people who professed to have been robbed by her republican neighbor of the immense territory of Texas. The men in charge of the military on the Río Grande appreciated the situation. The Benavides family did the Confederacy an immense favor by declaring for her. The trade that later sprang up at Matamoros completed the reasons for the neutrality of Mexico. One false move on the part of the Confederate officers on the Río Grande would have changed the face of affairs, and might have precipitated the hosts of Mexico upon the soil of Texas. The foreign complications affecting Mexico, no doubt, had an effect on the action of her rulers and assured peace with the Confederates.

Ford issued an address to the sovereign people of Texas explanatory of the views and intentions of the Confederate military. He explained the different sentiments of the Americans on the slavery question, insisted that the states represented in the convention of the United States in 1787 formed a constitution which recognized slavery. Opposition to African slavery had originated as an afterthought. He insisted that should the struggle end in the establishment of two governments—one ignoring and the other sustaining that institution—it would be an evidence simply of a difference in sentiment; each government would be independent and republican in its theory and practice. He addressed the Mexicans in Texas as Southern people in every sense of the word: in interest, in climate, and otherwise.

He well knew the Texas Revolution, the war with the United States brought about by the annexation of Texas, and the contrariety of sentiment emanating from the difference in the opinions entertained by Americans and the descendants of the hidalgos of Spain were of themselves sufficient to create a revulsion of feeling and an indisposition to agree upon questions of great political importance. Ford's efforts were to keep disagreements out of sight, to build up and encourage fraternity in thought and in action, and above all to live in peace and to exercise towards each other the duties of comity and good neighborhood.

In an official report made to Edward Clark, governor of Texas, Colonel Ford says: "I have endeavored to cultivate a friendly feeling between the military authorities of Texas, and those of Mexico. I am happy to state, that acts of friendship and good neighborhood have transpired between the authorities of Matamoros and ourselves. If the same sentiments prevail throughout Mexico it is quite possible there would be little difficulty in negotiating an extradition treaty." This bore date of April 16, 1861.

The possibility that Matamoros might become a market for a lucrative Confederate-European trade was an inducement to the authorities of Mexico to turn a deaf ear to the representations of the United States to allow the use of the territory of Mexico for moving troops from California against Texas. [Benito] Juarez is reported to have insisted that Mexico was too small a power to incur the enmity and hostility of either of the American belligerents. In any event he was averse to breaking up the great trade with the Confederates.

2

After the Federals had gone, Ford's regiment had been accepted into the service of the Confederate States. Ford remained on the lower part of the Río Grande and sent Lieutenant Colonel [John R.] Baylor and Major [Ed] Waller to control affairs on the upper portion of the river.

The Texas troops under Captain Nolan, Captain [John] Donelson, and Captain Griffin were sent up the Río Grande after Indians. Captain Nolan occupied Fort McIntosh, near Laredo. Captain Donelson was reported to have had a fight with Indians. It is impossible to give details: all reports of these and earlier affairs were burned in the state capitol in 1881, if memory serves.

In March or the early part of April, 1861, a Mexican named Ochoa, at the instigation of Cortina, pronounced against the Confederate government. The first trouble was in Zapata County, Texas. The *pronunciados* seized and hanged Señor Vela, the county judge. Major William Edwards' command, which was stationed at Ringgold Barracks, fought the Mexicans twice. Lieutenant Henry fought them at Clareno Ranch, between the county seat of Zapata County and Río Grande City, killing ten. Then Captain Nolan moved against them and struck them about daylight near Río Grande City around the fifteenth of April, 1861. Nolan's men fired eleven shots and killed eleven of Cortina's men. Nolan reported the skirmish and wrote a private letter to Colonel Ford reiterating the activities.

Captain Santos Benavides, afterwards a colonel in the service of the Confederacy, made a forced march from Laredo, attacked Cortina near Redmond's Ranch, now the town of Carrizo, and defeated him. This ended hostilities for the time being. All these small engagements, except that of Benavides, occurred previous to the bombardment of Fort Sumter. Colonel Ford published an order complimenting Captain Benavides and command on their successful battle with General Cortina.

The victory of Captain Benavides had an excellent effect, particularly on the population of the lower Río Grande. Benavides met with General García, who commanded the line of the Bravo, and requested him to use his influence in thwarting the efforts of Cortina to cause a war between Mexico and the Confederacy. García passed up the Río Grande and was in consultation with Cortina, or reputed to be. Cortina retired from the border; the men led by him abandoned his nefarious service and gave the people of that section a breathing spell. Cortina's subordinates, aiders, and abettors were probably quite sensible that the Confederate troops were rather too strong for them to make raids and carry plunder into Mexico without incurring danger.

The action of General García indicated a desire on his part to aid the Confederate troops in suppressing the insurrectionary efforts of Cortina and Ochoa. It must not be forgotten that Cortina expressed a strong determination to reconquer Texas, which was popular in Mexico. It was also at a time when the general government of Mexico was much weaker than General [Porfirio] Díaz made it in later years. General García had to treat such men as Cortina with more indulgence than would be evinced now.

3

About April 18, 1861, Captain Joe Love, Ford's adjutant, returned from Galveston with the news of the fall of Fort Sumter. War was now upon us. It was anticipated. The people of the North and the South had traduced and villified each other until they seemed to have lost sight of the fact that they were one people, governed by the same Constitution and the same laws. They were, however, people of diverse sentiments and diverse opinions and were as hostile as the citizens of two distinct governments could be. War was the inevitable result. The two peoples hated each other with a devilish feeling scarcely human. This hellish discord was inflamed by the wicked devices, artifices, and cunning craft of politicians, or more properly, by the machinations of unprincipled demagogues and others who should have practised and preached peace and love. War came with all its calamities, its rendings of family ties, its sacrifice of life, its hardening influences, and its extravagant expenditure of treasure. Demoniac passions crazed the North and the South alike. The South spent the hoarded wealth of centuries and the North created a debt of billions of dollars before either seemed disposed to consider the awful consequences of a war between brothers. Exhaustion on the part of the South in men and means demanded a surrender, and politicians of the North who had never fought passed the laws of reconstruction and oppressed the men who had valiantly faced the Northern soldiers in battle and had never dishonored their cause or themselves. But this is getting ahead of the story.

The question now requiring an answer is, what did you do to meet this terrible ordeal of fraternal war?

During the summer and early fall of 1861 Colonel Ford was commander of the Military District of the Río Grande, which extended from the mouth of the river for more than one thousand miles to above El

Paso. There was a great deal to do and the difficulties were compounded because the section was almost isolated from the remaining portion of Texas. It was almost one hundred and sixty-five miles from Brownsville to Corpus Christi by land. The country between these points was very sparsely settled. The sand district was located between the two towns. The Río Grande valley was settled mostly by Mexicans and by a small minority of Americans. It was one hundred miles from Brownsville to Río Grande City, a little more than two hundred miles on to Laredo, about three hundred on to Eagle Pass, and finally some three hundred and not quite fifty miles on up to Fort Clark. This may be termed the lower Río Grande country.

Seven companies of Ford's regiment were stationed in the upper Río Grande country around El Paso. Lieutenant Colonel John R. Baylor and Major Edwin Waller performed good service on the upper Río Grande. These men were mustered into service in the interior of Texas, marched to the neighborhood of El Paso, and there had several affairs with the Union troops, all of which have been mentioned in Colonel Baylor's reports and will not be repeated in these memoirs. Circumstances compelled Colonel Ford to remain on the lower Río Grande. He never saw a great many of the officers and men in the companies on the upper part of the river; consequently, he was a stranger to them. This state of affairs requires no comment. It speaks for itself.

The action in regard to the commencement of hostilities is thus described in Ford's report of April 21, 1861, to Governor Clark:

On the evening of the 18th inst. Capt. Love arrived here, from Galveston, bringing intelligence of the opening of hostilities between the Confederate States and Mr. Lincoln's government, and the sailing of the expedition for the coast of Texas, supposed to be destined for Brazos Santiago. . . . I very soon determined upon a course of action, but in order to have the opinion of my officers, and to enable them to understand matters fully, and to know my determination, I called a council of war. It was the opinion of all that Brazos Santiago is not defensible, that the post should be abandoned for the present, and that we concentrate and make a stand at this point. Captain [Stephen] Powers, who was here on business, left at midnight, accompanied by Mr. Lawton of the Engineer Department. To the captain was assigned the task of superintending the withdrawal of men, ordnance, and supplies of every kind from Brazos Island, and their transportation to this post by steamboats and waggons.

It may not be amiss to say, that there is no water on Brazos Island, save beach water of an unhealthy character—there are no rations—it is isolated. . . . There are no guns of long range on the island. A war vessel could shell a force out of Brazos Island without ever coming within reach of any gun we have there. One revenue cutter could make the place utterly useless to us.

On the 19th the men were put to work to repair Old Fort Brown, and they are progressing rapidly. In a short while it will be capable of offering a strong and protracted resistance to an investing force. It is easy of communication from the interior of the State, from which quarter we must now look for reinforcements and supplies. It cannot be approached without subjecting an enemy to serious annoyance . . . in reaching it from the coast or from any other direction. In the neighborhood mounted troops can be subsisted, and it answers the double purpose of defending Brownsville against the inroads of Black Republicans, and keeping Matamoros within due bounds. I shall be able to place within it about 10 heavy siege pieces and ammunition for siege purposes. . . . I called upon the Mayor of Brownsville, officially requesting aid. He expressed willingness to co-operate, and with that object in view a committee from the Board of Aldermen called upon me yesterday evening, and notified me of their desire to render every assistance within their power in consummating measures of defense.[1]

Mr. Galvan very promptly offered to place any thing in his mercantile establishment at the command of the State. Rations can be had here, and will be needed, if the enemy land soon. The citizens will furnish hands to work in the trenches, and volunteer companies will be organized. However, it would be improper not to state, that the preparations are not only being made to meet an invading force from the coast, but an anticipated raid from Cortina.

Old Fort Brown lies just below the town of Brownsville. The walls of the old fort had been diminished by time, by the weather, and by non-usage. The surroundings were overgrown with mesquite trees and bushes. These Judge [Israel B.] Bigelow superintended cutting down. He hired Mexicans to do the work and paid them. Everything was done by the people of Brownsville, within their power, to aid the military in preparing for defense. The city authorities and Colonel Ford met and consulted as to the propriety of what should be done next. The troops were put to work on Fort Brown. Judge Galvan had in his warehouse several barrels of pure, good whiskey, which once belonged to the United States. To encourage the workmen on Fort Brown, the "jigger" bucket was sent around at stated times.

The gentleman superintending the repairs of Fort Brown was a civil engineer. His name I do not now remember. He erected a work for the

---

[1] Not all of Brownsville's 3,000 people were loyal, law-abiding Confederate citizens. In 1861 it was still a frontier town with plenty of gunmen and drunks roaming the streets and brawling in saloons. Controlling these demanded a great deal of the commanding officer's time. Fremantle, who visited Brownsville a little later, remarked that it "was the rowdiest town of Texas, which was the most lawless state in the Confederacy." In Brownsville "the shooting-down and stringing-up systems are much in vogue." (Arthur James Lyon Fremantle, *The Fremantle Diary*, pp. 10, 17–18.)

protection of the besieged against cannon shot. It extended across the fort on the inside. A plan of the fort was forwarded to General Van Dorn, commanding the district of Texas with headquarters at San Antonio. Someone told Colonel Ford that Major [Thornton A.] Washington condemned the work. It may not have been true. Ford desired a friend to say to Major Washington that any criticism upon Fort Brown must be directed at General [Joseph K. F.] Mansfield, one of the most accomplished engineers in the Army of the United States.

4

In the effort to maintain the military power of the Confederate States, the writer was careful to direct his officers to aid, when necessary, the representatives of the civil law in the enforcement of its mandates. On April 15, 1861, Ford said: "It is always the duty of the military to aid the civil authorities, when called upon, in any legal way. I should have no hesitancy in using the whole force of this Military District to sustain a civil officer, and to aid him in the discharge of his duties. The laws must be enforced. Whoever sets them at defiance is an enemy to the state, and deserves to be treated as such. At the same time it is our duty to aid, yet we can not properly direct civil officers in the manner of their performance of official duties."

Similar instructions were given to each officer having a separate command.

It was a difficult matter to subsist the men on duty on the lower Río Grande after the Federal blockade sealed off Texas from the balance of the world. The writer remembers to have been endeavoring to trade for powder and percussion caps, which were in a vessel at the mouth of the Río Grande. Some gentleman of the intense Confederate stamp, who had become a resident of Matamoros, came to Brownsville to inform Ford the articles were of Yankee make, and not to purchase them. The reply was:

"I do not care if the powder and caps were made in hell and smelt of brimstone, I will buy them if I can."

Colonel Ford had reported to Governor Clark that he had on hand for the troops at Fort Brown a supply of provisions for about one month. Colonel Ford, in order to supply his troops, called upon the assessor and collector of Cameron County to turn over the money he had collected to Ford's quartermaster and commissary, providing to return the same, if possible. It has been claimed that Ford on this occasion violated his own orders that no military man could "direct" a civil authority. Ford did not view the act as violative of law. He deemed it a matter of economic necessity.

5

When the United States blockaded Brazos Santiago, Colonel Ford visited the merchants of Matamoros, particularly those of foreign countries, and insisted upon steps being taken at once to open trade with Europe and the Confederate States through Matamoros. He addressed General Van Dorn on the subject, also Major Guy M. Bryan and others. The consuls of Great Britain and Germany promised to aid in the matter, and they did. Cotton was hauled across Texas to Matamoros where it was traded for foodstuffs and war matériel. An immense trade opened up in a short while. Matamoros was soon crammed with strangers and filled with goods of every class.

In the meantime, King & Kenedy felt cramped in their transporting operations. They could not visit Brazos Santiago without being captured by the blockader. They consulted Ford in regard to placing their boats under the Mexican flag. Ford advised them to do so. The boats of that firm were then allowed to navigate the waters of the Gulf of Mexico and the Río Grande. They were laden with freight intended for the government and the citizens of the Confederate States, and no one interfered. After Ford had been ordered to another point, Colonel [Philip N.] Luckett was on duty at Brownsville. He sent a communication to Texas headquarters complaining that Colonel Ford had allowed the boats of King & Kenedy to be registered under the Mexican flag, and they could not be controlled by orders from Confederate officers. This was referred to Colonel Ford. He replied that in the first place the boats in question were owned by private citizens, and Confederate officers had no right to control their ownership and employment; secondly, that he favored their registration under the Mexican flag to render them free from capture by Federals; third, that they were just as much at the service of the Confederate commander at Fort Brown as they ever had been. Ford heard no more of it.

In the fall of 1861 Ford was ordered to turn over his command to Colonel Luckett and to retire to San Antonio for a much needed rest. At the same time Governor Clark sent Colonel [Charles Grimus Thorkelin de] Lovenskiold to the Río Grande to muster out all of Ford's soldiers who had not transferred from State service to the Confederate Army.

Lovenskiold had come to Texas at rather an early day. He was a brother to Field Marshal Lovenskiold of Denmark. Colonel Lovenskiold was

engaged for some years as a schoolteacher in Corpus Christi. He afterwards became a lawyer. He was a gentleman of fine mind and of great
acquirements. He managed nearly all of his cases outside the courts by
compromise and so on. But he usually satisfied his clients and secured a
heavy practice. When the clash of arms came he was known as a firm
secessionist. He labored under an affection of the nose which affected his
pronunciation and which was painful and distressing.

When Lovenskiold entered upon the duty of mustering out Ford's
State troops, he did not call upon Ford for information in regard to anything; in fact he declined Ford's proffered assistance. It was said by some
who professed to know that Lovenskiold attached censure and blame to
Ford, but for what Ford did not know and probably never will, as all the
papers were said to have burned in the old capitol fire.

Later in the Civil War Lovenskiold wrote to Ford expressing a desire
to be considered a friend. Ford answered him, saying that he understood
that Lovenskiold had expressed unfriendliness to him in the muster-out
report. Ford said that he had not seen the report and was willing to pass
it by. He said his services in Texas had been long and arduous, and he
thought the inimical expressions of no one man would be sufficient to
cause his fellow citizens to ignore and condemn him. He insisted that
the South was waging a war for the observance of her rights and her
friends ought to stand together. Lovenskiold answered that he was rather
surprised at Ford's determination but said nothing about the reported
charges. There the matter of the muster-out report ended.

XXVII

>>>

RICH MAN'S WAR, POOR MAN'S FIGHT!

When Ford was relieved from duty on the Río Grande, he visited San Antonio and remained there about two months. General [Henry E.] McCulloch then ordered him back to Fort Brown. In a few months Ford was again directed to return to San Antonio. This was in the spring of 1862. General [Hamilton P.] Bee was in command at San Antonio. Ford remained there some time—about two months.

The troops of the Second Texas Cavalry had been concentrated, or nearly so, in the interior of Texas. The Confederate Secretary of War ordered that all volunteer regiments should be reorganized so far as the election of field officers went. Ford declined to stand again for colonel, as he had not been elected previously by the men of the regiment, but had been appointed by the Texas secession convention. This position was perhaps not well founded. But Ford still persisted in not being a candidate in an election in the Second Texas Cavalry for field officers. General [P. O.] Hébert, just before leaving Texas, passed through Austin and conferred on Ford the appointment of major, which he did not accept. Hébert paid Ford as a colonel. When General [J. Bankhead] Magruder assumed command of Texas, he addressed Ford an official order as colonel and paid him as such.

In June, 1862, Ford was ordered to take charge of the Bureau of Conscription of the State. He visited the city of Houston, then went to Austin to enter upon the discharge of conscript duty. The conscript law had not yet reached Texas. Ford issued an order on the subject.

He did not favor the rich man. He exempted the ferryman—a poor man—and sent the owner of the ferry—a rich man—to the field. The overseer of Negroes was exempted and the owner taken, and so on through the different kinds of employers and employees.

Soon the conscript law reached Austin. It exempted the rich man and made the poor man a soldier by force of law. It was an unfortunate enactment. Very soon the cry went up from our armies: "The rich man's war and the poor man's fight." It did great harm. A man sent a communication to Austin saying that he had so many Negroes and so many cattle. "Does that exempt me from conscription?" Ford answered in substance, yes, but where a man has so much he ought to fight for it.

2

When Ford was ordered from the Río Grande the second time, he left his wife in Brownsville at the house of Major Eliju Smith, her father. She gave birth to Mary Louise on August 15, 1862. She has since become Mrs. Joseph W. Maddox. During the month of September George W. Morris was employed to conduct Mrs. Ford from Brownsville to Austin. Unfortunately the yellow fever prevailed on the lower Río Grande, and Morris fell victim to it. He was a friend whom circumstance could not swerve and brought the writer's family to Austin anyway. Invulnerable to the shafts of criticism, of irony, and of hatred, he was one of Nature's noblemen, brave and generous.

While on conscript duty, Ford had as his adjutant, Harry Trask of New York. Ford was ably assisted by Captain William C. Walsh, who was disabled by a wound at Gaines' Mill. He has since been twice elected as commissioner of the general land office. Lieutenant [William] Stowe was quartermaster and commissary. Lieutenant Archie McFarland was on duty at Austin. He later settled at Kerrville, and has been clerk of the district and county court of Kerr County for about twenty years. Ford established a branch office at Tyler in eastern Texas. Placed on duty there were Captain William G. Thomas and Lieutenant John Q. Sinclair. At San Antonio Jacob Waelder and Captain Jesse M. Bell were on duty.

Colonel Ford made it a point to assist Major [Simeon] Hart, the quartermaster at San Antonio and the purchasing agent of the Confederate government. The colonel induced him to employ Major Ed Burleson in purchasing mules. Burleson was at the time out of the service of the Confederate States. He had been major of General Henry E. McCulloch's frontier regiment and had resigned. The position assigned him by Major Hart exempted him from conscription. Burleson purchased for Major Hart a large number of mules which were much needed in the service.

The writer feels that he honestly and faithfully administered the conscript law. He always made an effort not to render the execution of the law onerous or unjust. A rule of the commandant was never, if possible to avoid it, to place a Union man in the Confederate ranks. He protested against the idea of drawing unwilling recruits from among those who differed from us in opinion. The war was caused by a wide difference in sentiments; the man of one party could not honestly serve in the ranks of the other.

Sometimes the enrolling officers would assign a Union man to a command, and in that case Ford felt unable to interfere. An old friend wrote to him and inveighed bitterly against what he had done. Ford replied that we were waging a war based on our opinion of the provisions of the Constitution of the United States. In the event we forced men into our ranks who believed we were wrong, would they not desert us at a critical period and carry news to their friends—our enemies—calculated to cause our defeat, or at least to ensure an abandonment of our plans? No more was heard of the matter.

John Hancock was a Union man. It was said that he declared his Union sentiments to anyone desiring to employ him as an attorney, thus allowing the visitor the privilege of withdrawing his request for Hancock's services. One day Mr. Coffee came into the office of Colonel Ford and presented a paper containing about fifteen names. It was signed. It was an exemption, granted because those exempted were to engage in making salt at a spring on the Colorado above Austin. Judge Hancock's name was prominent on the list. They were all Unionists.

The policy of kindly treatment was apparent. To a right-minded man, it was the sure means of securing neutrality in action and to a degree in feeling. Judge Hancock early in 1864 asked a private interview with the writer. It was granted. The judge said there was a determination on the part of the Confederate authorities to force him into their ranks. He seemed to believe the papers he held from Colonel Ford would not be respected. Hancock represented it to have been his intention to remain in the South as a non-combatant. He declared that the undoubted intention of the enrolling officer was to force him into the Confederate Army. For that reason he was going to leave the South. He then asked for the privilege of accompanying Colonel Ford who was on his way to the Río Grande. This was promptly refused.

"I can take no responsibility in the affair," Ford said. "I cannot guard you, as it were, to the Confederate boundary and allow you to pass out and over to the Unionists. That course would hardly be in keeping with my oath to the Confederate Constitution. If you are determined to go North, go at your own risk. As you have pledged yourself not to bear arms against the South I shall not endeavor to stop you."

He went to Mexico sometime after and did not return to Texas until after the surrender of General Lee. It was questioned whether the judge adhered to the noncombative principles advanced previous to leaving Texas. He certainly abandoned the idea of not fighting. It is just to say that he did a great deal for Confederates in the dark hours of reconstruction.

3

During 1862 and 1863 Texas Confederates in Virginia procured furloughs and came home. It was reported, by men who knew, that the wives of soldiers wrote to their husbands urging them to come home. In some instances the impatience of the writers induced them to exaggerate small affairs most egregiously. Truth compels the admission that in some few letters of wives the conduct of respectable men was grossly misrepresented. The soldiers to whom these communications were addressed frequently became incensed. Many of them made strong promises to redress these imaginary grievances when they returned to Texas.

There were a number of men of conscriptible age who managed to keep out of the army by reason of small offices they managed to hold and by other sharp practices well-known to the ardent patriot who stayed at home with his wife. These gentlemen were the most eloquent accusers of those men who came home and of those officers who lost fights, no matter what the difference in numbers or in position. These gentlemen abused everything and everybody wearing the Confederate uniform. From the lips out they were excelsior soldiers. These censorious citizens did great harm to the Confederate cause.

In order to prevent the dangers arising from men streaming home from the fronts and from the draft exempts who criticized mercilessly, Colonel Ford originated and wrote the system of the Order of the Sons of the

South. It was a disquisition on the principles enunciated in the Constitution of the Confederate States. It taught that the supreme authority was really inherent in the people, but was vested in the Confederate government by articles in the Constitution. The army, created by law, was subordinate to the civil authority. A soldier could not draw a ration, or an article of clothing, except by authority of civil law. The bayonet when acting in obedience to law was the defender of right and of liberty and, when not supported by law, was simply the despotic instrument of tyranny and oppression. In the latter case, it violated and suppressed the natural rights and privileges of free men. Among other things, Ford pointed out, in the Order, that he was

utterly opposed to violations of the Constitution and the laws, and the usurpation of power by any officer, civil or military, State or Confederate. It is the duty of all good citizens to resist, without delay, encroachment upon their liberties, and not to permit those who invade and trample upon their rights to do so with impunity, and to plead a passive endurance of wrongs as a precedence to justify the further exercise of arbitrary power, and more flagrant infractions of the supreme law of the land.

All power is inherent in the people—they are supreme. They alone can establish and ordain constitutions, or forms of government. The processes of government are delegated by the people, and are held in trust for the people. Officers are only agents of the people, and derive the authority to exercise certain powers from the constitution and the laws made in pursuance thereof. Any officer who may transcend his authority and presume to exercise power not delegated, is, to the extent of his usurpation, a tyrant. He has betrayed his trust, violated his oath of office and of allegiance to the sovereign power—the people. He can not offer in extenuation of the crime, that his motives were patriotic; that, in his opinion, the public good, and necessity, required his assumption of powers not vested by the constitution. These are the pleas of despots. They have been made to mislead almost every people who have lost their liberties.

The constitution is competent for all the purposes for which it was established and ordained. It is adequate to secure the people in the exercise and enjoyment of all their rights. Under its broad shield we have been, and will be, protected from all dangers which have assailed us, or may threaten us in the future. If this be [not] true, our government is a failure, and we are fighting for we know not what.

If the public good, and necessity, are the limitations of power, and the officers who exercise it are to be the judges of its extent, a constitution and laws would be useless. The will of officers would be the law.

The men who advocate these dangerous principles place themselves upon the platform of Seward and Lincoln. They tacitly admit the higher-law doctrine as true, and they justify the Black Republicans in all their inroads upon the constitution, and their outrages of every character, because they have perpetrated all these enormities as measures dictated by necessity and vindicated by the public good.

We have proclaimed to the world that we are struggling for liberty, against violations of the constitution, and against usurpations of power. But, if this doctrine of necessity, of public good, that the end justifies the means, be correct, and we permit it to supersede and over-ride the constitution, then we are wrong. We must recall our armies and say to them: "The battles you have fought are wholesale murders. Mr. Lincoln is right—ask his pardon, and submit to his rule."

The public good, in the proper sense of the term, never did require a violation of the constitution, and it never will.

It is never expedient to violate principle. Principle and expediency go hand in hand. It is a mistake to suppose they can be separated without the commission of error or crime.

Mr. Calhoun has well said, there can be no liberty without a constitution. That instrument is the ark of freedom. It is the duty of every patriot to defend it against attacks from any quarter. But in protecting it from encroachments by our own officers the means of defense and redress must not be mistaken. They consist in holding the aggressor to a strict accountability in arraigning him before the tribunals of the country, in holding him up for the execration of an indignant people, and the various remedies known to those accustomed to the workings of a democratic representative government.

There is no doubt but, that those who have withheld their services, and refused their support to the Confederate Government in the dark hours of peril would be pleased to institute other measures of pretended redress. To open wide the floodgates of disorder, confusion, and violence, and to introduce anarchy would be to them a labor of love. Against the machinations and the insidious suggestions of these people we cannot be too watchful.

The Government at Richmond has given us no just cause of complaint. The infractions of the Constitution, the disregard of law, and the evils they have created and may inflict upon us, have had their origin from other sources. They have not weakened our confidence in our Government nor our devotion to our cause. The man whose blood is so cold as not to appreciate the bond of love which unites us to our sister States, who from disapproval of the acts of subordinate officers, from disappointed ambition, or from any selfish motive, could counsel his countrymen to withdraw Texas from the Confederacy, or to prepare for a separation from a brotherhood endeared by so many glorious recollections, and common dangers, has no claims to patriotism which deserve the recognition of a generous and gallant people.[1]

---

[1] The editor has added the quoted portion of Ford's dissertation on the Order of the Sons of the South. It was published originally in the *Texas Almanac—Extra* (Austin), March 17, 1863.

The writer also believed that the Constitution inculcated the propriety of assisting disabled Confederate soldiers, of getting control of the meat markets and reducing prices within reason, of creating a fund to be used in purchasing marketable articles, of issuing these articles to those unable to purchase them, of seeking employment for soldiers' wives and children in need, in fact to make the members of the Sons of the South the friends and the assistants of the poor and the distressed. There were families in Austin who were furnished with provisions and wood and who did not know, for a time, from whom the supplies came. The meat market was controlled and prices reduced to a rate enabling the poor to buy.

The Sons of the South obtained a dissemination quite general throughout Texas, and as the writer understood, it was introduced into the Army of the Texas-Mississippi Department. When the United States Army occupied Texas after the war, the pamphlets of the order were generally destroyed or hidden. The writer would not have destroyed a single pamphlet. He would have avowed the authorship and faced the music. He was the fabricator of the whole matter, but received the assistance of Captain John J. Dix in the preparation of a portion of the Order.

4

There were a number in Texas who avoided conscription. Some of them occupied thinly-inhabited districts in northern Texas. They received attention by General H. E. McCulloch. In Cooke County Colonel William C. Young was shot by a man whom he had befriended and fed. Colonel Young was a gentleman of great popularity. He had filled many responsible positions, was an old Texian, an Indian fighter of note, and the friend of every good man. His death caused great excitement in northern Texas, and was the occasion of the killing of several men.

Other draft dodgers congregated in the hilly country above Austin. They formed camps and lived by hunting and by the kindness of friends. A murder was committed in Gonzales County. A company of citizens was organized and marched to the neighborhood of Austin, with the avowed object of arresting the Union men encamped westward of that point. Colonel Ford got together a few soldiers and some citizens. They moved at night, and were conducted to where the Unionists were sleeping. In the after part of the night a man, evidently opposed to the violence he supposed would be offered to the campers, discharged his gun twice. They were awakened. After a brief consultation the Union men abandoned their camp, passed over a creek, and near the space occupied by the Gonzales company. They ascended a bluff several hundred feet high and moved off. The name of the officer commanding the Gonzales company is not remembered. The object of the writer in accompanying this expedition was to prevent the commission of acts in violation of law. The man who fired the gun was well known. He is now dead. To mention his name would be useless.

In the fall of 1863 the Unionists were on the Colorado above Austin. A number of violations of the law were perpetrated in Travis County. The Union men were saddled with all the odium of these wrongdoings. Captain Dorbant, commanding a company in Burnet County, was consulted. He moved down the country; Colonel Ford moved up. A plan was formed to send scouts in every direction to scour the entire section, after which all the different bodies were to surround the residence of Mr. Priest, a Union man, at a designated hour that evening. The different places used as encampments were visited. The campers were either captured or run off. They all left that locality.

The plan formed to disperse the Unionists about Austin was productive of no bloodshed; no laws were violated and no one was mistreated. It is a good thing for an officer to so demean himself, on such occasions, as not to be afraid or ashamed to meet any of those who were affected by his actions. (The writer was told one of these Union men had threatened to kill him. After the war Ford met the man on the Colorado River opposite from Austin. He pronounced the report groundless.)

Elsewhere in the state loyal Confederates took it upon themselves to punish draft dodgers. After the war Governor Throckmorton expressed the opinion that men were executed as traitors to the Confederacy who were more remarkable for ignorance than for anything else. These were deplorable affairs; ones which may be regretted, and yet be accounted for as a result of the passions engendered by an unfortunate Civil War.[2]

---

[2] Unionist uprisings were widespread in eastern and northern Texas throughout 1863 and 1864. There were, for example, a large number of deserters and draft dodgers who hid out in the "Big Thicket" in Hardin County, skirmishing with Confederate scouts in the swampy wastelands around "The Blue Hole," "Panther's Den," "Doc Trull Hammock," and "Deserter's Island." During the winter of 1863–1864 Henry E. McCulloch had a great deal of trouble with angry Unionist mobs around Bonham up in the northern subdistrict who terrorized peaceful communities and threatened to tar and feather enrolling officers. For a time violence was so rampant there that Confederates lamented "the question is whether they or we shall control."

Unionism was strongest around San Antonio and Fredericksburg. These areas had a heavy population of German immigrants who had not been assimilated into the Southern culture and who therefore felt little loyalty to the Confederacy. When enrolling officers began conscripting young Germans in the summer of 1862, many of their fathers sent to the governor a petition denouncing the draft as a "despotic decree" and asking that the Texas government protect their "indisputable rights" as "free citizens" and refuse to comply with the draft laws.

5

During Ford's control of conscript affairs in Texas, he had his letters
and orders copied so that he could have in his possession a record of his

---

Then in July, 1862, with other Unionists in the area they held a meeting on Bexar
Creek and organized three military companies for protective purposes and set up an
advisory board.

When word of this meeting reached General H. P. Bee, commanding a sub-district of
Texas, he declared the counties of Gillespie, Kerr, Kendall, Medina, Comal, and Bexar
in a state of open rebellion against the Confederacy and dispatched Captain James
Duff's veterans to enforce martial law and protect enrolling officers. Duff, a cruel, hard-
driving officer, set up headquarters in Fredericksburg, whose inhabitants were "unionists
to a man," and promptly hanged anyone he suspected of having anti-Confederate sentiment.

Because of the violence, hundreds left the area. Among them were some 80 Unionist
men who met at the headwaters of Turtle Creek on July 31, 1862, and started for
Mexico. With them was a Confederate spy who left signs along the way for a body of
pursuers—a Confederate cavalry patrol under Lieutenant C. D. McRae—which was about
a day's ride behind.

On the morning of August 9, the Unionists, ignorant of their pursuers, reached
the Nueces River, followed its sinuous course for a few hours, then encamped in a
grassy clearing that afternoon. The sun was hot and several of the men napped while
two separate parties went out to shoot their dinner. At dusk one party returned very
much excited, explaining breathlessly that they had seen figures moving about in the
woods upstream. At that moment the other party came running into camp to report
that they also had seen strange movements in the brush. The men might have panicked
had one sturdy fellow not pointed out between chuckles that no enemy was out there:
the hunters had merely stalked one another. There was a moment of silence, then everyone laughed heartily and, still joking about it, prepared dinner. Afterward the leader,
Major Tegener, led a discussion ranging over topics such as the "Fatherland," "citizenship," "Civil War," and "refugeeing in Mexico."

After the guard was stationed and the others were in their pallets, a man named
John William Sansom called the major aside.

"Are you entirely satisfied, Major, that our boys saw no strangers around this
evening?"

"Of course I am," the major said. "Why do you ask?"

"Because . . ." And Sansom paused to wipe his brow. "Because I fear they did see
strangers and if they did, it meant harm to us."

The major laughed, assured Sansom that he was just jumpy, told him to get some
rest, and then went to his own pallet. Sansom went to bed too, but not to sleep. He
tossed and turned for a time, then rolled over to stare at the stars and the moon over-
head. A full moon. Ambushes were usually executed by the full of the moon—the
Indian way. He jumped from his pallet and ran after one of the guards, who had just disappeared behind a cedar-brake.

BEE-YOWWWWWW!

The man in front of him dropped to the ground.

BEE-YOWWWWWWW!

And the shot ricocheted off a tree just over Sansom's head. He fired three times as he
fell and rolled behind a cedar-brake. Suddenly, from somewhere off to his left came
the bloodcurdling Texas yell. He listened in horror at the popping of revolvers and the
screams of dying men in the direction of the camp.

Scrambling up he sprinted through singing bullets, dove behind a tree, crawled
through a patch of prickly pear, then dashed into camp. There he found his comrades

acts in that matter. After he was relieved from that duty, Captain William C. Walsh performed them for a period of time. When the Confederacy collapsed, he carried the official documents away from Austin, and they have been lost sight of. There is nothing in these records of which the

---

battling desperately with the Confederates, who had surrounded them. Sansom pleaded with the major, who was mortally wounded, to order the men to run for it.

But before they could move, the soldiers charged in with pistols blazing. Again Sansom sprinted through the gunfire, made it to the woods, and kept on running until he collapsed on the bank of the Nueces some distance away. For a while he heard the swearing and muffled shouts of men, then tensed at the rapid crack of cavalry carbines. They were shooting the prisoners!

Hours later, when the Confederates had gone, Sansom, suffering from shock, wandered over the battleground talking to the corpses. After the war he published an account of the massacre, placing the total dead at 34: 19 killed in the actual fighting, 9 murdered afterward, and 6 trampled by cavalry as they tried to escape through the woods. The Nueces River ambush was in Sansom's opinion one of the most hideous, cold-blooded crimes that had ever occurred in Texas.

Back at Fredericksburg Lieutenant McRae reported to Captain Duff that "they offered the most determined resistance and fought with desperation, asking no quarter whatever; hence I have no prisoners to report."

This massacre was probably the worst of those "deplorable affairs" that Ford mentioned in connection with Unionism in Texas. It precipitated Unionist uprisings in the Fredericksburg area and especially in San Antonio, where men cried out in protest, threatening to resist by force of arms and posting notices around the city:

NEWS

German brothers, are your eyes not opened yet? After the rich took every picayune away from you, and the paper is worth only one-half what you so hard earned, now that you have nothing left, now they go about and sell you, or throw you out of employment for Dunhauer, who left his wife and children, wants to do the same with you to the poor you might leave. Now is the time to stay the heads of Dunhauer, Maverick, Mitchel, and Menger to the last bone. We are always ready. If the ignorant company of Newton fights you, do as you please. You will always stay the God damn Dutchman. Do away with that nuisance, and inform everybody the revolution is broke out.

It is a shame Texas has such a brand. Hang them by their feet and burn them from below.

Unionists then marched through the streets singing "John Brown's Body" and the Yankee marching song, "We'll Hang Jeff Davis on a Sour-Apple Tree." Confederate troops captured and hanged a number of these troublemakers. As a result, there ensued a street war in which Unionists in hotel rooms and on roof tops took pot shots at soldiers by night or day. Violence prevailed in the Alamo City and in other German communities until the end of the war.

Some 2,132 Unionist sympathizers, rather than risk a hanging, left their homes to join the Federal Army. At least 1,500 of these enlisted in Union forces beyond the Texas borders. The others remained in the state to form their own Federal commands—the First and Second Texas Cavalry Regiments (Union)—which fought Rip Ford along the Río Grande in 1864 and which Ford mentions in the two chapters that follow.

(Arthur James Lyon Fremantle, *The Fremantle Diary*, pp. 32, 43–44; U.S. War Department, *The War of the Rebellion: A Compilation of the Official Records of the*

writer feels ashamed. There are errors of course—the incidents of fallible human nature.

Judge Oran M. Roberts praised Ford for his services as "the head of conscription in the State of Texas" and says

he was well fitted for that position. But still I am tempted to say, it is a shame that he has been placed, and kept there. I regard him as unquestionably the best military man that we had in Texas at the time of the war, and so I believe he was generally regarded by those who were well acquainted with him. He should have been in the field, and "Old Rip," as his frontier boys called him, would have made his mark. For unlike most of our frontier officers he had studied war as a science, has a fine military library, and had for years devoted himself to it. And then he had system, good business habits. Was a man of action, not of words, of caution in devising, and of intrepidity in execution.

The position of conscript commander offered to a man of covetous disposition the facilities for the acquisition of immense wealth. There were men who offered considerable sums of money to be exempted from conscription. These offers Ford simply refused. According to memory no answer was returned to the applicant. The law was executed.

Cotton was plentiful in Texas. The price was about ten cents per pound in Confederate currency. One hundred and fifty thousand dollars was turned over to Colonel Ford at one time for the purchase of mules. This money he could have expended in the purchase of cotton. For the purpose of transporting such cotton outside the limits of the Confederate States Ford could have exempted men of conscript age and hired them and their teams at a small price. In Mexican territory the cotton could have been sold at a fabulous price, sometimes as high as fifty cents per pound. The certainty of a return freight for the team was always an assured thing. Merchandise of almost any description was high priced within Texas. Teams were in great demand. The writer adopted none of the many facilities for the acquisition of wealth. He held a receipt for the money entrusted to his disposition, and has no qualms of conscience on that score.

Union and Confederate Armies, ser. I, vol. IX, pp. 614–616, 705, 706 [hereafter cited as Official Records]; Texas Almanac—Extra [Austin], December 18, 1862; John W. Sansom, Battle of the Nueces River, in Kinney County, Texas, August 10th, 1862, pp. 1–15; Robert W. Shook, "The Battle of the Nueces, August 10, 1862," Southwestern Historical Quarterly, LXVI [July, 1962], 31–42.)

XXVIII

>>

THE CAVALRY OF THE WEST

During the winter of 1863 the Federals had possession of the lower Río Grande. Matamoros was the point from which Texas, and really the country this side of the Mississippi River, received supplies which could not be obtained at home. The fact that wagons engaged in transporting these supplies had to proceed up the Río Grande to Eagle Pass before they could cross into Texas rendered the trip long and laborious. It was almost twice as far by way of Eagle Pass to Austin as it was by the direct route, that is, to cross the Río Grande at Brownsville and proceed directly. It was estimated that this out-of-the-way route at the lowest calculation added fifty per cent to the cost of articles. It was a consumption of additional time and a great hardship imposed upon the persons engaged in the carrying trade. The citizens compelled to travel over this line, more than three hundred miles through a foreign land, were greatly inconvenienced, losing both time and money. This was a matter which interested the military and the residents of a large scope of the Confederate States.

2

When General Magruder assumed command of the District of Texas, he evinced a determination to defend the State. Everything was done to create enthusiasm among the people. The battalions of Mr. Lincoln were met with success. Texas was again ready to do and die. To repeat what has been said elsewhere: "The advent of General Magruder was equal to the addition of 50,000 men to the forces of Texas." His motto was "Ready."[1]

On December 22, 1863, General Magruder addressed Ford a letter suggesting that he undertake a campaign on the lower Río Grande, having for its object the dispossession of the Federals and the restoration of the former line of traffic through Brownsville.[2] Several letters passed between them. Ford was keen to make an effort to clear the Texas mainland of Federals. He was relieved of conscript duty and authorized to raise a command to operate on the lower Río Grande. He left conscript matters in charge of Captain William Walsh and made his headquarters at San Antonio.

---

[1] Thomas North, who had seen Magruder in the fall of 1862 when he replaced P. O. Hébert as commander of Texas, remarked that the "gay, dashing, festive Magruder" was precisely the kind of man that "suited Texas." Hébert had been removed because

he proved to be a man of no military force or practical genius, though a West Pointer, and had enjoyed the advantages of military associations in Europe, the reflex of which appeared rather to damage his usefulness than otherwise. He brought with him so much European red-tapeism, and being a constitutional ape, that he preferred red-top boots, and a greased rat-tail moustache, with a fine equipage, and a suite of waiters, to the use of good, practical common sense. . . . Everybody became tired and disgusted with the General and his policy. He was too much of a military coxcomb to suit the ideas and ways of a pioneer country; besides, he was suspected of cowardice.

But now with Magruder in command, Texas could expect only action and victory.
(North, *Five Years in Texas: or, What You Did Not Hear during the War from January 1861 to January 1866*, pp. 105–106, 107.)

[2] Magruder specifically ordered Ford to "create the impression among all persons, your men as well as others, that you are coming to Indianola, via Goliad, to meet the enemy, and, after you have left San Antonio, you can strike off to the west. You will be very particular, and will not let a soul know of your intended movements. By making a sudden and rapid movement, you may be able to create a panic among the enemy; and, if so," there was an an excellent chance of winning a decisive victory. Ford hastily wrote him back that "there is no doubt of success. The results from an expulsion of the Yankees from the Rio Grande would be almost equal to those following the recapture of Galveston."
(Edmund P. Turner to Ford, December 22, 1863, *Official Records*, ser. I, vol. XXVI, pt. II, pp. 525–526; Ford to Turner, December 25, 1863, *ibid.*, pp. 534–535.)

As soon as he had received the order, Ford had issued a call to the people of Texas. In that he appealed to the men who were exempt from conscript duty, and implored them to come to the front and aid in expelling the enemy from the soil of Texas.

> Headquarters Cavalry of the West
> San Antonio, December 27, 1863

Persons desiring to go into service will report to me at San Antonio, without delay, where they will be subsisted and their horses foraged. Those not belonging to companies will be organized here. Companies already organized are requested to report for duty immediately.

It is highly important that the expedition be organized and placed in the field at once.

The people of the West are invited to turn out. They will be defending their own homes. Shall it be said that a mongrel force of Abolitionists, negroes, plundering Mexicans, and perfidious renegades have been allowed to murder and rob us with impunity? Shall the pages of history record the disgraceful fact, that Texians have tamely and basely submitted to these outrages, and suffered the brand of dishonor to be inflicted upon an unresisting people? For the honor of the State, for the sake of the glorious memories of the past, the hopes of the future, you are called upon to rally to the standard and to wash out the stains of invasion by the blood of your ruthless enemies.

> John S. Ford
> Col. Comdg.

These were the days when strong passions ruled. A family quarrel is usually the bitterest of all others. To take the expressions used on both sides it would be supposed that the belligerents could never be appeased, could never live together in harmony. Fortunately the sequel would prove differently, a great many expressions of hatred would be forgotten, some regretted, and we would become again one people.

The reasons in favor of the expedition into the lower Río Grande country were apparent, and the appeal met with a hearty and favorable response. When Ford reached San Antonio in December, several applications were already on hand asking for authority to raise companies. At this point Major [A. G.] Dickinson was in command, and aided the colonel in every way he possibly could.

The work of enlisting men was entered upon heartily. On December 27, 1863, in a report to General Magruder, the following was said of recruiting:

I have learned that the major general commanding has ordered him [Captain Thomas C. Cater] to report at Houston. His company is full to the minimum, and was not mustered into service. His men are of the very best class, and peculiarly adapted to the service assigned me, and I particularly request that they be allowed to remain under my command.

There will be another company from Travis County, one from Williamson and Burnet, and there are three being organized in Gonzales and adjacent counties. Captain John Littleton has reported a company from Karnes, and a company has been reported from Guadalupe County.

A company of 80 to 90 men has been raised in Caldwell County, but has not been reported. Companies and detachments are being raised in various localities, and at present it is impossible to say what number of volunteers will take the field.

Colonel Ford found considerable difficulty in securing funds to fit out the men of his command. On December 29, 1863, he wrote General Magruder as follows: "I have arranged to procure Mexican rope, which I can exchange for manilla with Major Hart."

(Ford had made it a rule when operating against Indians to have the horses of his command staked with strong ropes to prevent them from being stampeded. It was a favorite matter with the red men to slip in among the horses of Americans, scare them, and get them to running. They succeeded, on some occasions, in clearing American camps of quite all the horses. In Texas there was a saying: "It is better to tie your horse and count his ribs than to count his tracks." A horse can do good service on Texas grass, if he is properly moved and attended to. A cavalry soldier who has to go out and hunt his horse is generally too late for the fight.)

I have negotiated for some 260 Mexican blankets, weighing 6 pounds each, [Ford continued in his report to Magruder] I am to pay 50 pounds of cotton per blanket.

I have sent Col. E. R. Horde to Fort Merrill to contract for horses, mules, and pack-saddles, &c., and to procure rations of subsistence and forage.

I would respectfully suggest that, inasmuch as no arrangement has been made to furnish funds for the expedition, the major-general commanding allow the cotton bureau to turn over to my quartermaster 200 bales of cotton, to be sold at Piedras Negras for specie, to be used for the purchase of supplies.

Had I control of specie funds, I am satisfied I could secure the services of many Mexicans. I am intimately acquainted with many of that nation who could, and I think would, perform valuable service in our cause. . . .

Four pieces of artillery have been sent here. They were transported by an insufficient number of horses, and are not manned.

In the event the major-general commanding wishes me to take them to the front, I would respectfully request him to assign for duty with me at least 2 good artillery officers and an ordnance officer. . . .

I respectfully suggest the major-general commanding to assign for duty with me Captain [W. G. M.] Samuels.

Captain Samuels is an old resident of San Antonio. At that time he was an efficient and zealous ordnance officer.

A company of Federal cavalry took possession of Captain [Richard] King's ranch of Santa Gertrudis and made William Gregory a prisoner. In order to protect this exposed portion of Texas, Ford forwarded companies to the Nueces as fast as they were mustered into service. This happened about January 1, 1864. Captain James A. Ware and, afterwards, Major Mat Nolan controlled things in that quarter.

On January 14, 1864, Colonel Ford wrote to Colonel George W. White, commissary agent, to appoint [James S.] Holman to become his agent for the purchase of beef for the expeditionary forces. The appointment was made.

Colonel [Spruce M.] Baird was directed to report to Colonel Ford for duty. Baird raised a question of rank, but it was decided against him.[3] He eventually left his regiment under the command of Lieutenant Colonel [Daniel] Showalter and retired from the battlefront.

On February 5, 1864, Ford wrote Major General Magruder: "I regret not having been able to take the field ere this. I have had serious obstacles to surmount. Exhausted resources, a population almost drained of men subject to military duty, opposition from rivalry, and the nameless disagreeable retardations incident to an undertaking of this character, are all too well known to the major-general commanding not to be understood and appreciated. With the help of God, the kind offices of the major-general commanding, and persevering industry, I hope to render efficient service."

On February 17, 1864, in a report to General Magruder, Colonel Ford announced his readiness to move to the front in a few days. In conclusion he said: "I have received many favors from the major-general commanding, for none of which was I more grateful than the permission for Major D[ickinson] to cooperate with me. To lose him now when I am on the eve of making a forward movement is like depriving me of my right arm. I hope the exigencies of the service will not prevent the

---

[3] As Ford pointed out in Chapter XXVII, there was some question as to his actual military rank. When his regiment entered Confederate service, Ford automatically lost his appointment of colonel of state forces. For some reason he twice refused to hold regimental elections which would have made him colonel. He was never commissioned by the Confederate War Department. On March 1, 1864, the governor appointed him brigadier general of a reactivated state corps to command Brigade District No. 11. Ford, however, claimed throughout the war the rank of colonel of cavalry, C.S.A., and Hébert, Magruder, and John G. Walker, successive commanders of the state, recognized him and paid him as such.
(*Official Records,* ser. I, vol. XXVI, pt. II, pp. 47, 65, 382, 517, and vol. XXXIV, pt. II, p. 1011.)

major-general commanding from allowing Major D[ickinson] to accompany me."

Unfortunately Major Dickinson was ordered to remain on duty in San Antonio. About this time Lieutenant William H. Elliott was assigned to duty as assistant adjutant general. He is now dead. May God bless him. He was a good man, and a proper soldier. He was friendly to everyone, and lived without guile.

3

Here it may be as well to mention the deserters. There were at this time a goodly number of these men in Mexico who professed to have come away from the Confederate Army on account of bad treatment from officers. They communicated with Colonel George H. Giddings at Eagle Pass, expressing a devotion to the cause of the Confederacy and a desire to fight for their friends. The matter was referred to General Magruder, and he authorized their pardon and reception again into Confederate service. This order became known and hundreds of men left their commands with the declaration that they were going to join Ford. Very few of them ever found him. They managed to cross the Río Grande and to remain in Mexico until the war ended. The belief gained general acceptance that the expeditionary forces consisted largely of men who had abandoned their flag and fellow soldiers. Men came and applied confidently for deserters. They seldom found the men they desired to see.

As evidence of the writer's opinion of deserters, the following communication to Major L. M. Rogers and Captain J. A. Ware on February 10, 1864, is given:

You must endeavor to arrest any [deserters] who come within your reach. There can be no apology for the man who deserts while in front of the enemy. I understand these men have been deluded into the belief, that I would accept them into my command. God forbid, that I should ever encourage, in any way, conduct prejudicial to good order and discipline, and calculated to do our cause incalculable injury. I reprobate their course, and shall discountenance any proposition they may make to serve in my ranks. I desire you to give this all the publicity you can conveniently.

4

One of the major obstacles to the success of the expedition was the remarkable drought that had plagued the lower Río Grande country for the past two years. In a communication dated February 7, 1864, Major L. M. Rogers said: "You cannot imagine how desolate, barren, and desert-like this country is; not a spear of grass, nor a green shrub, with nothing but moving clouds of sand to be seen on these once green prairies."

Around water holes, then dry, could be seen hundreds of domestic animals, dead, their flesh seemingly dried upon their bones. To move cavalry across the region between the Nueces and the Río Grande was an undertaking of great moment. The greater part of the water found between the two rivers at that date was in wells. It is easy to be perceived how much labor, time, and patience were required to draw water enough from a deep well to satisfy the thirst of a regiment of men and all the animals they are compelled to have. The wells remind one of the scenes described in the Bible, and the contentions around the wells. In Texas, water and grass do not always occupy contiguous grounds. To travel over the country in question during a drought is a thing to be acquired by practice, and not from theory or books. The Nueces River was reported dry for miles.

The commander of the expeditionary forces knew the hardships he would be compelled to encounter in marching across the drouth-ridden regions. He had served there when the Indians came down for wild horses, "beauty and booty," back in '49, '50, and '51. At that period the country between the two rivers was covered by immense numbers of wild horses, and large herds of wild cattle were roaming over the prairies and woodlands.

5

Major [Albert] Walthersdorff was sent to the expeditionary forces on the lower Río Grande as instructor of tactics. He remained on that duty until the close of the war. He made many friends among the soldiers and people on the lower Río Grande. He was a gentleman of large frame and immense physical strength. He could take a man weighing more than two hundred pounds and, with apparent ease, hold him at arm's length.

During January, 1864, Major Walthersdorff had commanded a battalion of Texas State troops and had been very actively engaged in defending Blanco and adjoining counties against renegades and Indians. After he left, a detachment of Captain [Theodore] Heermann's company and Captain Dorbant's citizen company killed two renegades. Ford reported to General Magruder on January 28, 1864: "There is a considerable number of soldiers' families living in that region. They have not the means of transportation to move into the interior. They would feel as if they had been delivered helpless into the hands of the Indians and renegades should Major Walthersdorff's battalion be withdrawn.

The truth is the withdrawal would result in an immediate abandonment of that part of the frontier."

The Texas frontier suffered greatly from Indian depredations during the war. A tier of counties, at least three deep, was quite depopulated. The women and children had to be removed to the interior part of the state to protect them from being killed and made prisoners by cruel savages—a fate worse than death.

6

The recruiting of the men to fill up the ranks of the expeditionary forces, which we had styled "The Cavalry of the West," was pushed forward with zeal. The major general commanding gave every order to ensure success which he could issue without violating law and propriety. Colonel [Santos] Benavides, commanding at Laredo, was placed under Colonel Ford's authority. General Magruder anticipated that a portion of the Frontier Regiment would be ordered by Governor [Pendleton] Murrah to report for duty to Colonel Ford. Colonel Baird's regiment has been mentioned already. Captain James A. Ware was officially placed in charge of all the troops at or near San Patricio intended for service in the expeditionary forces. He was instructed to "appeal to the patriotism, the generosity, and the gallantry of the people." Lieutenant Colonel George H. Giddings was endeavoring to form a regiment. Major Hart, quartermaster, allowed Captain C. H. Merritt to report for duty to Colonel Ford. Major Dickinson of General Magruder's staff continued to assist Ford in every possible way. He was recommended to the proper authority as lieutenant colonel of the expeditionary forces. The application did not meet with approval and Major Dickinson was again ordered to remain in San Antonio.

Application was made for at least two pieces of rifled cannon, but was not complied with. Enrolling officers on conscript duty in various counties were instructed to turn over men to persons recruiting for the expeditionary forces. A great many bales of cotton were secreted between the Nueces and the Río Grande. The men of Ford's command were directed to hunt up these and turn them over to the officers of the cotton bureau. Cotton was the only sure means of obtaining money. Without money nothing could be purchased for the use of troops. Orders were issued prohibiting the transportation of cows, hogs, and other animals to Mexico. The conscript laws exempted men from being forced into the army if they owned a certain number of cattle. Should these men be allowed to drive their cattle into Mexico, the object of the law would be evaded. The policy of the Confederate government was to keep the means of subsistence within her own limits and to prevent men receiving the benefits of her laws from squandering the property conferring upon her citizens exemptions from military service. Selling this property in Mexico was for this reason strictly prohibited.

The following order was directed to Major Rogers, commanding a battalion of state troops on the Nueces: "The trade between the Nueces and lower Río Grande, if going on as reported, must be stopped. Men who furnish the Yankees are aiding and abetting the enemies of our country, and are committing treason. Such men can not claim to be our friends."

Camels once belonging to the United States were kept in San Antonio. Colonel Ford tried but failed to render them serviceable. He reported to General Magruder: "The camels have been sent to the Guadalupe for corn. Two are reported to have died on the trip. They can live best on grass, and it is not certain they will live on corn. Captain [William] Prescott will send them to Camp Verde for the present."[4]

On the twenty-seventh of January, 1864, Colonel Ford had requested Major General Magruder to place Major Felix Blucher under his command. Ford says: "He has been surveyor for many years in the country between the Nueces and the Río Grande, and is thoroughly acquainted with the geography and topography of that section." Also he was able to speak, read, and write four or five modern languages. He was the grand nephew of Field Marshal Blucher of the Prussian Army. Major Blucher, when he reached San Antonio, was indeed a valuable addition to The Cavalry of the West.

---

[4] Back in 1856 the United States Army Quartermaster devised an ingenious plan by which troops and supplies could be transported across Texas' abominable wastelands. The Inspector General heartily approved it, and in May of that year an American transport docked at Indianola and unloaded its strange cargo: an American officer with his regular staff, then two Turks, three Arabs, and of all things "a drove of camels of 34 in number, as follows,—1 Tunis Camel a mule, Bactrian Camels mules, 1 male Booghdee Camel a mule, 4 Arabian male Camels of burden, 14 Arabian female camels of burden, 1 Arabian male calf, 1 male Senaar Dromedary, 1 female Muscat dromedary, 2 male Siout dromedaries, 4 female Siout dromedaries, 1 male Mt Sinai dromedary, and 1 female and 1 male calfs."

The Inspector General was on hand to inspect the animals. He remarked that they were beyond a doubt "designed by the Creator for beasts of burthen." He felt sure that they were exactly what the army needed in making long marches over the desert lands of the southwest. The camels were later surrendered to Texas during the Civil War and afterwards, back in the service of the United States, were marched to Arizona, where they gradually perished (although in the next century tourists regularly reported having seen wild camels wandering about the illusory rocks and hills of Arizona).

(Paul Horgan, *Great River: The Rio Grande in North American History*, II, 809–810.)

7

Having been almost compelled to go to the front and not knowing what might happen on the line of march, Ford deemed it safest to send Mrs. Ford and our child, Lulu, by way of Eagle Pass. She had for company Don Manuel Treviño, his wife, and his sister-in-law, Miss Lu Estis. They left San Antonio early in March, crossed into Mexico, moved south, and arrived at Matamoros early in April, having consumed quite a month in making the trip. The journey was without any great misfortune in the way of accident, except the overturning of the ambulance at Camargo and the wounding of Lulu on the head. The wound caused her a great deal of suffering, but the skill of Dr. C. B. Combe relieved her.

When at Matamoros Mrs. Ford received polite attention from General Cortina, who was now governor of Tamaulipas and who offered her anything she might require. She thanked him, and told him she needed nothing. He attended to having her mail sent off, and did everything a gentleman could. These courtesies were extended in exchange for the kindness Colonel Ford had shown Cortina's mother in days gone by.

Mrs. Ford's father and mother and her sister, Miss Lu Smith, lived in Brownsville. Mrs. Ford's sister met her in Matamoros, and warned her not to go to Brownsville. The United States provost marshal had sent to their house to find out when Mrs. Ford would arrive. Miss Smith was sure of the determination to make Mrs. Ford a prisoner as soon as she arrived at her father's house. She was glad to remain in Matamoros.

Mrs. Ford's mother also visited her two or three times. One day Mrs. Smith went to the provost marshal for a pass to cross over to Matamoros. She was informed he had orders not to grant it. She waited on General Brown without delay. She told him if he could not give orders for her to go to Matamoros to see her own daughter that she demanded a pass to quit the United States. No more trouble was experienced in the procurement of passes.

United States officers visited Mrs. Ford on several occasions. One or two of them were old friends. Of course she had a lively interest in the events occurring on the other side of the Río Grande. It was August of 1864 before she met her husband again.

8

The rumors of an invasion by Federals from the direction of El Paso and another from Brownsville and of attack by renegades upon Eagle Pass were current almost every day. They were, no doubt, put out by the friends of the Federals. Our patrols had a number of skirmishes with the enemy all along the Nueces and out near Eagle Pass. The signs were ominous. Fear that a major Federal offensive might be in the making compelled Ford to hurry up with his preparations. He had on hand now about 1,000 volunteers; to stimulate the recruiting, he called upon the people "in the name of patriotism, of liberty, and all that is dear to man to shoulder their arms & defend their homes & property, their wives and their little ones against the brutal assaults of an enemy who respects neither age, sex or condition, who plunder alike the homstead, the halls of Legislation and the temples dedicated to the worship of almighty God. Submission is no protection against robbery and violence."

[On about March 17, 1864, Colonel Ford with almost 1,300 troopers moved out of San Antonio with high hopes of successful mission.[5]]

---

[5] Most of Ford's command consisted of draft exemptions, old men, and a great many youths between fifteen and seventeen. One of his captains reported "that in the last six months, fifty-seven children" had joined his battalion. When this became public, a newsman remarked that "Old Abe will find that he has undertaken an almost endless task to exterminate the seed of the rebellion. As fast as he kills one rebel, a dozen spring from his ashes."

(Houston *Daily Telegraph*, February 13, 1864.)

XXIX

>>>

CONFEDERATE REVIVAL

After nearly a week of hard riding, following the meandering Nueces River, the expeditionary forces reached San Fernando, a Confederate outpost west of Corpus Christi commanded by Major Mat Nolan.]

Nolan was a sprightly boy and well-liked by all the men. He had been a bugler in the Army of the United States and had accompanied the regular troops into Mexico. He was mustered into Ford's company as bugler early in 1850. In the history of the companies of 1850 and 1851 he was mentioned. During the Cortina war in 1860, he was a lieutenant in Ford's command. In 1861 he was captain of a company in Ford's regiment. He was first mustered into the service of the State of Texas and then in that of the Confederate States. During his state service he was very active in protecting the citizens against Indian forays. In April, 1861, he was engaged for a time in quelling the insurrectionary movement of General Juan Cortina.

In 1862 Nolan came to Corpus Christi to meet his wife, formerly Miss Macmahan. While there he witnessed the condition of affairs between the Nueces and the Río Grande, saw the whole scope of country without defense and the property of Confederate citizens at the mercy of their enemies. There were large cattle and horse ranches between the two rivers. Santa Gertrudis, the ranch of King & Kenedy, was about forty miles from Corpus Christi. It was very natural for Nolan to desire to act in defense of his relatives and friends. At that time Captain James A. Ware of Colonel [Augustus] Buchel's regiment was commanding the small Confederate force on the Nueces. Ware had been impelled by considerations similar to those actuating Nolan. His wife had been a resident of Corpus Christi. In these two officers—in fact, in many others which were coming to the front—the people felt that they had something tangible and firm on which they could depend in the hour of adversity and trial. Nolan and Ware had obtained leaves of absence from their respective commanders to remain in that section.

When Ford arrived at Nolan's camp, the major told him what all had happened in the area during the past few months. One of his first engagements was with Captain Cecilio Balerio, a Mexican bandit, at Patricio, about 50 miles southwest of Banquete.

I succeeded in coming up with a body of the enemy's cavalry posted in a dense mesquital, [Nolan said] attacked them at once, and, after a well-contested fight of some fifteen minutes' duration, dispersed and routed them completely. Owing to his position in the mesquital the exact number of the enemy could not be ascertained, but from appearances I believe that there were at least 125 men, completely armed with Burnside carbines, revolvers, and sabers, while my force, composed of detachments from Ware's, Cater's, Taylor's, [Henry] Scott's, [James] Richardson's, and [William] Tate's companies, numbered only 62, many of whom were most indifferently armed. The enemy was commanded by Cecilio Balerio and his son Juan Balerio in person, who, at the head of 80 men, charged and fought us most gallantly, and could only be repulsed after a desperate fight and at the cost of much blood and property.

Major Nolan went on to say that

among some papers found was a letter to Balerio, signed with initials only, dated Camargo, March 2, 1864, and informing him . . . that the forces under Col. John L. Haynes have left the Río Grande and are on the march to relieve and re-enforce the said Balerio. As a sufficient time had elapsed to enable said forces to have reached or be within striking distance of Balerio, considering the smallness of my force, the condition of my wounded (being without medical aid and without transportation), the impracticability of pursuit owing to the density and extent of the mesquital, and the distance from my support,

I . . . returned to camp on the San Fernando. The loss of the enemy must have been severe. Five dead bodies were found in the mesquital, but from the trails seen, showing that men had been dragged off when wounded, and pools of blood discovered, it is almost certain that at least 12 or 15 were killed or wounded. A large number of their horses were left on the ground either killed or wounded.[1]

Nolan's losses were three killed and one "slightly wounded." The defeat of Balerio was a great thing for the Confederates. He was an active officer, well acquainted with the country, brave and vigilant. It was understood that after his defeat he conducted his command to Brownsville, waited on Colonel Haynes, who refused to recognize him. One thing is sure: after Captain Balerio's departure from the waters of the Nueces, no one came to take his place.

Nolan's victory put a stop to Unionist activity in the Nueces River region. Before, Unionists had been in the habit of sending men into the cattle ranches along the Nueces for the purpose of procuring beef, for which, it was said, five dollars per head was paid. The troops heretofore on duty in that region had always opposed this method of supplying rations of fresh meat to the Yankees, but they were too few in number to effect much.

2

Colonel Ford had fixed his main camp a few miles from Captain King's ranch. [While encamped there, Ford received the report of a Federal raid on Laredo, which was at that time the center of the Mexican trade and the headquarters of Colonel Santos Benavides' command. The report, dated March 21, 1864, is given:]

SIR: I have the honor to report that the town of Laredo was attacked by the enemy on the 19th ultimo, about 3 o'clock in the afternoon. The news of the advance of the enemy on this town reached me only a short time before they were in view, and but little time was left to make preparations for our defense. I immediately collected my forces, only consisting of about 42 men of Captains Refugio and Cristoval Benavides' companies, and Captain Chapman's company, numbering about 30 men, and also a few American volunteers. All the citizens of the town rallied gallantly for the defense; and erecting barricades in the plaza, after I posted the citizens and Captain Chapman's company for the defense of the interior of the town, I proceeded with 42 men of

---

[1] In the original memoirs, Ford quoted Nolan's first report of his battle with Cecilio Balerio which was hastily written and incomplete; therefore, the editor has added Nolan's full report, dated Banquete, March 15, 1864, *Official Records*, ser. I, vol. XXXIV, pt. I, pp. 638–639.

my command to its outskirts, divided them in squads, and placed them in the adjacent houses to await the approach of the enemy. The Yankees, consisting of about 200 men (Americans and a few Mexicans), all regular soldiers and superiorly armed, halted when about a half mile from town, formed, and charged in squads, each numbering about 40 men. As soon as they came in reach of our guns my men gave the Texas yell, commenced firing on them, and compelled them to retreat to their main force, stationed a half mile from town. The Yankees, dismounting, then advanced on foot, keeping up a rapid fire. My men also maintained a steady fire, when the brave Major Swope and a Mexican named Juan Ivara charged right upon an advancing squad of 40 Yankees and compelled them to retreat. Major Swope stood there until he emptied the last shot of his six-shooter, which compelled him to retire for the purpose of reloading. While doing so his horse was shot three times, and also Juan Ivara's. The enemy advanced again, but were repulsed by the vigorous fire of my gallant men, who were full of fight. None of our men were killed or wounded. I am not positive that any of the enemy have been killed, but my men assert that a good many of the Yanks were wounded and that traces of blood have been found in various places. The firing was kept up until dark, when the Yankees thought best to skeedadle in their own peculiar style and give up their intention of walking into Laredo that day. They retreated about dark 3 miles below town and encamped, and our men kept by me in the same position described, expecting with every movement a new assault on the town. About 2 o'clock at night my re-enforcements arrived, which were stationed about 25 miles north from Laredo for the purpose of grazing our horses. On the arrival of my re-enforcements a general rejoicing took place among our little force, indicated by the ringing of church bells and blowing of trumpets, which I presume the Yanks must have heard and rather guessed that I received re-enforcements. Early next morning, Capt. Refugio Benavides, with about 60 well-mounted men, was sent to flank the enemy and get into their rear. He found, on reaching the enemy's camp, that they all had left in a stampede, throwing away some jackets and other things. He found, also, 5 horses branded U.S., which were left behind by the locomotive enemy in their hasty retreat.

Capt. R. Benavides started out again yesterday in pursuit of the enemy, to follow them up and find out all he can concerning them and their movements. To the best of my belief they are retreating towards Río Grande City, where the other portion of the enemy is stationed, and their strength at Río G[rande] City is supposed to be 300 (infantry) and two 12-pounder rifled guns. I think that the enemy will advance next time in a much larger force. They are well aware what my force is through their spies, and will undoubtedly bring a sufficient body next time to attack this place. I have written to Captain Giddings, commanding at Eagle Pass, to re-enforce me with all his available men as soon as possible, and would also suggest to you to send some re-enforcements to me if they can be spared from your command. I will do my best to hold the town as long as possible against any number of foes, but to do so I would beg of you to send me some ammunition, which I am in great need of. My requisition was not all filled at San Antonio last time. Please send me some Mississippi yagers, shotguns, minie rifle, Belgian musket, and navy-size six-shooter cartridges if possible before ten days.

This report was signed by Colonel Santos Benavides.[2]

During the fight Captain Cristóbal Benavides[3] was left in the plaza, with his company, as a reserve. Colonel Benavides gave him positive orders what to do in the event the enemy should defeat him.

"There are five thousand bales of cotton in the plaza. It belongs to the Confederacy. If the day goes against us fire it. Be sure to do the work properly so that not a bale of it shall fall into the hands of the Yankees. Then you will set my new house on fire. So that nothing of mine shall pass to the enemy. Let their victory be a barren one."

Colonel Benavides had recently built a rather large and costly house. It was on the west side of the plaza. He seemed determined that a victory of the Union troops should not be bloodless, and that in the amount of spoils acquired by it, it should be profitless. This spirit does honor to his memory.

The citizens of Laredo—men, boys, and even women—crowded the tops of the houses. Those possessing arms loaded them and prepared to fire. The services of the entire city were placed at the command of Colonel Benavides. There was no effort on the part of anyone to shirk. The enemy was in their presence. The desire of all, from the greatest to the least, was to defeat him. The soldiers were obedient, and those who have met them are always ready and willing to acknowledge them brave. The handful of them on duty at that hazardous period behaved as veterans. With the odds of more than three to one they drove off the Unionists, without cotton, without plunder, and without success. Their Laredo campaign was one of those feats they failed to avow with complacency. Being whipped by less than one-third their number was not a fact they were pleased to discuss.

It is not generally known that Colonel John L. Haynes made efforts to induce Colonel Benavides to take service in the Army of the United States. General H. P. Bee is authority for saying that E. J. Davis, colonel of a Texan cavalry regiment in the Union Army,[4] proffered a commission of

---

[2] The editor could make little sense out of the report of the Laredo engagement that Ford quoted in the original memoirs, so he has added Benavides' official report, dated Laredo, March 21, 1864, and followed it with Ford's own account, which was by the way based on a personal interview with Benavides a month after the battle. Benavides' report is in the *Official Records,* ser. I, vol. XXXIV, pt. I, pp. 647–649.

[3] Captain Benavides' first name is variously spelled Cristóbal and Cristóval.

[4] Colonel E. J. Davis' First Texas Cavalry, United States Army, was made up of Unionists, deserters, Mexicans, and a few soldiers of fortune. The outfit sailed to Louisi-

brigadier general to Colonel Benavides and that he declined to accept the position. He certainly deserves honor for his fidelity to the cause of the South. When the war ceased he willingly retired to the shades of private life. His actions in these premises may well be emulated by his countrymen.

It would appear invidious to close this account without making honorable mention of the officers and privates whose bravery and noble bearing, on this occasion, caused victory to perch on the banners of Texas, and who hurled from their firesides an enemy famed for his achievements by land and by sea.

3

Lieutenant Colonel Showalter with his regiment reached Camp Patterson on San Fernando Creek about March 30. The troops there had been engaged in making scouts in various directions, in drilling, and in getting ready to move to the front. The country between the Nueces and the Río Grande, as the writer said, was terribly dry, almost impossible to procure water for the men, to say nothing of the horses. Ford is confident an officer who had not seen service in that country could not have successfully conducted a mounted force across it.

It was decided to move to Los Ojuelos, forty miles from Laredo, on the Corpus Christi road. From that point the march toward Brownsville could be made by way of the Río Grande, where a supply of water was at all times available.

Major Nolan was directed to command the companies left near Corpus Christi. Major B. F. Fly reported to him with four companies of cavalry. He was to keep a good sized force on the Brownsville road, to watch the movements of the enemy at Corpus Christi and from the direction of Brownsville, and to drive them back, if strong enough. The major was ordered to his companies before Colonel Ford moved down the Río Grande. For some reason Fly's troops did not cooperate with Nolan. Major Creed Taylor, who was in command of the companies at the time Colonel Ford was on the march to Brownsville, recently affirmed that he had received no order to operate against the Federals or to cooperate with Nolan. Taylor is an old Texian and has never been in the habit of denying what is so.

Colonel Ford also directed Colonel Giddings to move to Los Ojuelos

---

ana in the late spring of 1864. It came back to Texas a year later quite proud of its dashing commander, who had just been commissioned a brigadier general. Colonel John L. Haynes' Second Texas Cavalry, United States Army, had similar personnel.

from Eagle Pass. Captain [Charles de] Montel was then ordered to move to Ford's headquarters.

Lieutenant [C. B.] Gardiner with a section of artillery was at Ford's camp on the eve of the forward movement. There was considerable trouble in procuring men to serve the artillery. They managed to let their horses stray away during the day and during the night.

Colonel Ford's column reached Laredo on April 17, 1864. Perhaps at this point it will be well to have a round-up of the various commands distributed over the Río Grande region. Lieutenant Colonel Showalter was with his command at Baroneño, sixty-four miles from Laredo; Captain Cater with part of Major Nolan's battalion, at Los Angeles, fifty-two miles from Laredo; Colonel Giddings with his incomplete regiment, still at Eagle Pass, one hundred miles above Laredo; and Major Nolan near Captain King's ranch, with several companies of his battalion. Major Walthersdorff was still west of San Antonio, operating against Indians.

4

The people inhabiting the Texas side of the Río Grande were generally friendly to the Confederate States. They were nearly all the while moving to take care of their domestic animals. Incessant troubles from hostile Indians had taught them to be always on the lookout and the alert. Hence they were vigilant guards for the Confederates.

The war in Mexico between the French Imperialists—who had come to Mexico in 1861, supported by Spain and Great Britain, to establish a government that would pay off Mexico's huge foreign debt—and the supporters of Benito Juárez' Republican government was raging at that time. General Vidauri was in Laredo at the house of Colonel Benavides. He was an Imperialist. He professed to have fifteen million percussion caps hidden in Mexico which Benavides and Ford tried to purchase.

Colonel Latham said that the Yankees sent a deputation to Monterey, asking the Juarez government to grant them leave of marching against Laredo by way of Camargo and Mier.

When Ford heard about this he wrote Magruder on April 17:

Would I not be justifiable in crossing the Río Grande to meet the enemy? It would almost be tantamount to a declaration of war on the part of the Juarez government against the Confederate States.

If President Juarez sees proper to transfer the theater of operations from Texas to Mexico he should be gratified. In that event the Vidauri and the French parties would be our allies, and I have never viewed the fact that we might be placed side by side with the French in Mexico as portending evil to our cause. I do not wish to be understood as intending to rashly plunge into complications. I shall await orders, unless impending danger and necessity render action a duty.

Lieutenant Colonel [J. J.] Fisher, an American of the Mexican Army, who afterwards joined the Confederates, was present during the interviews between Juarez and the United States officers. Part of the time Fisher interpreted for Mr. Juarez. Colonel Haynes of Texas was one of the deputies of the United States. Colonel Fisher said that Juarez did not grant the favor asked for. He spoke of the armies the belligerents had in the field, their battles, the power displayed by each, and told Haynes that Mexico was too small and weak a nation to wage war against either the United States or the Confederate States. In this manner he refused to grant permission to the request. Another strong incentive in refusing was in the fact of the immense amount of goods, war matériel, and cotton going out, and passing through the Mexican territory and giving employment to thousands of Mexicans. This trade left millions of monies in Mexico. It was spent in the war against imperialism and in internal and revolutionary dissensions.

5

A portion of Colonel Benavides' regiment, commanded by Captain Refugio Benavides, was directed to prepare to move. These men and the commands of Showalter and Cater were marched to Ringgold Barracks, where headquarters of the expeditionary forces were established. Here the different portions of the command intended for operations on the lower Río Grande were brought together and prepared for active service. At Ringgold Barracks several companies reported for duty, Giddings' regiment also.

The troops on duty in the expeditionary forces were thus spoken of by Colonel Ford:

The troops reporting here for duty were raised originally for my command or for the 4th Arizona regiment, and Benavides. I do not consider the order referred to by the major-general commanding as prohibiting the reception of that class of troops. The withdrawal of exempts upon the expiration of the term of service, and the absence of others without leave, have rendered it necessary to recruit some of my companies. I know of no just cause why I should be deprived of that privilege.

I have now, besides the companies which disbanded and went home from the San Fernando, material for the organization of two regiments. Those going home from Camp San Fernando were not deserters. With the recruits now on the march, and being raised, these regiments will be above the maximum strength.

The battalions are under the command of senior captains—but under instructions from District Headquarters of April 29, 1864, assurances have been given that regimental organizations would take place—everything subject of course to the approval of the major-general commanding. I shall, however, let the matter remain in *status quo* until further orders.

In justice to myself, I beg leave to remark that the most of the men now serving with me, and belonging to other commands, seemed disposed not to return to their commands. I placed them on duty, believing the good of the service justified it. Some of them acted well, and have been promoted. I ask that they be allowed to remain. There are others, who if left to themselves, would return to their commands whenever ordered, but as now situated, under the influences which would be brought to bear upon them, I am confident many of them would cross the Río Grande rather than go east. This is not the time, nor the place, for the execution of the order with any hope of remedying the evil.

As was said, many deserters came from Mexico to join our ranks. A great number of them had gotten into trouble in their respective commands, and saw no means of escaping punishment, except by leaving. An officer when prejudiced against a private can give him a lively foretaste of hell. In such a case it is a difficult matter for a superior officer, in fact, any officer, to discover the true state of the case. An officer is usually withheld from making a thorough investigation of such contingencies. The danger of encouraging conduct prejudicial to good conduct and military discipline confronts them and stops them. These military enemies and tyrants are found in many commands, from the fourth corporal to the major general.

While at Ringgold Barracks Colonel Ford purchased arms out of the secret service money furnished him. Colonel John Swisher was sent to Matamoros to purchase arms. He succeeded in sending us a goodly number. He sent us all the news he thought of moment. Eventually, he sent us Federal plans of the works at Fort Brown and of a fortified position above Brownsville, in the bend of the river known as Freeport. Captain Kenedy sent valuable information; so did other gentlemen. The Union force in the neighborhood of Brownsville was estimated at 7,000 men. The morning report at Fort Brown and vicinity called for over 5,000 men.

6

Everything was placed in a state of preparation at Ringgold Barracks. All the serviceable guns were obtained that could be. Ammunition for the different calibres of pieces was manufactured. All the provision we could haul conveniently was placed on wagons. Some pack mules were used. Pickets and scouts were well advanced towards the enemy. The news from the front was that Federal General [Francis J.] Herron had been ordered to abandon Texas, which he did, leaving only a skeleton force to defend Fort Brown and Brownsville.

Preparatory to moving, Captain A. C. Jones was placed in command of Ringgold Barracks. He was directed to take charge of all companies coming there until further ordered, to guard the line of the river as well as possible, to prevent the crossing of stock from this side, unless the party had a special order (the Mexicans were driving off stock, beginning a career which they afterwards made remarkable for infamy). Captain Penaloza's company remained on duty at Ringgold Barracks. This order was dated July 19, 1864, and was the last given at Ringgold.

The drought was very severe. There was not much grass on the road to Fort Brown. Ringgold Barracks was said to be one hundred miles above Fort Brown. The Palo Alto prairie was entirely nude of grass. Outside the river road the route to Fort Brown was hardly practicable for a force of any size. Our force was 1,500 men. That many were rationed. We had no artillery. The whole force was mounted.

A forward movement was made in the direction of Brownsville. Ford, with Giddings' regiment and other troops, proceeded directly by the river road. Colonel Showalter moved to the left and halted at the ranch of Como Se Llamo, some distance from the river valley. Ford proceeded to the ranch of John McAllen, some distance below the town of Edinburg, now called Hidalgo. Just below, Mr. [John] Webber lived. He was an old Texian, but had married a colored woman; notwithstanding, he was held in repute. A town was named after him—Webberville, sixteen miles below Austin. His house was visited. He closed the doors, refused admission until Ford came. His sons were made prisoners. One of them escaped and went to Fort Brown. He told the Federals that Ford had but sixty odd men. He saw no more. Accordingly, Federal authorities forwarded orders to Captain [Philip G.] Temple, commanding him to engage Ford and defeat him; and Temple could then have an easy time procuring supplies and equipments from loyal Confederate citizens in the area.

From McAllen's ranch Ford struck across country to the northward, marched down a branch of the Arroyo Colorado by way of Charles Stillman's ranch of Santa Rosa, and joined Colonel Showalter's command at Como Se Llamo. Having prepared dried beef for the trip, the command then started in the direction of the Río Grande. They struck the road from Río Grande City to Brownsville at Carricitos Ranch, just below Las Rucias, where Captain Temple's Federal company was encamped. We moved along a blind path through the chaparral to Las Rucias, sent Captain [James] Dunn and his company forward to feel out the enemy and cause them to develop. Dunn charged into their camp, and was shot dead from his horse. He had gone further than ordered. Others were killed too, among them Sergeant Cockerel of Showalter's command and Hijenio Sánchez of Captain Refugio Benavides' battalion. Showalter's men now moved forward and engaged the enemy. They fought from jacales— ordinary Mexican houses—from a large brick building, and from behind a large pile of bricks. Soon after Showalter was under fire, Cater and Benavides led their battalions into the thick of the fight.

The enemy was driven from every position. They retreated across the river into Mexico, many of them wounded, Captain Temple also. The force of the enemy was not accurately known. Companies A and C of Colonel E. J. Davis' Federal regiment were known to have been present. The enemy numbered 250 and over. We had about 200 men in the fight. They were reported to have lost several killed and ten wounded. We took thirty-six prisoners, two wagons, several horses, saddles, and other accoutrements. Our loss was three killed and four wounded. It is said to be true that but eight men of the Union companies ever reported at Fort Brown.

The loss of Captain Dunn was very much regretted by all the Texians. Lieutenant Colonel Showalter, Captain Refugio Benavides, Captain Ferrill, and Lieutenant Gardiner were complimented for gallantry, also Lieutenant Colonel Fisher, Major Blucher, chief of staff and the main guide, and Lieutenant [Edward] Duggan. Giddings' command was in the rear, marching in single file in a difficult section to pass over; hence the fight was almost over when they arrived.

We anticipated a force to come out against us. We were only twenty-four miles above Fort Brown. We moved slowly up the Río Grande, halted a day at Edinburg. No one came to offer us battle. We reached Ringgold without any difficulty. This fight occurred on June 25, 1864.

On July 12, 1864, the Major General issued an order of approval. Among other things he said: "Your course and efforts meets with . . . most perfect satisfaction. . . . none could have conducted the operations with greater success."

7

On July 22, 1864, we were less than 11 miles from Fort Brown, making preparations to move in that direction. A Mexican informed us a party of Union men were just below us at the Ebonal Ranch. We moved against them.

Some of the advance guard passed a small distance ahead and ascertained where the enemy were. Not knowing the strength of the party, we moved with about 800 men. A detachment was sent through the chaparral on foot with a view of passing around the Yankees. It met with more impediment in forcing its way through the dense underwood than was anticipated. When the time arrived for the main body to attack, they raised the Texas yell and went in. The Federals opened fire. Soon finding out they would be surrounded and captured, they mounted and fled. The pursuit was hot, and lasted to within the outer limits of Brownsville. At the ranch of Ramireno, some prisoners, horses, a wagon and team were taken. The ranch is in sight of Brownsville. Ford's scattered command was halted a while to allow of concentration and to ascertain whether the Federals would send out a force to meet us. None came and we moved off slowly. The detachment dispersed was small. We suffered no loss, and no one of the enemy was reported killed. Several were wounded, however.

On the march back our rear guard was attacked by the Federals. We supposed it to be a force sent to hold us in check until their main body could reach us. A company was posted across the road and received the Federals with a heavy fire. They fell back. Meantime we had formed a line and were determined to give battle. No enemy came, and we made camp sometime after dark. This affair occurred on July 22, 1864. It shows the caution of the enemy.

While in camp a Mexican came to the colonel and accused a soldier of having taken his blanket. The man came accompanied by several of his messmates. They lived in the interior of Texas, were near neighbors of the soldier having the blanket, saw it often, and knew he had brought it from home with him. Ford was convinced this was a tale manufactured for the occasion. He asked the Mexican the price of the blanket.

"Six dollars."

Ford handed the *caballero* the money, and all left satisfied. Ford told the boys to keep quiet about the incident; it would not bear repeating.

We were receiving supplies from Matamoros, where General Cortina was in command. He was known to be friendly to the Union men, yet he was not averse to allowing his friends to earn an honest penny by supplying the Confederates. He objected, however, to delivering supplies any nearer to Matamoros than Reynosa, opposite Edinburg. Our influences were brought to bear upon some to deliver freights opposite Carricitos.

8

On July 25, 1864, Ford's column moved down to the edge of Brownsville, and the colonel sent in troops near enough to engage the enemy at long range. Lieutenant Colonel Fisher commanded one battalion. All the officers were on the field and did their duty. Our main line was formed in "Dead Man's Hollow" just outside the city limits. Our advance drove the Federals into town. They had from fifteen to twenty wounded, and lost several horses. They would not move out and fight, and we would not march up near enough for them to use their artillery upon us and fight us under cover of their works, situated at Freeport above Brownsville and at Fort Brown below. We remained near them until we were sure they would not come out and fight. Late in the evening the Confederates withdrew.

At that time there were several thousand Confederates reported to be in Matamoros. We expected some recruits. It was the opinion of some that they would come booming over when there was a prospect of warm work. The recruits on this occasion were Colonel John M. Swisher, Dr. Charles B. Combe, and M. B. Anderson, usually called "Bob."

Colonel Swisher was a soldier at the memorable battle of San Jacinto. He was riding a horse of Dr. Combe's. A ball came inconveniently near Swisher.

Combe called out: "Take care, Swisher, or you will get my horse killed."

The old chap took fire at Combe's joke, and stammered out: "Damn your horse; don't you care if I get killed?"

We soon learned that the Federals had fixed up an ambuscade on the Brownsville road for our special entertainment. There were cannon, infantry, and cavalry prepared in fine style to kill us off. We did not go where they expected us.

On July 29 the Unionists evacuated Brownsville and Fort Brown and moved down the river to Brazos Island to embark for other points. The Yankee line of retreat was marked by articles of clothing that had been cast off.

The Confederates rode into Fort Brown on July 30, 1864. On entering we were at a loss to know whether the Union commander was really leaving or intended to return and attack us. We found Fort Brown in good condition, in better condition than we had been led to expect. We had not a single piece of artillery to place in it for defense. During all this period Colonel Ford was sick. He was frequently helped to mount his horse.

We learned General Herron was in camp eighteen miles below. Colonel Showalter with several hundred men was sent to look after our friends. When he discovered a body of them, he sent Captain Refugio Benavides forward to feel them out. Benavides executed the order, struck a party of the enemy, attacked, and drove them. For some reason Colonel Showalter failed to follow up with the remainder of the Confederate force. The following is the sum of a verbal report by Captain Benavides: "We captured a number of wagons, and fixed them to move off. We expected Colonel Showalter every moment. All at once we saw a heavy column of the enemy moving upon us. I then looked for Colonel Showalter, and saw his command going the other way, about a mile and a half off. The *carajos* came, and took all our wagons away from us."

Benavides was forced to run for it. The unfortunate failing of Colonel Showalter stood between him and success. When not under the influence of liquor, he was as chivalrous a man as ever drew a sword.

We still had no idea what the Federals were up to. As a precautionary measure, Colonel Ford called on Captain A. C. Jones and Colonel [Charles L.] Pyron to send him reinforcements. On August 4 a scout under Captain Robertson struck a party of the enemy some 15 miles below Brownsville, attacked the Federals vigorously, and succeeded in driving them back upon the main body, killing two and capturing two prisoners. From them we learned that the Federals planned to entrench on Brazos de Santiago. They were too weak to attack us.

In his official report to General Drayton, Ford said: "The families of our friends will be invited to return, and everything possible done to promote our cause, and to perpetuate the good understanding existing between ours and the Mexican authorities."

The vital trade was now resumed through Brownsville and Matamoros.

The families which had passed over the Río Grande to Matamoros during the Federal occupation now returned generally. Some of the Unionists remained in Brownsville. There was an effort made by one party—probably he represented others—to permit secessionists to occupy houses owned by Unionists, but Colonel Ford would not agree to prevent any family from occupying their own property, if it chose. If owners of property absented themselves and abandoned what they owned, it was used by the Confederate authorities and paid for, unless the owner was known to be a strong Unionist man. The plan concocted to put Unionists out of their houses, unless they would act as spies or would act outrageously as partisans, was not tolerated. In some instances families were divided, one part secessionist, another Unionist. The endeavor was to protect all who did not make themselves obnoxious; even then they had rights which must be respected.

XXX

>>

THE RING OF DECEIT

After capturing Fort Brown, Colonel Ford took prompt measures to reinstate Confederate rule. As was his practice, he did all in his power to aid the civil authorities in resuming the execution of the law.

The Federals were now strongly garrisoned on Brazos de Santiago. Our job was to drive them into the sea, while at the same time watching for a possible counterattack. Brazos Island could be approached by land, by passing down the Río Grande to a point known as the White House, then leaving the river by a deflection to the left cross-country, then by fording the Boca Chica, which separated Brazos Island from the mainland. The Boca Chica was narrow, but its waters were, at times, extremely swift. No bridge has ever stood across it. Another way to reach the island was by following the Río Grande to its mouth, turning at a small place called Clarksville and following the coast of the Gulf of Mexico northward to Brazos Island. The distance from the Mexican town of Bagdad at the mouth of the Río Grande was about eight miles.

Federal General Herron left Colonel [H. M.] Day on Brazos Island with 1,500 men. Day had instructions which fell into our hands. The blockader remained on duty. The Federals had works at the end of Brazos Island next to the Río Grande. During their occupation of the Brownsville area they had transported some large pieces of artillery from Fort Brown to the island. They had erected a railroad from the island to the White House, or White Ranch as some choose to call it. The cars had ceased to run when we reached Fort Brown. A bridge had been built over the Boca Chica, but had been washed away. Just outside the Boca Chica, on the Gulf side, was a sand bar which at ordinary tide was fordable. It was immediately under the guns of the fort and therefore passage over it to the island was rather perilous. The larger fort was not far from the port, and could be reached by artillery from the blockader.

The lighthouse was built on the mainland at Point Isabel, which stood on the bank of the Laguna Madre, directly across from Padre Island. By the wagon road which avoided the laguna it was more than twenty miles from the lighthouse to Brownsville. Ford nearly always kept troops near Point Isabel to prevent the Federals from steaming up from Brazos Santiago and attacking us in flank.

Not far from Point Isabel, to the right as you go to Brazos Santiago, there were shallows running quite all the way from the mainland to the gulf. At about half the distance across was an uninhabited island which could have been made a resting place for passing troops. We frequently discussed the possibility of attacking Brazos Island by way of the uninhabited island. The fact was, that the expedition would have been extremely dangerous, and if the fort was gained we could not reply to the long range guns on board the blockader, and the perilous undertaking would be attended by no advantageous results.

Colonel Ford was still ill. Field command of the Confederates devolved on Lieutenant Colonel Showalter. On or about August 8 Showalter captured a Yankee steamboat, the *Ark*. It was expected that the enemy would endeavor to recapture the vessel. Colonel Ford ordered Colonel Giddings to join Showalter and to "take every man with you." Word of the re-enforcement was then sent to Showalter: "Troops will at once be sent to your assistance. You will hold the boat as long as you can, and if the enemy come with too great [a] force, we will start to your assistance by daylight. Giddings should have reached you before this."

The Yankees made no effort to recapture the *Ark*. She was condemned as a prize by Confederate Judge Devine, and finally was sold to Thomas Gilgan of Matamoros for $23,000, if memory is correct.

2

The position of Colonel Ford was one requiring ability and circumspection. One mistake of his might have cost the Confederate cause a great deal. A war was raging in Mexico. A foreign power was sending troops into Mexico. They had to be made the friends of the Confederacy by fair and straight forward means.

Towards General Cortina Ford also extended a spirit of friendly fairness. Here is an example:

I have delayed addressing you officially, as the military representative of the Confederate States upon the lower Río Grande, until I could announce that the forces of Mr. Lincoln's government had retired from the mainland. They are confined to Brazos Island.

In again renewing official relations with the Mexican authorities, I take pleasure in reassuring them of my sincere desire to cultivate friendly relations, and to do all in my power to render our intercourse officially, commercially, and otherwise, pleasant and mutually advantageous.

I have to thank you and your government for many acts of kindness to our citizens while enjoying the security and protection of your flag, and your laws. Those generous acts will not be forgotten by us, and should the turn of events cause any of your countrymen to visit our shores we should be ungrateful not to reciprocate the kindly acts of our hospitable neighbors.

Of course this letter spoke more to the Juárez government than to General Cortina personally. We knew he was not friendly to the South. Still, Cortina, as was said, felt compelled to be more or less friendly. The immense trade existing between Mexico and the Confederate States was the prevailing reason. Many Americans—Union men and Confederates—were resident in Matamoros. Goods were sold to anyone having money or cotton. There was little thought of politics in the trading circles. The manner in which Cortina treated citizens of the United States and of Texas, while he was governor of Tamaulipas, is worthy of remembrance. There were Americans in Matamoros known to have been personally unfriendly to Cortina, yet he treated them kindly and honorably.

A French force landed at Bagdad on August 22, 1864. This was considered a rather good augury for the Confederates. They thought Louis Napoleon was well disposed to the Confederacy and hoped that by some turn of events the French troops in Mexico might be induced to aid the South: of course our treatment of the Frenchmen was something more considerate than it would have been had we hoped nothing from them.

A meeting was held at Matamoros that evening, at which the consuls and others representing foreign governments were represented. It was supposed the Juarez troops would be disbanded. In that event, if requested by foreign consuls, Colonel Ford would have sent troops into Matamoros for the protection of Confederate person and property. General Cortina, however, did not disband his men. Ford quickly addressed a note to Colonel F. W. Latham, who was collector of customs and representative of the Confederate States in Tamaulipas, requesting him to give Confederates there the protection of our flag, and should necessity require it, Ford indicated that he had a force sufficient to support Latham in the discharge of that important duty. Colonel Latham performed the duty.

The arrival of the French caused Colonel Ford to address a letter to Com. A. Veron of the French forces inquiring whether supplies for the Confederate government would be allowed to pass the mouth of the Río Grande, as heretofore. Ford then sent Lieutenant Colonel Fisher and Major [Waldermar] Hyllested, provost marshal general of Texas, to visit and confer with the French commander. Veron stated: "If the exigencies of war should take me to Matamoros you may rest assured that I shall see that all persons and property covered by the flag of your nation are duly respected."

Com. Veron's communication caused a great deal of satisfaction to the friends of the Southern cause. It gave General Cortina no great pleasure. About this time he began to give clear indications of an unfriendly character. One of these was in giving trouble to Americans in passing over to Matamoros, another in retiring the ferry boats early at night to the Mexican side and keeping them all night, and other tricks meant to give trouble and to annoy. He then complained that when his soldiers went down river to engage the French, Colonel Showalter's men, stationed at Palmito Ranch, fired across the river at the Mexicans. Colonel Showalter solemnly denied this.

On the contrary, Ford told Cortina on August 31: "Two shots were fired yesterday from the town of Matamoros upon my men at Freeport, and came near taking effect. . . . I shall cordially act in concert with you in speedily arranging a plan to check these outrages."

Ford then warned Showalter that an understanding seemed to exist between General Cortina and the Federals. On September 3, 1864, Cortina stopped the passage of forage from Matamoros for the Confederates. Ford wrote to Showalter to endeavor to obtain supplies from Bagdad. Ford also reported to General Drayton that Federal Colonel Day, commanding at Brazos Santiago, was trying to persuade Cortina to pass Mexican troops over the Río Grande and to attack the Confederates and capture Brownsville. Cortina "hates Americans, particularly Texians," Ford said. "He has an old and deep-seated grudge against Brownsville. . . . If he could cut his way through our lines, plunder our people, and get within the Yankee lines, it would be a finale he would delight in."

On September 6, 1864, General Cortina again opened fire on the Confederates, this time on Colonel Showalter at Palmito Ranch. The Mexicans used artillery and small arms, firing across the river. The Confederates behaved well. They silenced the artillery on several occasions, and were reported to have killed forty Mexicans. In addition, Cortina had despatched about 600 men with artillery up the Río Grande. They had orders to cross into Texas and attack Brownsville, supposing Ford would send all his troops below to Palmito. We had timely information of this move. We did not budge from the city or from Fort Brown. It had been raining hard and the rise in the river kept the Mexicans from crossing into Confederate territory.

Unfortunately, Colonel Showalter had recourse to the bottle. In the evening he retreated. His command moved to within eight miles of Fort Brown. He came to town in a maudlin condition, claimed to have lost from 15 to 150 men. According to his account large parties of Mexicans and Federals had driven him from his camp, a force of Federals was at that moment advancing by the Point Isabel road, and a heavy body of Mexicans had been sighted on the opposite bank of the Río Grande. We anticipated Cortina and the Federals would be on us early the next day.

Everything was done that night that could be to meet the assault, and every measure was adopted that possibly could be to restore the morale of Showalter's demoralized men. Ford reported to General Drayton:

I have sent a strong party under command of Capt Carrington to ascertain the position and strength of the enemy. I intend attacking him before he has concentrated his force.

They have cannon at several points. They have six pieces bearing upon this town.

I have organized the citizens and taken steps to use my whole force in the field.

We have no forage, and we are compelled to distribute the troops upon points where grass can be had.

On the night of September 6 Colonel Ford sent his wife and children to the convent in Brownsville. He did not know whether the Federals and Mexicans would attempt to move upon the town that night or not. He was not afraid for his wife and children to fall into the hands of the Federals, but he had doubts about how Cortina's men might treat them. The next morning Mrs. Ford came back to the house at an early hour.

"I am not going back to the convent," she said. "I am going to share the fortunes of my husband."

On the night of the sixth a terrible rain fell. It seemed that the roads would certainly be impassable to cannon and perhaps to anything else. We thanked God for it, believing we would have time to prepare for the reception of our enemies. A little before daylight Ford arose to visit the men and find what temper they were in. The first quarters he reached, he called out:

"Hallo boys, jump up and get ready. We have to go out and meet the enemy today."

He passed out the door and waited to see how the declaration was received.

One of the men jumped up, played the rooster, slapping his hands together and crowing: "Hurrah boys, by God, Old Rip is going to fight!"

This had more effect on Old Rip than a burst of eloquence could have produced. He knew his boys were all right and would fight.

In the morning haze, we could barely see the Mexicans advancing two pieces of artillery toward the ferry. The gunners were stationed and the portfires lighted. They had six other pieces not a great distance to the rear to aid them.

Ford acted quickly. He threw the main body of the Confederates forward in the direction of the Mexicans. Colonel Giddings, assisted by Major Hyllested, was in command of the Confederate advance. Ford then sent Captain [W. H. D.] Carrington forward with his company to reconnoitre the Yankee garrison at Brazos Island. On the eighth Carrington reported that the Federals had come onto the mainland and were now at Palmito Ranch. Cortina was still at Matamoros. Ford had learned that it was Cortina's intention to attack Brownsville as soon as Ford moved to meet the Federals at Palmito. Ford remained at the city. He addressed Cortina:

An unprovoked and unwarranted attack was made upon the command of Lt. Col. Showalter, at Palmito, on the sixth instant by Mexican troops. They are reported to have passed the Río Grande, and to have invaded the soil of the Confederate States.

Troops under your command are patrolling the banks of the Río Grande; your artillery is bearing upon the City of Brownsville; you stopped communication with this bank. I would respectfully inquire, if by these acts you intend to indicate that war exists between your government and that of the Confederate States?

To this missive General Cortina answered that he had received "the frank explanation you are pleased to offer with regard to the acts disapproved by you, and which for a moment could change the good understanding heretofore conserved in our official intercourse." The balance of his letter was in the same irrelevant and bombastic style.

On September 8, 1864, Colonel Ford addressed Com. Veron in regard to the September sixth affair at Palmito:

I am confident the commander of the French forces at Bagdad was not apprized of this movement on the part of Cortina, else in compliance with assurances, previously given, steps would have been taken to prevent it.

The Juarez Government is announced as no longer in existence, under the protection and guarantees of the Emperor Napoleon the Empire has been proclaimed in Mexico, such being the case the Imperial Government is in duty bound to prevent its subjects or residents from making war, or depredating upon the people, or invading the territory of a government with whom it is at peace. . . . I am assured every thing will be done on your part to repair the injury which has been inflicted upon the Confederate Government, and to withdraw the Mexican troops now invading our soil.

International law was favorable to the Confederacy. Com. Veron answered on the ninth. This one sentence discloses his whole position: "Our position of perfect neutrality towards the United States as well as towards the Confederacy prevents us from doing the service you request."

What had the United States to do with Com. Veron's forcing General Cortina to desist from attacking the Confederates? Cortina owed the United States no allegiance. He certainly violated Confederate neutrality when he fired upon us, and it was the duty of French officers to compel him to stop his cannonade. He was on the soil of the Imperial Government of Mexico, and the United States could do nothing in the matter.

We had now done everything within our power to meet the combined attack of the Yankees and Cortina's troops. Since it was known that Mexican troops were also stationed higher up the river, waiting to cross over to Texas and move down upon Brownsville, Colonel Ford deemed it necessary to have all the men that could be spared to defend the city.

The men left to defend Brownsville were kept on the move a great deal of the day. At one time a party would move out to be seen by Mexicans in Matamoros with coats on their backs. At another they would sally forth in their "shirt sleeves." Our purpose was to deceive as to numbers. Colonel Ford showed himself to the Mexicans quite often.

Every ten or fifteen minutes couriers were sent by Colonel Giddings, bearing information from the second front. Others were sent by Colonel Ford. He had heard again that as soon as he left to help Giddings, the Mexicans would swarm across the river to attack Brownsville.

Ford now considered a tricky plan: attack the Mexicans before they struck us. Such a movement was certainly justified by the Mexican hostilities committed upon us. They had invaded our territory. However, an important factor against such a move was the fact that Matamoros was the great city of supply for the Trans-Mississippi Department. If captured by Confederates the Federals could send an army there by way of the Gulf of Mexico, take the city, and close out every chance of receiving anything needful from Europe. The plan was dropped at the suggestion of General Drayton, who had come down the river to talk with Ford.

3

Giddings moved from Santa Rosalia on September 9, 1864, with 207 men of Lieutenant Colonel Showalter's late command under Major [F. E.] Kavanaugh and 164 men of his own regiment. Giddings engaged the Federals a few miles above Palmito Ranch. They were about 900 strong—600 Federals and 300 Mexicans—with two pieces of artillery. Captain Carrington led the attack, followed by the companies of Captains Carr and Sanders. They drove the enemy five or six miles, killing and wounding a great many. The main body of the enemy were found one mile below San Martín Ranch. Captains Owins, Sanders, and [John H.] Robinson were ordered to make a detour and engage the Federal right and rear. They failed to reach the proper point on account of the brush. Captain Benavides then arrived. He and Captain Carrington attacked the Federal center. Captain Carr moved on the enemy's right and did fine service, killing a great many. Our whole line was now engaged. The enemy retreated, with a loss of 80 or 90 killed and wounded; many of the Mexicans fled to Mexico. "In the pursuit," Giddings reported, "privates Drake and Dickson of my command followed [the enemy] so closely that their officer in command, Maj. [Edward J.] Noyes, threw aside his clothing, private papers, etc., to lighten his horse, all of which was captured."

The papers of Major Noyes contained a letter to a lady of Matamoros, in which he described an encounter with the Confederates commanded by Colonel Ford, in which Noyes' soldiers were victorious and chased the fleeing Confederates—a boast and a mistake.

Colonel Giddings followed the enemy to near the mouth of the Río Grande. He found them drawn up in line with four pieces of artillery, with about 800 men ready to fight, and another 250 on board the steamer *Matamoros*, lying in the water. Upon consultation the Confederates concluded not to attack. Leaving a force in observation, the main body fell back to Palmito Ranch.

On September 12, 1864, the Federals retired to Brazos Island. Colonel Giddings followed them to the Boca Chica.

Meanwhile word got out that General Cortina had been promised the position of brigadier general in the United States Army if he would attack and capture Brownsville for the United States. It was said that the authorities at Washington refused to assent, and Cortina decided to leave the Confederates alone.

The entire loss of the Federals in this short campaign was stated at 550. This included the killed, wounded, and missing. A great many of these crossed the Río Grande into Mexico. The Federal loss may have been overstated. Still, it was considerable. The Confederate loss was two or three killed, a few wounded, and three missing.

On September 22, in an official communication to Major [A. P.] Root of General Drayton's staff, Ford said: "I can not speak too highly of the gallant conduct of both officers and men in these affairs. In fact I feel that I can not do justice to the handful of badly armed men who met and defeated three or four times their number of well armed and disciplined troops."[1] These remarks applied specifically to the command of Colonel Giddings, who led the Confederates in the fighting done on these occasions.

Colonel Showalter, because of his conduct on the sixth, was arrested by order of General Drayton. Showalter was very mad when he found he was confined to the limits of Brownsville. Colonel Ford sent word to him, through a friend, that personally Ford had nothing against him. Ford was compelled to refer his case to a court-martial. General Drayton was acquainted with all the facts in the case, and he would have preferred charges against Ford if he allowed Colonel Showalter's case to

---

[1] Day's Federal command at Brazos Santiago was anything but "well-armed and disciplined," as Ford says. The only Yankees with any degree of discipline—the Nineteenth Iowa and the Ninety-First Illinois—had sailed for Louisiana back in August of 1864. This left Day with a force of perhaps 350 Negroes in the Sixty-Second United States Colored Infantry and the Eighty-First Corps d'Afrique Engineers and about 600 unpredictable ruffians in Haynes' Second Texas (Union) Cavalry—about 950 all told—to fight Ford's Texans.

Federal commanders reported their casualties at San Martín Ranch at 86 in killed, wounded, and missing. Ford's estimate of 550 Yankee casualties probably included losses sustained by the Mexican auxiliary. Even then the figure is impossibly high.

(*Official Records*, ser. I, vol. XLI, pt. I, p. 742; Stephen B. Oates, "John S. Ford: Prudent Cavalryman, C.S.A.," *Southwestern Historical Quarterly*, LXIV, 306–308.)

pass without calling him to account. The court was convened at San Antonio. Ford was summoned but did not go. Showalter was cleared. He was finally killed in a duel on the Pacific coast.

4

About the end of September, General Mejía, the commander of the Imperialists, arrived at Matamoros. A few days before, General Cortina came down to the ferry and invited Colonel Ford to come over and hold a friendly talk with him. By some means the Confederate soldiers learned of the proposition. They became excited, swore Ford should not go, that Cortina would kill him. After considerable expostulation Ford prevailed on them to occupy some houses in front of the ferry. He said to them:

"I will wear my pistols. If anything happens indicating bad faith, I will fire; then you can turn loose and kill every Mexican you can."

General Cortina came to the bank of the river, and when Ford landed he gave him a big hug, according to Mexican custom. They talked and arranged everything. They discussed the question of purchasing arms. We needed artillery and knew Cortina would be glad to sell his, if Ford could procure the money before General Mejía arrived. The Mexican and the Texian agreed to do business. Ford returned to the Confederate side.

In accordance with agreement Ford passed over to Matamoros a day or two afterwards. He was looking at the artillery. General Mejía was supposed to enter Matamoros the next day. All at once a messenger came and imparted the information that the French Imperial Guard was in the act of entering the city. Ford did not care to be seen engaged in looking at cannon. Mejía would not understand. Ford left in some haste, and made Brownsville in good time. The whole thing was fixed up by Cortina to let General Mejía find Ford in the hall where the artillery was. Cortina had previously told Captain Mifflin Kenedy he would see the last piece bursted before the Confederates should have them.

When the French entered Matamoros, Cortina deserted the cause of Juárez and took service with the Imperialists. But not all of his officers went with him. Colonel Canales and a few others, who were powerfully opposed to the Emperor Maximilian, rode for the hills.

On the evening of General Mejía's coming into Matamoros, the Texians saw a regiment of men approaching the ferry. The Confederates were assembled on the American side. A messenger told us it was Colonel Canales and his regiment escaping from General Mejía. They asked for the privilege of asylum in the Confederate States. They were told it would be granted, provided they yielded up their arms and disbanded, to which they agreed. They passed to this bank, and were disbanded.

Their arms, with the exception of those borne by officers, were taken possession of and were stacked. The whole command remained with us two or three days, departing when they chose. They were cautioned not to attempt to reorganize in Texas.

In the 1880's, Hubert Howe Bancroft published his *History of the North Mexican States and Texas,* in volume two of which he gave an account of what was supposed to have happened on the lower Río Grande in 1864. If Mr. Bancroft had employed writers who had regard for truth, rather than appealing to irresponsible men, he might have published a true account of things which occurred along the river during the Civil War. Not only does Bancroft erroneously state that the Mexicans actually captured Brownsville, over which they raised the United States flag, but he also makes Cortina the hero in his bungling and untruthful history of Texas. Given below is the statement of Colonel Canales and other distinguished officers of Mexico which completely disproves the allegations of Mr. Bancroft (to say nothing of the reports of Confederate officers who met and defeated the combined forces of Cortina, the arch-traitor, and his associates of Brazos Island).

Colonel [Ford]:—

The undersigned, officers of the Republican army of Mexico and at present residing in this city [of Brownsville] in voluntary exile beleiving [*sic*] it to be our duty to give a sufficient explanation of the late events which have occurred in the city of Matamoros, and the occasion [for] our departure from that country; and beleiving further that it is so much the more our duty to do so, because in the said city of Matamoros there are evil disposed, or perhaps ill-informed persons who . . . assume to calumniate those who, following the dictates of their consciences preferred to expatriate themselves before the occupation of the said city of Matamoros by the Imperial Forces,—have agreed by common consent to make in this manner the following statement:—

Towards the end of the month of August or the beginning of September last, Gen. Juan N. Cortina being in the city of Matamoros in command of the Brigade which bore his name, caused upon a certain day the officers of the garrison to be convened at the Government House for the purpose of deliberating in a council of war upon a topic of the highest importance. These being assembled, General Cortina took the floor to explain the object of the meeting stating that it was to ascertain the manner of conquering the cause of Mexico with that of the North in a solid & positive manner, and that for this purpose everything was prepared to contract a defensive & offensive alliance between the Government of Tamaulipas and the Commander of the forces of the U.S. then being at the port of Brazos Santiago. He stated further that as we were surrounded on all sides by hostile forces which would not long delay in attacking us, this step was the only one remaining to us to save the artillery & munitions of war in the garrison, asserting besides that the Commander of the U.S. troops had . . . the greatest willingness, not only to make the said agreement, but also to attack in concert with us the French forces already occupying the Mouth of the river. Therefore a deliberation ensued upon the above subject, and among the persons present who spoke thereon was José A. Puente Major of the Battalion of "The Faithful of Tamaulipas" who stated that in a matter of such grave importance it was necessary to act with great caution, inasmuch as it involved a great responsibility on our side, and that he believed that neither the Consul, nor the Commander of the U.S. Troops were sufficiently authorized to make such a treaty. He also stated that he was not unaware of the importance of this step, as regarded saving the artillery and munitions of war if it could be effected so that Mexico should not lose her right to the property, and so that this measure should not render worse the situation which was already sufficiently complicated. To these observations Gen Cortina himself answered;—that in convening a council of war he had done so out of pure formality, as he had anticipated every thing, and he would not do anything which might compromise or dishonor us;—that if we had confidence in him we ought to accept his measures, because they would only tend to better the situation which we then held, by making us doubly strong. These phrases, although stated in the language which is peculiar to him, seemed to calm a certain distrust manifested by a majority of the party by the apparent frankness with which they were expressed, and some stated that, although this was a matter which deserved to be considered with more deliberation, they confided in the patriotism & good faith of Genl. Cortina, in all things referring to the said treaty. After this Gen Cortina spoke again, saying that counting with the assent of the persons present to the making of such a treaty it was necessary to settle on some basis on which it should be framed, and he himself produced at the moment a general statement of the points which should therein be contained. The Committee appointed to frame the said basis consisted of Colonel Cerda Lieut. Col. Miguel Echazarrete & Major Commd'g Battalion José A. Puente. These refused at first to act, because the first . . . and last named officers had private reasons to do so, but all insisted saying that they were the most able to fullfil the task, and with no further remarks they retired to a separate apartment where they wrote out the above mentioned basis in conformity with the ideas of Gen. Cortina. The latter were:—that Genl. Cortina with the force under his command agreed in the most solemn manner to aid in every manner the forces of the U.S. and even to attack Brownsville if necessary provided that both did it simultaneously; the object of this being to cross the artillery and munitions of war from Matamoros to this city;— that upon the putting of these troops in the service of the U.S. [t]he commanders and other officers were to retain their ranks and privileges, and that Genl Cortina was still to hold . . . the command of his Brigade;—that the artillery and munitions of war were to be considered as belonging still to Mexico, to be returned to the Republic whenever the government thereof should demand the same. These, if we do not recollect wrong, were the principle articles of the said agreement, which was submitted to the council and approved by it although with apparent hesitation and disinclination;—all of us . . . impressed with the idea that the result of this deliberation would be communicated to each as soon as possible. After the adjournment of the . . . council, Colonel Canales, Colonel Cerda, Lieut Colonel Hidalgo and Major José A. Puente assembled in a private place to deliberate for themselves upon the matters just treated of, and . . . a long discussion ensued in which it was agreed that the policy adopted by all on the aforesaid occasion in appearing to conform to the desires of Cortina, had been the most proper, inasmuch as it enabled all to be informed of his designs & intentions and be cautioned in good time against the complications in which he wished to place them;—that it might have been better to have openly declared against the treaty but that this conduct would only have produced a rupture which was not convenient with a man who had as yet all the elements of war in his hands, whereas we had nothing upon which to base any movement whatever, notwithstanding the thousand improprieties Genl Cortina had committed towards all the members of this *junta,* notwithstanding that we were still entitled to refuse the engagements which might result from the said agreement, notwithstanding that we were convinced that it would not be carried into effect on account of the total want of authorization in both of the contracting parties[.] They resolved besides that as they could not reconcile their consciences with the acts in question, in case they . . . should be about to be carried out, it was necessary to impede the execution thereof, at all hazards, yet without causing any outbreak among ourselves until there should be a justifying cause. This was the determination of these officers, and up to this time they have not deviated from it for a single instant.

On the evening of the same day when the said junta took place, Major Puente was called to translate into English the basis of the agreement mentioned, for the purpose of presenting it to the Consul of the U.S. and the said officer did so with the greatest exactness. After this event some days elapsed without any further mention of the matter and many found cause to believe that the subject had been forgotten;—however, a few days after Major Puente was summoned before Genl. Cortina who requested him to serve as interpreter between him & the Consul of the U.S. who was going to determine upon the clauses of the basis. In effect, the Consul gave his statement, which was:— that neither he nor the Commander of the forces at Brazos Santiago were sufficiently empowered to make this treaty, and that he could only assure that, for his part, the Cortina Brigade would be well received and there would be no reason why Mexico should lose her right to her arms & munitions. This was the answer Genl. Cortina obtained, and upon its reaching the knowledge of Canales, Cerda and Hidalgo, the latter were confirmed in their determination not to take a single step in the hair-brained measures proposed by Cortina. Matters remained thus for a few days more. Nobody knew or could imagine the secret plans of the State Government, when, suddenly on the evening of

the 3rd, orders were issued that the Brigade should march the next day upon
the enemy then at the Boca del Rio. This was done; on the morning of the
4th of last month[.]

On the dawn of the 6th our artillery was firing severely upon the French
troops. If a serious attack was the intention, the movement was badly conceived, as we should have arrived at day-break within gun-shot of the enemy,
and not at artillery range from which we could not do any harm. However,
we all entertained the hope that this was merely a reconnoissance, and that at
night we would make a successful assault. Notwithstanding, after a few
cannon-shots, the artillery was ordered to retire outside of the enemy's range,
and then the cavarly [sic] also withdrew towards Burrita, there remaining only
to protect the pieces on the field the Battalion commanded by Canales, and
that commanded by Echazarrete. The Genl himself retired shortly afterwards
accompanied by his staff, taking the road to Burrita and leaving no other general instructions than those of guarding & watching the road to the Mouth of
the river. This took place at about 12 o'clock in the day, and matters remained
in this state till about three or four o'clock in the evening, at which time it
began to be whispered about that the forces of Cortina which had remained
behind with a piece of artillery had opened fire on a Confederate force on this
bank of the river. This news greatly alarmed us all, and particularly those of
us who had agreed not to follow Cortina to the left bank of the river, in case
he still persisted in doing so. However, nothing positive could be learned at
that moment, until at about sun-down an adjutant of Col Canales came to
inform him that Cortina had opened fire on the Confederate Troops, and
that the cavalry had crossed the river & were still fighting the forces of the
South. Upon this, Colonel Canales called around him the officers of his command, Colonel Cerda senior officer of the Brigade, and the Commander of the
"Union" Batallion [sic] Colonel [Echazarete], stating to them that Cortina had
just taken a wild & criminal measure, which on no account should be sanctioned
by us if we desired to preserve the good name of our State; that it was now
impossible to prevent the crossing of the cavalry, because that had already
been accomplished, but that it was very easy for us to refuse to cross over
however much it might displease Cortina. As might be expected we all
agreed not to cross the river if so ordered to do [so] by Cortina, and even
[Echazarrete] himself appeared to conform to this resolve. We were yet conferring upon this, when an order arrived from Cortina, that we should leave
our camp and retire to the Burrita;—this was complied with at about 7 o'clock
P.M. Having reached that place, the order was given for the troops to rest,
and Colonel Canales proceeded immediately to Cortina to know what plan
he entertained to carry out by a movement which had just destroyed every
hope of attacking the enemy. To this Cortina answered:—that his plan was to
pass all his force over to the other side of the river for the purpose of saving
them together with the artillery & munitions which had remained in Matamoros. At this answer Col. Canales was highly indignant and he knew that
the moment had arrived to express his sentiments on this subject. He there-

upon told Cortina that: . . . the step he was about to take was not only insane but criminal, that the people of Tamaulipas would not pardon him [for] such an act, and that it was a treacherous deed to set aside his own flag in order to array himself against a people fighting for its independence just as we were; that it was not too late yet for him to retrace his steps and that if it became absolutely necessary for us to save ourselves by crossing to the left bank of the river, we should join those who sustained a cause identical with our own, and among whom we all had numbers of friends, and, in fine, that his (Canales') followers repelled such a measure, and that though they would not prevent his (Cortina's) crossing because they did not wish to cause a scandal in the face of the enemy, yet they would not follow him and from that moment he considered himself absolutely independent. Cortina replied with the greatest cynicism that he knew his own business—that nothing should make him retrocede; that Canales might do as he chose since he had determined to lose himself and his followers. Canales replied that he feared nothing, and that with his conscience free he could find a place anywhere. Other words, of more or less bitterness, were exchanged by them, but without altering in any degree the determination of either. Colonel Canales then proceeded to withdraw with his battalion immediately, when Cortina sent for him to request him to remain there till next morning. Canales saw no objection to doing so, and he did not leave even on that day until all the force of Cortina had crossed with three pieces of artillery. He then withdrew with Colonel Cerda, who had agreed not to follow Cortina's designs. On the road from Burrita to Matamoros we overtook a party of fifty mounted men escorting the gun which had fired on the Confederate force. The commander of this party placed himself under Canales' orders stating that during the day he had received orders to cross the river, but that he had not wished to obey it & preferred to . . . retire.

The subsequent events, Colonel, however important they may be, are not believed by the undersigned to be unknown to you, and, through modesty you will permit us to pass them in silence.

We conclude this frank exposé of . . . well known facts, by stating that in this last expedition which started from Matamoros to attack a French force said to be coming up the river, the Batallion of Colonel Canales was placed in the rear, and neither he, or any of his command ever saw the . . . vessels. Colonel Cerda, who by that time was the senior officer of the Brigade embraces this opportunity to state that the force directly under Gen Cortina, was the only one which fired on the foremost vessel, and this by direct orders of the officer which could not be disobeyed even when it was found out that the said vessel carried a flag of truce; and further that whatever was done on this occasion was . . . by the express orders of Genl Cortina, without any person influencing him in any manner in his measures.

We are, Colonel, Your Obd't Serv't's

(Signed) Servando Canales
(Signed) Julian Cerda
(Signed) [?] G. Hidalgo
(Signed) José A Puente

Brownsville
Oct. 4/64

To/Col
   John S. Ford
   Commd'g Fort Brown
      Present

A true translation
   N. Maxan   Receiver C.S.A.

The statement of these gentlemen is conclusive as to the conduct of General Cortina on the occasion spoken of. According to the opinion of the signers of this declaration, Cortina was guilty of treason to his own country in attempting to transfer his whole command into the service of the United States. He violated the usages of civilized warfare when he ordered his men to fire on a vessel carrying a white flag, well knowing that the boat belonged to a government with whom the Republic of Mexico was at peace. In addition he fired on the soldiers of the Confederacy without orders from any superior officer, and invaded the territory of the Confederate States without authority. To these flagrant offences he added that of deserting his own flag and country, when he became an officer in the army of the Emperor Maximilian.

Strange as it may appear this man is the hero in Mr. Bancroft's so-called history! How completely does the narrative of the distinguished officers of Mexico disprove the allegations of Mr. Bancroft. He has the ill-starred credit of publishing as true, as veracious history, the untruthful allegations of a mendacious Mexican, whose name is not given, and of giving to the world an account of the capture of Brownsville by his hero, Cortina, an event which never happened during the Confederate War and is now disputed by General Cortina himself. The author now bids adieu to Mr. Bancroft's effort to convert the baseless, lying, and scurrilous productions of tricksters into history.

6

Colonel Canales was treated with every consideration. He had done us a friendly act, and we appreciated it highly. His refusal to enter our territory as a friend and ally of the Federals had helped us greatly, and probably enabled us to defeat the combination of Cortina and the Federals.

Colonel Canales remained a few days on the American side. He crossed the Río Grande and occupied Guerrero. Here he was recruiting and procuring arms from his followers. General Cortina commanded an expedition intended to defeat the force of Canales. Cortina had greatly the advantage in numbers and in the supply of arms and succeeded in worsting Canales. In this affair some of the best men on the Río Grande were killed. This battle effected an irreconcilable enmity between Canales and Cortina.

A note from the French commander announced the fact that they had watched us closely and felt that we had complied with the requirements of international law in regard to Colonel Canales.

The appearance of General Tomás Mejía upon the Río Grande was viewed with pleasure by Confederates. He was an Indian of rather rugged features who had fought his way up from a low position to the top of the ladder. He was honest, sincere, and truthful. There was no effort on his part to conceal his sentiments. He respected the feelings of others, and no one accused him of harsh and tyrannous conduct. He was kind and generous to his friends and was considerate and gentle to his enemies. In battle he was represented to be fearless, quick to perceive, and prompt to execute. It was difficult to tell when he was beaten. A tale was told of him in some of the military operations in Mexico, probably during the Empire. His army was routed. He had nothing left but a detachment of lancers. Placing himself at the head of these he boldly charged the advancing column of his adversaries, drove them back, and involved others in the backward movement. This sudden and unlooked-for attack caused a terror, a kind of panic which pervaded the whole army, and the fight became wild and wide-spread. Officers were not listened to and threatened with death if they attempted to check the disorderly rout. The Indian with his handful of lancers stood on the field, conquerors. Mejía reassembled his men, and they prepared to meet their opponents again. He was devoted to the Emperor Maximilian.

7

During the month of October, 1864, Lieutenant Colonel Mat Nolan came to the Río Grande as a member of Colonel Benavides' regiment with authority from Benavides to recruit men from Ford's command whose initial enlistments had expired. Colonel Ford warned Nolan that this would take men who otherwise might stay with Ford for another tour of duty.

Nolan, however, continued to beat for volunteers. Many were reported to have said that they had volunteered to serve under Colonel Ford, that they would not serve under anybody else, and marched away.

Again Ford warned Nolan that the "muster will very materially diminish my command at a time when every man should be in front of the enemy who are reported to be reinforcing. This diminution may be so great as to render the evacuation of the Río Grande a necessity should the enemy make a forward movement. This is a very serious consideration, and requires thought. I cannot believe such a contingency was contemplated when your instructions were issued. I would remark, however, that the reoccupation of the Río Grande by the Yankees would be paying very dearly for the filling up of" Benavides' command.

Lieutenant Colonel Nolan called at Ford's office, and they held a friendly conversation on the matter. Ford went with Nolan to Colonel Giddings' encampment; there Ford made a talk to the men, explaining what he conceived to be the object of the remuster ordered to be made by Nolan. Ford said that, if carried out, it would leave him without a command, but that it made no difference what became of him: the main object was to secure a successful issue to the Confederate cause, and in that view of the case, he was willing to be sacrificed. He advised the men to do any and everything for the good and the success of the South. Not a company, nor a man, was willing to remuster into Benavides' command. The two officials returned to Brownsville. Lieutenant Colonel Nolan said that he was satisfied the remuster could not be made without disorganizing the force and the turning of the Río Grande over to the Federals; he would have no more to do with the affair.[2]

---

[2] Ford and Nolan parted on cordial terms. As Rip said in Chapter XXIX, Lieutenant Colonel Mat Nolan had done more than any other man to keep order in the region around Corpus Christi while The Cavalry of the West campaigned along the Río Grande. On August 1, 1864, Nolan, though still in the army, was elected sheriff of Nueces County, and Ford apparently loaned him to the Corpus Christi area to keep order. On the night of December 22, 1864, Nolan and a horse trader named J. C. McDonald (sometimes called McFox) were talking in a lot across the street from Nolan's home. While they talked two men approached and asked if they might be Colonel Mat Nolan and McFox.

"Yes," Nolan said.

"We are the Gravis boys," and immediately one of them blasted Nolan with a double-barreled shotgun while the other one apparently shot at McDonald with a six-shooter, but missed. What happened after that isn't recorded, but at the inquest Mary Ann Shaw said she was inside the Nolan home when she heard firing, looked out the window and saw two men run across the street from the lot. She later testified that she was at home rather than at Nolan's place when she heard gunfire, then heard two men running past with another not far behind.

The men she heard were undoubtedly the Gravis boys chased by McDonald. Apparently he caught them about a block north of the Nolan residence and they gunned him down. He was hit several times but what killed him was a pistol shot behind the left ear.

By now several neighbors had rushed out of their houses to see what the commotion was about, had discovered Nolan, who was still alive, and carried him into his house where Dr. D. H. Lawrence examined the wound and told the colonel he was going to

In a short while Colonel Benavides called on Ford. They discussed the effort to remuster Ford's troops into Benavides' command. Ford explained the character of many of the men now in service on the Río Grande, pointing out that a large number were not subject to conscription, and therefore could not be stopped if they chose to leave. He called Benavides' attention to the number who would quit because they were deprived of the privilege of serving under the man of their choice. Benavides told of the many men in his regiment.

"Yes, you have them on paper," Ford said, "but I dare you to show more than 500 men in actual service. If you have in your regiment so great a number of men why do you wish to take men I have raised and mustered to fill out your regiment?"

Colonel Benavides denied having any such intention and avowed that he would have no more to do with the project. Had he been able to take into his regiment the companies of Ford's command, he would have had a brigade in the field and might have received the appointment of brigadier general. Several companies of his were raised by Ford anyway. In the event of turning Ford adrift, which he believes was the aim, many of these men would have returned to their homes. If a bee of the briga-

---

die. With his remaining energy Nolan described the shooting, naming the killers. "They"—the Gravis boys—had cause to kill him, he said only seconds before he died, but failed to relate what the cause was.

According to General James E. Slaughter, commanding the Río Grande District, Francis and Charles Gravis were really after McDonald, not Nolan, because the horse trader had seduced their sister. They shot Nolan along with him because Nolan would have been a witness. Local historian Ernest Morgan, in an article on the murder published in the Corpus Christi *Caller-Times* (July 30, 1961), dismissed Slaughter's statement as "a good story" but implausible and went on to say that the Gravis brothers "specifically asked for Nolan and McDonald. They killed Nolan and ran off. McDonald wasn't killed until afterward. Furthermore, if they had wanted to shoot only McDonald, they would hardly have picked as a time to do it an evening when he was strolling with the county sheriff." Others speculated that they killed Nolan because of an old grudge, or maybe because Nolan was well-known for his fighting abilities and the Gravis boys saw a chance to prove themselves better men. The best guess, however—as Morgan suggested—is that they murdered Nolan because he was planning some action against their stepfather, who, like a number of other Nueces County citizens hard-hit by the war, was cooperating with Yankee troops on Mustang Island. However that may be, it is true that the killers, though indicted, were never brought to trial. And when the war ended a few months later and Unionists took over the county government, they named the Gravis' stepfather sheriff, then gave one of the boys a job as deputy and also appointed him bailiff to the grand jury. Unionists dismissed the indictment for murder on December 6, 1866.

(I got the information on Nolan's slaying from the report of the coroner's jury and from the affidavit of Dr. D. H. Lawrence, located in the Nueces County Courthouse in Corpus Christi, Texas. Ernest Morgan's account in the *Caller-Times* is accurate and includes a biographical sketch of Nolan.)

dier general species got in Benavides' hat and stung him, and caused insanity, he deserves our sympathy. He has not our condemnation or ill-will.

8

A little after the middle of November, 1864, an effort was made to attack Brazos Island by crossing the Boca Chica from the mainland side, some distance from the small fort at the end of the island, then attacking that fort from the rear. We were of opinion that it could be reduced before it could be reached by reinforcements.

This project was being discussed when General [James E.] Slaughter was placed in command on the lower Río Grande. After investigating the matter, he concluded the plan was practicable. He suggested that Colonel Ford command, and he would accompany the expedition as a mere spectator. To which Ford objected. He said emphatically: if General Slaughter accompanies the men, he will command.[3]

The different commands were ordered to move to Palmito Ranch on about November 17. There is no record of the exact date when they concentrated at the ranch. They were on the ground and about 1,500 strong. A brisk norther commenced blowing the night of their arrival, and blew all the next day.

The second day, the command in part marched to the close proximity of the Boca Chica. The Federals were aware of our intentions. Mounted videttes were seen along the whole interior shore of the Boca Chica. During that day nothing was done in the way of an attack. The enemy were on the alert and ready.

Captain Carrington moved along the shore of the Gulf. He halted at about half a mile from the Federal fort, behind some small sand hills. The enemy opened fire upon him. They killed one of Carrington's privates. This was the only mishap.

The original plan was to cross the Boca Chica at night. This was not

---

[3] Ford and Slaughter disliked one another from the start. Probably what precipitated the feud that soon raged between the two was jealousy on the part of Rip Ford. Having done more than anyone else to keep the valley in Confederate control and to maintain the vital Mexican trade, the colonel no doubt wanted command of the sub-district and highly resented the appointment of Slaughter, who, in Ford's opinion, had done little for Texas or the Confederacy and who was not extremely popular with the soldiers. The two men feuded constantly over Mexican policy and military strategy, over problems of logistics and defense, even over such trivia as who should command patrols and where they should operate. It was fortunate for Confederate Texas that a Yankee offensive similar to Banks' invasion of November, 1863, did not come at this time.

(Oates, "John S. Ford: Prudent Cavalryman, C.S.A.," *Southwestern Historical Quarterly*, LXIV, 309–310.)

attempted, because the severe cold would have subjected those taking the water to considerable suffering. Nobody misbehaved and no one was blamed for the failure to get a fight. The command after a short time gave up the attempt and returned to Fort Brown. This more or less ended hostilities along the river until May of 1865.

9

In the course of life there are some acts of apparent insignificance which awaken feelings of thanks and pleasure later on. The annexed note of friends, many of whom have passed beyond the shores of time, revives sensations which their note produced during that troublous period in the history of the South. Its reproduction will convince those yet living that the present was not conferred upon one who was devoid of thankfulness.

Matamoros, Nov. 20th, '64

Col. John S. Ford
Dear Sir:

We your undersigned friends and acquaintances take great pleasure in presenting to you the accompanying *valise* as a small token of our admiration of you as a true patriot and soldier and our high esteem of your important services rendered the Rio Grande Country, as well as the entire Cause. *We have the honor to be your friends.*

T. W. Latham, Mas. Kleiber, E. H. Harris, J. B. Gallager, C. B. Combe, C. A. Darling, Wm. Brady, H. H. Beard, E. B. Nichols, Q. L. Williams, G. A. Wheat.

XXXI

>>

ANTHEM

Early in the month of March, 1865, Federal General Lew Wallace came to Brazos Santiago. He sent a communication to General Slaughter, inviting him to meet him at Point Isabel on the eleventh of that month. General Slaughter invited Colonel Ford to accompany him, which Ford did. At the meeting the matter of concluding a peace between the North and the South was discussed, and propositions were submitted by General Wallace. He suggested that it was useless to fight on the Río Grande, that if the contending parties met and slaughtered each other it would have no effect on the final result of the contest. We admitted the fact, but declined to entertain those propositions for want of authority from the Confederate government. The Confederates said that they could not act unless in conjunction with authorized agents of the Confederate government. The terms proposed actually included only the Trans-Mississippi Department; *i.e.*, Arkansas, Louisiana, Texas, and the Indian Territory.

Though nothing was decided of a formal nature, Ford and Slaughter left General Wallace expecting the peaceful coexistence along the river to continue. Both Confederate officers sent reports of the interview to General John G. Walker at Houston under the seal of secrecy. When General Walker received these documents he made some remarks of a rather unpleasant nature concerning the Confederates to whom the proposals were made, and published the papers. The writer did not care, for he felt the reports were not of a character to cause a Southern man displeasure.

2

At this time Lieutenant Colonel Showalter and his command had been ordered to another point in Texas. The companies of Colonel Benavides' regiment, on duty near Fort Brown, had been moved higher up the river, and were not accessible for inland service. The cessation of active hostilities on the lower Río Grande had been the cause for allowing many officers and men to visit their homes on furlough. Colonel Giddings with a portion of his regiment had been placed on picket duty at Palmito Ranch. He was now absent on leave.

On the twelfth of May, 1865, a report came in from Captain Robinson of Giddings' regiment that the Yankees had advanced, and he was engaged with them just below San Martín Ranch.

Colonel Ford directed him to hold his ground, if possible, and he would come to his aid as soon as men could be collected at Fort Brown. Couriers were sent to the different camps to hurry the men up. It was late in the evening when Robinson's report was received. In order to reach their destinations, the couriers had to ride at night.

It would be saying the mere truth to assert that Ford's orders found some of the detachments badly prepared to move. The artillery horses had to travel the most of the night of the 12th to reach Fort Brown. So had many of the men.

General Slaughter was not idle. We take his own account of his doings. He took supper at Ford's quarters. They were discussing the situation. The general gravely asserted that he had been hastily preparing to meet the unexpected emergency. He told of vechicles and other things he had caused to be impressed for the army. Among these he mentioned Dr. Austin's fine carriage. The doctor was from New Orleans.

Ford put the question: "General, what do you intend to do?"

"Retreat," the general said.

"You can retreat and go to hell if you wish!" Ford thundered. "These are my men, and I am going to fight."

Among other things Ford said was this: "I have held this place against heavy odds. If you lose it without a fight the people of the Confederacy will hold you accountable for a base neglect of duty."

The general finally agreed to move to the front. An hour was named to meet on the parade grounds at Fort Brown the next morning; from there we would march to meet the enemy. General Slaughter probably directed an order to be issued to march and engage the Unionists. Such a one is among my papers. It is dated May 12, 1865. I do not remember to have seen it before we engaged the Yankees.

Colonel Ford waited until 11 o'clock A.M. and General Slaughter failed to appear. The colonel placed himself at the head of the few troops present and marched to a short distance below San Martín Ranch.

He began to make dispositions to encounter the enemy. Captain O. G. Jones claimed to be in command by virtue of an order from General Slaughter. Colonel Ford placed him under arrest and under guard. After a few minutes Captain Jones, having abandoned his intention of commanding, asked for permission to "fight his battery." Colonel Ford granted it, assuring him there was nothing personal in the order of arrest.

When Colonel Ford saw the Federal lines some half a mile lower down below the ranch of San Martín, cutting the road at right angles, he felt badly.

"This may be the last fight of the war," he thought to himself, "and from the number of Union men I see before me, I am going to be whipped."

He buoyed up his spirits, made a short talk to the boys, and found them in such good fighting trim that he made haste to put them to work. It is but simple justice to them to say they fully met his expectations, and showed themselves worthy of the encomiums passed upon the gallant soldiers of a noble State.

Ford, having made reconnaissance and determined to attack, directed Captain Jones to place one section of his battery in the road under Lieutenant Smith, another under Lieutenant [William] Gregory on the left, supported by Lieutenant [Jesse] Vineyard's detachment. The other section was held in reserve. The guns were directed to move in advance of the line. Captain Robinson was placed in command of the main body of cavalry—Anderson's battalion under Captain D. W. Wilson on the right by consent, and Giddings' battalion on the left. Lieutenant Gregory had orders to move under cover of the hills and chaparral, to flank the enemy's right, and if possible to get an enfilading fire. Captain Gibson's and Cocke's companies were sent to the extreme left with orders to turn the enemy's right flank. Skirmishers were advanced.

Meanwhile one of King and Kenedy's boats came steaming up the river.

We could not satisfy ourselves as to the flag she bore. Two round balls were thrown at her from one of our cannons. Luckily she was missed.

The artillery opened fire before the enemy were aware we had guns on the field. Lieutenant M. S. Smith threw several well-directed shells and round shot into the enemy's lines. He was a promising young officer. Lieutenant Gregory's fire annoyed the enemy.

We had some volunteer French cannoneers. They had charge of the piece in front. Colonel Ford galloped past them a short distance above Palmito Ranch. He gave them a command to hurry up. After having gone two or three hundred yards, a ranger came up at full speed and informed Ford that the Frenchmen had halted and unlimbered the piece. Ford moved back at full speed and told the Frenchmen "Allons!" They limbered up briskly and went forward with celerity, but the chance of a good shot was missed. The colonel had not previously known of their presence.

Skirmish firing soon became brisk. Ford waited until he heard Gibson and Cocke open on his left. The colonel saw the enemy's skirmishers, which were well-handled, left without support by the retreating main body, and he ordered an advance. Very soon Captain Robinson charged with impetuosity. As was expected the Yankee skirmishers were captured and the enemy troops were retreating at a run.

Our guns pursued at the gallop; the shouting men pressed to the front. Occupying the hills adjacent to the road, Confederates fired in security from behind the crests. The enemy endeavored to hold various points, but were driven from them. The pursuit lasted for nearly seven miles, the artillery horses were greatly fatigued (some of them had given out), the cavalry horses were jaded. Ford was convinced the enemy would be reinforced at or near the White House. For these reasons he ordered the officers to withdraw the men. He said: "Boys, we have done finely. We will let well enough alone and retire."

After we had withdrawn a short distance, Brigadier General Slaughter, accompanied by Captain Carrington commanding Cater's battalion, arrived. Slaughter assumed command. He sent one of his staff, Captain W. R. Jones, to Colonel Ford directing him to resume the pursuit. This Colonel Ford declined to do, unless he could first see General Slaughter and explain to him the fatigued condition of the horses in his command. He particularly mentioned the horses of the artillery; several of these had been taken from the pieces because they were exhausted. The horses of the men had shown signs of failing. We were then too near Brazos Island not to expect Union reinforcements to be hastened to meet their retiring troops.

These reasons, if reported to General Slaughter, were ignored. Although it was now about dark, he ordered skirmishers to be thrown out. The Yankees also moved out in skirmish formation. They fired at each other. If anybody on either side was scratched, it was not mentioned.[1]

After General Slaughter had indulged in skirmish firing for a short time, perhaps ten minutes, he withdrew the Confederates, and rode up to where Colonel Ford was standing. We were then near Palmito.

The general said: "You are going to camp here tonight, are you not?"

"No sir."

"I have ordered down several wagons, loaded with subsistence and forage," said the general.

"I am not going to stop here in reach of the infantry forces on Brazos Island, and allow them a chance to 'gobble' me up before daylight."

"But remember the prisoners," the general said.

"I do sir. If we Confederates were their prisoners we would be compelled to march to a place of safety from attack by Confederates."

We moved about 8 miles higher up and encamped.

In this affair the enemy lost twenty-five or thirty killed and wounded, and 113 prisoners. Some were killed while swimming the river. A great many escaped into Mexico. In killed, wounded, and missing their loss approximated two hundred.[2]

They also lost two battle flags, one of which belonged to the Twenty-Fourth Indiana (the Morton Rifles). They abandoned many stands of arms, threw others into the Río Grande, and left clothing scattered on their whole line of retreat.

Our loss was five wounded, none of them supposed to be dangerous. Colonel Ford was indebted to the bravery and good conduct of both officers and men, and could not particularize where all did their duty. We must return to the Almighty for this victory, though small it may be, gained against great odds and over a veteran foe. This was the last land

---

[1] The way the story goes, as twilight fell the firing dwindled. An artillery shell burst near a youthful Confederate. Swearing loudly and shaking his fist—much to the delight of the old veterans—the youth aimed his rifle at the shadows of Brazos Island and fired the last shot in the Civil War.

(Carrington's account of the battle of Palmito Ranch in John Henry Brown, *History of Texas from 1685 to 1892,* II, 436.)

[2] With respect to the numbers engaged and the casualties, the accounts of Palmito Ranch come nowhere near general agreement. Federal losses out of about 800 engaged were probably 30 killed and wounded and 113 taken prisoner. Confederate casualties must have been more than five slightly wounded, as Ford said. Carrington himself stated in his report in Brown, *History of Texas,* II, 435, that after it was all over the Confederates took time out to bury their dead. It is likely that out of some 1300 engaged all told (this includes Cater's battalion which arrived late), the Confederates lost about the same number as the enemy in killed and wounded.

fight in the war.[3] It seems possible that the first blood of the war was spilt in Zapata County, Texas.

3

The readers will, perhaps, forgive me for again trespassing on their patience by asking them to lend their attention to matters connected with the last fight of the war.

In volume two of his miscalled *History of the North Mexican States and Texas,* Mr. Bancroft asserts:

Meantime on May 13, the engagement above alluded to, the last in the war, was fought near the old battlefield of Palo Alto, the scene of Taylor's victory over Arista. The Confederates were stationed at Palmetto and Colonel Theodore H. Barrett who was in command at Brazos Santiago, sent on the 11th 300 men under Lieutenant-Colonel Bronson [Branson] to attack them. Early in the morning of the 12th Bronson assaulted the enemy's camp, drove him from it, and captured a number of horses and cattle. He then fell back, and on the 13th was joined by Lieutenant-Colonel Morrison with 200 men. The Confederates had again assembled at Palmetto ranch in force, and were commanded by General J. E. Slaughter. Colonel Barrett now took command of the federal forces in person, and advanced against the foe, who was again driven from his position. About 4 o'clock in the afternoon, however, the federals were assailed in front by a strong body of infantry with six twelve pounders, while a squadron of cavalry succeeded, under cover of the chaparral, in flanking them. Barrett's position was critical, and retreat was his only alternative. For three hours a running fight was maintained without the Confederates being able to break the federal line, and at sunset they retired. The last shot in the great civil war had been fired.

Bancroft's allegation that Colonel Barrett caused the Confederates to abandon their position would do honor to the inventive genius of Baron Münchhausen.

The canard of the Federals being "assailed in front by a strong body of infantry" has not the slightest character of even probability. It is a false tale of whole cloth. There was no Confederate infantry on the lower Río Grande. Colonel Barrett and command ran from about 300 cavalry, and they were swift of foot, went like men who had important business at some other place. The Morton Rifles, the Sixty-Second Colored, a part of a Texas regiment, and, if memory is correct, the Forty-Sixth New York, proved themselves long-winded and swift-footed.

In regard to the claim that Lieutenant Colonel Branson drove Captain

---

[3] The memoirs account of Palmito Ranch was obscure and incomplete, so I integrated with it Ford's very detailed article covering the battle and its results and Bancroft's mistakes, printed originally in the San Antonio *Express,* October 10, 1890.

Robinson from his camp on the 12th, we will consult the short report made by the captain to Lieutenant Ed Duggan:

"I moved to the road at twelve m., found the enemy numbering 300 occupying Palmetto ranch. We commenced a skirmish with them and compelled them to fall back. I followed them to the White Ranch. I think they will return to the island to-night."

If Lieutenant Colonel Branson had defeated the Confederates and driven them from their camp, why was Lieutenant Colonel Morrison sent to him with 200 additional men? The Morton Rifles were an old veteran regiment and Lieutenant Colonel Morrison did, in all probability, rank Lieutenant Colonel Branson, who belonged to a colored regiment of more recent formation.

The writer has shown why General Slaughter was not with the Confederates in the affair of May 13, until the fight had been won, and they had withdrawn. He had important business somewhere else. What that was, let Captain L. G. Aldrich of General Slaughter's staff tell you in his own words:

Natchez, October 21, 1890

Colonel John S. Ford:

My Dear Friend: This morning's mail brought me evidence of kindly remembrance on the part of some distant friend in the shape of a copy of *The San Antonio Express* of the date of October 10, page 9, of which contained a most excellent article from your pen, and I hope for the truth of history, as well as full and well deserved justice to you, that Bancroft's works . . . may be corrected.

It affords me pleasure (unsolicited) to bear witness to the fact that General Slaughter never claimed the honor of the engagements of the 12th and 13th of May, 1865, but has always stood firmly upon the expressions and sentiments expressed in the congratulatory address issued by me to the troops under date of May 14, 1865, in obedience to his instructions. In fact General Slaughter did not reach the field until the battle was virtually over and the enemy in full and disorganized retreat.

That your article may be more complete I will state from personal knowledge that General Slaughter was necessarily delayed in his departure for the front by information, that suspicious movements on the part of Cortina, on the Mexican side of the river and above Brownsville, indicated an advance by him on our base of supplies—Brownsville—in conjunction with the movements of the Federals from Brazos Santiago. An event natural to expect in view of his (Cortina's) known intimacy with the Federal authorities.

Our force being limited in number and their presence being deemed essential to meet the advance of the Federals, some management was requisite to provide for protecting Brownsville against the probable attack of Cortina.

You may recollect that I, as assistant adjutant-general, was placed in command of the post. The citizens formed a home guard, pickets were established and all precautions possible taken to successfully baffle any effort of Cortina. One man in particular, General Slaughter, secured through the friendly aid of Señor Quintero an agreement with General Mejía that in case of an advance by Cortina his (Mejía's) cavalry would cross, in citizen's dress, and come to our assistance. And Señor Quintero remained with me throughout the night, ready to go to Matamoros with the summons upon which they were to move.

These negotiations were not completed until late, when placing me in command of Brownsville, General Slaughter proceeded to the front.

At the time Captain O. G. Jones, through the columns of the press, adorned himself with the plumes of victory, purloined from the chapeau of the true victor. I wrote a refutation of his claim and general charges. I sent [it] to the same paper for publication, in which I gave facts as herein recited.

Permit me, my dear colonel, to congratulate you upon the favorable consideration you have received from the hands of Providence, who has so long spared you as an honor and comfort to your family, to whom, as well [as] to yourself, I beg leave to tender assurances of profound esteem.

Very Truly Yours,
L. G. Aldrich
State Capt., and A.A.G.C.S.A.

This communication of Captain Aldrich has the appearance of settling the question of who commanded the Confederates at the last fight of the war. Colonel Ford considers the question closed and does not propose saying another word in the public prints on the subject, unless in answer to something which may be said by somebody else. The facts given above are submitted to a candid world more as a vindication of the truth of history, than as an act of justice to myself.

4

The prisoners taken in the battle of Palmito Ranch were conducted to Fort Brown and treated with kindness. Several of them were from Texas. This made no difference in their treatment. Some were taken who had deserted from the command on the lower Río Grande. The most of these were allowed to escape on the march up to Brownsville. The Confederate soldiers were unwilling to see them tried as deserters. Some of the Sixty-Second Colored Regiment were also taken. They had been led to believe that if captured they would either be shot or returned to slavery. They were agreeably surprised when they were paroled and permitted to depart with the white prisoners. Several of the prisoners were from Austin and vicinity. They were assured they would be treated as prisoners of war. There was no disposition to visit upon them a mean spirit of revenge.

The right to choose, to follow the yen of opinion, was recognized and accorded. All seemed to feel that, although engaged in terrible warfare, they were still brothers, still free-born Americans. The interchange of ideas between the Union men and the Confederates removed many causes of complaint, many bitter feelings, and much of the rancorous spirit of hostility engendered by four years of civil war. When the Union troops were set free, under the promise of not serving against the Confederate States again during the war, we feared that the United States authorities would not accept these terms. But we could not spare the money required to feed over one hundred prisoners and consequently had to turn them loose.

The fight of May 13 proved that the Confederate soldiers on the lower Río Grande would submit to nothing implicating their honor and manhood. They considered the advance of the Union troops as a violation of the terms of nonaction, as specified by General Lew Wallace, and they fought.[4]

A few days after the release of the prisoners, Lieutenant Magee came to Brownsville and gave notice that a number of United States officers were just outside the city of Brownsville and wished to pay the Confederate officers a friendly visit. General Slaughter was absent at the time. Colonel Ford directed the lieutenant to inform them: "They would be required not to converse with the Confederate officers and soldiers with a view to rendering them dissatisfied, and not to attempt acquiring a knowledge of the numbers of Confederates on duty." The terms were agreed to and a number of Union officers entered Brownsville as guests of the Confederates. The names of these officers are not remembered. The official account of their visit is not found. They were received kindly and their treatment was as hospitable as our means would permit. A major, whose name has passed out of memory, was at Colonel Ford's house. The major was partaking of a glass of egg-nog and remarked:

"If my wife knew I was now at the house of a Confederate colonel, and accepting his friendly hospitality, she would be so mad she would hardly speak to me."

---

[4] The Yankees claimed that, having received the news of Lee's surrender over a month before, they had come onto the mainland expecting Confederate capitulation. They had absolutely no intention of fighting. Ford and his lieutenants, who during the battle did not know about Appomattox, insisted that Union troops had come off Brazos Island looking for trouble, and certainly had found it. This dispute has never been settled to the satisfaction of both sides, but whatever brought about the last battle was actually insignificant as the final chapter of the Civil War came to a close. Texans who had fought hard to create a new nation based on slavery and states rights had now to face the long and dreary days of reconstruction under the flag of an indestructible union.

If memory is not at fault, there were about six of these Union officers. They went to Matamoros one Sunday morning, accompanied by Colonel Ford, Captain John J. Dix, and other Confederate officers. It was a big day. There was a military mass in the morning, a review of troops, and so forth. The mass had the firing of arms as a part of the programme. The review then came off. General Tomás Mejía, the reviewing officer, stationed himself on the north side of the plaza on a veranda or gallery of the second story of his residence. The United States officers were taken to the inside of the plaza opposite General Mejía. The troops marched past. Seeing United States and Confederate officers standing together, and apparently friendly, caused great surprise to the Mexicans. This spectacle produced quite an impression on the Mexican soldiery. Frequently there could be seen a curvature in a line, occasioned by an effort to secure a good sight of the Americans. The Mexicans marching on the outside made frequent inquiries: "Is it peace in the United States?" "What does it mean?"

"O it means nothing," Ford replied. "I am only trying to show these friends of mine something of the Mexican Empire."

After the review we concluded to hunt up a breakfast. The party proceeded to the restaurant of John Clinch. Ford knew the French officers; a great many of them boarded there; it was their breakfast hour. He called for the room in their rear. The Americans passed through the French dining room. These gentlemen rose to their feet while we passed. They appeared greatly surprised. About this time the military of France were expressing themselves much in favor of a war with the United States. If Louis Napoleon had made a war at the right time, it might have benefited the Confederacy.

5

When Ford returned to Brownsville, his troops expressed to him the idea that they had engaged in the war of secession upon their own sense of right and of duty, but now the time had arrived when they felt called upon to exercise their own ideas of what they owed to their families and to themselves. Since Confederate resistance had collapsed across the South, they decided to return to their homes and to abandon all hope of success in a contest which they believed had the sanction of God on the side of an indissoluble union. This resolution was formed after mature thought, without prejudice or passion, and they proceeded to execute it with the same sincerity and the same honesty of purpose which led them to become soldiers.

About the middle of May, while General Slaughter led a few of the men up the river to meet a Confederate column retiring into Mexico,[5] the main body of Ford's army rode away to the north, heading home. To part with these noble men was a sore trial. To see them leave and to reflect that this parting was in all probability our last on earth, brought with it a sad feeling none can express in words. It is one of those evidences of the weakness of human nature and the illusory character of all earthly ties and combinations. Many of those men have paid the last debt due to nature. May Almighty God in his infinite mercy have pardoned all their errors. The feeling of respect and admiration their commander then entertained for these worthy soldiers yet exists, undiminished and undimmed by time. It will resist successfully the aggressive effects of chance and change and will be stilled and subdued only by the all-powerful effects of death.

---

[5] Five hundred Missouri cavalry, determined never to submit to Yankee rule, rode down through Texas, picking up a few Texans along the way, and moved into Mexico. Leading them was a corps of hardened and pugnacious officers—men like Joe Shelby, "Old Pap" Sterling Price, Tom Hindman, and E. Kirby Smith, who had figured predominantly in the war in the West. It is said these troopers carried along their bullet-ridden flags, burying them in the Río Grande before crossing into Mexico.

(Stephen B. Oates, *Confederate Cavalry West of the River*, p. 221.)

BOOK **6** *The Desert and Beyond*

XXXII

>>

AFTERMATH OF DEFEAT

On the twenty-sixth day of May, 1865, Colonel Ford carried his family to Matamoros, Mexico. He had been on good terms with General Tomás Mejía, the Imperial commandant of the line of the Bravo, a man of character and of distinguished bravery.

A few days after the Fords acquired a house on the Mexican side, a French lieutenant rode up and addressed Mrs. Ford. He spoke Spanish so poorly that Mrs. Ford called out Mrs. [J. J.] Fisher, a French lady, to enable them to converse. The French officer stated that the house occupied by Colonel Ford's family was wanted for the occupation of French soldiers. He was told that we were renters, Americans who had been Confederates. It was distinctly stated that we took no part in the war existing in Mexico. He informed the ladies that all those things were of no moment to him. He named an hour, and not a far distant one, and if the house was not evacuated by that time, he would send a detachment of French soldiers to throw all the movables into the street. He seemed in bad humor, making no effort to speak politely to the ladies.

Mrs. Ford sent for her husband immediately. Without delay he waited on General Mejía, and informed him of what had occurred. The general sent for the French officer, informed him he had no authority for his action. Colonel Ford told General Mejía that if he had endorsed the doings of the French officer, Ford would have crossed the Río Grande at once, and the Imperialists would have been lucky to get good sleep for one night even.

In the course of a few months the city of Matamoros was threatened by the adherents of Juárez; a siege appeared imminent. Previously, General Mejía had applied to Colonel Ford for information concerning the position of the Republican forces on this side of Sierra Madre. Ford applied to the Juarezista officers, who for the time being were in Brownsville. They gave the location of their different commands, well knowing the same would be communicated to General Mejía, but not worrying about it because Mejía could not move against any command without his action being known. General Mejía, on account of this favor, promised to give Colonel Ford permission to cross his family and effects into Brownsville whenever requested.

2

A short while after Colonel Ford reached Matamoros, the commander of the United States forces on the Río Grande reached Brownsville. General [Frederick] Steele was a soldier and a gentleman. He was a cousin of General [William] Steele of the Confederate Army. One of the Federal commander's staff officers was Lieutenant Richard Strong, a cousin of Mrs. Ford's. He was a clever gentleman, and rendered communication between General Steele and Colonel Ford easy and agreeable.

In a short while authority was conveyed to Colonel Ford authorizing him to act as parole commissioner for the Confederates on the Río Grande. He had thought with care on the situation. He could see no future for an American outside the territory of the United States. He conceived there was more chivalry in sharing the fate of the men who were unable to leave the country where they had been reared than in seeking an asylum in a foreign land, and in thus eluding the disagreeable results of the late unfortunate war.

Major Blucher, Captain Kenedy, Captain King, Mr. Vance of San Antonio, and other gentlemen of note accompanied Ford to the headquarters of General Steele, where they were paroled.

"My opinion," General Steele told them, "is that the easiest and safest mode to reconstruct a state is to use its representative men in leading the people back to their allegiance."

All of the Confederates accepted the situation. They averred that they would observe the terms of parole because honor demanded it.

"General, we are now at your service in any matter involving the public good. If you desire information on any subject, couriers to convey dispatches, men to face any danger menacing the country, means of transportation, or supplies or anything in the line of your ordinary duty, we stand ready to respond to your call. We wish it distinctly understood, however, that we reserve our right to act for ourselves in political matters. In that connection we cannot be used."

The proffered offer of service was accepted. There were no concealments on either side. The interview was signalized by candor and fairness on both sides. This understanding rendered things clear and easy of perception. The people of the lower Río Grande and the military had no trouble with one another. The gentlemen who assumed control of civil affairs, however, caused considerable bad blood, and eventually defeated themselves.

Ford prevailed on every Confederate he found in Matamoros to accept a parole, return to his home, and perform the part of a good citizen of the United States. He argued that when the South exported the same quantity of cotton it did previous to the war, that would be an evidence of the restoration of her commercial affairs to the point she had attained in years gone by. He insisted that the Negro would vote, and so on.

Men of all classes had gone to Matamoros, the most of them with a view to speculate, some to avoid service, some from mere idleness and a disposition to wander listlessly through the world. It was a city of strange denizens, a motley crowd. There were millions of dollars worth of merchandise in the place. Every room, every niche capable of being occupied and of holding a man was rented at a large price. Never was a place of the same size crowded with more people, and made a display of more goods. When the Confederate war ended, there was a general dispersion of men, a hurry to leave a place once esteemed a sort of trader's Mecca. Goods were auctioned off for what they would bring. Rented houses were abandoned. Cotton was hurried off. Ere many months had passed, Matamoros had almost assumed its former appearance.

While there Colonel Ford became acquainted with a French officer, a count. In conversing one day the official informed the colonel there would soon be a state of war existing between France and the United States. He added:

"You are going to help us whip the United States, are you not?"

"France did not aid us in our struggle with the United States."

In reply to this he spoke of some matters preventing France from aiding the Confederates.

"It is too late now," Ford said. "I am a paroled prisoner. I would not fight for any government on earth with a rope around my neck, as it were, except my own."

"The United States has no money," the Frenchman observed.

Ford's American blood began boiling at this. "You forget, sir, that in a foreign war the United States can get every dollar its citizens can control."

"But we will blockade your coast, and destroy your commerce. Then where will your money come from?"

To this boast, Ford retorted: "Oh that is what I heard the United States officers say the other day that they would do with your commerce and your coast."

He became very much excited, and it was thought prudent to retire. The fact was, nothing had been said on the subject by the United States officers, but the count did not know it.

3

General Carbajal arrived at Brownsville from New York early in 1866. He began to operate against General Mejía. By inquiry the latter general ascertained he could expect nothing from the Americans in the way of facilities in the matter of retiring from Matamoros—it was understood he had been ordered by Maximilian to evacuate the city. Mejía soon moved down the Río Grande and embarked, as we learned, for Vera Cruz.

He had been very kind to Confederates. They respected him highly for his manly adherence to his word. It was generally conceded that in some of the revolutions occurring in Mexico he managed to save the life of General Escobedo. When it was known that the Emperor Maximilian and General Mejía suffered death together, after the French left Mexico, many blamed General Escobedo. He exculpated himself, however, as follows: The night before the tragic execution, General Escobedo entered the room occupied by General Mejía. He told him to go to a certain point, at a certain hour, and there he would find a man on guard, in whom he could confide. From that point he would be conducted to where he would see a horse already saddled. "Mount him and save your life." General Escobedo said he was astonished when the noble old Indian remarked: "No, I will stay and die with the Emperor." It was the expression of sentiment of devotion which few men have ever acted upon. It was evidence of a heroism which has never been exceeded.

4

After General Mejía evacuated Matamoros, General Carbajal entered it. He began at once to restore the Republican government. He raised soldiers, appointed officers, provided for the raising of funds. He performed all the functions rendered necessary by the situation and the urgency of public affairs. In order to have an American force in the field, he invited Colonel Ford to enter the service of the Republic of Mexico by assuming the position and command of brigadier general.

General [Philip] Sheridan was at that time in Fort Brown. Ford called upon him and told him about Carbajal's proposition. The general said that he was opposed to the disposition evinced by the Confederates. There was an enmity, a settled hostility, towards the government of the United States which ought not to be encouraged and which he would use every effort to defeat and suppress. He felt that men entertaining those unfriendly sentiments towards the Union ought not to be encouraged in going into Mexico.

"General," Ford said, "we have been defeated in a great war; of course the result has not satisfied us. To that extent we are dissatisfied, but you must remember that a great many of us surrendered to the armed forces of the United States with the same sense of honor and the same determination to observe the terms of surrender that governed us in the first instance. We feel bound by every honorable sentiment to observe the laws of the United States and to promote her interests, because our surrender inculcates these sentiments. I do not propose to engage a single man who is inimical to the United States, but I may engage some who are not satisfied with the results of the war."

"Well, go along, I suppose you will do right," the general replied. He was obeyed.

Men were enlisted and everything was done to advance the interests of the Juárez government. While the Confederate war lasted we had been friendly with the Imperialists, with the hope of benefiting our cause. When our Civil War ended, and we were declared a part of the Union, the question in Mexico then was simple. Shall we aid the cause of the Republic or the cause of Maximilian? In joining Juárez, we raised our voices in favor of a government for the people and by the people.

As affairs progressed, Ford's brigade was undergoing constant recruiting. General Carbajal furnished money for that purpose. The papers of the brigade unfortunately have all been lost or mislaid. Captain Seibert was acting adjutant general, Captain Miller was one of the captains, the rest of the officers have escaped memory.

General Carbajal appeared to place more reliance, in some respects, on his American than his Mexican troops. Colonel Ford noticed this and spoke to the general concerning it. Ford predicted trouble from it. It must not be forgotten that the Mexicans of that day were rather unfriendly to the Americans; consequently, favors shown Americans were sure to cause unpleasant feelings among the Mexicans.

As Ford had predicted, trouble soon began to brew. He saw demonstrations that convinced him a revolution against Carbajal was pending. Ford hurried to see General Lew Wallace, at General Carbajal's office, saying: "A revolution is on foot. In ten minutes we may have our throats cut." The general had a few moments to reflect on this consoling information. Then General Carbajal came running downstairs. He told me a revolution had definitely begun, and asked me to go to my fort. On the way out of the plaza Ford encountered Dr. Combe. We walked together till a carriage was met. Ford mounted and rode it to his fort.

Quite soon a body of Mexicans approached, watched the fort for a time, then retired. Then General Canales, who was leading the revolution against Carbajal, came to have a consultation with Ford. Canales said he adhered to the cause of Juárez. Ford indicated that these were his sentiments too. Before long Canales declared himself in command of Matamoros and the state of Tamaulipas and ordered Carbajal to leave the country.

The retiring of Carbajal was a peculiar affair. He had raised and educated General Canales. They were supposed to be friends.

5

In the course of time an officer was sent to take command of the line of the Bravo, whose name, if recollection is not at fault, was General [Actaviano] Zapata. General Canales refused to relinquish his command and placed Zapata under arrest. A good many of the soldiers, the Americans in particular, viewed this act to be in contravention to general orders and contrary to the wish of President Juárez. A German officer in the Mexican service who was unfriendly to Canales spoke of the arrest of General Zapata as an outrage against propriety. The German conversed with Captain Seibert and won him over. Very soon the whole brigade was ready to aid in releasing the imprisoned general. Seibert had been the prime mover in the matter in the brigade.

Although Ford was sick, he agreed to aid in the insubordinate movement against Canales and attended the meeting in which the plan of operations was contrived. The meeting was held on board a gunboat that had originally been fitted out by General Carbajal. While we were talking the boat moved from the upper fort on the river down to the end of the street leading to the northwest corner of the main plaza. At that point the conspirators disembarked. Since Colonel Ford for several hours now had labored under a chill, he deemed it imprudent to go in charge of the men.

It was now after dark and raining hard. At the designated hour the troops moved quickly into the main plaza, attacked the headquarters of General Canales, fired a short while, then returned. It is not probable that anybody on either side was hurt; no charge of bloodshed was registered against either party at the time.

The Americans boarded the gunboat; it moved down the river to the ferry landing, tying up on the American shore, where the Americans disembarked; then it moved to the Mexican side, where Canales' men took immediate possession of it.

Thus ended the attempt to unseat General Canales. Colonel Ford takes this occasion to say that the effort against General Canales was wrong, although the Juárez general maintained his liberty while the bloodless engagement was under progress. The writer is rather ashamed to make this statement, but he has promised to tell the truth.

XXXIII

>>>

CORTINA AGAIN

At the close of the Civil War in the United States, bad Mexicans who had been engaged with Cortina crossed into Texas and began depredating upon our people. They murdered men, robbed ranches, and were guilty of many cruel and atrocious acts. General Cortina was esteemed the head of these killing and plundering expeditions, though the evidences of the fact were not positive. Those operating on the lower Río Grande handed to him a certain percentage of their stealings. In this manner a reign of terror was created in the country between the Nueces and the lower Río Grande.

General Alexander McCook was placed in command of the valley of the lower Río Grande in 1867. McCook sent a company of cavalry to look after the evildoers. Colonel Ford with some citizens under civil authority accompanied the military. A Mexican named Juan Porras was one of Ford's party. He had engaged as a Confederate and, as was afterwards found out, he changed sides.

The command crossed the Arroyo Colorado and proceeded a few miles, when they met a drove of cattle, apparently between 500 and 1000. The Mexican went out and conversed with the men driving the horned stock. He came back and reported the cattle all right, said he knew the owners of them, and spoke of them as honest men of good character. At this we permitted the cattle to pass. We afterwards learned that the whole drove had been stolen, and our Mexican had not told the truth.

The command moved by way of Don Nepomuceno Cavazos' ranch and on the edge of the sand to Don Francisco Ytúrria's ranch, by the Old Sal del Rey, and to a point above the Old Salt Lake. At a ranch a few miles from Cavazos', Lieutenant Vernon, our commander, settled some trouble concerning cattle between Don Manuel Treviño and Don N. Cavazos.

The command marched from above the Great Salt Lake to near the house of Nepomuceno Cavazos and from there to Fort Brown in three days. Some stolen cattle were captured on the way and sent back by the citizens to Brownsville. They were sold and the money divided between the volunteers.

This expedition was an assurance that the military would endeavor to protect the property of citizens. It had a good immediate effect, though it did little, in the long run, towards checking the forays made by Mexicans upon our citizens.

2

A circumstance occurred in 1867 deserving attention. General [John] Sedgwick, then commanding Fort Brown and believing the American residents of Matamoros demanded protection against the probable action of the contending Mexican parties commanded by General Canales and General Escobedo, ordered into the city a force of United States troops. It was the general understanding that the contending parties on the Mexican side took great umbrage at the presence of the American troops, and consulted whether they should unite and attack the foreign interlopers, or fight each other. Be that as it may, one evening, when it was almost dark, news was received that General Cortina was making ready to cross the Río Grande and move upon Brownsville. The mayor of Brownsville, William Neale, was summoned to the quarters of the commanding general. He was requested to confer upon Colonel Ford and General West authority to raise and organize into companies a force of police, or police assistants, to aid the military in defending the city of Brownsville against the impending attack and pillaging operations of General Cortina.

Operations to render recruiting prompt and effective were adopted at

once. A large number of the influential citizens and residents of Brownsville were congregated at the markethouse. The greater part of the night
was spent in the matter. Arms and ammunition were furnished by the
government and issued to the different companies. Everything necessary
was done, and the command was given to break ranks. The order was to
be on the parade grounds at Fort Brown by daylight in the morning. A
small period of time was allowed for sleep and refreshments.

The appointed time was punctually observed by all. Several hundred
men were in line, and prepared for whatever might come. We were not
long in suspense. The booming of cannon, the rattle of musketry, and all
the confused and commingled sounds of battle were borne upon the
breeze. Escobedo had launched his army upon the fortifications of Canales.

We now thought Cortina would not come. The citizen command was
dismissed for the present, to be held in readiness to answer any call coming from the American commander.

The composition of the different companies was a convincing proof
that the Civil War had not rooted out and subdued the love of country.
The pride of being a free-born American, the proud feeling of being a
defender of the homes where liberty had "a local habitation and a name,"
was made pre-eminently conspicuous. Some of the officers were Unionists,
while others had faithfully followed the Southern cross. The rank and file
had similar diversity. Had an engagement taken place, the officers were
assured the only rivalry between the North and South, observable on that
occasion, would have been developed in the performance of duty and in
deeds of daring. A few Mexican-Americans had raised companies of
their countrymen. They were actuated by the same principles which governed men of American birth.

It was afterwards reported and currently believed that Cortina, when
he learned of the preparations made for his warm reception at Brownsville, felt a little averse to encountering them. This is problematical.

3

General McCook was in command of the lower Río Grande for some
time. This gentleman was very kind to the people of Texas. He endeavored to make them lose sight of the fact that they were a conquered
people and he the conqueror. He interfered as little as possible with civil
affairs, leaving them to a great extent in the hands of the men elected to
office by the voters. These constituted men who had opposed the South
in the late Civil War, the Northern men who had come South for profit

and pelf,[1] and the Negro. The men who had the honor and the hardihood to stand by the South in the great conflict, based upon a difference in the construction of the plain principles of the Constitution, were deprived of the right to vote, cyphers without value, human in form only. These men General McCook treated with respect and consideration. They had no right to complain, and did not complain that their rights and their franchises, as men who had been once free, had ever been curtailed, denied, or impinged upon by the action of General McCook. Notwithstanding the rigidity and the rigor of the reconstruction laws and the frequent forgetfulness of the fact that the people of the South still had rights, General McCook governed his military district mildly and pleasantly.

He was one of the people at all places of innocent amusement. He was a member of the club which met at Captain [Robert L.] Dalzell's new building on Elizabeth Street. He was one of the main originators of the fun had by all on St. Patrick's day. At public balls, private dinings, wherever people went to enjoy themselves, he was an attendant. Affable, accessible to all, polite and attentive to all, he was popular with all. In the way in which he governed there was no chance for dissatisfaction. Things moved along smoothly and pacifically. He was always found where duty bade.

General [Henry Boynton] Clitz superseded General McCook in command. Clitz was on the same character, only not so full of life. During his administration he made John S. Ford guide of the troops operating against cow-thieves and other disturbers of peace and quietude. Lieu-

---

[1] Ford's generation of white Texans greatly exaggerated the role, the influence, and the corruption of the so-called carpetbaggers—Northern immigrants who came to Texas during Reconstruction. Of the few carpetbaggers who helped found the state Republican party, one was Harvard-educated Edwin M. Wheelock of Massachusetts, a Presbyterian minister and a prewar abolitionist who favored civil and political rights for all men; another was George T. Ruby, born in New York City and educated in Maine, who came to Texas as a teacher with the Freedmen's Bureau and among other achievements served in the state senate during E. J. Davis' administration; Ruby's principal crime, in the eyes of native whites, was that he happened to be a Negro—and an outspoken, capable, distinctly unobsequious Negro at that. Of the ninety men who sat in the 1868 constitutional convention, only six to eight were carpetbaggers. According to Alywn Barr, *Reconstruction to Reform: Texas Politics, 1876–1906* (Austin: University of Texas Press, 1971), pp. 176–177, carpetbaggers "played only a limited role" in both the radical and conservative Republican factions. That they even remained in Texas after 1874 indicates that they had a permanent interest in the state. See also Carl H. Moneyhon, *Republicanism in Texas* (Austin: University of Texas Press, 1980), pp. 62, 66, and James M. Smallwood, *Time of Hope, Time of Despair: Black Texans during Reconstruction* (Port Washington, N.Y.: Kennikat Press, 1981), pp. 138–141, 146–148, 153–155.

tenant Vernon usually commanded the troops on these scouts. The depre-
dators had many friends on this side of the Río Grande. They were very
active, and kept the marauders well-apprised of the movements of the
military, and not many positive results sprang from the frequent marches
in search of the rascals. Some prisoners were made, and the presence of
the troops was effective.

4

In 1876 General Díaz came to Brownsville.[2] In a conversation with
Colonel Ford he stated that he had money enough to supply the wants of
a gentleman, but not sufficient to wage a war. He inquired if Americans
could be induced to loan him cash. The reply was:

"You are, no doubt, fully aware of the trouble General Cortina is
causing on this frontier. If measures are not taken to check his depredations, they are surely going to create hostilities between Mexico and the
United States. If you will give your word that, if successful in the revolution you are to inaugurate, you will order Cortina to be removed from
this frontier, Americans will loan you money."

General Díaz gave his word as requested. He obtained money from
American citizens. Don Savas Cavazos, a half brother of General Cor-
tina and a naturalized citizen of the United States, advanced Díaz money.
The sum was reported to be $50,000.

General Díaz afterwards took Matamoros. He moved to the interior of
Mexico. He was successful in various engagements.

Meantime General Cortina had declared for Díaz and the revolution-
ists. He was in command on the lower Río Grande. The commander of
President [Sebastián Lerdo de Tejada's] forces was Colonel Revueltas.
He held possession of Matamoros. Cortina occupied the country around
Matamoros, but did not engage his opponent. So it was asserted at least.

Colonel Ford was engaged in translating revolutionary documents and
having them published in Texas newspapers. He was the correspondent
of the Galveston News by letter and by telegrams. He was also in correspondence with the revolutionists, and was generally able to say what
would be their next movement. In this manner the Galveston News usually presented facts in relation to the doings of the combatants. General
Díaz succeeded in obtaining the presidency of Mexico. He has since convinced the world that at least one revolution in Mexico was set on foot

---

[2] Porfirio Díaz, an ex-*Juarezista* general, was getting up a revolution against President Sebastián Lerdo de Tejada.

for the welfare of the Mexican people. President Lerdo was an astute lawyer, with more brains than principles and less patriotism than selfishness. He was a cunning tyrant, and disregarded the Constitution and the laws of Mexico when they circumscribed his intended action.

General Servando Canales was an adherent of Díaz. He was an active friend, and did the principal fighting on this side of San Luis Potosí. After the accession of General Díaz to the presidency, Canales was made commander of the line of the Río Grande and military governor of Tamaulipas. The writer ascertained that General Cortina's conduct during the revolution was condemned and that he was accused of disobedience of orders. Under the agreement between General Cortina and Ford,[3] he considered himself justifiable in placing the general on his guard. He sent a man to him with the following advice: "Do not trust yourself in Matamoros. Sell off everything you have which can be moved."

When this warning came to Cortina, for such it really was, the old fellow is said to have remarked: "That old white-headed American thinks he knows Mexicans better than I do."

A few days thereafter the general rode into Matamoros; he had not reached the main plaza until he was made a prisoner. A court-martial was ordered. He was accused. The court, after trial and mature consideration, pronounced him guilty and worthy of death. Few were astonished. All knew that he had done as he pleased for many years and had probably wronged Canales and that the day of retribution had come.

Colonel Ford felt it a duty he owed to General Canales to warn him of his danger. Ford went to Matamoros and waited on the general.

"General Canales," Ford said, "it is known to everyone that yourself and General Cortina are deadly personal enemies. If you approve of the proceedings of the court-martial by which he was tried, and he is shot, it will be said that personal ill feeling actuated your approval. It will, in my opinion, be a stain on your memory for all time to come. Send the prisoner and the proceedings to President Díaz. Let him act as it may

---

[3] I could find no record of any personal agreement between Ford and Cortina. Hughes thinks that Captain S. H. McNally's testimony before a Congressional investigating committee in Washington may have the answer. McNally told the committee that once General Cortina returned some stolen stock "to a particular friend of his, one of his compadres on this side, who was an American." The American could have been Ford, whom Cortina begrudgingly admired and who upon receiving the stolen stock might have promised to help Cortina in some way.

(*U.S. House of Representatives, Index to Reports of Committees*, 44th Cong., 1st Sess., 1875–1876, p. 14; William John Hughes, "Rip Ford, Texan: The Public Life and Services of John Salmon Ford," ms., pp. 362–363.)

suit him. If he adjudges General Cortina worthy of death let him give the order or cause it to be done. If the contrary is his judgment let him turn Cortina loose."

After the writer had retired, a gentleman present reported that General Canales said: "Did you hear what that white-headed old man said? If there is a man in the world more opposed to Cortina's mode of doing things than Colonel Ford, I do not know him."

Canales sent Cortina to the City of Mexico where President Díaz has kept him under surveillance for nearly twenty years. Can any gentleman dare say that President Díaz has not fully redeemed his pledge?

XXXIV

>>

THE END OF INNOCENCE

P resident Grant ordered the election for governor of Texas to be held on November 30, 1869.[1] General [J. J.] Reynolds, the military commander of Texas, assigned three more days for the holding of said election—the first, second, and

---

[1] In 1869 two factions of the Republican party were campaigning against one another in the gubernatorial elections. The radical faction had met in Houston and nominated E. J. Davis. Soon after, the conservative Republicans had announced Andrew Jackson Hamilton—"Big Injun" or "Colossal Jack" to Texans—as their choice and urged President Grant to call early elections. The Davis faction, having a better chance of winning if the elections were late, sought delay.

Then Major General John J. Reynolds, commander of Texas and a close friend of the president, sided with Davis and persuaded Grant to set elections to begin in November. During the months that followed Reynolds stacked the registration boards with Davis men. With Grant's encouragement and Reynolds' aid the radicals managed to squeeze Davis into the capitol by a narrow margin of 800 votes. Davis won because most of the 37,370 blacks who voted cast their ballots for him. The Davis faction not only offered a program of reform but also sought to end white racial violence then sweeping the state.

third days of December. The courthouses of each county were mentioned as the places of voting. Voters were registered. These were Negroes and Union men who had not aided and assisted the Confederates in any manner during the Civil War. The leading and most intelligent men of the South were disfranchised. It was said during those days that General Reynolds manipulated the returns so as to enable him to declare E. J. Davis elected. Davis was installed as governor the twenty-eighth day of April, 1870.

In regard to events, George W. Paschal remarks in *A Digest of the Laws of Texas*: "Governor Davis was sworn in as provisional governor on the day that his election was declared; but in commissioning the senators, and signing the resolutions ratifying the amendments, he acted as governor; and, so I am told, he received the increased salary. Therefore the pretense that his tenure lasted from his public installment, on the 28th April, 1870, until the same day in 1874, rested on a very slender foundation."

He approved the law regulating elections on March 31, 1873, and was again a candidate for governor under the same law. He issued his proclamation ordering the election. It took place on December 2, 1873. The vote stood Richard Coke, the Democratic candidate, 85,549, Davis, 42,633—a difference of 42,916.

[On December 16 the Texas Supreme Court, in the infamous Rodríguez or "Semi-colon" case, declared in effect that the election of 1873 was invalid because the polls had remained open for three instead of four days, thus violating the constitution of 1869.] The action of the Supreme Court produced a lively sensation among the people generally.[2] They were satisfied the intention of the radicals of Texas was to hold on to office and power at all hazards. In this instance a large majority given at the polls was to be overridden and crushed. The people of Texas were to be held in serfdom. The Republican armies had freed the Negro, but the Republican despots of Texas were aiming to make dishonored slaves of thousands of Texians.

---

[2] In a long and rather discursive account of *Ex Parte Rodríguez* which I took out, Ford called the decision a "peculiar" one—an understatement in describing a case that lawyers still half-jokingly, half-disgustedly refer to as the "semi-colon" decision. Oran M. Roberts, an authority on Texas judicial affairs, remarked that "so odious has" the Rodríguez Case "been in the estimation of the bar of the State, that no Texas lawyer likes to cite any case from the volumes of the Supreme Court reports which contain the decisions of the court that delivered that opinion, and their pages are, as it were, tabooed by the common consent of the legal profession."

(Roberts, "The Political, Legislative, and Judicial History of Texas for Its Fifty Years of Statehood, 1845–1895," in Dudley G. Wooten [ed.], *A Comprehensive History of Texas*, II, 201.)

At the election of December, 1873, an amendment to the Constitution of Texas providing for the reorganization of the Supreme Court and the appointment of a chief justice and four associates had been adopted by a large vote of the people. This meant retirement to private life of the members of the Supreme Court of 1873. After their failure to defeat the will of the people, they were not considered in the appointments made by Governor Coke to fill the places vacant on the supreme bench.

[O. M.] Roberts, who was at a former time chief justice of the Supreme Court of Texas, was called upon by Mr. Coke for an opinion as to the constitutionality of his taking his seat if elected under the election law of 1873. This opinion was asked to ascertain whether Judge Roberts coincided with him in that question. Coke found that he did.

Judge Roberts decided that the length of time for which the governor and the members of the legislature were elected was not governed by the actual time. For instance, a member of the Thirteenth Legislature might have been a candidate for the Fourteenth and be defeated. If the law fixing the time of the meeting called them together one month before the two year term of the member of the Thirteenth Legislature had expired, he could not take his seat because he was not elected to the Fourteenth Legislature. The election of 1873 governed the time of the governor and the members of the legislature. It specified that the 13th of January was the day the Fourteenth Legislature must come together; it specified their action in the matter of counting the vote for governor and lieutenant governor; and it specified that after the inauguration of Governor Coke, Davis was a private citizen.

The people of Austin saw significant signs of trouble. They knew the previous decision of the Supreme Court and believed that Governor Davis was preparing to act on their opinion that the late election law was unconstitutional. There were movements among the colored folks. They were going to Austin on the Central Railroad. They would enter the cars and pass a town or so and then stop. A number would take passage at the point where the others stopped. This was to avoid attention. The members of the legislature from Cameron and other counties were on the train; the writer was with them. Judge Galvan, a Republican, was about the first man to speak of the movements of the colored men. He gave a shrewd guess as to their intent. We arrived at Austin and found the Democrats in a state of suspense. They were expecting a movement of Governor Davis of some character. They believed it would be in the direction indicated by the Supreme Court, or, in other words, a struggle to continue in power E. J. Davis and other Republican state officers, regardless of the will of the people expressed fairly and unequivocally at the ballot box. The Democrats very naturally were getting ready to counteract these revolutionary measures and to make the expressed will of the voters of Texas effective.

Governor Coke and Lieutenant Governor R. B. Hubbard were in Austin. They were endeavoring to ascertain the intentions of Davis and his radical supporters. The action of the radical members of the Supreme Court was an index to the whole matter. Before leaving their respective homes, Governor Coke and Lieutenant Governor Hubbard had telegraphed John H. Reagan, requesting him to come to Austin, and he did so.

Reagan was in communication with them most of the time. He went on three occasions to call on Governor Davis. On the first visit Colonel Word accompanied Reagan. He talked kindly, candidly, and firmly to Governor Davis, told him the inhabitants of Texas held him responsible for the condition affairs had assumed in the state, also that in the event fighting should unfortunately ensue, he would be sure to be killed.

Governor Davis still persisted in his course. He appeared to set on foot measures to induce the Texians to fire on the troops he had congregated at the capital. It will be seen the men serving the state avoided being the first to commit an aggressive act leading to civil war which would cause them to be again placed under military rule.

2

The struggle now assumed a somewhat different aspect. On January 12, 1874, the members of the legislature of Texas opposed to Governor Davis held a meeting. They elected John Ireland president and T. J. Bell secretary, and determined to meet on the 13th. [J. W.] Throckmorton waited on Governor Davis; Throckmorton assured the senators and representatives that Governor Davis and the radical members of the Thirteenth Legislature would not recognize the Fourteenth Legislature.

The legislature met on the day indicated. John Ireland was elected president *pro tem* of the senate and Guy M. Bryan was elected speaker of the house. A joint committee was sent by both houses to inform Governor Davis that the legislature was in session and ready to receive communications.

A large crowd of citizens from various sections of the state filled the lobbies. Expectations of trouble were lively and general. There was a feeling among influential and patriotic men to act with deliberation and great caution.

On January 12 Governor Davis received the following telegram from U. S. Grant:

Your dispatches and letters reciting the action of the supreme court of Texas, in declaring the late election unconstitutional, and asking the use of troops to prevent apprehended violence, are received. The call is not made in accordance with the constitution of the United States and the acts of congress under it, and cannot, therefore, be granted. The act of the legislature of Texas providing for the recent election having received your approval, and both political parties having made nominations, and having conducted a political campaign under its provisions, would it not be prudent, as well as right, to yield to the verdict of the people as expressed by their ballots?

John Hancock and Clinton Giddings, members of the United States Congress, had waited on President Grant and had assiduously and persistently represented the interests of Texas. The people of Texas should not forget the noble and necessary labors of those gentlemen, performed in one of the most important crises which has marked the history of the State. Judge James H. Bell, late of the Supreme Court of Texas, did effective work for Texas at Washington and other points. He wrote an able and unanswerable article, which was published in Colonel Forney's newspaper, and performed other services of great benefit to Texas. Bell had been a Union man during the war of secession and a Republican since, yet bore arms in the service of the Confederacy. Other gentlemen, besides those mentioned, showed themselves firm and true friends of Texas.

Senator [J. W.] Flanagan of Texas sent a telegram to Governor Davis' friend Colonel Flint, advising Davis to get out of the way. It was dated January 12, 1874.

On the same day Governor Davis issued the following:

Proclamation in the name and by the authority of the state of Texas. To all to whom these presents shall come, greeting:
Whereas the supreme court of the state, in a recent decision, declared the elections held on the 2nd day of December, 1873, in substance to be invalid, by reason of the unconstitutionality of the law under which said elections were held; and

Whereas great public injury and further dangerous complications of public affairs are likely to result from any attempt on the part of those claiming to have been chosen as members of the legislature, and other officers at said elections, to assume the positions they claimed; therefore,

For these and other reasons which it is not necessary to incorporate herein, it is deemed advisable, and it is so ordered, that those who have been chosen as legislators or other officers should not attempt to assume the positions they claim, unless by further action of adequate authority. Such election may hereafter be validated.

All good citizens are advised to abide by the decision of the competent tribunal, and aid in maintaining public order and moderate counsels.

In testimony whereof I have hereunto signed my name, and caused the great seal of the state to be affixed, at the city of Austin, this 12th day of January, A.D. 1874.

E. J. Davis, Governor

Nothing of importance was done officially on January 14. On January 15, said George W. Paschal in his *Digest of the Laws of Texas,*

in reply to the application of the joint legislative committee to Governor Davis for the election returns, Governor Davis replied that he did not think Mr. [D. U.] Barziza (the chairman of the committee, who presented the application in person,) the committee itself, or the body they represented, were entitled to them; but if Mr. Barziza would go to the secretary's office and take them of his own accord, he would not be resisted. Whereupon Mr. [Barziza] accompanied the secretary of State, [James P.] Newcomb, to his office, and Mr. Newcomb pointed to a desk where the returns were, and Mr. Barziza took them and asked him to seal the ends of the package, which Mr. Newcomb did. Mr. Newcomb declined to deliver or to allow him to find out where the constitutional amendments were, but they can easily be obtained after Coke's inauguration and the appointment of Captain George Clark as secretary of State. Mr. Newcomb drew up a protest against Mr. Barziza's action, and had it witnessed by the clerks of his department.

Mr. Paschal then says:

This evening General Britton had a number of armed men standing . . . in the basement of the capital, to prevent ingress and egress of the state officers. Some of the force were white and some negroes, all with muskets and bayonets fixed. General Britton appears in full dress uniform. It seems to be the determination of Governor Davis to resist taking possession of these rooms by force, unless greater force is used by his opponents.

On January 16, 1864, Richard Coke wrote Davis:

I have been on yesterday, the 15th day of January, duly and constitutionally declared and elected governor of the state of Texas, and having fully qualified as such, I have to ask of you the respectful delivery into my possession of the executive office of the state, with the papers, archives, and all property pertaining thereto, as well as the office of the secretary of state and its archives, papers, and property.

Davis replied the next day:

Acknowledging the receipt of your communication of yesterday, I have to say, in reply that I do not, as you know, regard you as the executive officer of this state, or entitled to the possession of the governor's office or any official records.

I am myself governor of the state until the 28th of April next. So much on this point. I will add, sir, to my view, and hope also to yours, that it becomes us, as citizens desirious of the peace of our state, that we should, without delay, concur in some plan for settling the question as to which is the legitimate state government, and of putting an end to the disturbed condition of the state.

As matters now stand, every day adds greatly to the injurious complication of our affairs. I therefore now propose to you to submit the question of recognition of the legitimate state government to the executive or congress of the United States, or both. As the executive of the United States is bound, under the constitution, to protect a legitimate government against domestic violence, this question is a proper one for him to decide.

I pledge myself to abide [by] the decision to be thus made, and will advise all good citizens to do the same. I also propose to join with you in adopting means best calculated to secure a prompt decision of this question.

Coke told Davis:

Sir: Yours of this instant, in reply to mine of yesterday, is to hand. By the will of the people of Texas, fairly and legally expressed at the polls, and the recognition of their representatives, the fourteenth legislature, now in session, it has been decided that I am constitutional governor of Texas, and as such I have been duly installed; and holding this decision absolute, and declining, under any circumstances, to consider your proposition to refer the matter to other authority, I respectfully renew the request made in my note of yesterday.

Seven men charged with the arrest of Mayor Wheeler of Austin were arrested this day—January 17. The party consisted of four Negroes and three whites.

Captain George Clark of Waco, having been appointed secretary of state by Governor Coke, demanded of James P. Newcomb the delivery into Clark's possession of the books and papers of the state department. Newcomb replied that he would be governed only by Governor Davis' action and orders and refused to deliver them to Coke.

The attorney general of the United States sent the following to Governor Davis.

Your telegram of yesterday, stating that, according to the constitution of Texas, you are governor until the 28th of April next, and that Hon. Richard Coke has been inaugurated and will attempt to seize the governor's office and buildings, and calling upon the President for military assistance, has been referred by him to me for answer; and I am instructed to say that, after considering the 4th section of article 4 of the constitution of Texas, providing that the governor shall hold his office for the term of four years from the date of his installment, under which you claim, and section three of the election declaration attached to said constitution, under which you were chosen, and which provides that the state and other officers elected thereunder shall hold their respective offices for the term of years prescribed by the constitution, beginning from the day of their election, under which the governor elect claims the office, and more than four years having expired since your election, he is of the opinion that your right to the office of governor at this time is, at least, so doubtful that he does not feel warranted in furnishing United States troops to aid you in holding further possession of it, and he therefore declines to comply with your request.

On January 16, 1874, Mr. [B. H.] Epperson introduced a resolution in the House of Representatives authorizing the speaker to appoint additional sergeants at arms. It was adopted. The speaker, Guy M. Bryan, appointed General William P. Hardeman, Captain William N. Hardeman, Colonel John S. Ford, and others. They were sworn in, and entered on duty at once.

3

Circumstances rendered it necessary to refer to Guy M. Bryan to speak relative to these matters. Annexed is his statement.

Quintama, Brazoria County, Texas
March 2, 1891

Austin, Texas
Dear General:
I cheerfully respond to your request. But writing from memory, and not having the journals of the House before me, I shall omit dates and many interesting details.

When the members elect of the Fourteenth Legislature met in Austin, in January, 1874, Gov. Davis refused to recognize the late election, and repudiated his own actions endorsing the same. The keeper of the keys of the Senate Chamber and Hall of Representatives was in sympathy with the people, opening the doors of the halls when the members of the Legislature came to the Capitol at the usual hour on the legal day of organization. In this way Senators and Representatives got possession of their respective halls and proceeded at once to organize. I was elected Speaker, and all the other officers were chosen without delay. The Senate organized, and Committees were appointed to wait on the Governor, and inform him of the organization of the two houses. He refused to recognize the Legislature. The Adjutant General proceeded under his directions to place the lower story of the Capitol in a state of defense, by erecting barricades at the four entrances of the ground floor, and placing armed men behind them and in the corridors, keeping them there on duty night and day. The Legislature proceeded to its work regardless of the position and attitude of the Governor.

Capt. Barziza, Chairman of the House Committee on Elections, called on the State Department for the election returns of the general officers, and the

Secretary refused to give them to him. He called on the Governor, and discussed the case with him, but the Governor was inflexible, and he reported these facts to the House. The Speaker finally told him to go to the Governor, and explain to him the situation, that the Legislature had duplicate returns, properly certified, and notorious testimony, sufficient to show that Coke and Hubbard were elected by large majorities, and that they would be inaugurated without the returns in his possession; to use all his address and ability to convince Gov. Davis of this fact, and that he only would be injured by his course, which could not prevent the inauguration. Barziza, who was courageous, able and eloquent, was successful. The Speaker announced the result to the House, and a resolution was passed to count the vote, and inaugurate the Governor and Lieutenant Governor elect at once.

Gov. Coke and Lieutenant Governor Hubbard were inaugurated late at night in presence of the Legislature and an enthusiastic mass of citizens packed on the floor and the galleries of the Hall of Representatives; that scene will never be forgotten by those who witnessed it.

Gov. Coke immediately retired to a committee room near the Senate Chamber, which he used as a temporary office, and made the necessary dispositions for the night, by placing Gen. Henry E. McCulloch in command of the Capitol, and grounds, and adjacent public buildings, accepting the services of the Travis Rifles, and placing them at his command.

Early after roll-call next morning the Speaker received a message from Gov. Coke to meet him without delay in his office, he complied at once. The Governor's room was filled with excited people, all standing. The Governor said: "Mr. Speaker, Gen. McCulloch has been up all night, and reports that he is sick, and can not attend to the duties that I assigned him to discharge; in consequence, I have decided that you must protect your portion of the Capitol and grounds, and Gov. Hubbard his, for I have so much to engage my attention I can not give it to these duties. The Legislature must protect itself and the Capitol." I turned to Gen. McCulloch and asked him if he could not retain the command given him by the Governor last night. He said he would like to do so, but was incapacitated by sickness, that he ought to be in bed, and that nothing but a sense of duty kept him up.

The Speaker left with head down thinking, as he pushed his way through the dense crowd in the lobby of the Senate and Hall between the two houses, how he could best meet this great responsibility so unexpectedly put upon him, when he met William N. Hardeman, the sight of whom suggested his cousin Gen. [William P.] Hardeman and Col. Ford. He turned to him and said: "Where is Old Gotch?" "He is here in the crowd." "Where is Old Rip?" "He too is here." "Find them, and bring them to me at the foot of the Speaker's stand." He told the Doorkeeper to admit them when they came. In a few minutes the three men were before him at the foot of the steps on the right of the Speaker's stand. The Speaker suspended proceedings for a few minutes, stepped down to the last step, immediately in front of the three, and said to them: "You love Texas, you have seen much service in her behalf during three wars, you are experienced and accustomed to command men. A great crisis is now upon Texas. Never has Texas needed your services more than now. I trust you fully, I know no men I would prefer to you for discharge of Arms for the protection of the Legislature, public buildings, and grounds. the duties I will entrust to you. I want to appoint you Assistant Sergeants at Under the resolution passed by the House I have the authority and I do confer upon you all the powers necessary to carry out your instructions. I wish you to take command outside of the Hall, protect the Legislature, preserve the peace, and prevent blood-shed, for if one drop is spilled—God only knows the consequences and the end. Order the Travis Rifles to their armory to remove their uniforms, but retain their guns and ammunition, and to act in the Capitol or outside as your posse. If you need a larger posse, acquaint me of your needs; and report to me from time to time the state of affairs; and call upon me for whatever you want, and I promise you shall have it. My place is here, I can not know of the necessities of the hour as you can, I rely upon you as equal to all emergencies, and I will be influenced by your reports."

The Speaker returned to his seat, and swore them in as Assistant Sergeants at Arms, and gave them written evidence of their authority. During the whole time that they were on duty, night and day, they showed tact, fidelity, and efficiency. Twice they prevented bloodshed. On one occasion an able and leading member of the House came to the Speaker and said: "I have just been to the window, and looked out on the grounds in front of the Capitol, and they are black with negroes. I hear they are swarming here from every direction to the assistance of Davis. Something should be done at once."

The Speaker said to him: "There is no occasion for anxiety I think; Gen. Hardeman and Col. Ford are in command, understand the situation, have all the necessary authority, and are competent to meet every requirement. They keep me informed, and I feel satisfied with what they do, and that every thing is being done for our protection, should any thing additional be required they will inform me."

When they reported to the Speaker that their services were no longer needed, the Speaker directed that the three should present themselves in open House, at the foot of the Speaker's stand, where they had been sworn as Assistant Sergeants at Arms. He addressed them as follows: "Faithful servants of Texas, I have asked you to come here, that in the presence of the Representatives of the people of Texas, in their name as Speaker, and in the name of every man, woman, and child in Texas to thank you for the invaluable services you have rendered them, for, but for you, Texas might have been drenched in blood, and remanded back to military rule, which in my humble judgment you have largely contributed to avert by your consummate tact, true courage and patriotism. You are now discharged."

At the conclusion of this address the members of the House manifested their approval by universal applause.

At this day one can not understand or appreciate the services rendered by you and your associates. But those who can recall the scenes of reconstruction,

and remember the "Semi-Coloned Supreme Court"; the acts of the military; and that the Chief Assistant Adjutant General of the Federal Commander of the Department came to Austin, and was there during the whole time of these proceedings, and that Gov. Davis was in communication with President Grant over the wires; saying that Grant would assist him, and had promised to do so, the gravity of the crisis in these piping times of peace may be faintly realized.

Your friend,
Guy M. Bryan

4

When we were sworn in as sergeants at arms, each one of us was impressed with the danger hovering over Texas and was determined, if possible, to keep the state strictly in the line of peace and prosperity, to resist if assaulted, but on no provocation to become the aggressors.

On January 17 the dangers of collision and bloodshed were imminent. The writer received notice that the citizens were coming together for the purpose of attacking the arsenal and releasing Mayor Wheeler from imprisonment. Ford proceeded down Congress Avenue and found the citizens in front of the house now occupied by Dr. Tobin as a drug store. The colonel mounted the steps and told them:

"Governor Coke is using every possible means to keep the peace and to administer the laws. We are acting under his orders. We are instructed by the governor to avoid being the aggressors under any circumstances; not to fire a shot unless fired upon. If the radicals and darkies attack us, we will give them the worst whipping ever inflicted on any set of men since the world began. If we fire the first shot, we will again be placed under a military government, and God only knows when we shall again be free."

Just then Major [Mart H.] Royston came along and announced that he had authority from General Hardeman to raise a company. The writer repeated Royston's declaration, and said:

"You gentlemen who wish to aid Governor Coke in sustaining himself in his constitutional and legal position as governor of Texas, and in the fair and impartial administration of the laws, will please fall in on Major Royston and obey his orders."

The men immediately formed in line behind Royston, and he marched them towards the capitol. As Major Royston was marching one of his men attempted to shoot a colored man. He was prevented. Royston dismissed him from the company.

Then we heard that Captain A. C. Hill had been despatched to the arsenal to prevent Lieutenant [Albert S.] Roberts from taking possession. Hill returned to the rear of the old capitol, waved his hat over his head and said they had been in luck—"no one killed or hurt." Our sentinel, at the head of the stairsteps, swore he would shoot Hill—"just to see him kick." General Hardeman was near, seized the gun, and kept the sentinel from firing.

Colonel Ford then went to a detachment of the Travis Rifles, inquired who was in command, and was answered by a sergeant. Ford told him that the Rifles were the custodians of the part of the capitol occupied by the governor and the legislature and told him to march his men to that point.

The streets were then about clear of armed men, and the danger of a collision between the armed citizens and radicals was averted for the time.

5

Matters dragged along, yet the Texians were lively in expecting something dangerous to be done by Governor Davis. General Hardeman inquired of Governor Coke whether he could go down to see and talk with Governor Davis. The governor assented and told the general to say what he thought suitable to the occasion. The following gentlemen accompanied the general: Captain William N. Hardeman, Mr. McLemore, a lawyer, Sheriff Zimpleman, and a gentleman from LaGrange.

In the course of the conversation Governor Davis referred to Governor Coke in a rather slighting manner: "The man whom you Democrats call *governor*."

"Yes," replied Mr. McLemore, "by virtue of a hundred thousand votes."

The general says Davis did not refer to Coke again during that interview. Davis agreed to send his troops away.

The general and others directed the saloons to be closed. The general remarked to Davis that his men were armed with guns and equipments belonging to the State of Texas, and insisted these should be turned over to the proper state officer. A considerable number of them were turned in.

General Hardeman left in a short while to see that the Democratic troops did not fire on the Davis men. Soon after he left the capitol, Davis' men huzzaed for "Governor Davis." As soon as the Democratic troops heard this outcry, not knowing what it meant, they started in the direction it came from. On reaching the front door of the old capitol, they encountered General Hardeman. He managed to put a gun across the side of the door which was then open and to prevent the men from passing through. He explained the cause of the shout. They heard the explanation, were perfectly satisfied, and returned to their quarters.

Governor Davis, as will be seen in Sheriff Zimpleman's statement below, left the capitol on the same night—January 23. The next day a legislative committee was raised and sent to the basement of the capitol to ascertain the situation. On approaching Davis' room they found the door locked and a man was despatched for the key. Captain Faulkner, an officer of the legislature, put his foot against the door and forced it open. They found the room unoccupied.[3]

6

Sheriff Zimpleman's Statement

Austin, Texas
February 11, 1892

Gov. Coke and Lieut. Gov. Hubbard came to Austin a few days before the time fixed for the meeting of the legislature. I was sent for and went to the City Hotel. There I found Gov. Coke, Lieut. Gov. Hubbard, John Ireland, and a few more. I think Hon. Claiborne Herbert was among them.

I was asked what interest I took in the inauguration of the democratic governor elect? Told them I was a peace officer and would endeavor to enforce the law. Asked if I knew what the law was in the case of Gov. Coke's inauguration? Told them from all accounts Coke had been elected by a majority of about 2 to 1. If in my power I would place Coke in the gubernatorial chair. In that matter, as far as able, I would endeavor to carry out any order from Gov. Coke, not in violation of law, and was assured he would give none of that character. They concluded to get the Senate Chamber and the House of Representatives in a position to enable them to enter them on the thirteenth of January, the day they were to convene. This was the eleventh of that month. It was urged that I should appoint a number of deputy-sheriffs, and place them in charge of the buildings. They had orders to admit no one, except on my authority.

For other purposes I appointed a number of other deputies. I considered them appointed, in regard to gubernatorial and legislative affairs, as deputies till the legislature met and organized, and no longer.

---

[3] White Texans opposed Davis and the radical Republicans mainly because of the radicals' commitment to black Texans. The radicals not only granted them civil and political rights but also enlisted them in the State Police and militia. Most white Texans believed that Negroes were inherently inferior and unfit for freedom and therefore that any attempt to give them political and civil rights was misguided. Out of that view came folk myths about the "boundless extravagance" and "lawless despotism" of the Davis administration—myths subsequent historians accepted as fact. Since the 1960s, scholarship has generally discredited the view of radical Reconstruction, pointing out its racist assumptions and attempting a fairer, more accurate assessment. As recent studies have stressed, Davis and his Republican colleagues accomplished many noteworthy things: in addition to safeguarding black voting rights, they outlawed discrimination on public carriers, established Texas' first public school system, and presided over a time of economic growth and prosperity "unparalleled in Texas history."

I continued to exert all my influence, as an officer and a citizen, in favor of the men who had been constitutionally chosen by the voters of Texas.

I called upon Gov. Davis twice the day he left the governor's office in the capitol. I told him the people were greatly exasperated by his attempt to continue to discharge the duties of Governor of Texas after having been beaten by a vote of the people, under a law he had solemnly approved, after having been decided against by Gen. Grant, and that I had every reason to believe they could no longer be controlled. I said: "I should not be surprised if the irritated people do not collect and in an infuriated mass hunt for you as the author of their wrongs." He asked what security would be given for his safety after he had left the office. I pledged myself to accompany him, and whoever endeavored to harm him would have to first render me lifeless. I went for a carriage. We entered it and drove to the governor's mansion, without any disturbance. It was then after night.

When we left the colored troops, occupying the basement of the capitol, huzzaed for Davis, or just before our leaving.

George B. Zimpleman

Sheriff Zimpleman was an able and active friend of Governor Coke, believing that his action was dictated by a love of law and right. At the same time Zimpleman was apprised of the necessity on the part of the Texians to be cool and ready to resist any armed aggression made by the radicals, but on no account to assume the offensive.

7

Lieut. Roberts' Statement

On the evening of January 15 [1874] Gen. A. S. Roberts was approached by Maj. George B. Zimpleman, then Sheriff of Travis county, and asked to arm himself, and report to him at the Capitol for assignment to duty as a peace officer. About four o'clock in the afternoon of the same day Gen. Roberts while engaged in conversation with Maj. Zimpleman was handed an order, by Lieut. L. E. Edwards, of the Travis Rifles, from Adjutant Gen. [F. L.] Britton, acting under orders of Gov. Davis, to Capt. M. D. Mather, then commanding the Travis Rifles, ordering him to report the company, under arms, immediately, to the Adjutant General.

Lieut. Edwards explained that Capt. Mather, for whom the order was intended, being sick, it was brought to Gen. Roberts for execution, he then being first lieutenant of the Travis Rifles. Lieut. Roberts proceeded at once to execute the order, but not until he had proposed and entered into a compact with Maj. Zimpleman, under which as soon as he should arrive at the Capitol, with the Travis Rifles, he should be summoned, with his command, by the Sheriff, as a *posse comitatus* to preserve the peace.

When Lieut. Roberts arrived at the Armory, the long roll was sounded, and very soon the company was under arms. Before leaving the Armory Lieut.

Roberts stated to the men that, if there were those among them who would hesitate to obey his orders, he hoped they would step out of the line, and leave their guns and accoutrements at the armory. Some three or four, who were republicans, stepped out—others, however, remained.

While these warlike preparations were being enacted the public interest was at the severest tension, and a struggle involving the shedding of blood and the loss of life appeared threatening and imminent. Many democrats who did not know of the conversation between the staunch and patriotic lieutenant of the Travis Rifles and the unflinching democratic Sheriff of Travis county, were alarmed, when they saw the company in full uniform and fixed bayonets march up the Avenue to the Capitol, excitement grew apace. Gov. Davis was calling on the Federal president to sustain him in his policy of force and usurpation. The leading democrats of Texas, conservative and cautious withal during the trying ordeal, were determined to resist to the end all efforts of the governor and his advisers to flagrantly disregard the results of an honest ballot. Among those most prominent in the party were Senator John Ireland and Gen. W. H. Mabry. These went to Lieut. Roberts and wanted to know to whom he proposed reporting his company. Lieut. Roberts answered he was acting under orders of the Adjutant General department, and refused to say more. He did not dare tell them of the understanding between himself and Maj. Zimpleman, for he well knew that, if Grant should sustain Davis, he would be court martialed and shot.

When the company marched to the basement of the Capitol, they were met by the Sheriff, and summoned as a *posse comitatus* to keep the peace. Lieut. Roberts immediately placed himself and command under the orders of the Sheriff; when they were marched to the hall separating the Senate from the House of Representatives; where they stacked arms.

At this exciting juncture a messenger came from General Britton to Lieut. Roberts [directing him] to report in person to him in the basement of the capitol. Lieut. Roberts refused to go, except upon assurances that he would not be arrested, but would be permitted to return. This assurance being given, he appeared before the disgruntled Adjutant General, who wanted to know if he had executed his order to Capt. Mather of the Rifles. The Lieutenant replied that he had. "Then why did you not report to me?" asked the Adjutant. "Because it did not suit me to do so" cooly rejoined the Lieutenant. "Then I understand you to refuse to obey my orders?" "I do, Sir" came the Lieutenant's answer. Gen. Britton then said: "I have no further use for you." To which Lieut. Roberts replied, with the query, "Am I permitted to pass your guard?" "Yes, Sir," said the General. Lieut. Roberts then returned to his post, and remained there, until the inauguration of Richard Coke, and the exciting, but peaceful restoration of the democratic party, in Texas, to the control of the State.

On the morning of the 17th Lieut. Roberts was ordered, by Adjutant Gen. Steele to proceed with a squad of men to the Arsenal, and take it in charge. T. B. Wheeler, then Mayor of the city of Austin, accompanied the squad. On arrival at the Arsenal the house was surrounded. The man in charge, Mr. Henry Cox, came out, and said: "I have one hundred negroes in that building," pointing to the Arsenal. "I wish you would remove your men. I am afraid they will be fired on by the men inside." Lieut. Roberts, for answer, took out his watch, and said: "I will give you three minutes to surrender, and, if a single man of my company is hurt I'll kill every man you have in that arsenal." Mayor Wheeler then interfered, and said: "I was sent here by the Adjutant General to see that there is no fighting done, and I therefore order Lieut. Roberts to with-draw." Lieut. Roberts had no alternative, but to obey. When he immediately despatched a messenger to the Adjutant General, to acquaint him with this situation, and asking for further orders. The messenger returned, bearing an order from Gen. Steele, ordering Lieut. Roberts, with his company, to report back to the Capitol. These facts clearly account for Lieut. Roberts' failure to arrest Henry Cox, and take possession of the Arsenal.

Lieut. Roberts' men were in the act of moving when a company of radicals were approaching the Arsenal. They had been sent from the Capitol. Capt. A. C. Hill was the commander, as we understood. Roberts moved backwards, with his sixshooter in his hand, to his command, and marched them to the Capitol, as ordered. Mayor Wheeler remained behind as a prisoner in the hands of the radicals. His statement will explain that incident. The detention of Mayor Wheeler caused great excitement in Austin. The citizens would have organized, and attempted to take the Arsenal, but for the timely interference of Col. Ford, which is mentioned [above].

The statement of Roberts was written at his dictation, by Mr. Wortham, who evidently made remarks the general would have omitted had he written them. They are, nevertheless, true.

The pupils of the military school, said to be 180 strong, came out and were very efficient in standing guard and performing other service. The school was in charge of General James and his brother.

Governor Coke was requested to give a statement concerning the actions of the friends of Texas in the early part of the affair; Governor Ireland also. Neither have replied up to the present date—May 1, 1892.

8

General McCulloch's Statement

San Antonio
June 29th, 1892

Col. John S. Ford
Dr Sir

Learning that you are getting up reliable information with regard to the acts of men, & in the organization of the Legislature and inauguration of Gov. Coke in January 1874, I wish to furnish you the following items. On the 16th of May 1892 Gov. Coke writes me "I am in receipt of your letter of May 10, as also one of some three or four weeks ago on the same subject. Your first letter is lying on my table now. Had been intending to answer it as soon as I got some leisure and could recall as far as possible the occurrences of the time when I was first inaugurated governor, about which you ask. My recollection about the whole matter is general and does not go into details. I remember distinctly that the whole business of arranging complications that might ensue in which force would have to be used to repel force which was threatened, was committed in the first instance informally to your hands, and that you managed everything in conjunction with George Zimpleman, Gen. Hardeman, Gen. Steele, Gen. Roberts and others with entire satisfaction to myself and the people assembled at Austin who were so much interested in the successful issue of the matter then in hand. I and, as I understood the members of the Legislature then in Session, confided in the prudence, firmness, and sagacity of yourself and associates in this matter; and I was not only satisfied but gratified with the manner in which the whole business was managed."

As Governor Coke had not been inaugurated, he and his councilors (who acted in council) were private citizens like myself, and could only commit these matters to my hands "informally," and I, in order to have legal authority to command armed men obtained a deputation from Geo. B. Zimpleman to act as his deputy sheriff in the matter, and for fear my word may be doubted, I quote here from his certificate to that effect "This is to certify that when Richard Coke was inaugurated governor of Texas Gen. Henry E. McCulloch was acting as Deputy Sheriff appointed by me" (as a great many others were at that time) Signed Geo B. Zimpleman Ex Sheriff Travis co Ap'l 18th, 1892.

I also make extracts from a long letter of Judge J. P. Richardson who was at that time Judge of the 27th Judicial District in which Austin was located. Speaking of matters in the basement of the Capitol he says on "entering the basement I was stopped by an armed sentinel, the hall was full of armed men. The sentinel called the officer of the guard, who in answer to my question said that Col. De Gress was in command. I asked to see Col. De Gress and he came forward and to my demand for his authority he presented the order of Governor Davis ordering him to call out the militia and station them in the Capitol. I then asked him to pass me through the guard to the upper hall which he did. I found there another armed force under the command (as I was given to understand of yourself). Both parties were eager for a fight, and both were only waiting the order for attack momentarily expected (Mr. Zimpleman accompanied me to your room and introduced me to you as commander of the forces in the upper part of the building) I asked you to give me your word that the Col. might come up to your room and that he should be free to return to his command without hindrance or delay, which word was given (I think I went down stairs and stated the case to Col. De Gress, who consented to come to your room which he did) [He] proposed that as both comman[ders] were present that they should [effect] a truce for the night, acting [upon] this suggestion it was agreed [between] you and Col De Gress that neith[er par]ty should make any aggressive [move]ment that night. This being done, Co[l. De] Gress returned to his command) [This] agreement was faithfully kept by bo[th] parties and the next day Gov. Da[vis] acting under the advice of Gen[eral] Grant President of the U.S. dis[missed] his forces and gave up the offic[e to] Governor Coke" and Col De Gress [endorses] what Judge Richardso[n has] written "I certify that the above s[tatement] of Hon J. P. Richardson is substantially [true as I] remember the circumstances" and [A. S.] Roberts writes "with regard to the tru[ce made] at the State House between Governor Coke and Davis. I was in [command] of the Travis Rifles ordered out by G[ov.] Davis on the eventful evening th[at] we expected the trouble. Marching at [the] head of the Company, arriving at the Capitol we were summoned by the sh[er]iff as a posse to keep the peace. [We] marched by him into the Hall [where] we stacked arms and posted senti[nels], remaining under orders of the sh[eriff], but yourself and Col. John S. Ford [were] there both seeming to be in authority. We spent the night in the ante room of the Senate Chamber. You remained as long as the company, or in other words was there when the company was withdrawn." This ought to satisfy you and every one else that I was on the ground and in command from the time the trouble was anticipated, until the armed force was withdrawn, although I was paid as a juror on the Federal Court for 22 days during that term (Jany 1874) but as the records do not show for what days I was paid, I will state for your information that my services commenced on the 5th day of Jany. and on the night of the 12th I was excused, and for the next five days I was at the Capitol working for Texas without pay or hope of reward, and at the end of that time, when all armed resistance had ceased and the officers fully in possession of their respective offices I returned to my place on the Federal jury. All through the early portion of this *dark* struggle I commanded as his Adjt General until Steele was installed on the 18th of Jany 1874

Respectfully
Henry E. McCulloch

General H. E. McCulloch has written several other letters claiming to have been the leader, or one of the prime movers, in resisting the efforts of Governor E. J. Davis to continue in charge of the gubernatorial office for a term longer than the law allowed. Ford disclaims the existence of any enmity or ill will against General McCulloch. Ford demands justice at the hands of his fellow citizens and nothing more.

General McCulloch was appointed adjutant general *pro tempore* on account, it is said, of the absence of Adjutant General William Steele. The Austin *Statesman* says General Steele received his appointment on January 16, 1874. He was certainly on duty on January 17 of that month. Lieutenant Roberts, commanding the Travis Rifles, avers as follows: "After the sixteenth of January General McCulloch ceased to be Adjutant General *pro tem.*"

Sheriff George B. Zimpleman made the statement: "The legislature met and organized January 13, 1874. After that day Gen. McCulloch was no longer a deputy-sheriff of Travis county."

McCulloch will please state under what appointment he acted?

We will quote again the declaration of Guy M. Bryan:

> The Governor's room was filled with excited people, all standing. The Governor said: "Mr. Speaker, Gen. McCulloch has been up all night, and reports that he is sick, and can not attend to the duties that I assigned him to discharge; in consequence, I have decided, that you must protect your portion of the Capitol and grounds, and Gov. Hubbard his, for I have so much to engage my attention I can not give it to these duties. The Legislature must protect itself and the Capitol." I turned to Gen. McCulloch and asked him if he could not retain the command given him by the Governor last night. He said he would like to do so, but was incapacitated by sickness, that he ought to be in bed, and, that nothing but a sense of duty kept him up.

Here Governor Coke withdrew any authority he had given McCulloch at his own declaration of inability to attend to the duties.

In one of his reiterated claims of having performed extraordinary duties he rather denies the account given by Guy M. Bryan and makes no effort to procure the evidence of Governor Coke that Bryan has failed to state the case as it was. That affair was transacted in the presence of many. Why not call on others to disprove Bryan's allegation?

General McCulloch says that General Steele did not assume discharge of the duties of the adjutant general's office until January 18; he is in opposition to the fact as many remember, and as stated by Roberts and by the Austin *Statesman*.

On January 17, 1874, Lieutenant Roberts marched his men to Shoal Creek, where the arsenal then was. Where was General McCulloch then?

General McCulloch affirms that General Steele took charge of the adjutant general's office on January 18; how did he convey orders to Lieutenant Roberts on January 17?

When General Hardeman prevented Mr. Callahan from shooting Captain Hill, where was General McCulloch? Where was he when Colonel Ford interfered and prevented citizens from marching against the arsenal? Where was he when Captain Royston dismissed a man from his company for attempting to shoot at a colored man in the capitol? Where was he when Sheriff Zimpleman went with Governor Davis to the governor's mansion? Where was he when the colored man let his gun go off by accident? When General Hardeman, Major McLemore, and others waited upon Governor Davis, where was General McCulloch? When Governor Davis dismissed the Republican force at the capitol, and they huzzaed for him, and the Texas force was prevented from assailing them by General Hardeman, where was General McCulloch? Echo asks "Where?"

If everything was arranged between the Davis men and the Texians and peace restored at the date mentioned by General McCulloch, how was it that Major Degress, an officer of Davis', swore out a process against J. E. Dillard and E. S. Shropshire for an assault upon him with force and arms, on January 18, 1874, while in lawful and peaceful possession of the office of superintendent of public instruction?

If General McCulloch was present at any one of the incidents above stated and attempted to exercise any authority, the writer was not conscious of the fact. If McCulloch had been clothed with the power of rendering himself invisible to human eyes, he may have been present at all the incidents recited.

General McCulloch, in his communication to Mr. Hollingsworth, says that the sergeants at arms—General Hardeman, Captain Hardeman, and Colonel Ford—drew pay, and underscores *pay*. We have been in Texas over fifty years, have filled many public offices, and this is the first time a charge of drawing too much pay has been made against either of us, and we have been made cognizant of the fact. If General McCulloch did not intend to convey that idea, what did he mean? Then the manner in which it was made, coming from the party it did, makes it show symptoms of an ungenerous endeavor to do us injury. Oh no, General McCulloch never drew pay for his services!

After the dismissal of the military, General Hardeman, Captain William Hardeman, and John S. Ford continued on duty. The papers furnished by Comptroller McCall show that John S. Ford was paid until February 7, 1874. The same amounts were paid to all three of the persons, though the receipts of payments to the two Hardemans were not found.

9

During this period the writer had acted as assistant editor to the Brownsville *Ranchero*, edited by Somers Kinney and owned by Kinney and Maltby, had afterwards written for the Brownsville *Courier*, owned and edited by E. P. Claudon, and then, in company with J. E. Dougherty, had started and published the Brownsville *Sentinel*. The paper was democratic, opposed the election of General Grant as President of the United States, the election of E. J. Davis as governor of Texas, and all the wild and oppressive measures of the Republican party in reference to the reconstruction of the Confederate States and other unconstitutional heresies they advocated and passed into laws. Ford had been for a period of time deprived of the right to vote. He thanks God that he has lived to see the Confederate States incontestibly Democratic, a majority of Democrats in the United States House of Representatives, and to have witnessed the four year administration of Grover Cleveland, a Democratic president.

Appendices

>>>

I   Shapley P. Ross and Times in Old Texas

II Richard King and Mifflin Kenedy:
    The Business Wizards of South Texas

>>>

The Appendices are biographical sketches which do not follow the chrono-logical design of the book.

Appendix I

>>

SHAPLEY P. ROSS AND
TIMES IN OLD TEXAS

SHAPLEY PRINCE ROSS was born in Jefferson County, Kentucky on January 18, 1811. In 1830 he married Miss Catherine Fulkerson, who had been born in 1812. He came to Texas in 1838 and stopped for some time near "Old Nashville," on the Brazos River. One of his nephews, Shapley Woolfolk, accompanied the family. Nearly every full moon the Indians paid the settlers a visit and carried off horses.

Ross traded two horses and a wagon for fifteen hundred acres of land, six hundred and forty acres of which were on Little River, not far below where the town of Belton now stands. The balance was situated elsewhere.

The object was to form a new settlement. This was effected by exchanges of land. Ultimately, Ross, Captain Dan Monroe, Matthew Jones, Giles O. Sullivan, the Reverend Lisle, Edward Wortham, and J. J. Turnham occupied lands on Little River, about where the town of Cameron now stands.

2

When General Woll invaded Texas in 1842, circumstances prevented Ross from turning out. He furnished Doc Sullivan, then about fourteen

years old, an outfit including the black horse. Sullivan was in the Somer-
vell Campaign when the order to fall back from the Río Grande was
given. Sullivan joined the Mier Expedition in February, 1843, was captured, and Ross lost his horse.

Shap Woolfolk came to Ross' place from the west. At his suggestion
Captain Ross sold some cows and bought a horse in order to join the
ranger command of Captain Jack Hays, the celebrated Texas Ranger.

The order of General Canalizo to the Mexicans to evacuate the country
between the Nueces and the Río Grande was promulgated in 1839. Many
Mexican residents left behind them large numbers of cattle and horses.
Armed parties of Texians went into the district between these rivers and
drove out the animals. War existed between the Republic of Mexico and
the Republic of Texas. The latter claimed the Río Grande as the boundary line between the two republics. Bands of armed Mexicans also entered the same region. Collisions occurred.

In 1843 Captain Hays made an expedition into the "debatable land."
He halted on the Arroyo Colorado—Red Creek—about thirty miles north
of Matamoros. He sent a scout to Los Indios, a lake about twenty-two
miles from where Brownsville was afterwards located. Hays had sixteen
men including Shapley Ross. They hid themselves in the chaparral and
emerged when an opportunity offered to effect anything. They captured
six Mexicans before returning to the command. The prisoners reported
500 cavalry in Matamoros. The rangers collected four hundred horses
and marched in the direction of San Patricio on the Nueces.

The command moved at a brisk gait to reach the river and, in this manner, strung out considerably. All at once eleven Mexicans, yelling and
firing, charged the rear of the column. Captain Ross and his nephew,
Woolfolk, were in danger of being cut off. Soon after the firing commenced, many of the rangers galloped back to assist their companions
in the rear. Captain Hays directed the horses to be driven to the timber.
The guide "threw off"; he and the prisoners, thus left almost alone,
managed to stampede the animals and run them towards the main body
of the enemy. The eleven Mexicans withdrew a short distance and began
firing again. Captain Hays told his men to remain where they were and
rode out to make a reconnaissance. He discovered more than a hundred
men within supporting distance of the eleven Mexicans—the whole constituting a force seven times larger than his own. By that time the drove
of captured horses was quite under the control of the Mexicans. Hays
moved off slowly and in good order. No effort was made to evade an
attack from the enemy. The horses had changed hands. Not a ranger was
hurt.

In galloping back and forth, Ross, Ad Gillespie, Guy Stokes, and

Shap Woolfolk had lost their hats. Captain Ross improvised a sort of tur-
ban made of an old calico shirt. He had been trading in horses and found
himself reduced down to a Mexican pony. The stampede had proved
rather rough upon the *caballado* he expected to drive home. The feelings
of the ranger on his ten-dollar, grass-fed charger, his head wrapped up
like a Turk's, his face scorched by the sun, and a pleasant prospect of a
long walk to his home, may be imagined, but not envied by any man outside of the lunatic asylum.

He had the good luck to reach Little River after meeting with some
adventures of a rather pleasant nature.

3

A short time after Captain Ross returned from the trip to the Río
Grande, five Indians made a foray in the settlement and stole his pony,
his only animal of the horse kind. They were not followed for want of
horses. This was almost the only instance of a failure to pursue marauders that occurred in that small community.

In 1842 George Barnard and David Torrey established a trading house
on Tahuacano Creek a few miles north of where the city of Waco now
stands. A treaty was made with the Indians in 1843 and John McLennan,
who had been captured by the Indians when a small boy, was recovered.
There was at this time a rather general cessation of troubles on the frontier.

In those days every man's house was open to the wayfarer and every
heart warmed towards the defenders of Texas.[1] There was not middle

---

[1] In the forties frontier entertainment consisted mainly of quiltings, dances, and house-
raising orgies in which neighbors for miles around came to help raise a home, then proceeded to get pleasantly drunk while the young danced and ate until they dropped.

Susan Turnham, Josiah's daughter, recalled a much quieter gathering—a quilting—at
Captain Shapley P. Ross' place.

Just after an early dinner at the Ross home the men were congregated at a spring
some distance below the Ross home which was in what is now the City Park. To
these men came a peddlar named Kattin Horn with the first barrel of whiskey ever
brought to Cameron. The men had no money, but by making a joint note they
secured all the whiskey they wanted. It was probably the first time in years that
these men had seen more than an occasional drink and so it did not require much
to floor them or rather ground them, as there were no floors even in the houses,
except dirt floors.

In some of the rude play Captain Ross fell in the water and his leather breeches
got soaking wet. He then went to sleep in the sun; and when he awoke a little later,
his pants were like boards, and a companion obligingly ripped the seams. The Captain took another drink and then concluded to go home and get another pair, and, as
walking in these he had on was difficult, he removed them and threw them across
his shoulder. Meanwhile someone had reported to the ladies that the men had
somehow got some whiskey and were drinking rather freely. Some of the ladies
became anxious, but Aunt Catherine [Ross] calmly continued her quilting as she
placidly remarked, "Well, I am not the least bit worried as Captain Ross never

ground for the cold, the calculating, and the mercenary: they were left severely alone. The demagogue and hypocrite did not roost high: they were unearthed contemptuously and their borrowed plumage stripped from them with as little remorse as a darky would feel in plucking the feathers from a fat gobbler.

4

A schoolhouse had been erected in the Ross neighborhood and a teacher had been employed. For some reason the school had not prospered. Captain Ross had gone hunting. He seated himself at a water hole and began pondering upon the situation. The unwelcome truth obtruded itself upon his mind that he was raising his children in ignorance. His memory brooded upon the predictions of his relatives when they were trying to dissuade him from going to Texas. Finally, one of them had remarked in derision:

"Ah well, let him go. In a few years he will come back from Texas in an old cart drawn by a crop-eared mule, and he will be followed by a gang of yellow dogs covered with mange. In that cart, and walking behind it, will sit a set of ignorant boobies, who would not know a schoolhouse from a hog pen or a schoolmaster from a Hottentot."

Ross determined to proceed to Austin and there to educate his children. He returned home and communicated his intention to Mrs. Ross. She simply remarked: "You have been a long time coming to that conclusion."

He went to Captain Monroe's place and told the captain what he intended to do. Monroe opposed the scheme. Ross assured him he was in earnest.

"I have 160 acres of land in the bottom and 130 acres here," Ross said. "Give me your wagon and that yoke of black oxen and you can have the land."

Monroe thought Ross might be funning. When the contrary became evident, the trade was made.

When the wagon had been loaded and a start about to be made, Armistead inquired in some trepidation:

---

drinks to excess." Almost at the same time the Captain, clad only in hunting shirt, with leather breeches across his shoulder was seen approaching. That quilting was immediately adjourned, and the Captain and his wife met alone, and no report of the meeting was ever published.

(Susan Turnham McCown [ed. by L. W. Kemp], "Early Days in Milam County: Reminiscences of Susan Turnham McCown," *Southwestern Historical Quarterly*, L, 372.)

"Which way now sir?"

"The way the heads of the oxen are turned," was the reply.

This reassured Armistead; he had no inclination to go any nearer the Indian camps.

When Captain Ross reached Austin, he met friends and acquaintances. Among the former was James B. Shaw, who was several years comptroller of Texas. Ross sold some hogs, clothed his family genteelly, and got employment. The children were placed in school, and they made good progress.

5

One day an officer of the United States Army with a file of soldiers came to the door of Ross' office and inquired:

"Is Mr. Ross here?"

"That is my name, sir. What will you have?"

"General Harney wishes to see you at the governor's office."

Ross wended his way to that point, wondering all the while what he had done to cause General [William S.] Harney to send for him. Ushered into the general's presence he was quite surprised to hear him say:

"I want you to raise a company of rangers. Can you do it in twenty days?"

"If I do not do it in ten days, I will report the failure to you."

The company was raised and led to a camp on Little River. On the twelfth day Captain Ross reported in person to General Harney at Austin. This prompt action inspired confidence at headquarters as well as among the people. Very soon, settlers occupied the country adjacent to the ranger camp.

The next encampment was on the San Gabriel and the one after that on Berry's Creek; the next move was to the Three Forks of Little River. To each place the pioneer settlers went. It was not the number of fights a command may have had or the number of Indians they may have killed, but the degree of confidence which they inspired that rendered them useful to the frontier.

In 1846 the company was ordered to Mexico under what is known as the "Curtis Call."[2] Ross' company was increased to one hundred men

---

[2] In 1846 Colonel Samuel R. Curtis, senior officer on the Río Grande with headquarters at Camargo, Mexico, requested that Washington raise 50,000 men for American forces in Mexico. Curtis then called on Governor Henderson to fill part of his requisition with Texan volunteers. This requisition was known as the "Curtis Call."

and was for a while stationed near San Antonio. Captain [Marshall S.] Howe of the United States Army was at the period in command of the Texas frontier. It is unpleasant to be compelled to say he was not popular. He was accused of ordering incomplete rations of subsistence to be issued to the Texas troops in camp near San Antonio. They were destined at that juncture for service in Mexico and were entitled to a battalion commander. Captain H. E. McCulloch and Captain Tom I. Smith were candidates for the office of major. Captain Howe refused to order an election. Captain Ross called at his office and requested him to do so. Captain Howe insisted the major-elect would assume command at once and order him off. Ross gave him his word of honor to the contrary, assuring him the battalion would be moved at once in the direction of Mexico. Captain Howe wrote an order for the election, but added a proviso that the major-elect should not assume command of the battalion until after it had crossed the San Pedro on the way to Mexico. Ross told him he could take his own order; Ross would not be the bearer of any such document.

Captain Howe became angry and hissed out: "Do you know who you are talking to, sir?"

"Yes, sir, I do. I am talking to Captain Howe."

"Well, sir, I will have you court-martialed and cashiered."

"Before you do that I will throw you into the river and drown you."

Suiting the action to the word, Ross seized the captain by the nape of the neck and the seat of the pants and carried him to the bannister. While the struggle was going on, Captain Smith and Captain McCulloch came into the office. They relieved Captain Howe and expostulated with Captain Ross, supposing the circumstance would get him into trouble and operate at the disadvantage of the ranger force.

The next day Captain Howe sent for Captain Ross. The latter went with some misgivings. The meeting was friendly. Captain Howe inquired of Ross what would satisfy the rangers.

"They wish to elect a major," Ross replied, "and proceed at once to Mexico. They are wasting time and rations here."

Captain Howe ordered an election. It came off the next day. Smith was elected major. The next day the battalion started for Camargo, Mexico.

The march was without many incidents. Two days before reaching Rancho Davis, a white flag was displayed on a hill to the right and west of the road. Major Tom I. Smith ordered Captain Ross to ascertain what it meant. He moved with a detachment. On nearing the flag he was met by Yellow Wolf, the celebrated Comanche chief. Yellow Wolf was anxious to know where the Texians were going. "To fight in Mexico" was the answer. He averred he was at war with Mexico and agreed not to molest the Americans.

That night the mustangs stampeded many of the rangers' horses and the quartermaster mules. The next day the Comanches returned the animals.

While at Rancho Davis, Major Smith received orders from General Taylor directing him to return to the Texas frontier and post the different companies of his battalion so as to give protection to the border settlers. Major Smith marched the command to Camargo to obtain supplies for the long march he had to make. Here General [George] Croghan ordered Major Smith to take his battalion and escort him to Monterey. The major took fifty men and accompanied the general to Cerralvo, where he was relieved by a regular officer and force.

Ross, as senior captain, marched the battalion to Guerrero, Mexico, and remained there until Smith and McCulloch returned from Cerralvo. The order to return to the Texas frontier was repeated. Major Smith moved the battalion to Laredo, turned in his wagons, retained the pack mules, and marched for the upper frontier.

6

After the Mexican War Captain Ross commanded an escort for Major Neighbors when he met the Anadarkoes and the Caddoes under José María in council at Fort Graham. The secretary of war announced his intention to continue the companies of Ross and H. E. McCulloch for another term of twelve months.

Captain Ross settled at Waco in 1847 with an understanding that he was to receive a certain quantity of land and the privilege of establishing and running a ferry across the Brazos River. He also started a farm. He took a part in the transaction of public affairs and always acted with the advocates of progress. He gave his sons a very good education and fitted each of them to play his part in the great drama of life. Mrs. Ross sent her daughters to school at the Baylor University. She was the first white woman ever in Waco.

During 1848, McLennan, Davis, and Richardson settled, by permission, on the Bosque River outside the line of posts. Ross with thirty men accompanied Major Neighbors to a point which is now in Palo Pinto County. There they met Hadebar's band of Caddoes. He said he had lived at that place twenty-one years. North of the Brazos from there, the Wichitas and Towakoni lived. At the distance of eight miles was a Waco village. The intention to visit these Indians was well nigh defeated. The

Brazos River rose very high and was therefore impassable. The rations being exhausted, the whites had to live on watermelons and roasting ears. The men grumbled and Major Neighbors directed Captain Ross to send them back to camp. Ross ordered twenty-five of them to return and put them in the charge of Alpheus D. Neal.

The Brazos fell in about a week. Neighbors ordered the party to accompany him to the other bank to visit White Feather, chief of the Wacoes. When the party came near White Feather's camp, he came forward and received them with great pomp. All were invited to enter a large wigwam. Captain Ross, Doc Sullivan, and Kirke went in with their pistols on. On observing this, White Feather commented on the peculiar appearance of men coming to hold a peace talk and wearing arms. This was interpreted by Leon Williams. Captain Ross said:

"Tell him our business is to fight and not to treat."

The chief averred his ignorance of the fact. Things looked dubious.

Jim Shaw expected trouble. He said: "Major Neighbors, the government of the United States pays me $500 a year to interpret and not to fight."

Ross called Leon Williams' attention to warriors who were coming in with sprung bows concealed under their blankets and robes and occupying scaffolds erected for bedding purposes. These scaffolds ran nearly two-thirds of the distance around the outer edges of the wigwams and were elevated several feet above the earthen floor where the fire was built.

During the council Major Neighbors accused the Wacoes of having violated the provisions of a treaty in not restraining their men from stealing horses from the people of Texas. Ahhedot inquired of the major to know "if he supposed people who had been raised to steal could be induced to stop all at once. It must be done little by little." He averred they had gathered up the horses which the Wacoes had stolen from the whites and that was all they could do. When the big talk ended the Indians delivered to the Texians eighteen horses.

The next move was an invitation from White Feather to be his guests at a feast. The whites were in no condition to refuse the alluring proposition. An immense kettle and a number of wooden bowls were brought in and set before us. White Feather's sergeant was the master of ceremonies. He had a long, sharp stick; this he would plunge into the kettle and bring it up with a dumpling made of corn meal on the end. He would carefully lick off any thick, watery substance adhering to the viand, then he would make a deposit in the wooden bowl. Leon Williams had the bad manners to express a hope that the sergeant would not lick his dumpling, but he reckoned without his host; the sergeant was equally polite to all. While the feast was progressing, a white man made his appearance in the festive crowd. Major Neighbors asked his name, residence, and business. He said that his name was Miller, that he was from the Indian Territory, and that he had come to trade with the Texas Indians.

"Trade what?" asked the major.

"Whiskey," said Miller.

"You know it is against the law to sell whiskey to Indians," the major said. "It is my duty to visit your camp and ascertain whether you have whiskey. I shall be there in the morning, and if I find things as you say, I shall hang you."

The visit was made and Miller was missing.

The whites left the next day and travelled down the country. When about opposite where Weatherford now stands, a party of four Cherokees —three men and a woman—were encountered. They were going to trade whiskey to Texas Indians for horses. Major Neighbors assured them the traffic was illegal and dangerous to the people of Texas because it impelled the Indians to kill them and steal their horses. He told them his duty compelled him to pour their five or six kegs of "busthead" on the ground. At this declaration Captain Ross saw one of the Cherokees inspecting his gun and knew he meant to fight. Ross, Sullivan, and Kirke with pistols in hand closed in on them and the others spilled the liquor without being molested. The proposition then was to ride fast that day, perhaps the next, and to camp in an out-of-the-way place. This was to be done to save their horses; the Cherokees would be almost sure to follow after and steal them to pay for the spilled whiskey.[3] Camp was made without any mishap.

The next trip was made with a view to visit the different tribes with which treaties had been made. Captain Ross took thirty men with him. While they were at a Caddo village, in what is now Palo Pinto County, considerable excitement was caused by the arrival of Mopochocupee—

---

[3] For years Major Neighbors had had considerable trouble with whiskey traders. Their liquor was considered a major factor in the decade of Indian uprisings. When drunk the Indians would paint themselves lavishly and then would gallop off to raid and plunder any settlement they happened upon. "In the absence of all law regulating intercourse with our wild bands," Neighbors wrote W. Medill on September 14, 1847, "and the serious difficulties attending the introduction of ardent spirits into their country, I shall be compelled, for self-preservation and the protection of our frontier settlers, to deal with the traders in the most summary manner." The worst troublemakers were the clandestine *Comancheros*—traders from Santa Fé who traveled among the Comanches exchanging whiskey and guns for horses. Neighbors, Ross, and Ford were convinced that these traders encouraged the red men to steal horses from the Texas settlers.

(Ford to Runnels, June 2, 1858, Governors' Letters, 1846–1860, ms.)

Owl—the principal or peace chief of all the bands of the Comanches. He was accompanied by two hundred old men, women, and youths. He had come to trade. His people did not plant anything, and they were anxious to procure anything in the shape of fruits and vegetables. The Owl exchanged a valuable horse for about sixty ears of corn. Fine skins were bartered for pumpkins, melons, and so on.

The Owl had an interview with Major Neighbors. He had the reputation of being an orator. He made a long speech in which he congratulated himself that the Great Spirit had permitted him to come there and see his friends and through them to hear from his great father at Washington. He said that he had told the Comanche women he knew they would steal but that they must not steal from the whites. In the event they disobeyed his orders he would give them a punishment not usual for a woman to bear. The Owl was rather a model Comanche. He usually talked to the point and expressed his sentiments. He kept his promises more faithfully than many of his countrymen.

From this chief, Major Neighbors learned that Santana and his Comanche band were on the Clear Fork of the Brazos; Toshaway and Porchanaquaheap—Buffalo Hump—were near the Double Mountain Fork of the Brazos. One of Major Neighbors' main objects was to secure the friendship of their powerful tribe and to ensure a permanent peace with them. They had done great injury to the border settlements in Texas.

The line of march was for Santanna's camp. On Hubbard's Creek the Texians met Ketumse, a war captain in Santanna's band. Ketumse had employed five Seminoles who were inclined to run off when the whites came in sight. They had assured Ketumse they were friendly with the Texians, but a flight proved to the contrary.

Ketumse accompanied the whites to Santanna's camp. That chief summoned a council. When it had met, Santanna informed Major Neighbors that he had fifty men in Mexico getting horses and mules. Neighbors informed him he had orders from Washington to put a stop to stealing from Mexico. He inquired whether Santanna would assist him in the matter. The chieftain returned a decided "no," saying: "We have made a treaty with you and we have observed its terms. We made a treaty with Mexico. Under the guise of friendship her troops surrounded a party of our people going among them to trade and fired into them. We will not treat with a people so treacherous."

Neighbors' efforts in this direction were made in compliance with an article in the treaty of Guadalupe Hidalgo concerning the restraining of our Indians in the matter of depredating upon the people of Mexico. The United States had to back down eventually, acknowledge herself unable to comply with the stipulations of the treaty, and enter into another arrangement.

In this connection it may be mentioned that Major Neighbors discussed the Mexican question with Buffalo Hump, who became indignant, declaring that he would never make peace with the Mexicans as long as water ran or grass grew. He accused the Mexicans of perfidy. "One of their officers had my daughter for his wife. She was taken by foul means from a man with whom they were at peace; and they have persistently and inhumanly refused to restore her to me."

Several months prior to this, Captain William G. Crump had command of a company on duty south and west of San Antonio. A difficulty occurred with the Lipan Indians, Captain Crump insisting that these Indians had stolen some of his company horses. The Lipans were attacked and a goodly number of them killed, probably thirty. The facts in the case were brought to light at the council with Santanna in this wise: Santanna spoke of the provisions of the treaty relative to the boundaries of the Indian hunting grounds in the direction of the white settlements, as designated by the line of stations or posts established first by Colonel Hays and later changed to suit the advancing line of settlers. He said no Indian could properly pass below that line unless he bore a written permission from the commander of a station; and he affirmed that the Comanches had not violated that regulation.

Carnebonahit, a war captain, arose to make a talk. He said he started for Mexico with a war party. He was careful to travel above the line of posts; notwithstanding a company of Americans which charged him, dispersed his men, and broke up his expedition. He followed after these men in order to learn whether they belonged below or above the line of posts and found they belonged below. On his way he found a man holding seven horses. Carnebonahit charged him and took the seven horses. He moved on, going northward, and struck the camp of Chiquito, the Lipan chief. That chief said at once:

"These are American horses."

"Yes," Carnebonahit replied.

"The Americans will follow the trail to my camp," Chiquito said, "and will fight me and my people for what you have done."

"I don't care. You and your men have piloted the Americans to the Comanche camps."

Carnebonahit then rode off.

Major Neighbors, finding nothing favorable to Mexico could be effected, returned to the trading house.

In order to clear up this matter, we will look ahead. In January, 1849,

Chiquito came to Ross at Bosque Station. When the Lipan chief learned Ross was no longer "a big captain" he refused to talk with Major [Ripley A.] Arnold of the United States Army. He solicited Ross to go with him to Barnard's Trading House to see Major Neighbors; he did so.

Chiquito assured Major Neighbors he had come to make peace and to stop the killing. He explained how he had gotten into trouble with Captain Crump, related the coming of Carnebonahit, the conversation, and the trailing of the seven horses into his camp. He said he saw the Americans coming and made an effort to explain, but the Americans were too mad to listen. They killed 25 or 30 of his people and carried off two hundred horses. If Captain Crump had opened his ears Chiquito would have told him all and would have gone with him after Carnebonahit. Chiquito took the remnant of his people and fled to Mexico. From there he made war upon the Americans.

"The last man I killed had saddlebags and appeared to live on York's Creek."

Neighbors and Ross recognized the dead man to be Captain York.

"That was not the last," Major Neighbors said. "You killed a man near where I live and cut him all to pieces."

"No, my people did not kill him; two of them saw two Tonks; each one had a man's thigh tied to his saddle. The Lipans do not eat their enemies."

He promptly agreed to face the Tonkawas. Major Neighbors saw him safely there and despatched a messenger for Major Arnold. He came.

Placido, the noble old chieftain, had his Tonks assembled. He informed his people of the tale Chiquito had circulated. If any of them killed the man in question, he earnestly besought them to come out and aver the fact and not let the innocent suffer. He told them he was resolved to carry out the treaty. Two Tonks rose to their feet and announced themselves as the slayers of that particular man. By way of extenuation they pleaded that he was not a *pavotivo*—white man—but a *moshotivo*—a bearded man, or German. They were liable to be held for murder under the treaty. Major Neighbors requested Major Arnold to take charge of them and keep them safely until they could be tried in accordance with the treaty.

"I am not subject to your orders," Major Arnold replied.

"Will you accede to the request if I reduce it to writing?" Major Neighbors inquired.

Major Arnold declined. He turned to Placido and Campo and notified them that he, Arnold, held them responsible for the two men and for the production of their bodies when called for. If they were not forthcoming he would have Placido and Campo in their stead. The two chiefs affirmed that they had no safe place to keep the men and that they might run off. They called Major Arnold's attention to the fact that he had a house in which to keep prisoners and had men to guard them. Major Arnold persisted in his decision.

After this affair, Placido and Campo had a consultation and concluded safety consisted in flight. How to go was the question. The killers had gone to the Comanches, and the chiefs felt sure they would hang in their places. They stole twenty-two horses from the neighboring settlers, Barnes, and others. They went to different tribes, but none were willing to protect them. After an absence of some months, Placido came back. He acknowledged that he had done wrong, dwelt on the temptation, and wound up by telling the Americans: "Here I am. Take me and do what you please with me." Nothing was done. The murderers were beyond reach, and no one felt that the chiefs were to blame. The settlers got back all the horses still alive and cared nothing for those lost. These were results flowing, in part, from the speech of Carnebonahit.

Mopochocupee never failed to respond when a circumstance occurred to test his fidelity to his pledges of friendship. On one occasion Major Neighbors was in Mopochocupee's camp; the Kiowas were encamped near by and manifested a feeling of hostility to the Texians. They marched by Neighbors' camp, displayed American scalps, and announced their intention to kill him. They sent him three messages of similar import. Six or eight Tonks, who were living with the Comanches, joined the major and assured him they would stand by him till death. Mopochocupee remonstrated with the Kiowas to no purpose. He then put himself squarely on the war path and said: "Before you can harm a hair on Neighbors' head, you will have to whip me and my Comanches."

This had the desired effect. To cut off all chance of treachery and surprise, when Neighbors left Mopochocupee furnished him with a strong escort to the white settlements.

7

The setting apart of four leagues of land on the Brazos and the same quantity on the Clear Fork for the establishment of two Indian agencies and reservations has been noticed. In 1855 Captain Ross received a communication from Supervising Indian Agent Robert S. Neighbors, then at

Washington City, requesting him to meet the Indians at the Brazos
Agency and hold them there until Neighbors could arrive with presents.
Captain Ross complied. Major Neighbors arrived with a commission for
Shapley P. Ross as Indian agent at the Brazos Agency. He entered on the
discharge of his duties on September 1, 1855. He relieved G. W. Hill,
who had been secretary of war of the Republic of Texas during President
Houston's second administration. Captain Ross expressed gratitude for
his kindness in aiding him to procure the appointment.

"You owe nothing to me," Hill replied. "The Indians through their
chiefs procured your appointment. They spoke of a tall man living on
the Brazos who had fought them four years and had treated them well;
he is brave, and brave men are not mean." Hill resigned on account of ill
health and died not long afterward.

The Indians under Captain Ross' charge were Delawares, Shawnees,
Caddoes, Wacoes, and others, all somewhat advanced in the habits of
civilized people. The agent's knowledge of the Indian sign language and
of the Caddo tongue and his long acquaintance with their race gave him
facilities for communication which few Americans possessed.

Not long after his appointment, Captain Ross was told by Jim Shaw,
the interpreter, that a Tahuacano Indian desired to speak with him in
private. Ross went into his office. A large Indian soon confronted him
there. His first salutation was "get up." Ross arose. The next expression
was: "You killed my brother."

Ross felt like a man who needed a revolver and a Bowie knife.

"He was the only brother I had, the bravest man on the frontier. Now
I want you to be my brother. If you consent I will do all you tell me—go
when you ask me and stay as long as you like." He produced a large mesquite thorn, raised the skin and muscle of his left side over his heart, ran
the thorn through the flesh, and cut out the thorn with his knife. He held
up the bloody token and called on the Great Spirit to witness his sincerity
in adopting Ross as his brother. Ross recognized him as the brother of
Big Foot, whom Ross had slain years before.

To the credit of the red man, he complied faithfully with his promise.
He wished to take the name of some grand American and expressed a
preference for George Washington. Human hopes and human vanity are
often consigned to the same grave.

In the year 1858 the writer remembers to have accidentally happened
into a wigwam where a dance of Indian ladies and gentlemen was progressing. He heard the irreverent boys exclaim: "Go it, Guts."

Looking into a corner, Ford saw Ross' brother making music by frantically shaking two gourds full of loose seeds; the dancers were keeping step to this cadenced sound.

8

In 1858 Captain Ross became an able assistant of the writer in making a campaign to the Canadian against the hostile Indians, which was noticed under that heading. The success of the expedition caused some unpleasant comments on the part of the regular officers on duty in Texas. They accused Captain Ross of partiality in favor of volunteer officers. He assured them he was ready to aid in rendering any expedition successful under a regular officer.

Placido and some other chiefs protested against their agent taking part in any other campaign.

"You might get killed and white people might think we had done it ourselves or had betrayed you to the enemy. You are as liable to be hit as any of us. Remember what your death might cost us. We depend on you as children do upon a father and should deplore your loss as sincerely as if we were your children."

Major Earl Van Dorn announced his intention to make an expedition against the hostile Comanches; Captain Ross promised him the co-operation of the Brazos Agency Indians. Major Van Dorn moved out to Salt Creek where he was joined by Captain Ross with about 100 Indians. They were almost the same men who had composed the Indian contingent in Ford's Canadian River Expedition. About this time Sul Ross arrived from school. He was then about twenty years old. Placido and others made a great ado. The old chief waited on Captain Ross and informed him:

"We have a young captain now. He will lead us into battle. We know he is brave, and we will follow him. You must stay and take care of our families while we are on the war path."

Ross' health admonished him to heed Placido's words. He assembled the Indians and addressed them:

"You have chosen this boy as your commander. I want you to promise to obey his orders as strictly as he will obey the orders of Major Van Dorn."

The promise was made and not broken.

In the engagement which occurred with the Comanches, Major Van Dorn and Captain Sul Ross were both wounded.

The Indians accompanied other regular officers on expeditions, but no results of much consequence were attained.

9

A belief was prevalent among the citizens of the counties below the reservations that the Indians residing there were implicated in the murders and robberies perpetrated on frontiersmen. Citizens organized and some skirmishing ensued. Matters assumed an aspect so threatening that Captain Ross reported to the commissioner of Indian affairs that, in his opinion, the Indians could not be retained on the Texas reservations without trouble and danger to life. He felt sad at the idea of putting a stop to the work of civilizing a people who might, in time, become useful as producers and capable of being made excellent irregular troops and first-class scouts and spies. He yielded to the inevitable. He consulted the chiefs and laid the facts before them. They agreed to accept homes on the Chickasaw lands in the Indian Territory.

The order for removal came in 1859. Captain Ross was in charge of the Indians. They were escorted by Major [George H.] Thomas in command of two hundred United States cavalry. The move cost the Indians considerably. Several years previous to this the government had given the Indians of the Brazos Agency three hundred cows; these had increased to about fifteen hundred. When preparations were being made to leave, these cattle were much scattered. Quite all of them were off the reservation. Captain [John Henry] Brown, commanding a company of State troops, said he had orders from the governor of Texas to shoot any Indian he found off the reservation. He had the credit of refusing to allow Indians with passes to gather their own stock. In this way they were compelled to abandon nearly all their cows. They also left horses.

Captain Ross bade adieu to the red men he had known and controlled so long. They loved him and were willing to confide everything—even life—to his keeping.[4]

---

[4] For Indian Agents Shapley P. Ross and Robert S. Neighbors, the removal of the Indians was a sad and sordid affair. These two men, more than anyone else, had tried their best to help the Indians who since 1836 had been cheated and deceived by the Texas government and by unruly settlers. When the last Indian had crossed the Red River into the Indian Territory (present-day Oklahoma), Neighbors wrote his wife:

I have this day crossed all the Indians out of the heather land of "Texas" and am now "out of the land of the Philistines."

If you want to hear a full description of our Exodus out of Texas read the "Bible" where the children of Israel crossed the Red Sea. We have had about the same show, only our enemies did not follow us to R. River. If they had—the Indians would have in all probability sent them back without the interposition of Divine Providence.

The enemies to whom he refers were John R. Baylor and Allison Nelson who, as I pointed out above, were hell-bent on destroying Neighbors and killing every Indian on the reservations.

(Kenneth Franklin Neighbours, "Robert S. Neighbors in Texas, 1836–1859: A Quarter Century of Frontier Problems," ms., II, 676.)

Soon after the removal, Major Neighbors was killed by Americans.[5] Not long afterward Captain Ross received an order to proceed to San Antonio to meet two clerks and aid them in settling the accounts of Major Neighbors. The labor was performed. The United States was indebted to Robert S. Neighbors, late supervising Indian agent in Texas, the sum of seven hundred dollars: an incontrovertible proof of his honesty in the administration of financial affairs.

Captain Ross received pay in full up to date. He continued to draw his salary up to the passage of the ordinance of secession by the people of Texas. His age precluded him from taking a very active part in the military operations. He was impressed with the importance of securing the neutrality of his old Indian wards, if their services could not be had in a manner not repugnant to humanity. For instance, they might have been used in procuring horses for the Confederate service. The chiefs had communicated with Ross and would have followed him. He visited Austin, procured an interview with the governor, and explained the matter. He did not propose an outlay of capital, but asked for some official recog-

---

[5] When he had the Indians safely established on their new reservation, Neighbors with great relief returned to Texas. "I have thank God got clear of the cares of the Indians," he wrote in the saddle, "and have sent my resignation as superintendent—and if I live to get home and keep my senses I think I will never hold another Indian appointment."

He stopped at the county and district clerk's office in Belknap to wind up Indian affairs. Just as he was leaving, he saw in the street about fifty yards away a young gunman who shouted:

"Neighbors, I understand that you have said that I am a horse-thief. Is it so?"

"No, sir, I never did," the major said, stepping into the street.

Suddenly the gunman made a play for his pistol and at the same moment a tremendous blast tore away the shoulders and the back of Neighbors' head—a man with a shotgun jumped from the roof of a nearby building, mounted his horse, and the two killers galloped out of town and into hiding, never to be brought to justice.

Neighbors died twenty minutes after the shooting. It is said that an old Indian who had seen it all limped up to the dying man, fell over him and wept for an entire day. When the reserve Indians heard about the killing, they wailed and moaned for days, even threatened revenge Indian style.

"Thus had the spirit of human envy and hatred found its fruition," grieved one of Neighbors' close friends, "not alone in the woes of unoffending Indians, but also in the untimely taking off of as gallant a knight as any who ever balanced a lance or drew a broadsword in behalf of the oppressed." The slaying of a man who had devoted his life to helping a backward and minority people "is but one more example of man's inhumanity to man" and forces one to "question the rightfulness of the claim" of the white race "to supremacy among the sons of men. It is to be hoped that the story of these men" —Indian Agents Neighbors, Shapley Ross, and Mat Leper—"who risked not only their personal standing by reason of their championship of an unpopular cause, but even life itself, may not be forgotten, while men would inspire their children with the example of unselfish service. If other men acquired fame in war, let it be remembered also that these wrought mightily for peace."

(Neighbours, "Neighbors," ms., II, 692–699.)

nition containing at least a shadow of authority on which to base his action. Governor [Francis R.] Lubbock replied that those Indians were outside of Texas, and that he had no authority to do anything in the premises. It is probable he did not fully comprehend the proposition of Captain Ross. In any event Ross abandoned the idea, though he continued to take a deep interest in the cause of the South.

After the close of the Civil War he remained at Waco and took part in the political doings of the times. His failing health induced him to try the climate of California. At the earnest solicitation of the children he had left behind, he returned to Texas in 1870. He no doubt felt unwilling to sever the ties binding him to the old pioneers with whom he had fought and suffered.

He was a man of good sense, candid in the expression of his opinions, willing to incur responsibility when backed by a sense of rectitude, a good friend and a fearless enemy, a useful citizen, charitable, and ever ready to assist the unfortunate. As a husband, a father, and a relative he bore himself blamelessly. He is now gone. If a useful life, a desire to assist his fellow men, and an undeviating honesty add anything to a man's chances to be blessed in the other world, we may feel an undoubted assurance that Captain Ross is enjoying unending bliss.

Appendix II

>>>

RICHARD KING AND
MIFFLIN KENEDY
The Business Wizards of South Texas

IN THE HISTORY OF A SECTION there are men who take the lead in affairs and control the actions of the people to a great extent. They impress upon all with whom they come in contact much of their own individuality. They appear not to rule, for much of their own action is produced by the men who act with them and much is produced by men who, while not under their control, sense the correctness of their views. In matters pertaining to the advancement of public affairs, their influence is felt and acknowledged. It may be truly said of such men that their works live after them. Such must be the verdict of the people of the lower Río Grande when they take into consideration the actions of Richard King and Mifflin Kenedy.

Mifflin Kenedy came to the lower Río Grande in 1846. He was then the commander of the *Corvette*, a steamboat belonging to the United States Quartermaster Department. She was plying between the mouth of the Río Grande and Camargo and Mier. Captain Kenedy had brought her from Pittsburgh, where she had been built. It is needless to say that he did his duty well and that he acquired the confidence and the esteem of all with whom he had transactions.

In the year 1847 Captain Richard King arrived on the Río Grande. He was employed as pilot on the *Corvette*. In this manner the names of these two gentlemen became associated. They remained associated until the close of the war between Mexico and the United States. They had won honor and the confidence of men who controlled affairs. They had won the confidence of the public.

In the year 1850 a company was formed. It was known as M. Kenedy & Co. and consisted of M. Kenedy, Richard King, Charles Stillman, and James O'Donnell. In 1852 Captain Kenedy purchased O'Donnell's interest. This firm continued in existence for about fifteen years. It was the main reliance for navigation from the port of Brazos Santiago to Roma, the center of navigation on the Río Grande in those days.

In 1850 the company had two boats on the Río Grande—the *Comanche* and the *Grampus*. Captain King and Captain Kenedy each commanded a boat. Whatever could be effected by prudence, foresight, and good management was done. Annually, millions of dollars worth of merchandise entered the customhouse of Brazos Santiago on Point Isabel. The merchandise was transported to Brownsville, Matamoros, Río Grande City, and other points along the river. A large proportion of it was carried into the northeastern States of Mexico. The carrying trade of the Río Grande was extremely lucrative, and those engaged in it soon amassed fortunes. Men possessing capacity, energy, and wealth were not likely to remain silent spectators of events they might control. M. Kenedy & Co. soon became an important factor in the affairs of the lower Río Grande. The firm possessed the requirements calculated to produce good results. It encouraged every enterprise calculated to promote the development of the natural resources of the country.

It must be remembered that in 1850 there was only a single family living on the road made by General Taylor from Corpus Christi to Brownsville—a distance of about one hundred and sixty-five miles. The country was infested with companies of Mexicans who frequently united the business of corralling wild mustangs and murdering and robbing travellers. The Comanches made descents into this district ostensibly to capture horses to ride and to eat, but really to kill the men and to make mistresses and slaves of women and children. In 1850 troops were stationed at various points to give protection to the settlers in the valleys of the Río Grande and the Nueces and to those engaged in mercantile pursuits. The writer has spoken of this matter elsewhere.

Life on the border of Texas was wild, rough, and dangerous. There were few points on the border where a family could locate without incurring dangers from which the boldest would recoil. The operations of the troops had inspired a degree of confidence, yet it remained to be seen who would be the first to make the venture to cast his fortunes in a district where life was menaced almost continuously and where property had no security beyond the range of the rifle and the six-shooter. It was Captain Richard King who made the first move in the matter of settling between the Río Grande and the Nueces. He came to the lands of the Santa Gertrudis and became one of the pioneers of that country. Of this more hereafter.

2

In 1851 the Carbajal Revolution occurred. He had the support of King and Kenedy and a majority of their friends on the Río Grande below Río Grande City. The object of the revolution was favorable to liberty as it was understood in the South. The question has been treated of in the chapter on Carbajal. M. Kenedy & Co. was the head and front of the movement. The course pursued by Mifflin Kenedy was mentioned above. He saw the condition of affairs in Mexico and was willing to do all in his power to avert disaster and to cause the Mexicans to do something to save themselves. What he suggested was discussed above. His suggestions are among the things of the past which cannot be portrayed; and hence they can only be judged of, and each man will be governed by his preconceived ideas. Had General Carbajal taken the position of president of the projected republic, it would have given power and respectability to the cause, but he preferred another course, and the cause was lost. It may have come to a bad end anyway. So let it pass.

In 1852 Captain Richard King, in company with Captain G. K. Lewis, better known as "Legs" Lewis, established a cattle ranch on the Santa Gertrudis Creek. They made their headquarters near where Captain Ford's old camp stood in 1849. This cattle camp became a stopping-place for wayfarers, a sort of city of refuge for all classes, the timorous and the hungry. The men who held it were of no ordinary mould. They had come to stay. It was no easy matter to scare them. The Indians still made descents upon the country. The regular troops were operating against them. In many of the fights the red men appeared to have been victorious. They fought in a manner at variance with that in which the drilled troops of the United States had been taught to fight. The savages had the advantage in numbers and in movement. But all this had no effect on the brave men who held the ranch of Santa Gertrudis. They had determined to make a ranch on the Santa Gertrudis or leave their bones to tell of their failure.

The company at Brownsville pursued the even tenor of its way. M. Kenedy & Co. aided enterprising men, encouraged the industrious, and was open-handed to the unfortunate and the afflicted. Kenedy and partners had extensive relations with Mexico and were always on the side of those who were struggling against the intolerable oppressions set on foot by the agents of a centralized military despotism, whose instincts and practices were prompted by unmitigated tyranny. On many occasions they took an active part in elections. In State and Federal campaigns they made it a rule to support the Democratic party. It was a difficult matter to be successful against them. They were zealously in favor of advancing the interests of the Río Grande region.

These were the palmy days of Brownsville. The trade of many of the northern states of Mexico came in by the way of the lower Río Grande. The quantity of goods entering by way of Brazos de Santiago and the mouth of the Río Grande was enormous. They represented $10,000,000 a year and sometimes $14,000,000 a year. Brownsville became a place noted for rich men. There were King and Kenedy, the firm of Stillman and Belden, W. H. Woodhouse, Don Francisco Ytúrria, Jeremiah Galvan, José San Román, and others who controlled hundreds of thousands of dollars. José San Román was a Spaniard who never had an evil thought. He amassed a large fortune and was never accused of having wronged anyone in its acquisition. He was reputed to be worth millions. It was said in 1859 that the businessmen of Brownsville and their friends in Matamoros could raise a million dollars on short notice. This might have been an exaggeration, yet it was never disputed.

The members of the firm of M. Kenedy & Co. were to a great extent the leaders of the people. Stillman, a millionaire, had little to learn. [Samuel]Belden was a man of parts. Jeremiah Galvan became a leader of the people in many things. To these Kenedy and King were sort of head men. They were really not exacting, and managed by their good sense and a knowledge of their sterling worth. What would have been impossible under other circumstances, they accomplished with ease.

The firm of M. Kenedy & Co. was often called upon by the military authorities of the United States to transport supplies for the troops stationed on the lower Río Grande. They did so on all suitable occasions for the state troops of Texas. It was their custom to extend aid and facilities to forces engaged in defending the frontier. They did the same for the civil authorities of the general and the state governments. Their readiness to procure trustworthy intelligence, to despatch trusty couriers, and to do all in their power to serve the public interests rendered them favorably and conspicuously known in many parts of the Union. They became a support to the citizens of their section and stood by them in prosperity and adversity. The charge was not made against them that they consulted their own interests in public matters and left the people to take care of themselves. They were with the people, and in all political matters they took the lead rather than avoided responsibility.

3

In 1852 Captain Kenedy established a cattle ranch at Valenio on the Nueces River. In 1854 he became the owner of another ranch at San Salvador del Tule, which was one of the first ranches in that country. It was destroyed by General Juan N. Cortina in 1859, when he made war upon the people of the United States and wreaked a bloody vengeance upon Americans whom he could not subjugate.

In 1856 Captain King moved his family from Brownsville to the ranch of Santa Gertrudis. It was an undertaking of great danger. The country between his residence and the Río Grande was thinly settled. The intervening country was raided by Indians. The Mexicans had not acknowledged the supremacy of the Americans. They expected to reconquer the country. For an American to carry his family into the wild country and settle fifty miles from Corpus Christi and one hundred and ten or twenty miles from the Río Grande was looked upon in those days as an act of extreme audacity.

It was the best move Captain King could have made. It gave him an opportunity to display the undaunted spirit he possessed. It raised the cattle ranch from a bachelor establishment to a first-class married establishment, indicating good sense and refinement.

The camp of Captain King had been the seat of hospitality. In it all found welcome. Much was due to the lady-like management of Mrs. King. The guest was reminded of the baronial halls of England which in days gone by were open to all well-behaved comers. On the part of the Texas rancher there was no attempt at display. The viands were easy of reach and abundant. There was a republican simplicity reigning supreme which made all feel comfortable and at home. All were treated as equals whose bearing gave guarantees of respectability. Had an unworthy pretender intruded, the air of respectability surrounding him would have awed him into respectful deportment and language.

Mrs. King was the daughter of the Reverend Hiram Chamberlain, a distinguished clergyman of the Presbyterian Church. He located at Brownsville just after the Mexican War. He was a prominent actor in every movement set on foot for the moral advancement of the people. He was a man who acted from good impulses and who was not afraid to advocate what he thought was right. His daughter was noted for her culture, her capacity, and her beauty. She was the wise counsellor of her husband, his faithful confidant in whom he placed implicit trust. In many cases she was the mentor whose judicious advice achieved success. Yet her demeanor was free from objection. She was meek in deportment, and in no instance did she seem to the observer to possess the power she sometimes employed in the affairs of her husband.

In days gone by, many people in the Northern and Southern states entertained an extremely unfavorable opinion of the people of Texas. Numerous people esteemed the Indian to be the superior of the Texian in many respects. Judge of the surprise of one of these deluded individuals, whose business had brought him to Texas to find men who did not butcher one another. If ever men loved each other, it was among the pioneers of Texas. Judge of the surprise of a man laboring under these mistaken opinions when he entered the residence of Captain King and received the courteous treatment he extended to all, when hospitality was lavished upon him and every aid rendered him which circumstances demanded. Think of his surprise when he was told it was all for good will and there was no charge.

It must be remembered that in those days Indian forays were frequent. The vast frontiers of Texas were peopled by men who feared not; but danger and death came unlooked for, and the women and children were often left unprotected. Santa Gertrudis was deemed a charmed spot on the sea of danger—once within its walls all risks vanished for the time being. The wayfarer felt he was in a circle that violence could not enter.

Two of the faithful friends and servitors of the ranch were Captain James Richardson and, on extraordinary occasions, Captain William Gregory. Richardson was at his post at all times. He was Captain King's head man, in whom he placed implicit trust. Richardson was brave and careful, a good and true man. He was a skilful opponent of Indians and made no mistakes in fighting them. Much in the shape of security to man and beast depended upon his good dispositions and his fearless bravery in meeting danger. Captain Gregory was equally brave upon all occasions and was always at the call of the owner of the Santa Gertrudis ranch when danger menaced.

In after times Hiram Chamberlain, Captain King's brother-in-law, was a manager of affairs on the ranch. Reuben Holbein, his trusted clerk, undeviating friend, and tried adviser, stayed with him till death parted them.

4

The operations of Texian troops in the Cortina War have been noticed previously. Captain Kenedy and Captain Francisco Ytúrria were active in the defense of Brownsville. To say the men of whom we are speaking were entitled to the grateful thanks of the people of that city would be stating the case mildly. Had they been remiss in duty every American and every Mexican who had taken up arms for them would have been slaughtered by Cortina's outlaws. The two gentlemen who commanded the citizen soldiers of Brownsville laid aside their swords in 1860 and returned to their duties as quiet citizens. The men of that time thank them, and their sons cannot refuse to laud them.

The raids of Cortina caused considerable loss to Captain Kenedy. His ranch of Tula was almost ruined. George and Mr. Cornelius Stillman suffered by the robbers. So did numerous others. Captain King promptly furnished all the supplies and all the intelligence needed by the United States and Texas troops. At that time there were some settlements on the road from King's ranch to Brownsville. It was strongly suspected that many Mexicans employed at the ranches were in collusion with Cortina.

After the Cortina War the vessels of M. Kenedy & Co. attained very respectable proportions. They transported vast quantities of merchandise from Brazos de Santiago to Brownsville and Matamoros and to all the places from the mouth of the Río Grande to Camargo on the San Juan River as well as to Roma on the Río Grande. For a long while Captain Kenedy and Captain King commanded steamboats themselves. Each boat had a full complement of officers and men. All the business of each boat was transacted on board. In process of time the number of boats in their service precluded this manner of transacting business; then it was done to a great extent in Brownsville.

In 1860 Captain Kenedy purchased an equal interest with Captain King in the ranch of Santa Gertrudis. Captain Walworth had an interest of 160 acres which the other partners bought and thus became full owners of the ranch. The firm name was Richard King & Co. The hospitalities extended to travellers and sightseers were undiminished. As genuine a welcome was extended to them as in the days gone by. The ranch on the broad bosom of the prairie maintained its celebrity as the resting place of the weary and as an asylum for the needy and distressed. It had won fairly the confidence and the esteem of the public, and has retained the respect of all classes up to date.

5

When the Civil War came, King and Kenedy were recognized as Confederates. They had made common cause with the people with whom they had relations of business, friendship, and affection. Their steamboats were at the use of the Confederate forces. They performed many useful purposes for the South. When the Yankees sent a blockader down to the mouth of the Río Grande, King and Kenedy registered their steamers under the Mexican flag and were thus able to navigate the Río Grande and the Gulf of Mexico unmolested. At this time the writer was in command of the Río Grande District, and he gave his commendation of this act. He was of opinion that the boats were not really under his command, and, even if they were, he could see no reason why they should not be placed under a neutral flag and thus be permitted to perform essential service for the Confederates. When once outside the waters of the Río Grande, the boats, if they had been flying the Confederate flag, would have been conquered or run back. As neutrals they felt bound to become the common carriers of both American belligerents. The war of intervention in Mexico, the advent of General Mejía, an ardent and steadfast supporter of the Maximilian government, the landing of French troops at Bagdad in 1864, and the occasional presence of Juárez' troops along the border rendered it difficult to steer clear of suspicion and some small trouble. Wise counsels prevailed. Everything seemingly disagreeable was successfully tided over, and the boats reaped an unusually rich financial harvest.

But for the services rendered by these boats it would have been a difficult matter to have procured the landing of Confederate supplies at Matamoros upon terms as fair as those granted by M. Kenedy & Co. Matamoros was the place where a large proportion of supplies for the troops and the people of the Trans-Mississippi Department were landed. It was at the time a place of immense business.

The Santa Gertrudis Ranch was visited by the Union troops in 1863, and not long thereafter it was abandoned by Captain King's family. Beef contractors in rounding up the cattle of King and Kenedy and of others acted for a while in safety. The cows were driven to Brownsville for the use of the Union army. In this and various other ways losses occurred to cattle owners living between the Río Grande and the Nueces.

These and other causes led Colonel Ford to undertake to aid the Confederates in the Río Grande country in 1864. On arriving at camp on the San Fernando, a creek some miles this side of King and Kenedy's ranch, Ford found Richard King serving as a private in Captain Richardson's company, if memory is right. King did his duty well, if the testimony of his officers can be taken as the truth.

Just after the close of the Civil War, General Fred Steele was sent to the Río Grande as commander of the troops of the United States. He sent for Colonel Ford, who was in Matamoros, and a good understanding was arrived at. In a short time the firm of King, Kenedy & Co.[1] was once again performing its accustomed duty. The promoters of disturbances were ferreted out and arrested.

When the District Court convened at Brownsville in 1867, Captain M. Kenedy and other prominent citizens served as grand and petit jury-men. Captain Kenedy was foreman of two grand juries. John S. Ford, at the request of Judge [John Charles] Watrous of the Federal court, also acted as foreman of a grand jury. Every proper effort was made to exe-cute the laws and to bring the offenders to justice. More than seventy offenders were convicted and sent to the penitentiary. The fact of Captain Kenedy's agreeing to serve two terms on the grand jury had a good effect on the citizens. All felt assured that he would not indict anyone without cause. His name to an indictment was esteemed a rather clear proof of guilt. At one—if not both—terms of the court, the grand and the petit jurors gave the county of Cameron their services free of cost.

6

At the early part of the Civil War, quite a number of stockraisers carried large herds of cattle south of the Nueces River. They squatted on the lands of others. Some of these men managed to purchase small tracts of land; others squatted wherever they could. Thus mere specks of earth were made the pretext for the right to graze their thousands of cattle upon thousands of acres of land upon which the stock owners had no right, not even so much as a lease or even the assent of the owners. Warm feelings, not devoid of bitterness, were engendered, but no scenes of vio-lence were enacted. The cessation of war in 1865 did not change the situation materially. The squatters remained. Those holding titles to these broad acres complained that they were deprived of the use of property they had owned for many years. For these and other reasons landholders in that part of Texas conceived the idea of enclosing their lands by fences. Captain Kenedy was a pioneer in the matter of building pasture fences. In 1868 he constructed a fence thirty-six miles in length. It stretched across the throat of a peninsula and enclosed 131,000 acres of land. This was the ranch of Laureles. This soon became a place of note. Other ranchers followed suit. The actuating motive was self-protection. In 1870 Captain King began to fence in the ranch of Santa Gertrudis. In circum-ference it was estimated to be one hundred and twenty miles.

---

[1] In the summer of 1866, the steamboat firm of M. Kenedy & Co. underwent a complete reorganization and took a new name: King, Kenedy & Co.

Just previous to this King and Kenedy had agreed to dissolve their partnership. In January 1869, they employed one hundred mounted men to "round up" their cattle. In November of that year the job was completed. They gathered 47,000 head. At the close of the war they had had 81,000 head. They averred that they had lost not only 34,000 head—the difference between the two totals, but they had lost in addition some 34,000 cows that would have been the natural increase over the past few years. These beeves had been taken into Mexico by her marauding citizens. The increase over that period was sworn to by numerous men of Texas. It was fixed at the rate of 33⅓ per cent per annum. Taking 81,000 as the number in 1865 the increase for the year 1866 would have amounted to 27,000; that would have made the total number 108,000. Take 33⅓ per cent as the natural increase at the end of 1867 and they would have had 144,000; for the year 1868 they should have had a total of 192,000 cows; and at the end of 1869 they should have been the owners of 256,000 cattle, allowing for accidental deaths and deaths occurring from disease.

It was very natural for these gentlemen to become restless under such losses. Captain Kenedy was at the head of the cattlemen on the lower Río Grande. They had a command in the field at the time which was paid by the cattle owners. They did all that men could do under the circumstances.

A large majority of the hands hired on cattle ranches were Mexicans. In many instances they were the neighbors and the friends of the bandits depredating upon the property of American citizens. They were unable to resist by force of arms even had they been so disposed. They received orders frequently from the raiders to say nothing. These orders were obeyed. The Federal Court in Brownsville appointed a grand jury to investigate cases as far as it could. But when a Mexican appeared before it and told it in plain terms that should he tell what he knew of cattle stealing, his life would be taken to pay the forfeit for what he had been constrained to promise the marauders, he was excused from swearing. It must be remembered that the cattle thieves were almost innumerable. They came from considerable distances in Mexico to engage in stripping those who had conquered them. It was a labor of love with the Mexicans. Officers of the Mexican Army engaged in the business of robbing those who claimed the protection of the United States. The Mexican who had taken the oath of allegiance to the Constitution of the United States was spotted. What chance had he to do anything but remain silent? A raiding party could cross the Río Grande and murder and rob, and nothing would be heard of it until it had crossed into Mexico. Beef was sold in Matamoros at very low prices.

Thus there was a reign of terror existing on the lower Río Grande. No one knew when he would fall a victim to the rage of incensed Mexicans who would put a man to death to secure themselves from being told upon. George Hill and others were killed to prevent them from telling where they had seen robbers with American cattle. Captain King had acted against the robbing Mexicans. They waylaid him more than once. They killed a young German sitting by his side in an ambulance on his return from Corpus Christi. An ambuscade was provided for him on the road from his ranch to Brownsville. He made an extraordinary drive and passed the spot where the murderers were to take his life before they reached it.

Among the causes rendering Captain Kenedy less exposed to the vengeful feelings of the raiding Mexicans was the fact of his having married Mrs. [Petra Vela de] Vidal, the widow of a captain in the regular army of Mexico. She possessed an intellect much above the ordinary and exerted great influence over her countrymen. It was natural for her to shield her husband as well as she could against the men who were systematically robbing the Texians and murdering those suspected of opposing them. It is true that Mrs. Kenedy did not meet any of the bandits, but she could reach them through others. In this manner her influence was exerted and bore good fruit. She did many charitable acts and had many warm friends who loved her. She was clear-headed and liberal in her views. She possessed none of the bigotry which causes many to persecute their neighbors and become firebrands in the community in which they live. Although a Catholic herself, she possessed too much good sense and too much kindness of heart to persecute those of a different opinion. Many of her friends were staunch Protestants, and no one ever accused her of making a difference in her treatment to anyone of a different religious belief. She was equally kind to all regardless of the church to which they belonged. She appeared to look more at the life and character of a person than at his mode of worship. In this manner she acquired the friendship of all classes. She deserved it.

During the existence of the "Cattle War"—for such it really was—the cattlemen of southern Texas, under the lead of King and Kenedy, instituted measures to protect their lives and property. They organized an association of stockmen, donated money to pay men for services in the field and to present their grievances to the public through the medium of newspapers and otherwise. They attempted to perform services for themselves that should have been performed by the United States government. The citizens of south and west Texas would not have been subjected to such outrages and indignities had the government claiming their allegiance taken measures of redress and retaliation. It might have been that the powers of government remembered the course of Texas during the Civil War and left her to take care of herself in the emergency brought about by the Mexican raiders.[2]

7

In 1869 Captain Kenedy moved his family from Brownsville to the ranch of Laureles. It must have been a movement dictated by interest. He left behind him children and friends. The firm of King, Kenedy & Co. was now virtually dissolved. Charles Stillman had gone to New York sometime previous to that, where he died. The other partners had found more lucrative employment. There had been an apathy among men of business hard to account for. They looked upon the business of Brownsville as there by nature. They sat idly by while Corpus Christi, San Antonio, and other points were offering inducements to secure the trade Brownsville had enjoyed. And they got it.

King and Kenedy proposed to build a railroad from Point Isabel to Brownsville. The only person who subscribed for shares in the road was Robert B. Kingsbury. They abandoned the undertaking, notwithstanding Charles Morgan proffered to advance them any sum of money they might need to accomplish the undertaking.

To make the decadence of Brownsville a fixed fact, Don José San Román moved back to Spain. Some dolorous wight might have properly stood on the steps of the market house and read to the inhabitants the lamentations of Jeremiah.

In 1875 [Uriah] Lott, the president of the road from Corpus Christi to Laredo, induced Captain Kenedy and Captain King to take an interest in the undertaking. He achieved all that could have been expected of a president. In 1881 they sold to the builders of the Mexican National Railway, whose headquarters were in New York, and the road has since remained in their charge. It occupies a position that in time may prove

---

[2] Because Mexican outlawry was so widespread along the border and because the Mexican central government was always too weak to stop it, Ford until his death consistently believed that to ensure peace the United States must extend its jurisdiction south of the great river. "Mexican affairs are unsettled and will no doubt remain so," he wrote O. M. Roberts on February 6, 1877. "The revolutions have paralyzed business and impeded industrial pursuits. The elements of reform, if there, can be made available with difficulty. A protectorate will become indispensable in my opinion." (Roberts Papers, ms.)

one of importance. If ever Corpus Christi succeeds in procuring deep water to the Gulf of Mexico by way of the lighthouse, or should a pass be cut through the islands off the coast to the Gulf, then Corpus Christi will become a seaport of great advantage. In that event she will be on the line of a short route to all the northern States of Mexico, and the commerce passing through her will be immense.

8

The health of Mrs. Kenedy became very bad. She received every attention which was possible. The faithful wife and mother, the dispenser of charities, the friend of the poor, saw her end approaching. She called her husband to her bedside and told him that she had reposed unlimited confidence in his love and trueness and that she left it to him to say what should be done with the property she had a right to claim. After her death on March 16, 1885, he gave to each of her children by a previous marriage the same amount allotted to his own children.

In 1882 Captain Kenedy had sold the Laureles Ranch to an English company. Soon afterward he had begun the establishment of a larger ranch called La Para—Grapevine Ranch—and fenced in all 400,000 acres. The location of the ranch was in the "sands," that reputed desert where, as some imagine, the genius of sterility presides. The care of the stock was entrusted to about 60 men. In "roundups" and on other occasions additional men were hired.

Soon Captain King had about 800,000 acres of land inclosed and had in his employment some 100 men.

Then Captain King's health began to fail. He endeavored to effect a recuperation, but in vain. He placed himself in the charge of Dr. [Ferdinand] Herff, but medical skill availed nothing. Captain King died on April 14, 1885, at the Menger House in San Antonio. He was not quite sixty years of age. The renowned pioneer of big rancheros in south Texas was no more. His death was mourned by all classes. He must be judged by the results he aided in achieving. He possessed financial ability of the first order, and he amassed a fortune of millions upon a theater of action where many failed. It is not upon the basis of a capitalist that his fame chiefly rests, but as a pioneer settler who stepped to the front, jeopardizing life and property, and who became instrumental in opening up thousands of square miles to settlement. The ranch of Santa Gertrudis became the center around which civilization clustered. Where the war whoop of the Comanche ascended, where the wild horse once pranced in unfettered liberty, Captain King introduced the arts of peace, and the song of praise ascended to the throne of God. Where an unpeopled region spread out before the eye of the traveller as a wild waste, where armed hosts of Mexicans and Americans once struggled for mastery, and where bloodshed and rapine prevailed, are now to be seen happy homes and contented people. The friends of the noble ranchero who made the risk which induced these changes can proudly affirm that these are results achieved by him and the men who labored with him. What a noble monument! It should be written indelibly upon the hearts of those now enjoying the fruits of the labors performed by him and others.

Captain King left his immense estate to the management of Mrs. King. This was the last and best evidence he could give of his devotion and confidence. Well it was deserved. The estate under her management is in good shape and prospering.

9

Captain Kenedy had invested largely in the San Antonio and Aransas Railroad, of which Uriah Lott was projector and president. This was one of the great enterprises calculated to develop the resources of west Texas and south Texas. In the future it will be an outlet for cattle by rail and by refrigerating vessels. If the project is pushed, as it should be, Texas beef can be offered in European markets at a figure comparatively low. The consummation of a matter of such vast importance would enable Texas cattle-growers to laugh at western quarantine cattle laws and leave the cattlemen of that section to take care of themselves.

This is probably the last public enterprise in which the only surviving member of the firm of King, Kenedy & Co. will engage. It is one of vast magnitude and indicates that the Pennsylvania Quaker has never lost sight of one of his generous impulses and has spent the main part of his life in laudable efforts to promote the interests of Texas. It must not be forgotten that he was Captain King's partner in the ranch of Santa Gertrudis. The writer can faithfully say that, after an acquaintance of forty years with Captain Kenedy, he has never known him to desert a friend or to quail before an enemy. He has been candid and outspoken, despising the arts of concealment and disguise. He has been a man of success, but that success has been the outcome of good sense and integrity. That he possesses talents of a high order none can deny. Let the man who writes of him after he has passed away speak of his mental acquirements. Let him do justice to a man who has made his mark in a country where thousands have failed to succeed and who never resorted to the arts of a flatterer.

General Bibliography

>>>

Manuscripts

Brown, Frank. "Annals of Travis County and of the City of Austin." Typescript. Archives Division of the Texas State Library, Austin.

Burleson, Ed. Papers. Archives Collection of the University of Texas Library, Austin.

Cortina, Juan N. Miscellaneous Papers. Archives Division of the Texas State Library, Austin.

Ford, John S. "Dr. John S. Ford's Medical Journal." San Augustine, Texas, February, 1844—May 11, 1844. Archives Collection of the University of Texas Library, Austin.

—. "John C. Hays in Texas." Typescript. Archives Collection of the University of Texas Library, Austin.

—. Letter Books. 3 vols. (vol. I, February 18 to April 24, 1864; vol. II, September 22 to November 29, 1864; vol. III, August 24 to December 30, 1864). Typescript. Archives Division of the Texas State Library, Austin.

—. Papers. Archives Division of the Texas State Library, Austin.

Goldfinch, Charles William. "Juan N. Cortina, 1824–1892: A Re-Appraisal." Master's thesis, University of Chicago, 1949.

Governors' Letters, 1846–1860. Archives Division of the Texas State Library, Austin.

Hughes, William John. "Rip Ford, Texan: The Public Life and Services of John Salmon Ford." Ph.D. thesis, Texas Technological College, 1958.

Indian Affairs Office, Letters Received. Washington, D.C. Photostatic copies in Archives Collection of the University of Texas Library, Austin.

Laroche, Clarence J. "Rip Ford: Frontier Journalist." Master's thesis, University of Texas, 1942.

Neighbours, Kenneth Franklin. "Robert S. Neighbors in Texas, 1836–1859: A Quarter Century of Frontier Problems." 2 vols. Ph.D. thesis, University of Texas, 1955.

Roberts, O. M. Lecture on San Augustine. Typescript. Archives Collection of the University of Texas Library, Austin.

—. Papers. Archives Collection of the University of Texas Library, Austin.

State of Texas vs. *Francis Gravis and Charles Gravis*. Indictment for Murder, Report of the Coroner's Jury, and Affidavit of Dr. D. H. Lawrence. Nueces County Courthouse, Corpus Christi, Texas.

Stuart, Ben C. "The History of Texas Newspapers From the Earliest Period to the Present." Beaumont, Texas, 1917. Typescript. Texas Collection of the University of Texas Library, Austin.

U.S. War Department. Records Group No. 94. National Archives, Washington, D. C.

Yager, Hope. "The Archive War in Texas." Master's thesis, University of Texas, 1939.

Newspapers

Caller-Times (Corpus Christi), 1961.
Daily Statesman (Austin), 1897.
Daily Telegraph (Houston), 1864.

Democratic Telegraph and Texas Register (Columbia and Houston), 1845, 1848, 1850.
Express (San Antonio), 1885, 1890.
Herald (Dallas), 1858.
Herald (San Antonio), 1857, 1865.
Northern Standard, The (Clarksville), 1843, 1845, 1849.
Picayune (New Orleans), 1847.
Red-Lander (San Augustine), 1840–1845.
Southern Intelligencer (Austin), 1857–1858.
Southwestern American (Austin), 1852–1854.
Texas Almanac—Extra (Austin), 1862–1863.
Texas Democrat (Austin), 1846–1849.
Texas National Register (Washington-on-the-Brazos and Austin), 1844–1846.
Texas Sentinel (Austin), 1857.
Texas State Gazette (Austin), 1849–1859.
Texas State Times (Austin), 1854–1857.
Tri-Weekly Telegraph (Houston), 1860.

Books

Baker, D. W. C. (ed.). *Original Narratives of Texas History and Adventure: A Texas Scrapbook, Made up of the History, Biography, and Miscellany of Texas and Its People.* New York: [no pub.], 1875.
Bancroft, Hubert Howe. *History of the North Mexican States and Texas.* 2 vols. San Francisco: The History Company, 1886–1889.
Biographical Directory of the Texan Conventions and Congresses. Austin: Book Exchange, Inc., 1941.
Biographical Souvenir of the State of Texas. Chicago: F. A. Battery & Company, 1889.
Blake, R. B. *Historic Nacogdoches, Texas.* Nacogdoches: The Nacogdoches Historical Society, 1939.
Brackett, Albert G. *General Lane's Brigade in Central Mexico.* Cincinnati: H. W. Derby & Co., 1854.
—. *History of the United States Cavalry, from the Formation of the Federal Government to the 1st of June, 1863.* New York: Harper & Brothers, 1865.
Brown, John Henry. *History of Texas from 1685 to 1892.* 2 vols. St. Louis: L. E. Daniell, 1893.
Carroll, Horace Bailey. *The Texan Santa Fe Trail.* Canyon, Texas: Panhandle-Plains Historical Society, 1951.
Crane, William Carey. *Life and Select Literary Remains of Sam Houston of Texas.* 2 vols. in 1. Philadelphia: J. B. Lippincott & Co., 1884.
Crocket, George Louis. *Two Centuries in East Texas.* Dallas: The Southwest Press, 1932.
Daggett, Ephraim M. "Adventure With Guerrillas," in Isaac George, *Heroes and Incidents of the Mexican War,* which see.
Daniell, L. E. *Personnel of the Texas State Government with Sketches of Representative Men of Texas.* San Antonio: Maverick Printing House, 1892.
De Shields, James T. *Border Wars of Texas.* Tioga, Texas: The Herald Company, 1912.
Domenech, Emmanuel. *Missionary Adventures in Texas and Mexico: A Personal Narrative of Six Years Sojourn in Those Regions.* London: Longman, Brown, Green, Longmans, and Roberts, 1858.
Ford, John S. *Annual Reports of the Superintendent of the Texas Institution for the Deaf and Dumb, 1879–1883.* Austin: State of Texas, 1880–1883.
—. *Origin and Fall of the Alamo, March 6, 1836.* San Antonio: Johnson Brothers Printing Company, 1895.
Freeman, Douglas Southall. *Lee's Lieutenants: A Study in Command.* 3 vols. New York: Charles Scribner's Sons, 1942.
—. *Robert E. Lee: A Biography.* 4 vols. New York: Charles Scribner's Sons, 1948.

Fremantle, Arthur James Lyon. *The Fremantle Diary.* Ed. by Walter Lord. Boston: Little, Brown & Company, 1954.

Friend, Llerena. *Sam Houston: The Great Designer.* Austin: University of Texas Press, 1954.

Gammel, H. P. N. (comp.). *The Laws of Texas: 1822–1897.* 10 vols. Austin: Gammel Book Company, 1898.

George, Isaac. *Heroes and Incidents of the Mexican War.* Greensburg, Pennsylvania: Review Publishing Co., 1903.

Green, Thomas J. *Journal of the Texian Expedition Against Mier.* New York: Harper & Brothers, 1845.

Greer, James Kimmins. *Colonel Jack Hays: Texas Frontier Leader and California Builder.* New York: E. P. Dutton & Co., Inc., 1952.

Handbook of Texas. Ed. by Walter Prescott Webb and H. Bailey Carroll. 2 vols. Austin: The Texas State Historical Association, 1952.

Hogan, William Ransom. *The Texas Republic: A Social and Economic History.* Norman: University of Oklahoma Press, 1946.

Horgan, Paul. *Great River: The Rio Grande in North American History.* 2 vols. New York: Rinehart & Company, Inc., 1954.

Jack Hays: the Intrepid Texas Ranger. Bandera, Texas: Frontier Times, [n. d.].

Johnson, Sidney Smith. *Texans Who Wore the Gray.* [Tyler, Texas: no pub., 1907].

Kendall, George Wilkins. *Narrative of the Texan Santa Fe Expedition.* 2 vols. New York: Harper & Brothers, 1844.

King, W. H. "The Texas Ranger Service and History of the Rangers, with Observations on Their Value as a Police Protection," in Dudley G. Wooten (ed.), *A Comprehensive History of Texas,* which see.

Lamar, Mirabeau B. *Letter of Gen. Mirabeau B. Lamar, Ex-President of Texas, on the Subject of Annexation, Addressed to Several Citizens of Macon, Geo.* Savannah: Printed by Thomas Purse, 1844.

Lea, Tom. *The King Ranch.* 2 vols. Boston: Little, Brown & Company, 1957.

Lubbock, Francis R. *Six Decades in Texas.* Austin: Ben C. Jones and Co., 1900.

McKay, S. S. *Debates in the Constitutional Convention of 1875.* Austin: University of Texas Press, 1930.

North, Thomas. *Five Years in Texas: or, What You Did Not Hear during the War from January 1861 to January 1866.* Cincinnati: Elm Street Printing Co., 1871.

Oates, Stephen B. *Confederate Cavalry West of the River.* Austin: University of Texas Press, 1961.

Overdyke, W. Darrell. *The Know-Nothing Party in the South.* Baton Rouge: Louisiana State University Press, 1950.

Paschal, George W. *A Digest of the Laws of Texas: Containing the Laws in Force, and the Repealed Laws . . . from 1754 to 1874.* 2 vols., carefully annotated. 4th ed. Washington, D.C.: W. H. & O. H. Morrison, 1874.

Pierce, Frank C. *A Brief History of the Lower Rio Grande Valley.* Menasha, Wisconsin: George Banta Publishing Company, 1917.

Reports of the Committee of Investigation Sent by the Mexican Government to the Frontier of Texas. Translated from the official edition made in Mexico. New York: Baker and Godwin, Printers, 1875.

Rister, Carl Coke. *Robert E. Lee in Texas.* Norman: University of Oklahoma Press, 1946.

Roberts, O. M. "The Political, Legislative, and Judicial History of Texas for Its Fifty Years of Statehood, 1845–1895," in Dudley G. Wooten (ed.), *A Comprehensive History of Texas,* which see.

—. "Texas," *Confederate Military History* (ed. by Clement A. Evans, 12 vols.) Volume XI. Atlanta: Confederate Pub. Co., 1899.

Roemer, Ferdinand. *Texas: With Particular Reference to German Immigration and the*

Physical Appearance of the Country. Translated from the German by Oswald Mueller. San Antonio: Standard Printing Company, 1935.

Rose, Victor M. *The Life and Services of Gen. Ben McCulloch.* Philadelphia: Pictorial Bureau of the Press, 1888.

Sansom, John W. *Battle of Nueces River in Kinney County, Texas, August 10th, 1862.* San Antonio, Texas: [no pub.], 1905.

Smithwick, Noah. *The Evolution of a State: or, Recollections of Old Texas Days.* Austin: Gammel Book Company, 1900.

Sweet, Alex E., and J. Armoy Knox. *On A Mexican Mustang through Texas: From the Gulf to the Rio Grande.* London: Chatto & Windus, 1884.

Texas (Republic). *Journals of the Constitutional Convention of 1845.* Austin: Miner & Gruger, Printers to the Convention, 1845.

—. *Journals of the House of Representatives of the Ninth Congress.* Washington-on-the-Brazos: Miller & Cushney, Public Printers, 1845.

Texas (State). *Journal of the Constitutional Convention of 1875.* Galveston: Printed for the Convention at the "News" Office, 1875.

U.S. House Exec. Docs., 36th Cong., 1st Sess., vol. II, Doc. 2; vol. VII, Doc. 52; vol. XII, Doc. 81. Washington, D.C.: Thomas H. Ford, Printer, 1860.

U.S. House of Representatives, Index to Reports of Committees, 44th Cong., 1st Sess., 1875–1876. Washington, D.C.: Government Printing Office, 1876.

U.S. Senate Exec. Docs., 36th Cong., 1st Sess., vol. I, Doc. 2; vol. IX, Doc. 21. Washington, D.C.: Thomas H. Ford, Printer, 1860.

U.S. War Department. *The War of the Rebellion: A Compilation of the Official Records of the Union and Confederate Armies.* 70 vols. in 128. Washington, D.C.: Government Printing Office, 1880–1901.

Van Horne, Thomas B. *The Life of Major-General George H. Thomas.* New York: Charles Scribner's Sons, 1882.

Wallace, Ernest, and E. Adamson Hoebel. *The Comanches: Lords of the South Plains.* Norman: University of Oklahoma Press, 1952.

Webb, Walter Prescott. *The Texas Rangers: A Century of Frontier Defense.* Boston and New York: Houghton Mifflin Company, 1935.

— and H. Bailey Carroll (eds.). *The Handbook of Texas,* which see.

Wilbarger, J. W. *Indian Depredations in Texas.* Austin: Hutchings Printing House, 1889.

Wilcox, Cadmus M. *History of the Mexican War.* Washington, D.C.: The Church News Publishing Company, 1892.

Winkler, E. W. (ed.). *Journal of the Secession Convention of Texas, 1861.* Austin: Austin Printing Company, 1912.

Wood, William D. *Reminiscences of Reconstruction in Texas; and Reminiscences of Texas and Texans Fifty Years Ago.* [n.p., no pub.], 1902.

Woodman, Lyman L. *Cortina: Rogue of the Rio Grande.* San Antonio: The Naylor Company, 1950.

Wooten, Dudley G. (ed.). *A Comprehensive History of Texas.* 2 vols. Dallas: William G. Scarff, 1898.

Yoakum, Henderson. *History of Texas from Its First Settlement in 1685 to Its Annexation to the United States in 1846.* 2 vols. New York: J. S. Redfield, 1855.

Articles

Barker, Eugene C. "The Annexation of Texas," *Southwestern Historical Quarterly,* L (July, 1946), 49–74.

Bender, A. B. "Opening Routes across West Texas," *Southwestern Historical Quarterly,* XXXVII (October, 1933), 116–135.

Bridges, C. A. "The Knights of the Golden Circle: A Filibustering Fantasy," *Southwestern Historical Quarterly,* XLIV (January, 1941), 287–302.

Carroll, H. Bailey. "Steward A. Miller and the Snively Expedition of 1843," *Southwestern Historical Quarterly,* LIV (January, 1951), 261–286.

Erath, George Bernard. (ed. by Lucy A. Erath). "Memoirs of George Bernard Erath," *Southwestern Historical Quarterly*, XXVI (January, April, 1923), 207–233, 255–279; XXVII (July, October, 1923), 27–51, 140–163.

Ford, John S. "Fight on the Frio, July 4, 1865," *Quarterly of the Texas State Historical Association*, I (October, 1897), 118–120.

Fornell, Earl W. "Texans and Filibusters in the 1850's," *Southwestern Historical Quarterly*, LIX (April, 1956), 411–428.

Greenwood, C. L. (comp.). "Opening Routes to El Paso, 1849," *Southwestern Historical Quarterly*, XLVIII (October, 1944), 262–272.

Hughes, W. J. " 'Rip' Ford's Indian Fight on the Canadian," *Panhandle-Plains Historical Review*, XXX (1957), 1–26.

Jewett, Henry J. "The Archive War of Texas," *De Bow's Review*, vol. I, no. 5 (New Series, May, 1859), 520–523.

Martin, Charles L. "The Last of the Ranger Chieftains," *The Texas Magazine*, IV (January, 1898), 33–41.

McCown, Susan Turnham (ed. by L. W. Kemp). "Early Days in Milam County: Reminiscences of Susan Turnham McCown," *Southwestern Historical Quarterly*, L (January, 1947), 367–376.

Middleton, Annie. "The Texas Convention of 1845," *Southwestern Historical Quarterly*, XXV (July, 1921), 26–62.

Neighbours, Kenneth F. "The Expedition of Major Robert S. Neighbors to El Paso in 1849," *Southwestern Historical Quarterly*, LVIII (July, 1954), 36–59.

Neighbors, Robert S. (ed. by Kenneth F. Neighbours). "The Report of the Expedition of Major Robert S. Neighbors to El Paso in 1849," *Southwestern Historical Quarterly*, LX (April, 1957), 527–532.

Oates, Stephen B. "John S. Ford: Prudent Cavalryman, C.S.A.," *Southwestern Historical Quarterly*, LXIV (January, 1961), 289–314.

"Organization and Objectives of the Texas State Historical Association, The," *Quarterly of the Texas State Historical Association*, I (July, 1897), 1–17.

Remington, Frederic. "How the Law Got into the Chaparral," *Harper's New Monthly Magazine*, XCIV (December, 1896), 60–69.

Rippy, J. Fred. "Border Troubles along the Rio Grande, 1848–1860," *Southwestern Historical Quarterly*, XXIII (October, 1919), 91–111.

Roberts, O. M. "President's Address," *Quarterly of the Texas State Historical Association*, I (July, 1897), 3–8.

Sandbo, Anna Irene. "The First Session of the Secession Convention of Texas," *Southwestern Historical Quarterly*, XVIII (October, 1914), 162–194.

Shearer, Ernest C. "The Carvajal Disturbances." *Southwestern Historical Quarterly*, LV (October, 1951), 201–230.

Shook, Robert W. "The Battle of the Nueces, August 10, 1862," *Southwestern Historical Quarterly*, LXVI (July 1962), 31–42.

Sowell, A. J. "Colonel Rip Ford and Rangers Battle with the Indians," *Frontier Times*, IV (June, 1927), 24–28.

Spellman, L. V. (ed.). "Letters of the 'Dawson Men' From Perote Prison, Mexico, 1842–1843," *Southwestern Historical Quarterly*, XXXVIII (April, 1935), 246–269.

Taylor, Bride Neill. "The Beginnings of the State Historical Association," *Southwestern Historical Quarterly*, XXXIII (July, 1929), 1–17.

Terrell, Alexander W. "The City of Austin from 1839 to 1865," *Quarterly of the Texas State Historical Association*, XIV (October, 1910), 113–128.

Trahern, George Washington (ed. by A. Russell Buchanan). "Texas Cowboy from Mier to Buena Vista," *Southwestern Historical Quarterly*, LVIII (July, 1954), 60–90.

Walsh, Captain W. C. "Austin in the Making," Austin *Statesman*, February 24, 1924.

Wheeler, T. B. "Reminiscences of Reconstruction in Texas," *Quarterly of the Texas State Historical Association*, XI (July, 1907), 56–65.

Winfrey, Dorman H. "The Texan Archive War of 1842," *Southwestern Historical Quarterly*, LXIV (October, 1960), 171–184.

Index

Young, William C.: at constitutional convention, 54; death of, 337

Ytúrria, Francisco: and Cortina War, 264, 463; ranch of, 409; success of, 460

Yuma, Arizona: death of John Glanton at, 64 n

Zacatal Ranch: 282

Zacualtipán, Mexico: battle at, 94–97, 98

Zambrano, ———: as guide for El Paso expedition, 127

Zapata, Colonel: death of, 186

Zapata, Actaviano; and Servando Canales, 406–407

Zapata County: anti-Confederates in, 324; Civil War in, 393

Zenobia, Colonel: as leader of guerrillas, 66, 68

Zimpleman, Sheriff George B.: and Coke-Davis controversy, 426–427, 427–428, 431, 433–434